ALCOHOL AND YOUTH

ALCOHOL AND YOUTH
A Comprehensive Bibliography

Compiled by Grace M. Barnes

With special assistance from Robert J. Brown

GREENWOOD PRESS
WESTPORT, CONNECTICUT • LONDON, ENGLAND

Library of Congress Cataloging in Publication Data

Barnes, Grace M.
    Alcohol and youth.

    Includes index.
    1.   Youth—Alcohol use—Bibliography. 2. Youth—North
America—Alcohol use—Bibliography. I. Brown, Robert J.
(Robert James),1958-   . II. Title.
Z7721.B37 1982   016.3622′92′088055   82-15397
[HV5824.Y68]
ISBN 0-313-23136-2 (lib. bdg.)

Library of Congress Catalog Card Number: 82-15397
ISBN: 0-313-23136-2

First published in 1982

Greenwood Press
A division of Congressional Information Service, Inc.
88 Post Road West, Westport, Connecticut 06881

Printed in the United States of America

10 9 8 7 6 5 4 3 2 1

Contents

Preface

Alcohol use and abuse among youth has been a topic of widespread public concern. In recent years there has been an increasing body of literature on various aspects of youthful drinking. Numerous studies have focused on the prevalence and social correlates of alcohol use in various clinical, institutional, and general population groups. Studies have addressed the causal factors and the prediction of problem drinking in youth by examining, for example, parental and peer influences on drinking. In addition the literature includes policy-related research pertaining to specific areas such as drinking and driving and changing drinking laws. There is a sizeable literature on program planning, ranging from strategies and goals for alcohol education and prevention to intervention issues for the young problem drinker.

The significance and scope of this area of investigation is represented in the present bibliography of nearly 5,000 citations directly related to the topic of youth and alcohol. Every attempt has been made to make this bibliography the most comprehensive one of its kind to date. This work is a result of an extensive search of published literature cited in *The Journal of Studies on Alcohol, Index Medicus, Current Contents*, as well as numerous other primary and secondary sources. In addition to books and journal literature, relevant theses, government reports, and popular literature have been included. References to literature published in languages other than English have been included, along with an English translation of each title. While this work is comprehensive, it is not necessarily exhaustive in that some newspaper articles, pamphlets, and unpublished manuscripts may have been omitted. The majority of the citations were included only after an informative abstract or the article itself was reviewed for its relevance to youth and alcohol.

Items in the bibliography are listed alphabetically by the last name of the author and are numbered consecutively. Journal titles have been listed in full. A subject index is provided in which articles are cataloged by item number.

The author gives very special thanks to Robert Brown for extensive researching of relevant titles and for the laborious task of carefully verifying and proofreading the references. Immeasurable thanks and appreciation are given to Cindy Britt, who tirelessly and cheerfully typed the camera-ready portions of this work. The author also gratefully acknowledges the assistance of Stephen Novick and Mark Scarbecz, Research Assistants, and Diane Augustino, Librarian at the Research Institute on Alcoholism, for their contributions to this effort.

Introduction

The frequent publicity on the topic of alcohol use among youth often has lead to the conclusion that drinking among teenagers is a relatively new phenomenon which has only recently reached "epidemic" proportions. Alcohol use *is* very prevalent among teenagers and young adults; in fact, it is the behavior of the majority of youth. However, the available research studies carried out over the past several decades indicate that drinking among youth has been a longstanding phenomenon. The growing number of research studies, along with improved methods of sampling and measurement, have resulted in increased knowledge regarding the prevalence and correlates of alcohol use and abuse among youth. The literature to date provides the basis for further research into the factors associated with problem drinking among teenagers and young adults, and it can serve as a foundation for the development of public policies and programs regarding youthful drinking.

PREVALENCE AND SOCIODEMOGRAPHIC CORRELATES

Surveys of adolescent drinking behaviors have been done with some regularity for over thirty years. They have been carried out among various groups of youth in a wide range of geographical locations. These studies have also used very different survey instruments and methods for measuring alcohol consumption. Thus it is difficult to compare drinking over time and across population groups. Nonetheless, there are some consistent findings in the literature on youthful drinking. Virtually all of the recent studies show that the vast majority of teenagers and young adults have had some personal experience using alcohol. For example, recent United States surveys carried out by the National Institute of Alcohol Abuse and Alcoholism indicate that 80 percent of American youth in grades seven through twelve have had a drink (not just a sip) at least once in their lives. The figures approach 90 percent for older adolescents in high school grades nine through twelve. Similarly, over 80 percent of the high school students reported having drinks two or more times.

Most studies of teenage alcohol use report a significant percentage of young people who drink heavily. For example, approximately 15 percent of high school students were classified as heavier drinkers in two recent United States national surveys. (Heavier drinking was defined as drinking at least once a week and having five or more drinks per drinking occasion.) It is important to note that although most adolescents drink, the majority of them drink moderately.

There are also some consistent findings with regard to the sociodemographic correlates of adolescent drinking behavior. In general, rates of drinking are higher among male adolescents than among female adolescents. The difference between the sexes is not as great for the overall prevalence of drinking as it is for heavier drinking. Studies show that the rates of heavier drinking are two to three times higher for males than for females. More specifically, reports indicate the average range of rates of heavier drinking to be between 5 percent and 15 percent for female adolescents and between 15 percent and 30 percent for male youth. Another widely reported finding is that the prevalence of drinking increases from younger adolescence to young adulthood, although there is often a plateau in the prevalence of drinking by the ages of fifteen and sixteen.

Relatively few studies have had sufficiently large and representative samples of minority youth to accurately establish their patterns of drinking. One recent nationwide United States study of students in grades seven through twelve sampled minority youth. The findings indicate that Black adolescents have the smallest proportions of drinkers and heavier drinkers in comparison to White students as well as other minority groups. In contrast to this finding, American Indian youth consistently show the largest proportion of heavier drinkers in comparison to other racial/ethnic groupings.

TRENDS IN DRINKING

There is a popular contention that drinking among teenagers has increased markedly in recent years. Unfortunately there are very few time-series surveys that use standardized measures of drinking in comparable samples over time. Despite this limitation, Blane and Hewitt have recently done an extensive review of the literature on youth and alcohol. This review considered 120 surveys carried out from the 1940s through 1975. The major findings indicated that there was a gradually "decelerating increase" in the prevalence of teenage alcohol consumption from World War II to the mid-1960s. However, there were no observable changes in drinking in the decade from the mid-1960s to the mid-1970s. Furthermore, new findings comparing United States national figures for 1974 and 1978 also show stable rates in the prevalence of drinking. Nonetheless, there are regional variations in drinking patterns. For example, trend studies in San Mateo County, California, show increases in drinking since 1970, but a plateau appears to have been reached in more recent years. Studies in Ontario, Canada, also show increases in drinking since the late 1960s. In areas with longstanding liberal social policies regarding alcohol use—such as New York State—reports indicate no evidence of an increase in teenage drinking or alcohol-related problems from the early 1950s to 1980. Indeed, rates have been relatively high for the thirty years since studies on alcohol and youth were first carried out.

Two other ideas popularly held are that girls' drinking behavior is becoming more similar to boys' drinking, and that adolescents are drinking at a younger age than they were at previous times. These ideas have failed to find support in the bulk of the empirical literature. Most studies still report a difference in the drinking behaviors of young males and females; and a recent review of the literature indicated no significant change in the mean age at first drink.

COLLEGE STUDENTS

Drinking among college students appears to be part of a continuum of drinking patterns begun in the high school years. From existing surveys of college students, the prevalence of drinking at least occasionally ranges from 80 percent to nearly all of the given student population. There are studies indicating that drinking does not necessarily increase throughout the college years. Rather, it appears that for a sizeable proportion of college students, heavier drinking patterns are already established during the high school years before entering college.

The correlates of drinking among college students are also similar to those observed among high school students. For example, heavy drinking is more characteristic of males than of females. Differences in drinking among racial groupings have also been observed: the rates of drinking and heavier drinking are considerably lower for Blacks than for White comparison groups. In general, drinking among college students is a reflection of the patterns of alcohol use among both adolescents and adults in a given societal context.

ALCOHOL-RELATED PROBLEMS

Although most youth drink during their teenage years, the majority drink moderately. However, surveys of alcohol use among youth report significant percentages of adolescents who drink heavily and experience various alcohol-related problems. Estimates of youthful problem drinking obviously vary greatly depending upon the definition used. One commonly-used definition sets the criteria for alcohol misuse as being drunk six or more times in the previous year, or having negative consequences two or more times in that year in at least three of the five problem areas (for example, trouble with school officials, friends, a date, or the police because of drinking, or driving after having too much to drink). According to this definition, national studies estimate that as many as 30 percent of tenth to twelfth grade students in the United States could be classified as misusing alcohol.

One alcohol-related problem area receiving added public attention is drinking and driving among youth. Young people generally have a low tolerance to alcohol, which appears to contribute to the occurrence of automobile accidents at lower blood alcohol levels than in other age groups. Thus inexperience with both driving and drinking put young people at a particularly high risk for traffic accidents.

Another area of concern when addressing alcohol-related problems among youth is delinquent or antisocial behavior. Those youth involved in delinquent acts are much more likely than other youth to be heavier drinkers. Whether excessive alcohol use precedes or leads to deviant behavior is still unresolved. The evidence to date indicates that there is not a simple causal link between excessive drinking and delinquent acts. Rather, it appears that for certain adolescents, problem drinking is only one factor in a complex network of problem behaviors. Research that has examined the extent of antisocial acts committed when teenagers were drinking and when they were not drinking reported that the adolescents who could be classified as heavier drinkers committed a disproportionate number of deviant behaviors even when they were completely sober. Thus it appears that drinking does not necessarily cause delinquency but should be examined as part of a total problem behavior syndrome.

Another issue illustrating this network of problem behaviors is the relationship between illicit drug use and alcohol. While alcohol remains the most widely used and abused drug among youth, multiple substance use is relatively common among young people of high school and college age. Frequent users of marijuana and other illicit drugs are significantly more likely than other youth to be heavy drinkers. Thus illicit drug users do not appear to curtail their use of alcohol.

There is a great deal of media attention devoted to the extent of "teenage alcoholism." Definition of alcoholism is critical for the accurate interpretation of such statements. If teenage alcoholism is defined as a pattern of drinking that causes any damage to the individual and/or society, then large numbers of adolescents can be identified as such. On the other hand, if alcoholism in teenagers is defined as a physical dependence with accompanying physiological damage (as it typically is for adult alcoholics in treatment), then there are very small percentages of youth who can be classified as alcoholics. There are actually very few reports in the literature documenting signs of physical dependence such as delerium tremens, alcohol-induced liver cirrhosis, and neurological damage among teenagers. These physical symptoms may take fifteen to twenty years of chronic drinking to develop, and therefore such late stage signs of alcoholism may indeed be rare among the general population of youth. Of course, this is not to minimize the severe effects of alcohol-related problems among youth such as family disruptions, school problems, and other social/psychological damage.

INFLUENCES ON YOUTHFUL DRINKING

The potential influences on the development of adolescent drinking behaviors are numerous and complex. Only recently has research been focused upon the relative importance of multiple factors influencing teenage alcohol use and abuse. At the broad societal level of analysis, drinking patterns vary according to sociocultural factors. Studies have found relationships between drinking and the level of urbanization, religious affiliation, and socioeconomic status. At the individual level, an adolescent's biological makeup and personality may also be determinants of drinking behavior. For example, some scientists have used twin studies to demonstrate that genetic factors are important in drinking even after controlling for environmental conditions. Also, some have presented data showing that certain personality characteristics may predispose a person to alcohol problems. Such factors may include a derogated self-image, alienation, sex-role conflict, and/or dependency conflict.

While both the sociocultural and individual systems are important for an understanding of youthful drinking, it is the joining of these two systems in the socialization process that strongly influences drinking behavior. It is through this process of socialization that the young person learns society's norms by associations with significant persons, particularly parents and peers. The first exposure to alcohol is usually within the home, where parents serve as role models for alcohol use among their children. Many studies indicate that among the best predictors of the drinking practices of youth are the attitudes and behaviors of their parents toward drinking. Thus adolescents who are infrequent or moderate drinkers are likely to come from homes where their parents are also moderate users of alcohol; and heavy drinking youth are more likely than others to have parents who are heavy drinkers themselves. Even experiencing the devastating effects of living with an alcoholic parent does not deter problem drinking in the young. In fact, children of alcoholic parents are at a very high risk for the development of problem drinking as well as other social/psychological problems.

While the similarities in the drinking attitudes and behaviors of parents and their adolescents can be explained in part by the child's imitation or modeling of parental behaviors, the family influences on developing drinking behaviors are undoubtedly more complex than simple modeling. The adolescent's psychosocial development occurs within the context of the family environment. Excessive drinkers are less likely to feel "very close" to their families. They are more likely to feel loosely controlled, specifically by the mother, and to feel rejected especially by the father, along with perceiving a great deal of psychological tension in their relationships with parents.

Retrospective studies of adult alcoholics also suggest that certain conditions in childhood and adolescence precede the onset of alcohol problems. For example, rebelliousness, hostility, and aggression, in addition to impulsivity and antisocial behavior, have been reported as being antecedent behavioral correlates of alcoholics.

From a somewhat different perspective it is possible, largely through case studies, to examine the children of alcoholics—a group thought to be at a particularly high risk for the development of alcohol problems. Important factors contributing to the high rate of problems in children of alcoholics have been described as the inadequate functioning of the family as a social unit. Inconsistent discipline, poor communication, and the social isolation that often characterizes alcoholic families, represent impediments to becoming a socialized adult. Thus the child of an alcoholic parent is very likely to have problems in developing a well-integrated self-image and in learning socially acceptable roles for his own behavior and that of others, as well as in establishing meaningful relationships with other people.

In addition to the family, the peer group constitutes another major socialization agent or influence on adolescent drinking. This topic has received considerable attention in the literature, yet perceived peer pressure to drink is only weakly related to adolescent drinking behavior. However, there is a fairly strong relationship between an adolescent's drinking and the drinking behavior of his/her friends. Rather than peers actually influencing drinking behavior, it may be that friends are chosen because of similar attitudinal and behavioral patterns. Certainly the peer group provides a social context for drinking and as such is important in determining where, when , and how alcohol is consumed.

PREVENTION AND PUBLIC POLICY ISSUES

Alcohol Education

Young people are seen as a prime focus for alcohol prevention efforts, since prevention or early intervention strategies are most effective before the severe, debilitating effects of chronic alcohol abuse have taken place. Alcohol education in the schools has been the most common alcohol prevention approach. Indeed, alcohol education has a rather long history dating from the temperance movement. At the present time, for example, all states in the United States mandate some form of alcohol education in the public school curriculum. This broad mandate may be fulfilled through a variety of approaches and emphases. Alcohol education may be offered as separate courses or integrated into other regular course work.

Not only does the amount of attention devoted to alcohol education vary greatly, but there is also a lack of consensus on the goals for alcohol education and prevention programs. Since alcohol education in the schools has its foundation in the temperance movement, an abstinence model continues to underlie much educational philosophy. This prohibition philosophy in secondary school education is also consistent with the laws allowing those who are eighteen years old or, in many localities, those nineteen, twenty, or twenty-one to legally purchase and consume alcoholic beverages. However, it is well recognized from general observation and the numerous studies of teenage drinking that by fourteen or fifteen years of age a majority of teenagers are drinking at least occasionally.

In recognition of the actual drinking practices of youth, a "responsible drinking" model has recently been adopted as the goal of many alcohol education/prevention efforts. This alternate model also lacks clarity due to conflicting definitions of "responsible" or "irresponsible" drinking. This perspective may include the related goals of reducing deviant drinking; clarifying one's values in an attempt to positively influence behavior; and improving one's coping skills so that alcohol does not become a mechanism for coping with social or psychological stress.

There have been a wide variety of methods used in alcohol education programs. These approaches range from simply conveying factual information about alcohol and its effect on the body to attempting to produce attitudinal changes and modification in drinking behavior. There have been a very limited number of systematic evaluation studies examining the effectiveness of these various methods. The available evidence indicates that students retain factual information about alcohol, but there are no observable changes in attitudes and behaviors over time as a result of education attempts.

Despite these problems inherent in alcohol education, it still has potential for prevention of alcohol problems among great numbers of young people. Public education remains an obvious means for facilitating prevention of alcohol abuse. Demonstration programs and evaluation research need to continue to determine the most effective approaches for the future.

Laws Defining the Legal Age of Drinking

The public policy issues surrounding the legal age for purchasing and consuming alcoholic beverages has received a considerable amount of attention by governmental and legislative bodies during the past decade. During the 1970s many areas of North America changed their laws to permit individuals under twenty-one years of age to purchase and drink alcoholic beverages. The Canadian provinces changed the laws between 1970 and 1974 to allow those eighteen or nineteen years old to drink legally. Half of the states in the United States also lowered the legal drinking age during the early 1970s.

These changes in the drinking laws did not happen in isolation but rather were a reflection of broader social policies defining the age of majority as eighteen years old. It was felt that because eighteen year olds could vote, pay taxes, drive, and join the military, they should also be legally able to buy and consume alcoholic beverages. In addition, it was thought that changing the drinking laws would serve to legalize what was already well-established, common behavior among older teenagers.

Prior to these changes in the drinking laws, there was no clear indication that these changes would significantly alter drinking patterns among youth. However, some Canadian studies subsequently showed increases in consumption levels after these laws were introduced. In the United States, studies of the impact of changes in the drinking laws have not been uniformly and systematically carried out. Research findings are mixed. Apparently some states experienced changes in consumption while others observed no changes in drinking rates.

One of the most critical public policy issues associated with the changing of drinking laws is the extent to which alcohol-related driving accidents have increased with lowering of the legal age for purchasing alcoholic beverages. There are studies indicating that the lowering of the age is associated with an increased rate of alcohol-related collisions among eighteen to twenty year old drivers. Because of these data, governmental bodies have been raising the drinking ages throughout the 1970s and 1980s. It remains to be seen whether or not raising the age of drinking will change either drinking patterns or drinking-related accidents. There is a considerable amount of controversy regarding causal implications in this area of research. Interpretation of findings is often complicated when laws are changed in conjunction with related measures such as establishing high penalties for serving alcohol to minors, instituting new packaging laws, or improving prevention/education measures. Thus even if changes are noted, it is difficult to attribute these to a change in the law per se. A related question is how much of a change in the drinking age is necessary for an impact on alcohol-related behaviors. For example, will raising the legal age of purchasing alcoholic beverages from eighteen to nineteen years old have any effect on alcohol-related behaviors. Well-designed empirical studies are needed before and after the laws are changed to assess the impact of such social policies.

Bibliography

A

1. Aaseth, J., Schwebs, R. and Sund, A. Alkohol- og Narkotika-
    problemer hos Vernepliktig Ungdom. (Alcohol and Drug
    Problems among Conscripted Youth.) Tidsskrift for den
    Norsk Laegeforening, Oslo, 97: 511-513, 1977.

2. ABC's of Drinking and Driving: Facts About America's No. 1
    Safety Problem. Pamphlet. Greenfield, Massachusetts:
    Channing L. Bete, 1976.

3. Abelson, H., Cohen, R. and Schrayer, D. A Nationwide Study of
    Beliefs, Information and Experience. In: Marihuana: A
    Signal of Misunderstanding. Vol. 2. National Commission
    on Marihuana and Drug Abuse. Washington, D.C.: U.S.
    Government Printing Office, 1972.

4. Abelson, H., Cohen, R., Schrayer, D. and Rappeport, M. Drug
    Experience, Attitudes and Related Behavior Among Adolescents
    and Adults. In: Drug Use in America: Problems in
    Perspective. Appendix. Vol. 1. Patterns and Consequences
    of Drug Use. U.S. National Commission on Marihuana and Drug
    Abuse. Washington, D.C.: U.S. Government Printing Office,
    1973, pages 489-867.

5. Abelson, H.I. and Atkinson, R.B. Public Experience with Psycho-
    active Substances: A Nationwide Study Among Adults and
    Youth. Princeton: Response Analysis Corporation, 1975.

6. Abelson, H.I., Fishburne, P.M. and Cisin, I. National Survey on
    Drug Abuse: 1977. A Nationwide Study--Youth, Young Adults
    and Older People. Vol. 1. Main Findings (DHEW Publ. No.
    ADM 78-618). Rockville, Maryland: National Institute on
    Drug Abuse, 1977.

7. Abelson, H.I., Fishburne,P.M. and Cisin, I. National Survey on
    Drug Abuse: 1977. A Nationwide Study--Youth, Young
    Adults and Older People. Vol. 2 (DHEW Publ. No. ADM
    78-618). Rockville, Maryland: National Institute on Drug
    Abuse, 1977.

8. Ablon, J. Family Structure and Behavior in Alcoholism: A Review
    of the Literature. In: The Biology of Alcoholism. Volume
    4. Social Aspects of Alcoholism. Eds. B. Kissin and
    H. Begleiter. New York: Plenum Press, 1976, pages 205-242.

9. Ablon, J. The Significance of Cultural Patterning for the
    "Alcoholic Family." Family Process, 19: 127-144, 1980.

10. Ablon, Joan. Family Behavior and Alcoholism. In: Cross-
     Cultural Approaches to the Study of Alcohol: An
     Interdisciplinary Perspective. Eds. Michael W. Everett,
     Jack O. Wadell and Dwight B. Heath. The Hague, Paris:
     Mouton Publishers, 1976, pages 133-160.

11. Ablon, Joan. Perspectives on Al-Anon Family Groups. In:
     Alcoholism: Development, Consequences and Interventions.
     Eds. Nada J. Este and M. Edith Heinemann. St. Louis:
     C.V. Mosby Company, 1977, pages 274-282.

12. Ablon, Joan and Cunningham, William. Implications of Cultural
     Patterning for the Delivery of Alcoholism Services. Journal
     of Studies on Alcohol, Suppl. No. 9: 185-206, 1981.

13. Abramo, C.T. Has Drug and Alcohol Education Quarantined Student
     Attitudes? Journal of Alcohol Education, 17(1): 29-36,
     1971.

14. Abrams, Lucille Annette, Garfield, Emily F. and Swisher, J.D.,
     Eds. Accountability in Drug Education: A Model for
     Evaluation. Washington, D.C.: Drug Abuse Council, 1973.

15. Abt Associates, Inc. Summary of Work Performed Pursuant to the
     Development of K-12 Alcohol and Alcohol Safety Curriculum
     Materials. Final Report. (DOT Publ. No. HS-800,726)
     Springfield, Virginia: U.S. National Technical Information
     Service, 1972.

16. Achenbach, T.M. and Edelbrock, C.S. The Child Behavior Profile:
     II. Boys Aged 12-16 and Girls Aged 6-11 and 12-16. Journal
     of Consulting and Clinical Psychology, 47: 223-233, 1979.

17. Acker, M.P. The Wets and the Drys (Drinking--What are the
     Risks?). New York: Scholastic Book Service, 1968.

18. Ackerman, J.M. Clinical Events Attending Father Loss in the
     Histories of V.A. Schizophrenic and Alcoholic Patients.
     Doctoral Dissertation (University Microfilms No. 68-12,386).
     Denver: University of Colorado, 1968.

19. Ackerman, Robert J. Children of Alcoholics: A Guidebook for
     Educators, Therapists, and Parents. Holmes Beach, Florida:
     Learning Publications, 1978.

20. Adair, L. Let's Take the Heat off Parents: Thoughts About
        Parents, Children, and Drugs. Addictions, 19(2): 60-71,
        1972.

21. Adams, C.C. The Cure. New York: Exposition Press, 1950.

22. Adams, D.B. Evaluation of an Educational Program for Juvenile
        Alcohol Offenders and Their Parents. Doctoral Dissertation
        (University Microfilms No. 76-15,573). University of Utah,
        1976.

23. Adams, L.T. Drinking and Student Understanding of Alcohol and
        Alcoholism in Selected High Schools of Southern Nevada.
        Master's Thesis. Utah State University, 1969.

24. Adams, V.E. The Effects of a Special Emphasis Class on the
        Perceived Self-Concept, Knowledge of Alcohol, Academic
        Achievement, and Attendance of a Selected Group of Middle
        School Students. Doctoral Dissertation (University
        Microfilms No. 8000001). East Texas State University, 1979.

25. Addeo, E.G. and Addeo, J.R. Why Our Children Drink. Englewood
        Cliffs, New Jersey: Prentice-Hall, 1975.

26. Addiction in the Young: I. Alcoholism. II. Drug Abuse.
        Journal of Practical Nursing, 29(7): 18, 1979.

27. Addiction Research Foundation. A.A.: Try to Understand How the
        Alcoholics Anonymous Program Works. Pamphlet. Toronto,
        Ontario, no date.

28. Addiction Research Foundation. Coffee, Tea and Me. Pamphlet.
        Toronto, Ontario, 1978.

29. Addiction Research Foundation. Interaction of Alcohol and Other
        Drugs: An Annotated Bibliography. 2nd ed. Compiled by
        E. Polacsek, T. Barnes, N. Turner, R. Hall and C.C. Weise.
        Toronto, Ontario, 1972.

30. Addiction Research Foundation. The Treatment of Alcoholics:
        An Ontario Perspective. The Report of the Task Force on
        Treatment Services for Alcoholics. Toronto, Ontario, 1978.

31. Addiction Research Foundation. North Bay Centre. Utilizing
        Students in the Presentation of Drug Education at Silver
        Birches Senior Elementary School, North Bay. Project H 130,
        Substudy No. 643. Toronto, Ontario, 1974.

32. Addictions Prevention Laboratory. Selected Reports of the
        Addictions Prevention Laboratory. Vol. 1. University Park,
        Pennsylvania: Pennsylvania State University, 1976.

33. Adler, P.T. and Lotecka, L. Drug Use Among High School Students:
    Patterns and Correlates. The International Journal of
    Addictions, 8(3): 537-548, 1973.

34. Adolescent Alcohol Abuse - Quarterly Notes. Journal of
    Alcoholism, 9(1): 42, 1974.

35. Adolescent Drinking - Quarterly Notes. Journal of Alcoholism,
    11(4): 117, 1976.

36. Age, Alcohol and Accidents. New Zealand Road Safety, 21(4): 6,
    1974.

37. Ahlfors, U.G. Alkoholpatienter i Öppen Vård. (Alcoholic
    Patients in Open Therapeutic Care.) Suom Lääkärilehti,
    Finland, 20: 2485-2489, 1965.

38. Ahlgren, Andrew and Norem-Hebeisen, Ardyth A. Self-Esteem
    Patterns Distinctive of Groups of Drug Abusing and Other
    Dysfunctional Adolescents. The International Journal of
    the Addictions, 14(6): 759-777, 1979.

39. Ahlström, S. Trends in Drinking Habits among Finnish Youth from
    the Beginning of the 1960's to the Late 1970's. (Social
    Research Institute of Alcohol Studies Report No. 128.)
    Helsinki: Social Research Institute of Alcohol Studies,
    1979.

40. Ahlström, S. Trenduntersuchung der Trinksitten Finnischer
    Jugendlicher von 1960 bis 1979. (Trends in Drinking Habits
    of Finnish Youth from 1960 to 1979.) Drogalkohol, 3(3):
    16-40, 1979.

41. Ahlström-Laakso, S. Changing Drinking Habits among Finnish
    Youth. In: Proceedings of the 31st International Congress
    on Alcoholism and Drug Dependence. Vol. 3. Eds. B. Blair,
    V. Pawlak, E. Tongue, and C. Zwicky. Lausanne:
    International Council on Alcohol and Addictions, 1975.

42. Ahlström-Laakso, S. Nuorison Juomatapojen Muuttuminen.
    (Changing Drinking Habits Among Youth.) Alkoholikysymys,
    43: 67-83, 1975.

43. Ahlström-Laakso, S. Ungdomens Alkoholbruk Förändras. (Changes
    in Alcohol Use among Youth.) Alkoholpolitik, Helsinki, 37:
    3-6, 1974.

44. Ahnsjö, S. Delinquency in Girls and Its Prognosis. Acta
    Paediatrica, Stockholm, 28, Suppl. No. 3, 1941.

45. Ahrens, E. Der Alkoholiker und Sein Soziales Umfeld aus der
     Sicht der Sozialberatung eines Grossbetriebes. (The
     Alcoholic and his Social Environment from the Standpoint of
     the Social Service in a Large Enterprise.) Arbeitsmedizin,
     Sozialmedizin, Praeventivmedizin, Stuttgart, 13: 47-49,
     1978.

46. Ahto, A. Om Psykopati och Alkoholmissbruk hos Unga Kvinnliga
     Förbrytare. (Psychopathy and Abuse of Alcohol Among Young
     Female Offenders.) In: Yearbook of the Northern
     Associations of Criminalists 1946-1947. Stockholm, 1948,
     pages 2-13.

47. Aitken, P.P. Ten-to-Fourteen-Year-Olds and Alcohol: A
     Developmental Study in the Central Region of Scotland.
     Vol. III. Edinburgh: Her Majesty's Stationery Office,
     1978.

48. Ajami, A.M., Jr. Drugs: An Annotated Bibliography and Guide to
     the Literature. Boston: G.K. Hall, 1973.

49. Akers, R.L. Teenage Drinking and Drug Use. In: Adolescents.
     Ed. D. Evans. Hinsdale, Illinois: Dryden Press, 1970.

50. Akers, R.L. Teenage Drinking: A Survey of Action Programs.
     Seattle, Washington: Northwestern Mutual Insurance Company
     of Seattle, 1967.

51. Akers, R.L., Krohn, M.D., Lanza-Kaduce, L. and Radosevich, M.
     Social Learning and Deviant Behavior: A Specific Test of a
     General Theory. American Sociological Review, 44: 636-655,
     1979.

52. Akers, Ronald L. Teenage Drinking: A Survey of Action Programs
     and Research. Journal of Alcohol Education, 13(4): 1-10,
     1968.

53. Akron Young Men's Christian Association. Beyond the Facts--
     Alcohol; A Value Education Approach. Pamphlet. Akron,
     Ohio, no date.

54. Akron Young Men's Christian Association. Youth Values Project.
     Valuing Youth. Akron, Ohio, 1974.

55. Akron Young Men's Christian Association. Youth Values Project.
     Valuing Youth, Valuing Families. (Revised edition). Akron,
     Ohio, 1975.

56. Alabama Department of Education. Alcohol and Traffic Accidents.
     (Drug Education Series, No. 3.) Pamphlet. Montgomery,
     Alabama, 1967.

57. Alabama Department of Education. Alcohol Facts for College Students. (Temperance Education Bulletin No. 7.) Montgomery, Alabama, 1955.

58. Alabama Department of Education. Building Wholesome Personalities. (Temperance Education Series No. 2.) Montgomery, Alabama, 1951.

59. Alabama Department of Education. Effects of Alcohol on People. (Drug Education Series, No. 4.) Pamphlet. Montgomery, Alabama, 1968.

60. Alabama Department of Education. Ideas: A Drug Educaton Resources Guide. Montgomery, Alabama, 1973.

61. Alabama Department of Education. Interdisciplinary Drug Education for Alabama Schools. Pamphlet. Montgomery, Alabama, 1972.

62. Alabama Department of Education. Our Alcohol Problem. (Temperance Education Series No. 1.) Montgomery, Alabama, 1951.

63. Alabama Department of Education. Relation of Alcohol to Social Problems. (Temperance Education Series No. 5.) Montgomery, Alabama, 1951.

64. Alabama Department of Education. Teacher's Guide for Instruction in Temperance Education. (Temperance Education Bulletin No. 6.) Montgomery, Alabama, 1953.

65. Alabama Department of Education. Drug Education Unit. The Classroom Teacher and Drug Education. Pamphlet. Montgomery, Alabama, 1972.

66. Alameda County School Department. Drug Education Center. Assessments of Student Drug and Alcohol Use and Drug Education Needs in Alameda County's Secondary Schools. Hayward, California, 1975.

67. Alameda County School Department. Drug Education Center. Student Drug Use Survey: San Leandro Unified School District. Hayward, California, 1975.

68. Al-Anon Family Group Headquarters. Al-Anon and Alateen, Groups at Work. The Basic Manual of Principles and Practices. Pamphlet. New York, 1976.

69. Al-Anon Family Group Headquarters. Al-Anon Faces Alcoholism. New York, 1965.

70. Al-Anon Family Group Headquarters. Al-Anon Fact File. Pamphlet.
        New York, 1969.

71. Al-Anon Family Group Headquarters. Alateen Do's and Don'ts.
        Card. New York, 1970.

72. Al-Anon Family Group Headquarters. Alateen: Hope for Children
        of Alcoholics. New York, 1973.

73. Al-Anon Family Group Headquarters. Facts About Alateen.
        Pamphlet. New York, 1969.

74. Al-Anon Family Group Headquarters. For Teenagers with an
        Alcoholic Parent. Pamphlet. New York, 1968.

75. Al-Anon Family Group Headquarters. A Guide for Sponsors of
        Alateen Groups. Pamphlet. New York, 1968 (revised
        edition, 1974).

76. Al-Anon Family Group Headquarters. How Can I Help My Children?
        Asks an Al-Anon Member. Pamphlet. New York, 1973.

77. Al-Anon Family Group Headquarters. If Your Parents Drink Too
        Much. Pamphlet. New York, 1974.

78. Al-Anon Family Group Headquarters. It's a Teenaged Affair.
        Pamphlet. New York, 1964.

79. Al-Anon Family Group Headquarters. Living With an Alcoholic.
        New York, 1960.

80. Al-Anon Family Group Headquarters. Living With an Alcoholic,
        With the Help of Al-Anon (revised edition). New York,
        1964. (Published in 1955 as: The Al-Anon Family Group:
        A Guide for the Families of Problem Drinkers.

81. Al-Anon Family Group Headquarters. Lois Remembers: Memoirs of
        the Co-Founder of Al-Anon and Wife of the Co-Founder of
        Alcoholics Anonymous. New York, 1979.

82. Al-Anon Family Group Headquarters. One Day at a Time in Al-Anon.
        New York, 1968.

83. Al-Anon Family Group Headquarters. Operation Alateen. Pamphlet.
        New York, 1962.

84. Al-Anon Family Group Headquarters. Purposes and Suggestions for
        Al-Anon Family Groups. Leaflet. New York, 1962.

85. Al-Anon Family Group Headquarters. A Teacher Finds Guidance in
        Al-Anon. Pamphlet. New York, 1973.

86. Al-Anon Family Group Headquarters. Youth and the Alcoholic
     Parent: A Message to Young People. Pamphlet. New York,
     1957 (revised 1966, 1972 and 1975).

87. Alaska Department of Education. Alcohol Education in Alaska
     Schools. Juneau, Alaska, no date.

88. Albas, Daniel, Albas, Cheryl and McCluskey, Ken. Anomie, Social
     Class and Drinking Behavior of High-School Students.
     Journal of Studies on Alcohol, 39: 910-913, 1978.

89. Albaugh, Bernard and Albaugh, Patricia. Alcoholism and
     Substance Sniffing among the Cheyenne and Arapaho Indians
     of Oklahoma. The International Journal of the Addictions,
     14(7): 1001-1007, 1979.

90. Alberta Department of Education. Teachers' Resource Book for
     Use with the Health and Personal Development Course.
     Edmonton, Saskatchewan, 1956.

91. Albrecht, Gary. The Alcoholism Process: A Social Learning
     Viewpoint. In: Alcoholism: Progress in Research and
     Treatment. Eds. P.G. Bourne and R. Fox. New York:
     Academic Press, 1973, pages 11-42.

92. Alcohol. Medical Journal of Australia, 2(21): 775, 1975.

93. Alcohol Abuse. People Helping People, 1(2): 2-14, 1974.

94. Alcohol Abuse Imperils Youth. Awake, 56(3): 16-18, 1975.

95. Alcohol Addiction in Young Men (The London Letter). Canadian
     Medical Association Journal, 100: 733, 1969.

96. Alcohol and Drug Problems Association of North America. Selected
     Papers Presented at the General Sessions of the 22nd Annual
     Meeting of the Alcohol and Drug Problems Association of
     North America, September 12-17, 1971, Hartford, Connecticut.

97. Alcohol and Highway Fatalities: A Study of 961 Fatalities in
     North Carolina During the Last Six Months of 1970. North
     Carolina Medical Journal, 33(9): 769-773, 1972.

98. Alcohol and the Young at School. New Zealand Medical Journal,
     90: 154, 1979.

99. Alcohol and Youth: Panelists Disagree on Education Methods.
     The Journal, 1: 8-9, 1972.

100. Alcohol/Drug Information Foundation. Alcohol and Accidents.
      Pamphlet. Lansing, Michigan, no date.

101. Alcohol, Drugs and Traffic Safety. Traffic Safety, 15-17, 1975.

102. Alcohol Education Service, Winnipeg, Manitoba, Canada. A Look at
     the New Teacher's Guide. Journal of Alcohol Education,
     13(1): 29-36, 1967.

103. Alcohol in Accidents and Crime. Editorial. Journal of
     Alcoholism, 9(1): 1-6, 1974.

104. Alcohol Studies: Youth No Drunker: Rand Impact Minor. Medical
     World News, 19(2): 14, 1978.

105. Alcohol Use "Growing Among Youth." American Issue, 80(2): 2,
     1973.

106. Alcoholics Anonymous. Student's Guide to Alcoholics Anonymous.
     Leaflet. New York: Alcoholics Anonymous World Services,
     1971.

107. Alcoholics Anonymous. Young People and A.A.. Pamphlet. New
     York: Alcoholics Anonymous World Services, 1953 (revised
     edition 1969).

108. Alcoholic Pancreatitis - Quarterly Notes. Journal of Alcoholism,
     11(2): 42, 1976.

109. Alcoholic Pancreatitis in a Boy of 15 - Quarterly Notes.
     Journal of Alcoholism, 11(1): 8, 1976.

110. Alcoholism. (Foreign Mail. Norway.) Journal of the American
     Medical Association, 177: 275, 1961.

111. Alcoholism and Women. Alcohol Health and Research World: 2-7,
     Summer, 1974.

112. Alcoholism as It Affects the Moral and Social Condition of the
     Child, the Home, and the Nation. International Congress
     Against Alcoholism, 12(114): 138-142, 1909.

113. Alcoholism Council of Orange County, Youth Services Program.
     Drinking Patterns and Problem Drinking Among Youth in Orange
     County. Santa Ana, California, 1976.

114. Alcoholism. Editorial. Royal Society of Health Journal, 99(6):
     223, 1979.

115. The Alcoholism Foundation of British Columbia. Both Sides Now.
     Pamphlet. Printed by the Narcotics Addiction Foundation of
     British Columbia. Distributed by the British Columbia
     Teachers' Federation (2235 Burrand Street, Vancouver,
     British Columbia). No date.

116. Alcoholism Foundation of Manitoba. Teenagers and Alcohol.
      (Foundation Report) Winnipeg, Manitoba, 1958.

117. Alcoholism in Women. Journal of the American Medical
      Association, 225(8): 988, 1973.

118. Alcoholism Misuse, the Family and Alcoholism Programs: Some
      Suggested Strategies of Intervention. Journal of Studies
      on Alcohol, 42(1): 172-179, 1981.

119. Alcoholism: New Victims, New Treatment. Time, 75-81, April 22,
      1974.

120. Alcoholism, 1941-1951: A Survey of Activities in Research,
      Education and Therapy. Quarterly Journal of Studies on
      Alcohol, 13(3): 421-511, 1952.

121. Alcoholism: Out in the Open. The Economist, 240(6675): 22-23,
      1971.

122. Alcoholism Research Information Center, Inc. Complete Education
      and Training Programs for Alcohol Abuse and Alcoholism.
      Virginia: Southern Area Alcohol Education and Training
      Program, Inc., 1977.

123. Aldoory, S. Research Into Family Factors in Alcoholism.
      Alcohol Health and Research World, 3(4): 2-6, 1979.

124. Alexander, C.N., Jr. Alcohol and Adolescent Rebellion. Social
      Forces, 45(4): 542-550, 1967.

125. Alexander, C.N., Jr. Consensus and Mutual Attraction in Natural
      Cliques: A Study of Adolescent Drinkers. American Journal
      of Sociology, 69: 395-403, 1964.

126. Alexander, C.N., Jr. and Campbell, E.Q. Balance Forces and
      Environmental Effects: Factors Influencing the Cohesiveness
      of Adolescent Drinking Groups. Social Forces, 46: 367-374,
      1968.

127. Alexander, C.N., Jr. and Campbell, E.Q. Normative Milieux and
      Social Behaviors: Church Affiliations and College Drinking
      Patterns. In: The Domesticated Drug: Drinking Among
      Collegians. Ed. G.L. Maddox. New Haven: College and
      University Press, 1970, pages 268-289.

128. Alexander, C.N., Jr. and Campbell, E.Q. Peer Influences on
      Adolescent Drinking. Quarterly Journal of Studies on
      Alcohol, 28(3): 444-453, 1967.

129. Alfars, Albert L. and Milgram, Gail. The Teenager and Alcohol.
      New York: Rosen, Richards Press, 1970.

130. Alibrandi, Tom. Turnabout - Mom and Dad are Getting Loaded and
     the Kids are on the Sauce. The Alcoholism Digest Annual, 5:
     35-39, 1976-77.

131. Alibrandi, Tom. Young Alcoholics. Minneapolis, Minnesota:
     CompCare Publications, 1978.

132. Alkohol: Einige Zahlen zum Referat von P. Plüss. (Alcohol:
     Some Numbers [to add] to the report by P. Plüss.)
     Fürsorger, 42: 22-24, 1974.

133. Alkohol, Zigaretten, Drogen bei Schülern. (Alcohol, Cigarettes,
     Drugs among School Children.) Therapie Gegenwart, 114:
     690, 1975.

134. Allardt, Erik. Drinking Norms and Drinking Habits. In:
     Drinking and Drinkers: Three Papers in Behavioral Science.
     Eds. Erik Allardt, Touko Marrkanen and Martti Takala.
     Stockholm, Sweden: Almquist and Wiksell, 1957, pages 7-110.

135. Allardt, Erik, Marrkanen, Touko and Takala, Martti. Drinking and
     Drinkers: Three Papers in Behavioral Science. Stockholm,
     Sweden: Almquist and Wiksell, 1957.

136. Allen, C. Teenage Drunkenness. (Correspondence.) British
     Medical Journal, 1: 1392-1393, 1961.

137. Allen, E.B. The Prevention of Alcoholism. Alcohol Hygiene,
     1(5): 11-13, 1945.

138. Allen, E.L. The Development of an Inventory to Identify the
     Attitudes of College and University Students Concerning
     Alcohol, Marijuana and Speed. Doctoral Dissertation
     (University Microfilms No. 76-25174). University of
     California, Los Angeles, 1976.

139. Allen, H.M. Some Hints for Public School Teachers. Leaflet.
     Evanston, Illinois: Signal Press, no date.

140. Allen, H.M. Teachers with the Know-How. Leaflet. Evanston:
     Illinois: Signal Press, no date.

141. Aller, L.F., Jr. Emotional Problems of Adolescents. II.
     Obesity, Suicide, School Problems, Drinking, Theft.
     Northwest Medicine, 65: 308-313, 1966.

142. Alltop, L.B., Lemley, D. and Williams, T. Do Children Seen in
     Mental Health Clinics Come from "Problem Drinking"
     Households? Inventory, 19(4): 9-11, 20, 1970.

143. Allworth, J.C. Adolescent Alcohol Abuse as a Symptom of Social
     Alienation and Identity Crisis. Doctoral Dissertation
     (University Microfilms No. 76-20960). United States
     International University, 1976.

144. Alsikafi, M., Globetti, G. and Christy, E.G. Abusive Alcohol
     Drinking: A Study of Social Attitudes of Youth in a
     Military Community. Drug Forum, 7: 317-328, 1978-79.

145. Althoff, S.A. and Nussell, E.J. Social Class Trends in the
     Practices and Attitudes of College Students Regarding Sex,
     Smoking, Drinking and the Use of Drugs. Journal of School
     Health, 41(7): 390-394, 1971.

146. Altman, H., Sletten, I.W. and Evenson, R.C. Childhood and
     Adolescent Problems of Adult Psychiatric Inpatients.
     Comprehensive Psychiatry, 16: 479-484, 1975.

147. Altman, Marjorie, Crocker, Ruth Whitcomb and Gaines, Donna.
     Female Alcoholics: The Men They Marry. Focus on Women,
     1(1): 33-41, 1980.

148. Amado, G. Des Enfants Préalcooliques? A Propos de la Prévention
     Précoce de l'Alcoolisme. (Prealcoholic Children? On Early
     Prevention of Alcoholism.) Evolution Psychiatrique: 133-
     153, 1959.

149. Amejko, E. Alcohol's Best Mixer: Understanding. Pamphlet.
     Cincinnati: Pamphlet Publications, 1977.

150. American Academy of Pediatrics. Committee on Youth and Canadian
     Pediatric Society. Committee on Adolescent Medicine.
     Alcohol Consumption: An Adolescent Problem. Pediatrics,
     55: 557-559, 1975.

151. American Alliance for Health, Physical Education and Recreation.
     A Monograph on Alcohol Education and Alcohol Abuse
     Prevention Programs at Selected American Colleges.
     Gainesville: University of Florida, Office for Student
     Services, 1978.

152. American Association for Health, Physical Education and
     Recreation. Resource Book for Drug Abuse Education.
     Washington, D.C.: U.S. Government Printing Office, 1969.

153. American Automobile Association. Teacher's Guide to Alcohol
     Countermeasures. Falls Church, Virginia, 1976.

154. American Automobile Association. You... Alcohol and Driving.
     Falls Church, Virginia, 1975.

155. American Colleges and Prohibition: A Survey of Opinion. The
     Intercollegiate Statesman, 19(7): 99-103, 108-112, 1922.

156. American Council on Alcohol Problems. Aspects of Alcohol and
     Alcoholism. Pamphlet. Washington, no date.

157. American Driver and Traffic Safety Education Association.
      Alcohol and Driving: A Curriculum for Driver Educators.
      Washington: U.S. National Highway Safety Administration,
      1971.

158. American Driver and Traffic Safety Education Association.
      Group Process in Alcohol Education with Strategies for the
      Classroom and Pilot Study Conducted in the Milwaukee Public
      Schools. Pamphlet. Washington, D.C., 1978.

159. American Driver and Traffic Safety Education Association.
      People Do Drink and Drive. Pamphlet. Washington, D.C.,
      1973.

160. American Legion. Children and Youth on the Rocks. Pamphlet.
      Indianapolis, Indiana, 1975.

161. The American School Health Association. A Statement Concerning
      the Use of Alcohol as Formulated by the Committee on Drugs
      of The American School Health Association. Journal of
      School Health, 42: 212, 1972.

162. American School Health Association. Teaching About Drugs: A
      Curriculum Guide, K-12. Kent, Ohio, 1971.

163. American Temperance Society and Narcotics Education. I Killed
      Winky Adams, and Other Stories. Pamphlet. Mountainview,
      California: Pacific Press, 1968.

164. Ames, M. Choose for Yourself: You and Alcohol. New York:
      Ramapo House, 1970.

165. Amini, F. and Burke, E. Acting Out and Its Role in the
      Treatment of Adolescents: An Objective Relations Viewpoint.
      Bulletin of the Menninger Clinic, 43: 249-259, 1979.

166. Andelković, A. and Banković-Simonović, R. Analiza Grupe
      Adolescenata Alkoholičara. (Analysis of a Group of
      Adolescent Alcoholics.) Alkoholizam, Beograd, 13(3-4):
      71-78, 1973.

167. Ander, A. Häufigkeitsverteilung der Blutalkoholwerte bei
      12,000 Strassenverkehrsunfällen in Baden-Württemberg.
      (Frequency Distribution of Blood Alcohol Levels in 12,000
      Traffic Accidents in Baden-Württemberg.) Hefte zur
      Unfallheilkunde, Berlin, 66: 83-90, 1961.

168. Andersen, I., Axelsen, F., Stehouwer, J. and Tonsgaard, O.
      Ungdom Tobak og Alkohol. (Youth, Tobacco and Alcohol.)
      Arhus: Akademisk Boghandel, 1966.

169. Anderson, B.G. How French Children Learn to Drink. Transaction, 5(7): 20-22, 1969. (Also in: Beliefs, Behaviors and Alcoholic Beverages: A Cross-Cultural Survey. Ed. M. Marshall. Ann Arbor: University of Michigan Press, 1979,pages 429-432.

170. Anderson, D.S. and Gadaleto, A.F. That Happy Feeling: An Innovative Model for a Campus Alcohol Education Program. Atlanta, Georgia: Southern Area Alcohol Education and Training Program, Inc., 1979.

171. Anderson, G.L. STADUS: Student Alcohol and Drug Use Survey: Guide Book and Survey Book. Pamphlet. Center City, Minnesota: Hazelden, 1979.

172. Anderson, S.C. Patterns of Identification in Alcoholic Women. Doctoral Dissertation (University Microfilms No. 77-7197). Rutgers University, 1976.

173. Ando, H. and Hasegawa, E. Drinking Patterns and Attitudes of Alcoholics and Nonalcoholics in Japan. Quarterly Journal of Studies on Alcohol, 31(1): 153-161, 1970.

174. Andorka, R. A Szeszesitalfogyaztási Szokások és Normák egy Közvéleménykutatás Alapján. (Habits and Norms of Alcoholic Beverages Consumption: Results of a Public Opinion Research.) Alkohologia, Budapest, 3: 147-150, 1972.

175. Andreini, M. and Green, S. Statistical Description of Cases Followed by the Anchorage Child Abuse Board, Inc., October, 1972 - March, 1975. Alaska: Anchorage Child Abuse Board, Inc., 1975.

176. Anhalt, H.S. and Klein, M. Drug Abuse in Junior High School Populations. American Journal of Drug and Alcohol Abuse, 3: 589-603, 1976.

177. Aniol, K., Przbylski, Z. and Marcinkowski, T. Utoniecia Wśród Młodzieży a Alkohol. (Drownings Among Youth, and Alcohol.) Problemy Alkoholizmu, Warsaw, 21(10): 10, 1973.

178. Anker, J. and Milman, D. Patterns of Nonmedical Drug Usage Among University Students. Student Attitudes Toward Drug Usage. In: Drug Abuse: Current Concepts and Research. Ed. W. Keup. Springfield, Illinois: Charles C. Thomas, 1972, pages 202-214.

179. Anker, J.L., Milman, D.H., Kahan, S.A. and Valenti, C. Drug Usage and Related Patterns of Behavior in University Students: I. General Survey and Marijuana Use. Journal of the American College Health Association, 19(3): 178-186, 1971.

180. Annis, Helen M. Adolescent Drug Use: The Role of Peer Groups
      and Parental Example. The Ontario Psychologist, 7(4): 7-9,
      1975.

181. Annis, Helen M. Patterns of Intra-Familial Drug Use. British
      Journal of Addiction, 69: 361-369, 1974.

182. Annis, Helen M. and Watson, Carol. Drug Use and School Dropout:
      A Longitudinal Study. Conseiller Canadien, 9: 155-162,
      1975.

183. Annotated Listing of Drug Abuse Films. In: Resource Book for
      Drug Abuse Education. American Association for Health,
      Physical Education and Recreation. Washington, D.C.: U.S.
      Government Printing Office, 1969, pages 95-98.

184. Antone, E.J., Jr. A Study of the Relationship of the Use of
      Various Drugs to the Visual-Motor Performance of College
      Students. Doctoral Dissertation (University Microfilms
      No. 72-27,619). Oregon State University, 1972.

185. Anumonye, A. Alcohol and Drug Use in Youth. In: Papers
      Presented at the 6th International Institute on the
      Prevention and Treatment of Drug Dependence, Hamburg,
      Germany, June 28-July 2, 1976. Lausanne: International
      Council on Alcohol and Addictions, 1979, pages 36-54.

186. Apostolov, M. Ispitivanje Raširenosti Uputrebe Alkohola Medu
      Učenicima. (The Effect of Alcohol on the Scholarship of
      Pupils.) Alkoholizam, Beograd, 7(1): 55-60, 1967.

187. Apperson, L.B. Childhood Experiences of Schizophrenics and
      Alcoholics. Journal of Genetic Psychology, 106: 301-313,
      1965.

188. Application of Dram Acts to Non-Commercial Suppliers of Liquor.
      Ross v. Ross, 294 Minnesota 115, 200 N.W. 2d 149, 1972.
      Washington University Law Quarterly, 1973(3): 708-715,
      1973.

189. Arafat, I. Drinking Behavior in High School, College and Adult
      Groups. Free Inquiry, 7: 87-91, 1979.

190. Araujo, R.L. Consideraciones Estadísticas Sobre el Consumo de
      Bebidas Alcohólicas por la Población de Venezuela.
      (Statistical Considerations on the Consumption of Alcoholic
      Beverages by the Population of Venezuela.) Revista de
      Sanidad y Asistencia Social, 20: 39-55, 1955.

191. Archer, Edith and Arundell, Rita. A Measuring Instrument for Use
      in Drug Education Programs: Development of the McLeod High
      Risk Inventory. Journal of Drug Education, 8(4): 313-325,
      1978.

192. Archibald, H.D. Alcoholism--A Public Health Problem. Canadian Journal of Public Health, 60: 415, 1969.

193. Arkansas Department of Education, A.W. Ford, Director. Drug Education: A Resource and Curriculum Guide, K-12. Little Rock, Arkansas, 1971.

194. Arizona Department of Education. Alcohol and Drug Division. Substance Abuse Resource Guide, K-12. Phoenix, 1976.

195. Armstrong, H.B. Drinking Patterns Among High School Students. Master's Thesis. Mississippi State University, 1963.

196. Aronson, H. and Gilbert, A. Preadolescent Sons of Male Alcoholics. An Experimental Study of Personality Patterning. Archives of General Psychiatry, 8(3): 235-241, 1963.

197. Arriëns, A. Alcohol and Education of the Young. International Congress Against Alcoholism, 22: 202-205, 1941.

198. Arthur, Gary, Sisson, P. Joe, and Nix, George. Three Year Follow-Up Drug Survey of High School Youth in a Typical Georgia School. Journal of Drug Education, 7: 43-52, 1977.

199. ASAP Gets Drinkers to Drive for Science. Crescent City Counterattack, 1(11): 1-2, 1973.

200. Asimi, A.A.D. Teenage Drinking Behavior: Report of a Survey in Northwestern Ontario, Lakehead University, 1971.

201. Asper, Samuel P. Self-Regulation in the Use of Alcohol. Maryland State Medical Journal, 23(12): 24-25, 1974.

202. Astor, G. Teenagers: How they Feel is How they Drive. New York Times Magazine, 6 (Part 1): 46, 48-49, March 2, 1975.

203. Atkins, A.J. and Gwynn, J. Minor. Alcohol Education for Teachers. New York: The Macmillan Company, 1959.

204. Atkinson, B. and Brugger, A.T. Do College Students Drink Too Much? Journal of Higher Education, 30: 305-312, 1959.

205. Ausubel, D.P. and Spalding, W.B. Alcohol and Narcotic Drugs: A Teacher's Manual. Springfield: Illinois Superintendent of Public Instruction, 1956.

206. Auto Accident Rate Soars for Drinkers Under 21 Years. The Union Signal, 99(5): 4, 1973.

207. Auvigne and Perrin. L'Alcoolisme des Buveurs de Vin en Loire-Inférieure. (The Alcoholism of Wine Drinkers in Loire-Inférieure.) Bulletin de l'Académie de Medecine, Paris, 123: 709-711, 1940.

208. Auwaerter, R. Drinking Problems Among Boys. California Youth
       Authority Quarterly, 17(4): 12-16, 1964.

209. Ayars, A.L. and Milgram, G.G. The Teenager and Alcohol. New
       York: Richards Rosen Press, 1970.

B

210. Babor, T.F. Goals, Expectations, and the Perceived
     Instrumentality of Alcohol Consumption as Related to
     Patterns of Drinking Behavior. Doctoral Dissertation
     (University Microfilms No. 71-11,455). University of
     Arizona, 1971.

211. Babor, T.F. and Berglas, S. Epidemiologie im Dienst der
     Prävention: Der Alkoholmissbrauch von Jugendlichen unter
     ökologischem Aspekt. (Epidemiology and Prevention: The
     Ecological Approach toward Alcohol Misuse Among Youth.)
     Drogalkohol, 3(3): 41-57, 1979.

212. Babor, T.F. and Berglas, S. Epidemiology in the Service of
     Prevention: Toward a Systematic-Ecological Approach to
     Adolescent Alcohol Abuse. In: Papers Presented at the 25th
     International Institute on the Prevention and Treatment of
     Alcoholism. Tours, France, June, 1979. Lausanne,
     Switzerland: International Council on Alcohol and
     Addictions, 1979, pages 2-13.

213. Babow, Irving. Alcohol, Youth and Traffic Accidents: A
     Sociological Perspective. Paper Presented at the Conference
     of the International Association for Accident and Traffic
     Medicine, London, England, September 1, 1975. (National
     Clearinghouse for Alcohol Information No. NCAI 021392)

214. Babow, Irving. Functions and Dysfunctions of Alcohol: A
     Sociological Perspective. Journal of School Health, 44(8):
     423-427, 1974.

215. Babst, D.V., Dembo, R. and Burgos, W. Measuring Consequences of
     Drug and Alcohol Abuse Among Junior High School Students.
     Journal of Alcohol and Drug Education, 25(1): 11-19, 1979.

216. Babst, D.V., Deren, S., Schmeidler, J. and Lipton, D. A Study of
     Family Affinity and Substance Use. Journal of Drug
     Education, 8: 29-40, 1978.

217. Babst, D.V., Koval, M. and Lipton, D.S. Attitudes of Youth Toward Drugs in Rural Areas of New York State. Drug Forum, 5(3): 267-282, 1977.

218. Babst, D.V., Uppal, G.S. and Schmeidler, J. Relationship of Youths' Attitudes to Substance Use in New York State. Journal of Alcohol and Drug Education, 23(2): 24-37, 1978.

219. Bachman, Jerald G., Johnston, Lloyd D. and O'Malley, Patrick M. Smoking, Drinking and Drug Use among American High School Students: Correlates and Trends, 1975-1979. American Journal of Public Health, 71(1): 59-69, 1981.

220. Bachman, Jerald G. and O'Malley, Patrick M. The Youth in Transition Series: A Study of Change and Stability in Young Men. In: Research in Sociology of Education and Socialization. Vol. 1. Greenwich, Connecticut: JAI Press, Inc., 1980, pages 127-160.

221. Bachrach, L.L. Characteristics of Diagnosed and Missed Alcoholic Male Admissions to State and County Mental Hospitals, 1972. Mental Health Statistical Note, 124: 1-12, 1976.

222. Backhouse, C.I. and James, I.P. The Relationship and Prevalence of Smoking, Drinking and Drug Taking in (Delinquent) Adolescent Boys. British Journal of Addiction, 64: 75-79, 1969.

223. Bacon, M. and Jones, M. Teen-Age Drinking. New York: Thomas Y. Crowell, 1968.

224. Bacon, M.K. The Dependency-Conflict Hypothesis and the Frequency of Drunkenness: Further Evidence from a Cross-Cultural Study. Quarterly Journal of Studies on Alcohol, 35: 863-876, 1974.

225. Bacon, S.D. Alcoholism and Social Isolation. In: Cooperation in Crime Control. Ed. M. Bell. New York: National Probation Association, 1945, pages 209-234.

226. Bacon, S.D. and Fillmore, K.M. Follow-Up Study of Drinkers in College: A Brief Statement of Progress and Proposed Research. New Brunswick, New Jersey: Rutgers Center of Alcohol Studies, April, 1973.

227. Bacon, Selden D. Alcohol Research Policy: The Need for an Independent Phenomenologically Oriented Field of Study. In: Research Priorities on Alcohol: Proceedings of a Symposium Sponsored by the Rutgers Center of Alcohol Studies and Rutgers University. Ed. Mark Keller. New Jersey: Journal of Studies on Alcohol, Suppl. No. 8: 2-26, 1979.

228. Bacon, Selden D. College Drinking: So What and What Next? In:
      The Domesticated Drug: Drinking Among Collegians.   Ed.
      G.L. Maddox. New Haven, Connecticut: College and
      University Press, 1970, pages 457-474.

229. Bacon, Selden D. Concepts. In: Alcohol and Alcohol Problems.
      Eds. W.J. Filstead, et al. Cambridge, Massachusetts:
      Ballinger, 1976, pages 57-134.

230. Bacon, Selden D. Defining Adolescent Alcohol Use: Implications
      for a Definition of Adolescent Alcoholism. Quarterly
      Journal of Studies on Alcohol, 37: 1014-1019, 1976.

231. Bacon, Selden D. Drug Abuse and Alcohol Abuse - The Social
      Problem Perspective. In: Drug Abuse: Psychology/
      Sociology/Pharmacology. Ed. Brent Hafen. Provo, Utah:
      Brigham Young University Press, 1973, pages 79-83.

232. Bacon, Selden D. Drug Abuse and Alcohol Abuse - The Social
      Problem Perspective. Prosecutor, 5(1): 32-36, 1969.

233. Bacon, Selden D. Education on Alcohol: A Background Statement.
      In: Secretary's Committee on Alcoholism, Alcohol Education.
      Proceedings of a Conference, March 29, 1966. U.S.
      Department of Health, Education and Welfare. Washington,
      D.C.: U.S. Government Printing Office, 1967, pages 7-15.

234. Bacon, Selden D. Our Thinking About Alcohol. Conference on
      Alcohol Education. Meeting Called by the Secretary of
      Health, Education and Welfare in March, 1966, Washington,
      D.C. Journal of Alcohol Education, 12(2): 2-15, 1966.

235. Bacon, Selden D. Relevance of the Social Problems of Alcohol for
      Coping with Problems of Drugs. In: Drugs and Youth. Eds.
      John R. Wittenborn, Henry Brill, Jean Paul Smith and
      Sarah Wittenborn. Proceedings of the Rutgers Symposium on
      Drug Abuse. Springfield, Illinois: Charles C. Thomas,
      1969, pages 44-51.

236. Bacon, Selden D. Social Settings Conducive to Alcoholism. New
      York State Journal of Medicine, 58: 3493-3499, 1958. (Also
      in: Journal of the American Medical Association, 164: 177-
      181, 1957.)

237. Bacon, Selden D., ed. Understanding Alcoholism. Annals of the
      American Academy of Political and Social Science, 315,
      January, 1958.

238. Bad Behavior at Football Matches: Quarterly Notes. Journal of
      Alcoholism, 8(1): 4, 1973.

239. Baden, M. Homicide, Suicide and Accidental Death Among Narcotic
      Addicts. Human Pathology, 3(1): 91-95, 1972.

240. Badonnel. Défaut de Soins et Mauvais Traitement des Enfants.
      (Neglect and Maltreatment of Children.) Revue Droit Pénal
      et de Criminologie (Brussels), 86(1): 39-42, 1962.

241. Baer, D.J. and Corroda, J. Age of Initial Drug Use and
      Subsequent Preference for Other Drugs. Psychological
      Reports, 32: 936, 1973.

242. Bahr, H.M. Family Size and Stability as Antecedents of
      Homelessness and Excessive Drinking. Journal of Marriage
      and the Family, 31(3): 477-483, 1969.

243. Bahr, H.M. Lifetime Affiliation Patterns of Early- and Late-
      Onset Heavy Drinkers on Skid Row. Quarterly Journal of
      Studies on Alcohol, 30: 645-656, 1969.

244. Bailey, B. Alcohol Today, a Workbook for Junior High Students.
      Dallas: Texas Alcohol Narcotics Education, 1964. (Revised
      edition, 1966.)

245. Bailey, J.P., Jr. and Wakely, J.T. Analysis of Education
      Programs for Primary Alcoholism Prevention. (Prepared for
      National Institute on Alcohol Abuse and Alcoholism.)
      (Research Triangle Institute Report Number 24-U-782-9.)
      Research Triangle Park, North Carolina: Research Triangle
      Institute Center for Health Studies, 1973.

246. Bailey, M.B. Alcoholism Treatment in Family Casework. Alcohol
      Health and Research World: 25-28, Summer, 1973.

247. Bailey, Margaret B. Alcoholism and Family Casework: Theory and
      Practice. New York: Community Council of Greater New York,
      1968.

248. Bailey, Margaret B. Alcoholism and the Family. In: Alcoholism
      and Family Casework: Theory and Practice. Ed. M.B. Bailey.
      New York: Community Council of Greater New York, 1968,
      pages 56-66.

249. Baird, K. Special Units Treat Problems of Teenagers. Hospitals,
      54(3): 50-53, 1980.

250. Bakal, Donald A., Milstein, Stephen L. and Rootman, Irving.
      Trends in Drug Use Among Rural Students in Alberta: 1971-
      1974. Canada's Mental Health, 23(4): 8-9, 1975.

251. Baker, D.P. Drinking by Teen-Agers Poses a Growing Problem Here.
      The Washington Post, pages A1, A7, March 30, 1975.

252. Baker, D.P. Lower Drinking Age Affects Schools. The Washington
      Post, pages A1, A4, March 31, 1975.

253. Baker, D.P. Parking Lots are Drinking Hangouts. The Washington
      Post, pages A1, A6, April 1, 1975.

254. Baker, D.P. Schools Offer Little Alcohol Education. The Washington Post, pages D1, D9, April 3, 1975.

255. Baker, D.P. Youth Programs Combat Alcohol Abuse. The Washington Post, pages A1, A12, April 2, 1975.

256. Baker, Joan M. Alcoholism and the American Indian. In: Alcoholism: Development, Consequences and Interventions. Eds. Nada J. Este and M. Edith Heinemann. St. Louis: C.V. Mosby Company, 1977, pages 194-203.

257. Baker, M. Inside Information. Pamphlet. Evanston, Illinois: Signal Press, no date.

258. Baker, M. Temperance Tales. Pamphlet. Evanston, Illinois. National WCTU Publishing House, 1959.

259. Baker M. The Three Partners and Other Scientific Temperance Lessons. Pamphlet. Evanston, Illinois: School and College Services, 1971.

260. Bako, G., Mackenzie, W.C., and Smith, E.S.O. The Effect of Legislated Lowering of the Drinking Age on Fatal Highway Accidents Among Young Drivers in Alberta, 1970-1972. Canadian Journal of Public Health, 67: 161-163, 1976.

261. Balain, P.R. Teenage Drinking, Abuse and Alcoholism. In: Proceedings of the International Conference on Alcoholism and Drug Abuse, San Juan, Puerto Rico, November 10-16, 1973. Eds. E. Tongue, R.T. Lambo, and B. Blair. Lausanne, Switzerland: International Council on Alcohol and Addictions, 1974, pages 141-145.

262. Baldwin, B.H. and Mathis, B.C. Teaching About Beverage Alcohol. Pamphlet. Springfield, Illinois: Superintendent of Public Instruction, 1969.

263. Balint, I. Recent Data on the Aetiology of Alcoholism. British Journal of Addiction, 60: 45-54, 1964.

264. Banks, E. and Smith, M.R. Attitudes and Background Factors Related to Alcohol Use Among College Students. Psychological Reports, 46: 571-577, 1980.

265. Baranowski, M.D. Adolescents' Attempted Influence on Parental Behaviors. Adolescence, 13: 585-604, 1978.

266. Bard, Bernard. The Failure of Our School Drug Abuse Programs. Phi Delta Kappan, 57: 251-255, 1975.

267. Bardan, J. and Leowski, J. Spozycie Alkoholu, Palenie Papierosów Oraz Opieka Spoleczna Nad Mlodzieza Szkolna. (Drinking, Smoking, and the Protection of Schoolchildren.) Warszawa: Prasowe Zaklody Graficzne RSW "PRASA", 1970.

268. Barker, M. L'approche des Usagers de Drogues Par un Service
        Multidisciplinaire pour Adolescents: Stratégie d'un
        Hôpital Universitaire. (An Approach to Drug Users by a
        Multi-Disciplinary Service for Adolescents: The Strategy
        of a University Hospital.) Toxicomanies, Quebec, 8: 249-
        253, 1975.

269. Barlow, T. Alcohol in Children. Medical Temperance Review, 4:
        166-168, 1901.

270. Barnard, G.W., Holzer, C. and Vera, H. A Comparison of
        Alcoholics and Non-Alcoholics Charged with Rape. Bulletin
        of the American Academy of Psychiatry and Law, 7(4): 432-
        445, 1979.

271. Barnes, C.P. and Olson, J.N. Usage Patterns of Nondrug
        Alternatives in Adolescence. Journal of Drug Education, 7:
        359-368, 1977.

272. Barnes, D.E. and Messolonghites, L. (Eds.). Preventing Drug
        Abuse: Ideas, Information, and Lines of Action for Parents,
        Young People, Schools, and Communities. New York: Holt,
        Rinehart, and Winston, 1972.

273. Barnes, Grace M. Adolescent and Adult Drinking Patterns: A
        Comparison of Values and Behavior Associated with Alcohol
        Use. Master's Thesis, State University of New York at
        Buffalo and Research Institute on Alcoholism, 1976.

274. Barnes, Grace M. The Development of Adolescent Drinking
        Behavior: An Evaluative Review of the Impact of the
        Socialization Process Within the Family. Adolescence,
        12(48): 571-591, 1977.

275. Barnes, Grace M. Drinking Among Adolescents: A Subcultural
        Phenomenon or a Model of Adult Behaviors. Adolescence,
        16(61): 211-229, 1981.

276. Barnes, Grace M. Drinking Patterns of Youth in Genesee County.
        Buffalo, New York: Research Institute on Alcoholism,
        1978.

277. Barnes, Grace M. Patterns of Drinking and Other Drug Use Among
        High School Males. Buffalo, New York: Research Institute
        on Alcoholism, 1980.

278. Barnes, Grace M. A Perspective on Drinking Among Teenagers with
        Special Reference to New York Studies. Journal of School
        Health, 45(7): 386-389, 1975.

279. Barnes, Grace M. A Perspective on Teenage Drinking. In:
        Alcohol Problems - Reviews, Research and Recommendations.
        Ed. David Robinson. London: Macmillan Press, 1979, pages
        93-100.

280. Barnes, Grace M. and Colvin, John J., Jr. Alcohol and Other
          Substance Use: Survey of a Western New York Suburban High
          School. Buffalo, New York: Research Institute on
          Alcoholism, 1979.

281. Barnes, Grace M. and Russell, Marcia. Drinking Patterns Among
          Adults in Western New York State: A Descriptive Analysis
          of the Sociodemographic Correlates of Drinking. Buffalo,
          New York: Research Institute on Alcoholism, 1977.

282. Barnes, Grace M. and Russell, Marcia. Drinking Patterns in
          Western New York State: Comparison with National Data.
          Journal of Studies on Alcohol, 39(7): 1148-1157, 1978.

283. Barnes, Judith, Benson, Carole, and Wilsnack, Sharon.
          Psychosocial Characteristics of Women with Alcoholic
          Fathers. In: Currents in Alcoholism. Vol. 6. Treatment
          and Rehabilitation and Epidemiology. Ed. M. Galanter. New
          York: Grune and Stratton, 1979, pages 209-222.

284. Barnett, J.H. College Seniors and the Liquor Problem. Annals of
          the American Academy of Political and Social Science: 130-
          146, 1932.

285. Barr, C.L., Fountain, A.W. and Klock, J.A. Student Drug and
          Alcohol Opinionnaire and Usage Survey, Grades 6, 7, 8, 9,
          10, 11, 12. Jacksonville, Florida: Duval County School
          Board, 1974.

286. Barr, Harriet, Cohen, Arie, Hannigan, Patricia and
          Steinberger, Henry. Problem Drinking by Drug Addicts and
          Its Implications. In: Currents in Alcoholism. Vol. 2.
          Psychiatric, Psychological, Social and Epidemiological
          Studies. Ed. F.A. Seixas. New York: Grune and Stratton,
          1977, pages 269-284.

287. Barrett, J.R. Social Impact of Implied Consent Laws.
          Transactions of the National Safety Council, (54th National
          Safety Congress), Chicago, 24: 82-83, 1966.

288. Barrett, M. Health Education Guide: A Design for Teaching
          (Kindergarten through Grade Twelve). Wynnewood,
          Pennsylvania: Health Education Associates, 1971.

289. Barron, F. Family Relationships, Problem Drinking and Antisocial
          Behavior Among Adolescent Males. Master's Thesis. Lansing:
          Michigan State University, 1970.

290. Barry, H., Jr., Barry, H. III, and Blane, H.T. Birth Order of
          Delinquent Boys with Alcohol Involvement. Quarterly
          Journal of Studies on Alcohol, 30: 408-413, 1969.

291. Barry, H. III, and Blane, H.T. Birth Order as a Method of
          Studying Environmental Influences on Alcoholism. Annals of
          the New York Academy of Sciences, 197: 172-178, 1972.

292. Barry, Herbert. Childhood Family Influences on Risk of
      Alcoholism. Progress in Neuro-Psychopharmacology, 3(6):
      601-612, 1979.

293. Barsby, Steve L. and Marshall, Gary L. Short-Term Consumption
      Effects of a Lower Minimum Alcohol-Purchasing Age. Journal
      of Studies on Alcohol, 38: 1665-1679, 1977.

294. Bärsch, W. Gefährdung Jugendlicher Durch den Alkohol. (The
      Endangering of Youth by Alcohol.) Offentliche
      Gesundheitswensen, Stuttgart, 37: 169-173, 1975.

295. Bärsch, W. Jugendliche und Alkohol. (Youth and Alcohol.)
      2nd Revised Edition. Hamburg: Neuland-Verlagsgesellschaft,
      1976.

296. Bartels, J. Jr. A Report to the Governor's Commission on Youth
      and Other Drug Use Among Youth in Oregon. Report.
      Olympia, Oregon, January 14, 1975.

297. Barth, J.T. and Sandler, H.M. Evaluation of the Randomized
      Response Technique in a Drinking Survey. Journal of Studies
      on Alcohol, 37: 690-693, 1976.

298. Bartoli, G. Les Enfants Victimes de L'alcool. (Children as
      Victims of Alcohol.) Revue D'Informatique, 30: 48-49, 1980.

299. Batchelor, I.R.C. Alcoholism and Attempted Suicide. Journal of
      Mental Science, 100: 451-461, 1954.

300. Baton Rouge Area Council on Alcoholism and Drug Abuse. Syllabus
      for Alcohol Education (7-12). Pamphlet. Baton Rouge,
      Louisiana, 1971.

301. Battegay, R. Alkohol, Tabak and Drogen im Leben des Jungen
      Mannes: Untersuchung an 4082 Schweizer Rekruten Betreffend
      Suchtmittelkonsum im Zivilleben und Wahren der
      Rekrutenschule. (Alcohol, Tobacco and Drugs in a Young
      Man's Life: Investigation of 4082 Swiss Recruits for
      Addictive Drug Consumption in Civil Life and During
      Training.) New York: Karger, 1977.

302. Battegay, R. Comparative Investigations of the Genesis of
      Alcoholism and Drug Addiction. Bulletin on Narcotics,
      13(2): 7-17, 1961.

303. Battegay, R. and Bergdol, A.M. Psychiatrische Aspekte des
      Alkoholismus: Ursachen und Entstehungsbedingungen.
      (Psychiatric Aspects of Alcoholism: Causes and
      Development.) In: Prophylaxe des Alkoholismus.
      (Prevention of Alcoholism.) Eds. R. Battegay and M. Wieser.
      Bern: Verlag Hans Huber, 1979, pages 94-111.

304. Battegay, R., Ladewig, D., Mühlemann, R. and Weidemann, M. The Culture of Youth and Drug Abuse in Some European Countries. International Journal of the Addictions, 11: 245-261, 1976.

305. Battegay, R., Mühlemann, R. and Zehnder, R. Comparative Investigations of the Abuse of Alcohol, Drugs and Nicotine for a Representative Group of 4082 Men of Age 20. Comprehensive Psychiatry, 16: 247-254, 1975.

306. Battegay, R., Mühlemann, R., Zehnder, R. and Dillinger, A. Konsumverhalten Einer Repräsentativen Stichprobe von 4082 Gesunden 20jährigen Schweizer Männern in Bezug auf Alkohol, Drogen und Rauchwaren. (Consumption Behavior of a Representative Random Sample of 4082 Healthy 20-Year-Old Swiss Men Regarding Alcohol, Drugs and Tobacco Products.) Schweizerische Medizinische Wochenschrift Journal Suisse de Medecine, Basel, 105: 180-187, 1975.

307. Battistich, Victor A. and Huffman, Scott. Psychoactive Drug Use in a Midwestern High School: Extent of Current Use and Future Trends. International Journal of the Addictions, 13(6): 975-980, 1978.

308. Battistich, Victor A. and Zucker, Robert A. A Multivariate Social-Psychological Approach to the Prediction of Psychoactive Drug Use in Young Adults. The International Journal of the Addictions, 15(4): 569-583, 1980.

309. Bauer, D.G. The Primary Prevention Project. Health Education Journal, 7(2): 9, 1976.

310. Bauer, W.W. and Dukelow, Donald A. What You Should Know About Smoking and Drinking. Booklet. Chicago: Science Research Associates, 1955.

311. Bauman, Karl E. and Bryan, Elizabeth S. Subjective Expected Utility and Children's Drinking. Journal of Studies on Alcohol, 41(9): 952-958, 1980.

312. Baumann, P. and Ligeti, R. Psychopathologisch Bewertete Beobachtungen bei Kindern von Trunksüchtigen Eltern. (Psychopathologically Evaluated Observations of Children of Alcoholics.) Alcoholism, Zagreb, 5: 63-68, 1969.

313. Baur, E.J. and McCluggage, M.M. Drinking Patterns of Kansas High School Students. Social Problems, 5: 317-326, 1958.

314. Baur, E.J. and McCluggage, M.M. Use of Alcoholic Beverages by Kansas High School Students. Unpublished Manuscript. Christian Social Relations Committee, Kansas Council of Churches, 1958.

315. Beal, L.E. Youth Education about Alcohol: Evaluation of a
         Multi-Level Program Conducted by Teachers and Peer Leaders.
         Doctoral Dissertation (University Microfilms No. 7809573).
         University of Pittsburgh, 1977.

316. Beattie, R.H. Youthful Problem Drinking and an Attempt at
         Alcohol Education. Journal of Alcohol Education, 14(3): 9-
         15, 1969.

317. Beauchamp, D.E. Beyond Alcoholism: Alcohol and Public Health
         Policy. Philadelphia, Pennsylvania: Temple University
         Press, 1980.

318. Becker, W. Alkoholbedingte Jugendkriminalität. (Juvenile
         Delinquency Due to Alcohol Abuse.) Therapie Gegenwart,
         119: 1631-1646, 1979.

319. Beckman, B., Carstensen, G. Pedagogues' Opinions on High School
         Instruction on the Alcohol Question. Tirfing, 35: 65-73,
         1941.

320. Beckman, H., Frank, R.R., Robertson, R.S., Brady, K.A. and
         Coin, E.J. Evaluation of Blood Pressure During Early
         Alcohol Withdrawal. Annals of Emergency Medicine, 10(1):
         32-35, 1981.

321. Beckman, Linda J. Alcoholism Problems and Women: An Overview.
         In: Alcoholism Problems in Women and Children. Eds.
         M. Greenblatt and M. Schuckit. New York: Grune and
         Stratton, 1976, pages 65-96.

322. Beckman, Linda J. Beliefs about the Causes of Alcohol-Related
         Problems among Alcoholic and Nonalcoholic Women. Journal
         of Clinical Psychology, 35(3): 663-670, 1979.

323. Beckman, Linda J. Psychosocial Aspects of Alcoholism in Women.
         In: Currents in Alcoholism. Vol. 4. Psychiatric,
         Psychological, Social and Epidemiological Studies. Ed.
         F.A. Seixas. New York: Grune and Stratton, 1978, pages
         367-379.

324. Beckman, Linda J. Women Alcoholics: A Review of Social and
         Psychological Studies. Journal of Studies on Alcohol,
         36(7): 797-824, 1975.

325. Beckman, Linda J. and Bardsley, Philip E. The Perceived
         Determinants and Consequences of Alcohol Consumption among
         Young Women Heavy Drinkers. The International Journal of
         the Addictions, 16(1): 75-88, 1981.

326. Bedworth, A.E. and D'Elia, J.A. Basics of Drug Education.
         Farmingdale, New York: Baywood, 1973.

327. Beech, Robert and Katz, Bernard. The Values of Middle Class Drug
      Users and their Perspective of the Values of Society.
      Journal of Drug Education, 10(1): 39-48, 1980.

328. Behrens, D. Teenage Drinking: On the Increase or Not? Newsday,
      pages 4A, 10A, December 11, 1973.

329. Beigel, A., Hunter, E.J., Tamerin, J.S., Chapin, E.H. and
      Lowery, M.J. Planning for the Development of Comprehensive
      Community Alcoholism Services: I. The Prevalence Survey.
      American Journal of Psychiatry, 131(10: 1112-1116, 1974.

330. Bell, D.S. and Champion, R.A. Deviancy, Delinquency and Drug
      Use. British Journal of Psychiatry, 134: 269-276, 1979.

331. Bell, D.S., Champion, R.A. and Rowe, A.J.E. Monitoring Alcohol
      Use among Young People in New South Wales 1971 to 1973.
      Australian Journal on Alcoholism and Drug Dependence, 3: 51-
      54, 1976.

332. Bell, J. and Testa, F. Smoking, Alcohol and Drugs: Three
      Resource Units. Grade Teacher, 87(3): 97-102, 105-106,
      1969.

333. Bell, R.G. Alcohol and Loneliness. Journal of Social Therapy,
      2: 171-181, 1956.

334. Bender, R.N. Why Methodist Colleges Ask their Students Not to
      Drink. Pamphlet. Washington: Methodist Church, General
      Board of Christian Social Concerns, no date.

335. Bendit, Emile A. Alcohol and Adolescence: What it Means, and
      What to Do. Primary Care, 2(4): 585-592, 1975.

336. Benforado, Joseph. Alcohol as the Primary Determinant of
      Hospitalization for Drug Abuse Problems in Wisconsin. In:
      National Council on Alcoholism. Papers Presented at the
      Annual Conference, Milwaukee, 1975. Eds. F. Seixas and
      S. Eggleston. Annals of the New York Academy of Science,
      263: 388-394, 1976.

337. Benjamin, Rommel and Benjamin, Mary. Sociocultural Correlates of
      Black Drinkers: Implications for Research and Treatment.
      Journal of Studies on Alcohol, Supplement No. 9: 241-245,
      1981.

338. Benjamin, Ruby R. and Fink, Raymond. Screening and Counseling:
      A Unique Approach to Adolescent Health. Adolescence,
      11(42): 181-193, 1976.

339. Bennet, J.L. and McAfee, D. Two Week Unit on Beverage Alcohol
      fou Use in Junior Year High School. Pamphlet. Ellensburg:
      Central Washington State College, 1970.

340. Bennett, J.A., Chafetz, M.E., Fitzsimmons, M., Fox, V. and
      Ottenberg, D.J. Who Will Help Teenage Alcohol Abusers?
      Patient Care, 9(16): 88-106 (passim), 1975.

341. Benos, Joannes. Die Klinische Dehandlung Jugendlicher
      Alkoholiker in Spezialeinrichtungen. (The Clinical
      Treatment of Adolescent Alcoholics in Special Settings.)
      In: Papers Presented at the 23rd International Institute
      on the Prevention and Treatment of Alcoholism. Dresden,
      June 6-10, 1977. Eds. E.J. Tongue and I. Moos. Lausanne:
      International Council on Alcohol and Addictions, 1977,
      pages 254-260.

342. Bentler, P. and Eichberg, R. A Social Psychological Approach to
      Substance Abuse Construct Validity: Prediction of
      Adolescent Drug Use from Independent Data Sources. In:
      Predicting Adolescent Drug Abuse: A Review of Issues,
      Methods and Correlates. NIDA Research Issues Series, Vol.
      11. Ed. D. Lettieri. Washington, D.C.: U.S. Government
      Printing Office, 1975, pages 129-146.

343. Berberian, R.M. Differential Rates of Drug Use Among Black and
      White, Affluent and Non-Affluent Adolescents. New Orleans:
      Paper presented to the Epidemiology Section of the Annual
      Meeting of the American Public Health Association,
      October 24, 1974.

344. Berberian, Rosalie M., Thompson, W., Douglas, Kasl,
      Stanislav, V., Gould, Leroy C., and Kleber, Herbert D. The
      Relationship Between Drug Education Programs in the Greater
      New Haven Schools and Changes in Drug Education and Drug-
      Related Beliefs and Perceptions. Health Education
      Monographs, 4: 327-376, 1976.

345. Berezin, F.C. and Roth, N.R. Some Factors Affecting the Drinking
      Practices of 383 College Women in a Coeducational
      Institution. Quarterly Journal of Studies on Alcohol, 11:
      212-221, 1950.

346. Bereznicki, M. Alkohol a Przestepczość Na Wsi (1). (Alcohol and
      Delinquency in the Countryside [1].) Problemy Alkoholizmu,
      Warsaw, 21(2): 7-9, 1973.

347. Berg, I.A. A Comparative Study of Car Thieves. Journal of
      Criminal Law and Criminology, 34: 392-396, 1944.

348. Bergman, H. and Agren, G. Cognitive Style and Intellectual
      Performance in Relation to the Progress of Alcoholism.
      Quarterly Journal of Studies on Alcohol, 35(4): Part A.,
      1242-1255, 1974.

349. Berka, J., Začátak Navykových Aktivit u Žáků Zdš. (Use of
      Addictive Substances by Students of 9-Year Schools.)
      (Prispevky z Praxe.) Protialkoholicky Obzor, Bratislava,
      14: 159-162, 1979.

350. Bernocchi, F. Contributo Allo Studio Dell'Alcoolismo Minorile.
      Risultati di Un'Inchiesta e Considerazioni. (Contribution
      to the Study of Alcoholism in Minors. Results of a
      Questionnaire and Discussion.) Annali di Neuropsichiatria
      Psicoanali, Naples, 8: 1-11, 1961.

351. Beschner, G.M. and Friedman, A.S., Eds. Youth Drug Abuse:
      Problems, Issues and Treatment. Lexington, Massachusetts:
      D.C. Heath, 1979.

352. Beschner, G.M. and Treasure, K.G. Female Adolescent Drug Use.
      In: Youth Drug Abuse: Problems, Issues and Treatment.
      Eds. G.M. Beschner and A.S. Friedman. Lexington,
      Massachusetts: D.C. Heath, 1979, pages 169-213.

353. Bewley, T.H. Patterns of Drug Abuse in London and the United
      Kingdom. In: The Pharmacological and Epidemiological
      Aspects of Adolescent Drug Dependence. Ed. C. Wilson.
      Oxford, England: Pergamon Press, 1968, pages 197-220.

354. Bickel, P., Bösch, H. and Uchtenhagen, A. Stoff und
      Applikationsart beim Drogenkonsum Jugendlicher: Eine
      Dimensionsanalytische Untersuchung von Konsumgewohnheiten.
      (Drugs and Their Modes of Application by Youth: A Factor
      Analytic Study of Consumption Patterns.) Sozial- und
      Praeventivmedizin, Zurich, 21: 31-37, 1976.

355. Biddle, Bruce J., Bank, Barbara J. and Marlin, Marjorie M.
      Parental and Peer Influence on Adolescents. Social Forces,
      58(4): 1057-1080, 1980.

356. Biddle, Bruce J., Bank, Barbara J. and Marlin, Marjorie M.
      Social Determinants of Adolescent Drinking: What They
      Think, What They Do and What I Think and Do. Journal of
      Studies on Alcohol, 41: 215-241, 1980.

357. Biener, K. Alkohol im Jugendalter. (Alcohol and Youth.)
      Medizinische Welt, Stuttgart, 187-193, 1966.

358. Biener, K. Bauernjugend und Alkoholkonsum. (Village Youth and
      Alcohol Consumption.) Suchtgefahren, Hamburg, 22: 92, 1976.

359. Biener, K. Die Einschätzung der 0,8 Promille Blutalkohol-
      Toleranzgrenze in der Bevölkerung. (Valuation of the 0.08%
      Blood Alcohol Limit by the Population.) Blutalkohol, 13,
      7-14, 1976.

360. Biener, K. Einflussfaktoren für das Rauchen der Jugend.
      (Motivation Factors for Smoking in Adolescents.) Bulletin
      der Schweizerischen Akademie der Medizinischen,
      Wissenschaften, 35: 111-117, 1979.

361. Biener, K. Gekoppelter Alkohol und Tabakkonsum Jugendlicher.
      (Combined Alcohol and Tobacco Consumption by Adolescents.)
      Schweizrische Rundschau fuer Medizin Praxis/Revue Suisse de
      Medecine, 65: 105-107, 1976. Also in: Zeitschrift fuer
      Allgemeinmedizen, Stuttgart, 52: 512-515, 1976.

362. Biener, K. Genussmittelprobleme bei Bauernmadchen. (Use of
      Alcohol, Tobacco, and Drugs by Rural Girls.) Medizinche
      Klinik, 72: 28-30, 1977.

363. Biener, K. Interventionsstudie zur Beeinflussbarkeit Jugendlicher
      im Genussmittel- und Drogenkonsum unter Besonderer
      Berücksichtigung der Präventiven Sportmizidin.
      (Intervention Study Aimed at Influencing Juveniles in the
      Use of Stimulants and Drugs with Special Reference to
      Preventive Sport Medicine.) Schweizerische Medizinische
      Wochenschrift, 104: 700-704, 1974.

364. Biener, Kurt. Jugend und Alkohol, Series "Helfen and Heilen".
      (Youth and Alcohol.) Klaukreuz - Verlag Bern, 1976.

365. Biener, K. Jugend and Drogen. (Youth and Drugs.) Derendingen-
      Solothurn: Habegger Verlag, 1978.

366. Biener, K. Tabakkonsum im Jugendalter. (Tobacco Use in
      Adolescence.) Fortschritte der Medizin, Leipzig, 95: 31-35,
      1977.

367. Biener, K. Varianzbreite des Drogenproblems der Jugend. (The
      Extent of Variance in the Drug Problem in Youth.)
      Suchtgefahren, Hamburg, 23: 162-169, 1977.

368. Biener, K. and Burger, C. Selbstmordversuche und Abschiedsbriefe
      Jugendlicher. (Suicide Attempts and Suicide Notes by
      Adolescents.) Nervenartz, 47: 179-185, 1976.

369. Biener, Kurt, J. The Influence of Health Education on the Use of
      Alcohol and Tobacco in Adolescence. Preventive Medicine, 4:
      252-257, 1975.

370. Bier, W.C., Ed. Alcoholism and Narcotics. New York: Fordham
      University Press, 1962.

371. Bieringer, G.M., Mülbert, F.M., Schmutz, E.W. and Schmidt, F.
      Drogen-, Tabak-, and Alkoholkonsum Mannheimer Oberschüler;
      Eine Repräsentativumfrage an Mannheimer Gymnasien und dem
      Gymnasium Buchen/Odenwald. (Drug, Tobacco and Alcohol
      Consumption of Secondary-School Students in Manneheim, A
      Representative Survey of the High Schools in Manneheim and
      in the High School Buchen/Odenwald.) Medizinische Welt,
      Stuttgart, 27: 1643-1647, 1976.

372. Bigger, W.G. Child Life and Alcohol. Medical Temperance Review,
      10: 52-57, 1907.

373. Biggs, D.A., Orcutt, J.B. and Bakkenist, N. Correlates of
      Marijuana and Alcohol Use Among College Students. Journal
      of College Student Personnel, 15: 22-30, 1974.

374. Bilodeau, L. Drug Use Among the Students in the Secondary
      Schools and CEGEP's on Montreal Island in 1969 and 1971.
      Quebec, Ontario: Office for the Prevention and Treatment
      of Alcoholism and Other Toxicomanias, 1971.

375. Binder, J., Sieber, M. and Angst, J. Entwicklung des
      Suchtmittelkonsums bei 19/20 Jährigen Jugendlichen. Ein
      Vergleich im Kanton Zürich 1971, 1974 und 1978.
      (Development of Drug Use Among Adolescents in the 19-20 Age
      Group. A Comparison in Canton Zurich Between 1971, 1974
      and 1978.) Schweizerische Medizinische Wockenschrift.
      Journal Suisse de Medecine, Basel, 109: 1331-1335, 1979.

376. Birdsall, Bergen. Teaching Unit on Alcohol Education. Los
      Angeles: California Temperance Federation, Inc., 1955.

377. Birdwood, George. The Willing Victim: A Parent's Guide to Drug
      Abuse. London: Secker and Waxburg, 1969.

378. Biron, Ronald, Carifio, James, White, Robert, DeCicco, Lena,
      Mills, Dixie, Deutsch, Charles and Reid, Gail Levine. The
      Critical Incident Approach to Assessing the Effects of an
      Alcohol Education Curriculum. Journal of Alcohol and Drug
      Education, 25(3): 20-27, 1980.

379. Birtchnell, J. Early Parent Death and Psychiatric Diagnosis.
      Social Psychiatry, 7: 202-210, 1972.

380. Biscogli, A.M.A., Lopez, A., Balducci, L. and Midulla, M.
      L'Intossicazione Alcoòlica Acuta nel Bambino: Studio su
      52 Casi. (Acute Alcohol Intoxication in Children: Study of
      52 Cases.) Minerva Paeditrica, Torino, 27: 1032-1036, 1975.

381. Bishop, Jim. The Glass Crutch: The Biographical Novel of
      William Wynn Wister. Garden City, New York: Doubleday,
      1945.

382. Björking, B. Scouter och Alkohol och Narkotika. (The Use of
      Alcohol and Narcotics Among Scouts.) Alkohol och Narkotica,
      68: 187-192, 1974.

383. Black, C. Alcohol Education: Children of Alcoholics, Part II.
      Oklahoma Nurse, 25(4): 2, 1980.

384. Black, Claudia. Children of Alcoholics. The Catalyst, 1(3): 15-
      21, 1980.

385. Black, Claudia. Children of Alcoholics. Alcohol Health and
      Research World, 4(1): 23-27, 1979.

386. Black, Claudia. Innocent Bystanders at Risk: The Children of
      Alcoholics. Alcoholism, The National Magazine, 1(3): 23-26,
      1981.

387. Black, Rebecca and Mayer, Joseph. Parents with Special Problems:
      Alcoholism and Opiate Addiction. Child Abuse and Neglect,
      4: 45-54, 1980.

388. Blacker, E., Demone, H.W., Jr. and Freeman, H.E. Drinking
      Behavior of Delinquent Boys. Quarterly Journal of Studies
      on Alcohol, 26(2): 223-237, 1965.

389. Blacker, Edward. Sociocultural Factors in Alcoholism. In:
      Alcoholism and Other Drugs: Perspectives on Use, Abuse,
      Treatment and Prevention. Eds. Paul C. Whitehead,
      Carl F. Grindstaff and Craig L. Boydell. Toronto, Montreal,
      Holt, Rinehart and Winston, 1973, pages 98-108.

390. Blacker, Edward. Sociocultural Factors in Alcoholism. In:
      Deviant Behavior and Social Reaction. Eds. C.L. Boydell,
      C.F. Grindstaff and P.C. Whitehead. Toronto: Holt,
      Rinehart and Winston, 1972, pages 310-320.

391. Blacker, Edward. Sociocultural Factors in Alcoholism.
      International Psychiatry Clinics, 3(2): 51-80, 1966.

392. Blackford, L. Five Mind-Altering Drugs (Plus One). San Mateo,
      California: San Mateo County Department of Public Health
      and Welfare, 1970.

393. Blackford, L. Nine Years of Research on Alcohol Use by Junior
      and Senior High School Students in San Mateo County,
      California. Paper presented at the Annual Forum of the
      National Council on Alcoholism, Milwaukee, Wisconsin, April,
      1975.

394. Blackford, L. San Mateo County, California, Surveillance of
      Student Drug Use: Alcoholic Beverages, Amphetamines,
      Barbiturates, Heroin, LSD, Marijuana, Tobacco - Levels of
      Use Reported by Junior and Senior High School Students,
      Trends Shown in Five Annual Surveys. San Mateo, California:
      San Mateo County Department of Public Health and Welfare,
      1972.

395. Blackford, L. San Mateo County California, Surveillance of
      Student Drug Use: Alcoholic Beverages, Amphetamines,
      Barbiturates, Heroin, LSD, Marijuana, Tobacco - Trends in
      Levels of Use Shown in Six Annual Surveys, Junior and Senior
      High School Students. San Mateo, California: San Mateo
      County Department of Public Health and Welfare, 1973.

396. Blackford, L. Student Drug Use Surveys - San Mateo County,
      California 1968-1975. San Mateo, California: San Mateo
      County Department of Public Health and Welfare, 1975.

397. Blackford, L. Student Trends in Drug Use - A Basis for
      Predicting the Future of Alcohol and Drug Related Problems
      Among Women. San Mateo, California: San Mateo County
      Department of Public Health and Welfare, 1975.

398. Blackford, L. Summary Report. Surveys of Student Drug Use, San
      Mateo County, California. San Mateo, California: San
      Mateo Department of Public Health and Welfare 1977.

399. Blackford, L. Summary Report - Surveys of Student Drug Use, San
      Mateo County, California - Alcohol, Amphetamines,
      Barbiturates, Heroin, LSD, Marijuana, Tobacco: Trends in
      Levels of Use Reported by Junior and Senior High School
      Students 1968-1976. San Mateo, California: San Mateo
      County Department of Public Health and Welfare, 1976.

400. Blackford, L. Surveillance of Levels of Drug Use in a Student
      Population. Drug Forum, 1: 307-313, 1972.

401. Blackford, L. Trends in Levels of Use Shown in Seven Annual
      Surveys - 1968-1974 Junior and Senior High School Students.
      San Mateo, California: San Mateo County Department of
      Public Health and Welfare, 1974.

402. Blackford, L.S. Summary Report - Surveys of Drug Use by Junior
      and Senior High School Students in San Mateo County, 1968-
      1976. San Mateo, California: Department of Public Health
      and Welfare, 1976.

403. Blackford, L.S. Trends in Student Drug Use in San Mateo County.
      California's Health, 27(5): 3-6, 11, 1969.

404. Blackford, Lillian. Surveys of Student Drug Use, San Mateo
      County, California. San Mateo, California: San Mateo
      Department of Public Health and Welfare, 1978.

405. Blackford, L.S. The Place of a Continuing Survey of Adolescent
      Alcohol Use in Defining "Alcoholism." Is It an Epidemic?
      In: Defining Adolescent Alcohol Use: Implications for a
      Definition of Adolescent Alcoholism. (Chairman) M. Keller.
      Symposium Presented at the Meeting of the National Council
      on Alcoholism, Washington, May 5-7, 1976.

406. Blair, B., Pawlak, V., Tongue, E. and Zwicky, C. Eds.
      International Congress on Alcoholism and Drug Dependence.
      February 23-28, 1975. 31st. Vol. III. Proceedings.
      Lausanne: International Council on Alcohol and Addictions,
      1975.

407. Blakeslee, A. and Sullivan, B. Alcohol: The New Teen-Age Turn-
      On. Pamphlet. New York: Associated Press, 1975.

408. Blane, H.T. and Chafetz, M.E. Dependency Conflict and Sex-Role
      Identity in Drinking Delinquents. Quarterly Journal of
      Studies on Alcohol, 32(4): 1025-1039, 1971.

409.   Blane, H.T. and Chafetz, M.E., Eds. Youth, Alcohol and Social
          Policy. New York: Plenum Press, 1979.

410.   Blane, H.T. and Greenwald, M.A.   Das MAP-Alkoholerziehungs-
          Projekt für Schüler. (The MAP Alcohol Education Project
          for Students.) Drogalkohol, 4(3): 33-47, 1980.

411.   Blane, H.T. and Hewitt, L.E. Alcohol and Youth: An Analysis of
          the Literature, 1960-1975. Rockville, Maryland: Prepared
          for the National Institute on Alcohol Abuse and Alcoholism;
          Alcohol, Drug Abuse and Mental Health Administration;
          Department of Health, Education and Welfare, 1977.
          (National Technical Information Service No. PB-268-698.)

412.   Blane, H.T. and Hewitt, L.E. Alcohol, Public Education and Mass
          Media: An Overview. Alcohol Health and Research World,
          5(1): 2-16, 1980.

413.   Blane, H.T., Hill, M.J. and Brown, E. Alienation, Self-Esteem
          and Attitudes toward Drinking in High-School Students.
          Quarterly Journal of Studies on Alcohol, 29: 350-354, 1968.

414.   Blane, Howard T. Alcohol Education and Traffic Safety. Paper
          presented at the NIMH-NHTSA Planning Meeting on a K-12
          Curriculum in Alcohol Abuse and Traffic Safety, Washington,
          D.C., February 23-24, 1971.

415.   Blane, Howard T. Current Approaches to Alcohol Problems Among
          Youth. In: Alcohol Problems Among Youth. Proceedings of
          a Workshop in Pittsburgh, Pennsylvania, December 2-3, 1976.
          Ed. Joseph Newman. Pennsylvania: Western Pennsylvania
          Institute of Alcohol Studies, September, 1977.

416.   Blane, Howard T. Education and the Mass Media in the Reduction
          of Alcohol Problems. Paper presented at the National
          Council on Alcoholism Region III Conference on Adolescent
          Alcohol Education, Lancaster, Pennsylvania, February 5-6,
          1975.

417.   Blane, Howard T. Education and Mass Persuasion as Preventive
          Strategies. In: The Prevention of Alcohol Problems:
          Report of a Conference. Eds. R. Room and S. Sheffield.
          Expert Conference on the Prevention of Alcohol Problems,
          Berkeley, California, December 9-11, 1974. Sacramento,
          California: California Health and Welfare Agency, Office of
          Alcoholism, 1976, pages 255-288.

418.   Blane, Howard T. Education and the Prevention of Alcoholism.
          In: The Biology of Alcoholism. Volume 4. Social Aspects
          of Alcoholism. Eds. B. Kissin and H. Begleiter. New York:
          Plenum Press, 1976, pages 519-578.

419.   Blane, Howard T. Issues in Preventing Alcohol Problems.
          Preventive Medicine, 5: 176-186, 1976.

420. Blane, Howard T. Middle-Aged Alcoholics and Young Drinkers. In: Youth, Alcohol and Social Policy. Eds. H.T. Blane and M.E. Chafetz. New York: Plenum Press, 1979, pages 5-38.

421. Blane, Howard T. The Personality of the Alcoholic: Guises of Dependency. New York: Harper and Row, 1968.

422. Blane, Howard T. Rediscovering Teen-Age Drinking in San Mateo: Comment on a Paper by L. St. C. Blackford. In: Defining Adolescent Alcohol Use: Implications for a Definition of Adolescent Alcoholism. (Chairman) M. Keller. Symposium Presented at the Meeting of the National Council on Alcoholism, Washington, May 5-7, 1976.

423. Blane, Howard T. Trends in the Prevention of Alcoholism. In: Frontiers of Alcoholism. Eds. M. Chafetz, H.T. Blane and M. Hill. New York: Science House, 1970, pages 258-267.

424. Blane, Howard T. Trends in the Prevention of Alcoholism. Psychiatric Research Reports of the American Psychiatric Association, 24: 1-9, 1968.

425. Blaney, R. and Radford, I.S. The Prevalence of Alcoholism in an Irish Town. Quarterly Journal of Studies on Alcohol, 34: 1255-1269, 1973.

426. Blechman, E.A., Berberian, R.M. and Thompson, W.D. How Well Does Number of Parents Explain Unique Variance in Self-Reported Drug Use? Journal of Consulting and Clinical Psychology, 45: 1182-1183, 1977.

427. Block, J.L. Your Child...An Alcoholic?. Pamphlet. Salt Lake City: Utah Alcoholism Foundation, no date.

428. Block, Jean L. Alcohol and the Adolescent. The Parents' Magazine, 26(12): 40-41, 87-92, December, 1951.

429. Block, J.R. Behavioral and Demographic Correlates of Drug Use Among Students in Grades 7-12. In: Predicting Adolescent Drug Abuse: A Review of the Issues, Methods and Correlates - Research Issues II. Ed. Dan Lettieri. Rockville, Maryland: National Institute on Drug Abuse, 1975, pages 265-276.

430. Block, J.R. and Goodman, Norman. Illicit Drug Use and the Consumption of Alcohol, Tobacco, and Over-the-Counter Medicine Among Adolescents. International Journal of the Addictions, 13(6): 933-946, 1978.

431. Block, Marvin A. Alcoholism Prevention and Reality: Comment on the Article by M.E. Chafetz. Quarterly Journal of Studies on Alcohol, 28: 551-553, 1967.

432. Block, Marvin A. Could Your Child Become an Alcoholic? Pamphlet. New York: American Medical Association, 1959.

433. Block, Marvin A. How Teenagers Set the Stage for Alcoholism.
      Today's Health, 40: 36-37, 66-69, 1962.

434. Block, Marvin A. Invest in Their Future. Pamphlet. New York:
      American Medical Association, Department of Alcoholism, no
      date.

435. Block, Marvin A. Teenage Drinking: Whose Responsibility?
      Leaflet. Buffalo, New York: Marvin A. and
      Lillian K. Block Foundation, 1961.

436. Block, Marvin A. What's a Parent to Do? Leaflet. Buffalo, New
      York: Marvin A. and Lillian K. Block Foundation, no date.

437. Block, Marvin A., Duttweiler, Dorthea C., Milich, Olga,
      Potter, Milton G. and Monnier, Dwight C. Problems of
      Alcoholism as Related to Health Education in the Secondary
      Schools: A Panel Discussion. Quarterly Journal of Studies
      on Alcoholism, 12: 495-516, 1951.

438. Blocker, Jack, Jr., Ed. Alcohol, Reform and Society: The
      Liquor Issue in Social Context. Westport, Connecticut:
      Greenwood Press, 1979.

439. Blom, G.E. and Snoddy, J.E. The Child, the Teacher and the
      Drinking Society: A Conceptual Framework for Alcohol
      Education in the Elementary School. In: Adolescence and
      Alcohol. Eds. J.E. Mayer and W.J. Filstead. Cambridge,
      Massachusetts: Ballinger, 1980, pages 257-272.

440. Blomberg, I. Alkoholfrågan I Grundskolans Läroböcker. (The
      Treatment of the Alcohol Problem in the Primary-School
      Textbooks.) Alkoholfrågan, 64, 304-311, 1970.

441. Blomberg, I. En Åsiktsändring I Fråga om Spritbuck har Inträffat
      Efter Motboksreformen. (A Change in Attitude Concerning the
      Use of Spirits after Rationing Reforms). Alkoholfrågan, 51
      229-232, 1957. (Also as Ruotsalaisten Mielipiteet
      Muuttuvat Väkijuomakysymyksessä. A Change in Attitude
      Concerning the Use of Spirits after Rationing Reforms.)
      Alkoholikysymys, 25: 199-201, 1957.

442. Blomberg, I. High School Students on Alcohol. Tirfing, 37: 125-
      144, 1943.

443. Blomberg, I. Hur Undervisar Skolan om Alkohol? (How do the
      Schools Teach About Alcohol?) Alkoholfrågan, 64: 194-205,
      1970.

444. Blomberg, I. Lärares Inställning till Kunskapsmoment i
      Alkoholfrågan. (Teachers Attitudes to the Educational
      Materials on the Alcohol Problem.) Alkoholfrågan, 54(1): 2-
      12, 1960.

445. Blomberg, I. Ungdomsfyllerister i Stockholm. En Jämförelse med
      Genomsnittsungdom. (Intoxicated Youths in Stockholm. A
      Comparison with the Average Youth.) Alkoholfrågan, No. 4-5,
      1960; No. 3-4, 1961. (Also in: Alkoholmissbruket Bland
      Ungdom. Stockholm: Centralförbundet för
      Nykterhetsundervisning, 1961, pages 17-30.)

446. Blomberg, I. and Marklund, U. Rapport fran Alkoholkongressin i
      Tours 1979: Om Alkohol-Information och Ungdomars
      Konsumption. (Report on Alcohol Information and Drinking
      among Youth.) Alkohol och Narkotica, 74(2): 6-13, 33, 1980.

447. Blouin, A.G., Bornstein, R.A. and Trites, R.L. Teenage Alcohol
      Use among Hyperactive Children: A Five-Year Follow-Up
      Study. Journal of Pediatric Psychology, 3: 188-194, 1978.

448. Blum, R. and Richards L. Youthful Drug Use. In: Handbook on
      Drug Abuse. Eds. R.I. Dupont, A. Goldstein and
      J. O'Donnell. Washington, D.C.: U.S. Government Printing
      Office, 1979, pages 257-269.

449. Blum, R.H., Aron, J., Tutko, T., Feinglass, S.G. and Fort, J.
      Drugs and High School Students. In: Students and Drugs:
      College and High School Observations. Ed. R.H. Blum. San
      Francisco, California: Jossey-Bass, Inc., 1970, pages 321-
      348.

450. Blum, R.H., Garfield, E.F., Johnstone, J.L. and Magistad, J.G.
      Drug Education: Further Results and Recommendations.
      Journal of Drug Issues, 8: 379-426, 1978.

451. Blum, Richard H. An Argument for Family Research. In: Drug
      Abuse from the Family Perspective. Ed. Barbara Gray Ellis.
      Washington, D.C.: U.S. Government Printing Office, 1980,
      pages 104-116.

452. Blum, Richard H. Drug Abuse and Alcoholism: Issues and
      Recommendations. Journal of Drug Issues, 8: 309-333, 1978.

453. Blum, Richard H. Drug Abuse Research: Some Personal
      Observations. Journal of Drug Issues, 7: 78-86, 1977.

454. Blum, Richard H. Drugs and America's Destiny: Trends and
      Predictions. In: Resource Book for Drug Abuse Education,
      2nd ed. Rockville, Maryland: National Clearinghouse for
      Drug Abuse Information, 1972, pages 19-23.

455. Blum, Richard H. Drugs and Personal Values. In: Resource Book
      for Drug Abuse Education. Washington, D.C.: U.S.
      Government Printing Office, 1969, pages 75-78.

456. Blum, Richard H. To Wear a Nostradamus Hat: Drugs and the
      American Future. Journal of Social Issues, 27(3): 89-106,
      1971.

457. Blum, Richard H. and Associates. Horatio Algers Children: The
      Role of the Family in the Origin and Prevention of Drug
      Risk. San Francisco, California: Josssey-Bass, 1972

458. Blum, Richard H. and Associates. Students and Drugs; Drugs II:
      College and High School Observations. San Francisco,
      California: Jossey-Bass, 1970.

459. Blum, Richard H., Blum, Eva and Garfield, Emily. Drug Education:
      Results and Recommendations. Lexington, Massachusetts:
      Lexington Books, 1976.

460. Blum, S.B., Rivers, P.C., Horvat, J. and Bellows, D. The Effect
      of Contracted Abstinence on College Students' Behavior
      Toward Alcohol Use. Journal of Alcohol and Drug
      Education, 25(3): 70-79, 1980.

461. Blumberg, H.H. Surveys of Drug Use among Young People.
      International Journal of the Addictions, 10(4): 699-719,
      1975.

462. Blume, Sheila B. Research Priorities in Alcohol Studies: The
      Role of Psychology. In: Research Priorities on Alcohol:
      Proceedings of a Symposium Sponsored by the Rutgers Center
      of Alcohol Studies and Rutgers University. Ed. Mark Keller.
      New Jersey: Journal of Studies on Alcohol, Supplement
      No. 8, 1979, pages 96-103.

463. Blumer, Herbert. The World of Youthful Drug Use. School of
      Criminology, University of California, Berkeley, 1967.

464. Bobley, R., Ed. The Family Guide to Good Living: A Practical
      Book of Often-Sought Advice on Common Personal Problems.
      Woodbury, New York: Bobley, 1977.

465. Bogg, R.A. Drinking as a Precursor to Hallucinogenic Drug Usage.
      Drug Forum, 5: 55-67, 1976.

466. Bogg, R.A. Drug Dependence in Michigan Including a Study of
      Attitudes and Actions of the Young People of Michigan.
      Detroit: Michigan State Department of Public Health, 1969.

467. Bogg, R.A. and Hughes, J.W. Correlates of Marijuana Usage at a
      Canadian Technological Institute. International Journal of
      the Addictions, 8: 489-504, 1973.

468. Bogg, R.A., Smith, R.G. and Russell, S.D. Drugs and Michigan
      High School Students: The Final Report of a Study
      Conducted for the Special Committee on Narcotics. Lansing,
      Michigan: Department of Public Health, 1969. (ERIC
      Document Reproduction Service No. ED 059 279). (Especially
      pages 37-41.)

469. Bogg, Richard. Marihuana Use by Michigan High School Students.
      Journal of Alcohol Education, 16(3): 7-15, 1971.

470. Boldt, Robert F., Reilly, Richard R. and Haberman, Paul W. A
        Survey and Assessment of the Current Status of Drug-Related
        Instructional Programs in Secondary and Elementary
        Educational Institutions. In: Drug Use in America:
        Problem in Perspective. Appendix. Volume II. Social
        Responses to Drug Use. U.S. National Commission on
        Marihuana and Drug Abuse. Washington, D.C.: U.S.
        Government Printing Office, 1973, pages 455-547.

471. Bonals, A. et al. Influencia del Alcoholismo Paterno en el
        Desarrollo Psiquico del Niño. (Influence of Paternal
        Alcoholism on the Psychological Development of the Child.)
        Commun Psiquiatria, 77(1): 369-382, 1978.

472. Bonney, M.E. Parents as the Makers of Social Deviates. Social
        Forces, 20: 77-87, 1942.

473. Booz-Allen and Hamilton, Inc. An Assessment of the Needs of and
        Resources for Children of Alcoholic Parents. Prepared for
        National Institute on Alcohol Abuse and Alcoholism. (Rep.
        No. PB-241-119; NIAAA/NCALI-75/13.) Springfield, Virginia:
        U.S. National Technical Information Service, 1974.

474. Borgstrom, S. Promotion of Total Abstinence Among Young People
        by Help of Students and the Universities. International
        Congress Against Alcoholism, 17: 84-94, 1924.

475. Boria, Maria C., Welch, Edward J. and Vargas, Anthony M. Family
        Life Theatre and Youth Health Services. American Journal
        of Public Health, 71(2): 150-154, 1981.

476. Borowitz, G.H. Some Ego Aspects of Alcoholism. British Journal
        of Medical Psychology, 37: 257-263, 1964.

477. Borunda, P. and Shore, J.H. Neglected Minority--Urban Indians
        and Mental Health. International Journal of Social
        Psychiatry, 24: 220-224, 1978.

478. Borzucki, H. Propaganda Przeciwalkoholowa Wśród Moldziezy i w
        Zakladach Pracy. (Propaganda for Alcoholism Prevention
        Among Youth and in Industry.) Problemy Alkoholizmu, Warsaw,
        20(5): 15-16, 1972.

479. Boscarino, J. Alcoholism in V.A. Inpatient Facilities: Some
        Implications of the V.A. Patient Census. American Journal
        of Drug and Alcohol Abuse, 7(2): 237-250, 1980.

480. Boscarino, Joseph. Isolating the Effects of Ethnicity on
        Drinking Behavior: A Multiple Classification Analysis of
        Barroom Attendance. Addictive Behaviors, 5(4): 307-312,
        1980.

481. Bosma, W.G.A. Alcoholism and Teenagers. Maryland State Medical
        Journal, 24(6): 62-68, 1975.

482.   Bosma, W.G.A.   Children of Alcoholics--A Hidden Tragedy.
       Maryland State Medical Journal, 21(1): 34-36, 1972.

483.   Bosma, William G.A.   Alcoholism and the Family.   Addictions,
       5(2): 11-12, 1976.

484.   Boulenger.   Alcoolisme Chronique Chez un Enfant.   (Chronic
       Alcoholism in Children.)   Journal of Neurologie, Brussels,
       13: 145-150, 1908.

485.   Boulin, Bertrand.   Children and Drugs.   Australian Journal of
       Alcoholism and Drug Dependence, 6: 7-11, 1979.   Reprinted
       from the United Nations Publication "Children and Drugs
       (Dossier)."   Prepared especially for the International Year
       of the Child.

486.   Boulogne, H.   Sociological Aspects of Alcohol and Drug Use in the
       Netherlands.   In: Papers Presented at the 18th
       International Institute on the Prevention and Treatment of
       Alcoholism, Seville, June, 1972.   Lausanne, Switzerland:
       International Council on Alcohol and Addictions, 1972, pages
       17-20.

487.   Bourgeois, M., Levigneron, M. and Delage, H.   Les Enfants
       d'Alcooliques; Une Enquête sur 66 Enfants d'Alcooliques d'un
       Service Pédopsychiatrique.   (Children of Alcoholics; A Study
       of 66 Children of Alcoholics in a Child Psychiatry Service.)
       Annales Medico-Psychologiques, Paris, 133(2): 592-609, 1975.

488.   Bourgeois, M. and Penaud, F.   Alcoolisme et Dépression: Enquete
       Statistique sur les Antécédents Familiaux de Dépression et
       d'Alcoolisme dans une Série d'Hommes Alcooliques et de
       Femmes Dépressives.   (Alcoholism and Depression:
       Statistical Study on Familial Antecedents of Depression and
       Alcoholism in a Series of Men Alcoholics and Women
       Depressives.)   Annales Medico-Psychologiques, Paris, 2: 686-
       699, 1976.

489.   Bourne, P.G.   Polydrug Abuse in the U.S.   In: International
       Conference on Alcoholism and Drug Abuse, San Juan, Puerto
       Rico, November, 1973.   Lausanne, Switzerland: International
       Council on Alcohol and Addictions, 1974, pages 249-257.

490.   Bourne, Peter.   Alcoholism in the Urban Black Population.   In:
       Alcohol Abuse and Black America.   Ed. F.D. Harper.
       Alexandria, Virginia: Douglass Publishers, 1976, pages 39-
       47.

491.   Bourne, Peter G.   Alcoholism in the Urban Negro Population.   In:
       Alcoholism, Progress in Research and Treatment.   Eds.
       Peter G. Bourne and Ruth Fox.   New York: Academic Press,
       1973, pages 211-226.

492.   Bourne, Peter G. and Fox, Ruth, Eds.   Alcoholism: Progress in
       Research and Treatment.   New York: Academic Press, 1973.

493. Bourneville, D.M. and Noir, J. Idiotie Congénitale-Atrophie Cérébraletics Nombreux: Recherches Cliniques et Thérapeutiques sur l'épilepsie, l'hystérie et l'idiotisme. (Cogenital-Atrophic Idiocy with Numerous Cerebral Tics: Clinical and Therapeutic Research on Epilepsy, Hysteria and Idiocy.) Information Psychiatrique, 54: 797-802, 1978.

494. Bovet, Lucien. Psychiatric Aspects of Juvenile Delinquency. (World Health Organization Monograph Series, No. 1.) Geneva: World Health Organization, 1951.

495. Bowen, B.D. and Kagay, M.R. The Impact of Lowering the Age of Majority to 18. (Report to the White House Conference on Youth.) Unpublished manuscript, 1973. (NCALI No. NCAI 018 027.)

496. Bowers, C. Troubled Teens. Pamphlet. Avon Park: Florida Bureau of Alcoholic Rehabilitation, 1974.

497. Bowers, E. For Troubled Teens with Problem Parents. Avon Park: Florida Bureau of Alcoholic Rehabilitation, 1971.

498. Bowers, W.J. Normative Constraints on Deviant Behavior in the College Context. Sociometry, 31: 370-385, 1968.

499. Bowers, W.J. Trends in College Campus Deviance. College Student Survey, 5(1): 20-30, 1971.

500. Bowker, Lee H. College Student Drug Use: An Examination and Application of the Epidemiological Literature. Journal of College Student Personnel, 16: 137-144, 1975.

501. Bowker, Lee H. Drug Use Among American Women, Old and Young: Sexual Oppression and Other Themes. San Francisco: R & E Research Associates, 1977.

502. Bowker, Lee H. The Influence of the Perceived Home Drug Environment on College Student Drug Use. Addictive Behaviors, Oxford, 1: 293-298, 1976.

503. Bowker, Lee H. Motives for Drug Use: An Application of Cohen's Typology. International Journal of the Addictions, 12: 983-991, 1977.

504. Bowker, Lee H. The Relationship between Sex, Drugs and Sexual Behavior on a College Campus. Drug Forum, 7: 69-80, 1978.

505. Bowker, Lee H. Student Drug Use and the Perceived Peer Drug Environment. The International Journal of the Addictions, 9(6): 851-861, 1974.

506. Bowles, C. Children of Alcoholic Parents. American Journal of Nursing, 68: 1062-1064, 1968.

507. Boyce, G.A. Alcohol and American Indian Students. Washington,
        D.C.: Bureau of Indian Affairs, Department of Interior,
        1965. (ERIC Document Reproduction Service No. ED 023 520.)

508. Boyd, J.E. A Multidimensional Explication of Popular Notions of
        Alcoholism. Quarterly Journal of Studies on Alcohol, 31:
        876-888, 1970.

509. Boydell, C.L., Grindstaff, C.F. and Whitehead, P.C., Eds.
        Deviant Behavior and Social Reaction. Toronto: Holt,
        Rinehart and Winston, 1972.

510. Boyle, B.L. and Stern, M.I. Myths About Drinking and Driving.
        Pamphlet. Toronto, Ontario: Addiction Research
        Foundation, 1977.

511. Boys' Clubs of America. Alcohol Abuse Prevention Project.
        Examining New Approaches to Alcohol Abuse Prevention.
        (Prepared by Jordan, D.K.) New York, 1977.

512. Boys' Clubs of America. Alcohol Abuse Prevention Project.
        Self-Awareness and Values Clarification Experiences for
        Boys' Clubs. (Prepared by Jordan, D.K.) New York, 1977.

513. Boys' Clubs of America, Project Team. Alcohol Abuse Prevention:
        A Comprehensive Guide for Youth Organizations. (Prepared
        by Jordan, D.K. and Windsor, B.K.) New York, 1978.

514. Bradford, D.E. Ethanol Poisoning in Children. British Journal
        on Alcohol and Alcoholism, 16(1): 27-32, 1981.

515. Bragg, T.L. Teen-Age Alcohol Abuse. Journal of Psychiatric
        Nursing, 14(12): 10-18, 1976.

516. Brain, Rioja, H. Tres Factores de la Delinquencia. (Three
        Factors in Delinquency.) Criminalia, Mexico, 13: 507-511,
        1947.

517. Braithwaite, J. and Braithwaite, V. An Exploratory Study of
        Delinquency and the Nature of Schooling. Australian and
        New Zealand Journal of Sociology, 14: 25-32, 1978.

518. Brajša, P. Obiteljska Patologija kod Kroničnih Alkoholičara.
        (Family Pathology in Chronic Alcoholics.) Alkoholizam,
        Beograd, 8(2/3): 32-49, 1968.

519. Brajša, P. and Kišić, T. Agresivitet Unutar Obiteljske Grupe.
        (Aggression Within the Family Group.) Lijecnicki Vjesnik,
        Zagreb, 91: 1265-1272, 1969.

520. Bramstang, G. Barnavårdslagen och de Underåriga
        Alkoholmissbrukarna. Några Gränsdragnings Spörsmål. (The
        Child Welfare Act and Juvenile Misusers of Alcohol. Some
        Differentiating Problems. Barnavard och Ungdomsskydd,
        37(3): 99-105, 1962.

521. Bratter, T.E. Reality Therapy: A Group Psychotherapeutic
      Approach with Adolescent Alcoholics. Annals of the New York
      Academy of Sciences, 233: 104-114, 1974.

522. Braucht, G.N. Preventing Teenage Problem Drinking: An Enticing
      Prospect, Tried but Unproven. Psychiatric Opinion, 12(3):
      22-25, 1975.

523. Braucht, G.N. A Psychosocial Typology of Adolescent Alcohol and
      Drug Users. In: Proceedings of the Third Annual
      Alcoholism Conference of the National Institute on Alcohol
      Abuse and Alcoholism. Washington, D.C.: U.S. Department
      of Health, Education, and Welfare, 1974, pages 129-144.
      (DHEW Publication No. ADM 75-137.)

524. Braucht, G.N., Brakarsh, D., Follingstad, D. and Berry, K.L.
      Deviant Drug Use in Adolescence: A Review of Psychosocial
      Correlates. Psychological Bulletin, 79: 92-106, 1973.

525. Braucht, G.N., Follingstad, D., Brakarsh, D. and Berry, K.L.
      Drug Education: A Review of Goals, Approaches and
      Effectiveness and a Paradigm for Evaluation. Quarterly
      Journal of Studies on Alcohol, 34(4): 1279-1292, 1973.

526. Braucht, G. Nicholas. Psychosocial Typology of Adolescent
      Alcohol and Drug Users. In: Proceedings of the Third
      Annual Alcoholism Conference. Rockville, Maryland:
      National Institute on Alcohol Abuse and Alcoholism, 1974,
      pages 129-144.

527. Brecher, E.M. and the Editors of Consumer Reports. Licit and
      Illicit Drugs: The Consumers Union Report on Narcotics,
      Stimulants, Depressants, Inhalants, Hallucinogens, and
      Marijuana--Including Caffeine, Nicotine and Alcohol.
      Boston, Massachusetts: Little, Brown, 1972.

528. Breckon, D.J. The Evolution of Alcohol Education in Michigan,
      1883-1968. Master's Thesis. University of Michigan, 1969.

529. Breed, Warren and DeFoe, James R. Themes in Magazine Alcohol
      Advertisements: A Critique. Journal of Drug Issues, 10(2):
      511-522, 1979.

530. Breg, W.R. An Activity Program in Alcohol Education. Journal
      of Health and Physical Education, 12: 561, passim, 1941.

531. Breg, W.R. Alcohol in Youth's World. Journal of the National
      Education Association, 26: 237, 1937.

532. Brehm, M. and Back, K. Self Image and Attitudes Towards Drugs.
      Journal of Personality, 36: 299-314, 1968.

533. Breitenfeld, D., Matas, D. , Pišpek, A. and Mataković, M.
        Gesundheitliche Vorbeugung Gegen den Alkoholismus der
        Jugendlichen am Lande. (Health Services to Prevent
        Alcoholism in Rural Youth.) Alcoholism, Zagreb, 9: 9-14,
        1973.

534. Brickman, William W. Adolescents and Alcohol Abuse. Intellect,
        103: 165, 1974.

535. Briddell, D.W. and Wilson, G.T. Effects of Alcohol and
        Expectancy Set on Male Sexual Arousal. Journal of
        Abnormal Psychology, 85:225-234, 1976.

536. Brigance, R.S. Family and Religious Factors in Problem Drinking
        Among High School Students. Master's Thesis. Mississippi
        State University, 1968.

537. Brightenbach, Lou. Some Observations on the Clergyman as a
        Resource Person in the Classroom. Journal of Alcohol
        Education, 15(3): 15-17, 1970.

538. Brill, N., Crumpton, E. and Grayson, H. Personality Factors in
        Marihuana Use. Archives of General Psychiatry, 24: 163-
        165, 1971.

539. Brisbane, F. Causes and Consequences of Alcohol Use Among Black
        Youth. Journal of Afro-American Issues, 4(2): 241-254,
        1976.

540. British Columbia. Department of Education. Manual of Reference
        for Alcohol Education. Victoria: King's Printer, 1949.

541. British Columbia. Department of Education, Division of Alcohol
        Education. Alcohol Education: Subject Integration in
        Grades 7 to 12. Victoria, British Columbia, 1949.

542. British Columbia. Department of Education, Division of Alcohol
        Education. Manual of Reference for Alcohol Education.
        Victoria, British Columbia, 1949.

543. Britton, W.L.S. Alcoholism and Youth: Some Questions Asked at
        School and Youth Meetings on Alcoholism and Suggested
        Answers. Wellington: National Society on Alcoholism of
        New Zealand, 1966.

544. Brodie, Keith. The Effects of Ethyl Alcohol in Man. In: Drug
        Use in America: Problems in Perspective. Appendix.
        Vol. I. Patterns and Consequences of Drug Use. U.S.
        National Commission on Marihuana and Drug Abuse.
        Washington, D.C.: U.S. Government Printing Office, 1973,
        pages 6-59.

545. Bron, B. Aktuelle Probleme des Alkoholmissbrauchs bei Kindern und Jugendlichen. (Current Problems of Alcohol Misuse in Children and Adolescents.) Zeitschrift fuer Allgemeinmedizin, 52: 505-511, 1976.

546. Bron, B. Alkoholmissbrauch bei Kindern und Jugendlichen. (Alcohol Misuse Among Children and Adolescents.) Suchtgefahren, Hamburg, 22: 41-52, 1976.

547. Brook, Judith S., Lukoff, Irving and Whiteman, Martin. Peer, Family and Personality Domains as Related to Adolescents' Drug Behavior. Psychological Reports, 41: 1095-1102, 1977.

548. Brooks, Cathleen. The Secret Everyone Knows. San Ygea: Kroc Foundation, 1980.

549. Brooks, Mark L., Walfish, Steven, Stenmark, David E. and Canger, Jonathan M. Personality Variables in Alcohol Abuse in College Students. Journal of Drug Education, 11(2): 185-189, 1981.

550. Brotman, R. A Functional Approach. International Journal of Psychiatry, 9: 349-354, 1970-71.

551. Brotman, Richard and Suffet, Frederic. The Concept of Prevention and Its Limitations. The Annals of the American Academy of Political and Social Science, 417: 53-65, 1975.

552. Brotman, Richard and Suffet, Frederic. Preventive Education: School Policy, Pressures and Presentation. In: Resource Book for Drug Abuse Education (2nd Edition). Rockville, Maryland: National Clearinghouse for Drug Abuse Information, 1972, pages 67-70.

553. Brown, Charles N. and Gunn, Alexander D.G. Alcohol Consumption in a Student Community. The Practitioner, 219: 238-242, 1977.

554. Brown, G.E. Alcoholism and Advertising. Congressional Record-- House of Representatives, 122(38): E1327-E1328, 1976.

555. Brown, George W. The Role of Alcohol in Iowa Motor-Vehicle Accidents. Journal of the Iowa Medical Society, 57(2): 130-133, 1967.

556. Brown, J., Matross, R. and Seaburg, D. Student Perceptions of Alcohol Policy Issues. University of Minnesota Office for Student Affairs Research Bulletin, 15(5): 1-9, 1974.

557. Brown, J.D. Illinois Trends in Elementary School Drug Education: Soft Sell. Journal of Drug Education, 3(2): 157-163, 1973.

558. Brown, J.M. Differences in Attitudes of Public School Students
      Toward Selected Drugs and the Relationship Between These
      Attitudes and Drug Knowledge. Doctoral Dissertation
      (University Microfilms No. 72-4065). North Texas State
      University, 1971. (Also see: University Microfilms, 1592.
      Ann Arbor, Michigan: Xerox University Microfilms, 1975.)

559. Brown, R.A. Educating Young People About Alcohol Use in New
      Zealand: Whose Side are We On? British Journal of Alcohol
      and Alcoholism, 13: 199-204, 1978.

560. Brown, R.A. A Preliminary Survey of Drug Use Among Law Students
      in New South Wales: Attitudes and Habits. Journal of Drug
      Issues, 7: 439-455, 1977.

561. Brown, S. Blood Alcohol in Poisoned Patients. European Journal
      of Toxicology, 3(6): 349-351, 1970.

562. Browning, D.H. and Boatman, B. Incest: Children at Risk.
      American Journal of Psychiatry, 134: 69-72, 1977.

563. Brozovsky, M. and Winkler, E. Glue Sniffing in Children and
      Adolescents. New York State Journal of Medicine, 65(15):
      1984-1989, 1965.

564. Brun-Gulbrandsen, S. and Irgens-Jensen, O. Abuse of Alcohol
      Among Seamen. British Journal of the Addictions, 62: 19-27,
      1967.

565. Bruno, J.E. and Doscher, L. Patterns of Drug Use Among Mexican-
      American Potential School Dropouts. Journal of Drug
      Education, 9: 1-10, 1979.

566. Brunswick, A.F. Health Needs of Adolescents: How the Adolescent
      Sees Them. American Journal of Public Health, 59(9): 1730-
      1745, 1969.

567. Brunswick, A.F. and Tarica, C. Drinking and Health: A Study of
      Urban Black Adolescents. Addictive Diseases, 1(1): 21-42,
      1974.

568. Brunswick, Ann F. Black Youths and Drug-Use Behavior. In:
      Youth Drug Abuse: Problems, Issues and Treatment. Eds.
      G.M. Beschner and A.S. Friedman. Toronto: Lexington Books,
      D.C. Heath and Co., 1979, pages 443-492.

569. Brunswick, Ann F. Health and Drug Behavior: A Study of Urban
      Black Adolescents. Addictive Diseases, 3(2): 197-214, 1977.

570. Brunswick, Ann F. Indicators of Health Status in Adolescence.
      International Journal of Health Services, 6: 475-492, 1976.

571. Brunswick, Ann F. Social Meanings and Developmental Needs: Perspectives on Black Youth's Drug Abuse. Youth and Society, 11(4): 449-473, 1980.

572. Brunswick, Ann F. and Boyle, John M. Patterns of Drug Involvement. Developmental and Secular Influences on Age at Initiation. Youth and Society, 11(2): 139-162, 1979.

573. Bruun, K. Drinking Patterns in the Scandinavian Countries. British Journal of the Addictions, 62: 257-266, 1967.

574. Bruun, K. Helsinkiläispoikien Alkoholin Käyttötavat. Tilastollisia Kuukausitietoja Helsingistä; Alkoholvanor Bland Helsingforspojkar. (Drinking Habits Among Boys Living in Helsinki.) Statistika Månadsuppgifter för Helsingfors, 12: 125-152, 1961.

575. Bruun, K. and Hauge, R. Drinking Habits Among Northern Youth. Helsinki: The Finnish Foundation for Alcohol Studies, 1963.

576. Bruun, K. and Hauge, R. Drinking Habits Among Northern Youth: A Cross-National Study of Male Teenage Drinking in the Northern Capitals. (Translated from Swedish and Norwegian by F.A. Fewster.) Helsinki: Alcohol Research in Northern Countries, 1963.

577. Bruyn, H.B. Alcohol and College Youth. Annals of the New York Academy of Sciences, 133(3): 866-872, 1966.

578. Bruyn, H.B. You've Got to Know the Territory. In: The Domesticated Drug: Drinking Among Collegians. Ed. G.L. Maddox. New Haven: College and University Press, 1970, pages 386-407.

579. Buckalew, L.W. Alcohol: A Description and Comparison of Recent Scientific vs. Public Knowledge. Journal of Clinical Psychology, 35(2): 459-463, 1979.

580. Buckalew, L.W. An Instructional Instrument for Increasing Alcohol Awareness. Journal of Alcohol and Drug Education, 25(2): 1-5, 1980.

581. Buckner, D.R. The Influence of Residence Hall Alcoholic Beverage and Study Hour Regulations on Student Behavior. Doctoral Dissertation (University Microfilms No. 68-2790). The American University, 1967.

582. Buckner, D.R. Restrictive Regulations and Catholic College Student Behavior. National Catholic Educational Association Bulletin, 65(4): 33-39, 1969.

583. Buda, B. A Család Szerepe a Deviáns Magatartásformák
     Kialakításában; Különös Tekintettel az Alkoholizmusra.
     (The Role of the Family in the Development of Deviant
     Behavior, with Special Reference to Alcoholism.)
     Alkohologia, Budapest, 3: 81-87, 1972.

584. Bueno, Dario. The Problem of Drug Addiction in Mexico. In:
     Drug Dependence. Eds. Robert Harris, William McIsaac and
     Charles Schuster. Austin, Texas: University of Texas
     Press, 1970, pages 305-314.

585. Buffington, L. Alcohol and Other Drug Use Patterns of Humboldt
     County Students, Grades 6 through 14. Humboldt County,
     California: Drug and Alcohol Abuse Program, 1973.

586. Bulteau, P. and Burns, D. Aborigines and Alcoholism: The Role
     of the General Hospital (Editorial). Medical Journal of
     Australia, 1(11): 593-594, 1978.

587. Bunce, R. San Mateo Annual High School Drug Census - 1975.
     Drinking and Drug Practices Surveyor, 11: 24-25, 1976.

588. Bunzel, R. The Role of Alcoholism in Two Central American
     Cultures. Psychiatry, 3: 361-387, 1940.

589. Burcat, W. Alcohol Education in Schools. Pamphlet. Trenton:
     New Jersey Department of Education, 1969.

590. Burck, C.G. Changing Habits in American Drinking. Fortune,
     94(4): 156-161, 164, 166, 1976.

591. Burdsal, C., Greenberg, G., Bell, M. and Reynolds, S. A Factor-
     Analytic Examination of Sexual Behaviors and Attitudes and
     Marihuana Usage. Journal of Clinical Psychology, 31(3):
     568-572, 1975.

592. Burgess, Louise Bailey. Alcohol and Your Health. Los Angeles:
     Charles Publishing, 1973.

593. Burk, E.D. Some Contemporary Issues in Child Development and the
     Children of Alcoholic Parents. Annals of the New York
     Academy of Sciences, 197:189-197, 1972.

594. Burkett, S.R. Interpersonal Relations and Their Effects on
     College Drinkers. Doctoral Dissertation (University
     Microfilms No. 69-12,595). University of Oregon, 1968.

595. Burkett, S.R. Religion, Parental Influence and Adolescent
     Alcohol and Marijuana Use. Journal of Drug Issues, 7: 263-
     273, 1977.

596. Burkett, S.R. Religiosity, Beliefs, Normative Standards and
     Adolescent Drinking. Journal of Studies on Alcohol, 41:
     662-671, 1980.

597.   Burkett, S.R.   Some Comments on a State-Wide Alcohol Education
        Program.   Journal of Alcohol and Drug Education, 21(2): 30-
        34, 1976.

598.   Burkett, S.R.   Youth, Violence and Alcohol.   Pullman, Washington:
        Washington State University, Department of Sociology, 1972.

599.   Burkett, S.R. and Carrithers, W.T.   Adolescent's Drinking and
        Perceptions of Legal and Informal Sanctions: A Test of
        Four Hypotheses.   Journal of Studies on Alcohol, 41: 839-
        853, 1980.

600.   Burkett, Steven R.   Youth, Violence and Alcohol.   In:
        Proceedings of the Joint Conference on Alcohol Abuse and
        Alcoholism, February 21-23, 1972.   (DHEW Publication No.
        73-9051.)   Washington, D.C.:   U.S. Government Printing
        Office, 1972, pages 1-12.

601.   Burkett, Steven R. and White, M.   School Adjustment, Drinking
        and the Impact of Alcohol Education Programs.   Urban
        Education, 11(1): 79-94, 1976.

602.   Burns, C.E. and Carman, R.S.   Validation of a Measure of
        Motivations for Alcohol Use.   Psychological Reports, 38:
        825-826, 1976.

603.   Burns, J.   Alcohol and Youth.   People, Human Resources, 1(2):
        28-30, 1972.

604.   Burns, T.   Al and His Friend Sam.   New York: Vantage Press,
        1979.

605.   Burns, T.   Getting Rowdy with the Boys.   Journal of Drug Issues,
        10: 273-286, 1980.

606.   Burtle, V.   Developmental/Learning Correlates of Alcoholism in
        Women.   In: Women Who Drink: Alcoholic Experience and
        Psychotherapy.   Ed. V. Burtle.   Springfield, Illinois:
        Thomas, 1979, pages 145-174.

607.   Burtsev, E.M.   O Provotsiruyushchei Roli Alkogolya v Patogeneze
        Narushenii Mozgovogo Krovoobrashcheniya u Molodykh Lyudei.
        (The Role of Alcohol in the Pathogenesis of Cerebro-Vascular
        Disorders in Young People.)   Sovetskaia Meditsina, Moskva,
        12: 91-95, 1975.

608.   Butejkis, J.   Młodziez i Alkohol.   (Youth and Alcohol.)   Problemy
        Alkoholizmu, Warsaw, 21(11): 14-15, 1973.

609.   Butler, F.O.   The Defective Delinquent.   American Journal of
        Mental Deficiency, 47: 7-13, 1942.

610. Butler, J.R., Reid, B.E. and Peek, L.A. Prediction of Drug Use
         Using Life History Antecedents with College Populations.
         Proceedings of the 81st Annual Convention of the American
         Psychological Association, 8: 303-304, 1973.

611. Byler, R., Lewis, G. and Totman, R. Teach Us What We Want to
         Know. New York: Mental Health Materials Center, 1969.

612. Byler, R.V. Alcohol Education in Connecticut. In: Secretary's
         Committee on Alcoholism, Alcohol Education, Proceedings of
         a Conference, March 29, 1966. Washington, D.C.: U.S.
         Government Printing Office, 1967.

613. Byler, W. Indian Children and Foster Care. Washington, D.C.:
         Statement by the Executive Director of the Association of
         American Indian Affairs, Inc., read into the record in
         testimony before the Subcommittee on Indian Affairs of the
         U.S. Senate, 1974.

614. Byrd, Oliver E., Ed. Health Instruction Yearbook. Stanford,
         California: Stanford University Press, 1950.

C

615. Cabral, S.L. "Time-Out": The Recreational Use of Drugs by Portugese-American Immigrants in Southeastern New England. Journal of Drug Issues, 10: 287-299, 1980.

616. Cabrini Health Care Center. 1974 Annual Report Accept Program. New York: Cabrini Health Care Center, 1975.

617. Caddy, G.R., Goldman, R.D. and Huebner, R. Group Differences in Attitudes Towards Alcoholism. Addictive Behaviors, 1: 281-286, 1976.

618. Cadoret, Remi J., Cain, Colleen A. and Grove, William M. Development of Alcoholism in Adoptees Raised Apart from Alcoholic Biologic Relatives. Archives of General Psychiatry, 37(5): 561-563, 1980.

619. Cadoret, Remi J. and Gath, A. Inheritance of Alcoholism in Adoptees. British Journal of Psychiatry, 132: 252-258, 1978.

620. Caffyn, L. Approaches to Alcohol Education. Pamphlet. Topeka: Kansas State Department of Public Instruction, 1961.

621. Cahalan, D. Comment on "Alcohol Misuse and Alcoholism Among Young People" by R.G. Smart. In: Defining Adolescent Alcohol Use: Implications for a Definition of Adolescent Alcoholism. (Chair) M. Keller. Symposium presented at the meeting of the National Council on Alcoholism, Washington, May 5-7, 1976.

622. Cahalan, D., Cisin, I.H. and Crossley, H.M. American Drinking Practices: A National Survey of Behavior and Attitudes. New Brunswick, New Jersey: Rutgers Center of Alcohol Studies, 1969.

623. Cahalan, D., Cisin, I.H. and Crossley, H.M. Demographic and Sociological Correlates of Levels of Drinking. In: Drug Use and Social Policy. Ed. J. Susman. New York: AMS Press, 1972, pages 3-49.

624. Cahalan, D. and Treiman, B. Drinking Behavior, Attitudes, and
      Problems in San Francisco. Berkeley, California: Social
      Research Group, University of California, 1976.

625. Cahalan, Don. Drinking Practices and Problems: Research
      Perspectives on Remedial Measures. Public Affairs Report,
      14(2): 1-6, 1973.

626. Cahalan, Don, Roizen, Ronald and Room, Robin. Attitudes on
      Alcohol Problem Prevention Measures: A Statewide
      California Survey. Prepared for Session on Prevention of
      Alcohol Problems, North American Congress on Alcohol and
      Drug Problems, Toyon Room, Hilton Hotel, San Francisco,
      California on December 17, 1974.

627. Cahová, D.K. K Výzkumu Názorů Mládeže Na Požívaní Alkoholu.
      (Views of the Youth of Southern Moravia on Alcoholism.)
      Protialkohoicky Obzor, Bratislava, 6: 37-40, 1971.

628. Cain, A.H. Young People and Drinking: The Use and Abuse of
      Beverage Alcohol. New York: John Day, 1963.

629. Cain, A.H. Young People and Drugs. New York: The John Day
      Company, 1969.

630. Cain, Vashti I. Alcohol Education in the Youth Community.
      Journal of Alcohol Education, 13(3): 28-36, 1968.

631. Caine, E. Two Contemporary Tragedies: Adolescent Suicide/
      Adolescent Alcoholism. Journal of the National Association
      of Private Psychiatric Hospitals, 9: 4-11, 1978.

632. Calanca, A. Alcoolisme des Jeunes. (Alcoholism in the Young.)
      Bulletin der Schweizerischen Akademie der Medizinischen
      Wissenschaften, 35: 221-225, 1979.

633. Caldwell, Dick. Bangkok and Back. Journal on Alcoholism, 10(2):
      78-82, 1975.

634. Calhoun, J.F. Attitudes Toward the Sale and Use of Drugs: A
      Cross-Sectional Analysis of Those Who Used Drugs. Journal
      of Youth and Adolescence, 3(1): 31-47, 1974.

635. Calhoun, J.F. Attitudes Toward the Sale and Use of Drugs--A
      Cross-Sectional Analysis. International Journal of the
      Addictions, 10: 113-126, 1975.

636. Calhoun, J.F An Examination of Patterns of Drug Use in Six
      Suburban Groups. The International Journal of the
      Addictions, 10(3): 521-538, 1975.

637. Calhoun, James F. Perceptions of the Use of Drugs--A Cross-
      Sectional Analysis. Adolescence, 11(41): 143-152, 1976.

638. California Auto Clubs Offer Junior High Alcohol Program. Traffic
        Safety, 79(4): 13, 1979.

639. California Department of Education. Alcohol, the Study of a
        Current Problem: A Manual of Basic Information for
        Teachers. Prepared by Jesse Feiring Williams, Sacramento,
        California: 1953.

640. California Department of Education. School Health Program
        Component, Alcohol Education Project. In: Criteria for
        Assessing Alcohol Education Programs. Sacramento,
        California, 1976.

641. California Department of Public Health. Alcoholic Rehabilitation
        Division. Alcohol, Alcoholism: Selected Annotated
        Bibliography for Teachers. Berkeley, California, 1961.

642. California Department of Public Health and Welfare. Mental
        Health Division. Summary Report--Surveys of Student Drug
        Use, San Mateo County, California. Pamphlet. San Mateo,
        California, 1976.

643. California Department of Rehabilitation. A Report on Statewide
        Conference on Alcohol Education and Prevention.
        (Conference Proceedings) Held June 24-25, 1970 at
        Sacramento, California. Prepared by L.M. Kent.
        Sacramento, California, 1970.

644. California Department of Rehabilitation. Alcoholism Program.
        Alcohol Education and Prevention. Prepared by L.M. Kent.
        Sacramento: California Office of Alcoholism, no date.

645. Calmes, Robert and Alexander, Sharon.   PAL, A Plan for
        Prevention of Alcohol Abuse - Some Evaluative Afterthoughts.
        Journal of Alcohol and Drug Education, 23(1): 2-7, 1977.

646. Campbell, D. and Watson, J.M. A Comparative Study of 18 Glue
        Sniffers. Community Health, 9: 207-210, 1978.

647. Campbell, E.J.M., Scadding, J.G. and Roberts, R.S. The Concept
        of Disease. British Medical Journal, 2: 757-762, 1979.

648. Campbell, E.Q. High School Drinking: A Preliminary Report on
        Research in Progress. Paper presented at the North
        Carolina Conference on Alcohol Education, Laurinburg, North
        Carolina, July, 1962.

649. Campbell, E.Q. The Internalization of Moral Norms. Sociometry,
        27: 391-412, 1964. (Also in: The Domesticated Drug:
        Drinking Among Collegians. Ed. G.L. Maddox. New Haven,
        Connecticut: College and University Press, 1970, pages 121-
        145.

650. Camps, F.E. The Pathological Aspects of Drug Dependence. In:
      The Pharmacological and Epidemiological Aspects of
      Adolescent Drug Dependence. Ed. C. Wilson. Oxford,
      England: Pergamon Press, 1968, pages 235-263.

651. Campus Alcohol Information Center and Bacchus (Students for the
      Prevention of. Alcohol Abuse). Drinking Fraternity Style.
      Leaflet. Gainsville, Florida: University of Florida,
      Campus Alcohol Information Center, no date.

652. Campus Alcohol Information Center and Bacchus (Students for the
      Prevention of Alcohol Abuse). Responsibility and Alcohol.
      Leaflet. Gainesville, Florida: University of Florida,
      Campus Alcohol Information Center, no date.

653. Canada. Commission of Inquiry Into the Mon-Medical Use of
      Drugs. Cannabis. Ottawa: Information Canada, 1972.

654. Canada. Final Report to the Commission of Inquiry Into the
      Non-Medical Use of Drugs. Ottawa: Information Canada,
      1973.

655. Canadian Researchers Urge Restricted Licenses and Higher
      Drinking Age for Teenage Drivers. Traffic Safety, 76(8):
      25, 37-38, 1976.

656. Canfield, Marsha. Disturbing Patterns in Drinking by County
      Students. St. Louis Globe-Democrat, pages A1, A6,
      November 1-2, 1975.

657. Cannell, M. Barry and Favazza, Armando, R. Screening for Drug
      Abuse Among College Students: Modification of the Michigan
      Alcoholism Screening Test. Journal of Drug Education, 8(2):
      119-123, 1978.

658. Cannon, C.J. Prohibition and the Younger Generation. North
      American Review, 222: 65-69, 1925.

659. Cantwell, D.P. Psychiatric Illness in the Families of Hyper-
      Active Children. Archives of General Psychiatry, 27(3):
      414-417, 1972.

660. Cappiello, Lawrence A. Prevention of Alcoholism--A Teaching
      Strategy. Journal of Drug Education, 7(4): 311-316, 1977.

661. Cappiello, Lawrence A. A Study of the Extent and Integration of
      Education on Alcoholism in the Public Secondary Schools of
      Western New York. Paper prepared for the Western New York
      Committee for Education on Alcoholism, Inc., Buffalo, 1954.

662. Care About Now, Inc. Alcohol and Drug Curriculum. Chelsea,
      Massachusetts, 1978.

663. Care About Now,Inc. Before You Drink, Think. Pamphlet.
      Chelsea, Massachusetts, no date.

664. Carek, D.J. Alcoholism in the Adolescent. Clinical Pediatrics,
      4: 252, 1965.

665. Carifio, James and Biron, Ronald. Collecting Sensitive Data
      Anonymously: The CDRGP Technique. Journal of Alcohol and
      Drug Education, 23(2): 47-66, 1978.

666. Carlhoff, H.-W. Ein Neuer Weg Durch Image-Umkehr: Aktion
      Jugendschutz Baden-Württemberg Initiiert Programm Gegen den
      Alkohol- und Nikotinmissbrauch Jugendlicher. (A New
      Approach Through Image Reversal: The Campaign "Youth
      Protection" in Baden-Württemberg Starts a Program Against
      Alcohol and Tobacco Misuse by Youth.) Jugendschutz, 20:
      173-176, 1975.

667. Carlisi, John A. Unique Aspects of White Ethnic Drug Use. In:
      Youth Drug Abuse: Problems, Issues and Treatment. Eds.
      G.M. Beschner and A.S. Friedman. Lexington, Massachusetts:
      D.C. Heath, 1979, pages 513-534.

668. Carlson, W.L. Age, Exposure and Alcohol Involvement in Night
      Crashes. Journal of Safety Research, 5(4): 247-259, 1973.

669. Carlson, William L. and Klein, David. Familial vs. Institutional
      Socialization of the Young Traffic Offender. Journal of
      Safety Research, 2(1): 13-25, 1970.

670. Carman, R.S. Internal-External Locus of Control, Alcohol Use
      and Adjustment Among High School Students in Rural
      Communities. Journal of Community Psychology, 2(2): 129-
      133, 1974.

671. Carman, R.S. Personality and Drinking Behavior Among College
      Students. Master's Thesis. University of Colorado, 1965.

672. Carp, Joel M. and Goldstein, Melvin. Better Living Without
      Chemistry: Some Program Alternatives to Drug Abuse.
      Journal of Drug Issues, 4: 149, 1974.

673. Carpenter, G. Alcohol and Children. Journal of State Medicine,
      12: 604-611, 1904.

674. Carroll, C.R. Application of the Taxonomy of Educational
      Objectives to Alcohol Education. Doctoral Dissertation
      (University Microfilms No. 65-13,210). Ohio State
      University, 1965.

675. Carroll, J.F., Malloy, F.E. and Kenrick, F.M. Alcohol by Drug-
      Dependent Persons: A Literature Review and Evaluation.
      American Journal of Drug and Alcohol Abuse, 4(3): 293-315,
      1977.

676. Caruana, S. Alcohol Education. Journal of Alcoholism, 4: 124-
      127, 1969.

677. Caruana, S. Alcohol: Education and the Adolescent. In: Notes
      on Alcohol and Alcoholism. Ed. S. Caruana. London:
      B. Edsall, 1972.

678. Caruana, S. and Buttimore, Anne. Nurses' Handbook on Alcohol
      and Alcoholism. London: Medical Council on Alcoholism,
      1974.

679. Caruana, S. and O'Hagan, Mary. Social Aspects of Alcohol and
      Alcoholism. London: Medical Council on Alcoholism, 1975.

680. Case, Helen E. Panel Discussion: Drug Education, Where It has
      Been, Where It is Going. Contemporary Drug Problems, 2(4):
      717-748, 1973.

681. Case Studies of Black Alcoholics. In: Alcohol Abuse and Black
      America. Ed. F.D. Harper. Alexandria, Virginia: Douglass
      Publishers, 1976, pages 61-78.

682. CASPAR Alcohol Education Program. Alcohol Education in the
      Classroom. Evaluation Report No. 8. Background and
      Summary of Selected Findings on the Impact of CASPAR
      Alcohol Education Program on Teacher Training and
      Curriculum Implementation, February, 1978. The Cambridge-
      Somerville Program for Alcoholism Rehabilitation (CASPAR,
      Inc.) December, 1979.

683. CASPAR Alcohol Education Program. The Somerville Story:
      Evolution of an Alcohol Education Program, July, 1974-
      June, 1976. Pamphlet. Somerville, Massachusetts, 1976.

684. CASPAR Alcohol Education Program in Conjunction with Somerville
      Public School Faculty Curriculum Team. Decisions About
      Drinking: A Sequential Alcohol Education Curriculum for
      Grades 3-12. Somerville, Massachusetts: CASPAR Alcohol
      Education Project, 1978.

685. Cassady, J.L. The Use of Parents and Contract Therapy in
      Rehabilitating Delinquent Adolescents Involved in Drug and
      Alcohol Abuse. Paper presented at meeting of Alcohol and
      Drug Problems Association of North America, 1975.

686. Casse, R.M., Jr. and Packwood, W.T. Drugs and the School
      Counselor. Washington, D.C.: APGA Press, 1972.

687. Cassel, Russell N. Drug Abuse Education. North Quincy,
      Massachusetts: Christopher Publishing House, 1971.

688. Cassel, Russel N. and Zander, Gail. Teach Me What I Want to
      Know About Drugs for Junior High School Students. The
      International Journal of the Addictions, 9(4): 541-567,
      1974.

689. Cassie, A.B. and Allan, W.R. Alcohol and Road Traffic Accidents.
      British Medical Journal, 2: 1668-1671, 1961.

690. Casswell, S. and Hood, M. Non-Medical Drug Use in Students.
      New Zealand Medical Journal, 85: 265-268, 1977.

691. Castile, A., Phipps, B. and Willis, R. Beyond the Facts:
      Alcohol - A Value Education Approach. Akron, Ohio: Youth
      Values Project, no date.

692. Castro, M.E., Valencia, M. and Smart, R.G. Drug and Alcohol Use,
      Problems and Availability Among Students in Mexico and
      Canada. Bulletin on Narcotics, 31: 41-48, 1979.

693. Catanzaro, Ronald C., Ed. Alcoholism: The Total Treatment
      Approach. Springfield, Illinois: Charles C. Thomas, 1968.

694. Cavan, R., Ed. Readings in Juvenile Delinquency. New York:
      J.B. Lippincott, 1969.

695. Cavan, Ruth Shonle. Juvenile Delinquency. New York:
      J.B. Lippincott, 1962.

696. Cawthon, Brenda. Many Teen Alcoholics Escape Detection.
      Buffalo Courier Express, page E-2, September 2, 1979.

697. Cekiera, C. Psychologiczne i Środowiskowe Determinanty
      Alkoholizmu Mlodziezy. II. (Psychological and
      Environmental Causes of Juvenile Alcoholism. II.)
      Problemy Alkoholizmu, Warsaw, 20(12): 9-10, 1972.

698. Center for Studies of Crime and Delinquency. Suicide, Homicide,
      and Alcoholism Among American Indians: Guidelines for Help.
      Washington, D.C.: U.S. Government Printing Office, 1973.
      (DHEW Publication No. 73-9124)

699. Centralförbundet för Nykterhetsundervisning: Alkoholvanor Bland
      Manlig Stockholmsungdom Mellan 15-24 år. (The Swedish
      Temperance Education Board: Drinking Habits Among Male
      Stockholm Youth Between 15 and 24 Years of Age.) Stockholm,
      1959.

700. Centro de Estudios Sobre Alcoholismo (CESA). Programa Escolar de
      Prevenció del Alcoholismo: Primero y Segundo Ciclos. Guia
      para el Estudio y el Manejo del "Programa Escolar de
      Prevencion del Alcoholismo. (School Program for the
      Prevention of Alcoholism: First to Sixth Grades and Guide
      for the Study and Management of the "School Program for the
      Prevention of Alcoholism.") San José, Costa Rica:
      Instituto Nacional Sobre Alcoholismo, 1978.

701. Chafetz, M. Why Drinking Can be Good for You. New York: Stein
      and Day, 1976.

702.   Chafetz, M.E.   Alcohol Excess.   Annals of the New York Academy
           of Sciences, 133(3): 808-813, 1966.

703.   Chafetz, M.E.   Alcoholism: Drug Dependency Problem Number One.
           Journal of Drug Issues, 4: 64-68, 1974.

704.   Chafetz, M.E.   Alcoholism Problems and Programs in Hungary,
           Yugoslavia, Rumania and Bulgaria.   New England Journal of
           Medicine, 266: 1362-1367, 1962.

705.   Chafetz, M.E.   Liquor: The Servant of Man.   Boston: Little,
           Brown, 1965.

706.   Chafetz, M.E.   The New Attack on Alcoholism.   Compact, 8(3): 5-
           6, 1974.

707.   Chafetz, M.E.   The Prevention of Alcoholism.   International
           Journal of Psychiatry, 9: 329-348, 1970-71.

708.   Chafetz, M.E.   Problems of Reaching Youth.   Journal of School
           Health, 43(1): 40-44, 1973.

709.   Chafetz, M.E.   Tippling American: On the Rocks.   PTA Magazine,
           67(9): 14-19, 1973.

710.   Chafetz, M.E. and Blane, H.T.   High School Drinking Practices
           and Problems.   Psychiatric Opinion, 16(3): 17-19, 1979.

711.   Chafetz, M.E., Blane, H.T. and Hill, M.J., Eds.   Frontiers of
           Alcoholism.   New York: Science House, 1970.

712.   Chafetz, M.E., Demone, H.W. and Solomon, H.C.   Alcoholism: Its
           Causes and Prevention.   New York State Journal of Medicine,
           62: 1614-1625, 1962.

713.   Chafetz, Morris E.   Alcohol Excess.   In: Frontiers of
           Alcoholism.   Eds. M. Chafetz, H.T. Blane and M. Hill.   New
           York: Science House, 1970, pages 296-305.

714.   Chafetz, Morris E.   Children of Alcoholics.   New York University
           Education Quarterly, 10(3): 23-29, 1979.

715.   Chafetz, Morris E.   The Crucial Challenge: Alcoholism and
           Prevention.   (Editorial, Introductory to Forum: The
           Prevention of Alcoholism, collected papers in Preventive
           Medicine.)   Preventive Medicine, 3(1): iii-iv, 1974.

716.   Chafetz, Morris E.   Prevention of Alcoholism in the United
           States Utilizing Cultural and Educational Forces.
           Preventive Medicine, 3: 5-10, 1974.

717.   Chafetz, Morris E., Ed.   Research on Alcoholism: Clinical
           Problems and Special Populations.   Proceedings of the
           First Annual Alcoholism Conference of the National
           Institute on Alcoholism and Alcohol Abuse.   Washington,
           D.C., June 25-26, 1971.

718. Chafetz, Morris E., Blane, Howard T. and Hill, Marjorie.
      Children of Alcoholics--Observations in a Child Guidance
      Clinic. Quarterly Journal of Studies on Alcohol, 32(3):
      687-698, 1971. (Also in: Drug Use and Social Policy. Ed.
      J. Susman. New York: AMS Press, 1972, pages 223-234.

719. Chambers, C.D., Inciardi, J.A. and Siegal, H.A. Chemical Coping:
      A Report on Legal Drug Use in the United States. New York:
      Spectrum, 1975.

720. Chambers, Carl. An Assessment of Drug Use in the General
      Population. In: Drug Use and Social Policy. Ed.
      J. Susman, New York: AMS Press, 1972, pages 50-123.

721. Chambers, Carl D. and Griffey, Michael S. Use of Legal
      Substances Within the General Population: Sex and Age
      Variables. Addictive Diseases, 2(1): 7-19, 1975.

722. Champion, H. Teach My Child the Facts About Alcohol. Leaflet.
      Bismarck, North Dakota: North Dakota Commission on
      Alcoholism, no date.

723. Champion, R.A. Monitoring Trends in Drug Use. International
      Journal of the Addictions, 15(3): 375-390, 1980.

724. Champion, R.A. and Bell, David. Attitudes Toward Drug Use:
      Trends and Correlations with Actual Use. International
      Journal of the Addictions, 15(4): 551-567, 1980.

725. Champion, R.A., Egger, G.J. and Trebilco, P. Monitoring Drug
      and Alcohol Use and Attitudes Among School Students in New
      South Wales: 1977 Results. Australian Journal of Alcohol
      and Drug Dependence, 5(2): 59-64, 1978.

726. Chanfreau, Diana, Fuhrmann, Inge, Lokare, Vaman G. and
      Montoya, Carlos. Drinking Behavior of Children in Santiago,
      Chile. Journal of Studies on Alcohol, 40(9): 918-922, 1979.

727. Channing, A. Alcoholism Among Parents of Juvenile Delinquents.
      Social Service Review, 1: 357-383, 1927.

728. Chapa, D., Smith, P.L., Rendon, F.V., Valdez, R. and Yost, M.
      The Relationship Between Child Abuse and Substance Abuse in
      a Predominantly Mexican-American Population. In: Child
      Abuse and Neglect: Issues on Innovation and Implementation.
      Proceedings of the Second National Conference on Child Abuse
      and Neglect, April 17-20, 1977. Vol. 1. Eds.
      M.L. Lauderdale, R.N. Anderson and S.E. Cramer. Washington,
      D.C.: National Center on Child Abuse and Neglect (OHDS
      78-30147) 1978, pages 116-125.

729. Chape, F.E. Beliefs and Attitudes of Recent High School
      Graduates on the Subject of Beverage Alcohol. Lansing:
      Michigan Department of Public Health, no date.

730. Chaplan, Abraham and Waldman, Ruth. An Adolescent Health
          Maintenance Clinic: A Community Mental Health Approach for
          Teenagers. Adolescence, 5: 53, 1967.

731. Chappell, M.N., Goldberg, H.D. Use of Alcoholic Beverages Among
          High School Students. New York: The Mrs. John S. Sheppard
          Foundation, 1953.

732. Chappell, M.N., Goldberg, H.D. and Campbell, W.J. Use of
          Alcoholic Beverages by High School Students in Nassau
          County Related to Parental Permissiveness. New York: The
          Mrs. John S. Sheppard Foundation, 1954.

733. Charlotte Council on Alcoholism. Decision Making (Alcohol).
          Pamphlet. Charlotte, North Carolina, no date.

734. Charlotte Drug Education Center, Inc. An Approach to Drug
          Education. Charlotte, North Carolina, 1973.

735. Charnley, J.R. Indications of a Potential Teenage Problem.
          Journal of Alcholism,7(2): 58-60, 1972.

736. Charnley, J.R. Profile of Alcohol Usage by Young Persons in
          Coventry. London: Coventry and Warwickshire Council on
          Alcoholism, 1976.

737. Chauncey, H.W. and Kirkpatrick L.A. Drugs and You. New York:
          Oxford, 1979, especially pages 119-135.

738. Chauncey, Robert L. New Careers for Moral Entrepreneurs:
          Teenage Drinking. Journal of Drug Issues, 10(1): 45-70,
          1980.

739. Cheek, F.E. Family Socialization Techniques and Deviant
          Behavior. Family Process, 5(2): 199-217, 1966.

740. Cheek, F.E., Sarett-Barrie, M., Holstein, C.M., Newell, S. and
          Smith, S. Four Patterns of Campus Marijuana Use: Part I.
          Drug Use. International Journal of the Addictions, 8(1):
          13-31, 1973.

741. Chegwidden, Michael J. Notes on an Alcohol Withdrawal Unit in
          Sidney. Journal of Drug Issues, 7: 391-397, 1977.

742. Child Study Association of America. You, Your Child and Drugs.
          New York: Child Study Press, 1971.

743. Children and Alcohol (Notes and News). Lancet, 1: 453, 1979.

744. Children on Licensed Premises (Editorial). Journal of
          Alcoholism, 10: 137-140, 1975.

745. Chilman, C.S. Lagey, J., Schiller, J. and Johnson, M. Social
     Psychological and Economic Aspects of Alcoholism.
     Washington, D.C.: U.S. Department of Health, Education and
     Welfare, 1966.

746. Chipman, D.A. and Parker, C.A. Characteristics of Liberal Arts
     College Marihuana Users. Journal of College Student
     Personnel, 13(6): 511-517, 1972.

747. Chisholm, C. Alcohol and Drug Addiction in Relation to Women and
     Children. British Journal of Inebriety, 26: 207-217, 1929.

748. Chng, Chwee Lye. The Goal of Abstinence: Implications for Drug
     Education. Journal of Drug Education, 11(1): 13-18, 1981.

749. Chopra, R.N., Chopra, G.S. and Chopra, I.C. Alcoholic Beverages
     in India. Indian Medical Gazette, 77: 224-232, 290-296,
     361-367, 1942.

750. Christiansson, G. and Karlsson, B. "Sniffing"--Berusningsätt
     Bland Barn. ("Sniffing"--Intoxication Among Children.)
     Svenska Läkartidningen, Stockholm, 54: 33-44, 1957.

751. Christensen, H.T. Student Views on Mate Selection. Marriage and
     Family, 9: 85-88, 1947.

752. Christiaens, L., Mizon, J.P. and Delmarle, G. Sur la Descendance
     des Alcooliques. (On the Offspring of Alcoholics.) Annales
     de Pediatrie (Semaine des Hospitaux, Paris), 36: 37-42,
     1960.

753. Christie, Nils and Hauge, Ragnar. Alkoholvaner blant
     Storbyungdom. Statens Institutt for Alkoholforskning.
     (Drinking Habits Among City Youth.) State Institute for
     Alcohol Research. Oslo: Universiretsforlager, 1962.
     (CAAAL Abstract No. 10906)

754. Churan, Charles. Redirecting Psychological and Social Patterns.
     Health Education, 6(2): 14-15, 1975.

755. Cider Drinking - Quarterly Notes. Journal of Alcoholism, 11(3):
     78, 1976.

756. Cisin, I.H. and Cahalan, D. American Drinking Practices: Some
     Implications for our Colleges. Paper presented at the
     American College Health Association Symposium on Alcohol and
     College Youth, Lake Tahoe, California, June 10, 1965.

757. Cisin, Ira. Formal and Informal Social Controls Over Drinking.
     In: Drinking: Alcohol in American Society - Issues and
     Current Research. Eds. J.A. Ewing and B.A. Rouse. Chicago:
     Nelson-Hall, 1978, pages 145-158.

758. Citron, P. Group Work with Alcoholic, Polydrug-Involved
     Adolescents with Deviant Behavior Syndrome. Social Work
     Groups, 1: 39-52, 1978.

759. Clarey, J.W. Drug Use and Its Relationship to Certain
      Activities for a Sample of Male Students in a Private High
      School. Doctoral Dissertation (University Microfilms No.
      75-9094). University of North Dakota, 1974.

760. Clark, C.D., Compton, M.J., Douglass, R.L. and Filkins, L.D. A
      Three Year Comparison of Alcohol Related Driving Behavior in
      Washtenaw County, Michigan. [Based on: Washtenaw County
      1971, 1972 and 1973 BAC roadside surveys. Final report.
      Prepared for Washtenaw County Alcohol Safety Action
      Programs. (Rep. No. UM-HSRI-AL-73-6; HS 801-041.) Ann
      Arbor; University of Michigan; Highway Safety Research
      Institute, 1973.] HIT Lab Report, 4(2): 1-14, 1973.

761. Clark, S.G. and Porter, J. Comparison of Recovered Alcoholic
      and Non-Alcoholic Communicators in Alcohol Education.
      Pamphlet. Springfield, Virginia: National Technical
      Information Service, 1979.

762. Clark, W.A. Black Pride, Drug Attitude, and Drug Use as They
      Relate to Black College Students. Doctoral Dissertation
      (University Microfilms No. 74-16,003). The Pennsylvania
      State University, 1973.

763. Clarke, D.W. Student Report. Teenage Drinking in New Hampshire:
      A Graphic Report, 16(3): 1-11, 1967.

764. Clarke, K.S., Ed. Drugs and the Coach. Washington, D.C.:
      American Alliance for Health, Physical Education and
      Recreation, 1972.

765. Clausen, John. Longitudinal Studies of Drug Use in the High
      School: Substantive and Theoretical Issues. In:
      Longitudinal Research on Drug Use: Empirical Findings and
      Methodological Issues. Ed. Denise B. Kandel. New York:
      John Wiley and Sons, 1978, pages 235-248.

766. Clausen, John A. Drug Addiction. In: Contemporary Social
      Problems (2nd edition). Eds. R.K. Merton and R.A. Nisbet.
      New York: Harcourt, 1966, pages 193-235.

767. Clay, M.L. A Sampling of the Attitudes and Knowledge of Macomb
      County High School Students About Alcohol and Its Uses.
      Lansing, Michigan: Michigan State Board of Alcoholism,
      1964.

768. Clay, Margaret L. Bringing a Lamp to the New Dark Ages. The
      Catalyst, 1(2); 51-57, 1980.

769. Clay, Margaret L. Macomb County Tackles Alcohol Education. The
      Michigan Alcohol Education Journal, 1(3): 25-33, 1964.

770.   Clayson, Christopher. The Role of Legislation in Diminishing
        the Misuse of Alcohol. In: International Conference on
        Alcoholism and Drug Dependence: Alcoholism and Drug
        Dependence, A Multidisciplinary Approach. Proceedings of
        the Third International Conference on Alcoholism and Drug
        Dependence, Liverpool, England, 1976. Eds. J.S. Madden,
        Robin Walker and W.H. Kenyon. New York: Plenum Press,
        1977, pages 401-408.

771.   Clayson, Christopher. The Role of Licensing Law in Limiting the
        Misuse of Alcohol. In: Alcoholism: New Knowledge and New
        Responses. Eds. Griffith Edwards and Marcus Grant. London:
        Croom Helm, 1977, pages 78-87.

772.   Clayton, Richard R. The Family and Federal Drug Abuse Policies--
        Programs: Toward Making the Invisible Family Visible.
        Journal of Marriage and the Family, 637-647, 1979.

773.   Clayton, Richard R. The Family Drug Abuse Relationship. In:
        Drug Abuse from the Family Perspective. Ed.
        Barbara Gray Ellis. Washington, D.C.: U.S. Government
        Printing Office, 1980, pages 86-103.

774.   Clemmons, P. Issues in Marriage, Family and Child Counseling in
        Alcoholism. In: Women Who Drink: Alcoholic Experience
        and Psychotherapy. Ed. V. Burtle. Springfield, Illinois:
        Thomas, 1979.

775.   Cleveland Public Schools, Division of Health Education.
        Instruction About Alcohol. Cleveland, Ohio: Board of
        Education, 1958.

776.   Clinard, Marshall B. The Public Drinking House and Society. In:
        Society, Culture and Drinking Patterns. Eds. D.J. Pittman
        and C.R. Snyder. New York: Wiley, 1962, pages 270-292.

777.   Clinebell, H.J. American Protestantism and the Problem of
        Alcoholism. Journal of Clinical Pastoral Work, 2: 199-215,
        1949.

778.   Clinebell, Howard J. Pastoral Counseling of the Alcoholic and
        His Family. In: Alcoholism. Ed. R.J. Catanzaro.
        Springfield, Illinois: Charles C. Thomas, 1968, pages 189-
        207.

779.   Cloninger, C. Robert. Psychiatric Illness in the Families of
        Female Criminals: A Study of 288 First-Degree Relatives.
        British Journal of Psychiatry, 122(571): 697-703, 1973.

780.   Cockerham, W.C. Drinking Attitudes and Practices Among Wind
        River Reservation Indian Youth. Journal of Studies on
        Alcohol, 36: 321-326, 1975.

781. Cockerham, W.C. Drinking Patterns of Institutionalized and Non-
      Institutionalized Wyoming Youth. Journal of Studies on
      Alcohol, 36: 993-995, 1975.

782. Cockerham, William C. Patterns of Alcohol and Multiple Drug Use
      Among Rural White and American Indian Adolescents.
      International Journal of the Addictions, 12: 271-285, 1977.

783. Coddington, R.D. and Jacobsen, R. Drug Use by Ohio Adolescents:
      An Epidemiological Study. The Ohio State Medical Journal,
      68(5): 481-484, 1972.

784. Cohen, Albert K. and Short, James F., Jr. Juvenile Delinquency.
      In: Contemporary Social Problems (2nd edition). Eds.
      R.K. Merton and R.A. Nisbet. New York: Harcourt, 1966,
      pages 84-135.

785. Cohen, A.Y. and Santo, Y. Youth Drug Abuse and Education:
      Empirical and Theoretical Considerations. In: Youth Drug
      Abuse: Problems, Issues and Treatment. Eds. G.M. Beschner
      and A.S. Friedman. Lexington, Massachusetts: D.C. Heath,
      1979, pages 229-254.

786. Cohen, Allan Y. Alternatives to Drug Abuse: Steps Toward
      Prevention. Pamphlet. National Clearinghouse for Drug
      Abuse Information, 1973. (NCDAI Publication No. 14, DHEW
      Publication No. [ADM] 75-197).

787. Cohen, Gary, Collins, Hugh and Susmilch, Charles. Personality
      Characteristics and Social Background of the Lysergic Acid
      Diethylamide User. In: New Aspects of Analytical and
      Clinical Toxicology. Eds. J. Singh and H. Lal. New York:
      Stratton, 1974, pages 263-271.

788. Cohen, M. and Klein, D. Age of Onset of Drug Abuse in
      Psychiatric Inpatients. Archives of General Psychiatry, 26:
      266-269, 1972.

789. Cohen, M. and Klein, D. Drug Abuse in a Young Psychiatric
      Population. American Journal of Orthopsychiatry, 40(3):
      448-455, 1970.

790. Cohen, S. Teenage Drinking: The Bottle Babies. Drug Abuse and
      Alcoholism Newsletter, 4(7): no pages, 1975.

791. Cohen, Sidney. The Drug Dilemma: A Partial Solution. In:
      Resource Book for Drug Abuse Education. American
      Association for Health, Physical Education and Recreation.
      Washington, D.C.: U.S. Government Printing Office, 1969,
      pages 14-17.

792. Cohen, Sidney, The Substance Abuse Problems. New York: The
      Haworth Press, 1981.

793. Colasuonno, T.M. Alcohol and Juvenile Delinquency. Portland,
         Oregon: Mental Health Division, Alcohol and Drug Section,
         1968. (NCALI No. NCAI 011252)

794. Cole, Steven, Cole, Elizabeth, Lehman, Wayne and Jones, Alvin.
         The Combined Treatment of Drug and Alcohol Abusers: An
         Overview. Journal of Drug Issues, 11(1): 109-122, 1981.

795. Cole, William. Are We Overlooking Our No. 1 Drug Problem.
         Parents and Better Family Living, 48(6): 42-43, 68, 1973.

796. Coleman, J.C. Who Leads Who Astray? Causes of Anti-Social
         Behavior in Adolescence. Journal of Adolescence, 2: 179-
         185, 1979.

797. Coleman, S.B. Sib Group Therapy: A Prevention Program for
         Siblings from Drug-Addicted Families. International Journal
         of the Addictions, 13: 115-127, 1978.

798. Coleman, Sandra. Siblings in Session. In: Family Therapy of
         Drug and Alcohol Abuse. Eds. E. Kaufman and P.N. Kaufman.
         New York: Gardner Press, 1979, pages 131-143.

799. A College President Faces the Alcohol Problem. American Issue,
         77(10): 4, 1970.

800. College-Student Drinking Since Prohibition. Literary Digest,
         90(2): 30-31, 45-73, 1926.

801. College Student Editors on College Drinking. The Literary
         Digest, 90(2):24-25, 44-57, 1926.

802. Collett, J. Fyllerisiffrorna 1972. (The 1972 Statistics on
         Drunkenness.) Alkohol och Narkotica, 67: 156-157, 1973.

803. Collett, J. Fyllerisiffrorna 1975. (Numerical Data on
         Drunkenness in 1975.) Alkohol och Narkotica, 70(4): 13-15,
         1976.

804. Collier, J.L. New Drug Menace: Teen-Age Drinking. New York:
         Reader's Digest, 109-113, April, 1975.

805. Collins, R. Lorraine and Marlatt, G. Alan. Social Modeling as a
         Determinant of Drinking Behavior. Implications for
         Prevention and Treatment. Addictive Behaviors, 6(3): 233-
         240, 1981.

806. Collins, W. A Study of Drinking Behavior at a College Drinking
         Spa. Journal of Alcohol Education, 13(2): 30-36, 1967.

807. Colorado Committee for Self-Regulation. Click? Pamphlet.
         Denver, Colorado, no date.

808. Colorado Committee for Self-Regulation. Lose Your Wheels?
         Pamphlet. Denver, Colorado, no date.

809.   Colorado Committee for Self-Regulation. A Square Thought About
       Your Wheels. Leaflet. Denver, Colorado, no date.

810.   Colorado Department of Public Health, Alcoholism Division.
       Alcoholism Education: An Annotated Bibliography for
       Educators. (Alcoholism Publication No. 3) Denver,
       Colorado, 1966.

811.   Colorado Facilitator Project. Resource Guide to Alcohol/Drug
       Prevention Programs in Colorado Schools. Pamphlet.
       Longmont, 1975.

812.   Coltoff, P. and Luks, A. Preventing Child Maltreatment: Begin
       With the Parent. An Early Warning System. New York: New
       York City Affiliate, Inc., 1978.

813.   Committee on Alcoholism and Drug Abuse of Greater New Orleans.
       Master Plan for Schools and General Data. Pamphlet. New
       Orleans, no date.

814.   Committee on Alcoholism for Greater New Orleans. Alcoholism--A
       High School Syllabus--Grades 9-12. Pamphlet. New Orleans,
       no date.

815.   Committee on Youth, American Academy of Pediatrics. Alcohol
       Consumption: An Adolescent Problem. Pediatrics, 55(4):
       557-559, 1975.

816.   Conger, John Janeway. Adolescence and Youth: Psychological
       Development in a Changing World. New York: Harper and
       Row, 1977.

817.   Conjeski, R., Casbeer, D., Welte, J., Russell, M., Barnes, G.
       and Greizerstein, H. Alcohol Consumption in New York State.
       Detailed Report and Supplement. Buffalo, New York:
       Research Institute on Alcoholism, 1980.

818.   Conley, J.J. Family Configuration as an Etiological Factor in
       Alcoholism. Journal of Abnormal Psychology, 89: 670-673,
       1980.

819.   Connecticut Department of Education. Suggested Approach to
       Alcohol Education in Connecticut Schools: A Guide to
       Action. Hartford, Connecticut, 1949.

820.   Connecticut Department of Education, Bureau of Elementary and
       Secondary Education, and Connecticut State Department of
       Mental Health, Alcoholism Division. Teaching About Alcohol
       in Connecticut Schools: A Guide for Teachers and
       Administrators. (Connecticut State Department of Education
       Bulletin No. 99.) Hartford, 1966. (Also as: Connecticut
       Department of Education and State Department of Mental
       Health. Teaching About Alcohol in Connecticut Schools.
       (Bulletin No. 99, 2nd printing.) Hartford, Connecticut,
       1966.

821. Connecticut General Assembly. Teenage Alcohol Use Study
      Commission. Teenage Drinking in Connecticut. Hartford,
      Connecticut, 1966.

822. Connor, Bernadette. An Evaluation of Alcohol Education Methods.
      Journal of Alcohol and Drug Education, 26(2): 39-42, 1981.

823. Connor, R. An Investigation of Parental Attitudes toward
      Drinking and Five Additional Factors in the Childhood
      Environment of Alcoholics. Master's Thesis. University
      of Washington, 1953.

824. Connor, W.D. Deviance in Soviet Society: Crime, Delinquency
      and Alcoholism. New York: Columbia University Press, 1972.

825. Conroy, Gladys E. and Brayer, Herbert O. Teen Involvement for
      Drug Abuse Prevention. Rockville, Maryland: U.S.
      Department of Health, Education and Welfare/National
      Institute on Drug Abuse, 1978.

826. Cooper, D.F. The Young Skid-Row Man. Doctoral Dissertation
      (University Microfilms No. 77-29904). University of
      Colorado at Boulder, 1977.

827. Cooper, Mitch A. and Sobell, Mark B. Does Alcohol Education
      Prevent Alcohol Problems?: Need for Evaluation. Journal
      of Alcohol and Drug Education, 25(1): 54-63, 1979.

828. Cooperative Commission on the Study of Alcoholism. Alcohol
      Problems: A Report to the Nation. (Prepared by
      Thomas F.A. Plaut.) New York: Oxford University Press,
      1967.

829. Corder, B.W. and Showalter, R.K. Health Science and College
      Life. Dubuque, Iowa: William C. Brown Co., 1972.

830. Corder, Brice W., Dezelsky, Thomas L., Toohey, Jack V. and
      Tow, Patrick K. An Analysis of Trends in Drug Use Behavior
      at Five American Universities. Journal of School Health,
      44(7): no pages, 1974.

831. Corder, Brice W., Smith, Ronald A. and Swisher, John D. Drug
      Abuse Prevention. Dubuque, Iowa: William C. Brown Co.,
      1975.

832. Cork, R.M. The Forgotten Children. Toronto: Addiction
      Research Foundation, 1969.

833. Cork, R.M., ed. The Forgotten Children: A Study of Children
      with Alcoholic Parents. In: The Forgotten Child. Ed.
      R.M. Cork. Toronto: Addiction Research Foundation, 1979,
      pages 19-41.

834. Cork, R.M. The Forgotten Children. Who are They? In: Deviant
      Behavior and Social Reaction. Eds. C.L. Boydell,
      C.F. Grindstaff and P.C. Whitehead. Toronto: Holt,
      Rinehart and Winston, 1972, pages 275-286. (Also in:
      Alcohol and Other Drugs: Perspectives on Use, Abuse,
      Treatment and Prevention. Eds. Paul C. Whitehead,
      Carl F. Grindstaff and Craig L. Boydell. Toronto,
      Montreal: Holt, Rinehart and Winston, 1973, pages 23-34.

835. Cornacchia, Harold, Bentel, David and Smith, David. Drugs in
      the Classroom. St. Louis: Mosby Company, 1973.

836. Cornacchia, Harold, J., Bental, David J. and Smith, David E.
      Drugs in the Classroom: A Conceptual Model for School
      Programs. St. Louis: C.V. Mosby, 1973 (2nd edition,
      1978).

837. Cornsweet, A.C. and Locke, B. Alcohol as a Factor in Naval
      Delinquencies. Navy Medical Bulletin, 46: 1690-1695, 1946.

838. Cosper, R., Mozersky, K. Social Correlates of Drinking and
      Driving. Quarterly Journal of Studies on Alcohol, 29
      (Supplement No. 4): 58-117, 1968.

839. Costly and Deadly. The Hidden Brook Current, 2(1): 1, 1973.

840. Cotroneo, Margaret and Krasner, Barbara R. Addiction,
      Alienation and Parenting. Nursing Clinics of North
      America, 11(3): 517-525, 1976.

841. Cotton, Nancy S. The Familial Incidence of Alcoholism. Journal
      of Studies on Alcohol, 40(1): 89-116, 1979.

842. Cowan, R. and Roth, R. The Turned-On Generation: Where Will
      They Turn To? Journal of Drug Education, 2: 39-47, 1972.

843. Cowley, J.C.P. Education About Alcohol--We have Been This Way
      Before. Royal Society Health Journal, 97(1): 26-28, 1977.

844. Cox, William F., Jr. and Luhrs, Joyce A. Relationship Between
      Locus of Control and Alcohol and Drug-Related Behaviors in
      Teenagers. Social Behavior and Personality, 6(2): 191-194,
      1978.

845. Craig, Robert. Characteristics of Inner-City Heroin Addicts
      Applying for Treatment in a Veteran Administration Hospital
      Drug Program (Chicago). International Journal of the
      Addictions, 15(3): 409-418, 1980.

846. Craig, S. and Brown, B.S. Comparison of Youthful Heroin Users
      and Nonusers from One Urban Community. International
      Journal of the Addictions, 10(1): 53-64, 1975.

847.   Cramer, M.J. and Blacker, E. "Early" and "Late" Problem
        Drinkers among Female Prisoners. Journal of Health and
        Human Behavior, 4: 282-290, 1963.

848.   Cramer, M.J. and Blacker, E. Social Class and Drinking
        Experience of Female Drunkenness Offenders. Journal of
        Health and Human Behavior, 7: 276-283, 1966.

849.   Cranford, V. and Seliger, R.V. Alcohol Psychopathology in a
        Family Constellation. Journal of Criminal Psychopathology,
        5: 571-583, 1944.

850.   Crawford, C.O., ed. Health and the Family: A Medical-
        Sociological Analysis. New York: Macmillan, 1971.

851.   Crawford, D.C. An Open Letter to Bill, the Bartender. Leaflet.
        Evanston, Illinois: Signal Press, no date.

852.   Crémieux, Albert, Cain, J. and Rabattu, J. Toxicomanie
        Alcoolique et Ortédrinique chez un Déséquilibré de la
        Sexualité. (Alcohol and Ortedrine Addiction in a Sexual
        Deviant.) Annales Médico-Psychologiques, Paris, 106: 497-
        501, 1948.

853.   Crisis Center Aids Youthful Clients. Journal of Alcohol and
        Drug Education, 20(3): 50-51, 1975.

854.   Crisp, Anthony D. Making Substance Abuse Prevention Relevant to
        Low-Income Black Neighborhoods. Journal of Psychedelic
        Drugs, 12(1): 13-19, 1980.

855.   Crisp, Anthony D. Making Substance Abuse Prevention Relevant to
        Low-Income Black Neighborhoods. II. Research Findings.
        Journal of Psychedelic Drugs, 12(2): 139-156, 1980.

856.   Critchley, C.H. and Gardner, J.M. A Pilot Study of the
        Relationship Between Need for Power and Drinking in 18 and
        21 Year old Males. Australian Journal of Alcoholism and
        Drug Dependence, 2: 86-88, 1975.

857.   Crites, J. and Schuckit, M.A. Solvent Misuse in Adolescents at a
        Community Alcohol Center. Journal of Clinical Psychiatry,
        40: 39-43, 1979.

858.   Cross, Herbert J. and Kleinhesselink, Randall R. Theoretical
        Speculations about Marijuana and Drug Issues. In:
        Differential Treatment of Drug and Alcohol Abusers. Eds.
        C.S. Davis and M.R. Schmidt. Palm Springs, California:
        ETC Publications, 1977, pages 45-53.

859.   Cross, Jay. Guide to the Community Control of Alcoholism. New
        York: American Public Health Association, 1968.

860. Cross, Wilbur. Kids and Booze: What You Must Know to Help Them.
      New York: E.P. Dutton, 1979.

861. Crossman, Leonard H. Rutgers Student Alcohol Project: Open
      Systems Perspective. Journal of Alcohol and Drug
      Education, 26(3): 23-29, 1981.

862. Crowthers, J.D. A History of Text-Book Teachings of Alcohol and
      Narcotics in Common Schools. Quarterly Journal of
      Inebriety, 24: 43-52, 1902.

863. Crumpton, E. and Brill, N.Q. Personality Factors Associated
      with Frequency of Marijuana Use. California Medicine,
      115(3): 11-15, 1971.

864. Cuarón, A.Q. Alcoholismo y Delincuencia. (Alcoholism and
      Delinquency.) Revista Mexicana Sociologia, 2: 41-53, 1940.

865. Cukalovic, T. Alcoholism and Juvenile Delinquency--Some
      Characteristic Cases from the Region of Niš. Alcoholism,
      Zagreb, 7: 38-41, 1971.

866. Cullen, K.J. and Woodings, T. Alcohol, Tobacco and Analgesics-
      Busselton, 1972. Medical Journal of Australia, 2(6): 71-
      79, 1975.

867. Cureton, L.M. Arrests for Drunkenness of Young Adults and Their
      Parents and Adolescent Behavior Problems. Palo Alto,
      California: American Institutes for Research, 1973.

868. Cureton, Louise. Project Talent: Arrests for Drunkenness of
      Young Adults and Their Parents and Adolescent Behavior
      Problems. Palo Alto, California: American Institutes for
      Research, 1973.

869. Cureton, Louise W. Parents' Police Records for Drunkenness and
      Behavior Problems of Their Children. In: Research on
      Alcoholism: Clinical Problems and Special Populations.
      Proceedings of the First Annual Alcoholism Conference of
      the National Institute of Alcoholism and Alcohol Abuse.
      Ed. Morris E. Chafetz. Washington, D.C., June 25-26, 1971,
      pages 262-265.

870. Curlee, Joan. Alcoholic Women: Some Considerations for Further
      Research. Bulletin of the Menninger Clinic, 31(3): 154-
      163, 1967.

871. Curlee-Salisbury, J. When the Woman You Love is an Alcoholic.
      St. Meinrad, Indiana: Abbey Press, 1978.

872. Curley, R.T. Drinking Patterns of the Mescalero Apache.
      Quarterly Journal of Studies on Alcohol, 28: 116-131, 1967.

873. Currie, Raymond, Linden, Rick and Driedger, Leo. Properties of
      Norms as Predictors of Alcohol Use among Mennonites.
      Journal of Drug Issues, 10(1): 93-107, 1980.

874. Curtis, L.R. Alcohol...or Highway Safety? Pamphlet. Dallas:
      Texas Alcohol Narcotics Education, 1970.

875. Curtis, R.H. Questions and Answers About Alcoholism. Englewood
      Cliffs, New Jersey: Prentice-Hall, 1976.

876. Custer, W. Early Drinking Behavior and Social Background of
      College Men. Master's Thesis. University of Montana, 1966.

877. Cutler, R. and Storm, T. Drinking Practices in Three British
      Columbia Cities: II. Student Survey. Vancouver:
      Alcoholism Foundation of British Columbia, 1973.

878. Cutler, R.E. and Storm, Thomas. Observational Study of Alcohol
      Consumption in Natural Settings: The Vancouver Beer
      Parlor. Quarterly Journal of Studies on Alcohol, 36(9):
      1173-1183, 1975.

879. Cutter, H.S. Conflict Models, Games, and Drinking Patterns.
      Journal of Psychology, 58: 361-367, 1964.

880. Cutter, Henry S.G. and Fisher, Joseph C. Family Experience and
      the Motives for Drinking. The International Journal of
      the Addictions, 15(3): 339-359, 1980.

881. Czeszejko-Sochacki, Z. Przestepstwo Rozpijania Maloletniego.
      (Drunkenness and Crime Among Children.) Warszawa: Wydawn.
      Prawnicze, 1975.

D

882. Dahlberg, G. Könssjukdomar och Alkohol. (Veneral Disease and Alcohol.) Svenska Läkartidningen, Stockholm, 46: 2436-2445, 1949. (Also in: Tirfing, 43: 92-100, 1949.

883. Dahlberg, G. Outlook on "Juvenile Inebriety." Tirfing, 41: 73-78, 1947.

884. Dahlgren, L. Female Alcoholics. III. Development and Pattern of Problem Drinking. Acta Psychiatrica Scandinavica, 57: 325-335, 1978.

885. Dahlgren, L. Special Problems in Female Alcoholism. British Journal of Addiction, 70 (Supplement 1): 18-24, 1975.

886. Dalgard, O.S. Unge Voldsforbrytere og Deres Senere Utvikling. (Young Assaulters and Their Later Development.) Nordisk Psykiatrisk Tidsskrift, Kungsbacha, Sweden, 18: 371-385, 1964.

887. Dalis, G.T. and Strasser, B.B. Teaching Strategies for Values Awareness and Decision Making in Health Education. Thorofare, New Jersey: Slack, 1978.

888. Dalla Volta, A. Accettazione e Rifiuto Delle Bevande Alcooliche nel Bambino. (Acceptance and Refusal of Alcoholic Beverages by the Child.) Archivo di Psicologia, Neurologia e Psichiatria, 16: 245-264, 1955.

889. Dalla Volta, A. Alcoolismo Infantile e Influenza Dell'Ambiente Familiare. (Alcoholism in Children and the Influence of the Family Environment.) Neuropsichiatria, 10: 1-8, 1954.

890. Dalla Volta, A. Aspetti Psicologici Dell'Alcoolismo Precocissimo
      e Precoce in Una Zona Vinicola Della Pianura Padana.
      (Psychological Aspects of Very Early and Early Alcoholism
      in a Wine-Growing Area of the Po Valley.) Archivio di
      Psicologia, Neurologia e Psichiatria, 16: 33-49, 1955.

891. Dalla Volta, A. L'Alcoolismo Iniziale nel Bambino. (Initial
      Alcoholism in Children.) Crianca Portugesa, Lisbon, 13:
      143-163, 1954.

892. Dalla Volta, A. New Aspects of the Psychological Problem of
      Alcoholism. Scientia Medica Italica, Rome, 5: 510-529,
      1957.

893. Dalla Volta, A. and Zecca, G. Aspetti Dell'Alcoolismo Infantile
      in Una Zona Circostante il Porto di Genova. (Aspects of
      Alcoholism in Children in the Neighborhood of the Port of
      Genoa.) Infanzia Anormale, Rome, 18: 1-15, 1956.

894. Dalzwell-Ward, A.J. Health Education. Journal of Alcoholism,
      8(2): 62-65, 1973.

895. Dalzwell-Ward, A.J. Tackling Problems at Source: Health
      Education. Journal of Alcoholism, 8: 62-65, 1973.

896. Dalzwell-Ward, A.J. A Textbook of Health Education. London:
      Tavistock Publications, 1974.

897. Damkot, David. Alcohol and the Rural Driver. In: Currents in
      Alcoholism, Vol. 6. Treatment and Rehabilitation and
      Epidemiology. Ed. M. Galanter. New York: Grune and
      Stratton, 1979, pages 319-325.

898. Daniel, Ralph. Alcohol or Alcoholism Education? Journal of
      Alcohol Education, 13(1): 44-45, 1967.

899. Daniels, Ralph M. Drug Education Begins Before Kindergarten:
      The Glen Cove, New York Pilot Program. Journal of School
      Health, 40(5): 242-248, 1970.

900. Danilova, E.A. O Roli Alkogolizma v Formirovianii Patologii
      Povendeniya u Detei Podrostkov. (On the Role of
      Alcoholism in the Development of Pathological Behavior in
      Children and Juveniles.) In: Tretii Vseros. S'yedz
      Nevropatologov i Psikhiatrov, Kazan'. Tom 3. Tezisy i
      Doklady. (The Third All-Russian Congress of
      Neuropathologists and Psychiatrists, Kazan'. Vol. 3.
      Thesis and Proceedings.) Moskva, 1974 pages 164-167.

901. D'Argenio, L. Sull'Alcoolismo Infantile. (On Alcoholism in
      Children.) Rassegna di Studi Psichiatrici, Siena, 48:
      879-898, 1959.

902. D'Argenio, L. Sull'Importanza Dell'Alcoolismo Infantile. (On
      the Importance of Alcoholism in Children. Rassegna di
      Studi Psichiatrici, Siena, 49: 680-684, 1960.

903. D'Augelli, J.F. and Weener, J.M. Communication and Parenting
      Skills: Leader Guide and Parent Workbook. University
      Park: Addictions Prevention Laboratory, Pennsylvania State
      University, 1977.

904. D'Augelli, J.F. and Weener, J.M. Do as I Do: The Parent's Role
      in Preventing Alcohol Abuse. Pamphlet. University Park:
      Pennsylvania State University, 1975.

905. D'Augelli, Judith Frankel. Parenting Skills for Alcohol Abuse
      Prevention: A Programmatic Approach. Paper Presented at
      the National Council on Alcoholism Region III Conference on
      Adolescent Alcohol Education, Lancaster, Pennsylvania,
      February 5-6, 1975.

906. David, Kenneth and Cowley, James. Pastoral Care in Schools and
      College. London: Edward Arnold, Ltd., 1980.

907. David, Lester. Alcohol: The New Trap for Teen-Agers. Good
      Housekeeping, 179(1): 63, 1974.

908. Davidson, F. and Choquet, M. Étude Épidémiologique du Suicide
      de L'Adolescent: Comparison Entre Suicidants Primares et
      Suicidants Récidivistes. (An Epidemiological Study of
      Adolescent Suicide: Comparison Between Primary Suicide
      Attempts and Repeaters.) Revue d'Épidemiologie, Medecine
      Sociale et de Sante Publique, 24: 11-26, 1976.

909. Davidson, F., Etienne, M., Piesset, J. Medico-Social Survey of
      662 Drug Users (April, 1971 - May, 1972). Bulletin on
      Narcotics, 25(4): 9-32, 1973.

910. Davies, D.L. Alcohol Education. In: Alcoholism: New
      Knowledge and New Responses. Eds. Griffith Edwards and
      Marcus Grant. London: Croom Helm, 1977, pages 345-351.

911. Davies, D.L., Ed. Aspects of Alcoholism. London: Alcohol
      Education Centre, Maudsley Hospital, 1977.

912. Davies, J. and Stacey B. Alcohol and Health Education in
      Schools. Health Bulletin, 29: 50-53, 1971. (Also in:
      Journal of Alcohol and Drug Education, 17(2): 1-7, 1972.

913. Davies, J. and Stacey, B. Drinking Behavior in Childhood and
      Adolescence. Journal of Alcohol and Drug Education, 17(3):
      1-11, 1972.

914. Davies, J. and Stacey, B. Teenagers and Alcohol: A
        Developmental Study in Glasgow. Vol. II: An Enquiry
        Carried Out on Behalf of the Health Education Unit of the
        Scottish Home and Health Department. London: Her
        Majesty's Stationery Office, 1972.

915. Davis, A.K., Werner, J.M. and Shutt, R.E. Positive Peer
        Influence: School Based Prevention. Health Education,
        8(4): 20-22, 1978.

916. Davis, C.S. and Schmidt, M.R., eds. Differential Treatment of
        Drug and Alcohol Abusers. Palm Springs, California: ETC
        Publications, 1977.

917. Davis, Donald I. Why Family Therapy for Drug Abuse? From the
        Clinical Perspective. In: Drug Abuse from the Family
        Perspective. Ed. Barbara Gray Ellis. Washington, D.C.:
        U.S. Government Printing Office, 1980, pages 63-70.

918. Davis, J.H. Alcohol as Precursor to Violent Death. Journal of
        Drug Issues, 5: 270-275, 1975.

919. Davis, R.D. The Traffic in Illicit Liquor. Police, 8(4): 6-9,
        1964.

920. Davis, R.E. Primary Prevention of Alcohol Problems. Alcohol
        Health and Research World, 1(1): 31, 1976.

921. Davis, R.E., Midalia, N.D. and Curnow, D.H. Illegal Drugs and
        Nutrition in Undergraduate Students. Medical Journal of
        Australia, 65(1): 617-620, 1978.

922. Davis, William. A Pilot Program to Help Alcoholics by
        Socializing their Power Needs. In: The Drinking Man. Eds.
        D.C. McClelland, W.N. Davis, R. Kalin and E. Wanner. New
        York: The Free Press, 1972, pages 316-331.

923. Dawkins, M.P. Alcohol Use among Black and White Adolescents.
        In: Alcohol Abuse and Black America. Ed. F.D. Harper.
        Alexandria, Virginia: Douglass Publishers, Inc., 1976,
        pages 163-175.

924. Dawkins, Marvin. Research Issues on Alcohol Abuse and Blacks.
        In: Alcohol Abuse and Black America. Ed. F.D. Harper.
        Alexandria, Virginia: Douglass Publishers, 1976, pages 141-
        152.

925. Dawkins, Marvin P. Alcohol Information on Black Americans:
        Current Status and Future Needs. Journal of Alcohol and
        Drug Education, 25(3): 28-40, 1980.

926. Dawkins, Marvin P. Alcohol Use Among Black and White
      Adolescents. In: Alcohol Abuse and Black America. Ed.
      Frederick D. Harper. Alexandria, Virginia: Douglass
      Publishers, Inc., 1976, pages 163-175.

927. Dax, E.C. Drug Dependency. Medical Journal of Australia,
      59(2): 1370-1373, 1972.

928. Day, B.R. Alcoholics and the Family. Journal of Marriage and
      the Family, 23: 253-258, 1961.

929. Dayton Ohio Public Schools. Developing Curriculum for Education
      of Youth in Meeting Modern Problems. Dayton, Ohio, 1973.

930. Dearden, Marlin H. and Jekel, James F. A Pilot Program in High
      School Drug Education Utilizing Non-Directive Techniques
      and Sensitivity Training. Journal of School Health, 41(3):
      118-124, 1971.

931. Dearing, M.D. Films on Alcoholism. American Librarian
      Association Bulletin, 43: 207-209, 1949.

932. De-Foe, J.R. and Breed, W. The Problem of Alcohol
      Advertisements in College Newspapers. Journal of the
      American College Health Association, 27: 195-199, 1979.

933. De-Foe, James and Breed, Warren. The Mass Media and Alcohol
      Education: A New Direction. Journal of Alcohol and Drug
      Education, 25(3): 48-58, 1980.

934. DeForest, John William, Roberts, Thomm Kevin and Hays, J. Ray.
      Drug Abuse: A Family Affair? Journal of Drug Issues, 4:
      130-134, 1974.

935. DeFuentes, Nanette. Teenage Alcoholism Program: A New Approach
      to Our Youth's Drinking Problem. The Alcoholism Digest
      Annual, 4: 14-21, 1975-76.

936. DeHaes, Willy and Schuurman, Johannes. Results of an
      Evaluation Study of Three Drug Education Methods.
      International Journal of Health Education, 28(4): 1-16,
      1975.

937. DeLint, J.E.E. Alcoholism, Birth Rank and Parental Deprivation.
      The American Journal of Psychiatry, 120(11): 1062-1065,
      1964.

938. DeLint, Jan E.E. Alcoholism, Birth Order and Socializing Agents.
      Journal of Abnormal and Social Psychology, 69: 457-458,
      1964.

939. Dembo, R., Farrow, D., Schmeidler, J. and Burgos, W. Testing a
        Causal Model of Environmental Influences on the Early Drug
        Involvement of Inner City Junior High School Youths.
        American Journal of Drug and Alcohol Abuse, 6: 313-336,
        1979.

940. Dembo, R. and Miran, M. Evaluation of Drug Prevention Programs
        by Youths in a Middle-Class Community. International
        Journal of the Addictions, 11: 881-903, 1976.

941. Dembo, R., Miran, M., Babst, D.V. and Schmeidler, J. The
        Believability of the Media as Sources of Information on
        Drugs. International Journal of the Addictions, 12: 959-
        969, 1977.

942. Dembo, R., Schmeidler, J., Lipton, D.S., Babst, D.V.,
        Diamond, S.C., Spielman, C.R., Bergman, P.J., Koval, M.,
        Miran, M.D. and Stephens, R.C. A Survey of Students'
        Awareness Toward Drug Abuse Prevention Programs in New York
        State, Winter, 1974-75. International Journal of the
        Addictions, 14: 311-328, 1979.

943. Dembo, Richard. Substance Abuse Prevention Programming and
        Research: A Partnership in Need of Improvement. Journal
        of Drug Education, 9(3): 189-208, 1979.

944. Dembo, Richard, Burgos, William, Babst, Dean V.,
        Schmeidler, James and LaGrand, Louis E. Neighborhood
        Relationships and Drug Involvement Among Inner City Junior
        High School Youths: Implications for Drug Education and
        Prevention Programming. Journal of Drug Education, 8(3):
        231-252, 1978.

945. Dembo, Richard, Burgos, William, Des-Jarlais, Don and
        Schmeidler, James. Ethnicity and Drug Use Among Urban
        Junior High School Youths. International Journal of the
        Addictions, 14(4): 557-568, 1979.

946. Dembo, Richard, Farrow, Dana, Schmeidler, James and
        Burgos, William. Testing a Causal Model of Environmental
        Influences on the Early Drug Involvement of Inner City
        Junior High School Youths. American Journal of Drug and
        Alcohol Abuse, 6(3): 313-336, 1979.

947. Dembo, Richard and LaGrand, Louis E. A Research Model for a
        Comprehensive, Health Service Orientated Understanding of
        Drug Use. Journal of Drug Issues, 8: 355-372, 1978.

948. Dembo, Richard, Pilaro, Leonard, Burgos, William,
        Des-Jarlais, Don C. and Schmeidler, James. Self-Concept
        and Drug Involvement Among Urban Junior High School Youths.
        The International Journal of the Addictions, 14(8): 1125-
        1144, 1979.

949. Dembo, Richard, Schmeidler, James, Babst, Dean V. and
        Lipton, Douglas, S. Drug Information Source Credibility
        Among Junior and Senior High School Youths. American
        Journal of Drug and Alcohol Abuse, 4(1): 43-54, 1977.

950. Dembo, Richard, Schmeidler, James and Burgos, William. Factors
        in the Drug Involvement of Inner City Junior High School
        Youths: A Discriminant Analysis. Presented at the Fifth
        National Drug Abuse Conference, Seattle, April, 1978.
        (Also in: The International Journal of Social Psychiatry,
        25(2): 92-103, 1979.

951. Dembo, Richard, Schmeidler, James and Burgos, William. Life-
        Style and Drug Involvement Among Youths in an Inner-City
        Junior High School. The International Journal of the
        Addictions, 15(2): 171-188, 1980.

952. Dembo, Richard, Schmeidler, James and Koval, Mary. Demographic,
        Value and Behavior Correlates of Marijuana Use Among Middle-
        Class Youths. Journal of Health and Social Behavior, 17:
        176-186, 1976.

953. Demorović, V. Alkohol Kao Faktor Delikventnog i Kriminalnog
        Ponsaňja. (Alcohol as a Factor in Delinquent and Criminal
        Behavior.) Medicinski Archiv, Sarajevo, 33: 75-80, 1979.

954. Demone, H. Do High School Boys Drink? Journal of Alcohol
        Education, 14(2): 20, 1969.

955. Demone, H.W. Teen-Agers and Alcohol. New Hampshire Bulletin on
        Alcoholism, 12(2): 1-11, 1962.

956. Demone, H.W., Jr. Drinking Attitudes and Practices of Male
        Adolescents. Doctoral Dissertation (University Microfilms
        No. 66-13637). Brandeis University, 1966. (Also see:
        Social Service Review, 40: 326-327, 1966.)

957. Demone, H.W., Jr. The Nonuse and Abuse of Alcohol by the Male
        Adolescent. In: Proceedings of the Second Annual
        Alcoholism Conference of the National Institute on Alcohol
        Abuse and Alcoholism, Rockville, Maryland, 1973, pages 24-
        32.

958. Demone, Harold. Implications from Research on Adolescent
        Drinking. In: Alcohol Education. U.S. Department of
        Health, Education and Welfare. Secretary's Committee on
        Alcoholism. Proceedings of the Conference, March 29, 1966.
        Washington, D.C.: U.S. Government Printing Office, 1967,
        pages 16-19.

959. Demone, Harold and Wechsler, Henry. Changing Drinking Patterns
        of Adolescent Since the 1960s. In: Alcohol Problems in
        Women and Children. Eds. M. Greenblatt and M. Schuckit.
        New York: Grune and Stratton, 1976, pages 197-210.

960.   Dennehy, C.M. Childhood Bereavement and Psychiatric Illness.
         British Journal of Psychiatry, 112: 1049-1069, 1966.

961.   Dennison, D., Prevet, T. and Affleck, M. Does Alcohol
         Instruction Affect Student Drinking Behavior? Health
         Education, 8(6): 28-30, 1977.

962.   Dennison, Darwin. The Effects of Selected Field Experiments
         Upon the Drinking Behavior of University Students. The
         Journal of School Health, 47(1): 38-41, 1977.

963.   Dennison, Darwin and Prevet, Thomas. Improving Alcohol-Related
         Disruptive Behaviors through Health Instruction. Journal
         of School Health, 50(4): 206-208, 1980.

964.   Densen-Gerber, J. and Baden, T.A. Drugs, Sex, Parents, and You.
         Philadelphia: Lippincott, 1972.

965.   Densen-Gerber, J. Hutchinson, S.F. and Levine, R.M. Incest and
         Drug-Related Child Abuse--Systematic Neglect by the Medical
         and Legal Professions. Contemporary Drug Problems, 6: 135-
         172, 1977.

966.   DeRicco, D.A. and Garlington, W.K. The Effect of Modeling and
         Disclosure of Experimenter's Intent on Drinking Rate of
         College Students. Addictive Behavior, 2: 135-139, 1977.

967.   DeRicco, Denise A. Effects of Peer Majority on Drinking Rate.
         Addictive Behaviors, 3(1): 29-34, 1978.

968.   Dervillée, P., L'épée, P., Lazarini, H.J. and Dervillée, E.
         Indications Statistiques sur les Relations Possibles Entre
         l'Alcoolisme et la Criminalité: Enquête dans la Région
         Bordelaise. (Statistical Indications of a Possible
         Relationship Between Alcoholism and Criminality: An Enquiry
         in the Bordeaux Region.) Revue de l'Alcoolisme, 7: 20-21,
         1961.

969.   Deshaies, G. L'Alcoolisme Héréditaire. (Hereditary Alcoholism.)
         Encéphale, 34: 446-468, 1941.

970.   Despotović, A. Alkoholizam, Narkomanije i Porodica.
         (Alcoholism, Drug Addictions and the Family.) Anali Zavoda
         za Mentalno Zdravje, Belgrade, 6(2-3): 191-202, 1974.

971.   Destits, Therese. A View Toward Prevention. Health Education,
         6(2): 2-4, 1975.

972.   Detoxification Without Benefit of Hospitals. Medical World News,
         14(30): 84-85, 1973.

973.   Deutsch, C. Mike and Tom. Pamphlet. Somerville, Massachusetts:
         CASPAR Alcoholism Education Program, 1978.

974. Deutsch, C., DiCicco, L. and Mills, D.   Reaching Children from
Families with Alcoholism: Some Innovative Techniques.   In:
Alcohol and Drug Problems Association of North America.
Proceedings Presented at the Twenty-Ninth Annual Meeting,
September 24-28, 1978, Seattle, Washington.   Washington,
D.C., 1978, pages 54-58.

975. Devečerski, M.   Rezultati Ispitivanja Zdravstvenog Stanja Kod
Grupe od 1000 Alkoholicara.   (Results of Investigation of
the Health Status in a Group of 1000 Alcoholics.)
Higijena, Beograd, 12: 254-260, 1960.

976. DeVillanueva, C.   Anomalías Congénitas Físicas y Psiquicas de
Origen Alcohólica.   (Congenital Physical and Psychological
Abnormalities of Alcoholic Origin.)   Revue Medico-
Chirurgicale, Barranquilla, 13(12a): 77-86, 1946.

977. Dezelsky, Thomas, Toohey, Jack and Kush, Robert.   A Ten-Year
Analysis of Non-Medical Drug Use Behavior at Five American
Universities.   Journal of School Health, 51(1): 51-55, 1981.

978. DiCicco, L.   The Health Educator.   In: Alcohol Education.
Proceedings of the Conference, March 29, 1966.   U.S.
Department of Health, Education and Welfare.   Secretary's
Committee on Alcoholism.   Washington, D.C.:   U.S. Government
Printing Office, 1967, pages 48-52.

979. DiCicco, L., Deutsch, C., Levine, G., Mills, D.J. and
Unterberger, H.   A School-Community Approach to Alcohol
Education.   Health Education, 8(4): 11-13, 1978.

980. DiCicco, L.M. and Unterberger, H.   Alcohol and Youth: Changing
Perspectives.   In: Alcohol Education for Teenagers:
Proceedings of a Workshop.   Newport, Rhode Island,
April 5-7, 1965, pages 21-25.

981. DiCicco, L.M. and Unterberger, H.   Does Alcohol Follow Drugs?
Bulletin of the National Association of Secondary School
Principles, 57(372): 85-91, 1973.

982. DiCicco, Lena and Unterberger, Hilma.   Correspondence--Drug
Education.   Quarterly Journal of Studies on Alcohol, 35:
291-292, 1974.

983. Dick, R.B. and Brown, L.T.   A Comparison of Drug Users and
Nonusers on a Midwestern University Campus.   The
International Journal of the Addictions, 9(6): 903-907,
1974.

984. Dickman, F.B. and Keil, T.J.   Public Television and Public
Health.   The Case of Alcoholism.   Journal of Studies on
Alcohol, 38(3): 584-592, 1977.

985. Dietz, P.E. and Baker, S.P. Drowning, Epidemiology and
      Prevention. American Journal of Public Health, 64: 303-
      312, 1974.

986. Dimas, G.C. Alcohol Education in Oregon Schools: A Topic
      Outline and Resource Unit for Teachers. Portland, Oregon:
      Oregon Mental Health Division, Alcohol and Drug Section,
      1968.

987. Dimas, G.C. Alcohol Education in Schools. Portland, Oregon:
      Mental Health Division, Alcohol Studies and Rehabilitation
      Section, 1967. (NCALI No. NCAI 011255)

988. Dimitrijevíc, D.T. Alkoholizam Roditelja u Patogenezi Dečijih
      Neuroza. (Alcoholism of the Parents in the Pathogenesis of
      Neuroses in Children.) Medicinski Archiv, Sarajevo, 12(1):
      81-85, 1958.

989. Dintcheff, C. L'Éducation Antialcoolique de la Jeunesse.
      (Temperance Education for Youth.) International Congress
      Against Alcoholism, 19: 134-141, 1930.

990. Diskind, Z.A. A Psycho-Cultural Investigation of Jewish
      Drinking Habits and Attitudes. Master's Thesis. Portland,
      Oregon, 1953.

991. Distilled Spirits Council of the United States. No One Answer:
      A Closer Look at Teenage Drinking. Pamphlet, Third
      Revised Edition. Washington, D.C., 1975.

992. Dodson, W.E, Alexander, D.F., Wright, P.F. and Wunderlich, R.A.
      Patterns of Multiple Drug Use Among Adolescents Referred by
      a Juvenile Court. Pediatrics, 47(6): 1033-1036, 1971.

993. Dizmang, L.H. Adolescent Suicide on an Indian Reservation.
      American Journal of Orthopsychiatry, 44(1): 43-49, 1974.

994. Doe, Jane. Alcoholism--One Family's Story. Pamphlet. Pastoral
      Services Commission. Independence, Missouri: Herald
      Publishing House, 1978.

995. Dohnány, L. Študentské Spolky Miernosti v Prvej Polovici 19
      Storočia na Solvensku. (Student Temperance Societies in
      the First Half of the 19th Century in Slovakia.)
      Protialkoholicky Obzor, Bratislava, 14: 155-158, 1979.

996. Dohner, J.A. Motives for Drug Use: Adults and Adolescents.
      Psychosomatics, 13(5): 119-123, 1972.

997. Do It Now Foundation. First International Action Conference
      Proceedings. Vol. 1-4. Phoeniz, Arizona, 1979.

998. Do It Now Foundation. You Got Any I.D., Kid? Pamphlet.
      Phoenix, Arizona, 1975.

999.   Dolan, J.S.   All in the Family: Understanding How we Teach and
       Influence Children About Alcohol.   Paper Presented at the
       Annual Meeting of the Alcohol and Drug Problems Association,
       Chicago, September 15, 1975.

1000. Dolan, Joseph.   Observations About the Responsible Drinking
       Theme and Threshold.   Journal of Alcohol and Drug
       Education, 21(2): 20-29, 1976.

1001. Dolan, M.   Alcoholism: The All-American Addiction.   American
       Pharmacy, 19(1): 26-29, 1979.

1002. Donadio, G. and LoCascio, A.   Impeigo del Test del Villaggio
       Immaginario in un Gruppo di Giovani Alcolisti: Note
       Preliminari Presentate al III Simposio Sull'Alcolismo di
       Zagabria.   (Use of the Imaginary-Village Test in a Group of
       Young Alcoholics: Preliminary Note Presented at the Third
       Symposium on Alcoholism in Zagreb.)   Lavoro
       Neuropsichiatrico, Rome, 37: 133-141, 1965.

1003. Donovan, Bruce.   The Brown Group on Alcohol Development of an
       On-Campus Education/Prevention/Treatment Forum.   Journal of
       Alcohol and Drug Education, 24(3): 56-65, 1979.

1004. Donovan, Bruce.   Studies of the Drinking Behavior of American
       White Male College Students: Implications of the Research
       for the Establishment of a College Alcohol Education
       Program.   Journal of Alcohol and Drug Education, 22(3): 5-
       16, 1977.

1005. Donovan, John E. and Jessor, Richard.   Adolescent Problem
       Drinking: Psychosocial Correlates in a National Sample
       Study.   Journal of Studies on Alcohol, 39(9): 1506-1524,
       1978.

1006. D'Orban, P.   Heroin Dependence and Delinquency in Women--A Study
       of Heroin Addicts in Holloway Prison.   British Journal of
       Addiction, 65: 67-68, 1970.

1007. Dordević-Banković, V. and Sedmak, T.   Primary Family and the
       Process of Socialization of Alcoholic-Sociopaths.
       Alcoholism, Zagreb, 8: 120-125, 1972.

1008. Dorn, Nick.   The Politics of Dependency Problems: Labor Market
       Failure, Youth and "Dependency Problems" in the United
       Kingdom.   Journal of Psychoactive Drugs, 13(1): 61-69, 1981.

1009. Dorn, Nick.   Standing Their Round: Teenage Drinking and the
       Transition to Work.   London: Croom Helm, 1982.

1010. Doucet, J.A., Finucan, Kerry and MacIntosh, Patricia.   Drug
       Education Programs: A Basis for Future Study.   Journal of
       Alcohol and Drug Education, 23(2): 26-75, 1978.

1011. Dough, Whitney J. Public Enemy Number One. Union Signal, 99(2): 11-13, 1973.

1012. Douglas, Frazier, Khavari, Khalil and Farber, Philip. Limitations of Scalogram Analysis as a Method for Investigating Drug Use Behavior. Drug and Alcohol Dependence, 7(2): 147-155, 1981.

1013. Douglass, R.L. The Consequences of Lower Legal Drinking Ages on Alcohol-Related Crash Involvement of Young People. Report on Alcohol, 34(3): 13-19, 1976.

1014. Douglass, R.L. The Effect of the Lower Drinking Age on Youth Crash Involvement. Doctoral Dissertation (University Microfilms No. 75-672). University of Michigan, 1974.

1015. Douglass, R.L. The Effect of the Lower Legal Drinking Age on Youth Crash Involvement - A Legal Impact Study. New Orleans, Louisiana: Paper Presented at the Annual Meeting of the American Public Health Association, 1974.

1016. Douglass, R.L. Results of a Legal Impact Study: The Lower Legal Drinking Age and Youth Crash Involvement. Hit Lab Reports, 5(2): 1-15, 1974.

1017. Douglass, R.L. and Filkins, L.D. The Effect of Lower Legal Drinking Ages on Youth Crash Involvement. Washington, D.C.: U.S. National Highway Traffic Safety Administration, 1974.

1018. Douglass, R.L., Filkins, L.D and Clark, F.A. The Effect of Lower Legal Drinking Ages on Youth Crash Involvement: Final Report, June, 1974. Ann Arbor, Michigan: Highway Safety Research Institute, 1974. (DOT Publication No. HS-031-3-754)

1019. Douglass, R.L., Filkins, L.D and Flora, J.D. Design Issues of a Legal Impact Study: The Lower Legal Drinking Age and Youth Crash Involvement. HIT Lab Reports, 4(10): 1-11, 1974.

1020. Douglass, Richard and Millar, Charles. Alcohol Availability and Alcohol-Related Casualties in Michigan, 1968-1970. In: Currents in Alcoholism. Vol. 6. Treatment and Rehabilitation and Epidemiology. Ed. M. Galanter. New York: Grune and Stratton, 1979, pages 303-317.

1021. Douglass, Richard L. The Legal Drinking Age and Traffic Casualties: A Special Case of Changing Alcohol Availability in a Public Health Context. Alcohol Health and Reseach World, 4(2): 18-25, 1979.

1022. Do You Remember Your First Drink? Journal of Alcohol and Drug Education, 17(3): 21-25, 1972.

1023. Drag, L.R. and Drucker, M.B. Undergraduate or Paraprofessional
       Training in the Treatment of Alcoholism and Drug
       Dependency. In: Alcohol and Drug Problems Association of
       North America. Selected Papers Presented at the General
       Sessions, Twenty-third Annual Meeting, September 10-15,
       1972. Atlanta, Georgia. Washington, D.C., 1972, pages 20-
       23.

1024. Dreszerowa, H. and Handelsman, J. Alcoholism Among School
       Children. Zdrowie Psychiatrisch, 2: 112-118, 1947.

1025. Drew, L.R.H. Alcoholic Offenders in a Victorian Prison.
       Medical Journal of Australia, 48(2): 575-578, 1961.

1026. Drewery, James. Social Drinking as a Therapeutic Goal in the
       Treatment of Alcoholism. Journal of Alcoholism, 9(2): 43-
       47, 1974.

1027. Dreyfus, Edward A., Beels, Carisse, Cook, Marcia,
       Faulkrod, Frances, Inocente, David, Morris, Robert,
       Murphy, Katherine, Speicher, Gloria, Vash, Peter,
       Widess, Karen, Ziiskin, Nina and Zunin, Ira. Adolescence:
       Theory and Experience. Columbus, Ohio:
       Charles E. Merrill, 1976.

1028. Drinkers at Record Level: Problems Increase for Youth, Adults.
       Bottom Line, 1(2): 2-4, 1977.

1029. Drinking at Lunch Time: Quarterly Notes. Journal of
       Alcoholism, 8(1): 4, 1973.

1030. The Drinking Driver. American Youth, 13(4): 19-21, 1972.

1031. The Drinking Question: Honest Answers to Questions Teenagers
       Ask About Drinking. Pamphlet. Washington, D.C.: National
       Institute on Alcohol Abuse and Alcoholism, U.S. Government
       Printing Office, 1975. (DHEW Publication No. ADM 76-286)

1032. Drug Abuse Council, Inc. Students and Drugs: A Report of the
       Drug Abuse Council. Washington, D.C.: Drug Abuse Council,
       Inc., 1975.

1033. Drug Abuse Council, Inc. Students Speak on Drugs. Washington,
       D.C.: Drug Abuse Council, Inc., 1974.

1034. Drug Abuse Prevention: Report of the Temporary State Commission
       to Evaluate the Drug Laws. Assemblyman Emeel S. Betros,
       Chairman. New York State Legislative Document No. 11,
       1974.

1035. Drug Education Through the News Media: Suggestions for
       Reporters and Drug Program Directors. Journal of Alcohol
       and Drug Education, 18(3): 30-35, 1973.

1036. Drug Use Still High Among American Youths, Latest Findings from
       Longitudinal Study Show. Institute for Social Research
       Newsletter, 3(3): 3, 1975.

1037. Drug Use Has Risen Among Young People; Alcohol Consumption Still
       High but Youths Decry Smoking. Institute for Social
       Research Newsletter, 4(3): 8, 1976.

1038. Drugs and the Educational Antidote. Nation's Schools, 85(4):
       49-52, 197, 1970.

1039. Drugs in Your Life. Book 2. Pamphlet. Columbus, Ohio: Xerox
       Education Publications, 1972.

1040. Dube, K.C., Kumar, A., Kumar, N. and Gupta, S.P. Prevalence and
       Pattern of Drug Use Amongst College Students. Acta
       Psychiatrica Scandinavica, 57: 336-356, 1978.

1041. Duckert, F. and Aasland, O.G. Rehabilitation of Alcoholics and
       Drug Addicts: An Experimental Approach. Journal of
       Studies on Alcohol, 41(3): 368-372, 1980.

1042. Duckert, M. Foreningsmedlemsskap og Rusmiddelbruk Blant Ungdom.
       (Organization Membership and Alcoholic Beverage Use Among
       Youth.) Tidsskrift EdruSpørsm, 31(4): 4-6, 1979.

1043. Duckert, M. Stoffbruk Blant Ungdom i Vest-Agder. (Drug Use
       Among Youth in Vest-Agder.) Tidsskrift EdruSpørsm, 30(1):
       20, 22, 1978.

1044. Duckert, M. Unge Stoffbrukeres Motiver for å Bruke Marihuana og
       Hasj. (Motives of Young Drug Users for Using Marihuana
       and Hashish.) Tidsrifft Edruspørsm, 30(2): 14-16, 1978.

1045. Duka, N. Protialkoholická Výchova na Školách v 19. Storočí.
       (Anti-Alcohol Education in Schools in the 19th Century.)
       Protialkoholicky Obzor, Bratislava, 8: 37-38, 1973.

1046. Dulfano, Celia. Family Therapy of Alcoholism. In: Practical
       Approaches to Alcoholism Psychotherapy. Eds. S. Zimberg,
       J. Wallace and S.B. Blume. New York: Plenum, 1978,
       pages 119-136.

1047. Dulfano, Celia. Recovery: Rebuilding the Family. Alcoholism,
       1(3): 33-36, 1981.

1048. Dull, R. Thomas and Williams III, Franklin P. Marihuana,
       Alcohol and Tobacco: Reassessment of a Presumed
       Relationship. Journal of Drug Education, 11(2): 129-139,
       1981.

1049. Duncan, Jane Watson. Persisting Psychotic States in Adolescent
       Drug Users. Child Psychiatry and Human Development, 5(1):
       51-62, 1974.

1050.   Dunnette, Marvin and Personnel Decisions Research Institute.
        Individualized Prediction as a Strategy for Discovering
        Demographic and Interpersonal/Psychosocial Correlates of
        Drug Resistance and Abuse. In: Predicting Adolescent
        Drug Abuse: A Review of Issues, Methods and Correlates -
        Research Issues II. Ed. Dan Lettieri. Rockville,
        Maryland: National Institute on Drug Abuse, 1975, pages
        97-128.

1051.   Dupont, R.L., Goldstein, A. and O'Donnell, J., Eds. Handbook on
        Drug Abuse. Washington, D.C.: U.S. Government Printing
        Office, 1979.

1052.   Dupont, Robert L. The Future of Primary Prevention. Journal of
        Drug Education, 11(1): 1-5, 1980.

1053.   Dupont, Robert L. Marihuana: A Review of the Issues Regarding
        Decriminalization and Legalization. In: Youth Drug
        Abuse: Problems, Issues and Treatment. Eds.
        G.M. Beschner and A.S. Friedman. Lexington,
        Massachusetts: D.C. Heath, 1979, pages 279-284.

1054.   Durning, K.P. and Jansen, E. Problem Drinking and Attitudes
        Toward Alcohol Among Navy Recruits. Journal of Alcohol
        and Drug Education, 22(10): 29-31, 1976.

1055.   Durrant, L.K. The Alcohol Problem from an Historical
        Perspective. Royal Society of Health Journal, 96(1): 42-
        44, 1976.

1056.   Duvall, E.M. and Motz, A.B. Are Country Girls so Different?
        Rural Sociology, 10: 263-274, 1945.

1057.   Dvorak, E.J. A Longitudinal Study of Nonmedical Drug Use Among
        University Students: A Brief Summary. Journal of the
        American College Health Association, 20: 212-215, 1972.

1058.   Dykeman, Bruce F. Teenage Alcoholism - Detecting Those Early
        Warning Signals. Adolescence, 14(54): 251-254, 1979.

E

1059. Easterling, M.G. and Clay, T.R. <u>A Knowledge and Opinion Survey of Phoenix High-School Students About Drinking and Driving</u>. Phoenix, Arizona: Phoenix Alcohol Safety and Action Project, 1973.

1060. Ebermann, H. Vergleichende Betrachtungen zur Drogenproblematik der Jugendlichen Nach Studienreisen in Ausserdeutsche Länder. (Comparative Observations of Drug Addiction Problems in Adolescents Based on Student Visits to Countries Outside Germany.) <u>Nervenarzt</u>, Berlin, <u>45</u>: 98-102, 1974.

1061. Eck, W.L. Classroom Methods of Teaching Alcohol Education. In: <u>Alcohol Education for Teenagers: Proceedings of a Workshop</u>. Newport, Rhode Island, April 5-7, 1965, pages 15-20.

1062. Eck, W.L. Some Current Forces in the U.S. That Impact on Alcohol Education Today. In: <u>Papers Presented at the 24th International Congress on the Prevention and Treatment of Alcoholism, Zurich, June, 1978</u>. Lausanne, Switzerland: International Council on Alcohol and Addictions, 1978, pages 272-282.

1063. Eck, William L. From the Classroom: A Master Teacher Reports. <u>Journal of Alcohol Education</u>, <u>13</u>(3): 37-39, 1967.

1064. Edmundson, W.F., Davies, J.E., Acker, J.D. and Byer, B. Patterns of Drug Abuse Epidemiology in Prisoners. <u>Industrial Medicine</u>, <u>41</u>(1): 15-19, 1972.

1065. Educating About Alcohol. <u>The Washington Post</u>, page A10, April 12, 1975.

1066. Educating Young People About Drugs (Notes and News). <u>WHO Chronicles</u>, <u>30</u>: 208-209, 1976.

1067.   Educating Youth Called Crucial in Alcoholism Fight. Alcohol
        and Health Notes: 1-2, May, 1973.

1068.   Education Commission of the States. Southeastern Regional
        Working Conference on the Prevention of Alcohol and Drug
        Abuse: A Report to the Education Commission of the States
        Task Force on Responsible Decisions About Alcohol.
        Knoxville, Tennessee, July 28-31, 1974. Pamphlet. Denver,
        Colorado, 1975.

1069.   Education Commission of the States. Task Force on Responsible
        Decisions About Alcohol: Interim Report Number 1 (A
        Summary). Pamphlet. Denver, Colorado, 1975.

1070.   Education Commission of the States. Task Force on Responsible
        Decisions About Alcohol: Interim Report Number 2 (A
        Summary). Pamphlet. Denver, Colorado, 1975.

1071.   Education Commission of the States. Task Force on Responsible
        Decisions About Alcohol: Interim Report Number 3 (A
        Summary). Pamphlet. Denver, Colorado, 1975.

1072.   Education Commission of the States. Task Force on Responsible
        Decisions About Alcohol: Interim Report Number 4 (A
        Summary). Pamphlet. Denver, Colorado, 1976.

1073.   Education Commission of the States. Western Regional Working
        Conference on the Prevention of Alcohol Misuse: A Report
        to the Education Commission of the States Task Force on
        Responsible Decisions About Alcohol. Long Beach,
        California, October 22-25, 1974. Pamphlet. Denver,
        Colorado, 1975.

1074.   Educational Research Council of America and the Participating
        School Systems - Dayton, Ohio and Lima, Ohio. Human-
        Persons and the Use of Psychoactive Agents: Student Rap
        Sheets. Cleveland, Ohio, 1973.

1075.   Educational Research Council of America and the Participating
        School Systems - Dayton, Ohio and Lima, Ohio. Human
        Persons and the Use of Psychoactive Agents: Teachers'
        Manual. Cleveland, Ohio, 1973.

1076.   Edwards, G., Hawker, A., Hensman, C. Peto, J. and Williamson, V.
        Alcoholics Known or Unknown to Agencies: Epidemiological
        Studies in a London Suburb. British Journal of Psychiatry,
        123(573): 169-183, 1973.

1077.   Edward, G., Williamson, V., Hawker, A., Hensman, C. and
        Postoyan, S. Census of a Reception Centre. British
        Journal of Psychiatry, 114(513): 1031-1039, 1968.

1078.   Edwards, Griffith. A Doubtful Prognosis. International Journal
          of Psychiatry, 9: 354-358, 1970-71.

1079.   Edwards, Griffith. Alternative Strategies for Minimizing
          Alcohol Problems: Coming Out of the Doldrums. Journal of
          Alcoholism, 10(2): 45-66, 1975.

1080.   Edwards, Griffith and Grant, Marcus, Eds. Alcoholism: New
          Knowledge and New Responses. London: Croom Helm, 1977.

1081.   Egan, K.E. Youth Experience "Drug/Alcohol Rehabilitation"--An
          Interactionist Perspective. Doctoral Dissertation
          (University Microfilms No. 7823617). Syracuse University,
          1978.

1082.   Egger, G.J., Parker, R. and Trebilco, P. Adolescents and
          Alcohol Use in New South Wales. Sydney, Australia: New
          South Wales Government Printer, 1976.

1083.   Egger, G.J., Webb, R.A.J. and Reynolds, I. Early Adolescent
          Antecedents of Narcotics Abuse. International Journal of
          the Addictions, 13: 773-781, 1978.

1084.   Ehlers, T. Alkoholbedingte Motivationsänderungen und
          Unfallgefährdung. (Changes in Motivation Due to Alcohol
          Intake and Accident Proneness.) Zeitschrift fur
          Experimentelle und Angewandte Psychologie, Gottingen, 13:
          1-18, 1966.

1085.   Ehline, D. and Tighe, P.O. Alcoholism: Early Identification
          and Intervention in the Social Service Agency. Child
          Welfare, 56: 584-592, 1977.

1086.   Ehrlich, D. Young Drinking Drivers Causing Worldwide Concern.
          The Journal, 2(12): 2, 1973.

1087.   Eilryyr, J.-A.L. Family Socialization and High School Social
          Climate Effects on Adolescent Alcohol and Marijuana Use.
          Doctoral Dissertation(University Microfilms No. 7812895).
          University of Maryland, 1977.

1088.   Einstein, R., Hughes, I.E. and Hindmarch, I. Patterns of Use of
          Alcohol, Cannabis and Tobacco in a Student Population.
          British Journal of the Addictions, 70: 145-150, 1975.

1089.   Einstein, S. and Allen, S., Eds. Proceedings of the First
          International Conference on Student Drug Surveys, 12-15
          September, 1971, Newark, New Jersey. Farmingdale, New
          York: Baywood, 1972.

1090.   Eisenthal, S. and Udin, H. Psychological Factors Associated
          With Drug and Alcohol Usage Among Neighborhood Youth
          Corps Enrolees. Developmental Psychology, 7(2): 119-123,
          1972.

1091. Eiser, J.R., Gossop, M. and Van-Der-Pligt, J.   Drug Attitudes and
        Discrimination Between Drugs Among a Group of English
        Schoolchildren. Drug and Alcohol Dependence, Lausanne, 5:
        57-62, 1980.

1092. Eisterhold, M.J., Murphy, P., Beneke, W. and Scott, G.   Multiple-
        Drug Use Among High School Students. Psychological
        Report, 44: 1099-1106, 1979.

1093. Eklund, L. and Nylander, I.   Risken för Återfall i Fylleri Bland
        Stockholmspojkar. (Risk of Repeated Intoxication in
        Stockholm Boys.) Socialmedicinsk Tidsskrift, Stockholm,
        42: 201-205, 1965.

1094. "El Alcoholismo"--Sección Sobre Alcoholismo para los Colegios,
        Utilizada por el Servicio de Alcoholicos y Toxicómanos del
        Hospital Psiquiátrico de Bétera. ("Alcoholism"--Session
        on Alcoholism for Students at the Alcoholism and Addiction
        Service of Bétera Psychiatric Hospital.) Drogalcohol, 4:
        147-156, 1979.

1095. El Centro Guidance Program: Youth Drinking Survey Completed.
        Eastside Sun, September 20, 1979.

1096. Elder, Thomas C. Alcoholism and Its Onset in a Population of
        Admitted Alcoholics (an AA Study). British Journal of
        Addiction, 68(4): 291-294, 1973.

1097. Eldred, D. Influence of Social Groups on the Drinking Behavior
        of Young People. In: Community Factors in Alcohol
        Education, 2nd Conference on Alcohol Education. Stowe,
        Vermont, October 16-18, 1961, pages 42-57.

1098. Elejalde, B.R. Marihuana and Genetic Studies on Columbia: The
        Problem in the City and in the Country. In: Cannabis and
        Culture. Ed. Vera Rubin. The Hague, Paris: Mouton
        Publishers, 1975, pages 327-343.

1099. El-Guebaly, N. and Offord, D.R. On Being the Offspring of an
        Alcoholic: An Update. Alcoholism: Clinical and
        Experimental Research, 3: 148-157, 1979.

1100. El-Guebaly, N., Offord, D.R., Sullivan, K.T. and Lynch, G.W.
        Psychosocial Adjustment of the Offspring of Psychiatric
        Inpatients: The Effect of Alcoholic, Depressive and
        Schizophrenic Parentage. Canadian Psychiatric Association
        Journal, 23: 281-290, 1978.

1101. El-Guebaly, Nady and Offord, David R. The Offspring of
        Alcoholics: A Critical Review. American Journal of
        Psychiatry, 134(4): 357-365, 1977.

1102. Eliminating Drinking Traditions at Yale. Intercollegiate
        Statesman: 100-101, 112, April/May, 1971.

1103.   Ellekjaer, E.F. and Lund, B.M.A. Sosiale Forhold og Stofforbruk
        Blant en Gruppe Unge Stoffmisbrukere i Oslo. (Social
        Conditions and Use of Drugs Among a Group of Young Addicts
        in Oslo.) Tidsskrift for den Norske Laegeforening, Oslo,
        93: 2081-2086, 1973.

1104.   Ellington, P.D. Critical Issues Facing Teenagers: Alcohol,
        Smoking and Drug Abuse. Journal of the Medical Association
        of Georgia, 64: 457-459, 1975.

1105.   Elliott, W.J. Intemperance and the N.S.P.C.C. British Journal
        of Inebriety, 26: 226-228, 1929.

1106.   Ellis, Barbara Gray. Report of a Workshop on Reinforcing the
        Family System as the Major Resource in the Primary
        Prevention of Drug Abuse. In: Drug Abuse from the Family
        Perspective. Ed. Barbara Gray Ellis. Washington, D.C.:
        U.S. Government Printing Office, 1980, pages 127-140.

1107.   Ellrod, J.G. Alcoholism in the Elementary Curriculum? Peabody
        Journal of Education, 47(2): 97-98, 1969.

1108.   Ellwood, L.C. Effects of Alcoholism as a Family Illness on Child
        Behavior and Development. Military Medicine, 145: 188-192,
        1980.

1109.   Elmer, A. Ungdomens Alkoholvanor--Ny Litteratur. (Drinking
        Practices Among Youth--Current Literature.) Alkohol och
        Narkotica, Stockholm, 73(1): 22-23, 1978.

1110.   Elseroad, H.O. and Goodman, S.M. Teenager's Attitudes Toward
        the Use of Drugs, Alcohol and Cigarettes. Rockville,
        Maryland: Montgomery County Public Schools, 1972.

1111.   Emerson, H. The Educational Approach to the Alcohol Problem.
        Scientific Temperance Journal, 52: 71-74, 82-85, 1944.

1112.   Encel, S., Kotowicz, K.C. and Resler, H.E. Drinking Patterns in
        Sydney, Australia. Quarterly Journal of Studies on
        Alcohol, (Supplement No. 6): 1-27, 1972.

1113.   The Encephalogram as Evidence Against Criminal Responsibility.
        (Foreign Letters.) Journal of the American Medical
        Association, 122: 190, 1943.

1114.   Engeset, A. and Idsøe, R. Alkoholmisbrukeres Foreldre og Brøde.
        Sammenhengen Mellom Foreldrenes Alkoholvaner og
        Alkoholmisbruk Blant Sønnene. (Misuse of Alcohol in
        Parents and Brothers. Connection Between the Drinking
        Habits of Parents and the Incidence of Alcohol Misuse Among
        Their Sons.) Oslo: Universitetsforlaget, 1958.

1115.   England, Ralph W.   A Theory of Middle Class Juvenile Delinquency.
        In: Readings in Juvenile Delinquency. Ed. R. Cavan. New
        York: J.B. Lippincott, 1969, pages 106-114.

1116.   Englebardt, Stanley L.   Kids and Alcohol, The Deadliest Drug.
        New York: Lothrop, Lee and Shepard, 1975.

1117.   Englebrecht, G.K.   Alcoholism as a Possible Factor in Suicide.
        In: Papers Presented at the 24th International Congress
        on the Prevention and Treatment of Alcoholism, Zurich,
        June, 1978. Lausanne, Switzerland: International Council
        on Alcohol and Addictions, 1978, pages 382-390.

1118.   Engs, R.C.   College Students' Knowledge of Alcohol and Drinking.
        Journal of the American College Health Association, 26:
        189-193, 1978.

1119.   Engs, R.C., Barnes, E. and Wantz, M.   Health Games Students Play:
        Creative Strategies for Health Education.   Dubuque, Iowa:
        Kendall-Hunt, 1975.

1120.   Engs, Ruth.   The Drug-Use Patterns of Helping-Profession
        Students in Brisbane, Australia.   Drug and Alcohol
        Dependence, 6(4): 231-246, 1980.

1121.   Engs, Ruth.   Let's Look Before We Leap: The Cognitive and
        Behavioral Evaluation of a University Alcohol Education
        Program.   Journal of Alcohol and Drug Education, 22(2):
        39-48, 1976.

1122.   Engs, Ruth and Mulhall, Peter.   Again--Let's Look Before We
        Leap: The Effects of Physical Activity on Smoking and
        Drinking Patterns.   Journal of Alcohol and Drug Education,
        26(2): 65-74, 1981.

1123.   Engs, Ruth C.   Drinking Patterns and Drinking Problems of College
        Students.   Journal of Studies on Alcohol, 38(11): 2144-
        2156, 1977.

1124.   Engs, Ruth C.   Training Manual for "Booze and You's" Group
        Leaders.   Bloomington, Indiana: Indiana University, 1975.

1125.   Engs, Ruth C., DeCoster, David A., Larson, Ralph V. and
        McPheron, Philip.   The Drinking Behavior of College
        Students and Cognitive Effects of a Voluntary Alcohol
        Education Program.   Bloomington, Indiana: Indiana
        University, 1976.

1126.   Ennis, Pamela.   Drinking and Driving Among Ontario Students in
        1977.   Toronto, Ontario, Canada: Addiction Research
        Foundation, 1978.

1127.   Ennis, Pamela. A Note on DWI Offenders of Illegal Drinking Age:
          Is Alcohol Really the Problem? Toronto, Ontario, Canada:
          Addiction Research Foundation, 1976.

1128.   Epstein, M.H., Crenshaw, C.S. and Albert V.M. High School Drug
          Survey: Washington County, Georgia. Journal of the
          Medical Association of Georgia, 65(1): 407-411, 1976.

1129.   Erickson, M.L. Group Violations, Socioeconomic Status and
          Official Delinquency. Social Forces, 52: 41-52, 1973.

1130.   Erickson, M.L. and Gibbs, J.P. Community Tolerance and Measures
          of Delinquency. Journal of Research in Crime and
          Delinquency, 16: 55-79, 1979.

1131.   Ericson, J.S. C.F.N.'s Instruction Courses for Teachers During
          the School Term 1936-37. Tirfing, 31: 106-112, 1937.

1132.   Ericson, J.S. Some Viewpoints Concerning Sobriety Information in
          Textbooks and High Schools. Tirfing, 35: 97-104, 1941.

1133.   Ericson, J.S. Temperance Education and Schoolbooks. Tirfing,
          26: 33-43, 1933.

1134.   Eriksson, M., Larsson, G. and Zetterström, R. Abuse of Alcohol,
          Drugs and Tobacco During Pregnancy Consequences for the
          Child. Paediatrician, 8: 228-242, 1979.

1135.   Eriksson, T. The Rise in Adolescents' Drinking. Tirfing, 36:
          57-60, 1942.

1136.   Eriksson, T. The Role of Alcohol in Juvenile Delinquency.
          Tirfing, 36: 93-99, 1942.

1137.   Erlick, A.C. Incidence of Drug Use and Issues of Prevention
          (Report of Poll 97 of the Purdue Opinion Panel). West
          Lafayette, Indiana: Purdue Research Foundation, 1973.

1138.   Erlick, A.C. and Van Horn, C. Current Views of High School
          Students Toward the Use of Tobacco, Alcohol, and Drugs
          or Narcotics (Report of Poll No. 86 of the Purdue Opinion
          Panel). West Lafayette, Indiana: Purdue Research
          Foundation, 1969.

1139.   Esche. Alkohol und Jugend. (Alcohol and Youth.) Alkoholfrage
          5: 355-358, 1908.

1140.   Esman, Aaron, H., Ed. The Psychology of Adolescence. New York:
          International Universities Press, Inc., 1975.

1141.   Esselström, J. and Nieminen, I. Vassan Nuoroisotutkimus 1954.
          (A Social Study of Youth in the City of Vassa in 1954.)
          Alkoholikysymys, Helsinki, 25: 12-62, 1957.

1142.   Esser, P.H. Conjoint Family Therapy for Alcoholics. British
        Journal of the Addictions, 63(3): 177-182, 1968.

1143.   Este, Nada J. and Heinemann, M. Edith. Alcoholism: Development,
        Consequences and Interventions. St. Louis, Missouri:
        C.V. Mosby Company, 1977.

1144.   Evangelista, O., Saforcada, E. and Marconi, J. Estudio de las
        Actitudes Hacia el Alcohol en Adolescents de Tres Estratos
        Sociales de la Ciudad de Córdoba. (A Study of Attitudes
        Toward Alcohol of Adolescents of Three Social Strata in the
        City of Córdoba.) Acta Psiquiátrica y Psicologia de
        América Latina, 21: 101-111, 1975.

1145.   Evans, G.B., Steer, R.A. and Fine, E.W. Alcohol Value
        Clarification in Sixth Graders: A Film-Making Project.
        Journal of Alcohol and Drug Education, 24(2): 1-10, 1979.

1146.   Evans, J.H. Attitudes of Adolescent Delinquent Boys.
        Psychological Reports, 34(3): 1175-1178, 1974.

1147.   Evans, Karen Loges and D'Augelli, Judith Franke. Role of
        Decision-Making Skills Training in Alcohol Abuse
        Prevention. Paper Presented at the National Council on
        Alcoholism Region III Conference on Adolescent Alcohol
        Education, Lancaster, Pennsylvania, February 5-6, 1975.

1148.   Evans, M. and Avril, M. Alcoholism--A Family Disease. Health
        Visitor, 42: 459-461, 1969.

1149.   Evans, Michael. Our Changing Laws: Can Teens Handle Liquor?
        Parade Magazine, pages 8-10, September 24, 1978.

1150.   Evans, P. The Education of Youth Concern. In: Summer School of
        Studies on Alcohol and Drugs, Melbourne, 1971. Symposium:
        Alcohol and Drugs--A Challenge for Education (and)
        Orientation. Courses: Alcohol and Drugs. Ed.
        Joseph H. Santamaria. Melbourne, University of Melbourne,
        Department of Medicine, St. Vincent's Hospital, 1971, pages
        23-26.

1151.   Evarts, P. Notes on Alcohol Education for Teachers. Department
        of Education, Bulletin No. 371. Lansing: Michigan
        Department of Education and Department of Public Health,
        Alcoholism Program, 1967.

1152.   Everett, M.W. et al. Anthropological Expertise and the Realities
        of White Mountain Apache Adolescent Drinking. Tucson:
        Paper Presented at the 32nd Annual Meeting of the Society
        for Applied Anthropology, 1973.

1153.   Everett, Michael W., Wadell, Jack O. and Heath, Dwight B., Eds.
        Cross-Cultural Approaches to the Study of Alcohol: An
        Interdisciplinary Perspective. The Hague, Paris: Mouton
        Publishers, 1976.

1154.   Ewing, J.A.   A Biopsychosocial Look at Drinking and Alcoholism.
        Journal of the American College Health Association, 25(3):
        204-208, 1977.

1155.   Ewing, J.A. and Rouse, B.A., Eds.   Drinking: Alcohol in
        American Society--Issues and Current Research.   Chicago:
        Nelson-Hall, 1978.

1156.   Ewing, John.   Social and Psychiatric Considerations of Drinking.
        In: Drinking: Alcohol in American Society - Issues and
        Current Research.   Eds. J.A. Ewing and B.A. Rouse.
        Chicago: Nelson-Hall, 1978, pages 93-115.

F

1157. Facts and Fancy About Teenage Drinking. Report on Alcohol,
13(2): 16-31, 1975.

1158. Fagerberg, S. A Comparative Study of Drug Use Patterns in Three
Academic Settings: University, Community College, and
High Schools. Journal of Alcohol and Drug Education,
20(2): 27-34, 1975.

1159. Fagerberg, Seigfried, Young, Marion, Sanders, Lowell,
McGoskill, Connie, Leardon, Robert and Beach, Laurie.
Illicit Drug Use in a Florida County. Journal of Alcohol
and Drug Education, 19(1): 9-17, 1973.

1160. Fago, D.P. and Sedlacek, W.E. A Comparison of Freshmen and
Transfer Student Attitudes and Behavior Toward Drugs.
Journal of College Student Personnel, 16(1): 70-74, 1975.

1161. Fahrenkrug, H. Zur Integration von Alkoholtrinken in das
Alltagsleben: Theorie und Methode Einer "Interpretativen
Alkoholsoziologie"--Dargestellt an Einer Explorativen
Studie zum Studentischen Trinkverhalten. (Integrating
Alcohol into Daily Life: Theories and Methods of a Study
of Student Drinking Behavior.) In: Alkoholkonsum und
Alkoholabhängigkeit. (Alcohol Consumption and Alcohol
Dependence.) Eds. H. Berger, A. Legnaro and K.-H. Reuband.
Stuttgart: W. Kohlhammer, 1979, pages 53-72.

1162. Fahrenkrug, H. Zur Sozialen Organisation Alltäglicher
Trinkhandlungen bei Studenten. Alkoholsoziologie auf der
Basis des "Interpretativen Paradigmas" Gegenwärtiger
Soziologie. (The Social Organization of Daily Drinking
Customs Among Students: Alcohol Sociology Based on
"Interpretative Paradigms" of Current Sociology.)
(Christian-Albrechts-Universität Soziologische
Arbeitsberichte 5) Kiel: Institut für Soziologie,
Christian-Albrechts-Universität, 1979

1163. Faigel, H.C. Where Have all the Junkies Gone? Clinical
       Pediatrics, 14: 703-705, 1975.

1164. Faigel, Harris C. Commentary: Why Our Children Drink. Clinical
       Pediatrics, 15(6): 509, 1976.

1165. Fairchild, D.M. Teen Group I: A Pilot Project in Group Therapy
       with Adolescent Children of Alcoholic Patients. Journal
       of Fort Logan Mental Health Center, 2: 71-75, 1964.

1166. Falewicz, J.K. Młodzi Robotnicy. (Young Workers.) Problemy
       Alkoholizmu, Warsaw, 18(10): 1-4; 18(11): 36, 1970.

1167. Falewicz, J.K. Studenci o Propagandzie Przeciwalkoholowej.
       (Students' Voice on the Anti-Alcohol Propaganda.)
       Problemy Alkoholizmu, Warsaw, 15(1): 5-7, 1967.

1168. Falewicz, J.K. Uwarunkowania Spoleczne Picia Wśród Młodziezy.
       (Social Conditioning of Drinking Among Youth.) Problemy
       Alkoholizmu, Warsaw, 26(78): 19-21, 44, 1979.

1169. Falkewicz, J.K. Wstepne Wyniki Badań Ankietowycn na Temat
       Spozycia Alkoholu w Srodowisku Studenckim. (Preliminary
       Reports of Studies of the Drinking Pattern in a Student
       Milieu.) Problemy Alkoholizmu, Warsaw, 15(4): 1-5, 1967.

1170. Falk, W. Die Akute Kindliche Alkoholintoxikation. (Acute
       Alcohol Intoxication in Children.) Zeitschrift fuer
       Allgemeinmedizin, 47: 1073-1075, 1971.

1171. Falstein, E.I. Juvenile Alcoholism: A Psychodynamic Case Study
       of Addiction. American Journal of Orthopsychiatry, 23:
       530-551, 1953.

1172. Fanai, F. Verlauf und Prognose der Verwahrlosung: Katamnesen
       Jugendlicher mit Gestörtem Sozialverhalten. (Progress and
       Prognosis of Degeneration: Catamnesis of Adolescents with
       Disturbed Social Behavior.) Psychiatria Clinica, 2(1):
       1-13, 1969.

1173. Fard, K., Hudgens, R.W. and Welner, A. Undiagnosed Psychiatric
       Illness in Adolescents: A Prospective Study and Seven-
       Year Follow-Up. Archives of General Psychiatry, 35: 279-
       282, 1978.

1174. Faris, Don. The Prevention of Alcoholism and Economic
       Alcoholism. Preventive Medicine, 3: 36-48, 1974.

1175. Farkasinszky, T., Simon, A., Wágner, A. and Szilárd, I.
       Entwicklungsstörungen der Persönlichkeit bei Kindern
       Alkoholiker. (Development of Personality Disturbances in
       Children of Alcoholics.) Alcoholism, Zagreb, 9: 3-8, 1973.

1176.   Farler, E.C., Santo, Y. and Speck, D.W.   Multiple Drug Abuse
        Patterns of Youth in Treatment.   In: Youth Drug Abuse:
        Problems, Issues and Treatment.   Eds. G.M. Beschner and
        A.S. Friedman.   Lexington, Massachusetts: D.C. Heath,
        1979, pages 149-168.

1177.   Farnsworth, D.L.   Drug Use for Pleasure? A Complex Social
        Problem. The Journal of School Health, 43(3): 153-158,
        1973.

1178.   Farnsworth, D.L.   Mental and Emotional Disturbances of the
        Secondary School-Age Student. Journal of School Health,
        45(4): 221-225, 1975.

1179.   Fatteh, A., Galbraith, W. and Mann, G.T.   Drink, Drive and Die.
        Virginia Medical Monthly, 96(6): 309-311, 1969.

1180.   Fatteh, A., Hudson, P. and McBay, A.   Highway Homicides and
        Suicides. North Carolina Medical Journal, 32(5): 184-185,
        1971.

1181.   Favazza, A.R. and Cannell, B.   Screening for Alcoholism Among
        College Students. American Journal of Psychiatry, 134(12):
        1414-1416, 1977.

1182.   Favazza, Armando.   Alcohol and Special Populations. Journal of
        Studies on Alcohol, (Supplement No. 9): 87-98, 1981.

1183.   Federn, E.   A Psycho-Social View of "Drug Abuse" in Adolescence.
        Child Psychiatry and Human Development, 3(1): 10-20, 1972.

1184.   Fee, D.   Drunk Driving: Outline of a Public Information and
        Education Program.   In: Alcohol, Drugs and Traffic Safety.
        Proceedings of the Sixth International Conference on
        Alcohol, Drugs and Traffic Safety, Toronto, September 8-13,
        1974. Eds. S. Israelstam and S. Lambert. Toronto,
        Ontario: Addiction Research Foundation, 1975, pages 789-
        798.

1185.   Feinglass, S.J. and Lappin M.   Alcoholism, Drug Abuse and
        Pregnancy: Causative Factors in Child Abuse and Neglect?
        In: Child Abuse and Neglect: Issues on Innovation and
        Implementation. Proceedings of the Second National
        Conference on Child Abuse and Neglect, April 17-20, 1977.
        Volume II. Eds. M.L. Lauderdale, R.N. Anderson and
        S.E. Cramer, Eds. Washington, D.C.: National Center on
        Child Abuse and Neglect (DHEW) pages 301-303, 1978.
        (OHDS) 78-30148.

1186. Feinglass, Sanford J. How to Plan a Drug Abuse Education
       Workshop. In: Resource Book for Drug Abuse Education.
       American Association for Health, Physical Education and
       Recreation, Washington, D.C.: U.S. Government Printing
       Office, 1969, pages 99-115. Also in: Research Book for
       Drug Abuse Education, 2nd Edition. Rockville, Maryland:
       National Clearinghouse for Drug Abuse Information, 1972,
       pages 91-104.

1187. Fejer, D., Smart, R. and Whitehead, P.C. Changes in the Patterns
       of Drug Use in Two Canadian Cities. In: Alcoholism and
       Other Drugs: Perspectives on Use, Abuse, Treatment and
       Prevention. Eds. Paul C. Whitehead, Carl F. Grindstaff and
       Craig L. Boydell. Toronto, Montreal: Holt, Rinehart and
       Winston, 1973, pages 156-164.

1188. Fejer, D., Smart, R.G. and Whitehead P.C. Changes in the
       Patterns of Drug Use in Two Canadian Cities: Toronto and
       Halifax. International Journal of the Addictions, 7: 467-
       479, 1972. Also in: Deviant Behavior and Social
       Reaction. Eds. C.L. Boydell, C.F. Grindstaff and
       P.C. Whitehead. Toronto, Ontario: Holt, Rinehart and
       Winston, 1972, pages 360-368.

1189. Fejer, Dianne and Smart, Reginald G. The Knowledge About Drugs,
       Attitudes Toward Them and Drug Use Rates of High School
       Students. Journal of Drug Education, 3(4): 377-388, 1973.

1190. Fejer, Dianne and Smart, Reginald G. Preferences of Students for
       Drug Education Programs and Program Elements. (Substudy
       No. 652) Toronto, Ontario: Addiction Research Foundation,
       1975. Also in: Journal of Alcohol and Drug Education,
       21(1): 11-20, 1975.

1191. Feldman, Ben H. and Rosenkrantz, Arthur L. Drug Use by College
       Students and Their Parents. Addictive Diseases, 3(2):
       235-242, 1977.

1192. Feldman, H. American Way of Drugging: Street Status and Drug
       Users. Society, 10(4): 32-38, 1973.

1193. Feldman, Harvey W. Street Status and the Drug Researcher:
       Issues in Participant-Observation. Pamphlet. Washington,
       D.C.: Drug Abuse Council, Inc., 1974.

1194. Felice, J.P. and Carolan, P.J. Tune in to Health, 2nd Edition.
       New York: CEBCO Standard Publishing, 1974.

1195. Feline, A. and Ades, J. Aspects Actuels de L'Alcoolisme du
       Sujet Jeune. (Present-Day Aspects of Alcoholism Among
       Youth.) Annales Médico-Psychologique, 138: 80-87, 1980.

1196. Female Under 21 Serving Drinks--Meaning of "Serve." Australian
       Law Journal, 17: 388, 1944.

1197.   Fenchel, M.S.   Sales to Minors.   Journal of Criminal Law, 29:
        743-745, 1939.

1198.   Ferdière, G. and Belfils.   Les Psychoses Alcooliques en France à
        L'Heure Actuelle.   (Alcoholic Psychoses in France at the
        Present Time.)   Praxis, Bern, 31: 516, 1942.

1199.   Ferguson, L.W.   Public-Service Drug-Use Scales: Rationale,
        Derivation and Norms.   Psychological Reports, 34: 871-876,
        1974.

1200.   Ferguson, Leonard W., Freedman, Marilyn and Ferguson, Edith P.
        Developmental Self-Concept and (Self-Reported) Drug Use.
        Psychological Reports, 41: 531-541, 1977.

1201.   Ferm, Vergilius.   A Dictionary of Pastoral Psychology.   New York:
        Philosophical Library, 1955.

1202.   Fernan, Joan.   Bartenders Seminars Held in Wisconsin.   Traffic
        Safety, 78(6): 16-17, 1978.

1203.   Fernandez, F.A.   The State of Alcoholism in Spain Covering Its
        Epidemiological and Aetiological Aspects.   British Journal
        of Addiction, 71(3): 235-242, 1976.

1204.   Ferrence, R.G.   Drinking, Driving and Age of Majority.   (Comment)
        Addictions, 24(1): 76-78, 1977.

1205.   Ferrence, R.G. and Whitehead, P.C.   Fatal Crashes Among Michigan
        Youth Following Reduction of the Legal Drinking Age.
        Journal of Studies on Alcohol, 36: 171-173, 1975.

1206.   Ferrier, W.K.   Alcohol Education in the Public School Curriculum.
        In: Alcohol Education for Classroom and Community: A
        Source Book for Educators.   Ed. R.G. McCarthy.   New York:
        McGraw-Hill, 1964, pages 48-66.

1207.   Festa, Michael, Snyder, Marilyn and Yurino, Lucia.   Final Report:
        Verona's Alcohol Education Program.   Verona, New Jersey:
        Public Health Department, 1975.

1208.   Feuerlein, W.   Alcohol Consumption Among the Youth in Bavaria.
        In: International Congress on Alcoholism and Drug
        Dependence, February 23-28, 1975, 31st Vol. III.
        Proceedings.   Lausanne: International Council on Alcohol
        and Addictions, 1975, pages 498-499.

1209.   Fields, M.G.   Drink and Delinquency in the USSR.   Problems of
        Communism, 4(3): 29-38, 1955.

1210.   Fields, B.L.   Adolescent Alcoholism: Treatment and
        Rehabilitation.   Family and Community Health, 2(1):61-90,
        1979.

1211. The Fight Against Alcoholism. Retail, Wholesale and Department
       Store Union, AFL-CIO, 16(22): 13, 1969.

1212. The Fight Against the Temperance School Books. Quarterly Journal
       of Inebriety, 25: 91-92, 1903.

1213. Fillmore, K.M. Abstinence, Drinking and Problem Drinking Among
       Adolescents as Related to Apparent Parental Drinking
       Practices. Master's Thesis. Amherst, Massachusetts:
       University of Massachusetts, 1970.

1214. Fillmore, K.M. Drinking and Problem Drinking in Early Adulthood
       and Middle Age: An Exploratory 20-Year Follow-Up Study.
       Quarterly Journal of Studies on Alcohol, 35: 819-840, 1974.

1215. Fillmore, K.M. Relationships Between Specific Drinking Problems
       in Early Adulthood and Middle Age: An Exploratory 20-Year
       Follow-Up Study. Journal of Studies on Alcohol, 36: 882-
       907, 1975.

1216. Fillmore, K.M., Bacon, S.D. and Hyman, M. The 27-Year
       Longitudinal Panel Study of Drinking by Students in
       College, 1949-1976. Final Report. (Report No. PB 300-302.)
       Springfield, Virginia: U.S. National Technical
       Information Service, 1979. Also as: The 27-Year
       Longitudinal Panel Study of Drinking by Students in
       College (1949-1976) (Final Report). U.S. Department of
       Health, Education and Welfare, 1979.

1217. Fillmore, Kaye M. and Marden, Philip W. Longitudinal Research at
       the Rutgers Center of Alcohol Studies. Alcoholism:
       Clinical and Experimental Research, 1: 251-257, 1977.

1218. Filstead, W.J., Rossi, J.J. and Keller, M., Eds. Alcohol and
       Alcohol Problems. Cambridge, Massachusetts: Ballinger,
       1976.

1219. Filstead, W.J. and Mayer, J.E. Adolescence and Alcohol: An
       Overview and Introduction. In: Adolescence and Alcohol.
       J.E. Mayer and W.J. Filstead. Cambridge, Massachusetts:
       Ballinger, 1980, pages 1-5.

1220. Filstead, W.J. and Mayer, J.E. Adolescence and Alcohol: Some
       Future Considerations. In: Adolescence and Alcohol.
       J.E. Mayer and W.J. Filstead. Cambridge, Massachusetts:
       Ballinger, 1980, pages 273-276.

1221. Filstead, W.J., Rossi, J.J. and Goby, M.J. Alcoholism and
       Alcohol Problems on College Campuses: Problems, Priorities
       and Recommendations. Journal of Alcohol and Drug
       Education, 21(2): 35-43, 1976.

1222. Filstead, William, McElfresh, Oru and Anderson, Carl. Comparing
       the Family Environments of Alcoholic and "Normal" Families.
       Journal of Alcohol and Drug Education, 26(2): 24-31, 1981.

1223. Fine, E.H., Yudin, L., Holmes, J. and Heinemann, S. Behavior
       Disorders in Children with Parental Alcoholism. Paper
       Presented at the Annual Conference of the National Council
       on Alcoholism, April 27-May 2, 1975, Milwaukee, Wisconsin.
       (Also as: Behavioral Disorders in Children with Parental
       Alcoholism. Annals of the New York Academy of Science,
       273: 507-517, 1976.)

1224. Fine, E.W. and Scoles, P. Secondary Prevention of Alcoholism
       Using a Population of Offenders Arrested for Driving While
       Intoxicated. Annals of the New York Academy of Science,
       273: 637-645, 1976.

1225. Fine, E.W., Scoles, P. and Mulligan, M. Under the Influence:
       Characteristics and Drinking Practices of Persons Arrested
       the First Time for Drunk Driving, with Treatment
       Implications. Public Health Reports, 90: 424-429, 1975.

1226. Fine, Eric. Social and Epidemiological Research. In: Currents
       in Alcoholism. Volume 2. Psychiatric, Psychological,
       Social and Epidemiological Studies. Ed. F.A. Seixas. New
       York: Grune and Stratton, 1977, pages 245-253.

1227. Fine, Eric, Scoles, Pascal and Mulligan, Michael. Alcohol Abuse
       in First Offenders Arrested for Driving While Intoxicated.
       In: Alcohol, Drugs and Traffic Safety. Proceedings of the
       Sixth International Conference on Alcohol, Drugs and
       Traffic Safety, September 8-13, 1974, Toronto. Eds.
       S. Israelstam and S. Lambert. Toronto, Ontario: Addiction
       Research Foundation of Ontario, 1975, pages 169-174.

1228. Fink, R., Chroman, P. and Clark, W. Parental Drinking and Its
       Impact on Adult Drinkers. Berkeley, California: Social
       Research Group, 1962.

1229. Finkle, Bryan S. Drugs in Drinking Drivers: A Study of 2,500
       Cases. Journal of Safety Research, 1(4): 179-183, 1969.

1230. Finland. Haminan Nuorkauppakamari Haminassa ja Vehkalahdella
       Opiskelevien Päihdeaineiden Käyttö Vuonna 1974:
       Yleisraportti. (The Use of Intoxicants Among Students in
       Hamina and Vehkalahdella During 1974: A General Report.)
       Hamina: Nuorkauppakamari, 1974.

1231. Finn, P. Alcohol Education in the School Curriculum: The
       Single Discipline vs. the Interdisciplinary Approach.
       Journal of Alcohol and Drug Education, 24(2): 41-57, 1979.

1232. Finn, P. Alcohol: You Can Help Your Kids Cope. Instructor,
       76-78, 83, November, 1975.

1233. Finn, P. Alcohol--You Can Help Your Kids Cope: A Guide for the
       Elementary School Teacher. Pamphlet. New York: National
       Council on Alcoholism, 1975.

1234. Finn, P. The Role of Attitudes in Public School Alcohol
       Education. Journal of Alcohol and Drug Education, 20: 23-
       42, 1975.

1235. Finn, P. The Role of Attitudes in Secondary School Alcohol-
       Traffic Safety Education. In: Alcohol, Drugs and Traffic
       Safety. Proceedings of the Sixth International Conference
       on Alcohol, Drugs and Traffic Safety, Toronto, September 8-
       13, 1974. Eds. S. Israelstam and S. Lambert. Toronto,
       Ontario: Addiction Research Foundation, 1975, pages 881-
       888. (Also in: Journal of Traffic Safety Education,
       22(3): 7-8, 12, 1975.

1236. Finn, P. Should Alcohol Education be Taught with Drug Education?
       Journal of School Health, 446-469, October, 1977.

1237. Finn, P. Surfacing and Exploring Attitudes Toward Alcoholics:
       Approaches and Techniques. Journal of Alcohol and Drug
       Education, 24(1): 58-72, 1978.

1238. Finn, P. and Platt, J. Alcohol and Alcohol Safety: A
       Curriculum Manual for Elementary Level. Volume 1.
       Washington, D.C.: U.S. Government Printing Office, 1972.
       (DOT Publication No. HS-800,707)

1239. Finn, P. and Platt, J. Alcohol and Alcohol Safety: A
       Curriculum Manual for Elementary Level. Volume 2. A
       Teacher's Activities Guide. Washington, D.C.: U.S.
       Government Printing Office, 1972. (DOT Publication No.
       HS-800,708)

1240. Finn, P. and Platt, J. Alcohol and Alcohol Safety: A
       Curriculum Manual for Junior High Level. Volume 1.
       Washington, D.C.: U.S. Government Printing Office, 1972.
       (DOT Publication No. HS-800,709)

1241. Finn, P. and Platt. J. Alcohol and Alcohol Safety: A
       Curriculum Manual for Junior High Level. Volume 2. A
       Teacher's Activities Guide. Washington, D.C.: U.S.
       Government Printing Office, 1972. (DOT Publication No.
       HS-800,710)

1242. Finn, P. and Platt, J. Alcohol and Alcohol Safety: A
       Curriculum Manual for Senior High Level. Volume 1.
       Washington, D.C.: U.S. Government Printing Office, 1972.
       (DOT Publication No. HS-800,705)

1243. Finn, P. and Platt, J. Alcohol and Alcohol Safety: A
       Curriculum Manual for Senior High Level. Volume 2. A
       Teacher's Activities Guide. Washington, D.C.: U.S.
       Government Printing Office, 1972. (DOT Publication No.
       HS-800,706).

1244.   Finn, Peter. The Development of Attitudinal Measures Toward
        Alcohol Education in the School and in the Home. Journal
        of Drug Education, 8(3): 203-219, 1978.

1245.   Finn, Peter. Institutionalizing Peer Education in the Health
        Education Classroom. Journal of School Health, 51(2): 91-
        95, 1981.

1246.   Finn, Peter. Teenage Drunkenness: Warning Signal, Transient
        Boisterousness, or Symptom of Social Change? Adolescence,
        14(56): 819-834, 1979.

1247.   Finn, Peter and Brown, James. Risks Entailed in Teenage
        Intoxication as Perceived by Junior and Senior High School
        Students. Journal of Youth and Adolescence, 10(1): 61-76,
        1981.

1248.   Finnell, W.S. A Study of the Relationship Between Academic
        Performance and the Use of Marijuana and Alcoholic
        Beverages Among Persisting College Students. Doctoral
        Dissertation (University Microfilms No. 73-6520). Memphis
        State University, 1972.

1249.   Finnell, W.S., Jr. and Jones, J.D. Marijuana, Alcohol and
        Academic Performance. Journal of Drug Education, 5: 13-21,
        1975.

1250.   Fischer, E. Beitrag zur Wirkung des Chron. Alkoholkonsums auf
        die Entwicklung des Kindes. (Contribution on the Effect
        of Chronic Alcohol Consumption in Child Development.)
        Archiv fuer Kinderheilkunde, 138: 199-211, 1950.

1251.   Fischer, Jay. Psychotherapy of Adolescent Alcohol Abusers. In:
        Practical Approaches to Alcoholism Psychotherapy. Eds.
        S. Zimberg, J. Wallace and S.B. Blume. New York: Plenum
        Press, 1978, pages 219-235.

1252.   Fischer, Jay and Coyle, Brian. A Specialized Treatment Service
        for Young Problem Drinkers (16-30 Years):   Treatment
        Results Obtained During the First Six Months of the
        Treatment Programme. British Journal of Addiction, 72(4):
        317-319, 1977.

1253.   Fischler, M.L. The Extent of and Socio-Psychological Factors
        Endemic to Drug Use-Abuse in a Section of Rural, Small Town
        New England. Doctoral Dissertation (University Microfilms
        No. 74-22337). University of Colorado, 1974.

1254.   Fisher, Margaret T., Jerrick, Stephen J. and
        VonLehmden-Maslin, Alys, (Eds.). Teaching About Drugs: A
        Curriculum Guide, K-12. Kent, Ohio: American School
        Health Association, 1972.

1255.   Fitzgerald, J.L. and Mulford, H.A.   The Prevalence and Extent of
        Drinking in Iowa, 1979.   Journal of Studies on Alcohol, 42:
        38-47, 1981.

1256.   Fitzpatrick, J.   Drinking and Young People.   In: Alcoholism.
        Ed. B. McCarthy.   Dublin: Impact, 1971.

1257.   Fitzpatrick, J.   Drinking and Young People: A Sociological
        Approach.   Journal on Alcoholism, 6(3): 90-94, 1971.

1258.   Fitzpatrick, J.   Drinking and Young People: A Sociological
        Study.   Master's Thesis.   National University of Ireland,
        1970.   (Also as: Report to the Irish National Council on
        Alcoholism.   Dublin, 1970.)

1259.   Fitzpatrick, J.   Drinking Among Young People in Ireland.   Social
        Studies, Irish Journal of Sociology, 1: 51-60, 1972.

1260.   Flanzer, J.P.   Alcohol-Abusing Parents and Their Battered
        Adolescents.   In: Currents in Alcoholism.   Volume 7.
        Recent Advances in Research and Treatment.   Ed.
        M. Galanter.   New York: Grune and Stratton, 1980,
        pages 529-538.

1261.   Flanzer, Jerry.   Alcohol Use Among Jewish Adolescents: A 1977
        Sample.   In: Currents in Alcoholism.   Volume 6.
        Treatment and Rehabilitation and Epidemiology.   Ed.
        M. Galanter.   New York: Grune and Stratton, 1979, pages
        257-268.

1262.   Flanzer, Jerry.   The Vicious Circle of Alcoholism and Family
        Violence.   Alcoholism, The National Magazine, 1(3): 30-32,
        1981.

1263.   Flanzer, Jerry and Gregory, M.   Family Focused Treatment and
        Management: A Multi-Discipline Training Approach.   In:
        International Conference on Alcoholism and Drug Dependence:
        Alcoholism and Drug Dependence, A Multidisciplinary
        Approach.   Proceedings of the Third International
        Conference on Alcoholism and Drug Dependence, Liverpool,
        England, April, 1976.   Eds. J.S. Madden, Robin Walker and
        W.H. Kenyon.   New York: Plenum Press, 1977, pages 239-261.

1264.   Flaum, T.K.   Teenage Drinking and Driving.   Leaflet.   Lansing,
        Michigan: Alcohol/Drug Information Foundation, 1964.

1265.   Fleck, Leon.   The Twelve-Year Struggle Against Alcoholism in
        France.   In: World Dialogue on Alcohol and Drug
        Dependence.   Ed. E.D. Whitney.   Boston, Massachusetts:
        Beacon Press, 1970, pages 20-40.

1266.   Fleming, R.J.   A Survey of Drinking Behavior Among Montana State
        University Students and the Potential for Problems with
        Alcohol: Implications for Counseling Services, Alcohol
        Education, and Student Personnel Services.   Doctoral
        Dissertation (University Microfilms No. 77-4972).   Montana
        State University, 1976.

1267.   Flint, R.   Teenage Drinking: A Cause for Concern?   Journal on
        Alcoholism, 9(3): 84-93, 1974.

1268.   Florida Bureau of Alcoholic Rehabilitation.   Man's Experience
        With Alcohol: A Curriculum Guide and Resource Manual.
        Prepared by K.H. Doig and S.G. Clarke.   Avon Park, Florida,
        1972.

1269.   Florida Department of Education.   Alcohol-Narcotics Education:
        A Handbook for Teachers.   Dallas: Tane Press, 1967.

1270.   Florida Department of Education.   Materials in the Florida State
        Adopted Textbooks and in Selected Supplementary Books
        Pertaining to the Field of Alcohol and Narcotics Education.
        With Suggested Teaching Aids.   Prepared at University of
        Florida and Stetson University (Katie Sue Echols,
        Consultant).   Tallahassee, Florida: 1947.

1271.   Florida.   Duval County School Board.   Research and Program
        Evaluation Section.   Student Drug and Alcohol Opinionnaire
        and Usage Survey, Grades 7, 8, 9, 10, 11, 12, Spring, 1971
        and 1972.   Jacksonville, Florida, 1972.

1272.   Florida.   Duval County School Board.   Test and Measurements
        Unit.   Student Drug and Alcohol Opinionnaire and Usage
        Survey, Grades 6, 7, 8, 9, 10, 11, 12, June, 1973 and
        January, 1974.   Jacksonville, Florida, 1974.

1273.   Florida.   Duval County School Board.   Test and Measurements
        Unit.   Student Drug and Alcohol Opinionnaire and Survey,
        Grades 6, 7, 8, 9, 10, 11, 12, January, 1975.
        Jacksonville, Florida, 1975.

1274.   Florida.   Duval County School Board.   Test and Measurements
        Unit.   Student Drug and Alcohol Opinionnaire and Usage
        Survey, Grades 6, 7, 8, 9, 10, 11, 12, January, 1976.
        Jacksonville, Florida, 1976.

1275.   Fogelman, K.   Drinking Among Sixteen-Year Olds.   Concern, 29:
        19-25, 1978.

1276.   Foggitt, R.H., Gossop, M.R. and Nicol, A.R.   Psychoneurotic
        Disturbance and Drug-Taking in Borstal Boys.
        Psychological Medicine, London, 6: 133-137, 1976.

1277. Fokina, E.N. Iz Istorii Bor'by s Alkogolizmom v Rossii--Raboty
       A.M. Korovina. (From the History of the Fight Against
       Alcoholism in Russia: The Work of A.M. Korovin.)
       Sovetskoe Zdravookhranenie, Moskow, 21(7): 60-64, 1962.

1278. Fontane, Patrick E. and Layne, Norman R. The Family as a
       Context for Developing Youthful Drinking Patterns. Journal
       of Alcohol and Drug Education, 24(3): 19-29, 1979.

1279. Football Hooliganism (Editorial). Journal of Alcoholism, 10(3):
       90-91, 1975.

1280. Football Supporters Drunk and Disorderly After Stealing Gin:
       Quarterly Notes. British Journal on Alcohol and
       Alcoholism, 12(1): 8, 1977.

1281. Forrai, M.S. and Anders, R. A Look at Alcoholism. Minneapolis:
       Lerner, 1978.

1282. Fors, Stuart W. On the Ethics of Selective Omission and/or
       Inclusion of Relevant Information in School Drug Education
       Programs. Journal of Drug Education, 10(2): 111-117, 1980.

1283. Forslund, M.A., Cockerham, W.C. and Raboin, R.M. Drug Use,
       Delinquency and Alcohol Use Among Indian and Anglo Youth in
       Wyoming. Laramie, Wyoming: Governor's Planning Committee
       on Criminal Administration, 1974.

1284. Forslund, M.A. and Gustafson, T.J. Alcohol and High-Schoolers.
       Bulletin of the National Association of Secondary School
       Principals, 53(338): 52-59, 1969.

1285. Forslund, M.A. and Gustafson, T.J. Influence of Peers and
       Parents and Sex Differences in Drinking by High-School
       Students. Quarterly Journal of Studies on Alcohol, 31:
       868-875, 1970.

1286. Forslund, M.A. and Gustafson, T.J. Relative Influence of Peers
       and Parents on Drinking by High-School Seniors.
       Albuquerque, New Mexico: Department of Sociology, The
       University of New Mexico, no date.

1287. Forslund, M. and Meyers, R. Delinquency Among Wind River Indians
       Reservation Youth. Criminology, 12: 97-106, 1974.

1288. Forslund, Morris A. Drinking Problems of Native American and
       White Youth. Journal of Drug Education, 9(1): 21-27, 1979.

1289. Foslund, Morris A. Functions of Drinking for Native American and
       White Youth. Journal of Youth and Adolescence, 7(3): 327-
       332, 1978.

1290. Forssman, H., Thuwe, I and Ericksson, B. Children with
       Supernumerary X-Chromosome: A Ten-Year Follow-Up Study of
       School Children in Special Classes. Journal of Mental
       Deficiency Research, 23: 189-193, 1979.

1291. Fort, Joel. The Pleasure Seekers: The Drug Crisis, Youth and
       Society. Indianapolis, Indiana: Bobbs-Merrill Co., Inc.,
       1969.

1292. Fort, Joel. Public Policy Reform. Journal of Drug Issues, 4:
       317-322, 1974.

1293. Fort, Joel. School: Our Biggest Drug Problem and Our Biggest
       Drug Industry. New York: McGraw-Hill, 1973.

1294. Fort, Joel. Youth, American Society and Drugs. In: The
       Pleasure Seekers. Joel Fort. Indianapolis: Bobs-Merrill,
       1969, pages 209-221.

1295. Fort, Joel. Youth: Drugs, Sex and Life. Current Problems in
       Pediatrics, 6(11): 1-42, 1976.

1296. Fort, L.M. Alcohol and You. Mountainview, California: Pacific
       Press, 1954.

1297. Fort, Twila and Porterfield, Austin L. Some Backgrounds and
       Types of Alcoholism Among Women. Journal of Health and
       Human Behavior, 2(1): 283-292, 1961.

1298. Foulds, G.A. The Significance of Age of Onset of Excessive
       Drinking in Male Alcoholics. British Journal of
       Psychiatry, 115: 1027-1032, September, 1969.

1299. Fox, Bernard and Borkenstein, Robert. Patterns of Blood Alcohol
       Concentrations Among Drivers. In: Alcohol, Drugs and
       Traffic Safety. Proceedings of the Sixth International
       Conference on Alcohol, Drugs and Traffic Safety, Toronto,
       September 8-13, 1974. Eds. S. Israelstam and S. Lambert.
       Toronto: Addiction Research Foundation of Ontario, 1975,
       pages 51-67.

1300. Fox, R. The Effect of Alcoholism on Children. In: Progress in
       Child Psychiatry. Proceedings of the Fifth International
       Congress of Psychotherapy, Vienna, 1961. Ed. B. Stokvis.
       Basel: Karger, 1963, pages 55-65. (Also as: The Effect
       of Alcoholism on Children. New York: National Council on
       Alcoholism, 1972.)

1301. Fox, Ruth. The Orientation of the Alcoholic to His Illness. In:
       Alcoholism: Group Psychotherapy and Rehabilitation. Eds.
       Hugh Mullan and Iris Sangiuliano. Springfield, Illinois:
       Thomas Publishing, 1966, pages 135-151.

1302.   Fox, Ruth.   Treating the Alcoholic's Family.   In: Alcoholism:
        The Total Treatment Approach.   Ed.   Ronald C. Catanzaro.
        Springfield, Illinois: Charles C. Thomas, 1968, pages 105-
        115.

1303.   Fox, V.   Alcoholism in Adolescence.   Journal of School Health,
        43: 32-35, 1973.

1304.   Framrose, R.   A Framework for Adolescent Disorder: Some Clinical
        Presentations.   British Journal of Psychiatry, 131: 281-
        288, 1977.

1305.   Frances, Richard J., Timm, Stephen and Bucky, Steven.   Studies of
        Familial and Nonfamilial Alcoholism.   Archives of General
        Psychiatry, 37: 564-566, 1980.

1306.   Frankel, G. and Whitehead, Paul.   Sociological Perspectives on
        Drinking and Damage.   In: Alcohol, Reform and Society:
        The Liquor Issue in Social Context.   Ed. Jack Blocker, Jr.
        Westport, Connecticut: Greenwood Press, 1979, pages 13-43.

1307.   Fredericks, J.   Community Alcohol Education and Prevention
        Program.   Doctoral Dissertation (University Microfilms
        No. 76-25605).   Utah State University, 1975.

1308.   Fredericks, J., Butler, J.G. and Nielsen, E.C.   Use of Local
        Statistics to Verify Conservatism Toward Drinking and
        Justify a Modern Position on Alcohol Education in a
        Conservative Community.   Journal of Alcohol and Drug
        Education, 21(1): 30-38, 1975.

1309.   Freed, E.   Opinions of Psychiatric Hospital Personnel and College
        Students Toward Alcoholism, Mental Illness and Physical
        Disability: An Exploratory Study.   Psychological Reports,
        15: 615-618, 1964.

1310.   Freed, E.X.   Drug Abuse by Alcoholics: A Review.   International
        Journal of the Addictions, 8: 451-473, 1973.

1311.   Freed, Earl X.   Reflections on Alcohol Miseducation.   Journal of
        Alcohol and Drug Education, 22(1): 1-4, 1976.

1312.   Freed, Earl X.   Some Interfaces Between Alcoholism and Mental
        Health.   Journal of Drug Issues, 6: 213-222, 1976.

1313.   Freeman, Don.   The Black Community and Marijuana Legalization.
        In: Drug Abuse: Modern Trends, Issues and Perspectives.
        Proceedings of the Second National Drug Abuse Conference,
        Inc., New Orleans, Louisiana, 1975.   Comp.: A. Schecter,
        H. Alksne and E. Kaufman.   New York: Marcel Dekker, Inc.,
        1978, pages 803-817.

1314.   Freeman, H.E. and Scott, J.F.   A Critical Review of Alcohol
        Education for Adolescents.   Community Mental Health
        Journal, 2(3): 222-230, 1966.

1315. Freeman, S. The Drinking Driver. British Medical Journal, 2:
          1634-1636, 1964. (Also in: American Heart Journal, 70:
          281-282, 1965.

1316. Freiová, E. Alkoholismus Rodiču a Mravní Narusěnost Mládeze
          Skolního Věku. (Alcoholism in Parents and the Moral
          Impairment of School-Age Children.) Ceskoslovenska
          Psychiatrie, 62: 188-192, 1966.

1317. Frenkel, S.I., Robinson, J.A. and Fiman, B.G. Drug Use:
          Demography and Attitudes in a Junior and Senior High School
          Population. Journal of Drug Education, 4(2): 179-186,
          1974.

1318. Freund, P.J. Armenian American Drinking Patterns. Alcohol
          Health and Research World, 5(1): 47-50, 1980.

1319. Friedman, Alfred S., Pomerance, Errol, Sanders, Richard,
          Santo, Yoav and Utada, Arlene. The Substance and Problems
          of Families of Adolescent Drug Abusers. Contemporary Drug
          Problems, 9(3): 327-356, 1981.

1320. Friedman, C. and Friedman, A. Drug Abuse and Delinquency. In:
          Drug Use in America. Problems in Perspective. Appendix,
          Volume 1. Patterns and Consequences of Drug Use. National
          Commission of Marihuana and Drug Abuse. Washington, D.C.:
          U.S. Government Printing Office, 1973, pages 398-484.

1321. Friedmann, A. Süchtigkeit im Kindes--und Jugendalter. (Drug
          Addiction in Children and Adolescents.) Acta
          Paedopsychiatrica, 36(8-10): 274-278, 1969.

1322. Fritzen, R.D. The Effects of Fear Appeal Communications and
          Communicators Upon Attitudes Toward Alcohol Consumption.
          Doctoral Dissertation (University Microfilms No. 74-20638).
          Western Michigan University, 1974.

1323. Fritzen, Robert and Mazer, Gil. The Effects of Fear Appeal and
          Communication Upon Attitudes Toward Alcohol Consumption.
          Journal of Drug Education, 5: 171-181, 1975.

1324. Fry, C.C. Drinking in College. Hygeia, 26: 710-711, 748, 1948.

1325. Fry, C,C, A Note on Drinking in the College Community.
          Quarterly Journal of Studies on Alcohol, 6: 243-248, 1945.

1326. Fullerton, M. A Program in Alcohol Education Designed for Rural
          Youth. Journal of Alcohol and Drug Education, 24(2): 58-
          62, 1979.

G

1327. Galanter, M. (Ed.). Currents in Alcoholism. Volume 5.
      Biomedical Issues and Clinical Effects of Alcoholism.
      New York: Grune and Stratton, 1979.

1328. Galanter, M. (Ed.). Currents in Alcoholism. Volume 6.
      Treatment and Rehabilitation and Epidemiology. New York:
      Grune and Stratton, 1979.

1329. Galanter, M. (Ed.). Currents in Alcoholism. Volume 7. Recent
      Advances in Research and Treatment. New York: Grune and
      Stratton, 1980.

1330. Galanter, M. Sociobiology and Informal Social Controls of
      Drinking: Findings from Two Charismatic Sects. Journal of
      Studies on Alcohol, 42: 64-79, 1981.

1331. Galanter, Marc. Young Adult Social Drinkers: Another Group at
      Risk. Alcoholism: Clinical and Experimental Research,
      4(3): 241-242, 1980.

1332. Galanter, Marc, Buckley, Peter, Deutsch, Alexander,
      Rabkin, Richard and Rabkin, Judith. Large Group Influence
      for Decreased Drug Use: Findings From Two Contemporary
      Religious Sects. American Journal of Drug and Alcohol
      Abuse, 7(3): 219-304, 1980.

1333. Galchus, Donna S. and Galchus, Kenneth E. Drug Use: Some
      Comparisons of Black and White College Students. Drug
      Forum, 6(1): 65-76, 1977.

1334. Gallagher, E. and Croake, E. Guidelines for School-Based Drug
      and Alcohol Abuse Prevention Programs. Mattituck, New
      York: TFL Press, 1977.

1335.   Gallagher, J.A.   Comparison Between Students' and Teachers'
        Attitudes Toward Adolescent Alcohol and Marijuana Users and
        Dogmatism.   Doctoral Dissertation (University Microfilms
        No. 73-29951).   St. John's University, 1973.

1336.   Galli, N.   Patterns of Student Drug Use.   Journal of Drug
        Education, 4(2): 237-248, 1974.

1337.   Galli, N.A.   A Comparative Analysis of the Attitudes and
        Behaviors of School Children (Selected Grades 4-12) and
        Their Parents Toward Drugs.   Doctoral Dissertation
        (University Microfilms No. 73-17211).   University of
        Illinois at Urbana-Champaign, 1972.

1338.   Gallup, George.   Seventh Annual Gallup Poll of Public Attitudes
        Toward Education.   Kappan, no pages, December, 1975.

1339.   Galvin, Katherine and Taylor, Richard.   Drug Education in
        Massachusetts.   In: Drug Use in America: Problems in
        Perspective.   Appendix.   Volume II.   Social Responses to
        to Drug Use.   U.S. National Commission on Marihuana and
        Drug Abuse.   Washington, D.C.: U.S. Government Printing
        Office, 1973, pages 411-454.

1340.   Gamage, James (Ed.).   Management of Adolescent Drug Misuse:
        Clinical, Psychological and Legal Perspectives.   Beloit,
        Wisconsin, STASH Press, 1973.

1341.   Gannon, J.A.   "...We Must Teach Scientific Truths": Outline of
        Proposed Public School Courses on Alcohol, Tobacco and
        Other Narcotics.   Medical Annals of the District of
        Columbia, 11: 409-412, 418, 1942.

1342.   Gantman, Carol A.   Family Interaction Patterns Among Families
        With Normal, Disturbed and Drug-Abusing Adolescents.
        Journal of Youth and Adolescence, 7(4): 429-440, 1978.

1343.   Garagliano, C.F., Lilienfeld, A.M. and Mendeloff, A.I.   Incidence
        Rates of Liver Cirrhosis and Related Diseases in Baltimore
        and Selected Areas of the United States.   Journal of
        Chronic Diseases, 32(8): 543-554, 1979.

1344.   Garfield, Emily and Blum, Richard.   Stanford University
        Evaluation Scales: Part I.   In: Accountability in Drug
        Education: A Model for Evaluation.   Eds.
        Lucille Annette Abrams, Emily F. Garfield and J.D. Swisher.
        Washington, D.C.: Drug Abuse Council, 1973, pages 57-72.

1345.   Garfield, Emily F. and Jones, Donald R.   Drug Education Group
        Process: Consideration for the Classroom.   Journal of Drug
        Education, 10(2): 101-110, 1980.

1346.   Garfield, Mark D. and Garfield, Emily F. A Longitudinal Study of
        Drugs on a Campus. International Journal of the
        Addictions, 8(4): 599-611, 1973.

1347.   Garitano, W.W. Youth and Drugs. Drug Forum, 1(2): 195-199,
        1972.

1348.   Garlie, N.W. Characteristics of Teenagers With Alcohol Related
        Problems. Doctoral Dissertation (University Microfilms
        No. 71-6010). Salt Lake City: University of Utah, 1971.

1349.   Garmon, W.S. The Many Faces of Ethyl. Nashville, Tennessee:
        Broadman Press, 1966.

1350.   Garrett, E.W. Special Purpose Police Forces. Annals of the
        American Academy of Political and Social Science, 291: 31-
        38, 1954.

1351.   Garrett, G.R. Drinking Bhavior of Homeless Women. Doctoral
        Dissertation. Washington State University, 1971.

1352.   Garrett, Gerald R. and Bahr, Howard M. Women on Skid Row.
        Quarterly Journal of Studies on Alcohol, 34(4): 1228-1243,
        1973.

1353.   Garriott, J. and Latman, N. Drug Detection in Cases of Driving
        Under the Influence. Journal of Forensic Sciences, 21:
        398-415, 1976.

1354.   Gates, E.M. and Bourdette, P.C. The Synanon Alternative to the
        Criminal Justice System. Journal of Drug Issues, 5: 233-
        241, 1975.

1355.   Gatti, Louis A. "Young People God's Beloved": Oklahoma Malt
        Beverage Association Pamphlet Hailed for Its Contribution
        to the Fight Against Alcohol Misuse. The Brewer's Digest,
        54(7): 16, 18, 48-49, 1979.

1356.   Gault, E.I. Aversion Therapy in Early Alcoholism. Medical
        Journal of Australia, 1(6): 278-280, 1967.

1357.   Gavaghan, Paul. The Liquor Industry's Perspective on Prevention
        of Alcohol Abuse. Journal of Alcohol and Drug Education,
        23(1): 63-69, 1977.

1358.   Gay, John E. Alcohol and Metropolitan Black Teenagers. Journal
        of Drug Education, 11(1): 19-26, 1981.

1359.   Gayford, J.J. Battered Wives. In: Violence and the Family.
        Ed. J.P. Martin. New York: Wiley, 1978, pages 19-39.

1360.   Gayford, J.J. Treatment of Young Alcoholics. Royal Society
        Health Journal, 97(1): 21-26, 1977.

1361. Gazda, Z. Ksztaltowanie Postaw Przeciwalkoholowych Mlodzieży
           Wiejskiej. (The Development of Antialcohol Attitudes
           Among Rural Youth.) Problemy Alkoholizmu, Warsaw, 19(11):
           11-12, 1971.

1362. Gedig, G.R. and Gedig, U.J. Alcohol Among the Youth in West
           Germany. Japanese Journal of Studies on Alcohol, 14: 118-
           126, 1979.

1363. Gedig, U. and Gedig, G. Die Alkoholfrage in Japan. (The Alcohol
           Question in Japan.) Suchtgefahren, Hamburg, 23: 97-106,
           1977.

1364. Gedig, U.J. Alkoholprävention im Allgemeinbildenden Schulwesen
           in der Bundesrepublik Deutschland. (Prevention of
           Alcoholism in the General Educational System of the
           Federal Republic of Germany.) Suchtgefahren, Hamburg, 25:
           122-129, 1979.

1365. Geikie, Y. Towards a Definition of Homelessness... Australian
           Journal of Alcoholism and Drug Dependence, 4: 16-18, 1977.

1366. Geis, G. and Seagren, L.W. A Model for Criminal Justice System
           Planning and Control. Long Beach, California: Digital
           Resources Corporation, 1971.

1367. Gelineau, V.A., Pearsall, D.T., Camp, J.M. and Zaks, L.A.
           Report of the Natick Youth Study. A Profile of Students
           Grades Nine Through Twelve. Boston: Massachusetts
           Department of Mental Health, Division of Drug
           Rehabilitation, April, 1972.

1368. Gentile, Donald. Liquor Laws Called Confusion on Rocks. The
           New York News, no pages, October 14, 1973.

1369. George, A. Survey of Drug Use in a Sydney Suburb. Medical
           Journal of Australia, 59(2): 233-237, 1972.

1370. Georgia Department of Public Health. Developing an Effective
           Alcohol Education Program in the Public Schools.
           Proceedings of Seminar. Athens, Georgia: University of
           Georgia, 1961.

1371. Geraty, T.S. The Role of the Educator in the Field of
           Prevention. In: Toward Prevention: Scientific Studies
           on Alcohol and Alcoholism. Ed. F.A. Soper. Washington,
           D.C.: Narcotics Education, 1971, pages 213-216.

1372. Gerchow, J. Jugendkriminalität und Alkohol unter
           Berücksichtigung Entwicklungspsychologischer und
           Soziokultureller Zusammenhänge. (Juvenile Delinquency and
           Alcohol: Its Relationship to Psychological Development
           and Sociocultural Aspects.) Suchtgefahren, Hamburg, 25: 1-
           11, 1979.

1373. Gergen, M., Gergen, K. and Morse, S. Correlates of Marijuana Use
       Among College Students. Journal of Applied Social
       Psychology, 2(1): 1-16, 1972.

1374. Geschwind, J.A. An Observational and Interview Study of Patterns
       of Alcohol Use Among Two Groups: College Males and
       Military. Journal of Alcohol and Drug Education, 25(3):
       59-69, 1980.

1375. Gewehr, J. and Feldmann, L. Alkohol-Prophylaxe in Schulen--
       Bericht aus der Praxis. (Alcohol Prevention in the
       School--A Clinical Report.) Suchtgefahren, Hamburg, 26:
       38-42, 1980.

1376. Ghadirian, A.M. Adolescent Alcoholism: Motives and
       Alternatives. Comprehensive Psychiatry, 20: 469-474, 1979.

1377. Gibbens, T.C. Drink, Drugs and Delinquency. Medicine, Science,
       and the Law, 12(4): 257-261, 1972.

1378. Gibbens, T.C.N. Trends in Juvenile Delinquency. (WHO Public
       Health Papers, No. 5.) Geneva: World Health Organization,
       1961.

1379. Gibbins, R.J., Israel, Y., Kalant, H., Popham, R.E., Schmidt, W.
       and Smart, R.G., (Eds.) Research Advances in Alcohol and
       Drug Problems. Volume 2. New York: Wiley and Sons, 1975.

1380. Gibbons, H.L., Ellis, J.W., Jr. and Plechus, J.L. Analysis of
       Medical Factors in Fatal Aircraft Accidents in 1965.
       Texas Medicine, 63(1): 64-68, 1967.

1381. Giel, R. and VanLuijk, J.N. Psychiatric Morbidity in 50
       Juvenile Delinquents in Addis Ababa. Social Psychiatry,
       5: 183-186, 1970.

1382. Gil, David G. Violence Against Children: Physical Child Abuse
       in the United States. Cambridge, Massachusetts: Harvard
       University Press, 1973.

1383. Gilpatrick, E.E. A Dram for Dreaming. Pamphlet. Cincinnati,
       Ohio: Pamphlet Publications, 1977.

1384. Ginzburg, Harold. Substance Substitution: Do Methadone
       Maintenance Patients Become Alcoholics? In: Currents in
       Alcoholism. Volume 2. Psychiatric, Psychological, Social
       and Epidemiological Studies. Ed. F.A. Seixas. New York:
       Grune and Stratton, 1977, pages 253-267.

1385. Ginzburg, Harold and Siguel, Eduardo. Alcohol and Marijuana:
       Mixed Substance Abuse. In: Currents in Alcoholism.
       Volume 4. Psychiatric, Psychological, Social and
       Epidemiological Studies. Ed. F.A. Seixas. New York:
       Grune and Stratton, 1978, pages 357-365.

1386. Giovannangeli, A.J. Alcohol Education for College Students. A
        Unit Based on Information Obtained at the 1946 Summer
        Session, "School of Alcohol Studies," Yale University.
        Keene, New Hampshire: Department of Science, Keene
        Teachers College, no date.

1387. Giovannangeli, A.J. Paradox of Teen-Age Drinking. New
        Hampshire Bulletin on Alcoholism, 15(4): 1-11, 1966.

1388. Giovannangeli, A.J. Study Workbook C₂H₅OH. Keene, New
        Hampshire: Giovannangeli, 1959.

1389. Girard, D.E. and Carlton, B.E. Alcoholism: Earlier Diagnosis
        and Definition of the Problem. Western Journal of
        Medicine, 129(1): 1-7, 1978.

1390. Girdano, D.A. and Girdano, D.D. Drug Education: Content and
        Methods. Reading, Massachusetts: Addison-Wesley, 1972
        (see especially pages 39-64).

1391. Girdano, D.A. and Girdano, D.D. Drug Usage Trends Among College
        Students. College Student Journal, 8(3): 94-96, 1974.

1392. Girdano, Dorothy Dusek and Girdano, Daniel A. College Drug Use--
        A Five-Year Survey. Journal of the American College
        Health Association, 25: 117-119, 1976.

1393. Glad, D.D. Attitudes and Experiences of American-Jewish and
        American-Irish Male Youth as Related to Differences in
        Adult Rates of Inebriety. Quarterly Journal of Studies on
        Alcohol, 8: 406-472, 1947.

1394. Glad, D.D. Attitude-Experience Characteristics of Male,
        American-Jewish and American-Irish Youth, With Reference
        to Use of Alcoholic Beverages. American Psychologist, 1:
        450, 1946.

1395. Glaser, H.H. and Massengale, O.N. Glue-Sniffing in Children:
        Deliberate Inhalation of Vaporized Plastic Cements.
        Journal of the American Medical Association, 181: 300-303,
        1962.

1396. Gläss, T. Die Bedeutung der Alkohol- und Tabakfrage für die
        Junge Generation. (The Meanings of the Problems of
        Alcohol and Tobacco for Youth.) Suchtgefahren, Hamburg,
        1(4): 10-20, 1956.

1397. Glassco, C.K., Jr. Drinking Habits of Seniors in a Southern
        University. Doctoral Dissertation (University Microfilms
        No. 72-25957). University of Mississippi, 1972. (Also
        see: Journal of Alcohol and Drug Education,21(1): 25-29,
        1975.

1398.   Glassner, Barry. Differences in Ethnic Drinking Habits.
        Alcoholism, 1(4): 19-21, 1981.

1399.   Glatt, M.M. Alcohol, Drugs, and the Adolescent. Public Health,
        London, 80: 284-294, 1966.

1400.   Glatt, M.M. Alcohol Misuse and Alcoholism Among the Young.
        Midwife Health Visit Community Nurse, 13(3): 77-79, 1977.

1401.   Glatt, M.M. Alcoholism, Crime and Juvenile Delinquency. British
        Journal of Delinquency, 9: 84-93, 1958.

1402.   Glatt, M.M. Crime, Alcohol and Alcoholism. Howard Journal of
        Penology and Crime Prevention, London, 11: 274-284, 1965.

1403.   Glatt, M.M. Drinking Habits of English (Middle Class)
        Alcoholics. Acta Psychiatrica Scandinavica, 37: 88-113,
        1961.

1404.   Glatt, M.M. A Guide to Addiction and Its Treatment. New York:
        Wiley, 1974.

1405.   Glatt, M.M. The Question of the Education of the Young About the
        Use and Abuse of Alcohol. British Journal of Addiction,
        56: 63-65, 1960.

1406.   Glatt, M.M. and Hills, D.R. Alcohol Abuse and Alcoholism in the
        Young. British Journal of Addiction, 63: 183-191, 1968.

1407.   Glatt, Max. The Alcoholic and the Help He Needs. New York:
        Taplinger, 1974.

1408.   Gleaton, Thomas J., Jr. and Smith, Sidney P. Drug Use by Urban
        and Rural Adolescents. Journal of Drug Education, 11(1):
        1-8, 1981.

1409.   Gliksman, Louis, Smythe, Padric C., Gorman, Jan and Rush, Brian.
        The Adolescent Alcohol Questionnaire: Its Development and
        Psychometric Evaluation. Journal of Drug Education, 10(3):
        209-227, 1980.

1410.   Globetti, G. Alcohol Abuse: Is Education the Answer?
        Morgantown, West Virginia: Paper Presented at the 7th
        Annual West Virginia School of Alcohol and Drug Abuse
        Studies, June 20-25, 1971.

1411.   Globetti, G. Alcohol Education in the School. Journal of Drug
        Education, 1(3): 241-248, 1971. (Also as: Alcohol
        Education in the School. Pamphlet. Farmingdale, New York:
        Baywood, 1971.

1412.   Globetti, G. An Appraisal of Drug Education Programs. In:
        Research Advances in Alcohol and Drug Problems. Volume 2.
        Eds. R.J. Gibbins, Y. Israel, H. Kalant, R.E. Popham,
        W. Schmidt and R.G. Smart. New York: Wiley and Sons,
        1975, pages 93-122.

1413.   Globetti, G. The Attitudes of High School Students Toward
        Alcohol Education in Two Mississippi Communities. Series
        No. 1. Mississippi: Mississippi State University,
        College of Arts and Sciences, 1966.

1414.   Globetti, G. Attitudes Toward Alcohol Education: A Comparative
        Study of Negro and White Community Members. Mississippi:
        Mississippi State University, 1967.

1415.   Globetti, G. A Comparative Study of White and Negro Teenage
        Drinking in Two Mississippi Communities. Phylon, 28(2):
        131-138, 1967.

1416.   Globetti, G. A Conceptual Analysis of the Effectiveness of
        Alcohol Education Programs. In: Research on Methods and
        Programs of Drug Education. Ed. M.S. Goodstadt. Toronto,
        Ontario: Alcoholism and Drug Addiction Research
        Foundation of Ontario, 1974.

1417.   Globetti, G. The Drinking Patterns of Negro and White High
        School Students in Two Mississippi Communities. Journal
        of Negro Education, 30: 60-69, 1970.

1418.   Globetti, G. Drinking Patterns of Young People in Abstinence
        Communities. Paper Presented at a Symposium on Law and
        Drinking Behavior, University of North Carolina Center for
        Alcohol Studies, Chapel Hill, North Carolina, 1971.

1419.   Globetti, G. The Effectiveness of Alcohol Education Programs.
        In: Research on Methods and Programs of Drug Education.
        Ed. M. Goodstadt. Toronto, Ontario: Addiction Research
        Foundation, Toronto, 1974.

1420.   Globetti, G. Problem and Non-Problem Drinking Among High School
        Students in Abstinence Communities. The International
        Journal of the Addictions, 7: 511-523, 1972.

1421.   Globetti, G. Problem Drinking Among Youth: Some Observations.
        In: Defining Adolescent Alcohol Use: Implications for a
        Definition of Adolescent Alcoholism. M. Keller (Chair.).
        Symposium Presented at the Meeting of the National
        Council on Alcoholism, Washington, May 5-7, 1976.

1422.   Globetti, G. Should They Be Taught to Drink? Frankfort,
        Kentucky: Kentucky Office of Alcoholism, no date.

1423.   Globetti, G. Social Adjustment of High School Students and
        Problem Drinking. Journal of Alcohol Education, 13(2):
        21-29, 1967.

1424.   Globetti, G. Student Attitudes Toward Alcohol Education.
        Journal of Alcohol Education, 16(2): 1-7, 1971.

1425. Globetti, G. A Survey of Teenage Drinking in Two Mississippi
       Communities. (Preliminary Report No. 3, Social Science
       Research Center). Mississippi: Mississippi State
       University, 1964.

1426. Globetti, G. Teenage Drinking in a Community Characterized by
       Prohibition Norms. British Journal of Addiction, 68(4):
       275-279, 1973.

1427. Globetti, G. Teenage Drinking in an Abstinence Setting. Kansas
       Journal of Sociology, 3: 124-132, 1967.

1428. Globetti, G. Trends in Youth Drinking. Paper Presented at the
       North American Congress on Alcohol and Drug Problems, San
       Francisco, California, December 12-18, 1974.

1429. Globetti, G. The Use of Alcohol Among High School Students in
       an Abstinence Setting. Pacific Sociological Review, 12:
       105-108, 1969.

1430. Globetti, G. The Use of Beverage Alcohol by Youth in an
       Abstinence Setting. Journal of School Health, 39: 179-183,
       1969.

1431. Globetti, G. Young People and Alcohol Education--Abstinence or
       Moderate Drinking? Drug Forum, 1(3): 269-273, 1972.

1432. Globetti, G. and Alsikafi, M. School-Age Drinking Patterns and
       Agencies of Socialization. Alabama: University of
       Alabama, 1976.

1433. Globetti, G., Alsikafi, M. and Christy, E.G. Children of the
       Military: Their Drinking Styles and Attitudes Toward
       Alcohol. Some Preliminary Findings. New Orleans,
       Louisiana: Paper Presented at the 27th Annual Meeting of
       Alcohol and Drug Problems Association, September 12-16,
       1976.

1434. Globetti, G., Alsikafi, M. and Christy, E.G. Permissive
       Attitudes Toward Alcohol Abuse Among Young Military
       Dependents. Journal of Drug Education, 7: 99-107, 1977.

1435. Globetti, G., Alsikafi, M. and Morse, R.J. Alcohol Use Among
       Black Youth in a Rural Community. Journal of Drug and
       Alcohol Dependence, Lausanne, 2: 255-260, 1977.

1436. Globetti, G. and Chamblin, F. Problem Drinking Among High School
       Students in a Mississippi Community. Mississippi:
       Mississippi State University, 1966.

1437. Globetti, G. and Cockrell, E. Selected Socio-Cultural Factors
       Associated with Favorable Attitudes Toward Alcohol
       Education. Mississippi: Mississippi State University,
       1965.

1438.   Globetti, G. and Harrison, D.E. Attitudes of High School
        Students Toward Alcohol Education. Journal of School
        Health, 40(1): 36-39, 1970.

1439.   Globetti, G., Harrison, D.E. and Oetinger, G. The Use and Misuse
        of Beverage Alcohol Among High School Students in Two
        Mississippi Communities. Mississippi: Mississippi State
        University, 1967.

1440.   Globetti, G. and McReynolds, M. A Comparative Study of the White
        and the Negro High School Students' Use of Alcohol in Two
        Mississippi Communities. Mississippi: Mississippi State
        University, 1964.

1441.   Globetti, G., Pomeroy, G.S. and Bennett, W.H. Attitudes Toward
        Alcohol Education. Pamphlet. Mississippi: Mississippi
        State University, 1969.

1442.   Globetti, G., Pomeroy, G.S. and Cain, V. Sourcebook in Alcohol
        Education. New York: Associated Educational Services,
        1969.

1443.   Globetti, G. and Windham, G.O. The Social Adjustment of High
        School Students and the Use of Beverage Alcohol. Sociology
        and Social Research, 51: 148-157, 1967.

1444.   Globetti, Gerald. Approaches to the Control of Alcoholic
        Beverages in the United States. Journal of Drug Issues,
        3(3): 260-266, 1973.

1445.   Globetti, Gerald. Factors Associated with a Favorable Attitude
        Toward Alcohol Education in Two Mississippi Communities.
        Journal of Alcohol Education, 13(1): 37-43, 1967.

1446.   Globetti, Gerald. Murray State University Center for Alcohol
        Education. Journal of Alcohol Education, 16(3): 1, 1971.

1447.   Globetti, Gerald. Prohibition Norms and Teenage Drinking. In:
        Drinking: Alcohol in American Society - Issues and Current
        Research. Eds. J.A. Ewing and B.A. Rouse. Chicago:
        Nelson-Hall, 1978, pages 159-170.

1448.   Globetti, Gerald. The Status of Alcohol Education in the School.
        In: International Conference on Alcoholism and Drug Abuse,
        San Juan, Puerto Rico, November, 1973. Lausanne,
        Switzerland: International Council on Alcohol and
        Addictions, 1974, pages 153-157.

1449.   Globetti, Gerald. Teenage Drinking. In: Alcoholism,
        Development, Consequences, and Interventions. Eds.
        Nada J. Estes and M. Edith Heinemann. St. Louis, Missouri:
        C.V. Mosby Company, 1977, pages 162-173.

1450. Globetti, Gerald, Alsikafi, Majeed and Morse, Richard. Black
       Female High School Students and the Use of Beverage
       Alcohol. The International Journal of the Addictions,
       15(2): 189-200, 1980.

1451. Globetti, Gerald, Alsikafi, Majeed and Morse, Richard. High
       School Students and the Use of Alcohol in a Rural
       Community: A Research Note. Journal of Drug Issues, 8:
       435-441, 1978.

1452. Globetti, Gerald and Pomeroy, Grace. Characteristics of
       Community Residents Who are Favorable Toward Alcohol
       Education. Mental Hygiene, 54(3): 411-415, 1970.

1453. Gmur, B.C., Fodor, J.T., Glass, L.H. and Langan, J.J. Making
       Health Decisions. Englewood Cliffs, New Jersey: Prentice-
       Hall, 1970.

1454. Godwod-Sikorska, C., Kiejlan, G., Młodzik, B., Pánkowska-
       Jurkowska, M. and Piekarska-Ekiert, A. Problemy
       Alkoholizmu Wśród Młodzieży z Wielodzietnych r Alkoholików
       na Podstawie Dziesiecioletnich Danych Katamnestycznych.
       (Problems of Alcoholism in Youngsters from Alcoholic
       Families with Many Children, Based on Data Spanning a 10-
       Year Follow-up Period.) In: Alkohol, Alkoholizm i Inne
       Uzależnienia. Przejawy, Profilaktyka, Terapia. Tom II.
       (Alcohol, Alcoholism and Other Addictions. Symptomatology,
       Prophylaxis and Therapy. Volume II.) Ed. J. Morawski.
       Warszawa: Wydawnictwo Prawnicze, 1977, pages 7-27.

1455. Goffin, J.L.C. Alcohol and the Adolescent. Health Education,
       8(40): 15-17, 1945.

1456. Golann, S.E. and Eisdorfer, C. (Eds.) Handbook of Community
       Mental Health. New York: Appleton-Century-Crofts, 1972.

1457. Gold, Martin. Delinquent Behavior in an American City. Belmont,
       California: Brooks/Cole Publishing Company, 1970.

1458. Gold, R.S., Duncan, D.F. and Sutherland, M.S. College Student
       Interests in Drug Education Go Further than Illicit Drugs.
       Journal of Drug Education, 10: 79-88, 1980.

1459. Goldenberg, M., Korn, F., Sluzki, C. and Tarnopolsky, A.
       Attitudes Toward Alcohol, Alcoholism, and the Alcoholic--
       An Exploratory Study. Social Science and Medicine, 2(1):
       29-39, 1968.

1460. Goldstein, B. Low Income Youth in Urban Areas: A Critical
       Review of the Literature. New York: Holt, Rinehart and
       Winston, 1967.

1461. Goldstein, Eleanor C., Morrissett, Irving and Cousins, Jack E.
       (Eds.) Alcohol. Volume 1. Gaithersburg, Maryland:
       Social Issues Resource Series, 1974.

1462.   Goldstein, G.S., Oetting, E.R., Edwards, Ruth and
        Garcia-Mason, Velma. Drug Use Among Native American Young
        Adults. The International Journal of the Addictions,
        14(6): 855-860, 1979.

1463.   Goldstein, J. Assessing the Interpersonal Determinants of
        Adolescent Drug Use. In: Predicting Adolescent Drug
        Abuse: A Review of Issues, Methods and Correlates. NIDA
        Research Issues Series, Volume 11. Ed. D. Lettieri.
        Washington, D.C.: U.S. Government Printing Office, 1975,
        pages 45-52.

1464.   Goldstein, J.W. Getting High in High School: The Meaning of
        Adolescent Drug Usage. New York: Paper Presented at
        Symposium on Students and Drugs at Annual Meeting of the
        American Educational Research Association, 1971.

1465.   Goldstein, J.W. Motivations for Psychoactive Drug Use Among
        Students. In: Readings in the Essentials of Abnormal
        Psychology. Ed. B. Kleinmutz. New York: Harper and Row,
        1974.

1466.   Goldstein, J.W. Students' Evaluations of Their Psychoactive Drug
        Use. Journal of Counseling Psychology, 22(4): 333-339,
        1975.

1467.   Goldstein, Joel W., Gleason, Terry C. and Korn, James H. Whither
        the Epidemic? Psychoactive Drug-Use Career Patterns of
        College Students. Journal of Applied Social Psychology,
        5(1): 16-33, 1975.

1468.   Goldstein, K.M. Note: A Comparison of Self- and Peer-Reports of
        Smoking and Drinking Behavior. Psychological Reports, 18:
        702, 1966.

1469.   Goldstein, Leon G. Youthful Drivers as a Special Safety Problem.
        Accident Analysis and Prevention, 4: 153-189, 1972.

1470.   Goldstein, M.S. Drinking and Alcoholism as Presented in College
        Health Textbooks. Journal of Drug Education, 5: 109-125,
        1975.

1471.   Gomberg, E.S. Etiology of Alcoholism. Journal of Consulting
        and Clinical Psychology, 32(1): 18-20, 1968.

1472.   Gomberg, E.S. Problems with Alcohol and Other Drugs. In:
        Gender and Disordered Behavior: Sex Differences in
        Psychopathology. Eds. E.S. Gomberg and V. Franks. New
        York: Brunner/Mazel, 1979, pages 204-240.

1473.   Gomberg, Edith S. Alcoholism in Women. In: The Biology of
        Alcoholism. Volume 4. Social Aspects of Alcoholism.
        Eds. B. Kissin and H. Begleiter. New York: Plenum Press,
        1976, pages 117-166.

1474.   Gomberg, Edith S.   Women with Alcohol Problems.   In: Alcoholism:
        Development, Consequences and Interventions.   Eds.
        Nada J. Este and M. Edith Heinemann.   St. Louis: C.V.
        Mosby Company, 1977, pages 174-185.

1475.   Gonzalez, G.M.   Procedures and Resource Materials for Developing
        a Campus Alcohol Abuse Prevention Program: A Tested Model.
        Gainesville, Florida: University of Florida, Alcohol Abuse
        Prevention Program, 1978.

1476.   Gonzalez, Gerardo M.   The Effect of a Model Alcohol Education
        Module on College Students' Attitudes, Knowledge and
        Behavior Related to Alcohol Use.   Journal of Alcohol and
        Drug Education, 25(3): 1-12, 1980.

1477.   Gonzalez, Gerardo M.   What Do You Mean--Prevention?   Journal of
        Alcohol and Drug Education, 23(3):14-23, 1978.

1478.   Goode, E.   The Drug Phenomenon: Social Aspects of Drug Taking.
        Pamphlet.   New York: Bobbs-Merrill, 1973.

1479.   Goode, E.   The Major Drugs of Use Among Adolescents and Young
        Adults.   In: Drugs and Youth: The Challenge of Today.
        Ed. E. Harms.   Elmsford, New York: Pergamon Press, 1973,
        pages 33-72.

1480.   Goode, Erich.   Drugs in American Society (First Edition).   New
        York: Alfred A. Knopf, Inc., 1972.

1481.   Goode, Erich.   Ideological Factors in the Marijuana Controversy.
        Annals of the New York Academy of Sciences, 191: 246-260,
        1971.

1482.   Goode, M.A.   The Relationship of Values, Career Choices and
        Attitudes Toward the Use of Alcohol of Eleventh and Twelfth
        Grade Students.   Doctoral Dissertation (University
        Microfilms No. 7922487).   The Ohio State University, 1979.

1483.   Goodlett, D. and Roberts, C.   The Effects of a Comprehensive
        Alcohol Education Curriculum on Student Knowledge and
        Attitudes About Alcohol in Grades Four, Five, Six, Junior
        High School, and Senior High School in Selected Schools in
        the Kent, Bellevue, and Lake Washington School Districts
        in King County, Washington.   Master's Thesis.   University
        of Oregon, 1975.

1484.   Goodman, A.B., Siegel, C., Craig, T., Wanderling J. and
        Haugland, G.   Inpatient Alcoholism Treatment Rates in a
        Suburban County, by Sex, Age, and Social Class.   Journal of
        Studies on Alcohol, 42(5): 414-420, 1981.

1485. Goodstadt, M.S.   Impact and Roles of Drug Information in Drug
         Education. Journal of Drug Education, 5: 223-233, 1975.

1486. Goodstadt, M.S., Sheppard, M.A. and Crawford, S.H. Appendices to
         Report: Development and Evaluation of Two Alcohol
         Education Programs for the Toronto Board of Education.
         (Substudy No. 942) Toronto, Ontario: Addiction Research
         Foundation, 1978.

1487. Goodstadt, M.S., Sheppard, M.A. and Crawford, S.H. Development
         and Evaluation of Two Alcohol Education Programs for the
         Toronto Board of Education. (Substudy No. 941) Toronto,
         Ontario: Addiction Research Foundation, 1978.

1488. Goodstadt, M.S., Sheppard, M.A., Kijewski, K. and Chung, L. The
         Status of Drug Education in Ontario: 1977. Toronto,
         Ontario: Addiction Research Foundation, 1977.

1489. Goodstadt, Michael. Drug Education - A Turn On or a Turn Off.
         Journal of Drug Education, 10(2): 89-99, 1980.

1490. Goodstadt, Michael (Ed.) Research on Methods and Programs of
         Drug Education. Toronto, Ontario: Addiction Research
         Foundation, 1974.

1491. Goodstadt, Michael and Gruson, Valerie. The Randomized Response
         Technique: A Test of the Procedure and the Validity of
         Self-Reported Drug Use. Toronto, Ontario: Addiction
         Research Foundation, no date.

1492. Goodstadt, Michael S. Alcohol and Drug Education: Models and
         Outcomes. Health Education Monographs, 6(3): 263-279,
         1978.

1493. Goodstadt, Michael S. Drug Education: Where Do We Go From Here?
         Toronto, Ontario: Addiction Research Foundation, 1974.

1494. Goodstadt, Michael S. Planning and Evaluation of Alcohol
         Education Programmes. Journal of Alcohol and Drug
         Education, 26(2): 1-10, 1981.

1495. Goodwin, D.W. Alcoholism and Heredity: A Review and Hypothesis.
         Archives of General Psychiatry, 36(1): 57-61, 1979.

1496. Goodwin, D.W. Genetic and Experiential Antecedents of
         Alcoholism: A Prospective Study. Alcoholism, 1(3): 259-
         265, 1977.

1497. Goodwin, D.W. Heredity Factors in Alcoholism. Hospital
         Practice, 13(5): 121-124, 127-130, 1978.

1498. Goodwin, D.W. Is Alcoholism Hereditary?. New York: Oxford
         University Press, 1976.

1499. Goodwin, D.W. Why People Do Not Drink: A Study of Teetotalers.
       Comprehensive Psychiatry, 10(3): 209-214, 1969.

1500. Goodwin, D.W., Davis, D.H. and Robins, L.N. Drinking Amid
       Abundant Illicit Drugs: The Vietnam Case. Archives of
       General Psychiatry, 32: 230-233, 1975.

1501. Goodwin, D.W., Schulsinger, F., Hermansen, L., Guze, S.B. and
       Winokur, G. Alcoholism and the Hyperactive Child Syndrome.
       Journal of Nervous and Mental Disorders, 160: 349-353,
       1975.

1502. Goodwin, D.W., Schulsinger, F., Hermansen, L., Guze, S.B. and
       Winokur, G. Alcohol Problems in Adoptees Raised Apart from
       Alcoholic Biological Parents. Archives of General
       Psychiatry, 28(2): 238-243, 1973.

1503. Goodwin, D.W., Schulsinger, F., Knop, J., Mednick, S. and
       Guze, S.B. Alcoholism and Depression in Adopted-Out
       Daughters of Alcoholics. Archives of General Psychiatry,
       34: 751-755, 1977.

1504. Goodwin, D.W., Schulsinger, F., Knop, J., Mednick, S. and
       Guze, S.B. Psychopathology in Adopted and Non-adopted
       Daughters of Alcoholics. Archives of General Psychiatry,
       34: 1005-1009, 1977.

1505. Goodwin, D.W., Schulsinger, F., Møller, N., Hermansen, L.,
       Winokur, G. and Guze, S.B. Drinking Problems in Adopted
       and Non-adopted Sons of Alcoholics. Archives of General
       Psychiatry, 31: 164-169, 1974.

1506. Goodwin, Donald. The Genetics of Alcoholism. Science and
       Alcohol Actions/Misuse, 1(1): 101-117, 1980.

1507. Goodwin, Donald W. The Cause of Alcoholism and Why It Runs in
       Families. British Journal of Addiction, 74: 161-164, 1979.

1508. Goodwin, Donald W. Family Studies of Alcoholism. Journal of
       Studies on Alcohol, 42(1): 156-162, 1981.

1509. Goodwin, Donald W. The Genetics of Alcoholism: A State of the
       Art Review. Alcohol and Health Research World, 2(3): 2-12,
       1978.

1510. Goodwin, Donald W. and Guze, Samuel B. Heredity and Alcoholism.
       In: The Biology of Alcoholism. Volume 3. Clinical
       Pathology. Eds. Benjamin Kissin and Henri Begleiter. New
       York: Plenum Press, 1974.

1511. Goodwin, Donald W., Powell, Barbara and Stern, John. Behavioral
       Tolerance to Alcohol in Moderate Drinkers. American Journal
       of Psychiatry, 127(12): 1651-1653, 1971.

1512.   Göransson, B.   Alkohol- och Narkotikainformation ett Fiasko?
        (Alcohol and Narcotics Information - A Failure?)
        Läkartidningen, Stockholm, 69: 3324-3327, 1972.

1513.   Gordis, E.N. and Sereny, G.   Effects of Prior Narcotic Addiction
        on Response to Treatment of Alcoholism.   Alcoholism, 4(1):
        34-39, 1980.

1514.   Gordon, A.   Open Letter to a Teenager.   Leaflet.   Des Moines,
        Iowa: Meredith, 1960.

1515.   Gordon, E.   Temperance Teaching in Europe.   Evanston, Illinois:
        Ernest Gordon, 1954.

1516.   Gordon, S.   You: The Psychology of Surviving and Enhancing Your
        Social Life, Love Life, Sex Life, School Life, Work Life,
        Home Life, Emotional Life, Creative Life, Spiritual Life,
        Style of Life, Life.   New York: Quadrangle/The New York
        Times Book Company, 1975.

1517.   Gorenstein, Ethan.   Relationships of Subclinical Depression,
        Psychopathy and Hysteria to Patterns of Alcohol Consumption
        and Abuse in Males and Females.   In: Currents in
        Alcoholism.   Volume 7.   Recent Advances in Research and
        Treatment.   Ed. M. Galanter.   New York: Grune and
        Stratton, 1980, pages 207-217.

1518.   Gorodetzky, B.L.   What You Should Know About Drugs: Teacher's
        Manual.   New York: Harcourt, 1971.

1519.   Gorodetzky, C.W. and Christian, S.T.   What You Should Know About
        Drugs: School Edition.   New York: Harcourt, 1971,
        especially pages 77-89.

1520.   Gorsuch, R.   The Impact of Drug Treatments on During-Treatment
        Criteria: 1971-1972 DARP Admissions.   American Journal of
        Drug and Alcohol Abuse, 2(1): 73-98, 1975.

1521.   Gorsuch, Richard L. and Arno, David H.   The Relationship of
        Children's Attitudes Toward Alcohol to Their Value
        Development.   Journal of Abnormal Child Psychology, 7(3):
        287-295, 1979.

1522.   Goshen, Charles E.   Drinks, Drugs and Do-Gooders.   New York:
        Free Press Division of Macmillan, Company, 1973.

1523.   Gosselin, N. and Parenteau, F.   L'Usage et L'Abus des Drogues au
        Québec: Apercu Global.   (Use and Misuse of Drugs in
        Quebec: A Global Outline.)   Toxicomanies, Québec, 11: 1-
        15, 1978.

1524. Gossett, J.T., Lewis, J.M. and Phillips, V.A. Extent and
       Prevalence of Illicit Drug Use as Reported by 56,745
       Students. Journal of the American Medical Association,
       216: 1464-1470, 1971.

1525. Gossett, J.T., Lewis, J.M. and Phillips, V.A. Psychological
       Characteristics of Adolescent Drug Users and Abstainers:
       Some Implications for Preventive Education. Bulletin of
       the Menninger Clinic, 36(4): 425-435, 1972.

1526. Gostyński, M., Marcinkowski, J.T. and Marcinkowski, T.
       Alkoholizm Wśród Młodzieży--w Świetle Danych z izb
       Wytrzeźwień w Poznaniu i Szczecinie. (Alcoholism Among
       Youth--in View of Data from Sobering-Up Stations in
       Poznan and Szczecin.) Wiadomosci Lekarskie, Warsaw, 28:
       1643-1648, 1975.

1527. Gottheil, Edward L., McLellan A. Thomas, Druley, Keith A. and
       Alterman, Arthur I. (Eds.) Addiction Research and
       Treatment: Converging Trends. New York: Pergamon Press,
       1977.

1528. Gould, A.P. Alcohol in Children. Medical Temperance Review, 4:
       165-166, 1901.

1529. Gould, George and Dickerson, Roy E. Digest of State and Federal
       Laws Dealing with Prostitution and Other Sex Offenses:
       with Notes on the Control of the Sale of Alcoholic
       Beverages as it Relates to Prostitution Activities. New
       York: The American Social Hygiene Association, Inc., 1942.

1530. Gould, L.C., Berberian, R.M., Kasl, S.V., Thompson, W.D. and
       Kleber, H.D. Sequential Patterns of Multiple-Drug Use
       Among High School Students. Archives of General
       Psychiatry, 34: 216-222, 1977.

1531. Grady, R.M. Survey of Student Opinion Concerning Drug Use.
       Colorado Springs, Colorado: Department of Research and
       Special Studies, Colorado Springs School District Eleven,
       1973.

1532. Grant, Marcus and Ginner, Paul (Eds.). Alcoholism in
       Perspective. Baltimore, Maryland: University Park Press,
       1979.

1533. Gray, Roy R. Guidelines for Comprehensive Health Education:
       A Conceptual Approach. Lincoln, Nebraska: State of
       Nebraska Department of Education, 1972.

1534. Great Boom in Student Drinking. The Literary Digest: 3-6,
       March 6, 1937.

1535.   Great Britain Board of Education. Syllabus of Lessons on
        "Temperance" for Scholars Attending Public Elementary
        Schools. London, England, 1909.

1536.   Great Britain Scottish Education Department. Syllabus of Lessons
        on "Temperance" for Use in Schools. London, England, 1910.

1537.   Great Britain Scottish Education Department. Syllabus of Lessons
        on "Temperance" for Use in Schools. London, England, 1920.

1538.   Great Falls Instructional and Library Materials Center. Tobacco,
        Drug and Alcohol Unit: Sixth Grade. Great Falls, Montana:
        Great Falls Public Schools, 1970.

1539.   Greater Hartford Council on Alcoholism. Information. Pamphlet.
        Hartford, Connecticut, 1969.

1540.   Greater St. Matthews Resource Committee. Not My Kid! A Survey
        of Drug Usage in Eastern Jefferson County, Kentucky. St.
        Matthews, Kentucky, 1973.

1541.   Greden, J.F., Frenkel, S.I. and Morgan, D.W. Alcohol Use in the
        Army: Patterns and Associated Behaviors. American Journal
        of Psychiatry, 132(1): 11-16, 1975.

1542.   Greeley, Andrew M., McCready, William C. and Theisen, Gary.
        Ethnic Drinking Subcultures. New York: Praeger
        Publishers, 1980.

1543.   Green, A.H. Child-Abusing Fathers. Journal of the American
        Academy of Child Psychology, 18: 270-282, 1979.

1544.   Green, B.E., Sack, W.H. and Pambrum, A. A Review of Child
        Psychiatric Epidemiology with Special Reference to American
        Indian and Alaska Native Children. White Cloud Journal of
        the American Indian, 2(2):. 22-36, 1981.

1545.   Green, J. Overview of Adolescent Drug Use. In: Youth Drug
        Abuse: Problems, Issues and Treatment. Eds. G.M. Beschner
        and A.S. Friedman. Lexington, Massachusetts: D.C. Heath,
        1979, pages 17-44.

1546.   Green, L.W. To Educate or Not to Educate: Is That the Question?
        American Journal of Public Health, 70(6): 625-626, 1980.

1547.   Green, Melvyn and Miller, Ralph. Cannabis Use in Canada. In:
        Cannabis and Culture. Ed. Vera Rubin. The Hague,
        Netherlands: Mouton Publishers, 1975, pages 497-520.

1548.   Greenberg, L.A. Is Alcoholism Inherited? Inventory, 7(2): 13-
        17, 1957.

1549.   Greenblatt, M. and Schuckit, M. (Eds.) Alcoholism Problems in
        Women and Children. New York: Grune and Stratton, 1976.

1550. Greenburg, Bradley S. Smoking, Drugging and Drinking in Top
        Rated TV Series. Journal of Drug Education, 11(3): 227-
        234, 1981.

1551. Greenburg, H.R. What You Must Know About Drugs. (Revised
        Edition.) New York: Scholastic, 1973.

1552. Greene County Council on Alcoholism. Objectives for Use in
        Teaching About Alcohol in Secondary Schools. Leaflet.
        Greene County, Ohio, 1969.

1553. Greensboro Public Schools Alcohol Education Workshop. Alcohol
        Education Curriculum Guide. Greensboro, North Carolina,
        no date.

1554. Gregory, D. Racial Differences in the Incidence and Prevalence
        of Alcohol Abuse in Oklahoma. Alcohol Technical Report, 4:
        37-41, 1975.

1555. Gregory, I. Alcoholism, Family Size and Ordinal Position.
        Canadian Psychiatric Association Journal, 10: 134-140,
        1965.

1556. Gregory, I. Family Data Concerning the Hypotheses of Heredity
        Predisposition Toward Alcoholism. Journal of Mental
        Science, 106: 1068-1072, 1960.

1557. Greist, J., Klein, M., Van Cura, L. and Erdman, H. Computer
        Interview Questionnaires for Drug Use/Abuse. In:
        Predicting Adolescent Drug Abuse: A Review of Issues,
        Methods and Correlates. NIDA Research Issues Series,
        Volume 11. Ed. D. Lettieri. Washington, D.C.: U.S.
        Government Printing Office, 1975, pages 147-164.

1558. Grey Advertising, Inc., New York. Research Department.
        Communications Strategies on Alcohol and Highway Safety.
        Volume II. High School Youth. Springfield, Virginia:
        National Technical Information Service, U.S. Department of
        Commerce, 1975.

1559. Griffin, John B., Jr. Introduction to Alcohol Abuse in
        Adolescents and Young Adults. In: Currents in Alcoholism.
        Volume 6. Treatment and Rehabilitation and Epidemiology.
        New York: Grune and Stratton, 1979, pages 229-231.

1560. Griffin, P.L. Drinking Behaviors and Attitudes Among Selected
        Adolescents of a Michigan Secondary School. Doctoral
        Dissertation (University Microfilms No. 76-19146).
        University of Michigan, 1976.

1561. Griffith, M. Knowledge and Usage of Drugs: A Study of Students'
        Attitudes in Grades Two through Twelve. Doctoral
        Dissertation (University Microfilms No. 74-2664). Indiana
        University, 1973.

1562. Grimm, D.L. Youth Wants to Know. Leaflet. Harrisburg,
       Pennsylvania Council on Alcohol Problems, no date.

1563. Grimm, H. Getränke für Kinder und Jugendliche im 16. bis 19.
       Jahrhundert, nach Zeitgenössischen Selbstzeugnissen.
       (Beverages of Children and Adolescents in the 16th to 19th
       Centuries According to Personal Accounts of
       Contemporaries.) Arzneimittel Jugendk., 68: 345-351, 1977.

1564. Grizzle, G.A. The Effects of a Drug Education Program Upon
       Student Drug Knowledge, Drug Usage, and Psychological
       States. Chapel Hill, North Carolina: University of North
       Carolina, Institute of Government, 1974.

1565. Gross, M.M., Rosenblatt, S.M., Lewis, E., Malenowski, B. and
       Broman, M. Hallucinations and Clouding of Sensorium in
       Alcohol Withdrawal. Some Demographic and Cultural
       Relationships. Quarterly Journal of Studies on Alcohol,
       32(4): 1061-1069, 1971.

1566. Grossman, H. Nine Rotten Lousy Kids. New York: Holt, Rinehart
       and Winston, 1972.

1567. Grossman, P.H. Drinking Motivation: A Cluster Analytic Study of
       Three Samples. Doctoral Dissertation (University
       Microfilms No. 66-2793). Denver: University of Colorado,
       1965.

1568. Groves, W. Eugene. Patterns of College Student Drug Use and
       Lifestyles. In: Drug Use: Epidemiological and
       Sociological Approaches. Eds. E. Josephson and
       E.E. Carroll. Washington, D.C.: Hemisphere Publishing,
       1974, pages 241-275.

1569. Gruber, K. Die Abstinenten Jugendorganisationen. (The Abstinent
       Youth Organization.) Alkoholfrage, 18: 113-120, 1922.

1570. Grunden, Grace. The Way It Is. Beaverton, Oregon: Peter George
       Books, 1973.

1571. Guinn, R. Attitudinal and Behavioral Aspects of Mexican-American
       Drug Use: Three Year Follow-Up. Journal of Drug
       Education, 8: 173-179, 1978.

1572. Guinn, R. Characteristics of Drug Use Among Mexican-American
       Students. Journal of Drug Education, 5(3): 235-241, 1975.

1573. Guinn, R. Self-Reported Attitudes and Behavior of Mexican-
       American Drug Use. International Journal of the
       Addictions, 14: 579-584, 1979.

1574. Guinn, R. and Hurley, R.S. A Comparison of Drug Use among
       Houston and Lower Rio Grande Valley Secondary Students.
       Adolescence, 11: 455-459, 1976.

1575.   Guinn, Robert. Alcohol Use Among Mexican-American Youth.
        Journal of School Health, 48(2): 90-91, 1978.

1576.   Gunderson, E.K.E. and Schuckit, M.A. Prognostic Indicators in
        Young Alcoholics. Military Medicine, 143: 168-170, 1978.

1577.   Gunderson, Ingrid. Incest and Alcoholism. Catalyst, 1(3): 22-
        25, 1980.

1578.   Gusfield, J.R. The Structural Context of College Drinking.
        Quarterly Journal of Studies on Alcohol, 22: 428-443, 1961.
        (Also in: The Domesticated Drug: Drinking Among
        Collegians. Ed. G.L. Maddox. New Haven, Connecticut:
        College and University Press, 1970, pages 290-306.)

1579.   Gusfield, Joseph. The Prevention of Drinking Problems. In:
        Alcohol and Alcohol Problems. Eds. W.J. Filstead,
        Jean J. Rossi and Mark Keller. Cambridge, Massachusetts:
        Ballinger, 1976, pages 267-291.

1580.   Gustafsson, K. Larmsiffror om Ungdomens Alkoholbruk--Värre Blir
        Det? (Alarming Figures on the Use of Alcohol Among Youth--
        Is It Getting Worse?) Alkohol och Narkotica, 70: 25-26,
        1976.

1581.   Gustar, Jahoda and Cramond, Joyce. Children and Alcohol: A
        Developmental Study in Glasgow. Volume 1. London: Her
        Majesty's Stationary Office, 1972.

1582.   Guze, S., Goodwin, D. and Crane, J. Criminal Recidivism and
        Psychiatric Illness. American Journal of Psychiatry
        127(6): 832-835, 1970.

1583.   Guze, S.B. Psychiatric Illness in Adopted Children of
        Alcoholics. Annals of the New York Academy of Sciences,
        197: 188, 1972.

1584.   Guze, S.B., Tuason, V.B., Gatfield, P.D., Stewart, M.A. and
        Picken, B. Psychiatric Illness and Crime, With Particular
        Reference to Alcoholism: A Study of 223 Criminals.
        Journal of Nervous and Mental Disease, 134: 512-521, 1962.

1585.   Guze, S.B., Wolfgram, E.D., McKinney, J.K. and Cantwell, D.P.
        Delinquency, Social Maladjustment and Crime: The Role of
        Alcoholism: A Study of First-Degree Relatives of Convicted
        Criminals. Diseases of the Nervous System, 29: 238-243,
        1968.

1586.   Gwaltney, F.W. Excessive Drinking of Alcohol--A Social,
        Psychiatric and State Problem. Mental Hygiene Survey, 5:
        17-20, 1943.

1587. Gwinner, P.D.V. The Young Alcoholic: Approaches to Treatment.
        In: International Conference on Alcoholism and Drug
        Dependence: Alcoholism and Drug Dependence, A
        Multidisciplinary Approach. Proceedings of the Third
        International Conference on Alcoholism and Drug Dependence,
        Liverpool, England, April, 1976. Eds. J.S. Madden,
        Robin Walker and W.H. Kenyon. New York: Plenum Press,
        1977, pages 263-269.

H

1588. H., Mary. *My Mother is an Alcoholic*. Leaflet. Carmel, New
       York: Guideposts Associates, 1960.

1589. Haag, J. *Health Education for Young Adults*. Austin, Texas:
       Steck-Vaughn, 1965.

1590. Haaranen, A. Vaikuttajan ja Kasvattajan Vastuu.
       (Responsibilities of Spokesmen and Educators in Alcohol
       Education.) *Alkoholipolitiikka*, Helsingfor, 44: 223-224,
       1979.

1591. Haastrup, S. and Thomsen, K. The Social Backgrounds of Young
       Addicts as Elicited in Interviews with Their Parents.
       Acta Psychiatrica Scandinavica, 48: 146-173, 1972.

1592. Haavio-Mannila, E. Alkoholijuomien Osuus Suomalaisissa
       Kylätappeluissa. (The Role of Alcohol in Village Fights in
       Finland.) *Alkoholipolitiikka*, Helsingfor, 2: 51-53, 1959.

1593. Haberman, P.W. Childhood Symptoms in Children of Alcoholics and
       Comparison Group Parents. *Journal of Marriage and the
       Family*, 28(2): 152-154, 1966.

1594. Haberman, P.W. Psycho-Physiologic and Childhood Symptoms in
       Alcoholics and Their Children. *Milbank Memorial Fund
       Quarterly*, 47(1): Part 2, 175-180, 1969.

1595. Haberman, Paul and Baden, Michael. *Alcohol, Other Drugs and
       Violent Death*. New York: Oxford University Press, 1978.

1596. Hádlík, J. and Mandlova, J. Abuse of Alcohol in Adolescents in
       the South Moravian Region. *Acta Facultalus Medicae
       Universitatis Brunensis*, (42): 91-103, 1973.

1597. Hádlík, J. and Mandlová, I. Epidemiologická Studie Abúzu
       Alkoholu a Jiných Drog u Dorostu a Mládeže v Jihomoravském
       Kraji v roce 1970. (Epidemiological Study of Abuse of
       Acohol and Other Drugs by Youth in Southern Moravia during
       1970.) Protialkoholicky Obzor, Bratislava, 7: 73-80, 1972.

1598. Haertzen, C.A. and Ross, F.E. Does the Frequency of Definitions
       for a Particular Drug in Slang Dictionaries Predict
       Quantity of Knowledge of the Slang. Psychological Reports,
       44(3): Part 2, 1031-1039, 1979.

1599. Hafen, B.Q. Alcohol: The Crutch that Cripples. St. Paul,
       Minnesota: West Publishing, 1977.

1600. Hafen, B.Q. and Peterson, B. Medicines and Drugs: Problems and
       Risks, Use and Abuse. Philadelphia, Pennsylvania, Lea and
       Febiger, 1978.

1601. Hafen, Brent Q. (Ed.) Drug Abuse: Psychology/Sociology/
       Pharmacology. Provo, Utah: Brigham Young University
       Press, 1973.

1602. Hagaman, Barbara L. Food for Thought: Beer in a Social and
       Ritual Context in a Western African Society. Journal of
       Drug Issues, 10: 203-214, 1980.

1603. Hagan, Terry A. Introduction to the Catalyst. The Catalyst,
       1(3): 3, 1980.

1604. Hager, Mary. Traditional View of Alcoholism Shaken. The
       Journal, 3(2): 9, 1974. (Toronto, The Addiction Research
       Foundation, 1974)

1605. Hagnell, O., Nyman, E. and Tunving, K. Dangerous Alcoholics:
       Personality Varieties in Aggressive and Suicidally-Inclined
       Subjects. Scandinavian Journal of Social Medicine, 1(3):
       125-131, 1973.

1606. Hahn, P.H. and O'Connor, J.P. The Juvenile Offender and the Law.
       Cincinnati, Ohio: W.H. Anderson, 1971.

1607. Hajduković, C., Hajduković, R and Čalovska, N. Maloletnicka
       Delinkvencija i Alkoholizam. (Juvenile Delinquency and
       Alcoholism.) Alkoholizam, Beograd, 18(3-4): 29-39, 1978.

1608. Halberstan, M. Ist Alkoholismus Erblich? (Is Alcoholism
       Hereditary? Fursorger, 47: 74-75, 1979.

1609. Hall, Leonard C. Facts About Alcohol and Alcoholism.
       Washington, D.C.: Superintendent of Documents, 1974.
       (DHEW Publication No. ADM 74-31).

1610. Hall, Malcolm. Illicit Drug Abuse in Australia - A Brief
       Statistical Picture. Journal of Drug Issues, 7: 311-318,
       1977.

1611. Halleck, Seymour. The Great Drug Education Hoax. The
       Progressive, 34: 30-33, 1970.

1612. Hallström, B. Missbruk på Folkhögskola Komplicerat Problem.
       (The Complicated Problem of [Alcohol and Drug] Misuse and
       Boarding School.) Alkohol och Narkotica, 68: 123-127,
       1974.

1613. Hallström, B. Ungdom Föräldrar Skolfork Diskuterar
       Alkoholforstran. (Young People--Parents--Teachers Discuss
       Alcohol Education.) Alkohol och Narkotica, 67: 92-95, 102,
       1973.

1614. Halmi, K.A. and Loney, J. Familial Alcoholism in Anorexia
       Nervosa. British Journal of Psychiatry, 123: 53-54, 1973.

1615. Halpern, F. Alcoholic "Potentials." Alcohol Hygiene, 1(7): 18-
       22, 1945.

1616. Halpin, G. and Whiddon, T. Drug Education: Solution or Problem?
       Psychological Reports, 40: 372-374, 1977.

1617. Halverson, G. The Liquor Industry: How Much Responsibility?
       Pamphlet. Boston, Massachusetts: Christian Science, 1972.

1618. Halverson, G. Teen-Agers Who Drink--What Can Be Done? Christian
       Science Monitor, Eastern Edition, 65(9): Section 2, 17,
       1972.

1619. Halverson, Guy. Shift from Pill-Popping to Alcohol. The Union
       Signal, 99(5): 24, 1973.

1620. Hamburg, B.A., Kraemer, H.C. and Jahnke, W. A Hierarchy of Drug
       Use in Adolescence: Behavioral and Attitudinal Correlates
       of Substantial Drug Use. American Journal of Psychiatry,
       132: 1155-1163, 1975.

1621. Hames, L.N. Can Alcohol Education Change the Role of Youth on
       Our Highways? In: Alcohol, Drugs and Traffic Safety.
       Proceedings of the Sixth International Conference on
       Alcohol, Drugs and Traffic Safety, Toronto, September 8-13,
       1974. Eds. S. Israelstam and S. Lambert. Toronto,
       Ontario: Addiction Research Foundation of Ontario, 1975,
       pages 861-868.

1622. Hames, L.N. Can Students be Taught to Mix Alcohol and Gasoline--
       Safely? Journal of School Health, 41(9): 481-488, 1971.
       (Also as: Can Students be Taught to Mix Alcohol and
       Gasoline--Safely? Pamphlet. Washington, D.C.: Distilled
       Spirits Council of the United States, 1971.

1623.   Hames, L.N.   The Case for Having the Public Schools Teach Our
        Youngsters How to Drink.   Clinical Toxicology, 11: 473-478,
        1977.

1624.   Hamilton, D.   Mari's Mountain.   Scottdale, Pennsylvania: Herald
        Press, 1978.

1625.   Hamlin, H.E.   Alcohol Talks to Youth: A Brief Scientific
        Discussion.   Pamphlet.   Evanston, Illinois: School and
        College Service, no date.

1626.   Hammen, C.L.   Depression in College Students: Beyond the Beck
        Depression Inventory.   Journal of Consulting and Clinical
        Psychology, 48: 126-128, 1980.

1627.   Hammond, R. (Ed.)   Facts and Fancy About Teenage Drinking.
        Report on Alcohol, 13(2): 16-31, 1975.

1628.   Hammond, R.L.   Legal Drinking at 18 or 21--Does it Make Any
        Difference?   Journal of Alcohol and Drug Education, 18(3):
        9-13, 1973.

1629.   Hampl, K. and Kejdanová, M.   Konzumace Alkoholických Nápojů Žáky
        Šestých a Devátých Tříd.   (Consumption of Alcoholic
        Beverages by Students in the Sixth and Ninth Grades.)
        Protialkoholicky Obzor, Bratislava, 7: 120-124, 1972.

1630.   Hanák, K.   Alkoholista Szülök--Állami Gondozott Gyerekek.
        (Alcoholic Parents--Children as Wards of the State.)
        Alkohologia, Budapest, 3: 98-107, 1972.

1631.   Hancock, D.C.   Points for Parents Perplexed About Drugs.
        Pamphlet.   Center City, Minnesota: Hazelden, 1975.

1632.   Hancock, David C.   Drugs, Alcohol and the Occult.   Journal of
        Alcohol and Drug Education, 20(1): 34-44, 1974.

1633.   Handbook for Parents About Drugs.   Toronto, Ontario: Photo Pix,
        1970.

1634.   Hannequin, T.   Isba Wytrzeżwień i Mlodziez.   (The Detoxification
        Station and Youth.)   Problemy Alkoholizmu, Warsaw, 20(8-9):
        12-13, 1972.

1635.   Hanson, D.J.   Anomie Theory and Drinking Problems: A Test.
        Drinking and Drug Practices Surveyor, Berkeley, (10): 23-
        24, 1975.

1636.   Hanson, D.J.   College Students' Reasons for Drinking: Twenty
        Year Trends.   College Student Journal, 9(3): 256-257, 1975.

1637.   Hanson, D.J.   Drinking Attitudes and Behaviors Among College
        Students.   Journal of Alcohol and Drug Education, 19(3):
        6-14, 1974.

1638. Hanover, Ronald E. Differential Treatment in High Risk Urban
       Areas. In: Differential Treatment of Drug and Alcohol
       Abusers. Eds. C.S. Davis and M.R. Schmidt. Palm Springs,
       California: ETC Publications, 1977, pages 45-53.

1639. Hanson, D.J. Norm Qualities and Deviant Drinking Behavior.
       Doctoral Dissertation (University Microfilms No. 73-19817).
       Syracuse, New York: Syracuse University, 1972.

1640. Hanson, D.J. A Note on Parental Attitudes and the Incidence of
       Drinking. Drinking and Drug Practices Surveyor, (8): 12-
       14, August, 1973.

1641. Hanson, David J. Alcohol Consumption Among College Students:
       1970-1975. College Student Journal, 11: 9-10, 1977.

1642. Hanson, David J. Drinking Problems: A Test of Alternative
       Explanations. Psychology, 14: 49-51, 1977.

1643. Hanson, David J. Social Norms and Drinking Behavior:
       Implications for Alcohol and Drug Education. Journal of
       Alcohol and Drug Education, 18: 18-24, 1973.

1644. Hanson, David J. Trends in Drinking Attitudes and Behaviors
       Among College Students. Journal of Alcohol and Drug
       Education, 22(3): 17-22, 1977.

1645. Hanson, J.R. and Simons, J.N. Alcohol-Related Highway Accidents:
       A Hospital Survey. Minnesota Medicine, 53(8): 905-907,
       1970.

1646. Hanson, Kathye J. and Este, Nada J. Dynamics of Alcoholic
       Families. In: Alcoholism: Development, Consequences and
       Interventions. Eds. Nada J. Este and M. Edith Heinemann.
       St. Louis: C.V. Mosby Company, 1977, pages 67-75.

1647. Hardy, R.E. and Cull, J.G. Fundamentals of Juvenile Criminal
       Behavior and Drug Abuse. Springfield, Illinois: Thomas,
       1975. (American Lecture Series Publication No. 955)

1648. Hardy, Richard E. and Cull, John G. (Eds.) Problems of
       Adolescents: Social and Psychological Approaches.
       Springfield, Illinois: Charles C. Thomas, 1974.

1649. Harford, T.C. Drinking Contexts: A Developmental Approach.
       Washington, D.C.: Paper Presented at the 84th Annual
       Convention of the American Psychological Association,
       September, 1976.

1650. Harford, T.C. Ecological Factors in Drinking. In: Youth,
       Alcohol and Social Policy. Eds. H.T. Blane and
       M.E. Chafetz. New York: Plenum Press, 1979, pages 147-
       182.

1651. Harford, T.C. Patterns of Alcohol Use Among Adolescents.
       Psychiatric Opinion, 12(3): 17-21, 1975.

1652. Harford, T.C. Teenage Alcohol Use. Postgraduate Medicine,
       60(1): 73-76, 1976.

1653. Harford, Thomas C. A National Study of Adolescent Drinking
       Behavior, Attitudes and Correlates. Journal of Studies on
       Alcohol, 37(11): 1747-1750, 1976.

1654. Harford, Thomas C. The NIAAA National Study: An Overview. In:
       Alcohol Problems Among Youth. Proceedings of a Workshop at
       Pittsburgh, Pennsylvania, December 2-3, 1976. Ed.
       Joseph Newman. Western Pennsylvania Institute of Alcohol
       Studies, September, 1977.

1655. Harford, Thomas C. and Mills, George S. Age-Related Trends in
       Alcohol Consumption. Journal of Studies on Alcohol, 39(1):
       207-210, 1978.

1656. Harman, C. Driver Education and Hazards of the Road. American
       Journal of Public Health, 71(2): 171, 1981.

1657. Harmony: A Community Alcohol Education Outreach Program:
       Training Manual. Hayward, California Drug Education
       Center, 1976.

1658. Harms, Ernest (Ed.). Drugs and Youth: The Challenge of Today.
       Elmsford, New York: Pergamon Press, 1973.

1659. Harmsworth, Harry C. A Survey of the Alcohol and Narcotics
       Problem in Idaho. Moscow, Idaho: Department of Social
       Sciences, University of Idaho, September 1, 1954.

1660. Harper, Edward O. The Problem of the Alcohol-Dependent
       Individual. Military Medicine, 139(6): 439-443, 1974.

1661. Harper, F.D. (Ed) Alcohol Abuse and Black America. Alexandria,
       Virginia: Douglass Publishers, 1976.

1662. Harper, Frederick D. Alcohol Education: The Role of the
       Teacher. Phi Delta Kappan, 57: 259, 1975.

1663. Harper, Frederick D. Overview: Alcohol and Blacks. In:
       Alcohol Abuse and Black America. Ed. Frederick D. Harper.
       Alexandria, Virginia: Douglass Publishers, Inc., 1976,
       pages 1-12.

1664. Harper, Frederick D. Summary, Issues and Recommendations. In:
       Alcohol Abuse and Black America. Ed. Frederick D. Harper.
       Alexandria, Virginia: Douglass Publishers, Inc., 1976,
       pages 187-200.

1665. Harper, Frederick D. and Dawkins, Marvin P.   Alcohol and Blacks:
       Survey of the Periodical Literature.   The British Journal
       of Addiction, 71(2): 327-334, 1976.

1666. Harriman, P.L.   The Alcohol Problem and the Small College.
       Alcohol Hygiene, 2(2): 3-8, 1946.

1667. Harris, Robert, McIsaac, William and Schuster, Charles (Eds.).
       Drug Dependence.   Austin, Texas: University of Texas
       Press, 1970.

1668. Harrison, D.E.   Emerging Drinking Patterns of Pre-Adolescents: A
       Study of the Influence of Significant Others.   Doctoral
       Dissertation (University Microfilms No. 71-8837).
       Mississippi: Mississippi State University, 1970.

1669. Harrison, D.E., Bennett, W.H. and Globetti, G.   Factors Related
       to Alcohol Use Among Pre-Adolescents.   Journal of Alcohol
       Education, 15(2): 3-10, 1970.

1670. Harrison, Dorrell.   Determining Knowledge and Attitudes on
       Alcohol, Tobacco, Drugs.   New York: Hoosick Falls Central
       School, March 17, 1975.

1671. Harrison, J.   Some Characteristics of Young Israeli Drug Users.
       Drug Forum, 7: 167-172, 1978-79.

1672. Harrison, J.B.   Should the Young be Educated in the Use and Abuse
       of Alcohol?   British Journal of Addiction, 56: 53-62, 1960.

1673. Harrison, V.M.   A Plea for the Early Instruction of Academic
       Students of Both Sexes as to the Dangers of Alcoholism and
       Its Associated Evils.   Charlotte Medical Journal, 62: 316-
       318, 1910.

1674. Hart, L.   Attitudes Toward Alcoholism and Drug Abuse Among a
       Group of High School Students.   Journal of Drug Education,
       5: 351-357, 1975.

1675. Hart, N.A. and Keidel, G.C.   The Suicidal Adolescent.   American
       Journal of Nursing, 79: 80-84, 1979.

1676. Hartmann, A.   Die Schnappsgefahr und ihre Bekämpfung.   (The
       Danger from Distilled Spirits and the Fight Against It.)
       Gesundheit und Wholfahrt, Zürich, 31: 330-340, 1951.

1677. Hartmann, D.   A Study of Drug-Taking Adolescents.   Psychoanalytic
       Study of the Child, 24: 384-398, 1969.

1678. Haskins, J.   Teenage Alcoholism.   New York: Hawthorn Books,
       1976.

1679. Haskins, J.B. Evaluating the Effect of a One-Day Drug Education
         Program on High School Journalists. Journal of Drug
         Education, 9: 263-271, 1979.

1680. Haško, L., Hrková, G. and Fridrich, J. Príspevok k Toxikománii
         Mladistvých. (Contribution to Toxicomania of Youth.)
         Protialkoholicky Obzor, Bratislava, 7: 117-120, 1972.

1681. Hassall, C. A Controlled Study of the Characteristics of Young
         Male Alcoholics. British Journal of Addiction, 63(3): 193-
         201, 1968.

1682. Hassall, C. Development of Alcohol Addiction in Young Men.
         British Journal of Preventive and Social Medicine, 23(1):
         40-44, 1969.

1683. Hassall, C. and Foulds, G.A. Hostility Among Young Alcoholics.
         British Journal of Addiction, 63: 203-208, 1968.

1684. Hauge, R. Alcohol Research in Norway. Olso, Norway: National
         Institute for Alcohol Research, 1978.

1685. Hauge, R. Drikkepress Blant Ungdom. (Pressures to Drink Among
         Youth. 3. Expectations and Reality.) Tidsskrift
         EdruSpørsm, 30(4): 10-11, 1978.

1686. Hauge, R. Drikkepress Blant Ungdom: Forventninger om Avhold og
         Bruk. (Pressure for Drinking Among Youth: Expectations of
         Abstinence and Drinking.) Tidsskrift EdruSpørsm, 30(2):
         33-35, 1978.

1687. Hauge, R. Drikkepress Bland Ungdom. 2. Forventninger og
         Atferd. (The Pressure to Drink Among Youth. 2.
         Expectations and Behavior.) Tidsskrift EdruSpørsm, 30(3):
         4-5, 20-21, 1978.

1688. Hauge, R. Ungdoms Holdning til Bruk og Misbruk av Alkohol. (The
         Attitude of Youth Concerning the Use and Misuse of
         Alcohol.) Tidsskrift EdruSpørsm, 29(4): 32-33, 1977.

1689. Hauge, R. Ungdom og Alkohol. (Youth and Alcohol.) Norsk
         Tidsskrift AlkSpørsm, 18: 1-63, 1966. (Also in: Statens
         Institutt for Alkoholforskning, Skr. No. 5. Oslo:
         Universitetsforlaget, 1966.)

1690. Hauge, R. Ungdom og Drikkepress. (Youth and Pressure to Drink.)
         Norsk Tidsskrift AlkSpørsm, 19: 34-49, 1967.

1691. Häussler, M., Mallach, H.J. and Mittmeyer, H.-J. Die Beteiligung
         Alkoholbeeinflusster Jüngerer Personen am Offentlichen
         Strassenverkehr. (Participation of Alcohol-Affected Young
         Persons in Public Road Traffic.) Blutalkohol, Hamburg,
         10: 335-341, 1973.

1692.   Havard, J.D.   Alcohol and Road Accidents.   In: Alcoholism: New
         Knowledge and New Responses.   Eds. G. Edwards and M. Grant.
         London: Croom Helm, 1977, pages 251-263.

1693.   Havassy-de Avila, B.   A Critical Review of the Approach to Birth
         Order Research.   Canadian Psychologist, 12(2): 282-305,
         1971.

1694.   Havighurst, R.J.   The Extent and Significance of Suicide Among
         American Indians Today.   Mental Hygiene, 55(2): 174-177,
         1971.

1695.   Hawker, A.   Adolescents and Alcohol.   Report of an Enquiry Into
         Adolescent Drinking Patterns Carried Out from October 1975
         to June 1976.   London: Edsall, 1978.

1696.   Hawker, A.   Alcohol and Adolescents.   British Journal on Alcohol
         and Alcoholism, 13: 2-5, 1978.

1697.   Hawker, A.   Problem of Young Alcoholics.   Health Visitor, 50:
         367, 1977.

1698.   Hawker, Ann.   Drinking Patterns of Young People.   In: Alcoholism
         and Drug Dependence: A Multidisciplinary Approach.
         J.S. Madden, Robin Walker and W.H. Kenyon.   New York:
         Plenum Press, 1977, pages 95-104.

1699.   Hawker, Ann.   Facts and Figures.   British Journal on Alcohol and
         Alcoholism, 13(1): 21-23, 1978.

1700.   Hawker, Ann.   Facts and Figures.   Poland.   British Journal on
         Alcohol and Alcoholism, 14(1): 18-19, 1979.

1701.   Hawkins, H.N.   Some Effects of Alcoholism of Parents on Children
         in the Home.   St. Louis, Missouri: Salvation Army,
         Midland Division, 1950.

1702.   Hayek, M.A.   Recovered Alcoholic Women With and Without Incest
         Experience: A Comparative Study.   Doctoral Dissertation.
         Reed University, 1980.

1703.   Hayes, R.W. and Tevis, B.W.   A Comparison of Attitudes and
         Behavior of High School Athletes and Non-Athletes with
         Respect to Alcohol Use and Abuse.   Journal of Alcohol and
         Drug Education, 23(10): 20-28, 1977.

1704.   Hays, J.R. and Winburn, G.M.   Drug Abuse Among Elementary School
         Students in a Suburban School Setting.   Journal of Drug
         Education, 2(4): 355-360, 1972.

1705.   Hays, J. Ray.   The Incidence of Drug Abuse Among Secondary School
         Students in Houston.   Medical Journal of St. Joseph
         Hospital, 7(4): 52-59, 72, 1972.

1706. Hays, J. Ray. The Incidence of Drug Abuse Among Secondary School
          Students in Houston, 1971. St. Joseph Hospital Medical
          Surgical Journal, 7(4): 146-152, 1972.

1707. Healy, P. Patterns of Drug Use in Australia, 1970-1977.
          Australian Journal of Alcoholism and Drug Dependence, 6:
          30-37, 1979.

1708. Healy, W. and Bronner, A.F. Youthful Offenders. American
          Journal of Sociology, 22: 38-52, 1916.

1709. Heath, R.W., Maier, M.H. and Remmers, H.H. Youth's Attitudes
          Toward Various Aspects of Their Lives. (Purdue Opinion
          Panel, Report of Poll No. 49.) Lafayette, Indiana:
          Division of Educational Reference, Purdue University,
          April 1957.

1710. Heather, Nick. Relationship Between Delinquency and Drunkenness
          Among Scottish Young Offenders. British Journal on
          Alcohol and Alcoholism, 16(2): 50-61, 1981.

1711. Hecht, C.A., Grine, R.J. and Rothrock, S.E. The Drinking and
          Dating Habits of 336 College Women in a Coeducational
          Institution. Quarterly Journal of Studies on Alcohol, 9:
          252-258, 1948.

1712. Hecht, M. Children of Alcoholics Are Children at Risk.
          American Journal of Nursing, 73(10): 1764-1767, 1973.

1713. Heesch, J.R. and Colyar, A.B. Drug Use in Anchorage, Alaska: A
          Survey of 15,634 Students in Grades 6 through 12--1971.
          Journal of the American Medical Association, 223: 657-664,
          1973.

1714. Heidenreich, C. Adrian. Alcohol and Drug Use and Abuse Among
          Indian-Americans: A Review of Issues and Sources. Journal
          of Drug Issues, 6: 256-272, 1976.

1715. Heilman, R.O. Early Recognition of Alcoholism and Other Drug
          Dependence. Maryland State Medical Journal, 25(9): 73-76,
          1976.

1716. Hein, F.V. Health Education and Drug Abuse. In: Teaching About
          Drugs: A Curriculum Guide, K-12 (2nd Edition). Kent,
          Ohio: American School Health Association, 1970.

1717. Hein, F.V. How Teens Set the Stage for Alcoholism. Leaflet.
          Chicago: American Medical Association, 1962.

1718. Hein, F.V., Farnsworth, D.L. and Richardson, C.E. Living,
          Health, Behavior and Environment (5th Edition). Glenview,
          Illinois: Scott, Foresman, 1970.

1719. Heine, T. Should You Teach Your Children to Drink? Pamphlet.
       Wisconsin Association on Alcoholism and Other Drug Abuse,
       Inc., Madison, Wisconsin, no date.

1720. Heinemann, M. Edith and Smith-DiJulio, Kathleen. Learning to
       Understand Alcoholism. Nursing Clinics of North America,
       11(3): 493-505, 1976.

1721. Helasvuo, K. Ungdomsfylleri i Helsingfors. (Juvenile Drinking
       in Helsingfors.) Nordisk Tidsskrift Kriminalvid, 51: 13-
       20, 1963.

1722. Helgason, T. and Ásmundson, G. Behaviour and Social
       Characteristics of Young Asocial Alcohol Abusers.
       Neuropsychobiology, Basel, 1: 109-120, 1975.

1723. Helin, I. Intoxikationer Med Alkohol och Läkemedel Bland
       Tonåringar i Malmö. (Poisionings with Alcohol and Drugs
       Among Teenagers in Malmö.) Läkartidningen, 69: 5095-5100,
       1972.

1724. Helm, Stanley T. Predisposition to Alcoholism. In: Resource
       Book for Drug Abuse Education. American Association for
       Health, Physical Education and Recreation. Washington,
       D.C.: U.S. Government Printing Office, 1969, pages 87-88.

1725. Helmick, E.F., McClure, W.T.and Mitchell, P.M. A Project to
       Analyze Risk to Alcohol Abuse Among Alaskan Native
       Students. In: Currents in Alcoholism. Volume 2.
       Psychiatric, Psychological, Social and Epidemiological
       Studies. Ed. F.A. Seixas. New York: Grune and Stratton,
       1971, pages 367-376.

1726. Help for Young Alcoholics Who Want Help. Patient Care, 106-117,
       September 15, 1975.

1727. Hemminki, E. Tobacco, Alcohol, Medicines and Illegal Drug
       Taking. Adolescence, 9(35): 421-424, 1974.

1728. Hemminki, E., Rissanen, A. and Mattila, A. The Opinions of
       Helsinki School Children on the Dangers of Drugs. The
       Health Education Journal, 31: 115-117, 1972.

1729. Henderson, S., Lewis, I.C., Howell, R.H. and Rayner, K.J.
       Mental Heath and the Use of Alcohol, Tobacco, Analgesics
       and Vitamins in a Secondary School Population. Acta
       Psychiatrica Scandinavica, 63: 186-189, 1981.

1730. Hendler, H. and Stephens, R. The Addict Odyssey: From
       Experimentation to Addiction. International Journal of the
       Addictions, 12(1): 25-42, 1977.

1731. Hennigan, L.P. The Patient's Attitude Toward the First
          Experience with Alcohol as a Diagnostic Tool. Maryland
          State Medical Journal, 29(10): 62-64, 1980.

1732. Henriksson, B. Aktiverad Narkotika- ock Alkoholinformation.
          (Active Drug and Alcohol Education.) Läkartidningen, 70:
          926-927, 1973.

1733. Henry, H.W. Advertising Alcohol--an ITV View. British Journal
          of Alcohol and Alcoholism, 15: 129-135, 1980.

1734. Hensel, B., Dunner, D.L. and Fieve, R. The Relationship of
          Family History of Alcoholism to Primary Affective
          Disorders. Journal of Affective Disorders, 1: 105-114,
          1979.

1735. Hercod, R. L'Évolution des Habitudes de Boisson en Suisse.
          (Evolution of Drinking Habits in Switzerland.)
          Gesundheitsen und Wohlfahrt, 26: 620-626, 1946.

1736. Herjanic, B., Herjanic, M., Wetzel, R. and Tomelleri, C.
          Substance Abuse: Its Effect on Offspring. Research
          Communications in Psychology, Psychiatry and Behavior, 3:
          65-75, 1978.

1737. Herjanic, B.M., Herjanic, M., Penick, E.C., Tomelleri, C.J. and
          Armbruster, R.B.S. Children of Alcoholics. Washington,
          D.C.: Paper Presented at the 7th Annual Medical-Scientific
          Session of the National Alcoholism Forum, May 1976.

1738. Herjanic, Barbara, Herjanic, Marijan, Penick, Elizabeth,
          Tomelleri, Carlos and Armbruster, Robert. Children of
          Alcoholics. In: Currents in Alcoholism. Volume 2.
          Psychiatric, Psychological, Social and Epidemiological
          Studies. Ed. F.A. Seixas. New York: Grune and Stratton,
          1977, pages 445-456.

1739. Hermann, H. Beskyttelseslovgivningen for Alkoholskadede.
          (Protective Legislation for the Alcohol Damaged.)
          Måanedsskrift for Praktisk Laegegering, Copenhagen,
          39: 155-166, 1961.

1740. Hermann, J. Die Katholische Kirche und die Alkoholfrage. (The
          Catholic Church and the Problem of Alcohol.) Fürsorger,
          14: 46-52, 1946.

1741. Herrera-Araya, M., Rivera-de-Solis, V., Valerio-Charpentier, E.
          and Venegas-Chinchilla, Y. Programa Escolar de Prevencion
          del Alcoholism: Primero and Segundo Ciclos. (A School
          Program for the Prevention of Alcoholism: First and
          Second Cycles.) San Jose, Costa Rica: Centro de Estudios
          Sobre Alcoholismo, 1974.

1742. Herrera-Hernandez, M. El Problema del Alcoholismo en la
         Infancia. (The Problem of Alcoholism in Childhood.) Acta
         Pediatrica Española, 23: 497-504, 1965.

1743. Herzog, E. Drug Use Among the Young: As Teenagers See It.
         Children, 17: 207-212, 1970.

1744. Hessberg, L.R. A Survey of the Statutes Affected by the
         Reduction of the Age of Majority in New York. Albany Law
         Review, 39: 493-520, 1975.

1745. Hetherington, E.M. and Wray, N.P. Aggression, Need for Social
         Approval, and Humor Preferences. Journal of Abnormal
         Social Psychology, 68: 685-689, 1964.

1746. Hetherington, R.W., Dickinson, J, Cipywnyk, D. and Hay, D.
         Drinking Behavior Among Saskatchewan Adolescents.
         Canadian Journal of Public Health, 69: 315-324, 1978.

1747. Hetherington, Robert W., Dickinson, Jane, Cipywnyk, Dmytro and
         Hay, David. Attitudes and Knowledge About Alcohol Among
         Saskatchewan Adolescents. Canadian Journal of Public
         Health, 70(4): 247-259, 1979.

1748. Heubner, W. and Hallermann, W. Zur Toxicität des Pyramidons.
         (The Toxicity of Pyramidon.) Archiv fuer Toxikologie,
         Berlin, 15: 157-158, 1954.

1749. Heuyer, G., Misès, R. and Dereux, J.-F. La Descendance des
         Alcooliques. (Offspring of Alcoholics.) Prensa Medica,
         Argentina, 65: 657-658, 1957.

1750. Hewitt, David and Nutter, Richard W. A Comparison of Three Drug
         Information Presentations. Journal of Drug Education,
         9(1): 79-90, 1979.

1751. Hibell, B. Angaende en Uppseendevackande Undersokning.
         (Concerning a Sensational Investigation. [Changes in the
         Drinking Customs Among Youth]). Alcohol och Narkotica,
         69: 316-319, 1975.

1752. Hibell, B. Utviklingen av den Svenske Ungdommens Alkoholvaner
         fra 1947 til 1976. (Drinking Habits Among Swedish Youth
         From 1947 to 1976.) Doctoral Dissertation. Lund, Sweden:
         Dox-Forlaget, 1977.

1753. Hibell, B. and Jonsson, E. Alcohol, Drug, Tobacco and Sniffing
         Practices Among Swedish Schoolchidren 1971-1974. British
         Journal of Addiction, 72: 117-127, 1977.

1754. Hibell, B. and Jonsson, E. Alkohol-, Narkotika- och Tobaksvanor
       i Grundskolan och Gymnasiet 1973. (The Use of Alcohol,
       Drugs and Tobacco in Elementary and High Schools in 1973.)
       Alkohol och Narkotica, 68: 170-180, 1974.

1755. Hibell, B. and Jonsson, E. Alkohol-, Narkotika-, Tobak- och
       Sniffningsvanor i Grund- och Gymnasieskolan 1974. (The Use
       of Alcohol, Drugs, Tobacco and Inhalants by Elementary and
       High School Students in 1974.) Alkohol och Narkotica, 69:
       28-36, 1975.

1756. Hibell, B. and Jonsson, E. Alkohol-, Tobaks-, Narkotika- och
       Sniffningsvanor i Grund och Gymnasieskolan 1975.
       (Drinking, Smoking and the Use of Narcotics and Inhalants
       in the Primary and Secondary Schools in 1975.) Alkohol
       och Narkotica, 70(6): 1-12, 1976.

1757. Hibell, B. and Jonsson, E. Alkohol-, Tobaks-, Narkotika- och
       Sniffningsvanor i Grundskolan 1977. (The Use of Alcohol,
       Tobacco, Drugs and Inhalants Among School Children in
       1977.) Alkohol och Narkotica, 72(6): 10-18, 1978.

1758. Hibell, B. and Jonsson, E. Skolelevers ANT-vanor 1972. (The Use
       of Alcohol, Narcotics and Tobacco Among Students in 1972.)
       Alkohol och Narkotica, 68: 345-348, 1974.

1759. Hibell, B. and Jonsson, E. Skolungdom och Mellanöl. (School
       Children and Medium Strong Beer.) Alkohol och Narkotica,
       68: 106-111, 1974.

1760. Hibell, B. and Jonsson, E. Skolungdomens Alkohol-, Narkotika-,
       Tobaks- och Sniffningsvanor 1978. (The Use of Alcohol,
       Drugs, Tobacco and Inhalants by School Children in Sweden
       in 1978.) Alkohol och Narkotica, 73(8): 19-27, 10, 1979.

1761. Hibell, B., Jonsson, E. and Svedugård, L. Alkohol-, Narkotika-
       och Rökvanor Bland Elever i Årskurserna 6 och 9 1971 och
       1972. (Drinking, Drug and Smoking Habits of Pupils in the
       6th and 9th Grades in 1971 and 1972.) Alkohol och
       Narkotica, 67: 122-129, 176-183, 1973.

1762. Higgins, Paul C., Albrecht, Gary L. and Albrecht, Maryann H.
       Black-White Adolescent Drinking: The Myth and the Reality.
       Social Problems, 25(2): 215-224, 1977.

1763. Higgins, R.L. The Manipulation of Interpersonal Evaluation
       Anxiety and Situational Control as Determinants of Alcohol
       Consumption in College Social Drinkers. Doctoral
       Dissertation (University Microfilms No. 73-32121).
       University of Wisconsin, 1973.

1764. Higgins, R.L. and Marlatt, G.A. Fear of Interpersonal Evaluation
       as a Determinant of Alcohol Consumption in Male Social
       Drinkers. Journal of Abnormal Psychology, 84: 644-651,
       1975.

1765. Hilgard, J.R. and Newman, M.F. Early Parental Deprivation as a
       Functional Factor in the Etiology of Schizophrenia and
       Alcoholism. American Journal of Orthopsychiatry, 33: 409-
       420, 1963.

1766. Hilgard, J.R. and Newman, M.F. Parental Loss by Death in
       Childhood as an Etiological Factor Among Schizophrenic and
       Alcoholic Patients Compared with a Non-Patient Community
       Sample. Journal of Nervous and Mental Disease, 137: 14-28,
       1963.

1767. Hill, H.E. The Social Deviant and Initial Addiction to Narcotics
       and Alcohol. Quarterly Journal of Studies on Alcohol, 23:
       562-582, 1962. (Also in: National Institute on Drug Abuse,
       Research Monograph Series 30. Rockville, Maryland: U.S.
       Department of Health, Education and Welfare (DHEW
       Publication Number ADM 79-882), 1980, pages 90-94.)

1768. Hill, H.H. Education as a Means of Prevention. In: Toward
       Prevention: Scientific Studies on Alcohol and Alcoholism.
       Ed. F.A. Soper. Washington, D.C.: Narcotics Education,
       1971, pages 217-225.

1769. Hill, Shirley Y., Cloninger, C. Robert and Ayre, Frederick R.
       Independent Familial Transmission of Alcoholism and Opiate
       Abuse. Alcoholism: Clinical and Experimental Research,
       1(4): 335-342, 1977.

1770. Hill, Thomas W. Lifestyles and Drinking Patterns of Urban
       Indians. Journal of Drug Issues, 10(2): 257-272, 1980.

1771. Hillbo, A. Ungdom och Ölförsäljning. (Young People and the Sale
       of Beer.) Alkoholfrågan, 63: 288-290, 1969.

1772. Hinckley, T.E. Jr. Analysis of Snowmobile Accidents Involving
       Young Operators in the State of New York. Doctoral
       Dissertation (University Microfilms No. 71-33,226).
       Michigan State University, 1971.

1773. Hindelang, M.J. The Social Versus Solitary Nature of Delinquent
       Involvements. British Journal of Criminology, 11: 167-
       175, 1971.

1774. Hindman, M. Child Abuse and Neglect: The Alcohol Connection.
       Lifelines, 19(3): 5-12, 1977.

1775. Hindman, M. Children of Alcoholic Parents. Alcohol Health and
       Research World, 1(3): 2-6, 1975-76.

1776. Hindman, Margaret H. Family Violence. Alcohol Health and
       Research World, 4(1): 2-11, 1979.

1777. Hindmarch, Ian, Hughes, Ian and Einstein, Rosemarie. Attitudes
          to Drug Users and to the Use of Alcohol, Tobacco and
          Cannabis on the Campus of a Provincial University.
          Bulletin on Narcotics, 27(2): 27-36, 1975.

1778. Hines, G.H. Attitudes and Practices of University Students
          Related to Tobacco, Alcohol and Marijuana Use. New Zealand
          Medical Journal, 80(519): 1-5, 1974.

1779. Hirayama, K., Watanabe, Y. and Chiba, K. (The Drinking Pattern
          of Boys and Girls--Students of Pharmaceutical Institute in
          Nihon University. [Japanese Text.] Japanese Journal of
          Studies on Alcohol, 5: 14-18, 1970.

1780. Hironimus, H. Survey of 100 May Act Violators Committed to the
          Federal Reformatory for Women. Federal Probation, 7: 31-
          34, 1943.

1781. Hirsh, Joseph. Alcohol Education: A Guide Book for Teachers.
          New York: Schuman, 1952.

1782. Hirsh, Joseph. Women and Alcoholism. In: Alcoholism and
          Narcotics. Ed. W.C. Bier. New York: Fordham University
          Press, 1962, pages 108-115.

1783. Hirsh, Joseph F. Alcohol Education: Its Needs and Challenges.
          American Journal of Public Health, 37: 1574-1577, 1947.

1784. Hislop, I.G. Childhood Deprivation: An Antecedent of the
          Irritable Bowel Syndrome. Medical Journal of Australia,
          66(1): 372-374, 1979.

1785. Hjort, L. and Irgens-Jensen, O. Bruk av Stoffer, Alkohol og
          Tobakk Blant Ungdom i Oslo 1968-1973. (Use of Drugs,
          Alcohol and Tobacco Among Youth in Oslo, 1968-1973.)
          Oslo: Statens Institutt for Alkoholsforskning, 1973.

1786. Hochbaum, G.M. Learning and Behavior: Alcohol Education for
          What? In: Alcohol Education. U.S. Department of Health,
          Education and Welfare. Washington, D.C.: U.S. Government
          Printing Office, 1967, pages 29-36.

1787. Hochbaum, G.M. Teaching Adolescents About Smoking, Drinking,
          Drug Abuse. Educational Digest, 34(5): 28-31, 1969.

1788. Hochbaum, Godfrey M. How Can We Teach Adolescents About
          Smoking, Drinking and Drug Abuse? Journal of Health,
          Physical Education, Recreation, 39: 34-38, 1968. (Also in:
          Resource Book for Drug Abuse Education. American
          Association for Health, Physical Education and Recreation.
          Washington, D.C.: U.S. Goverment Printing Office, 1969,
          pages 21-24.

1789. Hochhauser, M. Educational Implications of Drug Abuse. Journal of Drug Education, 8: 69-76, 1978.

1790. Hochhauser, Mark. Adolescent Drug Abuse and the Development of Behavior. International Journal of the Addictions, 13(6): 1013-1019, 1978.

1791. Hochhauser, Mark. Alcohol and Marijuana Consumption Among Undergraduate Polydrug Users. American Journal of Drug and Alcohol Abuse, 4(1):65-76, 1977.

1792. Hochhauser, Mark. Drug Education for Whom? Journal of Alcohol and Drug Education, 23(3): 24-33, 1978.

1793. Hochman, Joel Simon. Marihuana and Social Evolution. Englewood Cliffs, New Jersey: Prentice-Hall, 1972.

1794. Hocken, A.G. Driving Down Under. British Medical Journal, 2: 487-488, 1978.

1795. Hódosi, R. and König, É. Az Alkoholizmus Jelentösége a Gyermek-Ideggondozás Területén. (The Importance of Alcoholism in the Area of Child Psychiatry.) In: Tanulmányok az Alkoholizmus Pszichiátriai Következményeiröl. (Results of Psychiatric Study of Alcoholism.) Eds. I. Tariska, G. Geréby and G. Kardos. Budapest, Hungary: Alkoholizmus Elleni Orszagos Bizottság, 1969, pages 131-136.

1796. Hoff, E.C. Decisions About Alcohol. Greenwich, Connecticut: Seabury Press, 1961.

1797. Hoffman, A.M. Sociological Alienation and Drug Usage in Three Collegiate Settings. Doctoral Dissertation (University Microfilms No. 73-13,992). The Pennsylvania State University, 1972.

1798. Hoffman, H., Loper, R.G. and Kammeier, M.L. Identifying Future Alcoholics with MMPI Alcoholism Scales. Quarterly Journal of Studies on Alcohol, 35: 490-498, 1974.

1799. Hofsten, S. von. Gymnasisterna och Alkoholen. (High-School Pupils and Alcoholic Beverages.) Alkoholfrågan, 63: 151-161, 1969.

1800. Hofstra College Research Bureau, Psychological Division. Use of Alcoholic Beverages Among High School Students. New York: Sheppard Foundation, 1953.

1801. Hofstra College Research Bureau, Psychological Division. Use of Alcoholic Beverages by High School Students in Nassau County Related to Parental Permissiveness. New York: Sheppard Foundation, 1954.

1802.   Hogan, E.P.   Religious Affiliation, Norm Quality and Drinking
        Patterns of Adolescents.   Doctoral Dissertation (University
        Microfilms No. 79-23,486).   Washington State University,
        1979.

1803.   Hogue, R.C.   Drinking Behavior and Attitudes.   An Alcoholism
        Needs Assessment for the North Catchment Area of
        Hillsborough County.   Tampa, Florida: Northside Community
        Mental Health Center, Inc., 1977.

1804.   Höjer, J.A.   Drink in Adolescence as a Cause of Sickliness and
        Alcoholism.   Tirfing, 37: 1-9, 1943.

1805.   Holden, M.   Treatability of Children of Alcoholic Parents.
        Smith College Studies in Social Work, 16: 44-61, 1945.

1806.   Holland, Flint.   Secret in a Bottle, The Cause and Cure of
        Alcoholism.   New York: Pageant Press, 1952.

1807.   Holland, I.   Heads You Win, Tails I Lose.   Philadelphia,
        Pennsylvania: Lippincott, 1973.

1808.   Hollingshead, A.B.   Elmtown's Youth.   New York: Wiley and Sons,
        1949.

1809.   Hollister, William G.   Why Adolescents Drink and Use Drugs.   PTA
        Magazine, no pages, March 1969.   (Also in: Inventory:
        Quarterly Journal on Alcohol and Alcoholism, 20(4): 14-19,
        1971.

1810.   Holloday, Charles.   Alcohol Education in Public Schools.   In:
        Alcohol Education, Proceedings of a Conference, March 29,
        1966.   (Secretary's Committee on Alcoholism)   U.S.
        Department of Health, Education and Welfare.   Washington,
        D.C.:   U.S. Government Printing Office, 1967, pages 42-47.

1811.   Holloway, E.   Alcohol and Youth.   New York: Vantage Press, 1956.

1812.   Holloway, R.   Drinking Among Indian Youth.   Winnipeg, Manitoba:
        The Alcohol Education Service, 1966.

1813.   Holloway, R.   Student Drinking.   Winnipeg, Manitoba: Alcohol
        Education Service, 1964.

1814.   Hollstedt, C., Olsson, O. and Rydberg, U.   The Effect of Alcohol
        on the Developing Organism: Genetical, Teratological and
        Physiological Aspects.   Medical Biology, 55(1): 1-14, 1977.

1815.   Holmes, E., Jones, R. and Murphy, N.   Multi-Discipline Approach
        to Alcoholism.   Journal of the New York State School of
        Nursing and Teachers' Association, 6(3): 35-38, 1975.

1816. Holmes, S.J. Current Knowledge About Alcoholism--Treatment,
          Research and Prevention. In: Interpreting Current
          Knowledge About Alcohol and Alcoholism to a College
          Community. Proceedings of a Conference, May 28-30, 1963,
          Albany, New York. Ed. Richard Reynolds. Albany: New York
          State Department of Mental Health, 1963, pages 32-50.

1817. Holmila, M., Partanen, J., Piispa, M. and Virtanen, M.
          Alkoholerziehung und Alkoholpolitik. (Alcohol Education
          and Alcohol Politics.) Dragalkohol, 4(3): 13-32, 1980.

1818. Holmila, M., Partanen, J., Piispa, M. and Virtanen, M.
          Alkoholipoliittisen Tutkimuslaitoksen Tutkimusseloste.
          (Alcohol Education and Alcohol Policy.) An Interim
          Report of Alcohol Education of the 26th International
          Institute on the Prevention and Treatment of Alcoholism.
          Cardiff-Wales, June 9-14, 1980. Helsinki: Social Research
          Institute of Alcohol Studies, 1980.

1819. Holroyd, K.A. Effects of Social Anxiety and Social Evaluation on
          Beer Consumption and Social Interaction. Journal of
          Studies on Alcohol, 39: 737-744, 1978.

1820. Holsten, Fred. Repeat Follow-Up Studies of 100 Young Norwegian
          Drug Abusers. Journal of Drug Issues, 10: 491-504, 1980.

1821. Holzegreve, W. Frauen- und Jugendalkoholismus in der
          Bundesrepublik Deutschland Soziale Mobilität,
          Altersgliederung und Soziokulturelle Hintergründe.
          (Alcoholism in Women and Youth in the German Federal
          Republic--Social Mobility, Age Structure and Socio-Cultural
          Backgrounds.) In: Papers Presented at the 19th
          International Institute on the Prevention and Treatment of
          Alcoholism, Seville, Spain, June 5-10, 1972. Eds.
          E. Tongue and Z. Adler. Lausanne: International Council
          on Alcohol and Addictions, 1973, pages 47-52.

1822. Homer, M.M. Teaching Techniques for a Module in Alcohol
          Education and Traffic Safety for Junior High School.
          Doctoral Dissertation (University Microfilms No. 77-22259).
          Columbia University Teachers College, 1977.

1823. Homiller, Jonica. Alcoholism Among Women. Chemical
          Dependencies, 4(1): 1-31, 1980.

1824. Homonoff, E. and Stephen, A. Alcohol Education for Children of
          Alcoholics in a Boston Neighborhood. Journal of Studies
          on Alcohol, 40: 923-926, 1979.

1825. Honigmann, J.J. Dynamics of Drinking in an Austrian Village.
          Ethnology, 2: 157-169, 1963.

1826. Honigmann, J.J. and Honigmann, I. Drinking in an Indian-White
          Community. Quarterly Journal of Studies on Alcohol, 5:
          575-619, 1945.

1827. Hooliganism at Football Matches (Editorial). Journal of
            Alcoholism, 9(3): 81-82, 1974.

1828. Hoopa Alcohol Abuse Survey Program. A Study to Determine the
            Attitude of Youth in the Hupa Area Regarding the Usage of
            Drugs and Alcohol. Hoopa, California, 1975.

1829. Hoover, E.P. Incidents of Alcohol and Drug Related Arrests.
            Maryland State Medical Journal, 20(4): 99-101, 1971.

1830. Hoover, R.S. Youth and Chemical Dependence. Illinois Medical
            Journal, 156(1): 50-51, 1979.

1831. Hope, Earless H. A Study of Some Students' Opinions and
            Knowledge of Smoking and Drinking. Journal of the American
            College Health Association, 20: 219-227, 1972.

1832. Hoppe, K.D., Molnar, J. and Newell, J.E. Love- and Hate-
            Addiction in Delinquent Male Adolescents. Psychotherapy
            and Psychosomatics, Basel, 13: 271-277, 1965.

1833. Horan, J., D'Amico, M. and Williams, J.M. Assertiveness and
            Patterns of Drug Use: A Pilot Study. Journal of Drug
            Education, 5(3): 217-221, 1975.

1834. Horan, John J. Outcome Difficulties in Drug Education. Review
            of Educational Research, 44(2): 203-211, 1974.

1835. Horman, R.E. The Impact of Sociopolitical Systems on Teenage
            Alcohol Abuse. In: Youth, Alcohol and Social Policy.
            Eds. H.T. Blane and M.E. Chafetz. New York: Plenum Press,
            1979, pages 263-281.

1836. Horn, J.L. and Wanberg, K.W. Dimensions of Perception of
            Background and Current Situation of Alcoholic Patients.
            Quarterly Journal of Studies on Alcohol, 31(3): 633-658,
            1970.

1837. Horn, J.L., Wanberg, K.W. and Adams, G. Diagnosis of Alcoholism:
            Factors of Drinking, Background and Current Conditions in
            Alcoholics. Quarterly Journal of Studies on Alcohol, 35:
            147-175, 1974.

1838. Hornik, E.L. You and Your Alcoholic Parent. New York:
            Association Press, 1974. (Also as: Pamphlet. New York:
            Public Affairs Committee, 1974.)

1839. Hornstra, R.K. and Udell, B. Psychiatric Services and
            Alcoholics. Missouri Medicine, 70(2): 103-107, 1973.

1840. Horoshak, Irene. Teen-Age Drinking: A Growing Problem or a
            Problem of Growing? Registered Nurse, 39: 63-69, 1976.

1841.   Horton, J.M. and Annalora, D.J. Student Dropout Study of Ft.
        Wingate, New Mexico High School. Albuquerque, New Mexico:
        Bureau of Indian Affairs, 1974. (ERIC Document
        Reproduction Services NO. ED 096-084).

1842.   Hossack, Donald. The Investigation of Blood Alcohol Levels in
        967 Road Accident Fatalities. In: Alcohol, Drugs and
        Traffic Safety. Proceedings of the Sixth International
        Conference on Alcohol, Drugs and Traffic Safety, Toronto,
        September 8-13, 1974. Eds. S. Israelstam and S. Lambert.
        Toronto, Ontario: Addiction Research Foundation of
        Ontario, 1975, pages 825-830.

1843.   Housden, Leslie George. The Prevention of Cruelty to Children.
        New York: Philosophical Library, 1956, especially pages
        95-111.

1844.   How has Prohibition Affected Student Drinking in the American
        Colleges? The International Student, 27(7): 83-90, 1930.

1845.   Howard, B.A. and Sedlacek, W.E. Trends in Freshman Attitudes
        and Use of Drugs. College Student Journal, 295-301, 1975

1846.   Howell, John, Muehlberger, C.W., Rabin, Albert and
        McCarthy, Raymond G. Alcohol - Its Use and Abuse: Summary
        of Panel Discussion. In: Alcohol Education--Whose
        Responsibility? Proceedings of a Conference, May 1963,
        sponsored by Michigan Department of Mental Health; Michigan
        Department of Public Instruction, Michigan Department of
        Health; Michigan Congress of Parents and Teachers; Michigan
        State University; Michigan State Board of Alcoholism; and
        U.S. Public Health Service. Michigan Department of Health.
        Lansing, Michigan: Michigan State Board of Alcoholism,
        1963, pages 12-20.

1847.   Huang, Allen M. The Drinking Behavior of Educable Mentally
        Retarded and Non-Retarded Students. Journal of Alcohol
        and Drug Education, 26(3): 41-50, 1981.

1848.   Huba, G.J., Segal, B. and Singer, J.L. Consistency of
        Daydreaming Styles Across Samples of College Male and
        Female Drug and Alcohol Users. Journal of Abnormal
        Psychology, 86: 99-102, 1977.

1849.   Huba, G.J., Segal, B. and Singer, J.L. Organizatin of Needs in
        Male and Female Drug and Alcohol Users. Journal of
        Consulting and Clinical Psychology, 45: 34-44, 1977.

1850.   Huba, G.J., Wingard, J.A. and Bentler, P.M. Adolescent Drug Use
        and Intentions to Use Drugs in the Future: A Concurrent
        Analysis. Journal of Drug Education, 9: 145-150, 1979.

1851. Huba, G.J., Wingard, J.A. and Bentler, P.M. Beginning Adolescent
        Drug Use and Peer and Adult Interaction Patterns. Journal
        of Consulting and Clinical Psychology, 47: 265-276, 1979.

1852. Huba, G.J., Wingard, J.A. and Bentler, P.M. A Comparison of Two
        Latent Variable Causal Models for Adolescent Drug Use.
        Journal of Personality and Social Psychology, 40(1): 180-
        193, 1981.

1853. Huba, George J., Alkin, Marilyn S. and Bentler, Peter M. Is Coca
        Paste Currently a Drug of Abuse Among High School Students?
        Journal of Drug Education, 11(3): 205-212, 1981.

1854. Hubbard, H. Focus on Youth: The Prevention Model Replication
        Program. Alcohol Health and Research World, 3(2): 9-13,
        1978.

1855. Huber, C.B. Attitudes of Adolescent Offspring of Male
        Alcoholics: A Comparative Study. Doctoral Dissertation
        (University Microfilms No. 78-01684). California School
        of Professional Psychology, San Francisco, 1977.

1856. Huber, J. and Gain. Enfance en Danger Moral et Alcoolisme.
        (Children in Moral Danger and Alcoholism.) Bulletin de
        L'Academie Nationale de Medecine, Paris, 137: 377-378,
        1953.

1857. Huberty, Catherine E. and Huberty, David J. Treating the
        Parents of Adolescent Drug Abusers. Contemporary Drug
        Problems, 5(4): 573-592, 1975. (Also as: Treating the
        Parents of Adolescent Drug Abusers: The Necessity for
        Marriage Counseling. The Alcoholism Digest Annual, 5: 1-
        10, 1976-77.)

1858. Huberty, D.J. Drug Abuse: A Framework of Reference for
        Teachers. The High School Journal, 55(5): 234-240, 1972.

1859. Huberty, David J. and Malmquist, Jeffrey D. Adolescent Chemical
        Dependency. Perspectives in Psychiatric Care, 16: 21-27,
        1978.

1860. Huchner, David. "Water is Indeed Best". Temperance and the
        Pre-Civil War New England College. In: Alcohol, Reform
        and Society: The Liquor Issue in Social Context. Ed.
        Jack Blocker, Jr. Westport, Connecticut: Greenwood
        Press, 1979, pages 70-100.

1861. Huebner, P.B., Slaughter, Robert E., Goldman, Roy D. and
        Caddy, Glenn R. Attitudes Toward Alcohol as Predictors
        of Self-Estimated Alcohol Consumption in College Students.
        International Journal of the Addictions, 11(3): 377-388,
        1976.

1862. Hughes, J.M. Adolescent Children of Alcoholic Patients and the
          Relationship of Alateen to these Children. Journal of
          Consulting and Clinical Psychology, 45(5): 946-947, 1977.

1863. Hughes, P.A. Identificiation of Problem Drinkers Among Teenagers
          in Piedmont, North Carolina. Doctoral Dissertation
          (University Microfilms No. 72-20,280). Mississippi State
          University, 1972.

1864. Hughes, P.H., Schaps, E. and Sanders, C.R. A Methodology for
          Monitoring Adolescent Drug Abuse Trends. The International
          Journal of the Addictions, 8: 403-419, 1973.

1865. Hulbert, E.K. Restrictions: Not Where but What?. Leaflet.
          Evanston, Illinois: Signal Press, 1968.

1866. Humbert, F. Alcohol and the Child. World's Health, 9: 276-317,
          1928.

1867. Hundleby, John and Girard, Suzanne. Home and Family Correlates
          of Prior Drug Involvement Among Institutionalized Male
          Adolescents. International Journal of the Addictions,
          15(5): 689-699, 1980.

1868. Hunt, Leon G. Growth of Substance Use and Misuse: Some
          Speculations and Data. Journal of Drug Issues,
          257-265, 1979.

1869. Hunter, G.T. Identifying the Potential Problem Drinker in a
          College Mental Health Clinic. Journal of the American
          College Health Association, 17: 426-436, 1969.

1870. Huntwork, Dianne and Ferguson, Leonard W. Drug Use and Deviation
          from Self-Concept Norms. Journal of Abnormal Child
          Psychology, 5(1): 53-60, 1977.

1871. Hurster, M., Amerling, G., Myerson, N. and Pedraza, A. A
          Health Fair. Journal of School Health, 40(10): 539-541,
          1970.

1872. Husni-Palacios, M. and Scheur, P. The High School Student: A
          Personality Profile. Proceedings of the Annual Convention
          of the American Psychological Association, 7(2): 565-566,
          1972.

1873. Huszar, I. and Gabor I. Quelques Aspects Médico-Légaux Actuels
          de L'Alcoolisme Chronique. (Some Current Medicolegal
          Aspects of Chronic Alcoholism. Annales de Medicine Legale,
          46: 5-11, 1966.

1874. Hyde, M.O. Alcohol Abuse. In: Mind Drugs (4th Edition). Ed.
          M.O. Hyde. New York: McGraw-Hill, 1981, pages 53-65.

1875.   Hyde, M. (Ed.) Mind Drugs. New York: McGraw-Hill, 1968. (Also
        see Mind Drugs, 4th Edition, 1981.)

1876.   Hyde, M.O. Know About Alcohol. New York: McGraw-Hill, 1978.

1877.   Hyde, M.O. Mind Drugs and Driving. In: Mind Drugs (4th
        Edition). Ed. M.O. Hyde. New York: McGraw-Hill, 1981,
        pages 102-116.

1878.   Hyde, M.O. Mind Drugs: The Changing Scene. In: Mind Drugs
        (4th Edition). Ed. M.O. Hyde. New York: McGraw-Hill,
        1981, pages 3-8.

1879.   Hyde, Margaret. Addictions. New York: McGraw-Hill, 1978.

1880.   Hyde, Margaret O. Alcohol as a Mind Drug. In: Mind Drugs.
        Ed. M. Hyde. New York: McGraw-Hill, 1968, page 40.

1881.   Hyman, M.M. Accident Vulnerability and Blood Alcohol
        Concentrations of Drivers by Demographic Characteristics.
        Quarterly Journal of Studies on Alcohol, 29, Supplement
        No. 4: 34-57, 1968.

1882. Ianni, F. Attitudes Toward the Relationship Among Stress-Relief, Advertising and Youthful Drug Abuse in Two Recent Field Studies. In: National Commission on Marihuana and Drug Abuse. Drug Use in America: Problem in Perspective. Washington, D.C.: U.S. Government Printing Office, 1973, pages 612-623.

1883. Ibius, O. Neuvosto-Eestin Väkijuomaoloista. (On the Alcohol Problem in Soviet Estonia.) Alkoholikysymys, 25: 87-94, 1957.

1884. Idaho Department of Education. Survey of Drug Use Among Junior and Senior High School Students in the State of Idaho. Boise, Idaho, 1970.

1885. Ida Mae, D. Problem Children. Journal of the American Medical Association, 241: 167-168, 1979.

1886. Idänpään-Heikkilä, P. Berusning som Ungdomsproblem--Prevention och Behandling. (Intoxication as an Adolescence Problem--Prevention and Treatment.) Nordisk Medicin, Stockholm, 89: 61-63, 1974.

1887. Iglesias-Rodríguez, L. Factores Sociales en el Alcoholismo. (Social Factors in Alcoholism.) Actas Luso-Espanolas de Neurologia y Psiquiatria, 25: 26-32, 1966.

1888. Igra, Amnon and Moos, Rudolf H. Alcohol Use Among College Students: Some Competing Hypotheses. Journal of Youth and Adolescence, 8(4): 393-405, 1979.

1889. Ilic, A., Poleksic, J. and Deric, O. Problems of Prevention of Alcoholism. In: Papers Presented at the 19th International Institute on the Prevention and Treatment of Alcoholism, Belgrade, Yugoslavia, June, 1973. Lausanne, Switzerland: International Council on Alcohol and Addictions, 1973, pages 84-94.

1890.   Imre, P.D.   Drinking Habits of Church-Affiliated Teen-Agers.
        Quarterly Journal of Studies on Alcohol, 24(2): 320, 1963.

1891.   Indiana Department of Public Instruction.   Drug Abuse Education
        Resource Guide.   Indianapolis, Indiana, 1974.

1892.   Inebriety at Oxford.   Quarterly Journal of Inebriety, 28(1):
        85-86, 1906.

1893.   Ingersoll, R.L.   Socialization, Inconsistencies and Alcoholism:
        A Study of Attitudes.   Doctoral Dissertation (University
        Microfilms No. 65-6695).   University of Iowa, 1965.

1894.   Initial Impact of Raising Legal Drinking Age from 18 to 21.   The
        Bottom Line, 3(1): 16-20, 1979.

1895.   Insurance Institute for Highway Safety.   Narrative Summary of the
        IIHS Driver Education Study: Driver Education and Fatal
        Crash Involvement of Teenaged Drivers.   Eds.
        Leon Robertson and Paul Zador.   Washington, D.C., 1977.

1896.   Insurance Institute for Highway Safety.   To Prevent Harm.
        Washington, D.C., 1978.

1897.   International Conference on Alcoholism and Drug Dependence:
        Alcoholism and Drug Dependence, a Multi-Disciplinary
        Approach.   Proceedings of the Third International
        Conference on Alcoholism and Drug Dependence, Liverpool,
        England, April, 1976.   Eds. J.S. Madden, Robin Walker and
        W.H. Kenyon.   New York: Plenum Press, 1977.

1898.   International Council on Alcohol and the Addictions.
        International Conference on Alcoholism and Drug Abuse, San
        Juan, Puerto Rico, November, 1973.   Lausanne, Switzerland:
        International Council on Alcohol and Addictions, 1974.

1899.   International Council on Alcohol and Addictions.   Papers
        Presented at the 25th International Institute on the
        Prevention and Treatment of Alcoholism, Tours, France,
        June, 1979.   Lausanne, Switzerland: International Council
        on Alcohol and Addictions, 1979.

1900.   International Council on Alcohol and Addictions.   Papers
        Presented at the 24th International Congress on the
        Prevention and Treatment of Alcoholism, Zurich, June, 1978.
        Lausanne, Switzerland: International Council on Alcohol
        and Addictions, 1978.

1901.   International Council on Alcohol and Addictions.   Papers
        Presented at the 19th International Institute on the
        Prevention and Treatment of Alcoholism, Belgrade,
        Yugoslavia, June, 1973.   Lausanne, Switzerland,
        Internatinal Council on Alcohol and Addictions, 1973.

1902.   International Council on Alcohol and Addictions. Papers
         Presented at the 18th International Institute on the
         Prevention and Treatment of Alcoholism, Seville, June,
         1972. Lausanne, Switzerland: International Council on
         Alcohol and Addictions, 1972.

1903.   International Council on Alcohol and Addictions. Papers
         Presented at the 6th International Institute on the
         Prevention and Treatment of Drug Dependence, Hamburg,
         Germany, June 28-July 2, 1976. Lausanne, Switzerland:
         International Council on Alcohol and the Addictions, 1979.

1904.   International Council on Alcohol and Addictions. Papers
         Presented at the Fifth International Institute on the
         Prevention and Treatment of Drug Dependence, Copenhagen,
         Denmark, Volume II, July, 1974. Lausanne, Switzerland:
         International Council on Alcohol and Addictions, 1974.

1905.   International Council of Religious Education, Committee on
         Religious Education of Youth. Youth Action on the Liquor
         Problem: A Guide to Action for Christian Young People and
         Their Leaders in the New United Youth Movement.
         "Christian Youth Building a New World." Chicago, Illinois,
         1936.

1906.   Iowa Commission on Alcoholism. The Choice is Yours! Leaflet.
         Iowa, no date.

1907.   Iowa Commission on Alcoholism and State Department of Health.
         Iowa Teaching Guide on Alcohol. Des Moines, Iowa, 1967.

1908.   Iowa Department of Public Instruction. Alcohol and Other Drugs.
         (Prepared by D. Wright and M. Hays.) Des Moines, Iowa,
         1977.

1909.   Iowa Department of Public Instruction. Alcohol and Society: A
         Study of Some Socio-Economic Implications. Des Moines,
         Iowa, 1953.

1910.   Irgens-Jensen, O. Alkohol och Narkotika bland Oslo-Ungdom 1968-
         1973. (Alcohol and Other Drugs Among Oslo Youth 1968-
         1973.) Alkohol och Narkotica, 68: 54-62, 1974.

1911.   Irgens-Jensen, O. The Relationship Between Self-Reported Drunken
         Driving, Alcohol Consumption, and Personality Variables
         Among Norwegian Students. In: Alcohol, Drugs and Traffic
         Safety. Proceedings of the Sixth International Conference
         on Alcohol, Drugs and Traffic Safety. Toronto,
         September 8-13, 1974. Eds. S. Israelstam and S. Lambert.
         Toronto, Ontario: Alcoholism and Drug Addiction Research
         Foundation of Ontario, 1975, pages 159-168.

1912. Irgens-Jensen, O. and Burn-Gulbrandsen, S. Drugs in Norway:
         Attitudes and Use. International Journal of the
         Addictions, 6: 109-118, 1971.

1913. Irgens-Jensen, O. and Rud, M.G. Alkoholbruk blant Osko-Ungdom.
         (Use of Alcohol Among Youth in Oslo.) Tidsskrift
         EdruSpørsm, 30(2): 9-11, 16-17, 1978.

1914. Irgens-Jensen, O. and Rud, M.G. Alkoholbruk blant Oslo-Ungdom,
         Artikkel 2. (Alcohol Use Among Youth in Oslo, Part 2.)
         Tidsskrift EdruSpørsm, 30(3): 12-13, 16, 1978.

1915. Irgens-Jensen, Olav and Rud, Mons George. Changes in the Use of
         Drugs, Tobacco, and Alcohol Among Norwegian Youth from
         1968-1979. Journal of Drug Issues, 10(4): 405-420, 1980.

1916. Irvin, Donald B. Alcohol Education is Essential. New Jersey
         Council News, 28(2): 4, 1971.

1917. Irvine-Rivera, Edith M. The Dry Blockade. Philadelphia,
         Pennsylvania: Dorrance and Company, 1951.

1918. Irwell, L. Influence of Parental Alcoholism Upon the Human
         Family. Medical Times, 41: 114, 1913.

1919. Isaacs, Morton. College Student's Expectations of the Results of
         Drinking. Journal of Studies on Alcohol, 40(5): 476-479,
         1979.

1920. Isaacs, Morton. Stereotyping by Children of the Effects of
         Drinking on Adults. Journal of Studies on Alcohol, 38(5):
         913-921, 1977.

1921. Israelstam, S. and Lambert, S., Eds. Alcohol, Drugs and Traffic
         Safety. Proceedings of the Sixth International Conference
         on Alcohol, Drugs and Traffic Safety, Toronto, September 8-
         13, 1974. Toronto, Ontario: Addiction Research Foundation
         of Ontario, 1975.

1922. Issues in Child Protection and Substance Abuse: A Summary and
         Recommendations from the Wingspread Conference, December 6-
         8, 1979. The Catalyst, 1(3): 8-13, 1980.

1923. Istiphan, I. Drug Abuse in South Carolina 1975. Columbia,
         South Carolina: South Carolina Commission on Alcohol and
         Drug Abuse, 1975.

1924. Ivy, A.C., Ed. Really Living. New York: Narcotics Education,
         1962.

1925. Ivy, A.C. The Teaching of Scientific Information on Beverage
         Alcohol. Scientific Temperance Journal, 51: 41-42, 1943.

_____J

1926. J., Linda and L., David. Alcoholism: The Horror and the Pity.
      Pamphlet. Pleasantville, New York: Reader's Digest, 1974.

1927. Jackel, H.O., Lippert-Knobeloch, K., Herrmann, A., Leithoff, H.,
      Lippert, K., Mohr, U., Müller, H. and Rheindorf, P.
      Trunkenheitsgrad und Blutalkoholkonzentration nach Akutem
      Alkoholmissbrauch bei Volksfesten (Rosenmontag). (Degree
      of Drunkenness and Blood Alcohol Concentration Following
      Excessive Use of Alcohol at Festivals, Shrove Monday).
      Beitraege zur Gerichlichen Medizin, 31: 240-246, 1973.

1928. Jackson, B., Lange, W.R. and Lehmann, R.P. Teenage Drug Abuse in
      Middle-Class Milwaukee. Wisconsin Medical Journal, 71:
      210-212, 1972.

1929. Jackson, J.K. The Adjustment of the Family to the Crisis of
      Alcoholism. Quarterly Journal of Studies on Alcohol, 15:
      562-586, 1954. (Also as: The Adjustment of the Family to
      Alcoholism. Marriage and Family, 18: 361-369, 1956.)
      (Also as: Alcoholism and the Family. Annals of the
      American Academy of Political and Social Science, 315: 90-
      98, 1958.) (Also as: The Adjustment of the Family to the
      Crisis of Alcoholism. In: Sourcebook in Abnormal
      Psychology. Eds. L.Y. Rabkin and J.E. Carr. Boston:
      Houghton, Mifflin, 1967, pages 312-325.) (Also as: The
      Adjustment of the Family to the Crisis of Alcoholism. In:
      Deviance: The Interactionist Perspective. Eds.
      E. Rubington and M.S. Weinberg. New York: Macmillan,
      1968, pages 50-66, 1968.

1930. Jackson, J.K. Drinking, Drunkenness and the Family. In:
      Alcohol Education for the Classroom and Community: A
      Source Book for Educators. Ed. R.G. McCarthy. New York:
      McGraw-Hill, 1964, pages 155-166.

1931. Jackson, J.K. Driving Under the Influence of Alcohol. In:
       Alcohol Education for Classroom and Community: A Source
       Book for Educators. Ed. R.G. McCarthy. New York: McGraw-
       Hill, 1964, pages 173-189, 1964.

1932. Jackson, J.K. Family Structure and Alcoholism. Mental Hygiene,
       43: 403-406, 1959.

1933. Jackson, J.K. Social Adjustment Preceding, During and Following
       the Onset of Alcoholism. Doctoral Dissertation.
       University of Washington, 1955.

1934. Jackson, J.K. and Connor, R. Attitudes of the Parents of
       Alcoholics, Moderate Drinkers and Nondrinkers toward
       Drinking. Quarterly Journal of Studies on Alcohol, 14:
       596-613, 1953.

1935. Jackson, Javon and Calsyn, Robert. Evaluation of a Self-
       Development Approach to Drug Education: Some Mixed
       Results. Journal of Drug Education, 7: 15-28, 1977.

1936. Jackson, Joan K. Alcoholism and the Family. In: Society,
       Culture and Drinking Patterns. Eds. J. Pittman and
       R. Snyder. New York: John Wiley and Sons, Inc., 1962,
       pages 472-492.

1937. Jacob, Andre and Lavoie, Camil. A Study of Some of the
       Characteristics of a Group of Women Alcoholics. In:
       Selected Papers Presented at the General Sessions of the
       22nd Annual Meeting of the Alcohol and Drug Problems
       Association of North America, September 12-17, 1971.
       Hartford, Connecticut, no date, pages 25-32.

1938. Jacob, Theodore. An Introduction to the Alcoholic's Family. In:
       Currents in Alcoholism. Volume 7. Recent Advances in
       Research and Treatment. Ed. Marc Galanter. New York:
       Grune and Stratton, 1980.

1939. Jacob, Theodore, Favorini, Alison, Meisel, Susan S. and
       Anderson, Carol M. The Alcoholic's Spouse, Children and
       Family Interactions: Substantive Findings and
       Methodological Issues. Journal of Studies on Alcohol,
       39(7): 1231-1251.

1940. Jacob, Theodore, Ritchey, Diane, Cvitkovic, Joseph F. and
       Blane, Howard T. Communication Styles of Alcoholic and
       Nonalcoholic Families when Drinking and Not Drinking.
       Journal of Studies on Alcohol, 42(5): 466-482, 1981.

1941. Jacobs, S.H. Alcohol Abuse and Alcoholism Prevention Model
       Learning Systems: Preliminary Designs. Los Angeles,
       California: Sutherland Learning Associates, Inc., 1974.

1942.   Jacobson, L.D. Ethanol Education Today. Journal of School
            Health, 43(1): 36-39, 1973.

1943.   Jähnig, H.V. and Szewczyx, H. Alcohol Misuse Among Juvenile and
            Adolescent Delinquents. Psychiatrie, Neurologie und
            Medizinische Psychologie, Leipzig, 23: 26-33, 1971.

1944.   Jahoda, Gustav and Cramond, Joyce. Children and Alcohol: A
            Developmental Study in Glasgow. Volume I. An Enquiry
            Carried Out on Behalf of the Health Education Unit of the
            Scottish Home and Health Department. London: Her
            Majesty's Stationery Office, 1972. (Also as: Children and
            Alcohol: A Developmental Study in Glasgow. Health
            Bulletin, Edinburgh, 31: 314-317, 1973.

1945.   James, Willis. Addicts: Drugs and Alcohol Re-Examined. London:
            Pittman, 1973.

1946.   Jamieson, K.G. Alcohol and Driving: The Breathalyser Bogey.
            Medical Journal of Australia, 2(10): 425-434, 1968.

1947.   Janes, Cynthia L., Hesselbrock, Victor M., Myers, Darcy G. and
            Penniman, Janet H. Problem Boys in Young Adulthood:
            Teacher's Ratings and Twelve-Year Follow-Up. Journal of
            Youth and Adolescence, 8(4): 453-472, 1979.

1948.   Janson, Carl-Gunnar and Erland, Jonsson. Den Manliga
            Stockholmsungdomens Alkoholbeteende. En Deskriptiv och
            Explorativ Studie. (The Drinking Behaviour of Male
            Stockholm Youth. A Descriptive and Exploratory Study.)
            Manuscript in the Sociological Institute of the Stockholm
            University, no date.

1949.   Janz, H.W. Rehabilitation Alkoholkranker. (Rehabilitation of
            Alcoholics.) Zeitschrift fuer Allgemeinmedizin, 49: 969-
            973, 1973.

1950.   Janzen, Curtis. Family Treatment for Alcoholism: A Review.
            Social Work, 135-141, March, 1978.

1951.   Japan Society for Prevention of Alcoholism. (Alcohol Education
            Textbook for High School Students.) (Japanese Text.)
            Tokyo: Japan Society for Prevention of Alcoholism, 1979.

1952.   Jarema, M. Analysis of the Problem of Alcoholism Among the Young
            Secondary-School Students of the City of Szczecin.
            Roczniki Pomorskiej Academii Medycznej w Szczecinie,
            Warsaw, 22: 501-516, 1976.

1953.   Jarkka, J. Kouluissa Tapahtuvasta Raittiuso-Petuksesta. (The
            Teaching of Temperance in Schools.) Alkoholikysymys,
            Helsinki, 43: 93-95, 1975.

1954. Jarkka, J. Raittiuden Osuudesta Varusmieskasvatuksessa.
       (Temperance Education as a Part of Military
       Indoctrination.) Alkoholikysymys, Helsinki, 33: 227-237,
       1965.

1955. Jasinsky, M. Alkoholismus im Schulalter. (Alcoholism in School-
       Age Children.) Fortschritte der Medizin, Leipzig, 93:
       1511-1514, 1975.

1956. Jeffrey, E.C. Alcoholism Prevention and Reality: Comment on the
       Article by M.E. Chafetz. Quarterly Journal of Studies on
       Alcohol, 28: 546-548, 1967.

1957. Jenkins, P.M. When to Educate About Alcohol? Traffic Safety
       Education, 24(4): 9-27, 1977.

1958. Jenner, C. Die Heutige Daseinssituation als Herausforderung an
       die Alkoholerziehung. (The Current Existential Situation
       as Challenge to Alcohol Education.) In: Papers Presented
       at the 24th International Institute on the Prevention and
       Treatment of Alcoholism. Ed. E.J. Tongue. Lausanne:
       International Council on Alcohol and Addictions, 1978,
       pages 283-294.

1959. Jensen, G.R. Teenage Alcoholics. New Zealand Medical Journal,
       64: 230, 1965.

1960. Jesse, R.C. Children of Alcoholics: A Clinical Investigation of
       Familial Role Relationships. Doctoral Dissertation
       (University Microflims No. 77-32440). San Diego:
       California School of Professional Psychology, 1977.

1961. Jessor, R. Remarks on Drinking in Youth. In: Proceedings of
       the First Annual Alcoholism Conference. Ed. M. Chafetz.
       Rockville, Maryland: National Institute on Alcohol Abuse
       and Alcoholism, 1971, pages 258-261.

1962. Jessor, R., Carman, R. and Grossman, P.H. Expectations of Need
       Satisfaction and Drinking Patterns of College Students.
       Quarterly Journal of Studies on Alcohol, 29: 101-116,
       1968. (Also in: The Domesticated Drug: Drinking Among
       Collegians. Ed. G.L. Maddox. New Haven, Connecticut:
       College and University Press, 1970, pages 321-342.)

1963. Jessor, R., Collins, M.I. and Jessor, S.L. On Becoming a
       Drinker: Social-Psychological Aspects of an Adolescent
       Tradition. Annals of the New York Academy of Sciences,
       197: 199-213, 1972.

1964. Jessor, R., Cureton, L.W., Zucker, R.A. and Barron, F.H. Youth.
       In: Proceedings of the First Annual Alcoholism Conference
       of the National Institute on Alcohol Abuse and Alcoholism.
       Ed. M. Chafetz. Rockville, Maryland: National Institute
       on Alcohol Abuse and Alcoholism, 1974, pages 258-299.

1965.   Jessor, R., Graves, T.D., Hanson, R.C. and Jessor, S.L. Society,
         Personality, and Deviant Behavior: A Study of a Tri-Ethnic
         Community. New York: Holt, Rinehart and Winston, 1968.

1966.   Jessor, R. and Jessor, S.L. Adolescent Development and the Onset
         of Drinking. Pamphlet. New Brunswick, New Jersey:
         Rutgers Center of Alcohol Studies, 1975.

1967.   Jessor, R. and Jessor, S.L. Adolescent Development and the Onset
         of Drinking: A Longitudinal Study. Journal of Studies on
         Alcohol, 36: 27-51, 1975.

1968.   Jessor, S. and Jessor, R. Maternal Ideology and Adolescent
         Problem Behavior. Developmental Psychology, 10(2): 246-
         254, 1974.

1969.   Jessor, R. and Jessor, S. Problem Drinking in Youth:
         Personality, Social and Behavioral Correlates. In:
         Proceedings of the Second Annual Alcoholism Conference of
         the National Institute on Alcohol Abuse and Alcoholism.
         Ed. M. Chafetz. Rockville, Maryland: National Institute
         on Alcohol Abuse and Alcoholism, 1973, pages 3-23.

1970.   Jessor, R., Young, H.B., Young, E.B. and Tesi, G. Perceived
         Opportunity, Alienation and Drinking Behavior Among Italian
         and American Youth. Journal of Personality and Social
         Psychology, 15(3): 215-222, 1970.

1971.   Jessor, Richard. Alcohol and Youth: A Developmental
         Perspective. In: Alcohol Problems Among Youth.
         Proceedings of a Workshop at Pittsburgh, Pennsylvania,
         December 2-3, 1976. Ed. Joseph Newman. Western
         Pennsylvania Institute of Alcohol Studies, 1977, no pages.

1972.   Jessor, Richard. Discussion. In: Research on Alcoholism:
         Clinical Problems and Special Populations. Proceedings of
         the First Annual Alcoholism Conference of the National
         Institute of Alcoholism and Alcohol Abuse. Ed.
         Morris E. Chafetz. Washington, D.C., June 25-26, 1971,
         pages 297-299.

1973.   Jessor, Richard. Marijuana: A Review of Recent Psychosocial
         Research. In: Handbook on Drug Abuse. Eds R.I. Dupont,
         A. Goldstein and J. O'Donnell. Washington, D.C.: U.S.
         Government Printing Office, 1979, pages 337-355.

1974.   Jessor, Richard. Predicting Time of Onset of Marihuana Use: A
         Developmental Study of High School Youth. In:
         Predicting Adolescent Drug Abuse: A Review of Issues,
         Methods and Correlates - Research Issues II. Ed.
         Dan Lettieri. Rockville, Maryland: National Institute on
         Drug Abuse, 1975, pages 285-298.

1975. Jessor, Richard. Remarks on Drinking in Youth. In: Research on
       Alcoholism: Clinical Problems and Special Populations.
       Proceedings of the First Annual Alcoholism Conference of
       the National Institute of Alcoholism and Alcohol Abuse.
       Ed. Morris E. Chafetz. Washington, D.C., June 25-26, 1971,
       pages 258-261.

1976. Jessor, Richard, Chase, James A. and Donovan, John E.
       Psychosocial Correlates of Marijuana Use and Problem
       Drinking in a National Sample of Adolescents. American
       Journal of Public Health, 70: 604-613, 1980.

1977. Jessor, Richard and Jessor, Shirley L. Problem Behavior and
       Psychosocial Development: A Longitudinal Study of Youth.
       New York: Academic Press, 1977.

1978. Jessor, Richard and Jessor, Shirley. Theory Testing in
       Longitudinal Research on Marijuana Use. In: Longitudinal
       Research on Drug Use: Empirical Findings and
       Methodological Issues. Ed. Denise B. Kandel. New York,
       New York: John Wiley and Sons, 1978, pages 41-71.

1979. Jilek-Aall, Louise. Acculturation, Alcoholism and Indian-Style
       Alcoholics Anonymous. Journal of Studies on Alcohol,
       Supplement No. 9: 143-158, 1981.

1980. Joerger, K. Das Erleben der Zeit und seine Veränderurg durch
       Alkoholeinfluss: Eine Untersuchung über den
       Arbeitscharakter von Schülern an Weinorten. (The
       Experience of Time and Its Change Under the Influence of
       Alcohol: An Investigation of the Manner of Working by
       School Children in Viticultural Regions. Zeitschrift fur
       Experimentelle und Angewandte Psychologie, Gottingen, 7:
       126-161, 1960.

1981. Joffe, S.N., Thompson, W.O. and Imrie, C.W. A Juvenile with
       Alcohol-Associated Pancreatitis. Journal of Alcoholism,
       11(3): 96-97, 1976.

1982. Johansen, Bruce. The Tepees are Empty and the Bars are Full.
       Alcoholism, 1(2): 33-38, 1980.

1983. Johansson, K. Ungdomens Ölvanor. (The Beer-Drinking Habits of
       Young People.) Alkoholfragan, 65: 53-56, 1971.

1984. Johnson, Bruce. Toward a Theory of Drug Subcultures. In:
       Theories on Drug Abuse: Selected Contemporary Problems.
       (Research Monograph Series 30) Eds. Dan Lettieri,
       Mollie Sayers and Helen Pearson. Rockville, Maryland:
       National Institute on Drug Abuse, 1980, pages 110-119.

1985. Johnson, David W. Constructive Peer Relationship, Social
           Development and Cooperative Learning Experiences:
           Implications for the Prevention of Drug Abuse. Journal of
           Drug Education, 10(1): 7-24, 1980.

1986. Johnson, Elizabeth J. Family Counseling for Low Income Abusers.
           In: Drug Abuse from the Family Perspective. Ed.
           Barbara Gray Ellis. Washington, D.C.: U.S. Government
           Printing Office, 1980, pages 78-85.

1987. Johnson, Frank K. and Westman, Jack C. The Teenager and Drug
           Abuse. In: Readings in Adolescent Psychology. Eds.
           M. Powell and A.H. Frerichs. Minneapolis, Minnesota:
           Burgess, 1971, pages 292-301.

1988. Johnson, K.G., Donnelly, J.H., Scheble, R., Wine, R.L. and
           Weitman, M. Survey of Adolescent Drug Use. I. Sex and
           Grade Distribution. American Journal of Public Health,
           61(12): 2418-2432, 1971.

1989. Johnson, Kit, Donnelly, John, Scheble, Robert, Wine, Richard and
           Abbey, Helen. III - Correlations Among Use of Drugs.
           American Journal of Public Health, 62(2): 166-170, 1972.

1990. Johnson, M.W., DeVries, J.C. and Houghton, M.I. The Female
           Alcoholic. Nursing Research, 15: 343-347, 1966.

1991. Johnson, Roswell D. Alcohol and the College Campus. Journal of
           the American College Health Association, 22(3): 216-219,
           1974.

1992. Johnston, J. Alcoholism and the Wastage of Child Life. British
           Journal of Inebriety, 6: 179-185, 1909.

1993. Johnston, L. Drugs and American Youth. Ann Arbor, Michigan:
           Institute for Social Research, University of Michigan,
           1973.

1994. Johnston, L.D. Drug Use During and After High School: Results
           of a National Longitudinal Study. American Journal of
           Public Health, 64(1), Supplement No. 12: 29-37, 1974.

1995. Johnston, L.D. and Bachman, J.G. Monitoring the Future: A
           Continuing Study of the Lifestyles and Values of Youth.
           Washington, D.C.: Statement to the Press, October, 1975.

1996. Johnston, Lloyd D., Bachman, Jerald G. and O'Malley, Patrick M.
           Drug Use Among American High School Students 1975-1977.
           National Institute on Drug Abuse. Washington, D.C.: U.S.
           Govermnent Printing Office, 1977. (DHEW Publication No.
           ADM 78-619.)

1997. Johnston, Lloyd D., Bachman, Gerald G. and O'Malley, Patrick M.
       Drug Use Among American High School Students. In: The
       Yearbook of Substance Use and Abuse. Volume 2. Eds.
       Leon Brill and Charles Winick. New York: Human Sciences
       Press, 1980, pages 297-322.

1998. Joint Commission on Accreditation of Hospitals. Consolidated
       Standards for Child, Adolescent and Adult Psychiatric,
       Alcoholism and Drug Abuse Programs. Chicago, Illinois,
       1979.

1999. Joint Committee on Health Problems in Education. Organization
       Section. Journal of the American Medical Association,
       155: 40-42, 1954.

2000. Joint Meeting of the Fifth International Congress on Mental
       Health and the International Institute on Child Psychiatry;
       Alcoholism Symposium. Quarterly Journal of Studies on
       Alcohol, 15: 370-371, 1954.

2001. Jokiel, M. Młodzież o Alkoholu. (Youth and Alcohol.) Problemy
       Alkoholizmu, Warsaw, 22(10): 15-17, 1974.

2002. Jones, E. Student Drinking in the High Schools of Utah.
       Master's Thesis. University of Utah, 1957. (CAAAL
       Abstract No. 8217)

2003. Jones, G.C. Youth Deserves to Know. New York: Macmillan, 1958.

2004. Jones, Howard. Alcoholic Addiction: A Psycho-Social Approach to
       Abnormal Drinking. London: Tavistock, 1963.

2005. Jones, J.W. Acquisitional Processes Underlying Illicit Alcohol
       Abuse in Underage Children: An Observational Learning
       Model. Psychological Reports, 45: 735-740, 1979.

2006. Jones, K., Shainberg, L.W. and Byer, C.O. Drugs, Alcohol and
       Tobacco. San Francisco: Canfield Press, 1970.

2007. Jones, K.L., Shainberg, L.W. and Byer, C.O. Drugs and Alcohol.
       (3rd Edition) New York: Harper and Row, 1979.

2008. Jones, M.C. Personality Correlates and Antecedents of Drinking
       Patterns in Adult Males. Journal of Consulting and
       Clinical Psychology, 32: 2-12, 1968.

2009. Jones, M.C. Personality Antecedents and Correlates of Drinking
       Patterns in Women. Journal of Consulting and Clinical
       Psychology, 36: 61-69, 1971.

2010. Jones, R.S. Some Clues from Research. In: Alcohol Education.
       Proceedings of a Conference, March 29, 1966. Washington,
       D.C.: U.S. Government Printing Office, 1967, pages 25-28.

2011. Jones, Robert. Changing Patterns and Attitudes Toward Use of
       Alcoholic Beverages in the U.S. In: Interpreting Current
       Knowledge About Alcohol and Alcoholism to a College
       Community. Proceedings of a Conference, May 28-30, 1963,
       Albany, New York. Ed. Richard Reynolds. Albany: New York
       State Department of Mental Health, 1963, pages 9-20.

2012. Jones, T. Youth and Alcohol: A Study Prepared by the Ontario
       Youth Secretariat for the Cabinet of Ontario. Toronto,
       Ontario, 1976.

2013. Jones, T.L. Is Alcohol Education in Schools Necessary? In:
       Australian Foundation on Alcoholism and Drug Dependence.
       National Alcohol and Drug Dependence Multidisciplinary
       Institute. August 31-September 4, 1975. Burgmann College,
       Canberra. Canberra, 1975, pages 146-152.

2014. Jongman, R.W. and Veendrick, L. De Ernst van de Misdrijven
       Gepleedgd door Jongeren uit Verschillende Sociale Klassen.
       (Seriousness of Offenses Committed by Juveniles from
       Various Social Classes.) Nederlands Tijdschrift voor
       Criminologie, 15: 127-143, 1973.

2015. Jönsson, R. Folkhögskolan bör Diskutera Alkohol-Narkotika. (The
       Public High School Should Discuss Alcohol and Drugs.)
       Alkoholfragan, 65: 191-195, 1971.

2016. Jordan, Donald K. BCA Answers Alcohol Abuse Through the Values
       Revolution. Keynote, 4(2): 19-20, 1976.

2017. Jørgennsen, V. Noen Refleksjoner om Forebyggende Ungdomsarbeid
       på Edruskapssektoren. (Some Reflections on Work Done
       Among Youth on the Question of Sobriety.) Nordisk
       Tidsskrift AlkSpørsm, 26: 116-122, 1974.

2018. Jorris, E.H. Alcohol Involved in Most Driver Deaths. Wisconsin
       Medical Journal, 67(9): 417, 1968.

2019. Josephson, Eric. Problem Drinking Among Youth. In: An
       Assessment of Statistics on Alcohol-Related Problems. Ed.
       Eric Josephson. Columbia University School of Public
       Health. Prepared for the Distilled Spirits Council of the
       United States, Inc., May 5, 1980.

2020. Josephson, Eric. Adolescent Marijuana Use, 1971-1972: Findings
       from Two National Surveys. Addictive Diseases, 1(1): 55-
       72, 1974.

2021. Josephson, Eric. Trends in Adolescent Marijuana Use. In: Drug
       Use: Epidemiological and Sociological Approaches. Eds.
       E. Josephson and E.E. Carroll. Washington, D.C.:
       Hemisphere Publishing, 1974, pages 177-205.

2022.   Josephson, E. and Carroll, E.E., Eds. Drug Use: Epidemiological
        and Sociological Approaches. Washington, D.C.: Hemisphere
        Publishing, 1974.

2023.   Josephson, Eric and Rosen, Matthew. Panel Loss in a High School
        Drug Study. In: Longitudinal Research on Drug Use:
        Empirical Findings and Methodological Issues. Ed.
        Denise B. Kandel. New York: John Wiley and Sons, 1978,
        pages 115-133.

2024.   Jost, J. Wird die Gesundheits-, Sozial- und Jugendhilfe den
        Auswirkungen des Erhöhten Alkoholmissbrauch und dem Schutz
        der Familie Gerecht? (Are Health Education, Social Help
        and Youth Protection Adequate to Shield Families from
        Increasing Alcohol Abuse?) Gesundheitsfürsorge, Stuttgart,
        16: 85-86, 1966.

2025.   Jovanović, R. Omladina i Alkoholizam. (Youth and Alcoholism.)
        Alkoholizam, Beograd, 13(3-4): 25-26, 1974.

2026.   Jovanović, R. Stavovi Omladine o Alkoholizmu i Narkomanijama
        Sagledani Kroz Radove sa Nagradnih Konkursa. (Youth's
        Attitudes Toward Alcoholism and Drug Addictions Seen in
        Works Submitted for Prize Contests.) Alkoholizam, Beograd,
        12(2): 75-80, 1972.

2027.   Judd, L.L., Gunderson, E., Alexander, G.R., Attewell, P.,
        Buckingham, B., Blau, E., Crichton, J., Mandell, A.J. and
        Schuckit, J. Youth Drug Use Survey. In: Drug Use in
        America: Problems in Perspective. Volume I. Patterns
        and Consequences of Drug Use. U.S. National Commission on
        Marihuana and Drug Abuse. Washington, D.C.: U.S.
        Government Printing Office, 1973, pages 942-974.

2028.   Jugendliche Trinker. (Youthful Drinkers.) Sozial Arbeit,
        Berlin, 11(3): 133, 1962.

2029.   Jung, J. Drinking Motives and Behavior in Social Drinkers.
        Journal of Studies on Alcohol, 38: 944-952, 1977.

2030.   Jurek, K. Nĕkteré Přičiny Mravní Narušenosti Mládeže. (Some
        Causes of Moral Disorder in Youth.) Psychologia a
        Patopsychologia Dietata, Bratislava, 9: 171-176, 1974.

2031.   Juvenile Protective Association of Chicago. The Return of the
        Saloon. Chicago, Illinois, 1935.

K

2032. Kacavas, J. and Richardson, J. Utilizing the Vitalometer in Measuring One Aspect of Physical Fitness Among Short-Term Alcoholic Patients. American Corrective Therapy Journal, 30(4): 128-133, 1976.

2033. Kadushin, L.R. Drug Attitudes, Parental Child-Rearing Attitudes, and Youth's Perceptions of Parental Attitude Agreement. Doctoral Dissertation (University Microfilms No. 72-11362). University of Texas at Austin, 1971.

2034. Kahlström, K. Concerning Temperance Teaching in England's Primary and Secondary Schools. Tirfing, 26: 11-15, 1932.

2035. Kaij, L. Alcoholism in Twins. Studies on the Etiology and Sequels of Abuse of Alcohol. Stockholm: Almqvist and Wiksell, 1960.

2036. Kaij, L. and Dock, J. Grandsons of Alcoholics: A Test of Sex-Linked Transmission of Alcohol Abuse. Archives of General Psychiatry, 32: 1379-1381, 1975.

2037. Kaiser, G. Deliktformen und Typologie Junger Verkehrstäter. (Offenses and Typology of Young Traffic Offenders.) Blutalkohol, Hamburg, 15: 65-81, 1978.

2038. Kajubi, S.K. A Study on Alcoholic Coma. East African Medical Journal, 43(1): 21-25, 1966.

2039. Kalant, H. and Kalant, O.J. Drugs, Society, and Personal Choice. Don Mills, Ontario: General Publishing Company, 1971.

2040. Kalimo, Esko. Investigations on the Use of Alcohol Among Young People in Finland. Alkoholpolitikka, Helsingfor, 24: 122, 1961.

2041.   Kalin, R. Effects of Alcohol on Memory. Journal of Abnormal
            Social Psychology, 69: 635-641, 1964.

2042.   Kalin, R., McClelland, D.C. and Kahn, M. The Effects of Male
            Social Drinking on Fantasy. In: The Drinking Man. Eds.
            D.C. McClelland, W.N. Davis, R. Kalin and E. Wanner. New
            York: The Free Press, 1972, pages 3-22.

2043.   Kalin, Rudolf. Self Description of College Problem Drinkers.
            In: The Drinking Man. Eds. D.C. McClelland, W.N. Davis,
            R. Kalin and E. Wanner. New York: The Free Press, 1972,
            pages 217-231.

2044.   Kalin, Rudolf. Social Drinking in Different Settings. In: The
            Drinking Man. Eds. D.C. McClelland, W.N. Davis, R. Kalin
            and E. Wanner. New York: The Free Press, 1972, pages 21-
            44.

2045.   Kamiński, B. Nieprzystosowanie Pozytywne Dzieci z Rodzin
            Alkoholików. (Social Maladjustment of Children from
            Alcoholic Families.) Problemy Alkoholizmu, Warsaw, 23(12):
            5-6, 1976.

2046.   Kammeier, M.L. Adolescents from Families With and Without
            Alcohol Problems. Quarterly Journal of Studies on Alcohol,
            32: 364-372, 1971.

2047.   Kammeier, M.L. Biographic, Cognitive, Demographic and
            Personality Differences between Adolescents from Families
            with Identifiable Alcohol Problems and From Families
            without Identifiable Alcohol Problems. Doctoral
            Dissertation. Grand Forks, North Dakota: University of
            North Dakota, 1969.

2048.   Kammeier, M.L., Hoffman, H. and Loper, R.G. Personality
            Characteristics of Alcoholics as College Freshmen at Time
            of Treatment. Quarterly Journal of Studies on Alcohol, 34:
            390-399, 1973.

2049.   Kammeier, M.L., Loper, R.G. and Hoffman, H. Treatment and
            Pretreatment Personality Factors in Male Alcoholics.
            Pamphlet. (Hazelden Papers No. 1.) Center City,
            Minnesota: Hazelden, 1977.

2050.   Kammeier, Sister Mary Leo. Adolescents from Families with and
            without Alcohol Problems. Center City, Minnesota:
            Hazelden, no date.

2051.   Kampler, Hyman L. and MacKenna, Pat. Clinical Observations and
            Brief Family Therapy of Drug Abusing Adolescents and Their
            Families. Paper presented at the 52nd Annual Meeting,
            American Orthopsychiatric Association, Washington, D.C.,
            March 24, 1975.

2052. Kandel, D. Adolescent Marijuana Use: Role of Parents and Peers.
        Science, 181: 1067-1070, 1973.

2053. Kandel, D. Inter- and Intra-generational Influences on
        Adolescent Marijuana Use. Journal of Social Issues, 30(2):
        107-135, 1974.

2054. Kandel, D. Some Comments on the Relationship of Selected
        Criteria Variables to Adolescent Illicit Drug Use. In:
        Predicting Adolescent Drug Abuse: A Review of Issues,
        Methods and Correlates. Ed. D. Lettieri. NIDA Research
        Issues Series, Volume 11. Washington, D.C.: U.S.
        Government Printing Office, 1975, pages 343-361.

2055. Kandel, D. Stages in Adolescent Involvement in Drug Use.
        Science, 190(4217): 912-914, 1975.

2056. Kandel, D. and Faust, R. Sequence and Stages in Patterns of
        Adolescent Drug Use. Archives of General Psychiatry,
        32(7): 923-932, 1975.

2057. Kandel, D., Single, E. and Kessler, R.C. The Epidemiology of
        Drug Use among New York State High School Students:
        Distribution, Trends, and Change in Rates of Use.
        American Journal of Public Health, 66: 43-53, 1976.

2058. Kandel, Denise. Convergences in Prospective Longitudinal Surveys
        of Drug Use in Normal Populations. In: Longitudinal
        Research on Drug Use: Empirical Findings and
        Methodological Issues. Ed. Denise B. Kandel. New York:
        John Wiley and Sons, 1978, pages 3-38.

2059. Kandel, Denise. Developmental Stages in Adolescent Drug
        Involvement. In: Theories on Drug Abuse: Selected
        Contemporary Problems. (Research Monograph Series 30)
        U.S. National Institute on Drug Abuse. Eds. Dan Lettieri,
        Mollie Sayers and Helen Pearson. Rockville, Maryland:
        1980, pages 120-127. (DHEW Publication No. ADM 80-967)

2060. Kandel, Denise. Interpersonal Influences on Adolescent Illegal
        Drug Use. In: Drug Use: Epidemiological and
        Sociological Approaches. Eds. E. Josephson and
        E.E. Carroll. Washington, D.C.: Hemisphere Publishing,
        1974, pages 207-240.

2061. Kandel, Denise, Ed. Longitudinal Research on Drug Use:
        Empirical Findings and Methodological Issues. New York:
        John Wiley and Sons, 1978.

2062. Kandel, Denise. Reaching the Hard-to-Reach: Illicut Drug Use
        among High School Absentees. Addictive Diseases, 1(4):
        465-480, 1975.

2063. Kandel, Denise B. On Variations in Adolescent Subcultures.
       Youth and Society, 9: 373-384, 1978.

2064. Kandel, Denise B., Adler, Israel and Sudit, Myriam. The
       Epidemiology of Adolescent Drug Use in France and Israel.
       American Journal of Public Health, 7(3): 256-265, 1981.

2065. Kandel, Denise B., Kessler, R.C. and Margulies, Rebecca Z.
       Antecedents of Adolescent Initiation into Stages of Drug
       Use: A Developmental Analysis. Journal of Youth and
       Adolescence, 7(1): 13-40, 1978.

2066. Kandel, Denise B., Treiman, Donald, Faust, Richard and
       Single, Eric. Adolescent Involvement in Legal and Illegal
       Drug Use: A Multiple Classification Analysis. Social
       Forces, 55(2): 438-458, 1976.

2067. Kane, R.I. and Patterson, E. Attitudes and Behavior of High-
       School Students Toward Alcohol. Salt Lake City, Utah:
       University of Utah and the Department of Community and
       Family Medicine, no date.

2068. Kane, R.L. and Patterson, E. Drinking Attitudes and Behavior of
       High School Students in Kentucky. Quarterly Journal of
       Studies on Alcohol, 33: 635-646, 1972.

2069. Kannas, L. Raittiusliikkeen Nuorisotyön Koulutuksellisesta
       Suunnittelusta. (The Temperance Movement's Plans for
       Educating Adolescents.) Alkoholipolitiikka, Helsingfor,
       41: 99-103, 1976.

2070. Kansas Board of Health, Department of Public Instruction and
       National Institute of Mental Health. Proceedings of a
       Conference on Education, December 1-2, 1960, Topeka,
       Kansas. Topeka, Kansas, 1961.

2071. Kanter, Donald. Student Perceptions of Advertising's Role in
       Drug Usage and Attitudes. In: Communication Research and
       Drug Education. Ed. R.E. Ostman. Beverly Hills,
       California: Sage Publications, 1976, pages 117-132.

2072. Kapamadzija, B. and Backović, D. Middle School Youth and
       Alcohol: Results of an Enquiry. Alcoholism, Zagreb, 5:
       119-121, 1969. (Also as: Srednjoškolci i Alkohol:
       Rezultati Jednog Anketnog Ispitivanja. Annales Bolnice
       Stojanović, 8: 445-447, 1969. Also in: Alcoholizam,
       Beograd, 10(1): 66-70, 1970.)

2073. Kaplan, H.B. Self-Enhancing Functions of Alcohol Abuse Among
       Male Adolescents. In: Phenomenology and Treatment of
       Alcoholism. Eds. W.E. Fann, L. Karacan, A.D. Pokorny and
       R.L. Williams. New York: SP Medical and Scientific Books,
       1980, pages 151-166.

2074.   Kaplan, Howard and Pokorny, Alex. Alcohol Use and Self-
         Enhancement among Adolescents: A Conditional Relationship.
         In: Currents in Alcoholism. Volume 4. Psychiatric,
         Psychological, Social and Epidemiological Studies. Ed.
         F.A. Seixas. New York: Grune and Stratton, 1978, pages
         51-75.

2075.   Kaplan, Howard B. Antecedents of Deviant Responses: Predicting
         from a General Theory of Deviant Behavior. Journal of
         Youth and Adolescence, 6(1): 89-101, 1977.

2076.   Kaplan, Howard B. and Pokorny, Alex D. Self-Attitudes and
         Alcohol Use among Adolescents. In: Currents in
         Alcoholism. Volume 2. Psychiatric, Psychological, Social
         and Epidemiological Studies. Ed. F.A. Seixas. New York:
         Grune and Stratton, 1975, pages 285-298. (Also in: The
         Alcoholism Digest Annual, 5: 55-61, 1977.)

2077.   Kaplan, Mark S. Patterns of Alcoholic Beverage Use Among College
         Students. Journal of Alcohol and Drug Education, 24(2):
         26-40, 1979.

2078.   Karlsson, B. Thinner-, Alkohol, och Tabletmissbruk Bland Barn
         och Ungdom: Toxikologiska Synpunkter. (Thinner, Alcohol
         and Drug Misuse in Children and Adolescents: Toxicological
         Aspects.) Nordisk Medicin, Stockholm, 70: 893-896, 1963.

2079.   Karlstrom, G. and Olerud, S. The Management of Tibial Fractures
         in Alcoholics and Mentally Disturbed Patients. Journal of
         Bone and Joint Surgery, 56-B(4): 730-734, 1974.

2080.   Kárpáti, E. Adalékok a Magyarországi Alkoholkérdés Jogi
         Vonatkozásaihoz. II. Rész. (On the Legal Aspects of
         Alcohol Problems in Hungary. Part II.) Alkohologia,
         Budapest, 5: 39-52, 1974.

2081.   Karpio, V. Finsk Nykterhetsundervisning i Stöpsleven. (Finnish
         Abstinence Education Under Reform.) Tirfing, 40: 125-134,
         1946.

2082.   Karpman, Benjamin. The Hangover: A Critical Study in the
         Psychodynamics of Alcoholism. Springfield, Illinois:
         C.C. Thomas, 1957.

2083.   Kärre, K. Nykterhetsundervisningen. (Abstinence Education.)
         Tirfing, 41: 100-103, 1947.

2084.   Karsk, Roger S. Teenagers in the Next America: A Study of
         Teenage Life in Columbia, Maryland. Columbia, Maryland:
         New Community Press, 1977.

2085. Katz, Judith. Responsible Decision-Making. Health Education,
           6(2): 5-6, 1975.

2086. Katzper, Meyer, Ryback, Ralph and Hertzman, Marc. Alcohol
           Beverage Advertisement and Consumption. Journal of Drug
           Issues, 8: 339-353, 1978.

2087. Kaufman, E. Polydrug Abuse Problem in America. In: Proceedings
           of the 31st International Congress on Alcoholism and Drug
           Dependence, Bangkok, Thailand, February 23-28, 1975.
           Lausanne: International Council on Alcohol and
           Addiction, 1975, pages 507-515.

2088. Kaufman, E. and Kaufman, P.N. Family Therapy of Drug and Alcohol
           Abuse. New York: Gardner Press, 1979.

2089. Kaufman, Edward. Myth and Reality in the Family Patterns and
           Treatment of Substance Abusers. American Journal of Drug
           and Alcohol Abuse, 7(3): 257-279, 1980.

2090. Kaufman, Pauline. Family Therapy with Adolescent Substance
           Abusers. In: Family Therapy of Drug and Alcohol Abuse.
           Eds. E. Kaufman and P.N. Kaufman. New York: Gardner
           Press, 1979, pages 71-79.

2091. Kaye, S. Influence of Alcohol on Traffic Deaths in Puerto Rico
           1972. Boletin de la Asociacion Medica de Puerto Rico,
           65(6): 135-139, 1973.

2092. Kaye, Sidney. Alcohol, Drugs and Carbon Monoxide in Traffic
           Fatalities in Puerto Rico. In: Alcohol, Drugs and
           Traffic Safety. Proceedings of the Sixth International
           Conference on Alcohol, Drugs and Traffic Safety, Toronto,
           September 8-13, 1974. Eds. S. Israelstam and S. Lambert.
           Toronto, Ontario: Addiction Research Foundation of
           Ontario, 1975, pages 85-92.

2093. Kazimierski, J. Ksztaltowanie Pogladów Przeciwalkoholwych w
           Szkole. (Developing the Temperance Viewpoint in School.)
           Problemy Alkoholizmu, Warsaw, 20(6): 8-9, 1972.

2094. Kearney, T.R. and Taylor, C. Emotionally Disturbed Adolescents
           with Alcoholic Parents. Acta Paedopsychiatria, Basel,
           36: 215-221, 1969.

2095. Keeley, K.A. and Bell, R.A. Detoxification Units and the
           Prevention of Alcoholism. Annals of the New York Academy
           of Science, 273: 395-402, 1976.

2096. Keene, A. and Roche, D. Developmental Disorders in the Children
           of Male Alcoholics. Waterford, Ireland: Belmont Park
           Hospital, 1976.

2097. Keighley, B.D. Preventing Alcoholism in General Practice: Open
       Letter to High School Students from a Glasgow Family
       Doctor. British Journal of Alcohol and Alcoholism, 14: 14-
       18, 1979.

2098. Keil, Thomas. Social Correlates of In-Treatment Client Success.
       In: Drug Abuse: Modern Trends, Issues and Perspectives.
       Proceedings of the Second National Drug Abuse Conference,
       Inc., New Orleans, Louisiana, 1975. Comp.: A. Schecter,
       H. Alksne and E. Kaufman. New York: Marcel Dekker, Inc.,
       1978, pages 737-760.

2099. Keiner, F. Trinkgewohnheiten bei Jugendlichen. (Drinking
       Habits in Adolescents.) Therapie Gegenwart, 116: 1836-
       1850, 1977.

2100. Keituri, E. Alkoholistin Isä. (The Fathers of Alcoholics.)
       Alkoholikysymys, Helsinki, 22: 99-123, 1954.

2101. Kellam, S.G., Ensminger, M.E. and Simon, M.B. Mental Health in
       First Grade and Teenage Drug, Alcohol, and Cigarette Use.
       Drug and Alcohol Dependence, Lausanne, 5: 273-304, 1980.

2102. Keller, J.E. Alcohol, A Family Affair: Help for Families in
       Which There is Alcohol Misuse. Santa Ynez, California:
       Kroc Foundation, 1977.

2103. Keller, M. Alcohol and Youth. In: Adolescence and Alcohol.
       Eds. J.E. Mayer and W.J. Filstead. Cambridge,
       Massachusetts: Ballinger, 1980, pages 245-256.

2104. Keller, M. Alcoholism Among College Students. College Health
       Review, 12(4-6): 1, 5-7, 1948.

2105. Keller, M. Problems with Alcohol: An Historical Perspective.
       In: Alcohol and Alcohol Problems. Eds. W.J. Filstead,
       M. Keller and J.J. Rossi. Cambridge, Massachusetts:
       Ballinger, 1976, pages 5-28.

2106. Keller, Mark, Ed. International Bibliography of Studies on
       Alcohol. New Brunswick, New Jersey: Rutgers Center of
       Alcohol Studies, 1966.

2107. Keller, Mark, Ed. Research Priorities on Alcohol: Proceedings
       of a Symposium Sponsored by the Rutgers Center of Alcohol
       Studies and Rutgers University. New Jersey: Journal of
       Studies on Alcohol, Supplement No. 8, 1979.

2108. Keller, Oliver J., Jr. and Alper, Benedict. Halfway House:
       Community Centered Correction and Treatment. Lexington,
       Massachusetts: D.C. Heath, 1970.

2109.   Kellerman, J.L. AA--A Family Affair. Pamphlet. Charlotte,
        North Carolina: Charlotte Council on Alcoholism, 1974.

2110.   Kellerman, Joseph L. Guide for the Family of the Alcoholic.
        Long Grove, Illinois: Kemper Insurance Group, 1972.

2111.   Kelley, C.K. and King, G.D. Behavioral Correlates of the 2-7-8
        MMPI Profile Type in Students at a University Mental
        Health Center. Journal of Consulting and Clinical
        Psychology, 47: 679-685, 1979.

2112.   Kelley, D. Alcoholism and the Family. Maryland State Medical
        Journal, 22: 25-30, 1973.

2113.   Kelley, N.L. Social and Legal Programs in the United States.
        In: Alcohol Education for Classroom and Community: A
        Source Book for Educators. Ed. R.G. McCarthy. New York:
        McGraw-Hill, 1964, pages 11-31.

2114.   Kelley, P. and Conroy, G. A Promotive Health Plan Preventing
        Alcohol and Drug Abuse in the Schools. Arizona Medicine,
        29(1): 54-56, 1972.

2115.   Kellner, F.J. Drinking Sanctions in College. Master's Thesis.
        Rutgers University, 1967.

2116.   Kelly, Norbert L., Ed. Alcohol Education: A Reference Aid for
        Teachers. Raleigh: North Carolina Alcoholic
        Rehabilitation Program, 1957.

2117.   Kelly, Norbert L. Toward the Prevention of Alcoholism. Raleigh:
        North Carolina Department of Mental Health, 1970.

2118.   Kemény, L. Tájékoztató a KISZ Budapesti Bizottság
        Tevékenységéröl az Alkoholizmus Elleni Küzdelemben.
        (Information About the Activity of the Budapest Committee
        of the Young Communist League in the Fight against
        Alcoholism.) Alkohologia, Budapest, 6: 209, 1975.

2119.   Kendall, R.F. The Context and Implications of Drinking and Drug
        Use Among High School and College Students. Doctoral
        Dissertation (University Microfilms No. 76-19514). New
        York University, 1976.

2120.   Keniston, Kenneth. Drug Use and Student Values. In: Resource
        Book for Drug Abuse Education. American Association for
        Health, Physical Education and Recreation. Washington,
        D.C.: U.S. Government Printing Office, 1969, pages 70-74.

2121.   Kennedy, Dorothy. A Teacher: Help Me Stop Drug Abuse. Journal
        of Drug Education, 11(1): 9-11, 1981.

2122. Kennedy, E. On Becoming a Counselor: A Basic Guide for
      Nonprofessional Counselors. New York: Seabury, 1977.

2123. Kenney, Peter. Prospective Teachers' Attitudes Toward Alcohol
      Education. Journal of Alcohol and Drug Education, 24(1):
      14-30, 1978.

2124. Kenney, Peter. Prospective Teachers' Knowledge About Alcohol
      and Its Use. Journal of Alcohol and Drug Education,
      22(3): 49-63, 1977.

2125. Kent, P. An American Woman and Alcohol. New York: Holt,
      Rinehart and Winston, 1967.

2126. Kentucky Bureau for Health Services. 1974 Survey of Substance
      Use in Kentucky High School and College Populations.
      Frankfort, Kentucky, 1974.

2127. Kenyon, W.H. England's Problem. The Alcoholism Digest Annual,
      1: 31-34, 1972-1973.

2128. Kern, J.C., Schmelter, W.R. and Paul, S.R. Drinking Drivers
      Who Complete and Drop Out of an Alcohol Education Program.
      Journal of Studies on Alcohol, 38(1): 89-95, 1977.

2129. Kern, Joseph, Hassett, Carol, Collipp, Platon, Bridges, Carolyn,
      Solomon, Miriam and Condren, Raymond. Children of
      Alcoholics: Locus of Control, Mental Age and Zinc Level.
      Journal of Psychiatric Treatment and Evaluation, 3(2):
      169-173, 1981.

2130. Kern, Joseph C., Tippman, Joan, Fortgang, Jeffrey and
      Paul, Stewart R. A Treatment Approach for Children of
      Alcoholics. Journal of Drug Education, 7(3): 207-218,
      1977-1978.

2131. Kerr, K.B. A Program for Education about Alcohol in the Public
      Schools of Utah. Doctoral Dissertation (University
      Microfilms No. 59-1084). University of Utah, 1959.

2132. Keup, W., Ed. Drug Abuse: Current Concepts and Research.
      Springfield, Illinois: Charles C. Thomas, 1972.

2133. Keyserlingk, H. Jugendgefährdung durch Alkohol. (Youth
      Endangered by Alcohol.) Psychiatrie, Neurologie und
      Medizinische Psychologie, Leipzig, 15: 270-276, 1963.

2134. Khavari, K.A. and Farber, P.D. A Profile Instrument for the
      Quantification and Assessment of Alcohol Consumption.
      The Khavari Alcohol Test. Journal of Studies on Alcohol,
      39(9): 1525-1539, 1978.

2135. Kicking Up a Storm: 30 Proof Alcohol Milk-Shakes. Bottom Line,
          1(1): 21-24, 1977.

2136. Kieres, B. Małoletni w Izbie Wyrtrzeżwień. (Adolescents in
          Sobering-Up Stations.) Problemy Alkoholizmu, Warsaw,
          27(6): 15-16, 1980.

2137. Kiernan, Michael. An Actress on Alcohol's Problems. The
          Washington Daily News and Evening Star, A-1, A-16, May 22,
          1975.

2138. Kigel', D.G., Okulova, V.K., Devyaterikova, T.G. and Kirova, I.P.
          Nekotoryye Osobennosti Techeniya Alkogolizma i
          Alkogol'nykh Psikhozov v Yunosheskom. (Some Peculiarities
          of the Development of Alcoholism and the Alcoholic
          Psychoses in Youth.) Trudy Permskogo Meditsinskogo
          Instituta, USSR, 197: 52-55, 1972.

2139. Kikuchi, T., Kitamura, S. and Oyama, M. Rorschach Performance
          in Alcoholic Intoxication. Part I. Tohoku Psychologica
          Folia, 20: 45-71, 1961.

2140. Kikuchi, T., Kitamura, S., Sato, I. and Oyama, M. Rorschach
          Performance in Alcoholic Intoxication. Part II. Tohoku
          Psychologica Folia, 21: 19-46, 1962-1963.

2141. Killeen, John. U.S. Military Alcohol Abuse Prevention and
          Rehabilitation Programs. In: Youth, Alcohol and Social
          Policy. Eds. H.T. Blane and M.E. Chafetz. New York:
          Plenum Press, 1979, pages 355-381.

2142. Kime, R.E., Schlaadt, R.G. and Tritsch, L.E. Health Instruction:
          An Action Approach. Englewood Cliffs, New Jersey:
          Prentice-Hall, 1977.

2143. Kimes, W.T. Alcohol and Drug Abuse in South Carolina High
          Schools. Columbia, South Carolina: Department of
          Education, 1969.

2144. Kimes, Winter and Maher, Robert. South Carolina High School
          Students View Knowledge and Experience Related to the Use
          of Beverage Alcohol and Drugs. In: Selected Papers
          Presented at the General Sessions of the 22nd Annual
          Meeting of the Alcohol and Drug Problems Association of
          North America, September 12-17, 1971. Hartford,
          Connecticut, 1971, pages 3-6.

2145. Kimmel, C.K. A Prevention Program with Punch--The National PTA's
          Alcohol Education Project. Journal of School Health, 46:
          208-210, 1976.

2146. Kimmel, C.K. PTA Involvement in Alcohol Programs. In:
       Proceedings of the Fourth Annual Alcoholism Conference of
       the National Institute on Alcohol Abuse and Alcoholism.
       Washington, D.C.: U.S. Department of Health, Education and
       Welfare, 1975. (DHEW Publication No. ADM 76-284)

2147. Kinder, Bill N. Attitudes Toward Alcohol and Drug Use and Abuse:
       I. Demographic and Correlational Data. International
       Journal of the Addictions, 10(5): 737-760, 1975.

2148. Kinder, Bill N. Attitudes Toward Alcohol and Drug Abuse. II.
       Experimental Data, Mass Media Research and Methodological
       Considerations. International Journal of the Addictions,
       10(6): 1035-1054, 1975.

2149. Kinder, Bill N., Pape, Nance E. and Walfish, Steven. Drug and
       Alcohol Education Programs: A Review of Outcome Studies.
       The International Journal of the Addictions, 15(7): 1035-
       1054, 1980.

2150. King, Albion Roy. Basic Information on Alcohol. Revised
       Edition. Mount Vernon, Iowa: Cornell College Press,
       1957.

2151. King, Albion Roy. The Psychology of Drunkenness. Mount Vernon,
       Iowa: 1943.

2152. King, F.W. Users and Nonusers of Marihuana: Some Attitudinal
       and Behavioral Correlates. Journal of the American
       College Health Association, 18: 213-217, 1970.

2153. King, James A., Muraco, William S. and Vezner, Karl O.
       Adolescent Drug Use: The Problem in Perspective. Toledo,
       Ohio: The Bridge, 1974.

2154. King, James A., Muraco, William A. and Vezner, Karl O. Drug Use
       in Toledo Area Schools: How Serious is It? Toledo, Ohio:
       The Bridge, 1975.

2155. King, L.J., Murphy, G.E., Robins, L.N. and Darvisch, Harriet.
       Alcohol Abuse: A Crucial Factor in the Social Problems of
       Negro Men. American Journal of Psychiatry, 125: 1682-
       1690, 1969.

2156. King, L.J. and Pittman, G.D. A Six-Year Follow-Up Study of 65
       Adolescent Patients: Natural History of Affective
       Disorders in Adolescence. Archives of General Psychiatry,
       22(3): 230-236, 1970.

2157. King, Rufus. Drug Abuse and the Idioms of War. Journal of Drug
       Issues, 8: 221-232, 1978.

2158.   King, Sharon E.   Young Alcohol Abusers: The Challenge of
          Prevention.   Journal of Drug Education, 10(3): 233-238,
          1980.   (Also in: The Catalyst, 1(2): 233-238, 1980.

2159.   Kinney, J. and Leaton, G.   Loosening the Grip: A Handbook of
          Alcohol Information.   St. Louis, Missouri: C.V. Mosby Co.,
          1978.

2160.   Kinsey, Barry A.   Psychological Factors in Alcoholic Women from a
          State Hospital Sample.   The American Journal of Psychiatry,
          124: 1463-1466, 1968.

2161.   Kipperman, A. and Fine, E.   The Combined Abuse of Alcohol and
          Amphetamines.   American Journal of Psychiatry, 131: 1277-
          1280, 1974.

2162.   Kirk, J.   Alcoholism and Child Welfare.   Medical Press and
          Circular, 154: 70-72, 1917.

2163.   Kirk, J.   Alcoholism and Child Welfare in War Time.   British
          Journal of Inebriety, 14: 141-155, 1917.

2164.   Kirk, Raymond S.   Drug Use Among Rural Youth.   In: Youth Drug
          Abuse: Problems, Issues and Treatment.   Eds. G.M. Beschner
          and A.S. Friedman.   Lexington, Massachusetts: D.C. Heath,
          1979, pages 379-407.

2165.   Kirk, Raymond S.   Use of Alcohol and Other Drugs by Rural
          Teenagers.   In: Currents in Alcoholism.   Volume 6.
          Treatment and Rehabilitation and Epidemiology.   Ed.
          M. Galanter.   New York: Grune and Stratton, 1979, pages
          233-237.

2166.   Kirk, Robert G.   The Beverage Industry and Alcohol Education.
          Health Education, 6(2): 11-13, 1975.

2167.   Kirke, Peadar, Gough, Cora, Wilson-Davis, Keith, O'Rourke, Angus
          and Dean, Geoffrey.   Drugs--A Study of Irish Rural Post-
          Primary School Children 1970-71.   Journal of the Irish
          Medical Association, 66(9): 231-237, 1973.

2168.   Kirschenbaum, H., Ed.   The First Catalogue for Humanizing
          Education: 1978-1979 Edition.   Saratoga Springs, New York:
          National Humanistic Education, 1978.

2169.   Kissin, B. and Begleiter, H., Eds.   The Biology of Alcoholism.
          Volume 4.   Social Aspects of Alcoholism.   New York: Plenum
          Press, 1976.

2170.   Kissin, B. and Begleiter, H., Eds.   The Biology of Alcoholism.
          Volume 5.   Treatment and Rehabilitation of the Chronic
          Alcoholic.   New York: Plenum Press, 1977.

2171. Kissin, B., Milman, D.H. and Wey-Su, Huen. Patterns of Alcohol
       and Illicit Drug Usage Among Secondary School and
       University Students. Amsterdam: Paper presented at the
       30th International Congress on Alcoholism and Drug
       Dependence, September 1972.

2172. Kissin, Benjamin. Biological Investigations in Alcohol Research.
       In: Research Priorities on Alcohol. Proceedings of a
       Symposium Sponsored by the Rutgers Center of Alcohol
       Studies and Rutgers University. Ed. Mark Keller, New
       Jersey: Journal of Studies on Alcohol, Supplement No. 9,
       1971, pages 146-181.

2173. Kithie, Nicholas, Weaver, Juanita, Trencher, William,
       Wolfgang, Joan, Dahlke, Arnold and Tro, Joseph. The
       Juvenile Drug Offender and the Justice System. In:
       Drug Use in America: Problems in Perspective. Appendix.
       Volume III. The Legal System and Drug Control.
       Washington, D.C.: U.S. National Commission on Marihuana
       and Drug Abuse, 1973, pages 686-797.

2174. Kitzing, E. Alkohol und Jugend. (Alcohol and Youth.)
       International Congress Against Alcoholism, 22: 191-197,
       1941.

2175. Kivowitz, J. Alcoholic Adolescents. Medical Insights, 5(9): 22,
       26-27, 1973.

2176. Kjølstad, T. Alkoholisme hos Sjømenn. (Alcoholism Among
       Sailors.) Tidsskrift for den Norske Laegeforening, Oslo,
       84: 1243-1248, 1964.

2177. Klassen, D. and Hornstra, R.K. Prevalence of Problem Drinking in
       a Community Survey. Missouri Medicine, 73: 81-84, 1976.

2178. Klein, A., Davis, J. and Blackbourne, B. Marihuana and
       Automobile Crashes. Journal of Drug Issues, 1(1): 18-26,
       1971.

2179. Klein, D. An Important Question. Pamphlet. Lansing: Michigan
       Alcohol Education Foundation, 1966.

2180. Klein, J. and Phillips, D. From Hard to Soft Drugs: Temporal
       and Substantive Changes in Drug Usage Among Gangs in a
       Working-Class Community. Journal of Health and Social
       Behavior, 9(2): 139-145, 1968.

2181. Kleinfeld, J. and Bloom, J. Boarding Schools: Effects on the
       Mental Health of Eskimo Adolescents. American Journal of
       Psychiatry, 134: 411-417, 1977.

2182. Kleinman, P. and Lukoff, I. Generational Status, Ethnic Group
       and Friendship Networks: Antecedents of Drug Use in a
       Ghetto Community. New York: Columbia University School of
       Social Work, Center for Socio-Cultural Studies in Drug Use,
       1975.

2183. Kline, F. Gerald, Miller, Peter, Morrison, Andrew and
       Fredin, Eric. The Basis for Adolescent Information
       Acquisition about Drugs and Alcohol--A Uses and
       Gratification Approach. In: Papers presented at the
       Fifth International Institute on the Prevention and
       Treatment of Drug Dependence, Copenhagen, Denmark
       Volume II, July, 1974. International Council on Alcohol
       and the Addictions. Lausanne, Switzerland, 1974, pages
       310-321.

2184. Kline, J.A. Evaluation of a Multimedia Drug Education Program.
       Journal of Drug Education, 2(3): 229-239, 1972.

2185. Kline, J.A. and Roberts, A.C. A Residential Alcoholism Treatment
       Program for American Indians. Quarterly Journal of Studies
       on Alcohol, 34(3): 860-868, 1973.

2186. Klinge, Valerie and Vaziri, Habib. Characteristics of Drug
       Abusers in an Adolescent In-Patient Psychiatric Facility.
       Diseases of the Nervous System, 38: 275-279, 1977.

2187. Klock, J.A., Fountain, A.W. and Barr, C.L. Student Drug and
       Alcohol Opinionnaire and Usage Survey: Grades 7, 8, 9
       10, 11, 12. Jacksonville, Florida: Duval County School
       Board, 1972.

2188. Kluge, K.-J. and Strassburg, B. Wollen Jugendliche durch
       Alkoholkonsum Hemmungen Ablegen, Kontakte Knüpfen Bzw. Ihre
       Probleme Ertränken? (Alcohol Abuse in Adolescents - A
       Means of Discarding Inhibitions, of Establishing Contacts,
       or of Drowning One's Problems.) Praxis der
       Kinderpsychologie und Kinderpsychiatrie, 1: 24-32, 1981.

2189. Kmošková, L. and Matějček, Z. Děti v Alkoholické Rodině.
       (Children in the Alcoholic Family.) Protialkoholicky
       Obzor, Bratislava, 7: 171-174, 1972.

2190. Kneist, W. and Petermann, A. Rauch- und Trinkgewohnheiten 14-
       bis 18jähriger Jungen und Mädchen. (Smoking and Drinking
       Habits of 14- to 18-Year-Old Boys and Girls.) Zeitschrift
       fuer die Gesamte Hygiene und Ihre Grenzgebiete, Leipzig,
       10: 737-748, 1964.

2191.   Kneist, W. and Taubert, E. Die Verhutung von Alkoholmissbrauch
        durch Bildungs- und Erziehungsmassnahmen in Kindes- und
        Jugendalter. (Prevention of Alcohol Misuse by Training and
        Educational Measures in Childhood Adolescence.) In:
        Papers Presented at the 23rd International Institute on the
        Prevention and Treatment of Alcoholism, Dresden, June 6-10,
        1977. Eds. E.J. Tongue and I. Moos. Lausanne:
        International Council on Alcohol and Addictions, 1977,
        pages 213-216.

2192.   Knight, James A. The Family in the Crisis of Alcoholism.   In:
        Alcoholism: A Practical Treatment Guide. Eds.
        Stanley E. Gitlow and Herbert S. Peyser. New York: Grune
        and Stratton, 1980, pages 205-228.

2193.   Knipping, Paul A. and Maultsby, Maxie C., Jr. Rational Self-
        Counseling: Primary Prevention for Alcohol Abuse.
        Alcohol Health and Research World, 2: 31-35, 1977.

2194.   Knupper, Genevieve. Ex-Problem Drinkers. In: Life History
        Research in Psychopathology. Volume 2. Eds. M. Roff,
        L.N. Robins and M. Pollack. Minneapolis: University of
        Minnesota Press, 1972, pages 256-280.

2195.   Kobus, A. and Morawski, J. Sprezedaż Alkoholu w Gastronomii a
        Prżestepczość. (Sale of Alcohol in Restaurants and
        Delinquency.) Problemy Alkoholizmu, Warsaw, 21(2): 11-13,
        1973.

2196.   Kocsis, Louis, Clark, James, Meyers, Frank and Nolan, Robert.
        Integrating Alcohol Education in the Curriculum--Summary
        of Panel Presentation. In: Alcohol Education--Whose
        Responsibility? Proceedings of a Conference, May, 1963,
        sponsored by Michigan Department of Mental Health,
        Michigan Department of Public Instruction, Michigan
        Department of Health, Michigan Congress of Parents and
        Teachers, Michigan State University, Michigan State Board
        of Alcoholism, and U.S. Public Health Service. Lansing:
        Michigan State Board of Alcoholism, 1963, pages 29-31.

2197.   Kohler, Mary Conway and Dollar, Bruce. An Antidote to
        Alienation. The Center Magazine, 9(3): 3-30, 1976.

2198.   Kohn, P.M. and Annis, H.M. Drug Use and Four Kinds of Novelty-
        Seeking. British Journal of Addiction, 72: 135-141, 1977.

2199.   Koivukangas, K. Raittiustyö Evijärven Kansaja
        Kansalaiskouluissa. (Temperence Education in the Schools
        of Evijarvi.) Alkoholikysymys, Helsinki, 3: 85-91, 1969.

2200. Kołakowska-Przełomiec, H. Alkoholizowanie sie Nieletnich
       Przestepców a ich Późniejsze Przystosowanie Społeczne.
       (Alcoholization of Juvenile Delinquents and their
       Subsequent Social Functioning.) Problemy Alkoholizmu,
       Warsaw, 21(6): 4-6, 1973.

2201. Kolarova, D., Apostólov, M. and Panev, B. Štúdium Miery
       Sporteby Alkoholu a Jeho Dôsledkov Medzi Ziakami Jednej
       Desat'ročnek Skoly v Sofii. (Study on the Extent of
       Alcohol Consumption and its Consequences Among Pupils in
       a 10-Year School in Sofia.) Protialkoholicky Obzor,
       Bratislava, 8: 1-5, 1973.

2202. Kolbe, Lloyd J. To Educate or Not to Educate is Not the
       Question. American Journal of Public Health, 71(2): 171,
       1981.

2203. Koller, K.M. and Castanos, J.N. Family Background and Life
       Situation in Alcoholics: A Comparative Study of Parental
       Deprivation and Other Features in Australians. Archives
       of General Psychiatry, 21: 602-610, 1969.

2204. Konstantinović, I., Licht, A. and Vidaković, J. Alkoholizam kod
       Školske dece na Teritoriji Sreza Subotice. (Alcoholism in
       School Children in the Subotica District.) Higijena,
       Beograd, 9(2-3): 147-153, 1957.

2205. Kooi, Ronald Charles Vander. An Analysis of Drinking Practices
       and Problems among Male Undergraduates at a Midwestern
       University. Master's Thesis, Western Michigan University.
       Lansing: Michigan State Board of Alcoholism, 1961.

2206. Kopplin, D.A., Greenfield, T.K. and Wong, H.Z. Changing
       Patterns of Substance Use on Campus: A Four-Year Follow-
       Up Study. International Journal of the Addictions, 12:
       73-94, 1977.

2207. Kopteff, P. Päihteiden Väärinkäytön Kasautumisen Ongelma. (The
       Problem of Polydrug Misuse.) Alkoholikysymys, Helsinki,
       46: 13-16, 1978.

2208. Kopteff, Pekka. A Survey of the Abuse of Medicines and Illicit
       Drugs by Finnish Students. International Journal of the
       Addictions, 15(2): 269-275, 1980.

2209. Korcok, Milan. Alcoholism Treatment: Good and Getting Better.
       Focus on Alcohol and Drug Issues, 4(3): 4-5, 1981.

2210. Korcok, Milan. Another Candle to Light the Darkness: Some New
       Facts on Adolescent Use of Mood Modifying Substances.
       Journal of Alcohol Education, 14(3): 21-24, 1969.

2211. Korcok, Milan. Lalonde Proposes Preventive Medicine to Combat
       Alcohol Abuse. Canadian Medical Association Journal,
       115(3): 260-262, 1976.

2212. Korczak, C.W. and Leowski, J. Problem Alkoholizmu w Szkolach
       Warszawskich. II. Relacje Rodziców o Czestosci Picia
       Napojow Alkoholowych Przez Uczniów. (Problem of Alcoholism
       in the Schools of Warsaw. II. Parent's Report on
       Frequency of Drinking of Alcoholic Beverages by School
       Children.) Roczniki Panstwawego Zaklad Higieny, Warsaw,
       17: 345-350, 1966.

2213. Korn, J.H. and Goldstein, J.W. Psychoactive Drugs: A Course
       Evaluation. Journal of Drug Education, 3(4): 353-368,
       1973.

2214. Kostuj, E. Przestepczosc Nieletnich a Alkohol. (On Juvenile
       Delinquency and Alcohol.) Problemy Alkoholizmu, Warsaw,
       26(3): 11-12, 1979.

2215. Kosugi, Y. and Tanaka, M. (Parental Deprivation, Birth Order and
       Alcoholism) [Japanese Text] Japanese Journal of Studies
       on Alcohol, 10: 70-77, 1975.

2216. Kosviner, A., Hawks, D. and Webb, M.G.T. Cannabis Use Amongst
       British University Students. 1. Prevalence Rates and
       Differences between Students Who Have Tried Cannabis and
       Those Who Have Never Tried It. British Journal of the
       Addictions, 69: 35-60, 1974.

2217. Kraack, T.A. Beer in the Student Union. Brewer's Digest,
       50(2): 22-25, 1975.

2218. Kraft, D.P. Alcohol-Related Problems Seen at the Student Health
       Services. Journal of the American College Health
       Association, 27(4): 190-194, 1979.

2219. Kraft, D.P. College Students and Alcohol: The 50 + 12 Project.
       Alcohol Health and Research World, 3: 10-14, 1976.

2220. Kraft, D.P. Strategies for Reducing Drinking Problems Among
       Youth: College Programs. In: Youth, Alcohol and Social
       Policy. Eds. H.T. Blane and M.E. Chafetz. New York:
       Plenum Press, 1979, pages 311-353.

2221. Kraft, David P. Alcohol Education and Prevention: Implications
       for Programming at the University Level. Presentation at
       the Symposium on Drinking among College Students. Boston,
       Massachusetts, 1978.

2222. Kraft, S.P. Typology of Family Social Environments for Families
       of Alcoholics. Doctoral Dissertation (University
       Microfilms No. 77-25112). George Peabody College for
       Teachers, 1977.

2223. Kraft, T. and Al-Issa, I. Alcoholism Treated by Desensitization:
       A Case Report. Behaviour Research and Therapy, 5: 69-70,
       1967.

2224. Kraft, T. and Al-Issa, I. Desensitization and the Treatment of
       Alcohol Addiction. British Journal of Addiction, 63: 19-
       23, 1968.

2225. Kraus, A.S., Steele, R., Ghent, W.R. and Thompson, M.G. Pre-
       Driving Identification of Young Drivers with a High Risk
       of Accidents. Journal of Safety Research, 2(2): 55-60,
       1970.

2226. Kraus, J. Alcoholism and Drug Dependence as Factors in
       Psychiatric Hospital Admissions. Australian and New
       Zealand Journal of Psychiatry, 7(1): 45-50, 1973.

2227. Krauthamer, Carole. Maternal Attitudes of Alcoholic and
       Nonalcoholic Upper Middle Class Women. The International
       Journal of the Addictions, 14(5): 639-644, 1979.

2228. Krauthamer, C.M. The Personality of Alcoholic Mothers and Their
       Children: A Study of Their Relationship to Birth Order,
       Mother-Child Attitude, and Socioeconomic Status. Doctoral
       Dissertation (University Microfilms No. 74-8798). Rutgers
       University, 1973.

2229. Krimmel, H.E. The Alcoholic and His Family. In: Alcoholism:
       Progress in Research and Treatment. Eds. P.G. Bourne and
       R. Fox. New York: Academic Press, 1973, pages 297-310.

2230. Krimmel, H.E. Thinking Straight About Drinking. Pamphlet.
       Chicago, Illinois: National Congress of Parents and
       Teachers, no date.

2231. Krippner, S., Goldsmith, M., Lenz, G., Goldsmith, M. and
       Washburn, B. Alternatives in Consciousness among High
       School Students Produced by Ingestion of Illegal Drugs.
       The International Journal of the Addictions, 6(3): 419-
       442, 1971.

2232. Kristiansson, R. Alkohol- och Narkotikafrågor i Skolans
       Läroplaner. (Alcohol and Narcotics Study in the School's
       Curriculum.) Alkoholfrågan, 62: 158-160, 1968.

2233. Kristiansson, R. Folkhögskoleelevernas Alkoholvanor: Några
       Kommentarer Till en Undersökning. (Drinking Habits of
       Public High School Students: Some Comments on a Survey.)
       Alkoholfrågan, 65: 181-184, 1971.

2234. Krupinski, Jerzy, Stroller, Alan and Graves, Gwen D. Drug Use
       among the Young Population of the State of Victoria,
       Australia: A Metropolitan and Rural City Survey. Journal
       of Drug Issues, 7: 365-376, 1977.

2235. Krynak, D.T., Larsen, B.M. and Pettijohn, T.F. Alcohol and Other
       Drug Use among Rural Adolescents: Some Implications for
       Rural Drug-Programming. In: Papers presented at the 24th
       International Institute on the Prevention and Treatment of
       Alcoholism, Zurich, June, 1978. Ed. E.J. Tongue.
       Lausanne: International Council on Alcohol and
       Addictions, 1978, pages 184-202.

2236. Krystal, Henry, Moore, Robert A. and Dorsey, John M. Alcoholism
       and the Forces of Education. Personnel and Guidance
       Journal, 45: 134-139, 1966.

2237. Kubička, L. Postoje k Funkcím Alkoholu jako Prediktory
       Konzumace u Mladych Lidi: Předběžné Sdělení. (Attitudes
       Toward the Functions of Alcohol as Predictors of Alcohol
       Consumption in Young Adults: Preliminary Report.)
       Protialkoholicky Obzor, Bratislava, 13: 129-136, 1978.

2238. Kuehnle, J.C., Anderson, W.H. and Chandler, E. First Drinking
       Experience in Addictive and Nonaddictive Drinkers.
       Archives of General Psychiatry, 31(4): 521-523, 1974.

2239. Kulsiewicz, T. Alkohol a Młodzież: Przyczynek do Problematyki
       Alkoholizowania sie Młodziezy. (Alcohol and Youth: A
       Case of Problem Drinking among Youth.) Problemy
       Alkoholizmu, Warsaw, 22(12): 3-6, 1974.

2240. Kullander, T. Alkoholmissbrukets Problematik. (The Problem of
       Alcohol Abuse.) Socialmedicinsk Tidsskrift, Stockholm,
       38: 175-182, 1961.

2241. Kumar, A. and Desai, H.G. Aetiology of Indian Childhood
       Cirrrhosis: A New Hypothesis. Indian Journal of Medical
       Science, 30: 215-217, 1976.

2242. Kunkle-Miller, Carole and Blane, Howard T. A Small Group
       Approach to Youth Education About Alcohol. Journal of
       Drug Education, 7: 381-386, 1977.

2243. Kuttner, R.E. and Lorincz, A.B. Alcoholism and Addiction in
       Urbanized Sioux Indians. Medical Hygiene, 51(4): 530-542,
       1967.

2244. Kuusijärvi, Irja, Ed. Raittiuskasvatusken Kentältä, Kokemuksia
        ja Toimintavälähdyksiä Soumen Opettajain Raittiusliiton
        Työsaralta 1906-1956. (Concerning the Field of Temperance
        Education, Experiences and Glimpses of Activities. From
        the Proceedings of the Finnish Teachers Temperance League,
        1906-1956.) Vammala, Finland: Vammalan Kirjapaino Oy,
        1956.

2245. Kuznik, A. The Effect of the Lowered Age of Majority and
        Relaxed Dormitory Policies on Drug Usage by Dormitory
        Residents. Contact: The Journal of the Minnesota College
        Personnel Association, Spring, 1974-1975. (ERIC
        Document Reporduction Service No. ED 105 956)

2246. Kvapilík, J. and Petricék, B. Use of Alcohol, Tobacco, Caffeine
        and Drugs by Undergraduates. Activitas Nervosa Superior,
        Prague, 14(2): 140, 1972.

L

2247. Lachnit, V. and Taschner, H. Alkoholschäden und Ihre
Sozialmedizinische Bedeutung: 6-Jahres-Statistik einer
Internen Abteilung. (Alcohol-Induced Damages and Their
Sociomedical Significance: 6-Year Statistics of an
Internal Medicine Department. Wiener Medizinische
Wochenschrift, 124: 639-643, 1974.

2248. La Criminalité. Les Infractions. L'Enfance Délinquante.
(Criminality. Infractions. Delinquent Youth.) In:
Alcool, Alcoolisme, Alcoolisation. Données Scientifiques
de Caractère Physiologique, Economique et Social.
(Alcohol, Alcoholism, Alcoholization. Scientific
Information of Characteristics [in] Physiology, Economics
and Social.) Paris: Presses Universitaires de France,
1956, pages 217-226.

2249. Laessig, R.H. and Waterworth, K.J. Involvement of Alcohol in
Fatalities of Wisconsin Drivers. Public Health Reports,
85: 535-549, 1970.

2250. La Fe Youth Hostel. Alcoholic Beverage Use and Family Drinking
Patterns among Students in Santa Fe High School. Santa Fe,
New Mexico, 1975.

2251. Laignel-Lavastine. Retentissement de l'Alcoolisme sur la Famille
et l'Enfant. (The Repercussions of Alcoholism on the
Family and the Child.) Archives Internationale de
Neurologie, 60: 165-187, 207-211, 1941.

2252. Laiho, K., Isokoski, M. and Alha, A. Tod in der Sauna nach
Einnahme von Chinen und Alkohol. (Death in the Sauna
Following Ingestion of Quinine and Alcohol.) Archive of
Toxikology, Berlin, 21: 352-354, 1966.

2253.   La Lutte Contre l'Alcoolisme en Pologne.   (The Campaign Against
             Alcoholism in Poland.) Warsaw: Editions Médicales d'Etat,
             1956.

2254.   Lambert, G.B. Adolescence: Transition from Childhood to
             Maturity, 2nd Edition. Monterey, California: Brooks/Cole,
             1978.

2255.   Lamontagne, Y., Tétreault, L. and Boyer, R. Consommation
             d'Alcool et de Drogues Chez les Étudiants.
             I. Consommation, Effets et Raisons d'Utilisation d'Alcool
             Chez des Étudiants au Niveau Collegial (CEGEP). (Drinking
             and Drug Use Among Students. I. The Reasons for Drinking
             and Its Effects on Students at the College Level [CEGEP].)
             Union Médicale du Canada, 108: 219-228, 1979.

2256.   Lamontagne, Y., Tétreault, L. and Boyer, R. Consommation
             d'Alcohol et de Drogues Chez les Étudiants:
             II. Consommation et Raisons d'Utilisation de Drogues Chez
             les Étudiants au Niveau Collégial (CEGEP). (Consumption
             of Alcohol and Drugs by Students. II. Consumption and
             Reasons for the Use of Drugs among Students at the College
             Level [CEGEP].) Union Médicale du Canada, 108: 408-411,
             1979.

2257.   Lamontagne, Y., Tétreault, L. and Boyer, R. Consommation
             d'Alcool et de Drogues Chez les Étudiants:
             III. Milieu Familial, Secteurs d'Étude Impliqués et
             Comparaison entre Étudiants et Étudiantes Alcooliques au
             Niveau Collégial (CEGEP). (Alcohol and Drug Consumption
             in Students. III. Family Environment, Areas of Study and
             Comparison of Men and Women Alcoholics Enrolled in
             Colleges [CEGEP].) Union Médicale du Canada, 108: 573-757,
             1979.

2258.   Lander, Nathan. The Social Patterns of the Teen-Age Drug Abuser.
             In: Drugs and Youth: The Challenge of Today. Ed.
             E. Harms. Elmsford, New York: Pergamon Press, 1973,
             pages 131-135.

2259.   Landers, A. Booze and You: For Teenagers Only. Pamphlet.
             San Francisco, California: Field Enterprises, 1967.

2260.   Landman, R.H. Studies of Drinking in Jewish Culture:
             III. Drinking Patterns of Children and Adolescents
             Attending Religious Schools. Quarterly Journal of Studies
             on Alcohol, 13: 87-94, 1952.

2261.   Landrum, James and Windham, Gerald. A Comparison of DWI
             Repeaters and Non-Repeaters Who Attended a Level 1
             Rehabilitation Program. Journal of Alcohol and Drug
             Education, 26(2): 11-23, 1981.

2262. Lane County, Juvenile Department. Alcohol Education Program.
      Eugene, Oregon, 1976.

2263. Lang, A.R., Goeckner, D.J., Adesso, V.J. and Marlatt, G.A.
      Effects of Alcohol on Aggression in Male Social Drinkers.
      Journal of Abnormal Psychology, 84: 508-518, 1975.

2264. Langan, J.J. Alcohol Education Information and Content Flip
      Chart: Instructor's Manual. San Diego, California:
      Winston Products for Education, no date.

2265. Lange, E. and Trübsbach, G. Entwicklungsbesonderheiten,
      Soziales Bezugsfeld und Familienstruktur bei 100 Jungen,
      Straffällig Gewordenen Gewohnheits-Geselligkeitstrinkern
      der Stadt Dresden. (Developmental Peculiarities, Social
      Environment and Family Structure of 100 Juvenile
      Delinquent Habitual Social Drinkers in Dresden.)
      Psychiatrie, Neurologie und Medizinische Psychologie,
      Leipzig, 21: 311-317, 1969.

2266. Langone, John. Bombed, Buzzed, Smashed or...Sober: A Book
      About Alcohol. Boston, Massachusetts, Little Brown and
      Company, 1976.

2267. Lanu, K.E. Poikkeavan Alkoholikäyttäytymisen Kontrolli.   The
      Control of Deviating Drinking Behavior.) Helsinki,
      Finland: Publication No. 2, Finnish Foundation for
      Alcohol Studies, 1955.

2268. Laquer, B. Student und Alkohol. Alkoholfrage, 17: 241-242,
      1921.

2269. Larsen, B. and Larsen, L.N. Alcohol in Our Society. Bismarck,
      North Dakota: North Dakota Division of Alcoholism and
      Drug Abuse, 1972.

2270. Larsen, Bernard. Education as a Tool in Preventing Drug Abuse.
      Journal of Alcohol Education, 15(3): 35-39, 1970. (Also
      in: Inventory: A Quarterly Journal on Alcohol and
      Alcoholism, 20(4): 2-4, 1971.)

2271. Larsen, Bradley M. Female Adolescent Drinking, Problem Drinking
      and Sex Role Orientation: A Test of Adler's Propositions.
      San Francisco, California: R & E Research Associates,
      Inc., 1978.

2272. Larsen, E. Not My Kid! Liguori, Missiouri: Liguorian Books,
      1970.

2273. Larsen, Levi N. Alcohol Education to Meet the Needs of
      Children Today. Inventory: A Quarterly Journal on
      Alcohol and Alcoholism, 20(4): 10-13, 1971.

2274.   Larsen, Levi N.   Drug Education vs. Alcohol Education.   Journal
        of Alcohol and Drug Education, 16(2): 26-28, 1971.

2275.   Larsson, S.O. and Sundkvist, G.   Acute Intoxication: A
        Comparative Investigation at a General City Hospital for
        the Years 1951, 1961 and 1971.   Acta Medica Scandinavica,
        195(6): 515-520, 1974.

2276.   Lasky, D.I. and Ziegenfuss, J.T., Jr.   Anomie and Drug Use in
        High School Students.   International Journal of the
        Addictions, 14: 861-866, 1979.

2277.   Lassey, Marie L. and Carlson, John E.   Drinking Among Rural
        Youth: The Dynamics of Parental and Peer Influence.   The
        International Journal of the Addictions, 15(1): 61-75,
        1980.

2278.   Lassey, Marie L. and Carlson, John E.   Drinking Among Teenagers:
        Rural--Urban Comparison in Peer Influence.   Journal of
        Alcohol and Drug Education, 24(3): 8-18, 1979.

2279.   The Latest Teen Drug: Alcohol.   Newsweek: 68, March 5, 1973.

2280.   Laudeman, K.A.   Personality, Drinking Patterns and Problem
        Drinking among Young Adult Offenders.   Journal of Drug
        Education, 7: 259-269, 1977.

2281.   Lavenhar, M.A. and Sheffet, A.   Recent Trends in Nonmedical Use
        of Drugs Reported by Students in Two Suburban New Jersey
        Communities.   Preventive Medicine, 2(4): 490-509, 1973.

2282.   Laverty, S.G.   Reported Levels of Ethanol Consumption Related to
        the Development of Drinking Problems.   Addictive Diseases,
        2(3): 441-448, 1976.

2283.   Lavin, T.J., III.   The Alcohol Problem--More of the Same?
        Journal of the American College Health Association, 29:
        96-99, 1980.

2284.   Lawrence, E.A.   Teenage Alcoholism.   California Highway
        Patrolman, 40(8): 22-23, 82-83, 1976.

2285.   Lawrence, F.E.   Alcoholism on the College Campus.   Student
        Medicine, 4: 3-12, 1955.

2286.   Lawrence, J.R.   Drug Problems in Australia--An Intoxicated
        Society? (Leading Articles) Medical Journal of
        Australia, 65(2): 94-95, 1978.

2287.   Lawrence, T.S. and Velleman, J.D.   Correlates of Student Drug Use
        in a Suburban High School.   Psychiatry, 37(2): 129-136,
        1974.

2288. Laws in the U.S., A.D. 1903, Relating to Compulsory Instruction in Schools in Physiology and Hygiene with a Special Reference to the Effects of Alcoholic Drinks and Narcotics on the Human System. Bulletin of the American Academy of Medicine, 6: 635-637, 1904.

2289. Lawton, J.J., Jr. and Malmquist, C.P. Gasoline Addiction in Children. Psychiatric Quarterly, 35: 555-556, 1961.

2290. Laycock, S.R. Is Alcohol Education a Mental Hygiene Problem? Understanding the Child, 17: 89-91, 1948.

2291. Lazar, J.C. and Lazar, J. Youthful Drunk Drivers: A Mushrooming Crisis. Proceedings of the American Association of Automotive Medicine, 20: 52-59, 1976.

2292. Leake, R. and Pearce, J. Knowledge about, Attitudes toward, and Use or Non-Use of Drugs by Utah Secondary School Students. Doctoral Dissertation (University Microfilms No. 74-21245). University of Utah, 1974.

2293. Learning about Alcohol. Pamphlet. Washington, D.C.: Narcotics Education, no date.

2294. Learning to be a Drinker. British Medical Journal, 1: 309-310, 1973.

2295. Leary, Stephanie. In Defense of Alcoholism Counseling for the Family. Alcoholism, 1(2): 47-48, 1980.

2296. LeCroy, M.B. Alcohol and School Problems. Leaflet. Evanston, Illinois: Signal Press, 1972.

2297. Leczenie i Rehabilitacja Mlodocianych Alkoholikow. I. Stan Swiadczen dla Alkoholikow w Finlandii. (Treatment and Rehabilitation of Adolescent Alcoholics. I. The Health Sevice System for Alcoholics in Finland.) Problemy Alkoholizmu, Warsaw, 27(1): 19-21, 1980.

2298. Ledwidge, L. At the End of the Bottle: A Disturbing Account of the Alcoholic Parents' Effect on Children. ALK Organization, 1977.

2299. Lee, Betty Lou. Young Drinkers Provide Sobering Thoughts. The Journal, 1: 1, 3, 1974.

2300. Lee, E.E. The Counselor's Role in Alcohol Education Programs. The School Counselor, 23(4): 289-292, 1976.

2301. Lee, E.E. Female Adolescent Drinking Behavior: Potential Hazards. Journal of School Health, 48: 151-156, 1978.

2302. Lee, Essie E. Alcohol Education and the Elementary School
           Teacher. Journal of School Health, 46(5): 271-272, 1976.

2303. Lee, Essie E. Alcohol - Proof of What?. New York: Julian
           Messner, 1976.

2304. Lee, Essie E., Fishman, Ross and Shimmel, Gilbert M. Emerging
           Trends of Alcohol Use and Abuse Among Teenagers. New
           York: Hunter College, School of Health Sciences, 1975.

2305. Lee, Essie E. and Israel, Elaine. Alcohol and You. New York:
           Julian Messner, 1975.

2306. Lee, J.P. What Shall We Tell Our Children about Drinking?
           Pamphlet. New York: National Council on Alcoholism, no
           date.

2307. Lee, P.D.K. and Latta, R.J. Adolescent Alcohol Abuse in Hawaii.
           Hawaii Medical Journal, 36: 11-15, 1977.

2308. Leech, K. and Jordan, B. Drugs for Young People: Their Use and
           Misuse. Oxford: Religious Education Press, 1967.

2309. Lefkowitz, L.J. A Reponse to Substance Abuse in New York State.
           Journal of Drug Issues, 8: 247-254, 1978.

2310. Lehman, Walter. A Unique Method of Therapy for the Adolescent
           Drug User. In: Papers Presented at the Fifth
           International Institute on the Prevention and Treatment of
           Drug Dependence, Copenhagen, Denmark, Volume II, July,
           1974. Lausanne, Switzerland: International Council on
           Alcohol and Addictions, 1974, pages 355-360.

2311. Lehmann, W.X. The Devastating Effects of Alcohol Being Noted in
           Teenagers of Today. In: International Congress on
           Alcoholism and Drug Dependence, February 23-28, 1975,
           31st. Volume III. Proceedings. Eds. B. Blair, V. Pawlak,
           E. Tongue and C. Zwicky. Lausanne: International Council
           on Alcohol and Addictions, 1975, pages 516-618.

2312. Leiker, Louise. More Young Hit the Bottle. Buffalo Courier
           Express, no pages, October 26, 1974.

2313. Leite, E. To Be Somebody. Center City, Minnesota: Hazelden,
           1979.

2314. Leite, E. When Daddy's a Drunk--What to Tell the Kids.
           Pamphlet. Center City, Minnesota: Hazelden, 1979.

2315. LeMay, M. College Disciplinary Referrals for Drinking.
           Quarterly Journal of Studies on Alcohol, 29: 939-942, 1968.

2316.   Lemere, F., Voegtlin, W.L., Broz, W.R., O'Hollaren, P. and
        Tupper, W.E. Heredity as an Etiologic Factor in Chronic
        Alcoholism. Northwest Medicine, 42: 101-111, 1943.

2317.   Lenartowicz, Z. and Piekarski, W. Psychoterapia Nieletnich
        Przestepców-Alkoholików. (Psychotherapy of Alcoholic
        Juvenile Delinquents.) Problemy Alkoholizmu, Warsaw,
        25(2): 18-19, 1978.

2318.   Lender, Mark E. The Role of History in Early Alcohol Education:
        The Impact of the Temperance Movement. Journal of Alcohol
        and Drug Education, 23(1): 56-62, 1977.

2319.   Lento, A.G. Drugs, Drugs, Drugs: A Workbook. Albany, New York:
        CASDA--Capital Area School Development Association, State
        University of New York at Albany, 1977.

2320.   Lento, A.G. Teaching about the Nature and Abuse of Alcohol,
        Drugs and Tobacco. (Second Edition) Albany, New York:
        CASDA--Capital Area School Development Association, State
        University of New York at Albany, 1978.

2321.   Leon, Jeffrey. Trends in Drug Use Among Young People in Oshawa:
        Prevalence and Responses. Canada's Mental Health, 25(3):
        6-10, 1977.

2322.   Leopold, D. Alkoholdelikte und Lebensalter. (Alcohol-Related
        Crimes and Age.) Alcoholism, Zagreb, 10(1-2): 3-12, 1974.

2323.   Leowski, J. and Korczak, C.W. Problem Alkoholizmu w Szkolach
        Warszawskich. (Problems of Alcoholism in the Schools of
        Warsaw.) Roczniki Panstwawego Zaklad Higieny, Warsaw,
        17: 127-132, 1966.

2324.   Leowski, J., Saplis-Krasowska, L. and Korczak, C.W. Spozycie
        Alkoholu Przez Mlodziez Szkolna Województwa Warszawskiego.
        (Alcohol Drinking by School Children in the Provice of
        Warsaw.) Zdrowie, 79: 153-159, 1968.

2325.   Leowski, J., Saplis-Krasowska, L. and Korczak, C.W. Warunki
        Spoleczno Bytowe a Czestość Picia Napojów Alkoholowych
        Przez Mlodziez, Szkolna Województwa Warszawskiego.
        (Socioeconomic Conditions and the Frequency of Alcohol
        Drinking among School Children in the Provice of Warsaw.)
        Zdrowie, 79: 161-167, 1968.

2326.   Lerer, L. and Miller, S.M. Area Alcohol Education and Training
        Program Evaluation. Volume 1. Summary Findings and
        Recommendations. (Prepared for the U.S. National Institute
        on Alcohol Abuse and Alcoholism. Rep. No. PB-267-130.)
        Springfield, Virginia: National Technical Information
        Service, 1977.

2327. Lerner, A. Some Fundamentals of Alcohol and Drug Education.
        Health Education Journal, 17(4): 14, 23, 1954.

2328. Lerner, Richard M. Adolescent Development: Scientific Study
        in the 1980s. Youth and Society, 12(3): 251-275, 1981.

2329. Lerner, S. and Linder, R. Birth Order and Polydrug Abuse among
        Heroin Addicts. Journal of Drug Education, 5(3): 285-
        291, 1975.

2330. Lerner, S.E. and Burns, R.S. Youthful Pencyclidine (PCP) Users.
        In: Youth Drug Abuse: Problems, Issues and Treatment.
        Eds. G.M. Beschner and A.S. Friedman. Lexington,
        Massachusetts: D.C. Heath, 1979, pages 315-352.

2331. Lerner, S.E. and Linder, R.L. Drugs in the Elementary School.
        Journal of Drug Education, 4(3): 317-322, 1974.

2332. Lerner, S.E., Linder, R.L. and Burke, E.M. Drugs in the Junior
        High Schools. Journal of Psychedelic Drugs, 6(1): 51-56,
        1974.

2333. Lerner, S.E., Linder, R.L. and Drolet, J.C. Drugs in the High
        School. Journal of Drug Education, 4: 187-195, 1974.

2334. Leroy, D. Young People and Alcohol: The 'Youth Factor' in
        Road Accidents. Journal of Alcoholism, 9(1): 14-17, 1974.

2335. Lester, D. and Beck, A.T. Age Differences in Patterns of
        Attempted Suicide. Omega, 5: 317-322, 1974.

2336. Lettieri, Dan, Ed. Predicting Adolescent Drug Abuse: A Review
        of Issues, Methods and Correlates--Research Issues II.
        Rockville, Maryland: National Institute on Drug Abuse,
        1975.

2337. Leukefled, G.C. and Clayton, R.R. Drug Abuse and Delinquency:
        A Study of Youths in Treatment. In: Youth Drug Abuse:
        Problems, Issues and Treatment. Eds. G.M. Beschner and
        A.S. Friedman. Lexington, Massachusetts: D.C. Heath,
        1979, pages 213-227.

2338. Levanthal, H. An Analysis of the Influence of Alcoholic
        Beverage Advertising on Drinking Customs. In: Alcohol
        Education for Classroom and Community: A Source Book for
        Educators. Ed. R.G. McCarthy. New York: McGraw-Hill,
        1964, pages 267-297.

2339. Leven, R. and Vandre, V. A California Study of Relationships
        between Drinking and Crime. Police, 6(1): 18-21, 1961.

2340. Levine, Carol. When Alcoholism is a Family Problem. Parents Magazine and Better Family Living, 46(2): 75-106, 1971.

2341. Levine, Edward M. and Kozak, Conrad. Drug and Alcohol Use, Delinquency and Vandalism among Upper Middle Class Pre- and Adolescents. Journal of Youth and Adolescence, 8(1): 91-101, 1979.

2342. Levy, C.M. and Murphy, P.H. The Effects of Alcohol on Semantic and Phonetographic Generalization. Psychonomic Science Section on Human Experimental Psychology, 4: 205-206, 1966.

2343. Levy, Dave. Interview with Senator Howard Hughes. Alcoholism, 1(2): 6-9, 1980.

2344. Levy, Jerrold E. and Kunitz, Stephen J. Economic and Political Factors Inhibiting the Use of Basic Research Findings in Indian Alcoholism Programs. Journal of Studies on Alcohol, Supplement No. 9, 60-72, 1981.

2345. Levy, Marc. Community-Wide Prevention Strategies. In: Drug Abuse: Modern Trends, Issues and Perspectives. Proceedings of the Second National Drug Abuse Conference, Inc., New Orleans, Louisiana, 1975. Comp.: A. Schecter, H. Alksne and E. Kaufman. New York: Marcel Dekker, Inc., 1978, pages 1003-1011.

2346. Levy, Susan and Rasher, Sue Pinzur. Relationship of Intensity and Frequency of Student Drug Use to Reasons for Use. Journal of School Health, 51(5): 341-346, 1981.

2347. Lévy-Leboyer, C. and Moser, G. Les Motivations à ne pas Boire: Étude Comparative d'un Groupe de Buveurs et d'un Groupe de Non-Buveurs. (Reasons for Not Drinking: Comparative Study of a Group of Drinkers and a Group of Abstainers.) Toxicomanies, Quebec, 11: 103-122, 1978.

2348. Lewis, A.P.R. Alcohol and Abnormal Behavior in Head Injury Cases. British Journal of Addiction, 45: 15-38, 1948.

2349. Lewis, A.P.R. Alcohol as an Alleged Cause of Loss of Memory in Young Delinquents. British Journal of Inebriety, 42: 21-43, 1944.

2350. Lewis, David C. Drug Abuse Education: Principles and Practices. Toward Relevant Drug Education: A Personalized Approach. In: Resource Book for Drug Abuse Education (2nd Edition). Rockville, Maryland: National Clearinghouse for Drug Abuse Information, 1972, pages 63-66.

2351.   Lewis, David C.   Drug Education.   The Bulletin of the National
        Association of Secondary School Principals, 53(341): 87-
        98, 1969.

2352.   Lewis, P.C. and Rayner, K.G.   The Changing Scene: Dieting,
        Vitamins, Analgesics, Alcohol, Smoking in Hobart Secondary
        School Students.   Medical Journal of Australia, Sydney,
        65(2): 632-635, 1978.

2353.   Lewis, Pat.   Addicts at a Younger Age.   The Washington Evening
        Star and Daily News, (Now Section): 8-9, August 3, 1974.

2354.   Lewis, Pat.   From the Joint to the Jug.   The Washington Star-
        News: 8, August 11, 1973.

2355.   Lewis, Peter W. and Patterson, David W.   Acute and Chronic
        Effects of the Voluntary Inhalation of Certain Commercial
        Volatile Solvents by Juveniles.   Journal of Drug Issues,
        4: 162-175, 1975.

2356.   Lewis-Steere, Cindy, with Ewing, Ronelle.   ...But I Didn't Make
        Any Noise About It.   Pamphlet.   Minneapolis, Minnesota:
        CompCare Publications, 1981.

2357.   Lewke, L., Keller, M. and Palter, T.   Alcohol Education in Texas.
        Health Education, 6(2): 7-8, 1975.

2358.   Lex, Barbara.   Introduction: The Recreation and Social Use of
        Dependency-Producing Drugs in Diverse Social and Cultural
        Contexts.   Journal of Drug Issues, 10: 159-164, 1980.

2359.   Ley, H.A., Jr.   The Incidence of Smoking and Drinking Among
        10,000 Examinees.   Proceedings of the Life Extension
        Examinations, 2: 57-63, 1940.

2360.   Liberty Mutual Insurance Company.   Teen Drinkers: New Hazard in
        Highway Crisis.   Boston, Massachusetts, 1973.   (DOT
        Publication No. HS-013-824)

2361.   Licensed Beverage Industries, Inc.   Accurate and Unbiased
        Information about Alcohol Beverages is Essential to the
        Total Education of Youth.   New York, no date.

2362.   Licensed Beverage Industries, Inc.   Alcoholic Beverages: Their
        Effects on the Individual and Their Role in Society.   New
        York, no date.

2363.   Licensed Beverage Industries, Inc.   A Digest of State Laws and
        Available Materials in the Field of Alcohol Education and
        of the Educational Responsibilities and Activities of
        State Commissions on Alcoholism.   Paper.   New York, 1959.

2364. Licensed Beverage Industries, Inc. A Digest of State Laws and Available Materials in the Field of Alcohol Education and of the Educational Responsibilities and Activities of State Commissions on Alcoholism. New York, 1960.

2365. Licensed Beverage Industries, Inc. If You Choose To Drink, Drink Responsibly (Second Edition). New York: Distilled Spirits Council of the United States, Inc., 1973. (Third Edition, 1974).

2366. Licensed Beverage Industries, Inc. State Programs on Alcoholism and Their Relationships to Programs of Alcohol Education in Publicly Supported Schools. New York, 1957.

2367. Licensed Beverage Industries. Women's Division. No One Answer. Pamphlet. New York, 1965.

2368. Lichko, A. Ye., Aleksandrov, A.A., Vdovichenko, A.A., Ivanov, N. Ya. and Ozeretskovskii, S.D. Podrostki s Povyshennym Riskom Alkogolizatsii: K Probleme Psikhoprofilaktiki Alkogolizma. (Alcohol-Endangered Adolescents: The Problem of Psychological Prophylaxis in Alcoholism.) Trudy Leningradskii Nauchno-Issedovatelskii Psikhoneverologicheskii Institut Im. V. M. Bekhterva, Leningrad, 84: 50-54, 1977.

2369. Lichtman, G. Alcohol: Facts for Decisions. Pamphlet. Syracuse, New York: New Readers Press, 1974.

2370. Lieberman, F., Caroff, P. and Gottesfeld, M. Before Addiction: How to Help Youth. New York: Behavioral Publications, 1973.

2371. Lied, Erik R. and Marlatt, G. Alan. Modeling as a Determinant of Alcohol Consumption: Effects of Subject Sex and Prior Drinking History. Addictive Behaviors, 4: 47-54, 1979.

2372. Liepman, Michael R. Some Theoretical Connections between Family Violence and Substance Abuse. The Catalyst, 1(3): 37-42, 1980.

2373. Light, P.K. Let the Children Speak: A Psychological Study of Young Teenagers and Drugs. Lexington, Massachusetts, D.C. Heath, 1975.

2374. Lille, Mildred, L. Drinking and Domestic Relations. In: Toward Prevention: Scientific Studies on Alcohol and Alcoholism. Washington, D.C.: Narcotics Education, Inc., 1971, pages 97-105.

2375. Linck, K. Alter, Letale Dosis und Blutalkoholbefunde bei der
       Tödlichen Aethylalkoholvergiftung. (Age, Lethal Dosage
       and Blood Alcohol in Fatal Ethyl Alcohol Poisoning.)
       Medizinische Klinik, 45: 570-572, 1950.

2376. Lind, L. and Krabill, W. Alcohol and Your Life. Pamphlet.
       Scottsdale, Pennsylvania: Mennonite Publishing House,
       1963.

2377. Lindbeck, V.L. The Woman Alcoholic: A Review of the Literature.
       International Journal of the Addictions, 7(3): 567-580,
       1972.

2378. Lindelius, R. and Salum, I. Alcoholism and Crime: A Comparative
       Study of Three Groups of Alcoholics. Journal of Studies on
       Alcohol, 36(11): 1452-1457, 1975.

2379. Lindelius, R. and Salum, I. Alcoholism and Criminality.   Acta
       Psychiatrica Scandinavica, 49(3): 306-314, 1973.

2380. Linden, A.V. A Preliminary Evaluation of the Materials Suggested
       for Alcohol Education Found in Available Syllabi Prepared
       by Public School Systems in the United States. AAAIN
       Newsletter, 5(3): 3-19, 1959.

2381. Linden, A.V. and Macero, F.D. An Analysis of Available Syllabi
       Used for Alcohol Education in the Public Schools of the
       United States. Journal of School Health, 28: 166-171,
       1958.

2382. Linden, Arthur V. What is Being Done About Alcohol Education?
       The Journal of School Health, 27: 291-302, 1957.

2383. Linder, R.L. and Lerner, S.E. Birth Order and Psychoactive Drug
       Use among Students. Drug Forum, 5(1): 1-3, 1975-1976.

2384. Linder, R.L. and Lerner, S.E. Self-Medication and the Only
       Child. Journal of Drug Education, 2(4): 361-370, 1972.

2385. Linder, R.L., Lerner, S.E. and Burke, E.M. Drugs in the Junior
       High School. Journal of Psychedelic Drugs, 6(1): 43-49,
       1974.

2386. Linder, R.L., Lerner, S.E. and Drolet, J.C. Drug Use by Students
       of Drug Abuse. Journal of Drug Education, 3(3): 309-314,
       1973.

2387. Lindgren, A. Some Results from an International Series of
       Drinking Surveys. The Drinking and Drug Practices
       Surveyor, 8: 34-45, 1973.

2388. Link, A.D. Alcohol and Drugs: Their Use and Abuse by South
       Carolina Public School Students. Columbia, South Carolina,
       1973.

2389. Lint, J.D.E. and Schmidt, W. Mortality from Liver Cirrhosis and
       Other Causes in Alcoholics: A Follow-Up Study of Patients
       with and without a History of Enlarged Fatty Liver.
       Quarterly Journal of Studies on Alcohol, 31(3): 705-709,
       1970.

2390. Liong-A-Kong, H.P. Kort Onderzoek naar Misdragingen Surinamers
       en Antillainen. (A Brief Study of Delinquency in Natives
       of Surinam and the Netherlands Antilles.) Maanderschrift
       Gevangeniswezen, 18: 6-15, 1966.

2391. Lipscomb, W.R. Drug Use in a Black Ghetto. American Journal of
       Psychiatry, 127(9): 1166-1169, 1971.

2392. Lipscomb, W.R. and Holden, J. Risk of Being Labeled "Alcoholic":
       Significance of Psychiatric Status and Nationality. In:
       Sociological Aspects of Drug Dependence. Ed. C. Winick.
       Cleveland, Ohio: Chemical Rubber Company, 1974, pages 15-
       34.

2393. Lipton, Douglas S., Stephens, Richard C., Babst, Dean V.,
       Dembo, Richard, Diamond, Sharon C., Spielman, Carol R.,
       Schmeidler, James, Bergman, Phyllis and Uppal, Gopal S.
       A Survey of Substance Use among Junior and Senior High
       School Students in New York State, Winter 1974-75.
       American Journal of Drug and Alcohol Abuse, 4(20): 153-164,
       1977.

2394. Lipton, Douglas S., Stephens, Richard, Kaestner, Elisabeth,
       Diamond, Sharon and Spielman, Carol. Current Problems in
       Large Scale Drug Abuse Surveys. In: Drug Abuse: Modern
       Trends, Issues and Perspectives. Proceedings of the
       Second National Drug Abuse Conference, Inc., New Orleans,
       Louisiana, 1975. Compiled by: A. Schecter, H. Alksne and
       E. Kaufman. New York: Marcel Dekker, Inc., 1978, pages
       16-24.

2395. Lipton, H.R. The Prevention of Alcoholism. Alcohol Hygiene,
       1(5): 19-21, 1945.

2396. Liptow, W. Das Alkoholbehinderte Kind. (The Alcohol-Impeded
       Child.) Hamburg: Neuland-Verglasgesellschaft, 1977.
       (Also as: Das "Alkoholbehinderte" Kind. [The Alcohol-
       Handicapped Child.] In: Papers presented at the 23rd
       International Institute on the Prevention and Treatment of
       Alcoholism, Dresden, June 6-10, 1977. Eds. E.J. Tongue and
       I. Moos. Lausanne: International Council on Alcohol and
       Addictions, 1977, pages 240-252.)

2397. Liquor Licensing and Public Health. British Medical Journal,
          4(5841): 625-626, 1972.

2398. Lisansky, Edith S. Alcoholism in Women: Social and
          Psychological Concomitants. I. Social History Data.
          Quarterly Journal of Studies on Alcohol, 18: 588-662, 1957.

2399. Lisansky, Edith S. The Woman Alcoholic. The Annals of the
          American Academy of Political and Social Science, 315:
          73-81, 1958.

2400. Lisansky-Gomberg, E.S. Etiology of Alcoholism. Journal of
          Consulting and Clinical Psychology, 32: 18-20, 1968.

2401. Listiak, Alan. "Legitimate Deviance" and Social Class: Bar
          Behavior During Grey Cup Week. Sociological Focus, 7(3):
          13-44, 1974.

2402. Litt, I.F. and Schonberg, S.K. Medical Complications of Drug
          Abuse in Adolescents. Medical Clinics of North America,
          59: 1445-1452, 1975.

2403. Little, K. Survival for Youth in a Cocktail Culture. In:
          First International Action Conference on Substance Abuse,
          November 9-13, 1977, Volume I. Alcohol: Use and Abuse.
          Phoenix, Arizona: Do It Now Foundation, 1979, pages 9-19.

2404. Little, Kent. Options--A Program of Alcohol/Substance Education
          and Abuse Prevention. In: Papers Presented at the 25th
          International Institute on the Prevention and Treatment
          of Alcoholism, Tours, France, June, 1979. Lausanne,
          Switzerland: International Council on Alcohol and
          Addictions, 1979, pages 28-35.

2405. Littman, G. Alcoholism, Illness and Social Pathology among
          American Indians in Transition. American Journal of
          Public Health, 60(9): 1769-1787, 1970.

2406. Littunen, Y. Opintoympäristön Vaikutus Korkeakouluopiskelussa.
          (The Influence of Academic Environment in University
          Students.) Masters Thesis. Suomey Ylioppilaskuntien
          Liitto, 1956.

2407. Livitnov, P.N. Osobennosti Kliniki i Techeniya Alkogolizma v
          Molodom Vozraste. (Peculiarities in the Clinical
          Development of Alcoholism in Young Adults.) Trudy
          Moskovskago Nauchno-Issledovatel'skogo Instituta
          Psikhiatrii, USSR, 53: 19-32, 1968.

2408.   Logewall, B. Alkoholfrågan Studieobjekt i Skolklasser: Försök
        Med Integrerad Undervisning om Alkohol, Tobak, Narkotika i
        Västerås. (The Alcohol Question Subject for Study in
        Class: Experiment with Integrated Alcohol, Tobacco and
        Narcotics Study in Vasteras.) Alkoholfragan, 62: 147-150,
        1968.

2409.   Lolli, G. Alcoholism and Obesity Both Problems of Hunger.
        Connecticut Review of Alcoholism, 5: 1, 3-4, 1953.

2410.   Lolli, G. Alcoholism in Women. Connecticut Review of
        Alcoholism, 5: 9-11, 1953.

2411.   Lolli, G. Assets Outweigh Liabilities. International Journal of
        Psychiatry, 9: 358-368, 1970-71.

2412.   Lolli, G. Tuned In or Turned Off: A Noted Physician Addresses
        Youth on Sex, Drugs, Alcohol and Tobacco. New York: Lion
        Press, 1969.

2413.   Lolli, G. La Mujer Alcohólica. (The Alcoholic Woman.) Día
        Médico, 25: 969-975, 1953.

2414.   Lolli, G., Serianni, E., Golder, G., Mariani, A. and Toner, M.
        Relationship between Intake of Carbohydrate-Rich Foods and
        Intake of Wine and Other Alcoholic Beverages. A Study
        among Italians and Americans of Italian Extraction.
        Quarterly Journal of Studies on Alcohol, 13: 401-420, 1952.

2415.   Lolli, Giorgio. The Addictive Drinker. In: An Outline of
        Abnormal Psychology. Eds. Gardner Murphy and
        Arthur J. Bachrach. New York: Random House, 1954, pages
        295-310.

2416.   Lolli, Giorgio, Serianni, Emidio, Golder, Grace M. and
        Luzzatto-Fegiz, Pierpaolo. Alcohol in Italian Culture.
        Food and Wine in Relation to Sobriety Among Italians and
        Italian Americans. (Monographs of the Yale Center of
        Alcohol Studies, No. 3.) New Haven, Connecticut:
        Publications Division, Yale Center of Alcohol Studies and
        Glencoe, Illinois: Free Press, 1958.

2417.   Lomask, M. First Report on High-School Drinking. Better Homes
        and Gardens, no pages, March, 1954.

2418.   London, J. John Barleycorn. New York: Greenwood, 1968.

2419.   Loney, Jan. The Iowa Theory of Substance Abuse Among Hyperactive
        Adolescents. In: Theories on Drug Abuse: Selected
        Contemporary Problems. (Research Monograph Series 30)
        U.S. National Institute on Drug Abuse. Eds. Dan Lettieri,
        Mollie Sayers and Helen Pearson. Rockville, Maryland,
        1980, pages 132-136.

2420. Longclaws, Lyle, Barnes, Gordon E., Grieve, Linda and
          Dumoff, Ron. Alcohol and Drug Use Among the Brokenhead
          Ojibwa. Journal of Studies on Alcohol, 41(1): 21-36, 1980.

2421. A Look at a New Teachers' Guide. Journal of Alcohol Education,
          13(1): 29-36, 1967.

2422. Looney, J., Oldham, D. and Blotcky, M. Assessing Psychologic
          Symptoms in Adolescents. Southern Medical Journal, 71:
          1197-1202, 1978.

2423. Looney, M.A. Alcohol Use Survey on Campus: Implications for
          Health Education. Journal of the American College Health
          Association, 25: 109-112, 1976.

2424. Loper, R.G., Kammeier, M.L. and Hoffman, H. MMPI Characteristics
          of College Freshman Males Who Later Become Alcoholics.
          Journal of Abnormal Psychology, 82: 159-162, 1973.

2425. Lopuski, J. Od Najmłodzych Lat: Jak Ustrzec Dziecko Przed
          Alkoholem, 2nd Edition. (From the Earliest Age: How to
          Guard a Child from Alcohol.) Warszawa: Panstwowy Zaklad
          Wydawn. Lekarskich, 1972.

2426. Los Angeles County Department of Health Services. Nature and
          Scope of Alcoholism and/or Drug Addiction and Serious
          Substance Abuse Involving Minors. Los Angeles, California,
          1975.

2427. Losciuto, L. and Karlin, R. Correlates of the Generation Gap.
          Journal of Psychology, 81: 253-262, 1972.

2428. Lourie, R.S. Alcoholism in Children. American Journal of
          Orthopsychiatry, 13: 322-338, 1943.

2429. Love, Harold D. Youth and the Drug Problem: A Guide for
          Parents and Teachers. Springfield, Illinois:
          Charles C. Thomas, 1971.

2430. Lowe, G.D., Hodges, H.E. and Johnson, A.B. Deaths Associated
          with Alcohol in Georgia, 1970. Quarterly Journal of
          Studies on Alcohol, 35(1): 215-220, 1974.

2431. Lower Alcohol Content, Eliminating Advertising "More Realistic
          Approach". The Journal, 1(2): 1, 5, 1972.

2432. Lowering of Canadian Drinking Age: Quarterly Notes. Journal of
          Alcoholism, 11(1): 6, 1976.

2433. Lubotskaja-Rossel's, E.M. Alkogol' i Deti. (Alcohol and Youth.)
          Moskva: Meditsina, 1965.

2434. Lucero, R.J., Jensen, K.F. and Ramsey, C. Alcoholism and
       Teetotalism in Blood Relatives of Abstaining Alcoholics.
       Quarterly Journal of Studies on Alcohol, 32(1-A): 183-185,
       1971.

2435. Ludi, G.F. A Research Documentary Report: Third Quarter and
       A Research Documentary Report: Fourth Quarter. Santa Fe,
       New Mexico: Le Fe Youth Hostel, 1975.

2436. Ludwig, A.M., Wikler, A. and Stark, L.H. The First Drink:
       Psychobiological Aspects of Craving. In: Emerging
       Concepts of Alcohol Dependence. Eds. E.M. Pattison,
       M.B. Sobell and L.C. Sobell. New York: Springer, 1977,
       pages 71-95.

2437. Ludwig, S. Quellen des Alkoholmissbrauchs Jugendlicher Werden
       Energisch Bekämpf. (Vigorous Campaigns Against Sources
       of Juvenile Alcohol Abuse.) Forum Kriminalogie, Berlin,
       4: 169, 1968.

2438. Lukáči, J., Kardosóvá, V. and Halušková, A. Etylizmus detí a
       Mládeže. (Alcoholism in Children and Youth.)
       Protialkoholicy Obzor, Bratislava, 9: 158-160, 1974.

2439. Lukaszkiewicz, Z. Niepelnoletni Jako Przedmiot Przestepstwa z
       Art. 24 Ustawy o Zwalczaniu Alkoholizmu. (Offenses by
       Juveniles Under Article 24 of the Law for Combating
       Alcoholism.) Nowe Prawo, Warsaw, 19: 1022-1027, 1963.

2440. Lund, C.A. and Landesman-Dwyer, S. Pre-Delinquent and Disturbed
       Adolescents: The Role of Parental Alcoholism. In:
       Currents in Alcoholism. Volume 5. Biomedical Issues and
       Clinical Effects of Alcoholism. Ed. M. Galanter. New
       York: Grune and Stratton, 1979, pages 339-348.

2441. Lund, D. The Relation Between the Alcoholism of Parents and the
       Moral Degeneration of the Children. Tirfing: 77-83, 1920.

2442. Lundin, R.W. and Sawyer, C.R. The Relationship Between Test
       Anxiety, Drinking Patterns and Scholastic Achievement in a
       Group of Undergraduate College Men. The Journal of General
       Psychology, 73: 143-146, 1965.

2443. Lundquist, G.A. Alcohol Dependence. Acta Psychiatrica
       Scandinavica, 49(3): 332-340, 1973.

2444. Lüpke, H. von, Mebs, D. and Gerchow, J. Weitere Untersuchungen
       Zur Alkoholbedingten Delinquenz Jugendlicher und
       Heranwachsender. (Additional Studies on Alcohol-Related
       Delinquency in Youth and Adolescence.) Suchtgefahren,
       Hamburg, 24: 59-62, 1978.

2445. Lusby, E.P.   The Social Adjustment of High School Problem
            Drinkers in a Mississippi Community.   Master's Thesis.
            Mississippi State University, 1969.

2446. Lustig, B.   Über Alkoholismusprobleme in Sowjetischer und
            Europäischer Sicht.   (Problems of Alcoholism in Soviet and
            European Views.)   Wiener Medizinische Wochenschrift, 115:
            400-403, 1965.

2447. Lutheran Church.   Commission on Research and Social Action.
            Alcohol Problems--In Bits or as One?   Pamphlet.   Columbus,
            Ohio, 1968.

2448. Lyles, J.S.   Youth and Alcoholic Beverages.   Pamphlet.   Richmond,
            Virginia: John Knox, 1966.

M

2449. Maas, P. La Juenesse et l'Antialcoolisme. (Youth and Anti-Alcoholism.) International Congress Against Alcoholism, 19: 132-133, 1930.

2450. Maas, Paula, Shaffer, Gary P., Oliaro, Paul and Alderink, Jerry J. Alcohol Education on the College Campus: Coping with Change. The Catalyst, 1(2): 66-75, 1980.

2451. McAlister, Alfred, Perry, Cheryl, Killen, Joel, Slinkard, Lee Ann and Maccoby, Nathan. Pilot Study of Smoking, Alcohol and Drug Abuse Prevention. American Journal of Public Health, 70(7): 719-721, 1980.

2452. MacAndrew, C. Evidence for the Presence of Two Fundamentally Different, Age-Independent Characteriological Types Within Unselected Runs of Male Alcohol and Drug Abusers. American Journal of Drug and Alcohol Abuse, 6(2): 207-221, 1979.

2453. MacAndrew, C. On the Possibility of the Psychometric Detection of Persons who are Prone to the Abuse of Alcohol and Other Substances. Addictive Behaviors, 4: 11-20, 1979.

2454. McCabe, T.R. Victims No More. Center City, Minnesota: Hazelden, 1978.

2455. McCall, A.B. Whiskey and Clay Poultice in Snake-Bite. Medical Standard, 3: 100-101, 1888.

2456. McCarthy, R.G. Alcohol and the Adolescent. Journal of School Health, 30(3): 99-106, 1960.

2457. McCarthy, R.G., Ed. Alcohol Education for Classroom and Community: A Source Book for Educators. New York: McGraw Hill, 1964.

2458. McCarthy, R.G. Drinking and Intoxication. Glencoe, Illinois:
           Free Press, 1959.

2459. McCarthy, R.G. Drinking Patterns in the United States. In:
           Alcohol Education for Classroom and Community: A Source
           Book for Educators. Ed. R.G. McCarthy. New York:
           McGraw-Hill, 1964, pages 125-131.

2460. McCarthy, R.G. Drinking Practices in High School. In:
           Drinking and Intoxication. Ed. R.G. McCarthy. Glencoe,
           Illinois: Free Press, 1959.

2461. McCarthy, R.G. The Fellowship of Alcoholics Anonymous:
           Alcoholism in Industry. In: Alcohol Education for
           Classroom and Community. A Source Book for Educators.
           Ed. R.G. McCarthy. New York: McGraw-Hill, 1964, pages
           226-240.

2462. McCarthy, R.G. Teenagers and Alcohol: A Handbook for the
           Educator. New Haven, Connecticut: Publications Division,
           Yale Center of Alcohol Studies, 1956.

2463. McCarthy, R.G. and Douglass, E.M. Alcohol and Social
           Responsibility. New York: Thomas Y. Crowell and Yale
           Plan Clinic, 1949.

2464. McCarthy, R.G. and Douglass, E.M. Instruction on Alcohol
           Problems in the Public Schools. Quarterly Journal of
           Studies on Alcohol, 8: 609-635, 1948.

2465. McCarthy, Raymond. Summary of a Conference. In: Interpreting
           Current Knowledge About Alcohol and Alcoholism to a
           College Community. Proceedings of a Conference, May 28-
           30, 1963, Albany, New York. Ed. Richard Reynolds.
           Albany, New York: New York State Department of Mental
           Health, 1963, pages 74-79.

2466. McCarthy, Raymond G. Alcoholism, 1941-1951: A Survey of
           Activities in Research, Education and Therapy: Activities
           of State Department of Education Concerning Instruction
           about Alcohol. Quarterly Journal of Studies on Alcohol,
           13: 496-511, 1952.

2467. McCarthy, Raymond. High School Drinking Studies. In: Drinking
           and Intoxication: Selected Readings in Social Attitudes
           and Controls. Ed. Raymond G. McCarthy. New Haven,
           Connecticut: College and University Press, 1959, pages
           205-209.

2468. McCarthy, Raymond G., Ed. Drinking and Intoxication: Selected
           Readings in Social Attitudes and Controls. New Haven,
           Connecticut: College and University Press, 1959.

2469.   McCarthy, Raymond G. Exploring Alcohol Questions. New Haven,
          Connecticut: Yale Center of Alcohol Studies, 1956. (Also
          as: Pamphlet. New Brunswick, New Jersey: Rutgers Center
          of Alcohol Studies, 1970.)

2470.   McCarthy, Raymond G. Facts About Alcohol. Chicago, Illinois:
          Science Research Associates, 1951.

2471.   McCarthy, Raymond G. Instructor's Guide to "Facts about
          Alcohol". Chicago, Illinois: Science Research Associates,
          1951.

2472.   McCleary, R.D Child Alcoholism as Seen by the School in
          Illinois. International Journal of Offender Therapy and
          Comparative Criminology, 18(2): 182-186, 1974.

2473.   McClelland, D.C. The Power of Positive Drinking. Psychology
          Today, 4(8): 40-41, 78-79, 1971.

2474.   McClelland, D.C., Davis, W.N., Kalin, R. and Wanner, E., Eds.
          The Drinking Man. New York: The Free Press, 1972.

2475.   McClelland, David C. Examining the Research Basis for
          Alternative Explanations of Alcoholism. In: The
          Drinking Man. Eds. D.C. McClelland, W.N. Davis, R. Kalin
          and E. Wanner. New York: The Free Press, 1972, pages
          276-315.

2476.   McClintock, F.H. Criminological Aspects of Family Violence. In:
          Violence and the Family. Ed. J.P. Martin. New York:
          Wiley, 1978, pages 89-101.

2477.   McCluggage, M.M. and Baur, E.J. Attitudes Toward Use of
          Alcoholic Beverages: A Survey among High School Students
          in the Wichita Metropolitan Area and in the Non-
          Metropolitan Counties of Eastern Kansas. New York: The
          Mrs. John S. Sheppard Foundation, 1956.

2478.   McCluggage, Martin M., Baur, E. Jackson, Warriner, Charles and
          Clark, Carroll D. Summary of Essential Findings in the
          Kansas Study. In: Drinking and Intoxication: Selected
          Readings in Social Attitudes and Controls. Ed.
          Raymond G. McCarthy. New Haven, Connecticut: College and
          University Press, 1959, pages 211-219.

2479.   Maccoby, Michael. Alcoholism in a Mexican Village. In: The
          Drinking Man. Eds. D.C. McClelland, W.N. Davis, R. Kalin
          and E. Wanner. New York: The Free Press, 1972, pages
          217-231.

2480.   McConnell, J.T. More Myths About Drinking. Pamphlet. Lansing:
        Michigan Alcohol Education Foundation, 1969.

2481.   McConnell, John T. Issues in Alcohol Education. International
        Journal of Health Education, 12: 148-152, 1969. (Also as:
        Issues in Alcohol Education. Pamphlet. Lansing:
        Michigan Department of Public Health,1969.)

2482.   McCord, J. Alcoholism and Criminality: Confounding and
        Differentiating Factors. Journal of Studies on Alcohol,
        42: 739-748, 1981.

2483.   McCord, J. Etiological Factors in Alcoholism: Family and
        Personal Characteristics. Quarterly Journal of Studies on
        Alcohol, 33: 1020-1027, 1972.

2484.   McCord, J. Some Differences in Background of Alcoholics and
        Criminals. Annals of the New York Academy of Sciences,
        197: 183-187, 1972.

2485.   McCord, Joan and McCord, William. The Effects of Parental Role
        Model on Criminality. In: Readings in Juvenile
        Delinquency. Ed. R. Cavan. New York: J.B. Lippincott,
        1969, pages 176-186.

2486.   McCord, W. and McCord, J. Origins of Alcoholism. Stanford,
        California: Stanford University Press, 1960.

2487.   McCord, W., McCord, J. and Gudeman, J. Some Current Theories of
        Alcoholism: A Longitudinal Evaluation. Quarterly Journal
        of Studies on Alcohol, 20: 727-749, 1956.

2488.   McCord, William and McCord, Joan. A Longitudinal Study of the
        Personality of Alcoholics. In: Society, Culture and
        Drinking Patterns. Eds. D.J. Pittmann and C.R. Snyder.
        New York: Wiley, 1962, pages 413-430.

2489.   McCoy, Clyde B. and Watkins, Virginia McCoy. Drug Use Among
        Urban Ethnic Youth: Appalachian and Other Comparisons.
        Youth and Society, 12(1): 83-106, 1980.

2490.   McCracken, K. Alcohol Top Drug Problem in Minnesota. The
        Journal, 2(9): 12, 1973.

2491.   McCune, Donald. Drug Education in California. In: Drug Use in
        America: Problems in Perspective. Appendix. Volume II.
        Social Responses to Drug Use. U.S. National Commission on
        Marihuana and Drug Abuse. Washington, D.C.: U.S.
        Government Printing Office, 1973, pages 402-410.

2492.   McDaniel, R. Reference Group Influence on the Drinking Behavior
        of High School Students. Master's Thesis. Mississippi
        State University, 1965.

2493.   McDole, T.L., Pelz, D.C. and Schuman, S.S. Drinking and Age in
        Crashes Involving Youthful Drivers. Paper Presented at
        APHA Centennial Annual Meeting, Atlantic City, New Jersey,
        November 15, 1972.

2494.   MacDonald, A.P., Jr., Walls, R.T. and LeBlanc, R. College Female
        Drug Users. Adolescence, 8(30): 189-196, 1973.

2495.   MacDonald, Don. Startling Rise in Accidents - Researcher Blames
        Lower Drinking Age. The Chronicle Herald: 1-2, 1974.

2496.   McDonough, J. Irvin. A Guide to the Study of "Basic Information
        on Alcohol". Washington: TEM Press, no date.

2497.   McDuffie, Marjorie. A Way Back for Alcoholics. Christian
        Century, 90(1): 29-30, 1973.

2498.   McElfresch, O. Supportive Groups for Teenagers of the Alcoholic
        Patient: A Preliminary Report. Medical Ecology and
        Clinical Research, 3(1): 26-29, 1970.

2499.   McEwen, W.J. and Hanneman, G. The Depiction of Drug Use in
        Television Programming. Journal of Drug Education, 4:
        281-294, 1974.

2500.   McFadden, M. and Wechsler, H. Minimum Drinking Age Laws and
        Teenage Drinking. Psychiatric Opinion, 16(3): 22-23, 26-
        28, 1979.

2501.   McGeorge, J. Alcohol and Crime. Medicine, Science and the Law,
        3: 27-48, 1963.

2502.   McGerigle, P. Drugs and Alcohol and Their Effects on Health and
        Behavior. Boston, Massachusetts: Massachusetts Committee
        on Children and Youth, 1971. (NCALI Report NCAI 014211)

2503.   McGlothlin, W.H., Jamison, K. and Rosenblatt, S. Marijuana and
        the Use of Other Drugs. Nature, 228(5877): 1227-1229,
        1970.

2504.   McGlynn, B.M. Annotated Bibliography of Publications with
        General Relevance in the Area of Alcohol and Driving
        Research. (Rep. No. 47) State College, Mississippi:
        Mississippi State University Social Science Research
        Center, 1975.

2505.   McGuffin, S.J. Drinking Patterns of Young People in Northern
        Ireland. Ulster Medical Journal, 48: 160-165, 1979.

2506.   McIntosh, W.A., Fitch, S.D., Staggs, F.M., Jr. Nyberg, K.L. and
        Wilson, J.B. Age and Drug Use by Rural and Urban
        Adolescents. Journal of Drug Education, 9: 129-143, 1979.

2507.   MacKay, J.R.   Alcohol, Alcoholism and Youth.   Social Work, 10:
           75-80, 1965.   (Also in: New Hampshire Bulletin on
           Alcoholism, 14(2): 1965.)

2508.   MacKay, J.R.   Clinical Observations on Adolescent Problem
           Drinkers.   Quarterly Journal of Studies on Alcohol, 22:
           124-134, 1961.

2509.   MacKay, J.R.   Problem Drinking among Juvenile Delinquents.
           Crime and Delinquency, 9(1): 29-38, 1963.   (Also as:
           Problem Drinking among Juvenile Delinquents.   In: Crime
           in America.   Ed. B. Cohen.   Itasca, Illinois:
           F.E. Peacock, 1970, pages 197-202.

2510.   MacKay, J.R., Murray, A.E., Hagerty, T.J. and Collins, L.J.
           Juvenile Delinquency and Drinking Behavior.   Journal of
           Health and Human Behavior, 4(4): 276-282, 1963.

2511.   MacKay, J.R., Phillips, D.L. and Bryce, F.O.   Drinking Behavior
           among Teenagers: A Comparison of Institutionalized Youth.
           Journal of Health and Social Behavior, 8(1): 46-54, 1967.

2512.   MacKay, J.R., Phillips, D.L. and Bryce, F.O.   Drinking Behavior
           among Teenagers: A Comparison of Institutionalized and
           Non-Institutionalized Youth in New Hampshire.   Journal of
           Alcohol Education: 20-22, 1967.

2513.   McKechnie, R.J.   Parents, Children and Learning to Drink.   In:
           International Conference on Alcoholism and Drug Dependence:
           Alcoholism and Drug Dependence, a Multidisciplinary
           Approach.   Proceedings of the Third International
           Conference on Alcoholism and Drug Dependence, Liverpool,
           England, 1976.   Eds. J.S. Madden, Robin Walker and
           W.H. Kenyon.   New York: Plenum Press, 1977, pages 451-456.

2514.   McKechnie, R.J., Cameron, D., Cameron, I.A. and Drewery, J.
           Teenage Drinking in South-West Scotland.   British Journal
           of Addiction, 72(4): 287-295, 1977.

2515.   MacKenzie, R.G.   A Practical Approach to the Drug-Using
           Adolescent and Young Adult.   Pediatric Clinics of North
           America, 20(4): 1035-1045, 1973.

2516.   Mackerath, F.G.   The Drinking Child.   Lancet, 177: 414, 1909.
           (Also in: British Medical Journal, 2: 352, 1909.)

2517.   McKillip, J., Johnson, J.E. and Petzel, T.P.   Patterns and
           Correlates of Drug Use among Urban High School Students.
           Journal of Drug Education, 3(1): 1-12, 1973.

2518.   McKim, W.A.   Childhood Consciousness Altering Behavior and Adult
           Drug Taking.   Journal of Psychedelic Drugs, 9(2): 159-163,
           1977.

2519.   McKinley, R.A. and Moorhead, H.H.   Alcoholism.   Progress in
           Neurology and Psychiatry, 22: 459-468, 1967.

2520.   McLachlan, J.F.C., Walderman, R.L. and Thomas, S.   A Study of
           Teenagers with Alcoholic Parents.   (Monograph No. 3)
           Toronto, Canada: Donwood Institute, 1973.

2521.   McLeod, J.H. and Grizzle, G.A.   Alcohol and Other Drug Usage
           among Junior and Senior High School Students in Charlotte-
           Mecklenburg.   Charlotte, North Carolina, 1972.

2522.   McLeod, J.H. and McGuire, J.D.   Revisited: Alcohol and Other
           Drug Usage among Junior and Senior High School Students in
           Charlotte-Mecklenburg.   A Comparison of Three Surveys.
           Charlotte, North Carolina, 1975.

2523.   McLeod, W.R.   Alcoholism: The Drug Problem of the 1970's.   New
           Zealand Medical Journal, 79(507): 597-601, 1974.

2524.   McManus, John.   Some Applications of the Levinian Model to
           Community Mental Health: A Program of Differential
           Treatment and Research.   In: Differential Treatment of
           Drug and Alcohol Abusers.   Eds. C.S. Davis and
           M.R. Schmidt.   Palm Springs, California: ETC Publications,
           1977, pages 26-44.

2525.   Macnab, A.   Alcohol Education.   In: International Congress on
           Alcoholism and Drug Dependence, February 23-28, 1975,
           31st. Volume III.   Proceedings.   Eds. B. Blair,
           V. Pawlak, E. Tongue and Z. Zwicky.   Lausanne,
           Switzerland: International Council on Alcohol and
           Addictions, 1975, pages 72-74.

2526.   McNally, W.D.   Alcohol and Education.   Industrial Medical
           Surgery, 19: 67-68, 1950.

2527.   MacNicholl, T.A.   Alcohol and the Disabilities of School
           Children.   Journal of the American Medical Association,
           48: 396-398, 1907.

2528.   MacNicholl, T.A.   A Medical Study of the Effects of Alcohol on
           School Children.   New England Medical Monthly, 24: 305-307,
           1905. (Also in: Quarterly Journal of Inebriety, 27: 113-
           117, 1905.)

2529.   McPeek, F.W.   Youth, Alcohol and Delinquency.   Quarterly Journal
           of Studies on Alcohol, 4: 568-579, 1944.

2530.   McPherson, Kenard. Youth Alcohol Safety Education Curriculum
        for the Secondary School. Springfield, Virginia:
        National Technical Information Service, 1976.

2531.   Madden, J.S. Suggestions to a Regional Council on Alcoholism.
        Journal of Alcoholism, 11(4): 118-122, 1976.

2532.   Madden, J.S., Walker, R. and Kenyon, W.H., Eds. International
        Conference on Alcoholism and Drug Dependence: Alcoholism
        and Drug Dependence, A Multi-Disciplinary Approach.
        Proceedings of the Third International Conference on
        Alcoholism and Drug Dependence, Liverpool, England, April,
        1976. New York: Plenum Press, 1977.

2533.   Maddox, G.L. Adolescence and Alcohol. In: Alcohol Education
        for Classroom and Community: A Source Book for Educators.
        Ed. R.G. McCarthy. New York: McGraw-Hill, 1964, pages
        32-47.

2534.   Maddox, G.L. Alcohol Education: Clues from Research. In:
        Alcohol Education. U.S. Department of Health, Education
        and Welfare. Secretary's Committee on Alcoholism.
        Washington, D.C.: U.S. Government Printing Office, 1967,
        pages 20-24.

2535.   Maddox, G.L. Childhood and Alcohol: Some Roots of
        Pathological Drinking Behavior. In: Community Factors
        in Alcohol Education, 2nd Conference on Alcohol Education.
        Stowe, Vermont: October 16-18, 1961, pages 16-26.

2536.   Maddox, G.L. The Domesticated Drug: Drinking among Collegians.
        New Haven, Connecticut: College and University Press,
        1970.

2537.   Maddox, G.L. Drinking among Negroes: Inferences from the
        Drinking Patterns of Selected Negro Male Collegians.
        Journal of Health and Social Behavior, 9(2): 114-120, 1968.

2538.   Maddox, G.L. Drinking and Abstinence: Emergent Patterns among
        Selected Negro Freshmen. In: The Domesticated Drug:
        Drinking among Collegians. Ed. G.L. Maddox. New Haven,
        Connecticut: College and University Press, 1970, pages
        146-175.

2539.   Maddox, G.L. Drinking in High School. Pamphlet. New Brunswick:
        Rutgers Center of Alcohol Studies, 1958.

2540.   Maddox, G.L. Drinking in High School: An Interpretative
        Summary. A.A.I.A.N. Newsletter, 4(3): 3-14, 1958.

2541.   Maddox, G.L.   Drinking Prior to College.   In: The Domesticated
        Drug: Drinking among Collegians.   Ed. G.L. Maddox.   New
        Haven, Connecticut: College and University Press, 1970,
        pages 107-120.

2542.   Maddox, G.L.   High-School Student Drinking Behavior: Incidental
        Information from Two National Surveys.   Quarterly Journal
        of Studies on Alcohol, 25: 339-347, 1964.

2543.   Maddox, G.L.   Research Relating to Alcohol Education: A Review
        and Some Suggestions.   Selected Papers Presented at the
        Fifteenth Annual Meeting of the North American Association
        of Alcoholism Programs, 1964.   Washington, D.C.:   North
        American Association of Alcoholism Programs, 1964, pages
        29-45.

2544.   Maddox, G.L.   Role-Making: Negotiations in Emergent Drinking
        Careers.   Social Science Quarterly, 49(2): 331-349, 1968.

2545.   Maddox, G.L.   A Study of High School Drinking: A Sociological
        Analysis of a Symbolic Act.   Doctoral Dissertation
        (University Microfilms No. 57-2607).   Michigan State
        University, 1956.

2546.   Maddox, G.L.   Teenage Drinking and Planned Social Change.   In:
        Alcohol Education: What Does a Teacher Need to Know to
        Teach? Conference on Alcohol Education, Stowe, Vermont:
        October 14-16, 1959, pages 36-52.

2547.   Maddox, G.L.   Teenage Drinking in the United States.   In:
        Society, Culture and Drinking Patterns.   Eds. D.J. Pittman
        and C.R. Snyder.   New York: Wiley, 1962, pages 230-245.

2548.   Maddox, G.L.   Teenagers and Alcohol: Recent Research.   Annals
        of the New York Academy of Science, 133: 856-865, 1966.

2549.   Maddox, G.L. and Borinski, E.   Drinking Behavior of Negro
        Collegians: A Study of Selected Men.   Quarterly Journal of
        Studies on Alcohol, 25: 651-668, 1964.

2550.   Maddox, G.L. and McCall, B.C.   Drinking among Teenagers: A
        Sociological Interpretation of Alcohol Use by High-School
        Students.   New Brunswick, New Jersey: Rutgers Center of
        Alcohol Studies, 1964.

2551.   Maddox, G.L. and Williams, J.R.   Drinking Behavior of Negro
        Collegians.   Quarterly Journal of Studies on Alcohol, 29:
        117-129, 1968.

2552.   Maddox, George L. and Allen, Bernice.   A Comparative Study of
        Social Definitions of Alcohol and Its Uses among Selected
        Male Negro and White Undergraduates.   Quarterly Journal of
        Studies on Alcohol, 22: 418-427, 1961.

2553. Madeddu, A. and Malagoli, G. Drug Dependence in Italy: Some
         Statistical, Clinical and Social Observations. Bulletin
         on Narcotics, 22(4): 1-11, 1970.

2554. Mader, R. [Alcoholism in Adolescent Criminals: A Comparative
         Study, 1965-66 - 1969-70.] Acta Paedopsychiatrica, Basel,
         39(1): 2-11, 1972.

2555. Madsbad, S. Er Forekomsten af Alkoholisk Levercirrose hos Yngre
         Stigende? (Is the Incidence of Alcoholic Liver Cirrhosis
         in Young People Increasing?) Ugeskrift for Laeger,
         Copenhagen, 139: 1648-1650, 1977.

2556. Maida, P.R. Parent-Peer Group Relationships and Teenage Drug
         Use. Rockville, Maryland: National Institute of Mental
         Health, 1973.

2557. Mail, P.D. and McDonald, D.R. Tulapai to Tokay: A Bibliography
         of Alcohol Use and Abuse among Native Americans of North
         America. New Haven, Connecticut: HRAF Press, 1980.

2558. Maisto, S.A. and Rachal, J.V. Indications of the Relationship
         among Adolescent Drinking Practices, Related Behaviors,
         and Drinking-Age Laws. In: Minimum-Drinking-Age Laws.
         Ed. H. Wechsler. Lexington, Massachusetts: D.C. Heath
         and Co., 1980, pages 155-176.

2559. Maisto, Stephen, Connors, Gerard and Sobell, Mark. Effect of
         Instructional and Physiological Variables on Preference
         for Alcohol. International Journal of the Addictions,
         16(1): 89-96, 1981.

2560. Majewska, A. Recydywa Mlodych w Izbie Wytrzezwien. (Relapses of
         the Young in the Sobering-Up Station.) Problemy
         Alkoholizmu, Warsaw, 16(6): 1-2, 1968.

2561. Major, A. and Krajcsovics, P. Alkoholgenuss der Kinder und
         Jugendlichen in Ungarn. (Alcohol Consumption among
         Children and Adolescents in Hungary.) Beitraege zur
         Gerichtlichen Medizin, 32: 132-135, 1974.

2562. Majundar, Mahbubon and Bhatia, Pritam. Effective Family Position
         and Likelihood of Becoming an Alcoholic. Journal of
         Alcohol and Drug Education, 25(2): 19-31, 1980.

2563. Makela, Klaus. Consumption Levels and Cultural Drinking Patterns
         as Determinants of Alcohol Problems. Journal of Drug
         Issues, 5: 344-357, 1975.

2564. Malfetti, J.L., Simon, K.J. and Horner, M.M. AL-CO-HOL for
         Junior High School. Falls Church, Virginia: American
         Automobile Association, 1978.

2565.   Malfetti, James L. and Stewart, Ernest I. DWI Profiles. In:
        Drunken Driving: The Twelve Hours Before Arrest and What
        to Do About Them. New York: Teachers College, Columbia
        University, 1973, pages 111-135.

2566.   Malhotra, M.K. Alkohol bei Schülern im Kreis Mettmann. (Alcohol
        among Students in the Mettmann Region.) Öffentliche
        Gesundheitsweson, Stuttgart, 38: 226-245, 1976.

2567.   Malhotra, M.K. Rauschmittelkonsumenten im Urteil der
        Gymnasiasten. (Consumers of Intoxicating Substances as
        Seen by High School Students.) Suchtgefahren, Hamburg,
        24: 49-58, 1978.

2568.   Malignac, G. Délinquance Juvénile et Alcoolisme. (Juvenile
        Delinquency and Alcoholism.) Rééducation, 8(53): 27-31,
        1954.

2569.   Mallory, Aileen. Pop Wines - More Than Soda Pop. Listen, 28(6):
        6-7, 1975.

2570.   Mally, M.A. A Study in Family Patterns of Alcoholic Marriages.
        American Journal of Orthopsychiatry, 35: 325-326, 1965.

2571.   Maloff, Deborah, Becker, Howard, Funaroff, Arlene and
        Rodin, Judith. Informal Social Controls and Their
        Influence on Substance Abuse. Journal of Drug Issues,
        9(2): 161-184, 1979.

2572.   Maloney, S.K. A Guide to Alcohol Programs for Youth. Rockville,
        Maryland: National Clearinghouse for Alcohol Information/
        National Institute on Alcohol Abuse and Alcoholism, 1976.

2573.   Malzberg, B. Statistical Study of the Prevalence and Types of
        Mental Disease among Children and Adolescents.
        Psychiatric Quarterly, 5: 511-537, 1931.

2574.   Mandell, W. Youthful Drinking. Staten Island, New York:
        Wakoff Research Center, 1962.

2575.   Mandell, W., Cooper, A., Silberstein, R.M., Novick, J. and
        Koloski, E. Youthful Drinking: New York State 1962.
        Staten Island, New York: Wakoff Research Center, Staten
        Island Mental Health Society, 1963.

2576.   Mandell, Wallace and Ginzburg, Harold. Youthful Alcohol Use,
        Abuse and Alcoholism. In: The Biology of Alcoholism.
        Volume 4. Social Aspects of Alcoholism. Eds. B. Kissin
        and H. Begleiter. New York: Plenum Press, 1976, pages
        167-204.

2577. Mandlová, I. and Hádlík, J.   Abuzus Alkoholu u Mladistvych v
        Jihomoravskem Kraji.   (Alcohol Abuse among Youths in
        Southern Moravia.)   Protialkoholicky Obzor, Bratislava, 7
        3-9, 1972.

2578. Mandlová, I. and Viewegh, J.   Akutní Alkoholické Intoxikace u
        Dětí Vyšetřovaných po Časovém Odstupu.   (A Follow-Up
        Investigation of Acute Alcohol Intoxication in Children.)
        Psychologia a Patopsychologia Dietata, Bratislava, 3: 65-
        81, 1967.

2579. Manitoba Department of Education.   A Manual of Alcohol Studies
        for Schools.   Regina, Saskatchewan: The Saskatchewan Book
        Bureau, 1951.

2580. Manitoba Minister of Education.   Teaching Guide for Alcohol
        Education in the Secondary Schools.   Pamphlet.   Winnipeg,
        Manitoba, 1966.

2581. Mann, Marty.   Marty Mann Answers Your Questions about Drinking
        and Alcoholism.   New York: Holt, Rinehart and Winston,
        1970.

2582. Mannello, Timothy.   Primary Prevention Education.   Journal of
        Alcohol and Drug Education, 24(1): 39-57, 1978.

2583. Manning, William O. and Vinton, Jean.   Harmfully Involved.
        Center City, Minnesota: Hazelden Literature, 1978.

2584. Mantere, O.U.   The Renewal of Abstinence Teaching in Higher
        Schools.   Alkoholikysymys, Helsinki, 14: 101-115, 1946.

2585. Marden, P.G. and Kolodner, K.   Alcohol Abuse among Women: Some
        Differences and Their Implications for the Delivery of
        Services.   Prepared for the Special Treatment and
        Rehabilitation Programs, National Institute on Alcohol
        Abuse and Alcoholism.   (Report No. PB 295633)   Springfield,
        Virginia: U.S. National Technical Information Service,
        1979.

2586. Marden, P.G. and Kolodner, K.   Alcohol Use and Abuse among
        Adolescents.   Appleton, Wisconsin: St. Lawrence
        University, 1976.

2587. Marden, Philip, Zylman, Richard, Fillmore, Kay Middleton and
        Bacon, Selden D.   Comments on "A National Study of
        Adolescent Drinking Behavior, Attitudes and Correlates."
        Journal of Studies on Alcohol, 37(9): 1346-1358, 1976.

2588. Mareček, Josef.   Alkoholismus a Škola.   (Alcoholism in School.)
        Mariánske Lázně: Protialkoholní Poradnu OUNZ, 1956.

2589. Marek, Z., Widacki, J. and Zwarysiewicz, W.   Suicides Committed
          by Minors. Forensic Science, 7: 103-108, 1976.

2590. Margulies, Rebecca Z., Kessler, Ronald C. and Kandel, Denise B.
          A Longitudinal Study of Onset of Drinking among High School
          Students. Journal of Studies on Alcohol, 38(5): 897-912,
          1977.

2591. Marin, Gerardo. Social-Psychological Correlates of Drug Use
          among Colombian University Students. International
          Journal of the Addictions, 11: 199-207, 1976.

2592. Markell, W.A. Alcohol Abuse Prevention through Group Work with
          Elementary Age Children and Their Families. In:
          Proceedings of the Fourth Annual Alcoholism Conference of
          the National Institute on Alcoholism and Alcohol Abuse.
          Ed. M. Chafetz. Rockville, Maryland, 1975, pages 470-475.

2593. Marketing, Sales Promotions Keyed to Youth Market as Wine Sales
          Boom across U.S. Report on Alcohol, 33(1): 29-36, 1975.

2594. Marković, B. Prijedlog za Proučavanje Alkoholizma Kod Nas.
          (An Approach to the Study of Alcoholism in Yugoslavia.)
          Higijena, Beograd, 4: 184-190, 1952.

2595. Markovic, Bodizar. Principles of Health Education Underlying
          Education of Alcoholism. Quarterly Journal of Studies on
          Alcohol, 15: 631-642, 1952.

2596. Marlatt, G.A. Training Responsible Drinking with College
          Students. Paper presented at the Annual Convention of the
          American Psychological Association, Chicago, September,
          1975.

2597. Marlatt, G.A., Kosturn, C.F. and Lang, A.R. Provocation to
          Anger and Opportunity for Retaliation as Determinants of
          Alcohol Consumption in Social Drinkers. Journal of
          Abnormal Psychology, 84: 652-659, 1975.

2598. Marsden, Dennis. Sociological Perspectives on Family Violence.
          In: Violence in the Family. Ed. J.P. Martin. New York:
          Wiley, 1978, pages 103-133.

2599. Marshall, M. The Politics of Prohibition on Namoluk Atoll.
          Journal of Studies on Alcohol, 36(5): 597-610, 1975.

2600. Marshall, M. Weekend Warriors: Alcohol in a Micronesian
          Culture. Palo Alto, California: Mayfield, 1979.

2601. Marshall, S. Young, Sober and Free. Center City, Minnesota:
          Hazelden, 1978.

2602.   Martin, B.   Juvenile Liquor Arrests are Up.   Montgomery County
          Sentinel, November 15, 1973.

2603.   Martin, Felix.   Effects of Grade Level and Sex Upon Self-Reported
          Delinquency and Drug Usage.   Peabody Journal of Education,
          53: 115-120, 1976.

2604.   Martin, J.   Alcohol and the Family: Three Sure Ways to Solve
          the Problem.   Liguori, Missouri: Liguori Publications,
          1978.

2605.   Martin, J.P.   Family Violence and Social Policy.   In: Violence
          and the Family.   Ed. J.P. Martin.   New York: Wiley,
          1978, pages 199-254.

2606.   Martin, J.P., Ed.   Violence and the Family.   New York: Wiley,
          1978.

2607.   Martin, Roger D.   Reduction of Adolescent Drug Abuse through
          Post-hypnotic Cue Association.   Conseiller Canadien, 8(3):
          211-216, 1974.

2608.   Martindale, D.A. and Martindale, E.   The Social Dimensions of
          Mental Illness, Alcoholism and Drug Dependence.   Westport,
          Connecticut: Greenwood, 1971.

2609.   Maryland Department of Education.   ASAP Curriculum.   Baltimore,
          Maryland, 1972-1973.

2610.   Maryland Department of Health and Mental Hygiene.   Special
          Report on Alcohol Usage from the 1973 Survey of Drug Abuse
          among Adolescents.   Baltimore, Maryland, 1974.

2611.   Mascalo, Alison.   The Role of the College Counselor in Alcohol
          Abuse Counseling and Education.   Journal of Alcohol and
          Drug Education, 24(3): 52-55, 1979.

2612.   Mason, P.   Mortality among Young Narcotic Addicts.   Journal of
          Mount Sinai Hospital, 34: 4-10, 1967.

2613.   Massachusetts Department of Education.   Health Education
          Curriculum Guide, Grades 1-12.   Boston, Massachusetts,
          1971, 1972.

2614.   Massachusetts, University.   Summary of Alcohol Task Force Report:
          1974-1975.   Amherst, Massachusetts, 1975.

2615.   Mass-Observation.   Mass-Observation Report on Juvenile Drinking.
          London: Livesey-Clegg Youth Club, 1943.

2616.   Masten, F.   Missouri Acts to Reduce Teen Drinking and Driving.
          Traffic Safety,79(2): 16, 28, 1979.

2617.   Masten, F.L.   The Effects of a Three-Day Mini-Course on
            Knowledge and Attitudes about Drinking and Driving of High
            School Driver Education Students.   Doctoral Dissertation
            (University Microfilms No. 791-8414).   University of
            Missouri-Kansas City, 1979.

2618.   Matějček, Z.   Výzkum Dětí z Rodin Alkoholiků.   (Study of
            Children from Families of Alcoholics.)   Protialkoholicky
            Obzor, Bratislava, 13: 201-205, 1978.

2619.   Mathews, Jay.   Alcohol Making Strong Comeback.   The Washington
            Post, : A1, A3, June 11, 1973.

2620.   Matross, R., Brown, J. and Seaburg, D.   The Drinking Practices
            of Students at the University of Minnesota.   Minneapolis:
            University of Minnesota, Office for Student Affairs,
            August, 1974.   (ERIC Document Reproduction Service No. ED
            098 453)

2621.   Matthew, E.   The Alcohol Problem in Relation to Child-Life.
            British Journal of Inebriety, 4: 203-209, 1907.

2622.   Matthews, M.   Adolescent Home School for the Alcoholic and Poly-
            Drug User in Delaware.   In: Proceedings of the 31st
            International Congress on Alcoholism and Drug Dependence,
            Bangkok, Thailand: February 23-28, 1975.   Lausanne,
            Switzerland: International Council on Alcohol and
            Addictions, 1975, pages 519-521.

2623.   Matz, R., Christodoulou, J., Vianna, N. and Ruwitch, J.   Renal
            Tubular Dysfunction Associated with Alcoholism and Liver
            Disease.   New York State Journal of Medicine, 69(10):
            1312-1314, 1969.

2624.   Mauss, A.L. and Hopkins, R.H.   A Manual of Evaluation Guidelines
            for "Here's Looking at You":   A Model Program in Alcohol
            Education.   Prepared for National Institute on Alcohol
            Abuse and Alcoholism.   (PB 80-210560.)   Springfield,
            Virginia: National Technical Information Service, 1979.

2625.   Maust, Robert N.   Legal Implications of Alcoholic Beverages on
            the College Campus.   The Catalyst, 1(2): 59-65, 1980.

2626.   May, Gerald and Baker, William.   Human Environmental Factors in
            Alcohol-Related Traffic Accidents.   In: Alcohol, Drugs
            and Traffic Safety.   Proceedings of the Sixth International
            Conference on Alcohol, Drugs and Traffic Safety, Toronto,
            September 8-13, 1974.   Eds. S. Israelstam and S. Lambert.
            Toronto, Ontario: Addiction Research Foundation of
            Ontario, 1975, pages 129-145.

2627.   May, J. Drinking in a Rhodesian African Township. Salisbury:
            University of Rhodesia, Institute for Social Research,
            1973.

2628.   May, M. Violence in the Family: An Historical Perspective. In:
            Violence and the Family. Ed. J.P. Martin. New York:
            Wiley, 1978, pages 135-167.

2629.   Mayer, J.E. The Personality Characteristics of Adolescents Who
            Use and Misuse Alcohol. Doctoral Dissertation (University
            Microfilms No. 7927404). Northeastern University, 1979.

2630.   Mayer, J. and Black, R. An Investigation of the Relationship
            Between Substance Abuse and Child Abuse and Neglect.
            Boston, Massachusetts: National Center on Child Abuse and
            Neglect, 1975.

2631.   Mayer, John and Filstead, William J. The Adolescent Alcohol
            Involvement Scale. Journal of Studies on Alcohol, 40(3):
            291-300, 1979.

2632.   Mayer, John and Filstead, William J. The Adolescent Alcohol
            Involvement Scale: An Instrument for Measuring Adolescent
            Use and Misuse of Alcohol. In: Currents in Alcoholism.
            Volume 7. Recent Advances in Research and Treatment. Ed.
            M. Galanter. New York: Grune and Stratton, 1980, pages
            169-181.

2633.   Mayer, John E. Adolescent Alcohol Misuse: A Family Systems
            Perspective. Journal of Alcohol and Drug Education, 26(1):
            1-11, 1980.

2634.   Mayer, John E. and Filstead, William J., Eds. Adolescence and
            Alcohol. Cambridge, Massachusetts: Ballinger Publishing
            Company, 1980.

2635.   Mayer, John E. and Filstead, William J. Adolescence and Alcohol:
            A Theoretical Model. In: Adolescence and Alcohol. Eds.
            J.E. Mayer and W.J. Filstead. Cambridge, Massachusetts:
            Ballinger, 1980, pages 151-164.

2636.   Mayer, John E. and Filstead, William J. Empirical Procedures for
            Defining Adolescent Alcohol Misuse. In: Adolescence and
            Alcohol. Eds. J.E. Mayer and W.J. Filstead. Cambridge,
            Massachusetts: Ballinger, 1980, pages 51-68.

2637.   Mayer, Joseph and Black, Rebecca. Child Abuse and Neglect in
            Families with an Alcohol or Opiate Addicted Parent.
            Boston, Massachusetts: Washingtonian Center for
            Addictions, 1976.

2638. Mayer, Joseph and Black, Rebecca. The Relationship between
       Alcoholism and Child Abuse/Neglect. Paper presented at
       the 7th Annual Medical-Scientific Session of the National
       Alcoholism Forum, Washington, D.C., May 7, 1976.

2639. Mayer, Joseph and Black, Rebecca. The Relationship between
       Alcoholism and Child Abuse and Neglect. In: Currents in
       Alcoholism. Volume 2. Psychiatric, Psychological, Social
       and Epidemiological Studies. Ed. F.A. Seixas. New York:
       Grune and Stratton, 1977, pages 429-444.

2640. Mayer, Joseph, Black, Rebecca and MacDonall, James. Child Care
       in Families with an Alcohol-Addicted Parent. In:
       Currents in Alcoholism. Volume 4. Psychiatric,
       Psychological, Social and Epidemiological Studies. Ed.
       F.A. Seixas. New York: Grune and Stratton, 1978, pages
       329-338.

2641. Mazel, P., Girard, P.F. and Bourret, J. Trois Aspects Médico-
       Légaux du Problème de l'Alcoolisme. Délinquance Juvénile
       et Alcoolisme; Pathologie des Prisons et Alcoolisme;
       Accidents de la Rue et Alcoolisme. (Three Medical-Legal
       Aspects of Alcoholism. Juvenile Delinquency and
       Alcoholism; Prison Pathology and Alcoholism; Street
       Accidents and Alcoholism.) Lyon Medicale, 167: 51-56,
       1942.

2642. Meacher, M. Opening Address to the Conference. In:
       International Conference on Alcoholism and Drug Dependence:
       Alcoholism and Drug Dependence, A Multi-Disciplinary
       Approach. Proceedings of the Third International
       Conference on Alcoholism and Drug Dependence, Liverpool,
       England, April, 1976. Eds. J.S. Madden, Robin Walker and ·
       W.H. Kenyon. New York: Plenum Press, 1977, pages xv-xix.

2643. Means, Richard K. Drug Abuse Education: Many Hands of Help.
       Journal of Alcohol Education, 16(1): 20-27, 1970.

2644. Mebs, D., Lüpke, H. von and Gerchow, J. Alkoholbedingte
       Delinquenz Jugendlicher und Heranwachsender. (Alcohol-
       Related Delinquency of Adolescents and Young Adults.)
       Blutalkohol, Hamburg, 14: 331-345, 1977.

2645. Mecca, Andrew M. Primary Prevention: An Ode to the Future.
       Contemporary Drug Problems, 5(1): 21-27, 1976.

2646. Mečíř, J. Alkoholabusus bei Jugendlichen. (Alcohol Abuse by
       Young People.) Acta Paedopsychiatrica, Basel, 27: 108-112,
       1960.

2647. Mečíř, J. Schopnost Mládeže Rozeznat Netoxikomanické a
Toxikomanické Stadium Rozvoje Alkoholismu. (The Ability of
Young People to Differentiate between Stages of Nonaddicted
and Addicted State in the Development of Alcoholism.)
Československa Psychiatrie, 76: 55-58, 1980.

2648. Mečíř, J. Tisíc Pacientů Protialkoholní Poradny pro Mladistvé v
Praze. (A Thousand Patients from the Alcoholism Clinic
for Youth in Prague.) Českoslavenska Psychiatrie, 72: 41-
44, 1976.

2649. Mečíř, J. Vliv Skupin Mladistvých na Rozvoj Požívání
Alkoholichkých Nápoju Nezletilými. (Effect of the Group
on the Development of Drinking of Alcoholic Beverages by
Minors.) Československa Psychiatrie, 57: 16-21, 1961.

2650. Medhus, A. Conviction for Drunkenness--A Late Symptom among
Female Acoholics. Scandinavian Journal of Social Medicine,
3(1): 23-27, 1975.

2651. Medhus, A. and Hansson, H. Alcohol Problems among Female
Gonorrhoea Patients. Scandinavian Journal of Social
Medicine, 4(3): 141-143, 1976.

2652. Mehl, D. You and the Alcoholic in Your Home. Minneapolis,
Minnesota: Augsburg, 1979.

2653. Mellado-Cot, M.S. Las Drogas en los Colegios: Resumen de
Tesina. (Drugs in the Colleges: Research Summary.)
Drogalcohol, 4: 216-221, 1979.

2654. Melville, Joy. Some Violent Families. In: Violence and the
Family. Ed. J.P. Martin. New York: Wiley, 1978, pages
9-18.

2655. Melville, Joy. Women in Refuges. In: Violence and the Family.
Ed. J.P. Martin. New York: Wiley, 1978, pages 293-309.

2656. Member of the Community of St. Mary the Virgin. The Moral,
Mental and Physical Background of Female Inebriates.
British Journal of Inebriety, 42: 3-20, 1944.

2657. Memphis State University, College of Education, Department of
Special Education and Rehabilitation. Alcohol Abuse
Training Relevant to Minority Populations: Handbook:
Youth. Atlanta, Georgia: Southern Area Alcohol Education
and Training Program, 1977.

2658. Memphis State University, College of Education, Department of
Special Education and Rehabilitation. Alcohol Abuse
Training Relevant to Minority Populations: Trainer
Manual/Trainee Handbook and Pre/Post Test. Atlanta,
Georgia: Southern Area Alcohol Education and Training
Program, 1977.

2659. Memphis State University, College of Education, Department of
       Special Education and Rehabilitation. Youth, Alcohol
       Awareness Training for Health Educators, School
       Counselors, Youth Workers: Trainer/Trainee Manual and
       Pre/Post Test. Atlanta, Georgia: Southern Area Alcohol
       Education and Training Program, 1977.

2660. Mendelsohn, B. and Richards W. Alaskan Native Adolescents'
       Descriptions of their Mental Health Problems. Phoenix,
       Arizona: Paper presented at the Eighth Joint Meeting of
       the Professional Associations of the U.S. Public Health
       Service, May 1973.

2661. Mendelson, J.H. Another Doubtful Prognosis. International
       Journal of Psychiatry, 9: 368-371, 1970-71.

2662. Mendelson, Jack. Some Comments on College Drinking, and,
       Consequently, Alcohol Education. Journal of Alcohol
       Education, 14(2): 16, 1968.

2663. Mendonca, M. de. L'Usage des Boissons Alcooliques chez
       l'Enfant. (Consumption of Alcoholic Beverages by
       Children.) Toxicomanies, Québec, 5: 255-261, 1972.

2664. Meng, R. Psychische Hygiene des Alkoholismus als Psycho-
       Analytisches Problem. (Mental Hygiene of Alcoholism as a
       Psychoanalytic Problem.) Schweizerische Medizinische
       Wochenschrift Journal Suisse de Medecine, Basel, 71: 669-
       672, 1941.

2665. Menninger, W.C. Blueprint for Teenage Living. New York:
       Sterling Publishing, 1958.

2666. Mercer, G.W. A Model of Adolescent Drug Use. Doctoral
       Dissertation. Toronto, Ontario: York University, 1975.

2667. Mercer, G.W., Hundleby, J.D. and Carpenter, R.A. Adolescent
       Drug Use and Attitudes toward the Family. Canadian
       Journal of the Behavioral Science, 10: 79-90, 1978.

2668. Mercer, G.W. and Hundleby, J.D. Patterns of Adolescent Drug Use.
       British Journal of Addictions, 73: 323, 1978.

2669. Mercer, G.W. and Kohn, P.M. Child-Rearing Factors,
       Authoritarianism, Drug Use Attitudes, and Adolescent Drug
       Use: A Model. Journal of Genetic Psychology, 136: 159-
       171, 1980.

2670. Mercuri, G. Alcune Osservazioni su Alcoolismo e Criminalità.
       (Some Observations on Alcoholism and Crime.) Lavoro
       Neuropsychiatrico, Rome, 59(3): 117-123, 1977.

2671.   Merrick, Michael, Blakeley, James L. and Bongiovanni, Shelley.
        Report on Alcohol Use and Abuse of Junior and Senior High
        School Students in Fresno County. Fresno, California:
        Fresno County Health Department, no date.

2672.   Merriman, B. Advertising and Teenage Behaviour. British
        Medical Journal, 1: 1686-1687, 1961.

2673.   Merry, J. Causes and Prevention of Alcohol Abuse. Lancet, 1:
        421, 1973.

2674.   Merton, R.K. and Nisbet, R.A. Contemporary Social Problems,
        2nd Edition. New York: Harcourt, 1966.

2675.   Mésková, H., Mečiř, J. and Pihrtová, S. Otcovský Prvek u
        Chlapců Evidovaných v Protialkoholni Poradně v Praze.
        (On the Fathers of Boys Treated at the Antialcohol Clinic
        in Prague.) Československa Psychiatrie, 74: 402-405,
        1978.

2676.   Metropolitan Atlanta Council on Alcohol and Drugs. Teenage
        Alcohol Abuse. Prepared for Georgia PTA Institute,
        Athens, Georgia, June 10, 1975.

2677.   Metts, W. Deep River. Denver, Colorado: Accent Books, 1978.

2678.   Meyer, M.-L. Counselling Families of Alcoholics. Health
        Visitor, 50: 136-142, 1977.

2679.   Meyer, S.R. and Hookstead, S.A. Characteristics of Adolescent
        Users and Non-Users of Drugs. Journal of Alcohol and Drug
        Education, 21(3): 47-54, 1976.

2680.   Michael, M.M. and Sewall, K.S. Use of the Adolescent Peer Group
        to Increase the Self-Care Agency of Adolescent Alcohol
        Abusers. Nursing Clinic, 15(1): 157-176, 1980.

2681.   Michigan Accidents Skyrocket among Drinking Teenagers.
        Automotive News, (4431): 44, 1973. (Also in: American
        Association of Automotive Medicine Quarterly, (2): 25,
        1973.

2682.   Michigan Board of Alcoholism. Report of Alcoholism Education
        and Clinic Institute (Sponsored by the Michigan State
        Board of Alcoholism, May 14-15, 1956, Michigan Education
        Association Camp, St. Mary's Lake). Lansing, Michigan,
        1956.

2683.   Michigan Congress of Parents, Teachers and Students. Alcohol
        Alley. Chicago, Illinois: National Congress of Parents
        and Teachers, 1977.

2684. Michigan Department of Education. The Age of Majority:
       Guidelines for Local Districts. Lansing, Michigan, 1971.

2685. Michigan Department of Education. A Curriculum Guide on Alcohol
       Education for Teachers, 1970. Pamphlet. Lansing,
       Michigan, 1970.

2686. Michigan Department of Mental Health. Alcohol Education--Whose
       Responsibility? (Proceedings of a Conference, May, 1963,
       sponsored by Michigan Department of Mental Health;
       Michigan Department of Public Instruction; Michigan
       Department of Health; Michigan Congress of Parents and
       Teachers; Michigan State University; Michigan State Board
       of Alcoholism; and U.S. Public Health Service.) Lansing:
       Michigan State Board of Alcoholism, 1963.

2687. Michigan Department of Public Health. Is There Room for Ethyl?
       Pamphlet. Lansing, Michigan, 1963.

2688. Michigan Department of Public Health. Notes on Alcohol
       Education for Teachers. Pamphlet. Lansing, Michigan,
       1970.

2689. Michigan Department of Public Instruction. Education and
       Alcohol. Lansing, Michigan, 1957.

2690. Michigan Department of Public Instruction and State Board of
       Alcoholism. The Teacher's Role in Alcohol Education.
       Pamphlet. Lansing, Michigan, 1958.

2691. Michigan, Ontario Studies Show Lower Legal Drinking Age Affects
       Youthful Drinking Habits, Problems. Report on Alcohol,
       32(4): 30-40, 1974.

2692. Michigan's Office of Substance Abuse Services and Liquor Control
       Commission. Recommendations on Implementation of the
       Raise in Michigan's Legal Drinking Age. The Catalyst,
       1(2): 6-29, 1980.

2693. Michigan's 79th Legislative Regular Session of 1978. Act No. 531
       of Public Acts of 1978. The Catalyst, 1(2): 33-49, 1980.

2694. Michigan's State Police Report on Cost of Legal Drinking at 18.
       The New Jersey Council News, 30(3): 4, 1973.

2695. Mieroslawski, W., Obidzińska, Z. and Zaleska, A. Spożywanie
       Alkoholu Przez Dzieci w Wieku 7-14 Let. (Consumption of
       Alcohol by Children Aged 7-14.) Pediata Polska, Warsaw,
       37: 315-317, 1962.

2696. Mik, G. Sons of Alcoholic Fathers. British Journal of
       Addiction, 65: 305-315, 1970.

2697. Mikes, G. Hazai Komplex Vizgálat az Alkoholizmus Okainak és
        Artalmainak Megismerésére. (A Complex Investigation of
        the Causes and Harmful Effects of Alcoholism in Hungary.)
        Alkohologia, Budapest, 3: 107-111, 1972.

2698. Miketić, B. The Influence of Parental Alcoholism in the
        Development of Mental Disturbances in Children.
        Alcoholism, Zagreb, 8: 135-139, 1972.

2699. Miles, S.A., Ed. Learning about Alcohol: A Resource Book for
        Teachers. Washington, D.C.: American Association for
        Health, Physical Education and Recreation, 1974.

2700. Milgram, G. A Historical Review of Alcohol Education Research
        and Comments. Journal of Alcohol and Drug Education,
        21(2): 1-16, 1976.

2701. Milgram, G. Teenage Drinking and Alcohol Education. New Jersey
        Educational Association Review, 48(3): 24-25, 1974.

2702. Milgram, G.G. Alcohol Education Materials 1973-1978: An
        Annotated Bibliography. New Brunswick, New Jersey:
        Publications Division, Rutgers Center of Alcohol Studies,
        1980.

2703. Milgram, G.G. Comment on "Problem Drinking among Youth: Some
        Observations," by Gerald Globetti, Ph.D. In: Defining
        Adolescent Alcohol Use: Implications toward a Definition
        of Adolescent Alcoholism. Proceedings of a Conference,
        Washington, D.C., 1976. Eds. P.A. O'Gorman,
        S. Stringfield and I. Smith. New York: National Council
        on Alcoholism, 1977.

2704. Milgram, G.G. A Descriptive Analysis of Alcohol Education
        Materials. Journal of Studies on Alcohol, 36:416-421,
        1975.

2705. Milgram, G.G. Student Library Use of Alcohol Education
        Materials. Journal of Alcohol and Drug Education, 20(1):
        1-3, 1974.

2706. Milgram, G.G. Teenage Drinking Behavior and Alcohol Education
        in High School Perceived by Selected Reference Groups.
        Doctoral Dissertation (University Microfilms No. 70-3363).
        Rutgers University, 1969.

2707. Milgram, Gail G. Alcohol Education for Teenagers. In: Alcohol
        Problems among Youth. Proceedings of a Workshop at
        Pittsburgh, Pennsylvania, December 2-3, 1976. Ed.
        Joseph Newman. Pennsylvania: Western Pennsylvania
        Institute of Alcohol Studies, 1977.

2708. Milgram, Gail G. Alcohol Education Materials: An Annotated
        Bibliography. New Brunswick, New Jersey: Publications
        Division of Rutgers Center of Alcohol Studies, 1975.

2709. Milgram, Gail G. Alcohol Education in the Schools Perceived by
        Educators and Students. Journal of Alcohol and Drug
        Education, 20(1): 4-12, 1974.

2710. Milgram, Gail G. A Descriptive Analysis of Alcohol Education
        Materials, 1973-1979. Journal of Studies on Alcohol,
        41(11): 1209-1216, 1980.

2711. Milgram, Gail G. and Pandina, Robert J. Educational Implications
        of Adolescent Substance Use. Journal of Alcohol and Drug
        Education, 26(3): 13-22, 1981.

2712. Milgram, Gail Gleason. Analysis of Alcohol Education Curriculum
        Guides. New Brunswick, New Jersey: Center of Alcohol
        Studies, Rutgers University, 1975. (Also in: Journal of
        Alcohol and Drug Education, 20: 13-16, 1975.)

2713. Milgram, Gail Gleason. Current Status and Problems of Alcohol
        Education in the Schools. The Journal of School Health,
        46(6): 317-320, 1976.

2714. Milgram, Gail Gleason. Implications of College Policy on Campus
        Drinking Practices. The Alcoholism Digest Annual, 5: 70-
        72, 1976-1977.

2715. Milgram, Gail Gleason. What is Alcohol? and Why do People Drink?
        New Brunswick, New Jersey: Center of Alcohol Studies,
        Rutgers University, 1975.

2716. Millan, E. Prophylaxie Éducative de l'Alcoolisme dans les
        Écoles Mexicaines. (Educational Prophylaxis against
        Alcoholism in Mexican Schools.) Gazette des Hôpitaux
        Civils et Militaires, Paris, 127: 779-781, 1954.

2717. Miller, D. The Medical and Psychological Therapy of Adolescent
        Drug Abuse. International Journal of Psychotherapy, 2(3):
        309-330, 1973.

2718. Miller, D. and Jang, M. Children of Alcoholics: A 20-Year
        Longitudinal Study. Social Work Research Abstracts, 13:
        23-29, 1977.

2719. Miller, J.L. and Wahl, J.R. Attitudes of High School Students
        toward Alcoholic Beverages. New York: The Mrs. John S.
        Sheppard Foundation, 1956.

2720. Miller, K.D. and Williams, A.F. Blood Alcohol Concentrations of
        Patrons Leaving a College Pub. Journal of Studies on
        Alcohol, 42: 676-679, 1981.

2721. Miller, M. Task Force--Genesis of a Change. Nursing Clinics of
          North America, 14: 347-356, 1979.

2722. Miller, P.M. An Analysis of Chronic Drunkenness Offenders with
          Implications for Behavioral Intervention. International
          Journal of the Addictions, 10: 995-1005, 1975.

2723. Miller, P.M. Behavioral Strategies for Reducing Drinking among
          Young Adults. In: Youth, Alcohol and Social Policy.
          Eds. H.T. Blane and M.E. Chafetz. New York: Plenum Press,
          1979, pages 384-408.

2724. Miller, Sheldon, Helmick, Edward and McClure, William.
          Adolescent Alcoholism: A Relationship to Other Mental
          Health Problems. In: Currents in Alcoholism. Volume 4.
          Psychiatric, Psychological, Social and Epidemiological
          Studies. Ed. F.A. Seixas. New York: Grune and Stratton,
          1978, pages 77-85.

2725. Mills, G.S. Alcohol and Teenagers in Montgomery County,
          Maryland (Working Paper No. 4). Rockville, Maryland:
          National Institute on Alcohol Abuse and Alcoholism, 1975.

2726. Milman, D.H. and Anker, J.L. Patterns of Drug Abuse among
          University Students: IV. Use of Marijuana, Amphetamines,
          Opium, and LSD by Undergraduates. Journal of the American
          College Health Association, 20: 96-105, 1971.

2727. Milman, D.H. and Su, Wen-Huey. Patterns of Drug Usage Among
          University Students: V. Heavy Use of Marihuana and
          Alcohol by Undergraduates. Journal of the American
          College Health Association, 21(3): 181-187, 1973.

2728. Milman, D.H. and Su, Wen-Huey. Patterns of Illicit Drug and
          Alcohol Use among Secondary School Students. Journal of
          Pediatrics, 83(2): 314-320, 1973.

2729. Milman, Doris H. and Anker, Jerry L. Patterns of Drug Usage
          among University Students. Multiple Drug Usage. In:
          Drug Abuse: Current Concepts and Research. Springfield,
          Illinois: Charles C. Thomas, 1972, pages 190-201.

2730. Milne, L.D. and Vincent, M.L. Survey of Drug Use among South
          Carolina High School Students. Columbia, South Carolina:
          Commission on Narcotics and Controlled Substances, 1971.

2731. Milner, Gerald. Drug Awareness, Drugs and Drink: Awareness and
          Action. Melbourne, Australia: Perfect Publishing
          Company, 1979.

2732. Milner, Wayne M. Treatment at Henwood Multi-Dimensional.
          Rapport, 1(5): 4, 1972.

2733. Milstead, Robin J. Systematic Planning for Services to the
       Families of Alcoholic Persons in Rural Areas. The
       Alcoholism Digest Annual, 5: 40-45, 1976-1977.

2734. Milt, H. The Revised Basic Handbook on Alcoholism. Maplewood,
       New Jersey: Scientific Aids Publications, 1977.

2735. Minnesota Council on Alcohol Problems. Alcohol Education.
       Minneapolis, Minnesota, 1966 (2nd Edition, 1967).

2736. Minnesota Department of Education. A Guide for Instruction in
       Alcohol, Tobacco and Narcotics Education. St. Paul,
       Minnesota, 1957.

2737. Minnesota Department of Education, Curriculum Development Unit.
       Concepts of Chemicals: Drug Education Guidelines K-12.
       St. Paul, Minnesota, 1972.

2738. Miraglia, P.J. Selected Correlates of Self-Reported Alcohol Use
       in Catholic College Women. Doctoral Dissertation
       (University Microfilms No. 76-3203). University of
       Pennsylvania, 1975.

2739. Missbruket av Alkohol Bland Ungdom: CFN Föreslås Samordna
       Upplysning. (Misuse of Alcohol among Youth: CFN Proposes
       Coordinated Instruction.) Alkoholfrågan, 62: 182-183,
       1968.

2740. Missik, T. Stellungnahme der Adoleszenten zum Alkohol und
       Alkoholismus. (The Attitudes of Adolescents toward
       Alcohol and Alcoholism.) Alcoholism, Zagreb, 8: 40-45,
       1972.

2741. Mississippi Department of Education. Alcohol Education Handbook.
       Jackson, Mississippi, 1956.

2742. Mississippi Department of Education. Alcohol Education Handbook
       (Mississippi School Bulletin No. 141). Jackson,
       Mississippi, 1957.

2743. Mississippi Department of Education. Manual for Teaching Health
       for the Schools of Mississippi (Mississippi School
       Bulletin No. 118). Jackson, Mississippi, 1947.

2744. Mitchell, J.E., Hong, K.M. and Corman, C. Childhood Onset of
       Alcohol Abuse. American Journal of Orthopsychiatry, 49:
       511-513, 1979.

2745. Mitchell, K.R., Kirkby, R.J. and Mitchell, D.M. Drug Use by
       University Freshmen. Journal of College Student
       Personnel, 2(5): 332-336, 1970.

2746.   Mitchell, R.E. Personality Correlates of Frequent Marijuana and
        Alcohol Use in a College Male Population. Doctoral
        Dissertation (University Microfilms No. 72-15,260). Ohio
        State University, 1971.

2747.   Mitic, Wayne R. Alcohol Use and Self-Esteem of Adolescents.
        Journal of Drug Education, 10: 197-208, 1980.

2748.   Mivelaz, M. Alcoolisme et Délinquance. (Alcoholism and
        Delinquency.) Médecine et Hygiene, Genève, 23: 459-460,
        1965.

2749.   Mixing Mandrax and Alcohol (An Questions?) British Medical
        Journal, 2: 45, 1973.

2750.   Mizruchi, E.H. and Perrucci, R. Prescription, Proscription and
        Permissiveness: Aspects of Norms and Deviant Drinking
        Behavior. In: The Domesticated Drug: Drinking among
        Collegians. Ed. G.L. Maddox. New Haven, Connecticut:
        College and University Press, 1970, pages 234-253.

2751.   Mohan, D., Rustagi, P.K., Sundaram, K.R. and Prabhu, G.G.
        Relative Risk of Adolescent Drug Abuse: Part I.
        Sociodemographic and Interpersonal Variables. Bulletin on
        Narcotics, 33(1): 1-8, 1981.

2752.   Mohan, D., Sharma, H.K., Darshan, S., Sundaram, K.R. and
        Neki, J.S. Prevalence of Drug Abuse in Young Rural Males
        in Punjab. Indian Journal of Medical Research, 68: 689-
        694, 1978.

2753.   Mohan, D., Thomas, M.G., Sethi, H.S. and Prabhu, G.G.
        Prevalence and Patterns of Drug Use among High-School
        Students: A Replicated Study. Bulletin on Narcotics,
        31(3-4): 77-86, 1979.

2754.   Mohatt, Gerald. The Sacred Water: The Quest for Personal Power
        through Drinking among the Teton Sioux. In: The
        Drinking Man. Eds. D.C. McClelland, W.N. Davis, R. Kalin
        and E. Wanner. New York: The Free Press, 1972, pages
        261-275.

2755.   Monnier, Dwight Chapin. An Experiment in the Development of a
        Unit for Education on Alcoholism in Health Classes, at
        Three New York State Secondary Schools. Master's Thesis.
        Buffalo, New York: University of Buffalo, 1952.

2756.   Monoz, Ricardo F. The Prevention of Problem Drinking. In:
        How to Control Your Drinking. Eds. William R. Miller and
        Ricardo F. Munoz. Englewood Cliffs, New Jersey: Prentice-
        Hall, Inc., 1976, pages 236-242.

2757.   Monroe, J.J. and English, G.E. Ascription of Favorable and
        Unfavorable Attributes to Substance Abusers by College Age
        Males. Psychological Reports, 32: 875-882, 1973.

2758.   Monroe, Margaret E. and Stewart, Jean. Alcohol Education for
        the Layman: A Bibliography. New Brunswick, New Jersey:
        Rutgers University Press, 1959.

2759.   Montague, R.B. and Victor, J.B. Using a Differential Treatment
        Approach with High Risk High School Students. In:
        Differential Treatment of Drug and Alcohol Abusers. Eds.
        C.S. Davis and M.R. Schmidt. Palm Springs, California:
        ETC Publications, 1977, pages 70-87.

2760.   Montana, E. and O'Neill, C. Prevalence of Tobacco, Marijuana
        and Alcohol Usage among High School Students: A Local
        Survey and Comments on Current Patterns of Usage. Journal
        of the Medical Association of Georgia, 67: 211-214, 1978.

2761.   Montgomery County Public Schools. A Survey of Secondary School
        Students' Perceptions of and Attitudes toward Use of Drugs
        by Teenagers. Volume I. General Overview of Survey
        Findings; Volume II. Marijuana Use; Volume III
        Comparison of Teenagers in Different Geographic Areas and
        Schools and Survey of Secondary School Teachers.
        Rockville, Maryland: Montgomery County Public Schools,
        no date.

2762.   Moon, J.R. Alcoholism in Australia in 1975. In: National
        Council on Alcoholism. Papers Presented at the Annual
        Conference, Milwaukee, 1975. Eds. F. Seixas and
        S. Eggleston. Annals of the New York Academy of Science,
        263: 47-77, 1976.

2763.   Moore, M. A Note on Alcoholism. Rhode Island Medical Journal,
        25: 101-104, 1942.

2764.   Moore, R.A. and Wood, J.T. Alcoholism and Its Treatment in
        Yugoslavia. Quarterly Journal of Studies on Alcohol,
        24(1): 128-137, 1963.

2765.   Moore, Robert A. Drug X: Another Point of View. In: The
        Substance Abuse Problem. Ed. Sidney Cohen. New York:
        The Hawarth Press, 1981, pages 107-112.

2766.   Moorhead, H.H. Study of Alcoholism with Onset Forty-Five Years
        or Older. Bulletin of the New York Academy of Medicine,
        34: 99-108, 1958.

2767.   Moorhead, S.W. Acute Alcoholism in Children with Report of Two
        Cases. Archives of Pediatrics, 24: 108-111, 1907.

2768.   Moos, Rudolph H., Moos, Bernice S. and Kulik, James A.
        Behavioral and Self-Concept Antecedents and Correlates of
        College-Student Drinking Patterns. International Journal
        of the Addictions, 12(4): 603-615, 1977.

2769.   Moos, Rudolph H., Moos, Bernice S. and Kulik, James. College-
        Student Abstainers, Moderate Drinkers and Heavy Drinkers:
        A Comparative Analysis. Journal of Youth and Adolescence,
        5(4): 349-360, 1976.

2770.   Morando-Ratto, E. L'Adolescenza e la Droga. (Adolescence and
        Drugs.) Minerva Medica, Torino, 69: 3044-3053, 1978.

2771.   Morehouse, E.R. Working in the Schools with Children of
        Alcoholic Parents. Health and Social Work, 4(4): 144-
        162, 1979.

2772.   More Women and Young People are Joining A.A. Medical World News,
        19(21): 81, 1978.

2773.   Morrell, W.B. The Steering Group on Alcoholism of the Joseph
        Rowntree Trust. British Journal of Addiction, 61: 295-
        299, 1966.

2774.   Morrison, Andrew, Kline, F. Gerald and Miller, Peter. Aspects
        of Adolescent Information Acquisition about Drugs and
        Alcohol. In: Communication Research and Drug Education.
        Ed. R.E. Ostman. Beverly Hills, California: Sage
        Publications, 1976, pages 133-154.

2775.   Morrison, J. Adult Psychiatric Disorders in Parents of
        Hyperactive Children. American Journal of Psychiatry,
        137: 825-827, 1980.

2776.   Morrison, John A., Kelly, Kathe, Mellies, Margot, deGroot, Ido,
        Khoury, Philip, Gartside, Peter S. and Glueck, Charles J.
        Cigarette Smoking, Alcohol Intake and Oral Contraceptives:
        Relationships to Lipids and Lipoproteins in Adolescent
        School Children. Metabolism, 28(11): 1166-1170, 1979.

2777.   Morrison, J.R. and Stewart, M.A. A Family Study of the
        Hyperactive Child Syndrome. Biological Psychiatry, 3(3):
        189-195, 1971.

2778.   Morrison, J.R. and Stewart, M.A. The Psychiatric Status of the
        Legal Families of Adopted Hyperactive Children. Archives
        of General Psychiatry, 28(6): 888-891, 1973.

2779.   Morrissey, E.R. Alcohol-Related Problems in Adolescents and
        Women. Postgraduate Medicine, 64(6): 111-113, 116-199,
        1978.

2780.   Mortimer, R.G.   Drug Use and Driving by a University Student
         Sample.   Proceedings of the American Association of
         Automotive Medicine, 20: 198-210, 1976.

2781.   Moses, Donald A. and Burger, R.E.   Are You Driving Your Children
         to Drink? Coping with Teenage Alcohol and Drug Abuse.
         New York: Van Nostrand Reinhold, 1975.

2782.   Mosher, J.   The Prohibition of Youthful Drinking.   The Drinking
         and Drug Practices Surveyor, (9): 40-44, August, 1974.

2783.   Mosher, J.F.   The Prohibition of Youthful Drinking: A Need for
         Reform (Working Paper No. 29).   Berkeley, California:
         Social Research Group, 1973.   (Also in: Children and the
         Law Seminar: 1-45, Fall, 1973.) (Also in: Contemporary
         Drug Problems, 6: 397-436, 1977.)

2784.   Mount Diablo Unified School District.   First Annual Secondary
         School Survey of Drug Use, May 1971.   Secondary School
         Survey of Drug Use, May 1972, Secondary School Survey of
         Drug Use, May 1973.   Contra Costa County, California, no
         date.

2785.   Movchan, N.G., Butorina, N Ye. and Kazakov, V.S.   Opyt
         Organizatsii Raboty po Profilaktike Zloupotreblenii
         Alkogolem Sredi Podrostkov.   (Accomplishments in the
         Prevention of Alcohol Misuse among Adolescents.)
         Zdravookhranenie Rossiiskoi Federatsii, Moskav, (2): 39-
         40, 1980.

2786.   Movies Made on Alcoholism for Schools.   NIAAA Information and
         Feature Service: 3, December 28, 1976.

2787.   Moyer, David H. and Simon, Robert K.   Middle School Curriculum
         Change: An Action-Oriented Cooperative Drug Education
         Pilot Project.   Adolescence, 10(39): 313-326, 1975.

2788.   Mucha, V.   Úspešný boj Proti Alkoholismu je Jedným z
         Najhodnotnejších Darov Dospelých a Maládeže.   (Adolescent
         Welfare in Relation to Control of Alcoholism.)   Boj
         Zdravookhranenie, 25: 53-56, 1950.

2789.   Mueller, K.   Some Behavioral and Attitudinal Patterns of Alcohol
         Use from Selected Primary and Secondary Schools in Eight
         Communities.   In: A Multicultural View of Drug Abuse.
         Proceedings of the National Drug Abuse Conference, 1977.
         Eds. D.E. Smith, S.M. Anderson, M. Buxton, N. Gottlieb,
         W. Harvey and T. Chung.   Cambridge, Massachusetts:
         G.K. Hall/Schenkman Publishing Company, 1978, pages 477-
         478.

2790.   Mueller, Kurt.   Survey of Alcohol Use.   San Francisco,
         California: Social Advocates for Youth, 1976.

2791.   Mueller, S. and Ferneau, E.   Attitudes toward Alcoholism among a
        Group of College Students.   International Journal of the
        Addictions, 6(3): 443-451, 1971.

2792.   Muhlemann, R., Sommerauer, M. and Bergdol, A.-M.   Die Bedeutung
        der Verschiedenen Alkoholischen Getranke für Junge Männer
        de Verschiedenen Sprachgebiete der Schweiz.   (The
        Significance of Different Alcoholic Beverages for Young
        Men in the Various Linguistic Regions of Switzerland.)
        Schweizer Archiv fur Neurologie, Neurochirurgie und
        Psychiatrie, Zurich, 121: 165-173, 1977.

2793.   Mulford, H.A.   Education and Drinking Behavior.   In: The
        Domesticated Drug - Drinking Among Collegians.   Ed.
        G.L. Maddox.   New Haven, Connecticut: College and
        University Press, 1970, pages 81-97.

2794.   Mullan, Hugh and Sangiuliano, Iris, Eds.   Alcoholism: Group
        Psychotherapy and Rehabilitation.   Springfield, Illinois:
        Thomas Publishing, 1966.

2795.   Müller, R.   Alkoholkonsum von Kindern als Problem Abweichenden
        Verhaltens.   (Alcohol Consumption by Children as a Problem
        of Deviant Behavior.)   Suchtgefahren, Hamburg, 25: 114-121,
        1979.

2796.   Müller, R.   Gesamtschweizerische Repräsentativuntersuchung über
        den Alkohol- und Tabakkonsum der Schüler des 6., 7. und 8.
        Schuljahres (1978).   1. Teil.   (A Representative Study in
        Switzerland of the Drinking and Smoking Habits of Students
        in the 6th, 7th and 8th Grades [1978].   Part 1.)
        Lausanne: Schweizerische Fachstelle für Alkohol-probleme,
        1979.

2797.   Müller, R. and Abelin, T.   Grundlagen von Alkohol- und
        Tabakerziehungsprogrammen: Ähnlichkeiten und Kontraste.
        (The Basics for Health Education Programs on Alcoholism
        and Smoking: Similarities and Contrasts.)   Sozial- und
        Präeventivmedizin, Zurich, 22: 321-327, 1977.

2798.   Mullin, Lawrence S.   Alcohol Education: The School's
        Responsibility.   The Journal of School Health, 38: 518-
        522, 1968.

2799.   Munoz, L.C. and Parada-H., A.   Ensenanza Sobre Alcohol en las
        Escuelas.   (Teaching about Alcoholism in the Schools.)
        Archivos de Biologica y Medicine Experimentales, Santiago,
        Supplement No. 3: 312-319, 1969.   (Also as: Teaching
        about Alcoholism in the Schools.   In: Alcohol and
        Alcoholism.   Ed. R. Popham.   Toronto, Ontario:
        Addiction Research Foundation, 1970, pages 360-367.

2800. Munter, Preston. The College Community and Alcohol. In:
       Interpreting Current Knowledge about Alcohol and Alcoholism
       to a College Community. Proceedings of a Conference,
       May 28-30, 1963, Albany, New York. Ed. Richard Reynolds.
       Albany, New York: New York State Department of Mental
       Health, 1963, pages 51-61. (Also in: AAIAN Bulletin,
       10(1): 26, 1964.)

2801. Murata, Z. A Biological Study of Alcoholic Criminals.
       [Japanese Text] Seishin Shinkeigaku Zasshi (Psychiatria
       et Neurologia Japonica), Tokyo, 62: 1013-1045, 1960.

2802. Murphee, Henry. Some Possible Origins of Alcoholism. In:
       Alcohol and Alcohol Problems. Eds. W.J. Filstead,
       J.J. Rossi and M. Keller. Cambridge, Massachusetts:
       Ballinger, 1976, pages 135-165.

2803. Murphy, A.J. A Test Survey into the Alcohol and Drug Use Trends
       of Transient Youth at Sauble Beach, July and August, 1972.
       Toronto, Ontario: Addiction Research Foundation, 1972.

2804. Murphy, Gardner and Bachrach, Arthur J., Eds. An Outline of
       Abnormal Psychology. New York: Random House, 1954.

2805. Myers, J. Martin and Appel, Kenneth E. Drugs and Dependency:
       Who and Why. In: Mind Drugs. Ed. M. Hyde. New York:
       McGraw-Hill, 1968, pages 96-113.

2806. Myers, V.H. and Bates, J.M. Youth, Ethnicity and Drugs: Reports
       from the Job Corps. Los Angeles, California: J-Squared,
       B-Squared Consultants, Inc., 1973.

2807. Myers, Vincent. Drug Related Cognitions among Minority Youth.
       Journal of Drug Education, 7: 53-62, 1977.

2808. Myers, Vincent. Drug-Related Sentiments among Minority Youth.
       Journal of Drug Education, 8(4): 327-335, 1978.

2809. Myers, Vincent. Drug Use among Minority Youth. Addictive
       Diseases, 3(2): 187-196, 1977.

2810. Myerson, A. Alcoholism and Induction into Military Service.
       Quarterly Journal of Studies on Alcohol, 3: 204-220, 1942.

2811. Myerson, David J. A Therapeutic Appraisal of Certain Married
       Alcoholic Women. International Psychiatry Clinics, 3(2):
       143-157, 1966.

N

2812. Nace, E.P., O'Brien, C.P., Mintz, J., Ream, N. and Meyers, A.L.
       A Follow-up Study of Veterans Two Years after Vietnam.
       Paper presented at the 84th Annual Convention of the
       American Psychological Association, Washington, D.C.,
       September 7, 1976. (ERIC Report No. ED 141 694).
       Washington, D.C.: U.S. National Institute of Education,
       Educational Resources Information Center, 1976.

2813. Naeve, W. and Schulz, F. Zur Alkohol-Kriminalität der Frauen.
       (Alcohol Criminality of Women.) Suchtgefahren, Hamburg,
       25: 13-27, 1979.

2814. Nail, R., Gunderson, E. and Arthur, R. Black-White Differences
       in Social Background and Military Drug Abuse Patterns.
       American Journal of Psychiatry, 13(10): 1097-1102, 1974.

2815. Naor, E.M. and Nashold, R.D. Teenage Driver Fatalities
       Following Reduction in the Legal Drinking Age. Journal of
       Safety Research, 7: 74-79, 1975.

2816. Napier, Ted L., Carter, Timothy J. and Pratt, M. Christine.
       Correlates of Alcohol and Marijuana Use among Rural High
       School Students. Rural Sociology, 46(2): 319-332, 1981.

2817. National Center for Alcohol Education. The Community Health
       Nurse and Alcohol-Related Problems. Arlington, Virginia,
       1978.

2818. National Center for Alcohol Education. Planning a Prevention
       Program: A Handbook for the Youth Worker in an Alcohol
       Service Agency. Arlington, Virginia, 1976.

2819. National Center for Alcohol Education. Planning a Prevention
       Program: A Handbook for the Youth Worker in an Alcohol
       Service Agency. (DHEW Publication No. ADM 78-647).
       Washington, D.C.: U.S. Government Printing Office, 1978.

2820. National Center for Alcohol Education. You, Youth, and
       Prevention. Arlington, Virginia, 1978.

2821. National Children's Bureau. Britain's Sixteen-Year-Olds.   Ed.
       K. Fogelman. London: National Children's Bureau, 1976.

2822. National Clearinghouse for Alcohol Information. Alcoholism
       Prevention Guide to Resources and References. Rockville,
       Maryland, 1979.

2823. National Clearinghouse for Alcohol Information. Resource Book
       for Drug Abuse Education (2nd Edition). Rockville,
       Maryland, 1972.

2824. National Commission on Marihuana and Drug Abuse. Drug Use in
       America: Problems in Perspective. Appendix. Volume I.
       Patterns and Consequences of Drug Use. Washington, D.C.:
       U.S. Government Printing Office, 1973.

2825. National Commission on Marihuana and Drug Abuse. Second Report.
       Drug Use in America: Problem in Perspective. Washington,
       D.C.: U.S. Government Printing Office, 1973.

2826. National Committee for Education on Alcoholism. Report of First
       Six Months' Activities of the National Committee for
       Education on Alcoholism. Quarterly Journal of Studies on
       Alcohol, 6: 126-127, 1945.

2827. National Congress of Parents and Teachers. Alcohol: A Family
       Affair. Chicago, Illinois, 1974.

2828. National Congress of Parents and Teachers. The Infamous
       Booziometrograph (Sometimes Referred to as the Data
       Collection Guide). Chicago, Illinois, no date.

2829. National Congress of Parents and Teachers. The People to People
       Approach to Alcohol Abuse Intervention: A Handbook for
       PTA Leaders and Facilitators. Chicago, Illinois, 1976.

2830. National Council of the Churches of Christ in the U.S.A., Task
       Force on Alcohol Problems. Problem Drinking. Pamphlet.
       New York: Council Press, no date.

2831. National Council on Alcoholism. "Defining Adolescent Alcohol
       Use": Implications toward a Definition of Adolescent
       Alcoholism. New York, 1977.

2832. National Council on Alcoholism. Strictly for Teenagers.
       Pamphlet. New York, no date.

2833. National Council on Alcoholism. What is Alcohol Education?
       Leaflet. New York, 1975.

2834.   National Council on Alcoholism. Women and Alcoholism: NCA
        Position Statement. The Catalyst, 1(3): 70-74, 1980.

2835.   National Council on Alcoholism. Work in Progress on Alcoholism.
        Papers Presented at the Annual Conference, Milwaukee, 1975.
        Eds. F. Seixas and S. Eggleston. Annals of the New York
        Academy of Science, 273: 1-664, 1976.

2836.   National Education Association. People Do Drink and Drive.
        Washington, D.C., 1973.

2837.   National Highway Traffic Administration. Annual Report on the
        Public Information and Education Countermeasure of Alcohol
        Safety Action Projects. Washington, D.C.: U.S. Department
        of Transportation, 1975.

2838.   National Highway and Traffic Safety Administration.
        Communications Strategies on Alcohol and Highway Safety.
        Volume 2. High School Youth. Washington, D.C., 1975.

2839.   National Highway Traffic Safety Administration. Drinking and
        Driving. (NHTSA-151-75 BAB) Washington, D.C., 1974.

2840.   National Highway Traffic Safety Administration. How to Talk to
        Your Teenager about Drinking and Driving. Pamphlet.
        Washington, D.C.: U.S. Department of Transportation, with
        National Congress of Parents and Teachers, 1975.

2841.   National Highway Traffic Safety Administration. Results of
        National Alcohol Safety Action Projects. Washington, D.C.,
        1979.

2842.   National Highway Traffic Safety Administration. You...Alcohol
        and Driving: Students. Washington, D.C., 1977.

2843.   National Highway Traffic Safety Administration. You...Alcohol
        and Driving: Teacher Guide. Washington, D.C., 1977.

2844.   National Highway Traffic Safety Administration. Youth Alcohol
        Education Material Dissemination and Promotion.
        Springfield, Virginia: National Technical Information
        Service, 1977.

2845.   National Highway Traffic Safety Administration. Youth, Alcohol
        and Speeding: Their Joint Contribution to Highway
        Accidents. Washington, D.C., 1977.

2846.   National Institute for Drug Programs, Center for Human Services.
        Bibliography on Drug Abuse: Prevention, Treatment,
        Research. Washington, D.C.: Human Services, 1973.

2847. National Institute on Alcohol Abuse and Alcoholism. Alcohol Abuse and Alcoholism Prevention Model Learning Systems. (Developed by Sutherland Associates for the National Institute on Alcohol Abuse and Alcoholism.) Rockville, Maryland, 1974.

2848. National Institute on Alcohol Abuse and Alcoholism. Alcohol and American Indians. Rockville, Maryland: National Clearinghouse for Alcohol Information, 1980.

2849. National Institute on Alcohol Abuse and Alcoholism. Alcohol and Blacks. Rockville, Maryland: National Clearinghouse for Alcohol Information, 1980.

2850. National Institute on Alcohol Abuse and Alcoholism. Alcohol and the Chicano. Rockville, Maryland: National Clearinghouse for Alcohol Information, 1978.

2851. National Institute on Alcohol Abuse and Alcoholism. An Ounce of Prevention - A Course for Blacks. (ADM-77-454) Rockville, Maryland: U.S. Department of Health, Education and Welfare, Public Health Service: Alcohol, Drug Abuse and Mental Health Administration, 1977.

2852. National Institute on Alcohol Abuse and Alcoholism. Deviant Youths Should be Target of Prevention During Ages 11-14. NIAAA Information and Feature Service (IFS No. 25): 3, July 2, 1976.

2853. National Institute on Alcohol Abuse and Alcoholism. Drinking Myths. Pamphlet. (RSVP 44-102) Rockville, Maryland: U.S. Department of Health, Education and Welfare, with Operation Threshold, United States Jaycees, 1974.

2854. National Institute on Alcohol Abuse and Alcoholism. The Drinking Question: Honest Answers to Questions Teenagers Ask about Drinking. Pamphlet. Washington, D.C.: U.S. Government Printing Office, 1975.

2855. National Institute on Alcohol Abuse and Alcoholism. Education an Alternative for Young Offenders. NIAAA Information and Feature Service (IFS No. 22): 1, March 30, 1976.

2856. National Institute on Alcohol Abuse and Alcoholism. Guide to Alcohol Programs for Youth. Pamphlet. Rockville, Maryland, 1977.

2857. National Institute on Alcohol Abuse and Alcoholism. In Focus: Alcohol and Alcoholism Media. Washington, D.C.: U.S. Government Printing Office, 1977.

2858. National Institute on Alcohol Abuse and Alcoholism. Inner-City Youth Trained in Peer Prevention Skills. NIAAA Information and Feature Service (IFS No. 23): April 12, 1976.

2859.   National Institute on Alcohol Abuse and Alcoholism. Is Beer a
        Four Letter Word? Washington, D.C.: U.S. Government
        Printing Office, 1978.

2860.   National Institute on Alcohol Abuse and Alcoholism. A National
        Study of Adolescent Drinking Behavior, Attitudes and
        Correlates: Final Report. Research Triangle Park, North
        Carolina: Research Triangle Institute, 1975.

2861.   National Institute on Alcohol Abuse and Alcoholism. Proceedings
        of the Second Annual Alcoholism Conference of the National
        Institute on Alcohol Abuse and Alcoholism. Rockville,
        Maryland: U.S. Department of Health, Education and
        Welfare, 1973.

2862.   National Institute on Alcohol Abuse and Alcoholism. Reflections
        in a Glass - A Course for Women. Rockville, Maryland:
        U.S. Department of Health, Education and Welfare, Public
        Health Service; Alcohol, Drug Abuse and Mental Health
        Administration, 1977. (DHEW Publication No. ADM 77-453).

2863.   National Institute on Alcohol Abuse and Alcoholism. Teaching
        about Drinking. Pamphlet. Washington, D.C.: U.S.
        Government Printing Office, no date.

2864.   National Institute on Alcohol Abuse and Alcoholism. The Answer
        Book. Pamphlet. Washington, D.C.: U.S. Government
        Printing Office, 1975 (Revised 1978). (DHEW Publication
        No. 78-294)

2865.   National Institute on Alcohol Abuse and Alcoholism. The Power
        of Positive Drinking--A Course for Parents of Young
        Children. Rockville, Maryland: U.S. Department of
        Health, Education and Welfare, Public Health Service;
        Alcohol, Drug Abuse and Mental Health Administration,
        1977. (DHEW Publication No. 77-452).

2866.   National Institute on Alcohol Abuse and Alcoholism. The Unseen
        Crisis: Blacks and Alcohol. Washington, D.C.: U.S.
        Government Printing Office, 1977. (DHEW Publication No.
        ADM 77-478).

2867.   National Institute on Alcohol Abuse and Alcoholism. The Whole
        College Catalog about Drinking: A Guide to Alcohol abuse
        Prevention. Washington, D.C.: U.S. Government Printing
        Office, 1976. (DHEW Publication No. ADM 76-361).

2868.   National Institute on Alcohol Abuse and Alcoholism. Young People
        and Alcohol. Pamphlet. Washington, D.C.: U.S. National
        Highway Traffic Safety Administration, 1975.

2869.   National Institute on Alcohol Abuse and Alcoholism.   Youth Sees
        Drinking as a Symbol of Adulthood. NIAAA Information and
        Feature Service (IFS No. 20): 3, January 30, 1976. (Also
        in: Journal of Alcohol and Drug Education, 22(1): 22-23,
        1976.)

2870.   National Institute on Drug Abuse. An Approach for Casual Drug
        Users. (Technical Paper.) Pamphlet. Washington, D.C.:
        U.S. Government Printing Office, 1977.

2871.   National Institute on Drug Abuse. Drug Abuse from the Family
        Perspective. Ed. Barbara Gray Ellis. Washington, D.C.:
        U.S. Government Printing Office, 1980.

2872.   National Institute on Drug Abuse. Drug Abuse Prevention
        for Your Community. Pamphlet. Washington, D.C.: U.S.
        Government Printing Office, 1978.

2873.   National Institute on Drug Abuse. Drugs and Minorities
        (Research Issues 31). Eds. Gregory Austin, Bruce Johnson,
        Eleanor Carroll and Dan Lettieri. Rockville, Maryland,
        1978. (DHEW Publication No. ADM 78-507)

2874.   National Institute on Drug Abuse. Drug Use among American High
        School Students. Eds. L.D. Johnston, J.G. Bachman and
        P.M. O'Malley. Washington, D.C.: U.S. Department of
        Health, Education and Welfare, 1977. (DHEW Publication
        No. ADM 78-619)

2875.   National Institute on Drug Abuse. Drug Users and Driving
        Behavior (Research Issues 20). Eds. Gregory Austin,
        Robert Sterling-Smith, Mary Macari and Dan Lettieri.
        Rockville, Maryland, 1977. (DHEW Publication No. Adm.
        77-508)

2876.   National Institute on Drug Abuse. Drugs and Family/Peer
        Influence: Family and Peer Influences on Adolescent Drug
        Use. Eds. Patricia Ferguson, Thomas Lennox and
        Dan Lettieri. Washington, D.C.: U.S. Government Printing
        Office, 1975. (DHEW Publication No. ADM 75-186)

2877.   National Institute on Drug Abuse. Drugs and the Class of '78:
        Behaviors, Attitudes and Recent National Trends. Eds.
        Lloyd Johnston, Jerald G. Bachman and Patrick M. O'Malley.
        Rockville, Maryland: U.S. Department of Health, Education
        and Welfare. Public Health Service. Alcohol, Drug Abuse
        and Mental Health Administration, 1979, especially pages
        193-217.

2878.   National Institute on Drug Abuse. A Family Response to the Drug
        Problem: A Family Program for the Prevention of Chemical
        Dependence. Washington, D.C.: U.S. Government Printing
        Office, 1976.

2879.   National Institute on Drug Abuse. A Family Response to the Drug
         Problem: A Family Program for the Prevention of Chemical
         Dependence: Group Facilitator Guidelines. Washington,
         D.C.: U.S. Government Printing Office, 1976.

2880.   National Institute on Drug Abuse. Highlights from Drug Use
         among American High School Students 1975-1977. Pamphlet.
         Washington, D.C.: U.S. Government Printing Office, 1978.

2881.   National Institute on Drug Abuse. Predicting Adolescent Drug
         Abuse: A Review of Issues, Methods and Correlates--
         Research Issues II. Ed. Dan Lettieri. Rockville,
         Maryland, 1975.

2882.   National Institute on Drug Abuse. Teen Involvement for Drug
         Abuse Prevention: Manual and Administrator's Guide.
         Pamphlet. Washington, D.C.: U.S. Government Printing
         Office, 1978.

2883.   National Institute on Drug Abuse. Theories on Drug Abuse:
         Selected Contemporary Problems (Research Monograph
         Series 30). Eds. Dan Lettieri, Mollie Sayers and
         Helen Pearson. Rockville, Maryland, 1980. (DHEW
         Publication No. ADM 80-967)

2884.   National Institute on Drug Abuse. This Side Up: Making
         Decisions About Drugs. Washington, D.C.: U.S. Government
         Printing Office, 1979.

2885.   National Institute of Mental Health. Mental Health Aspects of
         Alcohol Education. Boston, Massachusetts: Office of the
         Massachusetts Commissioner on Alcoholism, 1959.

2886.   National Institute of Mental Health. Think about Drinking.
         Pamphlet. Washington, D.C.: Superintendent of Documents,
         1968. (Public Health Service Pub. No. 1683) (National
         Institute of Mental Health Children's Bureau Publication
         No. 456)

2887.   National Youth Council of Ireland. Teenage Drinking: A Cause
         for Concern. Dublin: Teenage Drinking Committee, 1976.

2888.   Nau, E. Kindesmisshandlung. (Child Abuse.) Monatsschrift fur
         Kinderheilkunde, Berlin, 115: 192-194, 1967.

2889.   Navarra, John G. Drugs and Man. Garden City, New York:
         Doubleday and Co., Inc., 1973.

2890.   Naylor, P.R. Alcohol, Alibis and Alateen. Leaflet. New York:
         Al-Anon Family Group Headquarters, 1964.

2891. Nebraska Department of Education. Guidelines for Comprehensive
       Health Education: A Conceptual Approach. Lincoln,
       Nebraska, 1972.

2892. Nebraska Division of Alcoholism. The Decision is Yours.
       Pamphlet. Lincoln, Nebraska, no date.

2893. Needle, R.H. and Hill, A.E. Basic Concepts of Alcohol. Second
       Edition. River Forest, Illinois: Laidlaw, 1975.

2894. Nehemskis, Alexis, Macari, Mary A. and Lettieri, Dan J. Drug
       Abuse Instrument Handbook: Selected Items for
       Psychosocial Drug Research. NIDA Research Issues Series,
       Volume 12. Washington, D.C.: U.S. Government Printing
       Office, 1976.

2895. Nelker, G. Alkoholvanor och Alkoholskador i Statistisk
       Belysning. (Drinking Habits and Alcohol Damages in Light
       of Statistics.) Svenska Läkartidningen, Stockholm, 52:
       1597-1609, 1955.

2896. Nelker, G. Nykterhetskommittens Undersökningar om Alkoholvanor
       och Alkoholskador. (Investigation by the Temperance
       Committee of Drinking Habits and of Damages Due to
       Drinking.) Tirfing, 46: 4-12, 1952.

2897. Nellis, M., Ed. Drugs, Alcohol and Women: A National Forum
       Source Book. Sponsored by the National Institute on Drug
       Abuse, Program for Women's Concerns, October 24-26, 1975,
       Miami Beach, Florida. Washington, D.C.: National
       Research and Communications Associates, Inc., 1976.

2898. Nelson, D.O. A Comparison of Drinking and Understanding of
       Alcohol and Alcoholism between Students in Selected High
       Schools of Utah and in the Utah State Industrial School.
       Journal of Alcohol Education, 13(4): 17-25, 1968.

2899. Nelson, D.O. Drinking and Student Understanding of Alcohol and
       Alcoholism in Selected High Schools in Utah. Logan, Utah:
       Utah State University, 1967.

2900. Nelson, Gaylord. Advertising and the National Health. Journal
       of Drug Issues, 6: 28-33, 1976.

2901. Nelson, L. Alcoholism in Zuni, New Mexico. Preventive Medicine,
       6(1): 152-166, 1977.

2902. Neubert, R. Jugend und Alcohol. (Youth and Alcohol.)
       Zeitschrift fur Aerztliche Fortbilting, 53: 626-629, 1959.

2903. Nevandomsky, J. Patterns of Self-Reported Drug Use among
       Secondary School Students in Bengal Sate, Nigeria.
       Bulletin on Narcotics, 33(1): 9-20, 1981.

2904.   Newton, J.E.   The Potential Drug Problem on Norfolk Island.
        Journal of Drug Issues, 7: 427-438, 1977.

2905.   Nevada Department of Education.   Comprehensive Health Education
        for Secondary Schools.   Carson City, Nevada, 1976.

2906.   Neville, E.C.   Garden of Broken Glass.   New York: Delacorte,
        1975.

2907.   New Association of Educators on Alcohol and Narcotics.
        Quarterly Journal of Studies on Alcohol, 12: 688-689, 1951.

2908.   New Hampshire.   Education on Alcoholism: A Report for the Fiscal
        Years July 1, 1952-June 30, 1954.   New Hampshire Bulletin
        on Alcoholism, III(6): no pages, January, 1955.

2909.   New Hampshire Department of Education.   Teaching about Alcohol:
        A Guide for Teachers.   Concord, New Hampshire, 1955.

2910.   New Hampshire Department of Education.   Teaching about Alcohol:
        A Guide for Teachers.   Pamphlet.   Curriculum Guide.
        Concord, New Hampshire, 1960.

2911.   New Hampshire Department of Health and Welfare.   Annual Report:
        New Hampshire Program on Alcohol and Drug Abuse.   Concord,
        New Hampshire, 1975.

2912.   Newman, H.W.   Variability in Tolerance to Depressant Drugs.
        Stanford Medical Bulletin, 5: 12-14, 1947.

2913.   Newman, T.M.   Promise Parent Study Groups: A Manual of
        Instruction: Techniques for Enhancing Parenting Skills.
        Chicago, Illinois: National Congress of Parents and
        Teachers, 1977.

2914.   New Mexico Commission on Alcoholism.   The Secondary School in
        the Prevention of Alcoholism.   Workshop Proceedings.
        Albuquerque, New Mexico, February 29, March 1, 2, 1960.
        Santa Fe, New Mexico, 1960.

2915.   New Mexico Commission on Alcoholism, Education Division.   A
        Topic Outline and Resource Unit for Teachers about Alcohol
        and Alcoholism.   Albuquerque, New Mexico, 1968.

2916.   Newmeyer, J. and Johnson, C.   Drug Emergencies in Crowds: An
        Analysis of "Rock Medicine", 1973-1977.   Journal of Drug
        Issues, 9: 235-245, 1979.

2917.   New Program of Alcohol Education of the Province of British
        Columbia, Canada.   Quarterly Journal of Studies on
        Alcohol, 9: 319-324, 1948.

2918.   Newton, John P. Alcoholic Beverage Buying Habits of University
         of Delaware Students. Journal of College Student
         Personnel, 19(4): 316-320, 1978.

2919.   New York City Police Department. A Survey of Police Incidents
         Involving Drinking by Youth in New York City. New York,
         1962.

2920.   New York Department of Education, Bureau of Drug Education.
         Annotated Resource Guide for Alcohol, Tobacco and Other
         Drug Abuse/Misuse Prevention Education Programs:
         Secondary Level. (Prepared by B.P. Thompson.) Albany,
         New York, 1979.

2921.   New York Department of Education, Curriculum Development Center.
         Health Curriculum Materials for Grades 7, 8, 9. Albany,
         New York, 1970.

2922.   New York Department of Education, Division of Health and Drug
         Education Services. Coordinating Strategies for Drug and
         Alcohol Abuse Prevention in the New York City Schools:
         An Invitational Conference. Pamphlet. New York, 1975.

2923.   New York Department of Mental Health, NIMH. Proceedings of a
         Conference, May 28-30, 1963, Albany, New York. In:
         Interpreting Current Knowledge about Alcohol and
         Alcoholism to a College Community. Ed. Richard Reynolds.
         Albany, New York, 1963.

2924.   New York Division of Substance Abuse Services. Drug Use among
         College Students in New York State. New York, New York,
         1981.

2925.   New York Interdepartmental Health Resources Board. Advisory
         Committee on Alcoholism. Problem Drinking and Alcoholism.
         Ed. H.D. Kruse. Albany, New York, 1957.

2926.   New York Office of Drug Abuse Services. Bureau of Social
         Science Research and Program Evaluation. A Survey of
         Substance Use among Junior and Senior High School Students
         in New York State. Report No. 1. Prevalence of Drug and
         Alcohol Use. New York, 1975.

2927.   New York Office of Drug Abuse Services. Bureau of Social
         Science Research and Program Evaluation. Drug Abuse
         Prevention: The Awareness, Experience and Opinions
         of Junior and Senior High School Students in New York
         State. (Report No. 2 of Winter 1974-1975 Survey.) New
         York, 1976.

2928.   New York Senate Committee on Mental Hygiene and Addiction
        Control. Why Nineteen: The Minimum Drinking Age and
        Related Initiatives to Combat Alcoholism, Drunk Driving
        and Teenage Alcohol Abuse. New York: Senate Mental
        Hygiene and Addiction Control Committee, 1981.

2929.   New York State University at Buffalo. Intoxicant Drugs: Survey
        of Student Use, Roles and Policies of the University.
        Buffalo, New York, 1968.

2930.   New York State University College, Buffalo. Professional
        Studies Research and Development Complex. Computer-Based
        Resource Unit: Alcohol. Buffalo, New York, 1972.

2931.   New York State University. Education Department, Bureau of
        Drug Education. Alcohol Education: A Teacher's
        Curriculum Guide for Grades 7-12. Albany, New York, 1976.

2932.   New York State University. State Education Department and
        Curriculum Development Center. Strand II, Sociological
        Health Problems, Grades 10, 11 and 12. Albany, New York,
        1970.

2933.   New York Temporary State Commission to Evaluate the Drug Laws.
        Education: Scaling the Problem Down to Size.
        Contemporary Drug Problems, 4(1): 83-92, 1975.

2934.   New York University of Education, Health, Nursing and Arts
        Professions. Health Education and Alcohol Problems: Case
        Histories of Three Workshops. Workshop I, Alcohol
        Problems and Adolescent Turmoil. New York, New York,
        December 10-11, 1976. New York, 1977.

2935.   Nielsen, J. Nogle Aspekter Vedrørende Alkoholisme og
        Alkoholforskning i Norden. (Some Aspects of Alcoholism
        and Alcohol Research in the Scandinavian Countries.)
        Nordisk Psykiatrisk Tidsskrift, 18: 500-520, 1964.

2936.   Nikolić, B. Osvrt na Trezvenjački Pokret u nas do 1941. Godine.
        (A Review of the Temperance Movement in Yugoslavia until
        1941.) Psihijatrija Danas, Belgrade, 11: 391-400, 1979.

2937.   Nilson-Giebel, M. Peer Groups Help Prevent Dependence among
        Youth in the Federal Republic of Germany. International
        Journal of Health Education, 23: 20-24, 1980.

2938.   Noe, R.W. Drinking and Student Understanding of Alcohol and
        Alcoholism in Selected High Schools of Missouri. Master's
        Thesis. University of Missouri, 1972.

2939.   Noel, Nora E. and Lisman, Stephen A. Alcohol Consumption by
        College Women Following Exposure to Unsolvable Problems:
        Learned Helplessness or Stress Induced Drinking.
        Behaviour Research and Therapy, Oxford, 18: 429-440, 1980.

2940.   Noel, W.M. Personality Characteristics and Attitudes of Male
        and Female High School Drinkers and Abstainers toward
        Alcoholic Beverages. Doctoral Dissertation (University
        Microfilms No. 8000242). United States International
        University, 1979.

2941.   Nolte, Ann. OK Miss, But Do You Drink? Journal of Alcohol
        Education, 14(2): 21-24, 1968.

2942.   Nolte, Ann. The Spirit of the Times. Journal of Alcohol
        Education, 15(3): 2-7, 1970.

2943.   Noordzij, P.C. Drinking and Driving in the Netherlands over a
        Four-Year Period. In: Alcohol, Drugs and Traffic Safety.
        Proceedings of the Sixth International Conference on
        Alcohol, Drugs and Traffic Safety, Toronto, September 8-13,
        1974. Eds. S. Israelstam and S. Lambert. Toronto:
        Addiction Research Foundation of Ontario, 1975, pages 33-
        39.

2944.   Nordland, K. Friluftsliv som Alternativ. (Outdoor Activities
        as an Alternative.) Tidsskrift EdruSpørsm, 30(4): 28-31,
        1978.

2945.   Norelle-Lickiss, J. Social Deviance in Aboriginal Boys.
        Medical Journal of Australia, 58(2): 460-470, 1971.

2946.   North American Association of Alcoholism Programs. Selected
        Papers Presented at the General Sessions of the 15th
        Annual Meeting, September 27-October 1, 1964, Portland.
        Washington, D.C., 1964.

2947.   North American Association of Alcoholism Programs. Selected
        Papers Presented at the General Sessions of the 20th
        Annual Meeting, September 14-19, 1969, Vancouver, British
        Columbia. Washington, D.C., no date.

2948.   North Carolina Health and Physical Education, Department of
        Public Instruction. Suggestions and Requirements for
        Alcohol Education in North Carolina Public Schools.
        Pamphlet. Raleigh, North Carolina, 1969.

2949.   North Dakota Commission on Alcoholism. The Role of Alcohol in
        Society: A Concise and Factual Study Guide on the
        Problems of Alcoholism. Bismarck, North Dakota, 1957.

2950. North Dakota Commission on Alcoholism. Supplement to "The Role of Alcohol in Society": Problems Involved in Alcohol Education. Bismarck, North Dakota, 1957.

2951. North Dakota Department of Public Instruction. Alcohol and Narcotics Education: Teacher Guide and Manual for North Dakota Schools. Bismarck, North Dakota, 1952.

2952. North, Robert and Orange, Richard. Teenage Drinking. New York: Macmillan Publishing Company, Inc., 1980.

2953. Northup, D.W. What to Tell Young People about Alcohol and Narcotics. West Virginia Medical Journal, 59(12): 374-377, 1963.

2954. Novak, D.G. Personality Traits and Family Interaction Patterns Associated with Alcoholism. In: Alcoholism: General Hospital Issues and Perspectives. Eds. D.G. Novak and R.L. Jones. Austin, Texas: Texas Hospital Association, 1976, pages 33-37.

2955. Now You're Living. Washington: Narcotics Education, 1964.

2956. Nowlis, H.H. Coordination of Prevention Programs for Children and Youth. Public Health Report, 96: 34-37, 1981.

2957. Nowlis, H.H. Drugs on the College Campus. Garden City, New York: Doubleday, 1969.

2958. Nowlis, H.H. Drugs on the College Campus: A Guide for College Administrators. Detroit, Michigan: National Association for Personnel Administrators, 1967.

2959. Nowlis, Helen H. Commonalities among Prevention Programs for Children and Youth: Executive Summary. In: Alcohol, Drug Abuse and Mental Health Administration, Conference on Prevention, September, 1979. Rockville, Maryland, 1980.

2960. Nowlis, Helen H. Communicating about Drugs. In: Resource Book for Drug Abuse Education. American Association for Health, Physical Education and Recreation. Washington, D.C.: U.S. Government Printing Office, 1969, pages 8-10.

2961. Nowlis, Helen H. Drugs Demystified. Paris: Unesco, 1975.

2962. Nowlis, Helen H. Strategies for Prevention. Contemporary Drug Problems, 5(1): 5-20, 1976.

2963. Nurco, D. Special Studies: Training Schools. Drug Abuse Study, 1969. Baltimore, Maryland: Department of Mental Hygiene, 1969.

2964.   Nurco, David. Etiological Aspects of Drug Abuse. In: Handbook
        on Drug Abuse. Eds. R.I. Dupont, A. Goldstein, and
        J. O'Donnell. Washington, D.C.: U.S. Government Printing
        Office, 1979, pages 315-324.

2965.   Nusbaumer, Michael R. and Zusman, Marty E. Autos, Alcohol and
        Adolescence: Forgotten Concerns and Overlooked Linkage.
        Journal of Drug Education, 11(2): 167-178, 1981.

2966.   Nuttall, E.V. and Nuttall, R.L. Parental Correlates of Drug Use
        among Young Puerto Rican Adults. American Journal of Drug
        and Alcohol Abuse, 6: 173-188, 1979.

2967.   Nuttall, E.V., Nuttall, R.L., Polit, D. and Clark, K. Assessing
        Adolescent Mental Health Needs: The Views of Consumers,
        Providers and Others. Adolescence, 12: 277-285, 1977.

2968.   Nutting, P.A., Price, T.B. and Baty, M.L. Non-Health
        Professionals and the School-Age Child: Early
        Intervention for Behavioral Problems. Journal of School
        Health, 49: 73-78, 1979.

2969.   Nye, L.J.J. Doctors and the Drink Traffic. Medical Journal of
        Australia, 29: 33, 1942.

2970.   Nylander, I. Children of Alcoholic Fathers. Acta Paediatrica
        Scandinavica, Stockholm, 49, Supplement 121, 1960.

2971.   Nylander, I. A 20-Year Prospective Follow-Up Study of 2164
        Cases at the Child Guidance Clinics in Stockholm. Acta
        Paediatrica Scandinavica, Stockholm, Supplement No. 276:
        1-45, 1979.

2972.   Nylander, I. "Thinner" Addiction in Children and Adolescents.
        Acta Paedopsychiatrica, Basel, 29: 273-283, 1962.

2973.   Nylander, I. Thinner-, Alkohol- och Tablettmissbruk Bland Barn
        och Ungdom: Kliniska Synpunkter. (Thinner, Alcohol and
        Drug Misuse in Children and Adolescents: Clinical
        Aspects.) Nordisk Medicin, Stockholm, 70: 896-899, 1963.

2974.   Nylander, I. and Rydelius, P. The Relapse of Drunkenness in
        Non-Asocial Teen-Age Boys. Acta Psychiatrica Scandinavica,
        Munksgaard, Copenhagen, 49: 435-443, 1973.

2975.   Nylander, Ingvar and Rydelius, P.A. Drunkenness in Children and
        Teenagers. International Journal of Mental Health, 7:
        117-131, 1979.

O

2976. Oberteuffer, D. and Kaplan, R. Health Instruction. Suggestions
         for Teachers. Outline of Content for Junior High School...
         Journal of School Health, 39(5A): 48-90, 1969.

2977. Obitz, F., Oziel, L. and Unmacht, J. General and Specific
         Perceived Locus of Control in Delinquent Drug Users.
         International Journal of the Addictions, 8(4): 723-727,
         1973.

2978. O'Brien, W.B. and Halpern, S. Drug Abuse and Alcoholism in
         Youth: A Perspective. Addiction Therapy, 2: 22-26, 1977.

2979. Obuchowska, I. Emotional Contact with the Mother as a Social
         Compensatory Factor in Children of Alcoholics.
         International Mental Health Research Newsletter, 16: 2, 4,
         1974.

2980. O'Connor. J. Parental Influences: A Tri-Ethnic Study on the
         Transmission of Drinking Behaviour from Parent to Child--
         Preliminary Communication. Irish Medical Journal, 69:
         152-158, 1976.

2981. O'Connor, J. Social and Cultural Factors Influencing Behaviour
         among Young People: A Cross National Study of the
         Drinking Behaviour and Attitudes Towards Drinking of Young
         People and Their Parents. Volumes I, II. Doctoral
         Thesis. National University of Ireland, 1976. (Also as:
         Report to the British Medical Council on Alcoholism, 1976.)

2982. O'Connor, Joyce. Annotation: Normal and Problem Drinking among
         Children. Journal of Child Psychology and Psychiatry,
         18(3): 279-284, 1977.

2983.   O'Connor, Joyce. Cultural Influences and Drinking Behavior.
        Drinking in Ireland and England: A Tri-Ethnic Study of
        Drinking among Young People and Their Parents. Journal of
        Alcoholism, 10(3): 94-121, 1975.

2984.   O'Connor, Joyce. The Young Drinkers. London: Tavistock
        Publications, 1978.

2985.   O'Day, J. Drnking Involvement and Age of Young Drivers in Fatal
        Accidents (Michigan). HIT Lab Reports, 13-14, October,
        1970.

2986.   Ödegard, Ö. Alcohol and Crime. An Investigation Concerning
        the Causes of Juvenile Delinquency. Tirfing, 34: 69-77,
        1940.

2987.   O'Donnell, J.A. and Clayton, R.R. Determinants of Early
        Marihuana Use. In: Youth Drug Abuse: Problems, Issues
        and Treatment. Eds. G.M. Beschner and A.S. Friedman.
        Lexington, Massachusetts: D.C. Heath, 1979, pages 63-110.

2988.   O'Donnell, J.A., Voss, H.L., Clayton, R.R., Slatin, G.T. and
        Room, R. Young Men and Drugs: A Nationwide Survey.
        (NIDA Research Monograph Series 5) Rockville, Maryland:
        National Institute on Drug Abuse, 1976.

2989.   O'Donnell, John. On Education to Prevent Marijuana Abuse. In:
        Communication and Drug Abuse: Proceedings of the Second
        Rutgers Symposium on Drug Abuse. Eds. J.R. Wittenborn,
        Jean Paul Smith and Sarah A. Wittenborn. Springfield,
        Massachusetts: Charles C. Thomas, 1970, pages 395-403.

2990.   Oetting, E.R., Edwards, Ruth, Goldstein, G.S. and
        Garcia-Mason, V. Drug Use among Adolescents of Five
        Southwestern Native American Tribes. The International
        Journal of the Addictions, 15(3): 439-445, 1980.

2991.   Oetting, E.R. and Goldstein, George S. Drug Use among Native
        American Adolescents. In: Youth Drug Abuse: Problems
        Issues and Treatment. Eds. G.M. Beschner and
        A.S. Friedman. Toronto, Ontario: Lexington Books,
        D.C. Heath and Company, 1979, pages 409-441.

2992.   O'Farrell, T.J., Harrison, R.H. and Cutter, H.S.G. Marital
        Stability among Wives of Alcoholics: An Evaluation of
        Three Explanations. British Journal of Addiction, 76(2):
        175-190, 1981.

2993.   Offenses of Drunkenness. (Command 5380) London: Her Majesty's
        Stationary Office, 1972.

2994.   Offer, Daniel, Marohn, Richard C. and Ostrov, Eric.   Delinquent
        and Normal Adolescents. Comprehensive Psychiatry, 13:
        347-355, 1972.

2995.   Offord, D.R. and Poushinsky, M.F.   School Performance, IQ and
        Female Delinquency. International Journal of Social
        Psychiatry, 27: 53-62, 1981.

2996.   Ogborne, A.C., Vingilis, E., Kijewski, K. and Salutin, L.
        Drinking Patterns and Problems among Adolescents Charged
        with Underage Drinking. (Substudy No. 1015) Toronto,
        Ontario: Addiction Research Foundation, 1978.

2997.   Ogden, M., Spector, M.I. and Hill, C.A., Jr.   Suicides and
        Homicides among Indians. Public Health Report, 85: 75-80,
        1970.

2998.   O'Gorman, P.   Prevention Issues Involving Children of Alcoholics.
        In: Services for Children of Alcoholics. Symposium held
        on September 24-26, 1979 at Silver Spring, Maryland.
        U.S. National Institute on Alcohol Abuse and Alcoholism.
        Research Monograph No. 4. Washington, D.C.: U.S.
        Government Printing Office, 1981, pages 81-100. (DHHS
        Publication No. ADM-1007)

2999.   O'Gorman, P.A.   Perception of Fathers in Adolescents from
        Alcoholic Homes. Vigo, Spain: Paper presented at 22nd
        International Institute on the Prevention and Treatment of
        Alcoholism, June 7-11, 1976.

3000.   O'Gorman, P.A.   Self-Concept, Locus of Control and Perception of
        Father in Adolescents from Homes with and without Severe
        Drinking Problems. Doctoral Dissertation (University
        Microfilms No. 76-4189). New York: Fordham University,
        1975.

3001.   O'Gorman, Patricia and Lacks, Hazel. Aspects of Youthful
        Drinking. New York: National Council on Alcoholism,
        1979.

3002.   O'Gorman, Patricia A., Stringfield, Sharon and Smith, Iris, Eds.
        Defining Adolescent Alcohol Use: Implications Toward a
        Definition of Adolescent Alcoholism. Proceedings of the
        National Council on Alcoholism 1976 Conference,
        Washington, D.C. New York: National Council on
        Alcoholism, 1977.

3003.   O'Hagan, M.   An Educational Approach to the Use and Abuse of
        Alcohol. Journal of Alcoholism, London, 7: 80-84, 1972.

3004.   O'Hagan, M.E.   Omladina, Alkohol, Prekomerno Pijenje--Irska
        Dilema. (Youth, Alcohol, Excessive Drinking--an Irish
        Dilemma.) Alkoholizam, Beograd, 13(3-4): 5-14, 1973.

3005. O'Hagan, M.E. Youth, Alcohol, Excessive Drinkers--An Irish
         Dilemma. In: Papers Presented at the 19th International
         Institute on the Prevention and Treatment of Alcoholism,
         Belgrade, Yugoslavia, June, 1973. Lausanne, Switzerland:
         International Council on Alcohol and Addictions, 1973,
         pages 66-74.

3006. Ohio Congress of Parents and Teachers and Ohio Department of
         Health. A Guide to Planning a Teenage Institute on Alcohol
         and Other Drugs. Pamphlet. Columbus, Ohio: Ohio PTA and
         Ohio Department of Health, no date.

3007. Ohio Congress of Parents and Teachers and Ohio Department of
         Health. A Teenage Institute on Alcohol and Other Drugs.
         Pamphlet. Columbus, Ohio: Ohio PTA and Ohio Department
         of Health, no date.

3008. Ohio Department of Education, the Educational Research Council
         of America and the Participating School Systems--Dayton,
         Ohio and Lima, Ohio. Drugs, Alcohol, Tobacco and Human
         Behavior: Student Book, Junior High School. Cleveland,
         Ohio: Educational Research Council of America, 1971.

3009. Ohio Department of Education, the Educational Research Council
         of America and the Participating School Systems--Dayton,
         Ohio and Lima, Ohio. Drugs, Alcohol, Tobacco and Human
         Behavior: Teacher Manual, Junior High School. Cleveland,
         Ohio: Educational Research Council of America, 1971.

3010. Ohio Department of Health. A Look into Teen-Age Drinking.
         Pamphlet. Columbus, Ohio, no date.

3011. Ohio Department of Health. Alcohol Education. Pamphlet.
         Columbus, Ohio, 1968.

3012. Ohio Department of Health: Alcoholism Program. Life is Real:
         1973 Teenage Institute on Alcohol and Other Drugs--A
         Summary of Recommendations, August 12-16, 1973. (Prepared
         by Paula E. Wead) Columbus, Ohio, 1973.

3013. Ohio Department of Health: Alcoholism Program. 1972 Teenage
         Institute on Alcohol and Other Drugs--A Summary of the
         Recommendations, August 6-9 and 13-16, 1972. Columbus,
         Ohio, 1972.

3014. Ohio Department of Health: Alcoholism Program. Teaching Unit
         on Alcohol and Alcoholism. Pamphlet. Columbus, Ohio,
         no date.

3015. Ohio Department of Liquor Control. A Look at Why People Drink.
         Pamphlet. Columbus, Ohio, no date.

3016.   Ohio Department of Liquor Control. Liquor Laws and the Teenager.
         Leaflet. Columbus, Ohio, no date.

3017.   Ohio Department of Liquor Control. Portrait of an American
         Drinker. Pamphlet. Columbus, Ohio, no date.

3018.   Ohio Department of Liquor Control. The Underage Drinking
         Problem. Pamphlet. Columbus, Ohio, no date.

3019.   Ohio Governor's Committee on Teenage Drinking. Summary of
         Recommendations from the 1968 Teenage Institute on
         Alcohol. (Report of the Institute held August 25-28, 1968
         at Kent, Ohio, sponsored by Governor's Committee on Teenage
         Drinking, Ohio Department of Health, Ohio Department of
         Liquor Control, Kent State University, Ohio Congress of
         Parents and Teachers and Ohio School Counselors
         Association.) Columbus, Ohio, 1968.

3020.   O'Hollaren, P. and Wellman, W.M. Alcoholism: Drinking Pattern
         and Birth Order of 738 Alcoholics. Northwest Medicine,
         56: 811-813, 1957.

3021.   Ohyama, M. The Changes of "Body-Image Boundary Scores" Under
         Condition of Alcoholic Intoxication. Tohoku Psychologica
         Folia, 22: 100-107, 1964.

3022.   Oklahoma Department of Education. Narcotic and Drug Education
         Curriculum Guide: An Approach to Drug Education K-6.
         Norman, Oklahoma, 1973.

3023.   Oksala, E. Ajattelemisen Aihetta. (Food for Thought.)
         Alkoholipolitiikka, Helsingfor, (4): 117-118, 1957.

3024.   Oksala, E. Något att Tänka På. (Food for Thought.)
         Alkoholipolitiikka, Helsingfor, (3): 73-74, 100-101, 1957.

3025.   O'Leary, D.E., O'Leary, M.R. and Donovan, D.M. Social Skill
         Acquisition and Psychosocial Development of Alcoholics:
         A Review. Addictive Behaviors, 1: 111-120, 1976.

3026.   O'Leary, D.E.H. Self-Disclosure in Heavy and Light Drinking Male
         College Students. Doctoral Dissertation (University
         Microfilms No. 7800959). University of Washington, 1977.

3027.   Oliver, J.S. and Watson, J.M. Abuse of Solvents "for Kicks":
         A Review of 50 Cases. Lancet, 1: 84-86, 1977.

3028.   Olkinuora, H. Kansa- ja Kansalaiskoulujen Opetussuunnitelmien
         ja Oppikirjojen Alkoholi-Informaation Sisällön Erittely:
         Alkoholitutkimussäätiön Raittiuskasvatusprojekti I.
         (Content Analysis of Alcohol-Information in Educational
         Plans and Textbooks of Public Schools: Temperance
         Education Project I of the Finnish Foundation for Alcohol
         Studies.) Research Report No. 30. Jyväskylä, Finland:
         University of Jyväskylä, Department of Education, 1971.

3029. Olkinuora, H. Raittiuskasvatustutkimuksen Antamat Viiteet
       Opetuksen Kehittämiselle. (Some Conclusions from a Study
       on Temperance Education in Schools.) Alkoholikysymys,
       Helsinki, 43: 3-14, 1975.

3030. Oltman, J.E. and Friedman, S. A Consideration of Parental
       Deprivation and Other Factors in Alcohol Addicts.
       Quarterly Journal of Studies on Alcohol, 14: 49-57, 1953.

3031. O'Malley, Patrick M., Bachman, Jerald G. and Johnston, Lloyd D.
       Drug Use and Military Plans of High School Seniors.
       Youth and Society, 10(1): 65-77, 1978.

3032. Only, Mark. High: A Fairwell to the Pain of Alcoholism.
       Englewood Cliffs, New Jersey: Prentice-Hall, 1974.

3033. Ontario Department of Education. A Teacher's Manual for
       Alcohol Education. (Prepared by N.R. Speirs.) Toronto,
       Ontario, no date.

3034. Operation Cork. Soft is the Heart of a Child: Film Discussion
       Kit. San Diego, California, 1979.

3035. Oppenheim, G. When Your Teenager Starts Drinking. Pamphlet.
       New York: National Council on Alcoholism, no date.

3036. Oppenheimer, J.L. Francesca, Baby. New York: Scholastic,
       1976.

3037. Orange County, California, Youth Services Program, Alcoholism
       Council. Drinking Patterns and Problem Drinking among
       Selected Youth in Orange County. Santa Ana, California,
       1976.

3038. Orcutt, J.D. Deviance as a Situated Phenomenon: Variations in
       the Social Interpretation of Marijuana and Alcohol Use.
       Social Problems, 22: 346-356, 1975.

3039. Orcutt, J.D. A Theoretical and Empirical Analysis of the Social
       Determinants of Recreational Drug Effects. Doctoral
       Dissertation (University Microfilms No. 73-18137).
       University of Minnesota, 1973.

3040. Orcutt, J.D. Toward a Sociological Theory of Drug Effects: A
       Comparison of Marijuana and Alcohol. Sociology and Social
       Research, 56(2): 242-253, 1972.

3041. Orcutt, J.D., Cairl, R.E. and Miller, E.T. Professional and
       Public Conceptions of Alcoholism. Journal of Studies on
       Alcohol, 41: 652-661, 1980.

3042.   Orcutt, James D. and Biggs, Donald A.   Perceived Risks of
        Marijuana and Alcohol Use: Comparisons of Non-Users and
        Regular Users. Journal of Drug Issues, 3: 355-360, 1973.

3043.   Orcutt, James D. and Biggs, Donald A.   Testing a Sociological
        Theory of Recreational Drug Effects. Sociology and Social
        Research, 59(2): 136-149, 1975.

3044.   Oregon Alcohol Education Committee. Oregon's Program of Alcohol
        Education and Rehabilitation. (A Report to Governor
        Mark Hatfield, Members of the State Legislature, State
        Officials and Citizens of Oregon. Activities of the
        Oregon Alcohol Education Committee. Biennium 1957-1959.)
        Portland, Oregon, 1959.

3045.   Oregon Alcohol Education Committee. A Resource Unit in Alcohol
        Studies for Secondary Teachers. Portland, Oregon, 1958.

3046.   Oregon Alcohol Studies and Rehabilitation Section. Alcohol
        Education in Oregon Public Schools. Revised Edition.
        Salem, Oregon, 1963.

3047.   Oregon Board of Higher Education, Division of Continuing
        Education. The School Counselor Faces Youth and Alcohol.
        (Proceedings of a Conference, February 1964, sponsored by
        Oregon State Division of Mental Health, Alcohol Studies
        and Rehabilitation Section; Oregon State System of Higher
        Education, Division of Continuing Education; and U.S.
        Department of Health, Education and Welfare, National
        Institute of Mental Health.) Portland, Oregon, 1964.

3048.   Oregon Department of Education. Alcohol Education in Oregon
        Public Schools. (Prepared under the auspices of the
        Oregon Alcohol Education Committee and the State Department
        of Education.) Salem, Oregon, 1956.

3049.   Oregon Mental Health Division. Alcohol Education in Oregon's
        Schools: A Topic Outline and Research Unit for Teachers.
        Portland, Oregon, 1964.

3050.   Orford, Jim. Alcohol and the Family. In: Alcoholism in
        Perspective. Eds. Marcus Grant and Paul Gwinner.
        Baltimore, Maryland: University Press, 1979, pages 77-89.

3051.   Orford, Jim. Impact of Alcoholism on Family and Home. In:
        Alcoholism: New Knowledge and New Responses. Eds.
        Griffith Edwards and Marcus Grant. London: Croom Helm,
        1977, pages 234-243.

3052. Orford, Jim, Waller, Seth and Peto, Julian. Drinking Behavior and Attitudes and Their Correlates among University Students in England. I. Principal Components in the Drinking Domain. II. Personality and Social Influence. III. Sex Differences. Quarterly Journal of Studies on Alcohol, 35: 1316-1374, 1974.

3053. Organisation for Economic Co-Operation and Development. Road Research. Young Driver Accidents. Paris, 1975.

3054. Organizatsiya i Soderhaniye Protivoalkogol'noi Raboty so Shkol'nikami. Metodicheskiye Materiyaly v Pomoshach' Lektoru. (The Organization and Scope of Education Anti-Alcohol Programs for School Children. Methods and Materials to Aid Lectures.) Moskva, 1979.

3055. Orive, Ruben and Gerard, Harold. Personality, Attitudinal and Social Correlates of Drug Use. International Journal of the Addictions, 15(6): 869-881, 1980.

3056. Orme, T.C. and Rimmer, J. Alcoholism and Child Abuse: A Review. Journal of Studies on Alcohol, 42: 273-287, 1981.

3057. O'Rourke, A., Gough, C. and Wilson-Davis, K. Alcohol--A Report on a Study in Dublin Post-Primary Schoolchildren, 1970. Journal of the Irish Medical Association, 67: 355-358, 1974.

3058. O'Rourke, A., Wilson-Davis, K. and Gough, C. Smoking, Drugs and Alcohol in Dublin Secondary Schools. Irish Journal of Medical Science, 140(5): 230-241, 1971.

3059. O'Rourke, T.W. Assessment of the Effectiveness of the New York State Drug Curriculum Guide with Respect to Drug Knowledge. Journal of Drug Education, 3(1): 57-66, 1973.

3060. Orring, J. Skola och Folkrörelser i Samverkan: Några Reflexioner Kring det Aktuella Läget på Alkoholoch Narkotikaområdet. (School and Popular Movements in Cooperation: Some Reflections on the Present Situation in Regard to Alcohol and Narcotics.) Alkoholfragan, 64: 315-321, 1970.

3061. Osborn, S.G. and West, D.J. Do Young Delinquents Really Reform? Journal of Adolescence, 3: 99-14, 1980.

3062. Oshodin, O.G. Alcohol Abuse among High School Students in Benin City, Nigeria. Doctoral Dissertation (University Microfilms No. 8105891. Columbia University Teachers College, 1980. (Also as: Alcohol Abuse among High School Students in Benin City, Nigeria. Drug and Alcohol Dependence, 7(2): 147-155, 1981.

3063. Osman, Jack D.   Value Growth Through Drug Education.   School Health Review, 5(1): 25-30, 1974.

3064. Österberg, I.   Barn och Fäder: en Alkoholpsykologisk Studie. (Children and Fathers: An Alcohol-Psychological Study.) Alkoholipolitiikka, Helsingfor, 22: 106-108, 123, 1959.

3065. Österberg, I.   Lapset ja Isät.   Alkoholipsykologista Taustaa. (Children and Fathers: An Alcohol-Psychological Study.) Alkoholipolitiikka, Helsingfor, 24: 244-246, 1959.

3066. Ostman, R.E., Ed.   Communication Research and Drug Education. Beverly Hills, California: Sage Publications, 1976.

3067. Ottenberg, D.J.   Teenage Alcohol Abuse: Focusing Our Concern. Psychiatric Opinion, 12(3): 6-11, 1975.

3068. Otterland, A.   Juvenile Workers in Sweden.   Industrial Medicine, 33: 201-208, 1964.

3069. Otterström, E.   Delinquency and Children from Bad Homes.   A Study of Their Prognosis from a Social Point of View. Acta Paediatrica, Stockholm, 33:   Supplement No. 5, 1946.

3070. Our Greatest Drug Problem--It's an Intensely Personal Thing. Listen, 28(5): 2-3, 1975.

3071. Overman, Everett F.   The Alcoholic Family: A Psychosocial Analysis.   American Archives of Rehabilitation Therapy, 24(2): 25-32, 1976.

3072. Owen, R.D.   Prevention of Alcoholism with Implication for Elementary and Secondary School Education.   Doctoral Dissertation (University Microfilms No. 77-4749). University of Oregon, 1976.

3073. Ozmon, Kenneth L., Desroches, Kenneth F. and MacDonald, Ian P. Using Community Resources: A Cooperative Approach to Drug Education for Teachers.   Journal of Alcohol and Drug Education, 19(3): 15-22, 1974.

P

3074. Packer, K.L. A Model Drug Policy for a School System. Health Education, 7(3): 34-35, 1976.

3075. Padilla, Eligio R., Padilla, Amado M., Morales, Armando, Olmedo, Esteban L. and Ramirez, Robert. Inhalant, Marijuana and Alcohol Abuse among Barrio Children and Adolescents. International Journal of the Addictions, 14(7): 945-964, 1979.

3076. Padovani, G. Considerazioni Sulle Condizioni Psicologiche dell' Alcoolismo e Deduzioni pro Filattiche e Terapeutiche. (The Psychological Conditions in Alcoholism and Prophylactic and Therapeutic Deductions.) Giornale Psiquiatria Neuropathologie, 76: 79-88, 1948.

3077. Page, J.D. Topic Outline for Classroom Teachers about Alcohol and Alcoholism. (Curriculum Guide) Pamphlet. Albuquerque: New Mexico Commission on Alcoholism, 1970.

3078. Pajka, S. Spozycie Alkoholu Przez Uczniów Klas VII w Powiecie Ostroleckim. (Consumption of Alcohol by 7th-Grade Primary-School Pupils and Their Families in the Town of Ostroleka and Surrounding Country.) Problemy Alkoholizmu, Warsaw, 14(3-4): 8-12, 1966.

3079. Palmer, R.H., Oulette, E.M., Warner, L. and Leichtman, S.R. Congenital Malformations in Offspring of a Chronic Alcoholic Mother. Pediatrics, 53(4): 490-499, 1974.

3080. Pandina, Robert. Adolescent Alcohol Use Project Description. New Brunswick, New Jersey: Rutgers Center of Alcohol Studies, 1977.

3081. Pandina, Robert J. and White, Helene Raskin. Patterns of Alcohol
         and Drug Use of Adolescent Students and Adolescents in
         Treatment. Journal of Studies on Alcohol, 42(5): 441-456,
         1981.

3082. Pandina, Robert, White, Helen Raskin and Yorke, Joseph.
         Estimation of Substance Use Involvement: Theoretical
         Considerations and Empirical Findings. International
         Journal of the Addictions, 16(1): 1-24, 1981.

3083. Pankau, Joseph W., Romer, Kenneth G., Mortimer, Rudolf G. and
         Stone, Donald B. An Educational Approach for Court
         Referred DWI Offenders: Diagnosis and Program Evaluation.
         Paper presented at the 50th Annual Convention of the
         American School Health Association, New Orleans, October,
         1976.

3084. Papanek, M.L. Excessive Drinking, a Factor in Family
         Disintegration. In: International Conference on
         Alcoholism and Drug Abuse, San Juan, Puerto Rico,
         November, 1973. Lausanne, Switzerland: International
         Council on Alcohol and Addictions, 1974, pages 183-193.

3085. Parent Drinking Often a Factor in Students' Behavior Problems.
         NIAAA Information and Feature Service (IFS No. 31): 6,
         December 28, 1976.

3086. Parents Misunderstand Kids' Switch to Alcohol. Listen, 26(12):
         20, 1973.

3087. Parfrey, P.S. Factors Associated with Undergraduate Alcohol
         Use. British Journal of Preventive and Social Medicine,
         28(4): 252-257, 1974.

3088. Park, P. College Drinking Profiles in Three Countries. In:
         The Domesticated Drug: Drinking among Collegians. Ed.
         G.L. Maddox. New Haven, Connecticut: College and
         University Press, 1970, pages 361-379.

3089. Park, P. Dimensions of Drinking among Male College Students.
         Social Problems, 14: 473-482, 1967.

3090. Park, Peter. Problem Drinking and Role Deviation: A Study in
         Incipient Alcoholism. In: Society, Culture and Drinking
         Patterns. Eds. D.J. Pittman and C.R. Snyder. New York:
         Wiley, 1962, pages 431-454.

3091. Parker, Douglas and Parker, Elizabeth. Status and Status
         Inconsistency of Parents on Alcohol Consumption of
         Teenage Children. International Journal of the
         Addictions, 15(8): 1233-1239, 1980.

3092.   Parker, F.B.   Sex-Role Adjustment and Drinking Disposition of
        Women College Students.   Journal of Studies on Alcohol,
        36(11): 1570-1573, 1975.

3093.   Parker, F.B.   Self-Role Strain and Drinking Disposition at a
        Prealcoholic Age Level.   Journal of Social Psychology,
        78(1): 55-61, 1969.

3094.   Parks, W.B.   Alcohol Education Nationwide as Reflected in
        Selected Curriculum Bulletins Issued by State Departments
        of Education.   AAIAN Newsletter, 4(2): 9-15, 1958.

3095.   Parland, O.   Alkoholism och Homosexualitet.   (Alcoholism and
        Homosexuality.)   Alkoholipolitiikka, Helsingfor, (3): 75-
        80, 101-102, 1957.

3096.   Parland, O.   Alkoholismi ja Homoseksualismi.   (Alcoholism and
        Homosexuality.)   Alkoholipolitiikka, Helsingfor, (4): 119-
        124, 1957.

3097.   Parnitzke, K.H. and Prüssing, O.   Kinder Alkoholsüchtiger Eltern.
        (Children of Alcoholic Parents.)   Psychiatrie, Neurologie
        und Medizinische Psychologie, Leipzig, 18: 1-5, 1966.

3098.   Parr, R.J.   Alcoholism and Cruelty to Children.   British Journal
        of Inebriety, 6: 77-81, 1908.   (Also in: Medical Press
        and Circular, 85: 659, 1908.

3099.   Parry, Hugh J.   Sample Surveys of Drug Abuse.   In: Handbook on
        Drug Abuse.   Eds. R.I. Dupont, A. Goldstein and
        J. O'Donnell.   Washington, D.C.:   U.S. Government Printing
        Office, 1979, pages 381-394.

3100.   Parsons, P.J.   A Study of Values of Spanish-Surname Undergraduate
        College Students at Five State Colleges in Colorado.
        Doctoral Dissertation (University Microfilms No. 71-4205).
        University of Northern Colorado, 1970.

3101.   Partanen, J., Bruun, K. and Markkanen, T.   Inheritance of
        Drinking Behavior: A Study on Intelligence, Personality
        and Use of Alcohol of Adult Twins.   (Finnish Foundation
        for Alcohol Studies, Publication No. 14)   Helsinki,
        Finland: Finnish Foundation for Alcohol Studies, 1966.

3102.   Pasciutti, John.   Current Emphasis in Instruction about
        Alcoholism.   In: Interpreting Current Knowledge about
        Alcohol and Alcoholism to a College Community.
        Proceedings of a Conference, May 28-30, 1963, Albany,
        New York.   Ed. Richard Reynolds.   Albany: New York State
        Department of Mental Health, 1963, pages 62-73.

3103. Pasciutti, John. The Need for Alcohol Education. In: Alcohol
        Education--Whose Responsibility? (Proceedings of a
        Conference, May, 1963, sponsored by Michigan Department of
        Mental Health; Michigan Department of Public Instruction;
        Michigan Department of Health; Michigan Congress of
        Parents and Teachers; Michigan State University; Michigan
        State Board of Alcoholism; and U.S. Public Health Service.)
        Lansing: Michigan State Board of Alcoholism, 1963,
        pages 22-26.

3104. Pasciutti, John J. Alcohol Education in the State of Vermont.
        Montpelier: Vermont Department of Education, 1956.

3105. Pasciutti, John J. Alcohol Education: Its Role in Prevention
        of Excessive Drinking. Journal of Alcohol Education,
        13(2): 2-9, 1967.

3106. Pasciutti, John J. The Role of the Elementary School in Alcohol
        Education. Leaflet. Montpelier: Vermont Department of
        Education, 1957.

3107. Pasciutti, John J. The Role of Parents in Alcohol Problems.
        Leaflet. Montpelier: Vermont Department of Education,
        1957.

3108. Pashchenkov, S.Z. O Klinicheskom Techenii Alkogolizma u
        Bol'nykh s Semeinoi Otyagoshchennost'yu. (The Clinical
        Evolution of Alcoholism in Patients with a Familial
        Taint.) Klinicheskaya Meditsina, Moskav, 52(3): 93-96,
        1974.

3109. Passey, G.E. and Pennington, D.F., Jr. Techniques for the
        Assessment of Selected Attitudes toward Alcohol and Its
        Use. Montgomery: Alabama Commission on Alcoholism, 1959.

3110. Paszkowska, H. Pciie i Nadużywanie Alkoholu Przez Młodociany
        ch Sprawców Przestepstw Przeciwko Mieniu. (Drinking and
        Alcohol Misuse among Juveniles Guilty of Crimes against
        Property. Problemy Alkoholizmu, Warsaw, 24(9): 9-10,
        1977.

3111. Paszkowska, H. Picie i Nadużywanie Alkoholu Przez Młodcianych
        Sprawców Przestepstw Przeciwko Mieniu. Cz. II. (Drinking
        and Intoxication among Juvenile Perpetrators of Property
        Offenses. Part II.) Problemy Alkoholizmu, Warsaw,
        24(10): 9, 1977.

3112. Patch, Vernon. Public Health Aspects of Adolescent Drug Use.
        In: Drug Use in America: Problems in Perspective.
        Appendix. Volume I. Patterns and Consequences of Drug
        Use. U.S. National Commission on Marihuana and Drug
        Abuse. Washington, D.C. : U.S. Government Printing
        Office, 1973, pages 975-1077.

3113. Patel, A.R., Roy, M. and Wilson, G.M. Self-Poisoning and
       Alcohol. Lancet, 2(787): 1099-1102, 1972.

3114. Paton, R.T. Drinking: Social and Otherwise: A Primer on Booze
       and Commonsense Guide to Self-Evaluation. Pamphlet.
       Arlington, Virginia: H/P Publishing Company, 1978.

3115. Patrick C. Relation of Childhood and Adult Leisure Activities.
       Journal of Social Psychology, 21: 65-79, 1945.

3116. Patterson, H.R. Drinking Patterns in Leicestershire. Journal
       of Alcoholism, 7(4): 118-130, 1972.

3117. Paty, J. A Comparative Report on the Non-Use or Use of Drugs
       by Secondary Students in Public Schools in Hawaii, 1971
       and 1974. Honolulu, Hawaii: Department of Education,
       Office of Instructional Services, 1975.

3118. Paul, A.M., Jr. Alcoholism--Prevention: Alcohol Education as
       Preventive Medicine. Journal of the Kansas Medical
       Society, 69(9): 418-420, 1968.

3119. Paul, D.L. An Evaluation of Alcohol Education Materials in
       Elementary, Junior High School and Senior High School
       Textbooks as Related to Student Needs. Master's Thesis.
       Kalamazoo, Michigan: Western Michigan University, 1964.

3120. A Peaceful "Rock" Festival. (Editorial) Journal of Alcoholism,
       11: 77, 1976.

3121. Peacock, P.B., Gelman, A.C. and Lutins, T.A. Preventive Health
       Care Strategies for Health Maintenance Organizations.
       Preventive Medicine, 4: 183-225, 1975.

3122. Pearce, J. and Garrett, H.D. A Comparison of the Drinking
       Behavior of Delinquent Youth Versus Non-Delinquent Youth
       in the States of Idaho and Utah. Journal of School Health,
       40: 131-135, 1970.

3123. Pearlman, S. Patterns of Doctoral Dissertations and Master's
       Theses Focused on Drug Usage among Students in Educational
       Settings. Journal of Alcohol and Drug Education, 20(2):
       1-4, 1975.

3124. Pearson, Gladys E. A Polydrug Society. The Alcoholism Digest
       Annual, 2: 35-39, 1973-1974.

3125. Peek, C., III. Drinking Regulations of Colleges and National
       College Fraternities. In: The Domesticated Drug:
       Drinking among Collegians. Ed. G.L. Maddox. New Haven,
       Connecticut: College and University Press, 1970, pages
       254-267.

3126. Peek, C.W. III. Consensus on Drinking Norms and Strength of
       Sanctions in Male Collegiate Friendship Groups. Doctoral
       Dissertation (University Microfilms No. 71-24198).
       Durham, North Carolina: Duke University, 1971.

3127. Peer Approach to Prevention in Philadelphia. Alcohol Health and
       Research World, 2: 10-13, 1974.

3128. Peltoniemi, T. Begreppet Familjevåld: Dess Anknytning till
       Alkohol och Andra Sociala Problem. (The Concept of Family
       Violence: Its Connection with Alcohol and Other Social
       Problems.) Alkohol och Narkotica, 74(5): 21-26, 1980.

3129. Peltoniemi, T. Kemin Koululaisten Keskioluen Käyttö. (The Use
       of Medium Beer among Students in Kemi.) Alkoholikysymys,
       Helsinki, 43: 84-89, 1975.

3130. Peltoniemi, T. Nuorten Alkoholijuomien Käytöstä Aiheutuvat
       Ristiriidat. (Social Conflicts Caused by Alcohol
       Consumption among Youth.) Alkoholikysymys, Helsinki, 43:
       90-92, 1975.

3131. Peltoniemi, T. Nuorten Alkoholijuomien Käyttö Pääkaupungissa ja
       Peräpohjolassa. (Drinking Habits of Youth in Helsinki and
       Northern Finland.) Alkoholikysymys, Helsinki, 46: 48-58,
       1978.

3132. Peltoniemi, T. Ungdomens Alkoholvanor i Torneå och Harparanda:
       Tornedalstraditionen. (The Drinking Habits of Youth in
       Torneå and Harparanda: Traditions in Tornedalen.)
       Alkoholipolitiikka, Helsingfor, 41: 135-145, 1978.

3133. Pelz, D.C., McDole, T.L. and Schuman, S.H. Drinking-Driving
       Behavior of Young Men in Relation to Accidents. Journal
       of Studies on Alcohol, 36: 956-972, 1975.

3134. Pelz, D.C. and Schuman, S.H. Drinking, Hostility and Alienation
       in Driving of Young Men. In: Proceedings of the Third
       Annual Alcoholism Conference of the National Institute on
       Alcohol Abuse and Alcoholism, Washington, D.C., June 20-
       22, 1973. Ed. M. Chafetz. Rockville, Maryland:
       National Institute on Alcohol Abuse and Alcoholism, 1973,
       pages 50-74. (DHEW Publication No. ADM 75-137)

3135. Pelz, D.C. and Schuman, S.H. What is the "Dangerous Age" for
       Young Drivers? Traffic Safety, 70(8): 24-25, 35-36, 1970.

3136. Penick, Elizabeth C., Read, Marsha R., Crowley, Patricia A. and
       Powell, Barbara J. Differentiation of Alcoholics by
       Family History. Journal of Studies on Alcohol, 39(11):
       1944-1948, 1978.

3137. Penn, J.R. College Student Life-Style and Frequency of Alcohol Usage. _Journal of the American College Health Association_, _22_(3): 220-222, 1974.

3138. Pennsylvania Department of Education. _Conceptual Guidelines for School Health Programs in Pennsylvania_. Harrisburg, Pennsylvania, 1970.

3139. Pennsylvania Liquor Control Board. _Underage Drinking: What's in it for You?_ Pamphlet. Philadelphia, Pennsylvania, no date.

3140. Penyazeva, G.A. Alkogolizm i Narusheniye Mozgovogo Krovobrashcheniya v Molodom Vostraste. (Alcoholism and Brain Circulation Disorders in Young People.) In: _Tretii Vseros. Syedz Nevropatologor i Psikhiatrov, Kazan._ _Tom 3. Tezisky Doklady._ (The Third All-Russian Congress of Neuropathologists and Psychiatrists, Kazan'. Volume 3. Thesis and Proceedings.) Moskva, 1974, pages 260-261.

3141. People Helping People. _Alcohol Abuse_, _1_(2); 2-14, 1974.

3142. Percey, L.R.N. Alcoholism and Attempted Suicide. _British Medical Journal_, _2_: 1167, 1954.

3143. Perčinkovski, R., Polenaković, M. and Cekov, G. Analitička Studija Protvalkoholonog Vaspitanja Omladine USSR Makedonjii. (Analytical Study of the Antialcohol Education of Youth in the Socialist Republic of Macedonia.) _Anali Bolince "Dr. M. Stojanović"_, Zagreb, _6_: 149-159, 1967.

3144. Perlstein, A. and Clifford, B. The Use of Drugs in the Treatment of Alcoholism in the Young. Paper Presented at the Fourteenth Annual Meeting of the North American Association of Alcoholism Programs, Miami Beach, Florida, October 27-31, 1963.

3145. Perrine, M.W. The Vermont Driver Profile: A Psychometric Approach to Early Identification of Potential High-Risk Drinking Drivers. In: _Alcohol, Drugs and Traffic Safety_. Proceedings of the Sixth International Conference on Alcohol, Drugs and Traffic Safety, Toronto, September 8-13, 1974. Eds. S. Israelstam and S. Lambert. Toronto: Addiction Research Foundation of Ontario, 1975, pages 199-223.

3146. Perry, M.E. How Teens are Switching from Dope to Alcohol: Too Many Parents are Saying "Thank God, Johnny's Only Drunk". _Washington Star_, A1, A5, February 25, 1975.

3147. The Persuasive Convert. _Human Behavior_, _5_(2): 48-49, 1976.

3148. Peters, H.B. Changes in Color Fields Occasioned by
        Experimentally Induced Intoxication. Journal of Applied
        Psychology, 26: 692-701, 1942.

3149. Peterson, Davis M., Beer, Elizabeth T. and Elifson, Kirk W.
        Student Drug Use: An Annotated Bibliography. Atlanta,
        Georgia: Department of Sociology, Georgia State
        University, 1975.

3150. Peterson, Robert C. Suggestions for Educators. In: Resource
        Book for Drug Abuse Education. American Association for
        Health, Physical Education and Recreation. Washington,
        D.C.: U.S. Government Printing Office, 1969, pages 4-7.

3151. Petit, M. and Lépine, J.-P. L'Enfant et l'Adolescent Devant
        l'Alcool. (The Child and the Adolescent with Respect
        to Alcohol.) Gazette Medicale de France, 85: 4123-4124,
        4126, 1978.

3152. Pettersen, J.R. Kulturkamp for Edruskap. (Cultural Struggle
        for Sobriety.) Tidsskrift EdruSpørsm, 30(4): 18, 25,
        1978.

3153. Petrován, O. Serdülökorúak Védelme az Alkoholizmus Veszélyei
        Ellen: Elözetes Megjegyzések egy Pályázathoz. (The
        Protection of Adolescents against the Hazards of
        Alcoholism: Preliminary Comments on a Competition.)
        Alkohologia, Budapest, 3: 161-167, 1972.

3154. Petzel, T.P., Johnson, J.E. and McKillip, J. Response Bias in
        Drug Surveys. Journal of Consulting and Clinical
        Psychology, 40(3): 437-439, 1973.

3155. Pharmacological Features of Drug Dependence, A Symposia. In:
        The Pharmacological and Epidemiological Aspects of
        Adolescent Drug Dependence. Ed. C. Wilson, Oxford,
        England, Pergamon Press, 1968, pages 241-288.

3156. Phelps, Donald G. Do Ethnic Minorities Need Special Alcoholism
        Programs? Addictions, 2(3): 7-9, 1973.

3157. Phelps, Donald G. Minority Treatment Programs? The Alcoholism
        Digest Annual, 1: 6-11, 1972-1973.

3158. Phillips, Julianne. Alcoholics Anonymous: An Annotated
        Bibliography, 1935-1972. London, Ohio: Central Ohio
        Publishing Company, 1973.

3159. Phillipson, R. Adolescent Alcohol Abuse. Drug Abuse and
        Alcoholism Newsletter, 2(8): 4, 1973.

3160. Phillipson, Richard V. Special Groups and Situations.
       1. Problem Drinking in Adolescents. In: The Substance
       Abuse Problems. Ed. Sidney Cohen. New York: The Haworth
       Press, 1981, pages 313-318.

3161. Phillipson, Richard V. Special Groups and Situations.
       2. Teenage Drinking: The Bottle Babies. In: The
       Substance Abuse Problems. Ed. Sidney Cohen. New York:
       The Haworth Press, 1981, pages 318-324.

3162. Phillipson, Richard V. Special Groups and Situations.
       3. Lowering the Drinking Age: Effects on Auto Accidents.
       In: The Substance Abuse Problems. Ed. Sidney Cohen.
       New York: The Haworth Press, 1981, pages 325-329.

3163. Piechaud, F. and Freour, P. L'éducation de la Jeunesse dans la
       Lutte Anti-Alcoolique. Rôle des Centres d'éducation
       Sanitaire. (Education of Youth in the Antialcohol Fight.
       The Role of Health Education Centers.) Annales D'hygiene
       Publique et de Médecine Légale, Paris, 28: 151-156, 1950.

3164. Pierson, W.L. Recommended Principles for Curriculum Development
       Derived from a Survey and Analysis of Alcohol and Drug
       Curricula in Selected Upper Great Plains School Systems.
       Doctoral Dissertation (University Microfilms No. 77-34530).
       University of South Dakota, 1976.

3165. Pinheiro Cintra. Sobre o Alcoolismo nas Criancas. (Alcoholism
       in Children.) Pediatria Pratica, San Paulo, 14: 249, 1943.

3166. Pinto, Leonard J. Alcohol and Drug Abuse among Native American
       Youth on Reservations: A Growing Crisis. In: Drug Use
       in America: Problems in Perspective. Appendix.
       Volume 1. Patterns and Consequences of Drug Use. U.S.
       National Commission on Marihuana and Drug Abuse.
       Washington, D.C.: U.S. Government Printing Office, 1973,
       pages 1157-1178.

3167. Pipher, J.R. An Evaluation of an Alcohol Course for Junior High
       School Students: An Examination of Differential Course
       Effectiveness as Associated with Subject Characteristics.
       Doctoral Dissertation (University Microfilms No. 78-3883).
       The University of Nebraska-Lincoln, 1977.

3168. Pittell, S.M. The Etiology of Youthful Drug Involvement. In:
       Drug Use in America: Problems in Perspective. Appendix.
       Volume I. Patterns and Consequences. U.S. National
       Commission on Marihuana and Drug Abuse. Washington, D.C.:
       U.S. Government Printing Office, 1973, pages 879-913.

3169. Pittman, D.J., Ed. Alcoholism. New York: Harper and Row,
       1967.

3170. Pittman, D.J. and Lambert, M.D. Alcohol, Alcoholism and
       Advertising: A Preliminary Investigation of Asserted
       Associations. St. Louis: Washington University, Social
       Science Institute, 1978.

3171. Pittman, David. An Overview of Social and Demographic Issues.
       In: Currents in Alcoholism. Volume 7. Recent Advances
       in Research and Treatment. Ed. M. Galanter. New York:
       Grune and Stratton, 1980, pages 341-349.

3172. Pittman, David J. Drinking and Alcoholism in American Society.
       In: Alcoholism. Ed. R.J. Catanzaro. Springfield,
       Illinois: Charles C. Thomas, 1968, pages 70-79.

3173. Pittman, David J. Skid Row and the Law. The Alcoholism Digest
       Annual, 2: 24-30, 1973-1974.

3174. Pittman, David J. and Gordon, C. Wayne. Revolving Door--A Study
       of the Chronic Police Case Inebriate. Glencoe, Illinois:
       The Free Press, 1958.

3175. Pittman, David J. and Snyder, Charles R., Eds. Society,
       Culture, and Drinking Patterns. New York: John Wiley and
       Sons, Inc., 1962.

3176. Pizer, Vernon. The Young Drunks. Washington Daily News (Sunday
       Star Magazine Section): 7, 19-25, A, 1973.

3177. Planar for Laerarutdanning i Obligatoriske Emne i Grunnskolen:
       Alkohol, Narkotika og Tobakk. (Planning Required Courses
       for Teacher Training in the Primary School: Alcohol,
       Narcotics and Tobacco.) Norsk Tidsskrift EdruSpørsm, 27:
       137-141, 1975.

3178. Plant, M.A. Young Drug and Alcohol Casualties Compared: Review
       of 100 Patients at a Scottish Psychiatric Hospital.
       British Journal of Addiction, 71: 31-43, 1976.

3179. Plant, Martin. Is Illegal Drugtaking a Problem? In:
       International Conference on Alcoholism and Drug Dependence:
       Alcoholism and Drug Dependence, a Multidisciplinary
       Approach. Proceeedings of the Third International
       Conference on Alcoholism and Drug Dependence, Liverpool,
       England, April, 1976. Eds. J.S. Madden, Robin Walker and
       W.H. Kenyon. New York: Plenum Press, 1977, pages 35-46.

3180. Plant, Martin A. Drugtakers in an English Town. London:
       Tavistock Publications, 1975.

3181. Plant, Martin A. Learning to Drink. In: Alcoholism in
       Perspective. Eds. Marcus Grant and Paul Gwinner.
       Baltimore: University Park Press, 1979, pages 34-41.

3182. Plat, P. Considerations Biologiques sur la Nutrition des Enfants
       Occidentaux. (Biological Considerations about the
       Nutrition of Western Children.) Infirmiere Francaise,
       Paris: (212): 31-32, 1980.

3183. Plaut, T.F.A. Prevention of Alcoholism. In: Handbook of
       Community Mental Health. Eds. S.E. Golann and
       C. Eisdorfer. New York: Appleton-Century-Crofts, 1972,
       pages 421-438.

3184. Plaut, Thomas. Alcohol Problems: A Report to the Nation by the
       Cooperative Commission on the Study of Alcoholism. New
       York: Oxford University Press, 1967.

3185. Pliner, P. and Cappell, H. Drinking, Driving and the
       Attribution of Responsibility. Journal of Studies on
       Alcohol, 38: 593-602, 1977.

3186. Plymat, W.N. How to Fortify Young People against Social
       Pressure to Drink. Leaflet. Des Moines, Iowa: Preferred
       Risk Mutual Insurance, 1965.

3187. Plymat, W.N. Should the Legal Drinking Age be Lowered? Report
       on Alcohol, 30(1): 3-30, 1972.

3188. Plymat, W.N. Total Education for the Prevention of Alcoholism.
       Report on Alcohol, 32(3): 3-35, 1974.

3189. Plumb, Marjorie, D'Amanda, Christopher and Tainter, Zebulon.
       Chemical Substance Abuse and Perceived Locus of Control.
       In: Predicting Adolescent Drug Abuse: A Review of Issues,
       Methods and Correlates--Research Issues II. Ed.
       Dan Lettieri. Rockville, Maryland: National Institute on
       Drug Abuse, 1975, pages 225-261.

3190. Plüss-Rüegg, P. Unterwegs zur Neuen Rangordnung der Werte.
       (Toward a New Ranking of Values.) Fürsorger, 42: 18-22,
       1974.

3191. Pogády, J. and Haško, L. Komprehenzívny Prístup k Problematike
       Alkoholizmu Mládeže. (A Comprehensive Approach to
       Problems of Juvenile Alcoholism.) Protialkoholicky Obzor,
       Bratislava, 12: 7-11, 1977.

3192. Poldrugo, F. and De-Vanna, M. La Farmacodipendenza e
       l'Alcoolismo nei Giovani. (Drug-Dependence and Alcoholism
       in Youth.) Minerva Psichiatrica e Psicologica, Turin,
       18: 99-102, 1977.

3193. Poldrugo, F., De-Vanna, M., Ottolenghi, F. and Verrienti, P.
       Alcohol and Drug Dependence in the Youth: A Comparative
       Study. Alcoholism, Zagreb, 14: 122-125, 1978.

3194.   Polich, J.M.   Alcohol Problems among Civilian and Military
        Personnel.   In: Youth, Alcohol and Social Policy.   Eds.
        H.T. Blane and M.E. Chafetz.   New York: Plenum Press,
        1979, pages 59-90.

3195.   Polk, K.   Drinking and the Adolescent Culture.   Eugene, Oregon:
        Lane County Youth Project, 1964.

3196.   Polk, K. and Burkett, S.R.   Drinking as Rebellion: A Study of
        Adolescent Drinking Patterns.   In: Schools and
        Delinquency.   Eds. K. Polk and W. Schafer.   Englewood
        Cliffs, New Jersey: Prentice-Hall, 1972, pages 116-128.

3197.   Polk, Kenneth.   Class Strains and Rebellion among Adolescents.
        In: Schools and Delinquency.   Eds. K. Polk and
        W.E. Schafer.   Englewood Cliffs, New Jersey: Prentice-
        Hall, 1972, pages 102-114.

3198.   Polk, Kenneth and Halferty, David.   School Cultures, Adolescent
        Commitments and Delinquency.   In: Schools and
        Delinquency.   Eds. K. Polk and W.E. Schafer.   Englewood
        Cliffs, New Jersey: Prentice-Hall, 1972, pages 71-90.

3199.   Polk, Kenneth and Schafer, Walter E., Eds.   Schools and
        Delinquency.   Englewood Cliffs, New Jersey: Prentice-
        Hall, 1972.

3200.   Pollack, D. and Shore, J.H.   Validity of the MMPI with Native
        Americans.   American Journal of Psychiatry, 137: 946-950,
        1980.

3201.   Pollack, J.H.   Teenage Drinking and Drug Addiction.   National
        Education Association Journal, 55(5): 8-12, 1966.

3202.   Pollack, M.B.   Mood-Altering Substances: A Behavior Inventory.
        Journal of Educational Measurement, 7(3): 211-212, 1970.

3203.   Pollack, Marion.   Construction of an Evaluation Instrument to
        Appraise Behavior in the Use of Stimulants and
        Depressants.   Journal of Alcohol Education, 13(4): 11-16,
        1968.

3204.   Poll Rates Teen Drinking No. 2 in Illinois Issues.   Journal of
        Alcohol and Drug Education, 24(2): 72, 1979.

3205.   Polo, Carol Jane Abernathy.   A Study of Alcohol Education for
        Pre-Adult Males Premised on the Methodology and
        Principles of Adult Education.   Doctoral Dissertation
        (University Microfilms No. 72-25056).   Kansas State
        University, 1975.

3206. Polo, Kenneth Ray. A Longitudinal Study of Alcohol Education
       for Pre-Adult Males Premised on the Methodology and
       Principles of Adult Education. Doctoral Dissertation
       (University Microfilms No. 75-25057). Kansas State
       University, 1975.

3207. Polyanskaya, T.C. I.M. Dogel'--Odin iz Bortsov s Alkogolizmom v
       Dorevolyutsionnoi Rossii. (I.M. Dogel'--One of the
       Fighters against Alcoholism in Prerevolutionary Russia.)
       Sovetskoe Zdravookhranenie, Moskow, 21(7): 56-60, 1962.

3208. Pomeroy, G.S. and Globetti, G. The Mississippi Story: A
       Demonstration Project in Alcohol Education. (Mississippi
       State University, Department of Sociology and Anthropology,
       Administrative Report No. 1) Mississippi: State College,
       1968.

3209. Popham, R.E., Schmidt, W. and De-Lint, J. The Effects of Legal
       Restraint on Drinking. In: The Biology of Alcoholism.
       Volume 4. Treatment and Rehabilitation of the Chronic
       Alcoholic. Eds. B. Kissin and H. Begleiter. New York:
       Plenum Press, 1972, pages 576-625.

3210. Popper, P. A Serdülők Alkoholizmusáról. (On the Alcoholism of
       Adolescents.) Alkohologia, Budapest, 3: 144-147, 1972.

3211. Poremba, Chet. Youth Treatment Complex: Other Health,
       Emotional, Social Needs Must be Met. Focus on Alcohol and
       Drug Issues, 4(3): 22, 1981.

3212. Porter, M.R., Vierira, T.A., Kaplan, G.J., Heesch, J.B. and
       Colyar, A.B. Drug Use in Anchorage, Alaska. A Survey of
       15,634 Students in Grades 6 through 12 in 1971. Journal
       of the American Medical Association, 223: 657-664, 1973.

3213. Portnoy, Barry. Effects of a Controlled-Usage Alcohol Education
       Program Based on the Health Belief Model. Journal of Drug
       Education, 10(3): 181-195, 1980.

3214. Posel, Z. and Tomczak, J.W. Alkoholizowanie sie Młodzieży.
       (Young People are Becoming Alcoholics.) Problemy
       Alkoholizmu, Warsaw, 23(4): 15-16, 22, 1976.

3215. Posel, Z. and Tomczak, J.W. Psychiatryczne Aspekty Relacji
       Miedzy Nadużywaniem Alkoholu i Innych Środków Odurzajacych
       Przez Młodziez. (Psychiatric Aspects of the Relation
       between the Misuse of Alcohol and that of Other Stupefying
       Agents by Young People.) In: Alkohol, Alkoholizm i Inne
       Uzależnienia. Przejawy, Profilaktyka, Terapia. Tom II.
       (Alcohol, Alcoholism and Other Addictions. Symptomatology,
       Prophylaxis and Therapy. Volume II.) Ed. J. Morawski.
       Warszawa: Wydawnictwo Prawnicze, 1977, pages 181-190,
       English Summary, page 190.

3216.   Pospišil-Završki, K. and Turčin, R.   Alkoholizam i čl. 196.
KZ--Zlostavljanje i Zapuštanje Maloljetnika.   (Alcoholism
and Article 196 of the Criminal Law--Abuse and Neglect of
Minors.)   Neuropsihijatrija, Zagreb, 16: 49-53, 1968.

3217.   Postoyan, S. and Orford, J.   Drinking Behaviour and Its
Determinants amongst University Students in London.   In:
Proceedings of the Third International Conference on
Alcoholism and Addictions, Cardiff, Volume I.   Ed.
M. Evans.   London: Welsh Hospital Board, 1970.

3218.   Poteat, W.H.   The Theological Student and the Liquor Question.
Quarterly Journal of Studies on Alcohol, 4: 195-198, 1943.

3219.   Potvin, Raymond H. and Lee, Che-Fu.   Multistage Path Models of
Adolescent Alcohol and Drug Use.   Journal of Studies on
Alcohol, 41(5): 531-542, 1980.

3220.   Poulsen, R.L.   Variables Discriminant of Problem Drinking
Behaviors among a Select Sample of Two-Year Multicultural
College Students in New Mexico and El Paso, Texas.
Doctoral Dissertation (University Microfilms No. 77-25070).
New Mexico State University, 1977.

3221.   Poulsen, Roger L., Pettibone, Timothy J. and Willey, Darrell S.
The Ethnic Variable and Problem Drinking in a Select
Sample of Southwestern Two-Year Multicultural College
Students.   American Journal of Drug and Alcohol Abuse,
5(4): 497-506, 1978.

3222.   Powell, David.   Needs Assessment Survey Reoport--Eastern Area
Alcohol Education and Training Program.   Journal of
Alcohol and Drug Education, 21(3): 1-7, 1976.

3223.   Powell, K.   Alcohol and the Adolescent Drinker.   Australian
Family Physician, Sydney, 7: 663-671, 1978.

3224.   Powell, M.   Youth: Critical Issues.   Columbus, Ohio: Merrill,
1972.

3225.   Powell, M. and Frerichs, A.H., Eds.   Readings in Adolescent
Psychology.   Minneapolis, Minnesota: Burgess, 1971.

3226.   Powledge, Fred.   Are We Raising a Generation of Alcoholics?
Family Circle: 74, 82, 160, 162, April, 1975.

3227.   Prendergast, T.J., Jr., Preble, M.R., Jr. and Tennant, F.S., Jr.
Drug Use and Its Relation to Alcohol and Cigarette
Consumption in the Military Community of West Germany:
Drugs, Alcohol, Cigarettes in a Military Setting.
International Journal of the Addictions, 8: 741-754, 1973.

3228. Prendergast, T.J., Jr. and Schaefer, E.S. Correlates of Drinking and Drunkenness among High-School Students. Quarterly Journal of Studies on Alcohol, 35: 232-242, 1974.

3229. Prescott, James. Somatosensory Affectional Deprivation (SAD) Theory of Drug and Alcohol Use. In: Theories on Drug Abuse: Selected Contemporary Problems. (NIDA Research Monograph Series 30). U.S. National Institute on Drug Abuse. Eds. Dan Lettieri, Mollie Sayers and Helen Pearson. Washington, D.C.: U.S. Government Printing Office, 1980, pages 286-296. (DHEW Publication No. ADM 80-967)

3230. Presnall, L.F. Alcoholism--The Exposed Family. Salt Lake City: Utah Alcoholism Foundation, 1977.

3231. Preston, J.D. Factors Related to Attitudes and Behavior toward Beverage Alcohol among High School Students. Master's Thesis. Mississippi State University, 1964.

3232. Preston, J.D. Religiosity and Adolescent Drinking Behavior. Sociological Quarterly, 10: 372-383, 1969.

3233. Preusser, D.F., Oates, J.F. and Orban, M.S. Identification of Countermeasures for the Youth Crash Problem Related to Alcohol. Springfield, Virginia: National Techinical Information Service, 1975. (DOT HS-801344)

3234. Prevet, T.E. The Effects of an Alcohol Instructional Model on Self-Reported Drinking Behavior of University Students. Doctoral Dissertation (University Microfilms No. 7732693). State University of New York at Buffalo, 1977.

3235. Price, G.B. Alcoholism and Childhood. British Journal of Inebriety, 8: 67-77, 1910.

3236. Prince, R., Greenfield, R. and Marriott, J. Cannabis or Alcohol? Observations on their Use in Jamaica. Bulletin on Narcotics, 24(1): 1-9, 1972.

3237. Priyadarsini, S. Public Perceptions of Drinking by Juveniles in India: A Case Study. Journal of Studies on Alcohol, 42: 594-603, 1981.

3238. Problems Related to Alcohol Consumption: The Changing Situation: Report of a WHO Expert Committee. Contemporary Drug Problems, 9(2): 185-207, 1980.

3239. Proceedings of the Jount Conference on Alcohol Abuse and Alcoholism, February 21-23, 1972. Washington, D.C.: U.S. Government Printing Office, 1972. (DHEW Publication No. HSM 73-9051).

3240. Proceedings of the Third Annual Alcoholism Conference of the
         National Institute on Alcohol Abuse and Alcoholism, June
         20-22, 1973, Washington, D.C. Alcoholism: A Multilevel
         Problem Treatment: Organization and Management.
         Rockville, Maryland, 1973. (DHEW Publication No. ADM
         75-137)

3241. Proface, D. Collegiate Drinking. Commonwealth, 25: 633-634,
         1937.

3242. Program on Alcohol Abuse Aimed at School Children. Public
         Health Reports, 89(6): 588, 1974.

3243. Protecting Your Health Series: Teacher's Manual. Fairfield,
         New Jersey: Cebco Standard, 1974.

3244. Prové, W. Sociologische Aspecten van het Alcoolisme: Onderzoek
         Naar Enkele Drinkgewoonten bij de Gentse
         Universiteitsstudent. (Sociological Aspects of Alcoholism:
         Investigation into Drinking Habits of Ghent University
         Students.) Archives Belges de Médecine Social, Hygiene,
         Médecine du Travail et Médecine Legal, Brussels, 11: 16-28,
         1965. (Also as: Enquête sur Quelques Comportements des
         Étudiants en Matière d'Usage de Boissons Alcoolisées à
         l'Université de Gand. [Investigation on Some Behaviors
         of Ghent University Students with Respect to Use of
         Alcoholic Beverages.] Revue de l'Alcoolisme, 11: 16-28,
         1965.

3245. Prys-Williams, G. Supermarket Off-Licenses and the Growth of
         Drunkenness among Young Women and Young Persons Since 1966.
         Pamphlet. (Prepared for the Christian Economic and Social
         Research Foundation) London: Alliance News, 1975.

3246. Psotka, J. and McKnight, A.J. Youth, Alcohol, and Driving:
         Subtle Attitude Measures. In: American Association for
         Automotive Medicine. Proceedings of the 23rd Annual
         Conference of the American Association for Automotive
         Medicine in Cooperation with the University of Louisville
         School of Medicine, held at Louisville, Kentucky,
         October 3-6, 1979. Morton Grove, Illinois, 1981.

3247. Psychology of Teenage Drinking. Journal of Alcohol Education,
         15(2): 16, 1970.

3248. PTA and HEW Act Against Alcoholism. National PTA Bulletin,
         Summer 1972.

3249. PTA Launches Media Campaign against Teen Alcohol Abuse. Brewers
         Digest, 52(10): 32-34, 1977.

3250. Pullar-Strecker, H. Is Juvenile Drunkenness Increasing? British
         Medical Journal, 2: 1354, 1954.

3251. Punnanitanond, S. Changing Patterns of Drug Use among Thai
           Youths, 1972-1976. Journal of Drug Issues, 10: 241-256,
           1980.

3252. Purdy, K. Young People and Driving. New York: John Day, 1967,
           especially pages 53-61.

3253. Purtell, T.C. Tonight is too Late. New York: Paul S. Erikson,
           1965, especially pages 105-121, 123-140.

3254. Pyramid Alternatives, Inc. Drinking Behavior, Attitudes and
           Problems among Seventh and Eighth Graders at the Laguna
           Salada Union School District. Pacifica, California:
           Pyramid Alternatives, Inc., 1977.

Q

3255. Questions for Teachers: Can the School Health Education Study
      Help You? Journal of Alcohol Education, 14(2): 30-33,
      1968.

3256. Quidu, M., Boschi, J.E. and Gautier, E. La Consommation
      Ethylique Excessive chez les Jeunes de Moins de 25 Ans.
      (Excessive Alcohol Consumption in Young People Under the
      Age of 25.) Revue de Neuripsychiatrie et d'Hygiene
      Mentale de l'Enfance, Paris, 20(6-7): 551-559, 1972.

3257. Quidu, M., Hellaouet, M., Lobrichon, M.-C., Soyer, Y. and
      Gautier, R. A Propos de Quelques cas d'Ivresse Publique
      chez des Mineurs Pénaux. (Concerning Some Cases of Public
      Drunkenness among Juvenile Delinquents.) Revue de
      Neuropsychiatrie Infantile et d'Hygiene Mentale de
      l'Enfance, Paris, 22: 737-751, 1974.

3258. Quirin, Dianne. Girls, Boys and Booze. A Local Look at the
      Nation's Newest Teenage Tragedy: The Adolescent Alcoholic.
      Courier Express (Magazine): August 17, 1975, no pages.

3259. Quiroga-de-García, S. Estudio de las Actitudes Frente al
      Alcohol en Dos Grupos de Niños de 13 Años. (Study of
      Attitudes toward Alcohol in Two Groups of 13-Year-Old
      Children.) Acta Psiquiátrica y Psicologia de America
      Latina, 22: 295-301, 1976.

_____ R

3260. Rabins, P., Swanson, W.C. and Gallant, D.M. A Comparison of Two
       Methods of Determining Drug Use among University Students.
       Journal of the Louisiana State Medical Society, 126(1): 1-
       4, 1974.

3261. Rachal, J.V. Defining Adolescent Alcohol Use: Measurements,
       Use, and Results from a National Study of Junior and
       Senior High School Students. Washington, D.C.: Paper
       presented at National Council on Alcoholism Conference:
       Defining Adolescent Alcohol Use, May 5-7, 1976. (Also in:
       Defining Adolescent Alcohol Use: Implications toward a
       Definition of Adolescent Alcoholism. Proceedings of a
       Conference, Washington, D.C., 1976. Eds. P.A. O'Gorman,
       S. Stringfield and I. Smith. New York: National Council
       on Alcoholism, 1977, pages 169-200.

3262. Rachal, J.V., Williams, J.R., Brehm, M.L., Cavanaugh, B.
       Moore, R.P. and Eckerman, W.C. A National Study of
       Adolescent Drinking Behavior, Attitudes and Correlates.
       (Prepared for National Institute on Alcohol Abuse and
       Alcoholism.) Springfield, Virginia: U.S. National
       Technical Information Service, 1975. (Report No. PB-246-
       002; NIAAA/NCALI-75/27)

3263. Rachal, J. Valley, Hubbard, Robert L., Williams, Jay R. and
       Tuchfeld, Barry S. Drinking Levels and Problem Drinking
       among Junior and Senior High-School Students. Journal of
       Studies on Alcohol, 37(11): 1751-1761, 1976.

3264. Radecki, W. Rozpijanie Maloletniego w Świetle Prawa Karnego.
       (Getting a Minor Drunk in the Light of Penal Law.)
       Problemy Alkoholizmu, Warsaw, 22(9): 4-6, 1974.

3265. Radecki, W. Wradzieckim Prawie Karnym Zwalcznie Razpijania
       Niepelnoletnich. (Fighting against Drunkenness in Minors
       as Reflected in the Soviet Penale Code.) Problemy
       Alkoholizmu, Warsaw, 25(12): 22-23, 1978.

3266. Radosevich, Marcia, Lanza-Kaduce, Lonn, Akers, Ronald L. and
       Krohn, Marvin D. The Sociology of Adolescent Drug and
       Drinking Behavior: A Review of the State of the Field:
       Part I. Deviant Behavior: An Interdisciplinary Journal,
       1: 15-35, 1979.

3267. Radosevich, Marcia, Lanza-Kaduce, Lonn, Akers, Ronald L. and
       Krohn, Marvin D. The Sociology of Adolescent Drug and
       Drinking Behavior: A Review of the State of the Field:
       Part II. Deviant Behavior: An Interdisciplinary Journal,
       1: 145-169, 1980.

3268. Radziejewski, U.F. 14-Åring på Diskotek Får Mellanöl på
       Roulette. (Fourteen Year Old at a Discotheque Wins Medium
       Strength Beer at Roulette.) Alkoholfragan, 65: 7-10,
       1971.

3269. Ragan, F.A., Jr., Samuels, M.S. and Hite, S.A. Ethanol Ingestion
       in Children: A Five Year Review. Journal of the American
       Medical Association, 242: 2787-2788, 1979.

3270. Raising the Drinking Age. (Quarterly Notes) Journal of
       Alcoholism, 11(3): 78, 1976.

3271. Rand, M.E., Graf, W. and Thurlow, C. Alcohol or Marijuana: A
       Follow-Up Survey at Ithaca College. Journal of the
       American College Health Association, 18(5): 366-367, 1970.

3272. Ramée, F. and Michaux, P. De Quelques Aspects de la
       Délinquance Sexuelle dans un Département de l'Ouest de la
       France. (Some Aspects of Sexual Offenses in a Province
       in Western France.) Archive Belges de Médecine, Social
       Hygiene, Médecine du Travail et Médecine Legal, Brussels,
       19: 79-85, 1966.

3273. Rankin, J.G., Moon, J. and Luby, B.F. Alcohol and Education:
       Some Questions Discussed. Educactional Magazine,
       Australia, (6506): 1-12, 1969.

3274. Rankin, William L., Tarnai, John, Fagan, Nancy J.,
       Mauss, Armand L. and Hopkins, Ronald H. An Evaluation of
       Workshops Designed to Prepare Teachers in Alcohol
       Education. Journal of Alcohol and Drug Education, 23: 1-13,
       1978.

3275. Rao, V. Nandini, Rao, V.V. Prakasa and Benjamin, Rommel. Sex,
       Parental Background, and Drinking Behavior of Black
       Collegians. International Journal of Sociology of the
       Family, 9: 47-66, 1979.

3276. Raoul, Walsh. Preventive Education in Apprentice Training.
       Australian Journal of Alcoholism and Drug Dependence, 3(2):
       45-46, 1976.

3277. Rappaport, L.J. Role and Context Interaction in Families of
       Alcoholics. Doctoral Dissertation (University Microfilms
       No. 77-9803). Boston College, 1976.

3278. Rappaport, M.B. Alcohol Education in New York State Schools.
       A.A.A.I.N. Newsletter, 4(2): 21-25, 1958.

3279. Rardin, D., Lawson, T. and Kruzich, D. Opiates, Amphetamines,
       Alcohol: A Comparative Study of American Soldiers.
       International Journal of the Addictions, 9: 891-898, 1974.

3280. Rash, J.K. Pathways to Health: Teaching Guide. Pamphlet.
       New York: Globe, 1975.

3281. Rathod, N.H. and Thomson, I.C. Women Alcoholics: A Clinical
       Study. Quarterly Journal of Studies on Alcohol, 32: 45-
       52, 1971.

3282. Ray, O. Drugs, Society and Human Behavior, 2nd Edition. St.
       Louis: Mosby, 1978.

3283. Ray, Oakley S. The Classification of Drug Users. Journal of
       Drug Issues, 6(2): 123-134, 1976.

3284. Read, D.A. and Greene, W.H. Creative Teaching in Health. New
       York: MacMillan Co., 1971, especially pages 246-276.

3285. Reagan, Michael V., Ed. Readings in Drug Education. Metuchen,
       New Jersey: The Scarecrow Press, Inc., 1972.

3286. Reason, A.J. Easing the Community Conscience--Alcoholic
       Treatment Programmes. Australian Journal on Alcoholism and
       Drug Dependence, 3: 6-9, 1976.

3287. Recommendations of Ontario Council of Women for Alcohol
       Education Program. Quarterly Journal of Studies on
       Alcohol, 11: 177-178, 1950.

3288. Recommendation of the Teenage Liquor Law Coordination Commission,
       State of Connecticut. Journal of Alcohol Education, 12(3):
       6-12, 1966.

3289. Red Cross Adds Alcohol Unit for Youth. NIAAA Information and
       Feature Service (IFS No. 31): 1, December 28, 1976.

3290. Reed, Archie C. The Price of Sobriety. Journal of Drug Issues,
       3(4): 313-317, 1973.

3291.   Reed, Celeste S.   Resources for the Prevention and Treatment of
           Child Abuse and Neglect (CA/N) Available to People in
           Michigan.   The Catalyst, 1(3): 48-53, 1980.

3292.   Reeves, W.C., Nanda, N.C. and Gramiak, R.   Echocardiography in
           Chronic Alcoholics Following Prolonged Periods of
           Abstinence.   American Heart Journal, 95(5): 578-583, 1978.

3293.   Reginister-Haneuse, G. and Hullebroeck, G.   Enquêtes Auprès
           d'Adolescents Belges.   Résultats et Conclusions por
           l'Education Saintaire.   (Survey of Belgian Adolescents.
           Results and Conclusions for Health Education.)   Archives
           Belges de Médecine, Social Hygiene, Médicine du Travail
           et Médecine Legale, Brussels, 36: 296-301, 1978.

3294.   Reid, Betty.   Apathy + Adolescence = Alcoholism.   Royal Society
           Health Journal, 97(1): 18-21, 1977.

3295.   Reilly, R.L.   "I'm Not an Alcoholic Because..."   Liguori,
           Missouri: Liguori Publications, 1978.

3296.   Reinhardt, J.M.   Alcoholism and Culture Conflict in the U.S.A.
           International Journal of Offender Therapy, 13(3): 177-181,
           1969.

3297.   Reiskin, H. and Wechsler, H.   Drinking among College Students
           Using a Campus Mental Health Center.   Journal of Studies
           on Alcohol, 42(9): 716-724, 1981.

3298.   Research Triangle Institute.   A National Study of Adolescent
           Drinking Behavior, Attitudes and Correlates.   (Report for
           the National Institute on Alcohol Abuse and Alcoholism.
           U.S. Department of Health, Education and Welfare, April,
           1975.)   Research Triangle Park, North Carolina: Research
           Triangle Institute, Center for the Study of Social
           Behavior, 1975.

3299.   Response Analysis Corporation.   Nonmedical Use of Psychoactive
           Substances.   Part I: Main Findings.   Princeton, New
           Jersey, 1976.

3300.   Response Analysis Corporation.   Public Experience with
           Psychoactive Substances.   Part I: Main Findings.
           Princeton, New Jersey, 1975.

3301.   Resource Unit Outlines for Alcohol Education.   Journal of
           Alcohol Education, 17(2): 19-22, 1972.

3302.   Retterstøl, N.   Bruk Av Alkohol og Tobakk Blant Ungdom i Oslo
           1968-1973.   (Use of Alcohol and Tobacco among Youth in
           Oslo 1968-1973.)   Tidsskrift for den Norske Laegeforening,
           93: 2260, 1973.

3303.   Retterstøl, N. Hvordan går det for de Unge Stoffbrukere? (How
        Does it Go for the Young Drug Users?) Tidsskrift
        EdruSpørsm, 32(3): 29-30, 1980.

3304.   Retterstøl, N. Mer Stoffbruk Blant Osloungdom? (Increased Drug
        Use among Youth in Oslo?) Tidsskrift for EdruSpørsm,
        31(4): 20, 1979.

3305.   Retterstøl, N. Om fyll Blant Ungdom. (Inebriety among Youth.)
        Tidsskrift EdruSpørsm, 30(3): 10-11, 1978.

3306.   Retterstøl, N. Use and Abuse of Dependency Producing Drugs in
        Norway. Journal of Drug Issues, 5: 22-32, 1975.

3307.   Retterstøl, Nils. Introduction: The Scandinavian Perspective.
        Journal of Drug Issues, 10: 401-404, 1980.

3308.   Retterstøl, Nils. Models for the Treatment of Young Drug
        Dependents. Journal of Drug Issues, 10: 433-440, 1980.

3309.   Reuband, K.-H. Devianz, Problemdefinition und Institutionelle
        Reaktion: Ergebnisse einer Trendalayze zum Exzessiven
        Alkoholkonsum Jugendlicher. (Deviance, Problem Definition
        and Institutional Reaction: Results of a Trend Analysis
        of Excessive Alcohol Consumption in Youth.) Kolner
        Zeitschrift fuer Sociologie und Socialpsychologie,
        Wiesbaden, 31: 56-78, 1979.

3310.   Reuband, K.-H. Exzessives Trinken bei Jugendlichen: Uber den
        Einfluss von Problemagen, Sozialier Partizipation und
        Lebensstil. (Excessive Drinking among Young: Influence
        of Problematic Circumstances, Social Participation and
        Life Style.) In: Jugend und Alkohol: Trinkmuster,
        Suchtentwicklung und Therapie. (Youth and Alcohol:
        Drinking Patterns, Addiction Development and Therapy.)
        Eds. H. Berger, A. Legnaro and K.-H. Reuband. Stuttgart:
        W. Kohlhammer, 1981, pages 76-93.

3311.   Reuband, K.-H. Konstanz und Wandel im Alkoholgebrauch
        Jugendlicher. (Constancy and Change in Regard to Alcohol
        Use among Youth.) In: Jugend und Alkohol: Trinkmuster,
        Suchtentwicklung und Therapie. (Youth and Alcohol:
        Drinking Patterns, Addiction Development and Therapy.)
        Eds. H. Berger, A. Legnaro, and K.-H. Reuband. Stuttgart:
        W. Kohlhammer, 1981, pages 22-41.

3312.   Reuband, Karl-Heinz. The Pathological and the Sub-Cultural
        Model of Drug Use - A Test of Two Contrasting Explanations.
        In: International Conference on Alcoholism and Drug
        Dependence: Alcoholism and Drug Dependence, A
        Multidisciplinary Approach. Proceedings of the Third
        International Conference on Alcoholism and Drug Dependence,
        Liverpool, England, April, 1976. Eds. J.S. Madden,
        Robin Walker and W.H. Kenyon. New York: Plenum Press,
        1977, pages 151-169.

3313. Reul, Myrtle. "Help I'm Confused" - Summary of Teen-Age Panel.
        In: Alcohol Education--Whose Responsibility? Proceedings
        of a Conference, May, 1963, sponsored by Michigan
        Department of Mental Health; Michigan Department of Public
        Instruction; Michigan Department of Health; Michigan
        Congress of Parents and Teachers; Michigan State
        University; Michigan State Board of Alcoholism; and U.S.
        Public Health Service. Lansing: Michigan State Board of
        Alcoholism, 1963, page 21.

3314. Reus, W. The Influence of Alcoholism on the Child. Enkrateia,
        65-80, 1934.

3315. Reynolds, J.C., Jr. Drug Education Gap. The Clearinghouse: A
        Journal for Modern Junior and Senior High Schools, 50(1):
        10-11, 1976.

3316. Rhoads, J. Rainbow Retreat, Inc., Phoenix, Arizona. In:
        Services for Children of Alcoholics. Symposium Held on
        September 24-26, 1979 at Silver Spring, Maryland. U.S.
        National Institute on Alcohol Abuse and Alcoholism.
        Research Monograph No. 4. Washington, D.C.: U.S.
        Government Printing Office, 1981, pages 164-176. (DHHS
        Publication No. ADM 81-1007)

3317. Rhode Island Department of Education. An Educational Program
        Dealing with Drug Abuse, Grades K-12. Washington, D.C.:
        U.S. Government Printing Office, 1970.

3318. Rhode Island Department of Social Welfare, Division of
        Alcoholism. Alcohol Education and Its Implications for
        the Youthful Driver. Proceedings of a Workshop, Newport,
        November, 1961. Providence, Rhode Island, 1962.

3319. Rhode Island Department of Social Welfare, Division of
        Alcoholism. Alcohol Education for Teenagers. Proceedings
        of a Conference, April, 1965, sponsored by U.S. Public
        Health Service, National Institute of Mental Health;
        Rhode Island State Department of Social Welfare. Division
        of Alcoholism; and Rhode Island Department of Education.
        Providence, Rhode Island, 1965.

3320. Rice, Thurman B. and Harger, Rolla N. Effects of Alcoholic
        Drinks, Tobacco, Sedatives, Narcotics. Chicago, Illinois:
        Wheeler Publishing Company, 1949.

3321. Richard, H. Youthful Offenders and Alcohol. California Youth
        Authority Quarterly, 19(4): 15-18, 1966.

3322. Richards, Louise G. Evaluation in Drug Education: Methods and
        Results. In: Resource Book for Drug Abuse Education,
        2nd ed. Ed. M. Ellis. Rockville, Maryland: National
        Clearinghouse for Drug Abuse Information, 1972, pages 87-
        90.

3323. Richards, Louise G. Evaluation in Drug Education--Notes on the
       State of the Art. Presented at the National Conference on
       Research in School Health, American Association for Health,
       Physical Education and Recreation. Detroit, Michigan,
       March 31, 1971.

3324. Richards, T.M. Kolmac Clinic, Silver Spring, Maryland. In:
       Services for Children of Alcoholics. Symposium held on
       September 24-26, at Silver Spring Maryland. U.S. National
       Institute on Alcohol Abuse and Alcoholism. Research
       Monograph No. 4. Washington, D.C.: U.S. Government
       Printing Office, 1981, pages 177-185. (DHHS Publication
       No. ADM 81-1007)

3325. Richards, T.M. Splitting as a Defense Mechanism in Children of
       Alcoholic Parents. In: Currents in Alcoholism. Volume 7.
       Recent Advances in Research and Treatment. Ed.
       M. Galanter. New York: Grune and Stratton, 1980, pages
       239-244.

3326. Richards, T.M. Working with Disturbed Children of Alcoholic
       Mothers. In: Currents in Alcoholism. Volume 7.
       Recent Advances in Research and Treatment. Ed.
       M. Galanter. New York: Grune and Stratton, 1980, pages
       521-527.

3327. Richards, W.T. Background and State-of-the-Art in K-12 Alcohol
       Education Curriculum Development. Pamphlet. Madison:
       State of Wisconsin Department of Education, 1971.

3328. Richards, W.T. Guidelines for the Development of K-12 Alcohol
       Education Curriculum in Traffic Safety. Pamphlet.
       Madison: Wisconsin State Department of Public Instruction,
       no date.

3329. Richards, W.T. Planning Meeting on a K-12 Curriculum in Alcohol
       Abuse and Traffic Safety. Presented at a Conference
       sponsored by the National Institute of Mental Health and
       the National Highway Traffic Safety Administration,
       Washington, D.C., February 23-24, 1971.

3330. Richardson, A.W. Temperance Teaching in Higher Schools.
       International Congress Against Alcoholism, 12: 81-84,
       1909.

3331. Richardson, Charles E. Drug Education: Some Insights and Some
       Analysis of a Conceptual Approach. Journal of Alcohol
       Education, 16(1): 1-7, 1970.

3332. Richardson, D.C. and Campbell, J.L. Alcohol and Wife Abuse:
       The Effect of Alcohol on Attributions of Blame for Wife
       Abuse. Personality and Social Psychology Bulletin, 6: 51-
       56, 1980.

3333. Richardson, H.K. Alcoholism, Its Nature and Prevention.
       Alcohol Hygiene, 1(5): 23-39, 1945.

3334. Richardson, J.J. A Study of the Relationship of Attitudes of
       College Students and Their Parents toward Consumption of
       Alcoholic Beverages. Doctoral Dissertation (University
       Microfilms No. 65-1335). Southern Illinois University,
       1964.

3335. Richman, L.A. Statewide Survey of Educators' Perceptions of
       Alcohol Education Programs in California Public Schools.
       Doctoral Dissertation. Berkeley: University of
       California, 1976.

3336. Richman, L.A. Teenagers, Alcohol and Education: An Annotated
       Bibliography of Journal Articles. Journal of Alcohol and
       Drug Education, 20(1): 18-27, 1974.

3337. Richter-Velander, J. The Alcohol Problem of the Child. Tirfing,
       Sweden, 5-8, 22-28, 1918.

3338. Riddle, P.C. Teenage Drinking...Impulse or Imitation? Minnesota
       Journal of Education, 43: 12-13, 1962.

3339. Riester, A.E. Adolescent Society and Drinking Customs. Doctoral
       Dissertation (University Microfilms No. 67-9454). Columbia
       University, Teachers College, 1967.

3340. Riester, A.E. and Zucker, R.A. Adolescent Social Structure and
       Drinking Behavior. Personnel and Guidance Journal, 47(4):
       304-312, 1968. (Also in Readings in Adolescent Psychology.
       Eds. M. Powell and A.H. Frerichs. Minneapolis, Minnesota:
       Burgess, 1971, pages 302-314.)

3341. Rigby, K. Drug Use in S.A. Schools: A Brief Report. Australian
       Journal of Alcoholism and Drug Dependence, 3: 88-89, 1976.

3342. Riggs, L. College Administration of Alcoholic Beverage
       Regulations. In: The Domesticated Drug: Drinking among
       Collegians. Eds. G.L. Maddox. New Haven, Connecticut:
       College and University Press, 1970, pages 408-436.

3343. Riggs, Lawrence. Alcohol on the College Campus. In: The
       President's Bulletin Board Supplement. Nashville,
       Tennessee: Division of Educational Institutions, The
       Board of Education, the Methodist Church, 1959.

3344. Riley, John W., Jr. and Marden, Charles F. Who, What, and How
       Often? In: Drinking and Intoxication: Selected Readings
       in Social Attitudes and Controls. Ed. Raymond G. McCarthy.
       New Haven, Connecticut: College and University Press,
       1959, pages 182-189.

3345. Riley, Matilda White and Waring, Joan. Age, Cohorts and Drug
       Use. In: Longitudinal Research on Drug Use: Empirical
       Findings and Methodological Issues. Ed. Denise B. Kandel.
       New York: John Wiley and Sons, 1978, pages 225-233.

3346. Rimmer, J. Psychiatric Illness in Husbands of Alcoholics.
       Quarterly Journal of Studies on Alcohol, 35(1): 281-283,
       1974.

3347. Rimmer, J. and Chambers, D.S. Alcoholism: Methodological
       Considerations in the Study of Family Illness. American
       Journal of Orthopsychiatry, 39: 760-768, 1969.

3348. Rimmer, John, Pitts, F.N., Reich, T. and Winokur, G. Alcoholism.
       II. Sex, Socioeconomic Status and Race in Two Hospitalized
       Samples. Quarterly Journal of Studies on Alcohol, 32:
       942-952, 1971.

3349. Rist, E. Le Vin et la Morale Sociale Selon Platon et Galien.
       (Wine and Social Mores According to Plato and Galen.)
       Presse Médicale, Paris, 62: 1119, 1954.

3350. Ritson, B. Review: Childen and Alcohol. Child Care, Health
       and Development, 1: 263-269, 1975.

3351. Ritson, Bruce. Alcohol and Education. In: International
       Conference on Alcoholism and Drug Dependence: Alcoholism
       and Drug Dependence, A Multidisciplinary Approach.
       Proceedings of the Third International Conference on
       Alcoholism and Drug Dependence, Liverpool, England, 1976.
       Eds. J.S. Madden, R. Walker and W.H. Kenyon. New York:
       Plenum Press, 1977, pages 457-463.

3352. Ritson, Bruce. Alcohol and Young People. Journal of
       Adolescence, 4: 93-100, 1981.

3353. Ritson, E.B. Drinking Among Young People. In: Notes on Alcohol
       and Alcoholism. Ed. S. Caruana. London: B. Edsall, 1972.

3354. Ritson, E.B. Psychological Medicine. Treatment of Alcoholism.
       British Medical Journal, 2(5963): 124-127, 1975.

3355. Rivers, William. Is There a Relationship between Drug Use and
       Academic Achievement? Journal of School Health, 51(3):
       171-173, 1981.

3356. Robbins, E.S., Robbins, L., Frosch, W.A. and Stern, M. College
       Student Drug Use. American Journal of Psychiatry, 126:
       1743-1750, 1970.

3357. Robbins, L., Robbins, E., Pearlman, S., Phillip A., Robinson, E.
       and Schmitter, B. College Students' Perceptions of Their
       Parents' Attitudes and Practices toward Drug Use. Journal
       of Alcohol and Drug Education, 18(2): 6-12, 1973.

3358.   Robbins, L., Robbins, E.S., Stern, M., Frosch, W.A. and David, J.
        Drug Use in Adolescents: Findings from a District-Wide
        Census of Junior High School and High School Students in
        New York State. Montreal: Paper presented at the annual
        meeting of the American Psychiatric Association,
        August 26-31, 1973.

3359.   Robbins, P.H., Tanck, R.H. and Meyersburg, H.A. Psychological
        Factors in Smoking, Drinking and Drug Experimentation.
        Journal of Clinical Psychology, 27(4): 450-452, 1971.

3360.   Robe, Lucy Barry. LICA of Nassau. Long Island Council on
        Alcoholism of Nassau, 1(4): 48-50, 1973.

3361.   Robe, Lucy, Robe, Robert and Wilson, P. Ann. Maternal Heavy
        Drinking Related to Delayed Onset of Daughters'
        Menstruation. In: Currents in Alcoholism. Volume 7.
        Recent Advances in Research and Treatment. Ed.
        M. Galanter. New York: Grune and Stratton, 1980, pages
        515-520.

3362.   Roberts, C. and Mooney, C. Here's Looking at You: A Teacher's
        Guide for Alcohol Education. (Revised Edition) Seattle,
        Washington: Comprehensive Health Education Foundation,
        1976.

3363.   Roberts, H.M. Arithmetic of the Familial Transmission of
        Alcoholism in Canada. Canadian Journal of Public Health,
        61: 179, 1970.

3364.   Roberts, K. Medical Education: A Model for Primary Prevention.
        In: Association of Labor-Management Administrators and
        Consultants on Alcoholism, Inc. Proceedings of the Seventh
        Annual Meeting, San Francisco, October 3-6, 1978.
        Arlington, Virginia, 1978, pages 189-192.

3365.   Robinson III, James. A Comparison of Three Alcohol Instruction
        Programs of the Knowledge, Attitudes and Drinking
        Behavior of College Students. Journal of Drug Education,
        11(2): 157-166, 1981.

3366.   Robertson, L.S. Facts and Fancy in the Formation of Public
        Policy. American Journal of Public Health, 70(6); 627,
        1980.

3367.   Robertson, Leon S. Crash Involvement of Teenaged Drivers When
        Driver Education is Eliminated from High School. American
        Journal of Public Health, 70: 599-603, 1980.

3368.   Robertson, Leon S. Robertson's Reply to Harman and Kolbe.
        American Journal of Public Health, 71(2): 172, 1981.

3369.   Robertson, Leon and Zador, Paul. Narrative Summary of the IIHS
        Driver Education Study. "Driver Education and Fatal Crash
        Involvement of Teenaged Drivers." Washington, D.C.:
        Insurance Institute for Highway Safety, 1977.

3370.   Robinovitch, L.G. Rapport Entre la Criminalité des Enfants et
        l'Alcoolisme des Parents. (Relationship between Juvenile
        Delinquency and Parental Alcoholism.) Internationale
        Congress de Medicine, Paris, 541-547, 1901.

3371.   Robins, L.N. An Actuarial Evaluation of the Causes and
        Consequences of Deviant Behavior in Young Black Men. In:
        Life History Research in Psychopathology. Volume 2. Eds.
        M. Roff, L.N. Robins and M. Pollack. Minneapolis,
        Minnesota: University of Minnesota Press, 1972, pages
        137-154.

3372.   Robins, L.N. Deviant Children Grown Up: A Sociological and
        Psychiatric Study of Sociopathic Personality. Baltimore:
        Williams and Wilkins, 1966.

3373.   Robins, L.N. et al. Adult Psychiatric Status of Black
        Schoolboys. Archives of General Psychiatry, 24: 338-344,
        1971.

3374.   Robins, L.N., Darvish, H.S. and Murphy, G.E. The Long-Term
        Outcome for Adolescent Drug Users - A Follow-Up Study of
        76 Users and 146 Nonusers. Proceedings of the American
        Psychopathological Association, 59: 159-180, 1970.

3375.   Robins, L.N., West, P.A., Ratcliff, K.S. and Herjanic, B.M.
        Father's Alcoholism and Children's Outcome. In: Currents
        in Alcoholism. Volume 4. Psychiatric, Psychological,
        Social and Epidemiological Studies. Ed. F.A. Seixas.
        New York: Grune and Stratton, 1978, pages 313-327.

3376.   Robins, Lee, Bates, William and O'Neal, Patricia. Adult
        Drinking Patterns of Former Problem Children. In:
        Society, Culture and Drinking Patterns. Eds.
        D.J. Pittman and C.R. Snyder. New York: Wiley, 1962,
        pages 395-412.

3377.   Robins, Lee N. The Natural History of Drug Abuse. In:
        Theories on Drug Abuse: Selected Contemporary Problems.
        (Research Monograph Series 30) U.S. National Institute
        on Drug Abuse. Eds. Dan Lettieri, Mollie Sayers and
        Helen Pearson. Rockville, Maryland, 1980, pages 215-224.
        (DHEW Publication No. ADM 80-967).

3378.   Robins, Lee N. Sturdy Childhood Predictors of Adult Antisocial
        Behaviour: Replications from Longitudinal Studies.
        Psychological Medicine, London, 8: 611-622, 1978.

3379. Robins, Lee N. and Guze, Samuel B. Drinking Practices and
       Problems in Urban Ghetto Populations. In: Recent Advances
       in Studies of Alcoholism: An Interdisciplinary Symposium.
       Washington, D.C., June 25-27, 1970. Sponsored by the
       National Center for Prevention and Control of Alcoholism.
       National Institute on Mental Health. Eds.:
       Nancy K. Mello and Jack H. Mendelson. Washington, D.C.:
       U.S. Government Printing Office, 1971, pages 825-842.

3380. Robins, Lee N., Murphy, George E. and Breckenridge, Mary B.
       Drinking Behavior of Young Urban Negro Men. Quarterly
       Journal of Studies on Alcohol, 29: 657-684, 1968.

3381. Robinson, D., Ed. Alcohol Problems - Reviews, Research and
       Recommendations. London: Macmillan Press, 1979.

3382. Robinson, David. Factors Influencing Alcohol Consumption. In:
       Alcoholism: New Knowledge and New Responses. Eds.
       Griffith Edwards and Marcus Grant. London: Croom Helm,
       1977, pages 60-77.

3383. Robinson, G.L. and Miller, S.T. Drug Abuse and the College
       Campus. Annals of the American Academy of Political and
       Social Science, 417: 101-109, 1975.

3384. Robinson, G.L., Young, L.R. and Duffy, M.E. Review of College
       and University Policies Concerning Illegal and Unprescribed
       Drugs and Narcotics. In: U.S. National Commission on
       Marihuana and Drug Abuse. Drug Use in America: Problem
       in Perspective. Appendix, Volume II. Social Responses to
       Drug Use. Washington, D.C.: U.S. Government Printing
       Office, 1973, pages 548-581.

3385. Robinson, M.S. The Place of Alcohol Education in Adult Life. Its
       Relationship to, and Effects on the Education of Youth.
       Second Annual Conference of Louisiana Council on Alcohol
       Education Held March 8-9, 1956. Baton Rouge, Louisiana:
       College of Education, Louisiana State University, and
       Agricultural and Mechanical College, 1956, no pages.

3386. Robinson, R. The Prospects of Adequate Education about Alcohol
       and Alcoholism. Journal of Alcohol Education, 14(2): 1-4
       1969.

3387. Robinson, R.R. Alcoholism Prevention and Reality: Comment on
       the Article by M.E. Chafetz. Quarterly Journal of Studies
       on Alcohol, 28: 553-554, 1967.

3388. Robinson, R.R. How About a Drink: The Pleasure and Problems of
       Alcohol. Philadelphia, Pennsylvania: Westminister, 1973.

3389. Robinson, R.R. On the Rocks. Richmond Hill, Ontario:
       Scholastic-TAB Publications, 1979.

3390. Robles, R.R., Martínez, R. Colon, A.I. and Moscoso, M.
       Variables Socioculturales Relacionadas con el Uso de
       Alcohol entre los Adolescentes de las Escuelas Secundarias.
       (Sociocultural Variables Associated with the Use of Alcohol
       among Adolescents at Secondary Schools in Puerto Rico.)
       Boletin de la Oficina Sanitaria Pan-Americana, 85: 220-
       231, 1978.

3391. Robles, Rafaela, Martínez, Ruth and Moscoso, Margarita. Drug
       Use among Public and Private Secondary School Students in
       Puerto Rico. International Journal of the Addictions,
       14(2): 243-258, 1979.

3392. Rockwell, Don A. Alcohol and Marihuana--Social Problem
       Perspective. British Journal of Addiction, 68(3): 209-214,
       1973.

3393. Rodriguez-Lopez, A. Ingesta Alcoholica en Escolares de Una
       Communidad Rural Gallega. (Alcohol Ingestion by Students
       of a Galician Rural Community.) Drogalcohol, 4(4): 195-
       199, 1979.

3394. Rodriguez-Martos-Dauer, A. Sobre la Etiologia del Habito
       Alcoholico. (On the Etiology of Habituation to Alcohol.)
       Drogalcohol, 3: 115-119, 1978.

3395. Rodriguez-Martos-Dauer, A. and Welsch-Pastor, T. Interrelaciones
       entre Alcoholismo y Dinamica Conyugal: Repercusion sobre
       los Hijos. (Interconnections between Alcoholism and
       Marital Dynamics: Their Repercussions on the Children.)
       Drogalcohol, 4: 13-22, 1979.

3396. Rodzinie i Dziecku w Trudnej Sytuacji. (Child and Family Aid in
       Alcohol-Related Crises.) Problemy Alkoholizmu, Warsaw,
       26(4): 1, 1979.

3397. Roe, A. The Adult Adjustment of Children of Alcoholic Parents
       Raised in Foster-Homes. Quarterly Journal of Studies on
       Alcohol, 5: 378-393, 1944.

3398. Roe, A. Alcohol Education in the Schools. Science Monthly,
       60: 51-54, 1945.

3399. Roe, A. Legal Regulation of Alcohol Education. Quarterly
       Journal of Studies on Alcohol, 3: 433-464, 1942.

3400. Roe, A. A Survey of Alcohol Education in Elementary and High
       Schools in the United States. New Haven, Connecticut:
       Quarterly Journal of Studies on Alcohol, 1943. (Reprinted
       in 1946.)

3401. Roe, A. A Survey of Alcohol Education in the United States.
       Quarterly Journal of Studies on Alcohol, 3: 574-662, 1943.

3402.   Roe, B.   Don't Ignore Alcohol.   National Association of Student
         Personnel Administrators Journal, 11(1): 27-33, 1973.

3403.   Roebuck, J. and Johnson, R.   The Negro Drinker and Assaulter as
         a Criminal Type.   Crime and Delinquency, 8(1): 21-33, 1962.

3404.   Roebuck, J. and Kessler, R.   The Etiology of Alcoholism:
         Constitutional, Psychological and Sociological Approaches.
         Springfield, Illinois: Charles C. Thomas, 1973.

3405.   Roff, J.D.   Adolescent Development and Family Characteristics
         Associated with a Diagnosis of Schizophrenia.   Journal of
         Consulting and Clinical Psychology, 44: 933-939, 1976.

3406.   Roff, M., Robins, L.N. and Pollack, M., Eds.   Life History
         Research in Psychopathology, Volume 2.   Minneapolis,
         Minnesota: University of Minnesota Press, 1972.

3407.   Rogers, E.M.   Group Influences on Student Drinking Behavior.
         In: The Domesticated Drug: Drinking among Collegians.
         Ed. G.L. Maddox.   New Haven, Connecticut: College and
         University Press, 1970, pages 302-320.

3408.   Rogers, E.M.   Reference Group Influences on Student Drinking
         Behavior.   Quarterly Journal of Studies on Alcohol, 19:
         244-254, 1958.

3409.   Rogers, J.F.   Instruction in the Effects of Alcohol and Tobacco.
         Leaflet.   Washington, D.C.: U.S. Office of Education,
         1934.

3410.   Rogers, J.F.   State-Wide Trends in School Hygiene and Physical
         Education.   Pamphlet.   Washington, D.C.: U.S. Office of
         Education, 1941.

3411.   Roizen, Ron.   A Sociological Look at Alcohol-Related Problems:
         A Talk Prepared for High-School Students.   Journal of
         Alcohol and Drug Education, 24(1): 31-38, 1978.

3412.   The Role of Alcohol in Urban Gang Violence.   New Jersey Council
         News, 28(5): 1+, 1971.

3413.   Rolleston, J.D.   Some Aspects of the Alcohol Problem.   British
         Journal of Inebriety, 39: 45-59, 1942.

3414.   Rollet, J.   Données Précises sur l'Alcoolisme Infantile en
         France.   (Exact Data on Drinking by Children in France.)
         Vie Médicale, Paris, 40: 825-828, 1959.

3415.   Rollins, J.H. and Holden, R.H.   Adolescent Drug Use and the
         Alienation Syndrome.   Journal of Drug Education, 2: 249-
         261, 1972.

3416. Roman, P.M. The Future Professor: Functions and Patterns of
           Drinking among Graduate Students. In: The Domesticated
           Drug: Drinking among Collegians. Ed. G.L. Maddox. New
           Haven, Connecticut: College and University Press, 1970,
           pages 204-217.

3417. Roman, Paul M. The Impact of Alcoholism on the Family. A
           Sociological View. In: Health and the Family: A Medical-
           Sociological Analysis. Ed. C.O. Crawford. New York:
           Macmillan, 1971, pages 217-241.

3418. Rombro, R.A. Minor's Capacity to Consent to Medical Treatment.
           Maryland State Medical Journal, 27(2): 43-46, 1978.

3419. Romine, Ray S. Alienation and the Use of Mind-Altering Drugs by
           College Students. Health Education, 7(3): 38-40, 1976.

3420. Rommeney, G. Zur Persönlichkeitswürdigung des Alkoholtäters.
           (On the Personality Evaluation of the Alcoholic
           Delinquent.) Beitraege zur Gerichlichen Medizin, 25: 105-
           109, 1969.

3421. Room, R. and Sheffield, S., Eds. The Prevention of Alcohol
           Problems: Report of a Conference. Expert Conference on
           the Prevention of Alcohol Problems, Berkeley, California,
           December 9-11, 1974. Sacramento, California: California
           Health and Welfare Agency, Office of Alcoholism, 1976.

3422. Room, Robin. The Case for a Problem Prevention Approach to
           Alcohol, Drug, and Mental Problems. Public Health Reports,
           96(1): 26-33, 1981.

3423. Room, Robin. Concepts and Strategies in the Prevention of
           Alcohol-Related Problems. Contemporary Drug Problems,
           9(1): 9-47, 1980.

3424. Room, Robin. Introduction: Drug and Alcohol Problems: Social
           Control and Normative Patterns. Journal of Drug Issues,
           10(1): 1-5, 1980.

3425. Room, Robin. Normative Perspectives on Alcohol Use and Problems.
           Journal of Drug Issues, 5: 358-368, 1975.

3426. Room, Robin. Priorities in Social Research on Alcohol. In:
           Research Priorities on Alcohol. Proceedings of a
           Symposium Sponsored by the Rutgers Center of Alcohol
           Studies and Rutgers University. Ed. Mark Keller. New
           Jersey: Journal of Studies on Alcohol, Supplement No. 8,
           1979, pages 248-268.

3427. Rooney, J.F. and Schwartz, S.M. The Effects of Minimum Drinking
           Age Laws Upon Adolescent Alcohol Use and Problems.
           Contemporary Drug Problems, 6: 569-583, 1977.

3428.   Rootman, I. and Oakey, J.   School and Community Correlates of
        Alcohol Use and Abuse among Alberta Junior High School
        Students.   Canadian Journal of Public Health, 64: 351-359,
        1973.

3429.   Rootman, Irving.   Drug Use among Rural Students in Alberta.
        Canada's Mental Health, 20(6): 9-14, 1972.

3430.   Rose, H.K. and Glatt, M.M.   A Study of Alcoholism as an
        Occupational Hazard of Merchant Seamen.   Journal of Mental
        Science, 107: 18-30, 1961.

3431.   Rosenbaum, M.   Sex Roles among Deviants: The Woman Addict.
        International Journal of Addiction, 16(5): 859-878, 1981.

3432.   Rosenberg, C.   Young Drug-Addicts: Addiction and Its
        Consequences.   Medical Journal of Australia, 24: 1031-1033,
        1968.

3433.   Rosenberg, C.M.   Determinants of Psychiatric Illness in Young
        People.   British Journal of Psychiatry, 115(525): 907-915,
        1969.

3434.   Rosenberg, C.M.   The Young Addict and His Family.   British
        Journal of Psychiatry, 118: 469-470, 1971.

3435.   Rosenberg, C.M.   Young Alcoholics.   British Journal of
        Psychiatry, 115: 181-188, 1969.

3436.   Rosenberg, C.M.   Young Drug Addicts: Background and Personality.
        Journal of Nervous and Mental Disease, 148: 65-73, 1969.

3437.   Rosenberg, C.M. and Dolinsky, H.   Drug and Alcohol Use by Young
        People Attending a Psychiatric Emergency Service.   British
        Journal of Addiction, 67(3): 189-194, 1972.

3438.   Rosenberg, J.S., Kasl, S.V. and Berberian, R.M.   Sex Differences
        in Adolescent Drug Use: Recent Trends.   Addictive
        Diseases, 1(1): 73-96, 1974.

3439.   Rosenberg, N., Goldberg, I.D. and Williams, G.W.   Alcoholism and
        Drunken Driving.   Evidence from Psychiatric and Driver
        Registers.   Quarterly Journal of Studies on Alcohol, 33(4):
        1129-1143, 1972.

3440.   Rosenberg, N., Laessig, R.H. and Rawlings, R.R.   Alcohol, Age
        and Fatal Traffic Accidents.   Quarterly Journal of Studies
        on Alcohol, 35: 473-489, 1974.

3441.   Rosenblitt, D.L. and Nagey, D.A.   The Use of Medical Manpower in
        a Seventh Grade Drug Education Program.   Journal of Drug
        Education, 3(1): 39-56, 1973.

3442.   Rosenbluth, J., Nathan, P.E. and Lawson, D.M. Environmental
        Influences on Drinking by College Students in a College
        Pub: A Behavioral Observation in the Natural Environment.
        Addictive Behaviors, 3: 117-121, 1978.

3443.   Rosett, H.L., Snyder, P., Sander, L.W., Lee, A., Cook, P.,
        Weiner, L. and Gould, J. Effects of Maternal Drinking on
        Neonate State Regulation. Developmental Medicine and
        Child Neurology, 21(4): 464-473. 1979.

3444.   Roskin, G., Kassnove, R. and Adams, J. Group Vocational
        Rehabilitation Counselling for Drug Abusers as an Outreach
        Technique in the Schools. Drug Forum, 7: 35-40, 1978.

3445.   Rosner, Bernard. A Family Problem. The Catalyst, 1(3): 45-47,
        1980.

3446.   Roth, R. Alcoholism and the Family: Putting the Pieces
        Together. Alcoholism: A National Magazine, 1(3): 19-22,
        1981.

3447.   Rouse, B.A. and Ewing, J.A. College Drinking and Other Drug Use.
        In: Drinking: Alcohol in American Society--Issues and
        Current Research. Eds. J.A. Ewing and B.A. Rouse.
        Chicago, Illinois: Nelson Hall, 1978, pages 171-202.

3448.   Rouse, B.A. and Ewing, J.A. Marijuana and Other Drug Use by
        Women College Students: Associated Risk Taking and Coping
        Activities. American Journal of Psychiatry, 130: 486-491,
        1973.

3449.   Rouse, B.A. and Ewing, J.A. Student Drug Use, Risk-Taking and
        Alienation. Journal of the American College Health
        Association, 22(3): 226-230, 1974.

3450.   Rouse, B.A. and Ewing, John. An Overview of Drinking Behaviors
        and Social Policies. In: Drinking: Alcohol in American
        Society--Issues and Current Research. Eds. J.A. Ewing and
        B.A. Rouse. Chicago, Illinois: Nelson-Hall, 1978, pages
        339-381.

3451.   Rouse, Beatrice. Johns Hopkins University National Survey of
        College Drug Use. Drinking and Drug Practices Surveyor,
        (4): 6-7, 1971.

3452.   Rouse, Beatrice A., Waller, Patricia F. and Ewing, John A.
        Adolescent's Stress Levels, Coping Activities and Father's
        Drinking Behavior. Proceedings of the American
        Psychological Association, 81: 681-682, 1973.

3453. Rouse, Beatrice A. and Ewing, John A. Student Drug Use, Risk-
        Taking and Alienation. In: Scientific Proceedings in
        Summary Form: The One Hundred and Twenty-Sixth Annual
        Meeting of the American Psychiatric Association.
        Honolulu, Hawaii, May 7-11, 1973. Summary of Paper
        No. 274. Washington, D.C.: American Psychiatric
        Association, 1973, pages 303-304.

3454. Roush, G.C., Thompson, W.D. and Berberian, R.M. Psychoactive
        Medicinal and Nonmedicinal Drug Use among High School
        Students. Pediatrics, 66: 709-715, 1980.

3455. Rouvillois, H. De l'Usage des Boissons Alcoolisées chez
        l'Enfant dans les Établissements Scolaires. (On the Use
        of Alcoholic Beverages by Children in Educational
        Institutions.) Bulletin de l'Academie Nationale de
        Médecine, Paris, 140: 71-73, 1956.

3456. Roy, Marjorie and Greenblatt, Elaine. Driving Under the
        Influence of Liquor: Follow-Up Study of Age, Sex and
        Simultaneous Offenses. Boston, Massachusetts: Office of
        Commissioner of Probation, 1979.

3457. Rozelle, G.R. Experiential and Cognitive Small Group Approaches
        to Alcohol Education for College Students. Doctoral
        Dissertation (University Microfilms No. 7913314). The
        University of Florida, 1978. (Also in: Journal of Alcohol
        and Drug Education, 26(1): 40-54, 1980.

3458. Rozelle, George and Gonzalez, Gerardo. A Peer-Facilitated
        Course on Alcohol Abuse: An Innovative Approach to
        Prevention on the College Campus. Journal of Alcohol and
        Drug Education, 25(1): 20-30, 1979.

3459. Rubin, Vera, Ed. Cannabis and Culture. The Hague: Mouton
        Publishers, 1975.

3460. Rudner, S. Changing Patterns of Drug Abuse in Nassau County.
        Journal of Drug Education, 2: 319-327, 1972.

3461. Rule, B.G. and Phillips, D. Responsibility Versus Illness
        Models of Alcoholism: Effects on Attitudes toward an
        Alcoholic. Quarterly Journal of Studies on Alcohol, 34:
        489-495, 1973.

3462. Rungelj, V. Teoretična in Practična Izrodisča za Skupinsko
        Druzinsko Zdravljenije Alkoholikov ob Delu. (Theoretical
        and Practical Prerequisites of Group and Family Therapy
        for Working Alcoholics.) Zdravstveni Vestník, Ljubljana,
        48(1): 37-41, 1979.

3463. Rush, T.V. Predicting Treatment Outcomes for Juvenile and
         Young-Adult Clients in the Pennsylvania Substance-Abuse
         System. In: Youth Drug Abuse: Problems, Issues and
         Treatment. Ed. G.M. Beschner and A.S. Friedman.
         Lexington, Massachusetts: D.C. Heath, 1979, pages 629-
         656.

3464. Rushing, W.A. Alcoholism and Suicide Rates by Status Set and
         Occupation. Quarterly Journal of Studies on Alcohol,
         29(2): 399-412, 1968.

3465. Russell, James A. and Bond, Catherine R. Individual Differences
         in Beliefs Concerning Emotions Conducive to Alcohol Use.
         Journal of Studies on Alcohol, 41: 753-759, 1980.

3466. Russell, James A. and Bond, Catherine R. Beliefs among College
         Students on Settings and Emotions Conducive to Alcohol and
         Marijuana Use. The International Journal of the
         Addictions, 14(7): 977-986, 1979.

3467. Russell, J.S. and Hollander, M.J. Drug Use among Vancouver
         Secondary School Students: 1970 and 1974. Vancouver:
         Narcotic Addiction Foundation of British Columbia, 1974.

3468. Russell, M. and Bigler, L. Screening for Alcohol-Related
         Problems in an Outpatient Obstetric-Gynecologic Clinic.
         American Journal of Obstetrics and Gynecology, 134(1): 4-
         12, 1979.

3469. Russell, M. and Welte, J.W. Estimation of Alcohol Consumption
         from the Health and Nutrition Examination Survey.
         American Journal of Drug and Alcohol Abuse, 7(4): 389-401,
         1980.

3470. Russell, R.D. Alcohol and Other Mood-Modifying Substances in
         Ecological Perspective: A Framework for Communicating and
         Educating. Quarterly Journal of Studies on Alcohol, 35:
         606-619, 1974.

3471. Russell, R.D. Alcoholism Prevention and Reality: Comment on
         the Article by M.E. Chafetz. Quarterly Journal of Studies
         on Alcohol, 28: 549-551, 1967.

3472. Russell, R.D. College Drinking: Students See It Many Ways.
         In: The Domesticated Drug, Drinking among Collegians.
         Ed. G.L. Maddox. New Haven, Connecticut: College and
         University Press, 1970, pages 176-203.

3473. Russell, R.D. Education about Alcohol for Real American Youth.
         Paper Presented at 28th International Congress on Alcohol
         and Alcoholism. Washington, D.C., 1968.

3474.   Russell, R.D.   Education about Alcohol in the University:
        Obligation and Opportunity. In: The Domesticated Drug:
        Drinking among Collegians. Ed. G.L. Maddox. New Haven,
        Connecticut: College and University Press, 1970, pages
        437-456.

3475.   Russell, R.D.   Philosophies for Educating about Alcohol and
        Other Mood-Modifying Substances: Personal and Social
        Controls. Leaflet. New Brunswick, New Jersey: Rutgers
        Center of Alcohol Studies, 1976. (Also in: Journal of
        Studies on Alcohol, 37(3): 365-374, 1976.

3476.   Russell, R.D.   Quelle Méthode d'Éducation Devrions-Nous Adopter
        en Matiere d'Alcool pour Prévenir les Problèmes de
        Demain? (Which Method of Alcohol Education Should We
        Adopt in Order to Prevent Future Problems?) Toxicomanies,
        Quebec, 8: 195-217, 1975.

3477.   Russell, R.D.   Some Meat on the Bones of an Important Concept:
        An Activity to Bring Forth a "Variety of Motivations."
        Journal of Alcohol and Drug Education, 21(2): 44-48, 1976.

3478.   Russell, R.D.   Teacher Education. In: Alcohol Education.
        Secretary's Committee on Alcoholism. U.S. Department of
        Health, Education and Welfare. Proceedings of a
        Conference, March 29, 1966. Washington, D.C.: U.S.
        Government Printing Office, 1967, pages 53-57.

3479.   Russell, R.D.   Teaching Learning Guide. Carbondale, Illinois:
        Southern Illinois University, 1966.

3480.   Russell, R.D.   What Shall We Teach the Young about Drinking?
        (Popular Pamphlets on Alcohol Problems, No. 5.) New
        Brunswick, New Jersey: Rutgers University Center of
        Alcohol Studies, 1970.

3481.   Russell, Robert.   Do You Remember Your First Drink? Journal of
        Alcohol and Drug Education, 17(3): 21-25, 1972.

3482.   Russell, Robert.   Guest Editorial. Journal of Alcohol and Drug
        Education, 19(2): 38-42, 1974.

3483.   Russell, Robert.   No Mood Modifying Substances: What It Would
        be Like. Journal of Alcohol Education, 14(3): 30-33, 1968.

3484.   Russell, Robert.   What Constitutes "Appropriate Control" of
        Alcoholic Beverages in the Community? Situations for
        Judgment and Discussion. Journal of Alcohol Education,
        15(3): 8-12, 1970.

3485.   Russell, Robert D.   Alcohol Education vs. Alcoholism Education.
        Journal of Alcohol Education, 13(1): 46-48, 1967.

3486.   Russell, Robert D. The Concept Approach to Alcohol Education.
         Quarterly Journal of Studies on Alcohol, 30: 158-160, 1969.

3487.   Russell, Robert D. Education about Alcohol...for Real American
         Youth. Journal of Alcohol Education, 14(3): 1-3, 1969.

3488.   Russell, Robert D. Educational Approaches to Developing
         Community Support. Address to Oklahoma City Council on
         Alcoholism, February 15, 1974.

3489.   Russell, Robert D. Listening to Youth: A Not-Altogether
         Enlightening Experience. Journal of Alcohol and Drug
         Education, 18(1): 1-3, 1972.

3490.   Russell, Robert D. A New Way of Thinking about Alcohol. Journal
         of Alcohol Education, 12(3): 25-28, 1966.

3491.   Russell, Robert D. What Constitutes Use and Misuse of Alcohol in
         the Home? Journal of Alcohol Education, 15(2): 11-16,
         1970.

3492.   Russell, Robert D. What Do You Mean--Alcohol Education? The
         Journal of School Health, 35: 351-355, 1965. (Also as:
         What Do You Mean--Alcohol Education? Pamphlet. Kent,
         Ohio: American School Health Association, 1965.)

3493.   Rustagi, P.K., Prabhu, G.G., Mohan, D. and Sundaram, K.R.
         Relative Risk of Adolescent Drug Abuse: Part II.
         Intrapsychic Variables. Bulletin on Narcotics, 18(2): 33-
         40, 1981.

3494.   Rutherford, D. Juvenile Drinking: Adolescence and Alcohol.
         Royal Society of Health Journal, 97(1): 14-17, 1977.

3495.   Ruton, N.G. A Follow-Up Survey of Alcohol and Drug Use by
         Transient Youth at Sauble Beach: July and August, 1973.
         Toronto, Ontario: Addiction Research Foundation, 1973.

3496.   Ryan, C., Siegel, F. and Williams, C. How to Talk with Children
         about Drinking: A Parent Guide to Alcohol Education: A
         Leader's Handbook. Lexington: Massachusetts Parent-
         Teacher-Student Association, 1977.

3497.   Ryback, R.S. Teen-Age Alcoholism and Drug Abuse. New England
         Journal of Medicine, 294: 56, 1976.

3498.   Ryback, R.S. Teen-Age Alcoholism, Medicine and the Law. New
         England Journal of Medicine, 293: 719-721, 1975.

3499.   Rydberg, U. Fylleri bland Ungdom. (Drunkenness among Youth.)
         Läkartidningen, Stockholm, 75: 1591, 1978.

3500. Rydelius, P.A. Alkoholmissbruk hos Barn och Ungdom. (Alcohol
           Misuse among Children and Young People.) Läkartidningen,
           Stockholm, 76: 2399-2401, 1979.

3501. Rydelius, P.A. Barnpsykiatriskt Omhändertagande av Unga
           Fyllerister. (Child-Psychiatric Care of Young Inebriates.)
           Läkartidningen, Stockholm, 75: 1607-1611, 1978.

3502. Rydelius, P.A. Methanol Intoxication--A Differential Diagnosis
           also of Current Interest in Child Psychiatric Practice.
           Acta Paedopsychiatrica, Basel, 43(5-6): 261-265, 1978.

3503.   Saarni, Carolyn. Adolescence and Alienation. In: Health
        Education and Alcohol Problems: Case Histories of Three
        Workshops. Workshop I: Alcohol Problems and Adolescent
        Turmoil. New York University School of Education, Health,
        Nursing and Arts Professions, New York, New York,
        December 10-11, 1976.

3504.   Sabey, Barbara and Codling, P.J. Alcohol and Road Accidents in
        Great Britain. In: Alcohol, Drugs and Traffic Safety.
        Proceedings of the Sixth International Conference on
        Alcohol, Drugs and Traffic Safety, Toronto, September 8-
        13, 1974. Eds. S. Israelstam and S. Lambert. Toronto:
        Addiction Research Foundation of Ontario, 1975, pages 73-
        83.

3505.   Sackin, Claire. Youthful and Aged Alcohol Abusers: Some Policy
        Implications. Journal of Alcohol and Drug Education,
        26(1): 69-75, 1980.

3506.   Sadava, S.W. Initiation to Cannabis Use: A Longitudinal Social
        Psychological Study of College Freshmen. Canadian Journal
        of Behavioral Science, 5(4): 371-384, 1973.

3507.   Sadava, S.W. and Forsyth, R. Decisions about Drug Use: An
        Application of the Choice-Shifts Paradigm. Psychological
        Reports, 38: 1119-1133, 1976.

3508.   Sadowska, A. Poradnia dla Młodzieży w Łodźi: Jedyna w Kraju.
        (An Alcoholism Dispensary for Youth in Lodz: The Only One
        in the Country.) Problemy Alkoholizmu, Warsaw, 23(4): 17,
        1976.

3509.   Saint, E.G. Alcohol and Society. Medical Journal of Australia,
        2(2): 69-76, 1969.

3510. Sales to Minors, Intoxicating Liquors. Detroit Law Review, 5:
       93-96, 1935.

3511. Salesi, R.A. Alcohol Consumption in Literature for Children and
       Adolescents: A Content Analysis of Contemporary Realistic
       Fiction. Doctoral Dissertation (University Microfilms
       No. 7730505). University of Georgia, 1977.

3512. Salgado, A. El Alcoholismo Paterno y la Delincuencia Juvenil.
       (Parental Alcoholism and Juvenile Delinquency.) Archivos
       Venezolanos de Puericultura y Pediatria, 8: 1711-1783,
       1946.

3513. Saltman, J. The New Alcoholics: Teenagers. (Public Affairs
       Pamphlet No. 499). New York: Public Affairs Committee,
       Inc., 1973.

3514. Samková, M. Vliv Rodinného Prostředí na Vznik Alkoholismu:
       Pokus o Rozbor Životopisů Léčených Alkoholiků. (The
       Influence of Family Environment on the Development of
       Alcoholism: Life History Analysis of Treated Alcoholics.)
       Protialkoholicky Obzor, Bratislava, 14: 177-182, 1979.

3515. Sanchez, M. and Moien, M. Utilization of Short-Stay Hospitals
       by Persons Discharged with Alcohol-Related Diagnoses.
       Vital Health Statistics, 13(47): 1-34, 1980.

3516. Sanchez-Dirks, R.D. Hispanic Drinking Practices: A
       Comparative Study of Hispanic and Anglo Adolescent
       Drinking Patterns. Doctoral Dissertation (University
       Microfilms No. 7818456). New York University, 1978.

3517. Sanchez-Dirks, Ruth. Drinking Practices among Hispanic Youth.
       Alcohol Health and Research World, 3(2): 21-27, 1978/79.

3518. Sandmaier, Marian. The Invisible Alcoholics: Women and Alcohol
       Abuse in America. New York: McGraw-Hill, 1980.

3519. Sandmaier, Marian. The Making of an Alcoholic Woman. Focus on
       Women, 1(1): 61-70, 1980.

3520. Sands, D. The College Teacher. In: Alcohol Education.
       Secretary's Committee on Alcoholism, U.S. Department of
       Health, Education and Welfare. Proceedings of a
       Conference, March 29, 1966. Washington, D.C.: U.S.
       Government Printing Office, 1967, pages 61-63.

3521. Sands, Edward S. Alcohol Education. Journal of Alcohol
       Education, 14(2): 9-15, 1969.

3522. Sanford, N. Personality and Patterns of Alcohol Consumption.
       Journal of Consulting and Clinical Psychology, 32(1): 13-
       17, 1968.

3523. Sanford, N. and Singer, S. Drinking and Personality. In: No
       Time for Youth--Growth and Constraint in College Students.
       Student Life and Its Problems. Ed. J. Katz. San
       Francisco, California: Jossey Bass, 1968. (ERIC
       Document Reproduction Service No. ED 026-699)

3524. Sanford, Nevitt. Is the Concept of Prevention Necessary or
       Useful? In: Handbook of Community Mental Health. Eds.
       S.E. Golann and C. Eisdorfer. New York: Appleton-
       Century-Crofts, 1972, pages 461-475.

3525. San Leandro Unified School District. Student Drug Use Survey.
       Alameda County, California: Alameda County School
       Department, 1975.

3526. Sanok, M. Alkoholizm Środowiska Rodzinnego Jako Jedna z Przczyn
       Drugoroczności i Niedostosowania Spolecznego Mlodzieży.
       (Alcoholism in the Family Environment as One of the Causes
       of Youngsters' Failure at School and Social Lag.)
       Problemy Alkoholizmu, Warsaw, 26(10): 9-10, 1979.

3527. Santamaria, J.N. The Social Implications of Alcoholism. Medical
       Journal of Australia, 2(10): 523-528, 1972.

3528. Santamaria, J.N. Social Patterns of Drinking in Young People and
       the Related Blood Alcohol Levels. In: Alcohol, Drugs and
       Traffic Safety. Proceedings of the Sixth International
       Conference on Alcohol, Drugs and Traffic Safety, Toronto,
       September 8-13, 1974. Eds. S. Israelstam and S. Lambert.
       Toronto: Alcoholism and Drug Addiction Research Foundation
       of Ontario, 1975, pages 384-387.

3529. Santo, Yoav. The Methodology of the National Youth Polydrug
       Study (NYPS). In: Youth Drug Abuse: Problems, Issues
       and Treatment. Eds. G.M. Beschner and A.S. Friedman.
       Lexington, Massachusetts: D.C. Heath, 1979, pages 129-145.

3530. Santo, Yoav and Friedman, Alfred S. Overview and Selected
       Findings from the National Youth Polydrug Study.
       Contemporary Drug Problems, 9(3):285-300, 1981.

3531. Santo, Yoav, Friedman, Alfred S. and Hooper, H. Elston. Patterns
       of Drug Use and Characteristics of Adolescent PCP Users in
       Drug Abuse Treatment. Contemporary Drug Problems, 9(3):
       369-390, 1981.

3532. Santo, Yoav, Hooper, H. Elston, Friedman, Alfred S. and
       Conner, William. Criminal Behavior of Adolescent Nonherion
       Polydrug Abusers in Drug Treatment Programs. Contemporary
       Drug Problems, 9(3): 301-326, 1981.

3533.   Sareyan, A. and Wilson, P.   Analysis of the Use of the Motion
           Picture in Alcohol Education.   In: Proceedings of the
           Joint Conference on Alcohol Abuse and Alcoholism,
           February 21-23, 1972. Washington, D.C.: U.S. Government
           Printing Office, 1972, pages 153-167. (DHEW Publication
           No. HSM 73-9051)

3534.   Sargent, M.   A Cross-Cultural Study of Attitudes and Behavior
           towards Alcohol and Drugs. British Journal of Sociology,
           22(1): 83-96, 1971.

3535.   Saskatchewan Department of Education. A Manual of Alcohol
           Studies for Schools. Regina, Saskatchewan, 1954.

3536.   Satchell, Michael.   Skid Row: The "Invisible" Women. The
           Washington Evening Star and Daily News: B4, February 19,
           1974.

3537.   Sauer, J. The Neglected Majority. Pamphlet. Milwaukee,
           Wisconsin: DePaul Rehabilitation Hospital, 1976.

3538.   Saunders, W.M. and Kershaw, P.W.   The Prevalence of Problem
           Drinking and Alcoholism in the West of Scotland. British
           Journal of Psychiatry, 133: 493-499, 1978.

3539.   Scarpitti, Frank R. and Datesman, Susan K., Eds. Drugs and the
           Youth Culture. Beverly Hills, California: Sage
           Publications, 1980.

3540.   Scarpitti, Frank R. and Datesman, Susan K. Introduction. In:
           Drugs and the Youth Culture. (Sage Annual Reviews of
           Drug and Alcohol Abuse. Volume 4.) Eds. F.R. Scarpitti
           and S.K. Datesman. Beverly Hills, California: Sage
           Publications, 1980, pages 9-29.

3541.   Schachter, M.   Examen Comparativo de las Perturbaciones Neuro-
           Psiquicas Observadas en los Ninos de Padres Tuberculosos,
           Sifiliticos, Paludicos o Alcoholicos. (Comparative
           Analysis of Neuropsychiatric Disturbances in Children of
           Tubercular, Syphilitic, Malarial and Alcoholic Fathers.)
           Revista Espanola de Pediatria, Zaragoza, 6: 823-826, 1950.

3542.   Schachter, M.G.   Contribution à l'Étude Clinico-Psychologique
           des Enfants Maltraités: Sévices Physiques et Moraux.
           (Contribution to the Clinicopsychological Study of
           Mistreated Children: Physical and Moral Cruelty.)
           Giornale di Psichiatria e di Neuropatologia, Ferrarra, 80:
           311-317, 1952.

3543.   Schaeffer, G.M., Schuckit, M.A. and Morrissey, E.R.   Correlation
           between Two Measures of Self-Esteem and Drug Use in a
           College Sample. Psychological Reports, 39: 915-919, 1976.

3544.   Schafer, Walter E. Participation in Interscholastic Athletics
        and Delinquency. In: Schools and Delinquency. Eds.
        K. Polk and W.E. Schafer. Englewoods Cliffs, New Jersey:
        Prentice-Hall, Inc., 1972, pages 91-101.

3545.   Schafer, Walter E. and Polk, Kenneth. School Conditions
        Contributing to Delinquency. In: Schools and Delinquency.
        Eds. K. Polk and W.E. Schafer. Englewoods Cliffs, New
        Jersey: Prentice-Hall, Inc., 1972, pages 181-238.

3546.   Schaps, Eric, Churgin, Shoshanna, Palley, Carol, Takata, Beverly
        and Cohen, Allan. Primary Prevention Research: A
        Preliminary Review of Program Outcome Studies.
        International Journal of the Addictions, 15(5): 657-679,
        1980.

3547.   Schaps, E., Cohen, A.Y., Resnik, H.S.; Schaps, E., Slimmon, L.R.;
        Schaps, E., Adams, W.T. and Resnik, H.S. Balancing Head
        and Heart: Sensible Ideas for the Prevention of Drug and
        Alcohol Abuse. Book 1. Prevention in Perspective. Book 2.
        Eleven Strategies. Book 3. Implementation and Resources.
        Lafayette, California: Prevention Materials Institute
        Press, 1975.

3548.   Schaps, Eric, DiBartolo, Russell, Moskowitz, Joel, Palley, Carol
        and Churgin, Shoshanna. A Review of 127 Drug Abuse
        Prevention Program Evaluations. Journal of Drug Issues,
        11(1): 17-43, 1981.

3549.   Scharff, N. Kids' Drinking has Police Tipsy with Frustration.
        Washington Star: B1, B4, August 3, 1975.

3550.   Schecter, A., Alksne, H. and Kaufmann, E., Eds. Drug Abuse:
        Modern Trends, Issues and Perspectives. Proceedings of the
        Second National Drug Abuse Conference, Inc., New Orleans,
        Louisiana, 1975. New York: Marcel Dekker, Inc., 1978.

3551.   Scheller-Gilkey, G., Gomberg, E.S. and Clay, M. College Students
        and Alcohol: An Exploration of Observations and Opinions.
        Journal of Alcohol and Drug Education, 24(3): 30-41, 1978.

3552.   Schenk, J. Die Bedeutung von Alkoholbewertung,
        Persönlichkeitsmerkmalen und Sozialen Umweltbedingungen
        für den Alkoholkonsum bei Jungen Männern. (The
        Significance of Attitudes toward Alcohol, Personality
        Characteristics and Social Conditions for Alcohol
        Consumption among Young Men.) In: Jugend und Alkohol:
        Trinkmuster, Suchtentwicklung and Therapie. (Youth and
        Alcohol: Drinking Patterns, Addiction Development and
        Therapy.) Eds. H. Berger, A. Legnaro and K.-H Reuband.
        Stuttgart: W. Kohlhammer, 1980, pages 61-75.

3553. Schenk, Josef. Structure of Drug Use and Drug Definition among
       Youth. International Journal of the Addictions, 12(4):
       459-469, 1977.

3554. Scherer, S.E. Hard and Soft Hallucinogenic Drug Users: Their
       Drug Taking Patterns and Objectives. International Journal
       of the Addictions, 8(5): 755-766, 1973.

3555. Scherer, S.E. and Mukherjee, B.N. "Moderate" and Hard Drug Users
       among College Students: A Study of Their Drug Use Patterns
       and Characteristics. British Journal of Addiction, 66:
       315-328, 1971.

3556. Schifferes, J.J. Healthier Living: A College Textbook in
       Personal and Community Health. (Second Edition) New York:
       Wiley, 1965, especially pages 181-196.

3557. Schilling, Martha and Carman, Roderick. Internal-External
       Control and Motivations for Alcohol Use among High School
       Students. Psychological Reports, 42: 1088-1090, 1978.

3558. Schlegel, Ronald P. Some Methodological Procedures for the
       Evaluation of Educational Programs for Prevention of
       Adolescent Alcohol Use and Abuse. Evaluation Quarterly,
       1(4): 657-672, 1971.

3559. Schlegel, Ronald P., Crawford, Craig A. and Sanborn, Margaret D.
       Correspondence and Mediational Properties of the Fishbein
       Model: An Application to Adolescent Alcohol Use. Journal
       of Experimental Social Psychology, 5(13): 421-430, 1977.

3560. Schlegal, Ronald P. and Sanborn, Margaret D. Religious
       Affiliation and Adolescent Drinking. Journal of Studies on
       Alcohol, 40(7): 693-703, 1979.

3561. Schmidt, E. and Sindballe, A.-M. Stoffer, Alkohol og Tobak:
       En Undersøgelse Blandt Unge: Roskildes Skoler: Rapport
       fra Forskningsunderudvalget. (Drugs, Alcohol and Tobacco:
       An Investigation among Youth in the Schools at Roskilde:
       A Report by the Research Subcommittee.) København:
       Kontaktudvalget Vedrørende Ungdomsnarkomanien, (eksp.,
       Store Kongensgade 1), 1974.

3562. Schmidt, M.T. and Hankoff, L.D. Adolescent Alcohol Abuse and Its
       Prevention. Public Health Review, 8: 107-153, 1979.

3563. Schmidt, W. A Note on the Effect of Lowering the Legal Drinking
       Age on the Consumption of Alcoholic Beverages. Toronto,
       Ontario: Addiction Research Foundation, 1972.

3564. Schmidt, W. and Kornaczewski, A. A Further Note on the Effect of Lowering the Legal Drinking Age on Alcohol Related Motor Vehicle Accidents. Toronto, Ontario: Addiction Research Foundation, 1973.

3565. Schmidt, W. and Kornaczewski, A. A Note on the Effect of Lowering the Legal Drinking Age on Alcohol Related Motor Vehicle Accidents. Toronto, Ontario: Addiction Research Foundation, 1973.

3566. Schmidt, W. and Kornaczewski, A. L'Abaissement de l'Âge Auquel la loi de l'Ontario Permet d'Absorber de l'Alcool et ses Effets sur les Accidents d'Automobiles Attribuables à l'Alcool. (Lowering the Legal Drinking Age in Ontario and Its Effects on Automobile Accidents Attributable to Alcohol.) Toxicomanies, Quebec, 8: 105-116, 1975.

3567. Schmidt, Wolfgang. Adolescent Alcohol Abuse. The Alcoholism Digest Annual, 2: 40-43, 1973-1974.

3568. Schmidt, Wolfgang and Kornaczewski, Alexander. The Effects of Lowering the Legal Drinking Age in Ontario on Alcohol-Related Motor Vehicle Accidents. In: Alcohol, Drugs and Traffic Safety. Proceedings of the Sixth International Conference on Alcohol, Drugs and Traffic Safety, Toronto, September 8-13, 1974. Eds. S. Israelstam and S. Lambert. Toronto: Addiction Research Foundation of Ontario, 1975, pages 763-770.

3569. Schmutte, G.T., Leonard, K.E. and Taylor, S.P. Alcohol and Expectations of Attack. Psychological Reports, 45: 163-167, 1979.

3570. Schmutte, G.T. and Taylor, S.P. Physical Aggression as a Function of Alcohol and Pain Feedback. Journal of Social Psychology, 110: 235-244, 1980.

3571. Schneider, K.A. Alcoholism and Addiction: A Study Program for Adults and Youth. Philadelphia, Pennsylvania: Fortress Press, 1976.

3572. Schneider, Robert J., Sangsingkeo, Phon and Punnahitanond, Serin. A Survey of Thai Student Use of Illicit Drugs. International Journal of the Addictions, 12: 227-239, 1977.

3573. Schnoll, Sidney H. Alcohol and Other Substance Abuse in Adolescents. In: Addiction Research and Treatment: Converging Trends. Eds. E.L. Gottheil, A.T. McLellan, K.A. Druley and A.I. Alterman. New York: Pergamon Press, 1979, pages 40-45.

3574.   Schomp, G.   Alcohol: Its Use, Abuse, and Therapy: Expert
        Practical Advise with Christian Insights. Huntington,
        Indiana: Our Sunday Visitor, 1977.

3575.   Schonberg, S. Kenneth and Litt, Iris F. Medical Treatment of the
        Adolescent Drug Abuse: An Opportunity for Rehabilitative
        Intervention. Primary Care, 3(1): 23-37, 1976.

3576.   Schonfeld, W.A. The Adolescent's Crises Today: Socioeconomic
        Affluence as a Factor. New York State Journal of Medicine,
        67: 1981-1990, 1967.

3577.   Schonfield, J. Differences in Smoking, Drinking and Social
        Behavior by Race and Delinquency Status in Adolescent
        Males. Adolescence, 1(4): 367-380, 1966.

3578.   Schoolboy Drunkenness - Quarterly Notes. British Journal on
        Alcohol and Alcoholism, 12(1): 9, 1977.

3579.   Schröder, U. Alkoholismus bei Kindern und Jugendlichen.
        (Alcoholism in Children and Adolescents.) Zeitschruft
        fuer Allgemeinmedizin, 52: 500-504, 1976.

3580.   Schuchard, Keith. The Floodtide of Drugs and the Very Young:
        Re-Building the Protective Dikes at Home and Abroad. In:
        Drug Abuse in the Modern World: A Perspective for the
        Eighties. Eds. G.G. Nahas and H.C. Frick II. New York:
        Pergamon Press, 1981, pages 316-322.

3581.   Schuckit, M., Pitts, F.N., Jr., Reich, T., King, L.J. and
        Winokur, G. Alcoholism. I. Two Types of Alcoholism in
        Women. Archives of General Psychiatry, 20: 301-306, 1969.

3582.   Schuckit, M., Rimmer, J. and Winokur, G. Alcoholism: Influence
        of Parental Illness. British Journal of Psychiatry,
        119(553): 663, 1971.

3583.   Schuckit, M.A. Alcohol and Youth. Advances in Alcoholism,
        1(13): 1-3, 1979.

3584.   Schuckit, M.A. Alcoholism and Sociopathy--Diagnostic Confusion.
        Quarterly Journal of Studies on Alcohol, 34(1): 157-164,
        1973.

3585.   Schuckit, M.A. Family History and Half-Sibling Research in
        Alcoholism. Annals of the New York Academy of Sciences,
        197: 121-125, 1972.

3586.   Schuckit, M.A. Overview of Alcoholism. Journal of the American
        Dental Association, 99(3): 489-493, 1979.

3587.   Schuckit, M.A. and Chiles, J.A. Family History as a Diagnostic
        Aid in Two Samples of Adolescents. Journal of Nervous and
        Mental Diseases, 166: 165-176, 1978.

3588.   Schuckit, M.A., Goodwin, D.A. and Winokur, G. A Study of
        Alcoholism in Half Siblings. American Journal of
        Psychiatry, 128(9): 1132-1136, 1972.

3589.   Schuckit, M.A., Goodwin, D.W. and Winokur, G. The Half Sibling
        Approach in a Genetic Study of Alcoholism. In: Life
        History Research in Psychopathology. Volume 2. Eds.
        M. Roff, L.N. Robins and M. Pollack. Minneapolis:
        University of Minnesota Press, 1972, pages 120-127.

3590.   Schuckit, M.A. and Morrissey, E.R. Propoxyphene and
        Phencyclidine (PCP) Use in Adolescents. Journal of
        Clinical Psychiatry, 39: 7-13, 1978.

3591.   Schuckit, M.A., Petrich, J. and Chiles, J. Hyperactivity:
        Diagnostic Confusion. Journal of Nervous and Mental
        Diseases, 166: 79-87, 1978.

3592.   Schuckit, Marc. A Theory of Alcohol and Drug Abuse: A Genetic
        Approach. In: Theories on Drug Abuse: Selected
        Contemporary Problems. (Research Monograph Series 30)
        U.S. National Institute on Drug Abuse. Eds. D. Lettieri,
        M. Sayers and H. Pearson. Rockville, Maryland, 1980,
        pages 297-302. (DHEW Publication No. ADM 80-967)

3593.   Schuckit, Marc and Morrissey, Elizabeth R. Alcoholism in Women:
        Some Clinical and Social Perspectives with an Emphasis on
        Possible Subtypes. In: Alcoholism Problems in Women and
        Children. Eds. M. Greenblatt and M. Schuckit. New York:
        Grune and Stratton, 1976, pages 5-25.

3594.   Schuckit, Marc and Morrissey, Elizabeth, R. Minor in Possession
        of Alcohol: What Does It Mean? In: Currents in
        Alcoholism. Volume 4. Psychiatric, Psychological, Social
        and Epidemiological Studies. Ed. F.A. Seixas. New York:
        Grune and Stratton, 1978, pages 339-356.

3595.   Schuckit, Marc, Morrissey, Elizabeth R., Lewis, Nancy and
        Buck, William. Adolescent Problem Drinkers. In: Currents
        in Alcoholism. Volume 2. Psychiatric, Psychological,
        Social and Epidemiological Studies. Ed. F.A. Seixas. New
        York: Grune and Stratton, 1977, pages 325-355, 1977.

3596.   Schuckit, Marc A. and Winokur, George. A Short Term Follow Up
        of Women Alcoholics. Diseases of the Nervous System,
        33(10): 672-678, 1972.

3597.   Schulz, F. and Naeve, W. Über den Panoramawandel der
          Alkoholkriminalität: Untersuchungen Anhand von
          Blutalkoholbefunden aus den Jahren 1965 und 1975 (Freie
          und Hansestadt Hamburg). (Change in the Panorama of
          Alcohol-Related Criminality: Analysis of Blood Alcohol
          Findings from 1965-1975 in Hamburg.) Zeitschrift fuer
          Rechtmedizin, Berlin, 82: 1-25, 1978.

3598.   Schuman, S.H., McConochie, R. and Pelz, D.C. Reduction of Young
          Driver Crashes in a Controlled Pilot Study: Two-Year
          Follow-Up in One Michigan High School. Journal of the
          American Medical Association, 218(2): 233-237, 1971.

3599.   Schuman, S.H. and Pelz, D.C. A Field Trial of Young Drivers:
          An Epidemiological Approach in Michigan. Archives of
          Environmental Health, 21(3): 462-467, 1970.

3600.   Schuman, S.H., Pelz, D.C., Erlich, N.J. and Selzer, M.L. Young
          Male Drivers: Impulse Expression, Accidents and
          Violations. Journal of the American Medical Association,
          200: 1026-1030, 1967.

3601.   Schuster, R. Ein Betrag zur Effektivitätsbeurteilung Einer
          Senkung des Gefahrengrenzwertes. (Evaluation of the
          Effectiveness of Lowering the Legal Limit.) Blutalkohol,
          Hamburg, 14: 78-80, 1977.

3602.   Schweitzer, H. Alkohol als Verkehrsunfallursache. (Alcohol as
          a Cause of Traffic Accidents.) Monatsschrift fuer
          Unfallheilkunde, 55: 257-271, 1952.

3603.   Scientific Temperance Federation. Temperance Education in
          American Public Schools. Boston, Massachusetts, 1930.

3604.   Sclare, A. Balfour. Alcohol Problems in Women. In:
          International Conference on Alcoholism and Drug
          Dependence: Alcoholism and Drug Dependence, A
          Multidisciplinary Approach. Proceedings of the Third
          International Conference on Alcoholism and Drug Dependence,
          Liverpool, England, April, 1976. Eds. J.S. Madden,
          R. Walker and W.H. Kenyon. New York: Plenum Press, 1977,
          pages 181-187.

3605.   Sclare, A. Balfour. Effecting Change in Alcoholism Service.
          Journal of Alcoholism, 11(4): 123-127, 1976.

3606.   Sclare, A. Balfour. The Epidemiology of Alcoholism. British
          Journal of Alcohol and Alcoholism, 13(2): 86-91, 1978.

3607.   Sclare, A. Balfour. The Female Alcoholic. British Journal of
          the Addictions, 65(2): 99-107, 1970.

3608.   Scotland's Drink Problem. British Medical Journal, 4(884): 64,
          1973.

3609. Scott, E.M. _Struggles in an Alcoholic Family_. Springfield, Illinois: Charles C. Thomas, 1970.

3610. Scott, E.M. Young Drug Abusers and Non-Abusers: A Comparison. _International Journal of Offender Therapy and Comparative Criminology_, 22: 105-114, 1978.

3611. Scott, Edward M. _The Adolescent Gap-Research Findings on Drug Using and Non-Drug Using Teens_. Springfield, Illinois: Charles C. Thomas, 1972.

3612. Scott, Joseph W. and Vay, Edmund W. A Perspective on Middle Class Delinquency. In: _Readings in Juvenile Delinquency_. Ed. R. Cavan. New York: J.B. Lippincott, 1969, pages 115-128.

3613. Scott, P.D. Offenders, Drunkenness and Murder. _British Journal of Addiction_, 63: 221-226, 1968.

3614. Sedláčková, J. and Widermannová, L. (The Influence of the Alcoholic Family Environment on the Neuropsychic Development of the Child.) (Czech text.) _Ceskoslovenska Psychiatrie_, Praha, 52: 272-277, 1956.

3615. Seffrin, John R. and Seehafer, Roger W. Multiple Drug-Use Patterns among a Group of High School Students: Regular Users vs. Nonusers of Specific Drug Types. _The Journal of School Health_, 46(7): 413-416, 1976.

3616. Seffrin, John R. and Seehafer, Roger W. A Survey of Drug Use Beliefs, Opinions and Behavior among Junior and Senior High School Students. Part One: Group Data. _The Journal of School Health_, 46(5): 263-268, 1976.

3617. Segal, B. Drug Use, Alcohol Use and Nonuse of Either as a Function of Personality. In: _Papers Presented at the Fifth International Institute on the Prevention and Treatment of Drug Dependence, Copenhagen, Denmark, Volume II, July, 1974_. International Council on Alcohol and Addictions. Lausanne, Switzerland, 1974, pages 360-371.

3618. Segal, B., Rhenberg, G. and Sterling, S. Self-Concept and Drug and Alcohol Use in Female College Students. _Journal of Alcohol and Drug Education_, 20(3): 17-22, 1975.

3619. Segal, B. and Rose, R. Sensation Seeking and Alcohol Use: A Correlate in Experience. _Journal of Alcohol Education_, 17(2): 8-12, 1972.

3620. Segal, B.M. The Effect of the Age Factor on Alcoholism. In: _Currents in Alcoholism. Volume 2. Psychiatric, Psychological, Social and Epidemiological Studies_. Ed. F.A. Seixas. New York: Grune and Stratton, 1977, pages 377-393.

3621.   Segal, Bernard. Drug Use and Stimulus Seeking. In: Drug Abuse: Modern Trends, Issues and Perspectives. Proceedings of the Second National Drug Abuse Conference, Inc., New Orleans, Louisiana, 1975. Comp.: A. Schecter, H. Alksne and E. Kaufman. New York: Marcel Dekker, Inc., 1978, pages 1194-1204.

3622.   Segal, Bernard. Locus of Control and Drug and Alcohol Use in College Students. Journal of Alcohol and Drug Education, 19(3): 1-5, 1974.

3623.   Segal, Bernard. Personality Factors Related to Drug and Alcohol Use. In: Predicting Adolescent Drug Abuse: A Review of Issues, Methods and Correlates - Research Issues II. Ed. D. Lettieri. Rockville, Maryland: National Institute on Drug Abuse, 1975, pages 167-191.

3624.   Segal, Bernard, Huba, George J. and Singer, Jerome L. Drugs, Daydreaming and Personality: A Study of College Youth. Hillsdale, New York: Erthurm and Associates, 1980.

3625.   Segal, Bernard, Huba, George J. and Singer, Jerome L. Prediction of College Drug Use from Personality and Inner Experience. The International Journal of the Addictions, 15(6): 849-867, 1980.

3626.   Segal, Bernard, Huba, G.J. and Singer, Jerome L. Reasons for Drug and Alcohol Use by College Students. The International Journal of the Addictions, 15(4): 489-498, 1980.

3627.   Segal, B. and Merenda, P.F. Locus of Control, Sensation Seeking, and Drug and Alcohol Use in College Students. Drug Forum, 4: 349-369, 1975.

3628.   Segal, Bernard and Singer, Jerome L. Daydreaming, Drug and Alcohol Use in College Students: A Factor Analytic Study. Addictive Behaviors, 1: 227-235, 1976.

3629.   Seidler, Gary. Alcohol Tops among Students. The Journal, 2(3): 1, 5, 1973.

3630.   Seixas, F.A., Ed. Currents in Alcoholism. Volume 2. Psychiatric, Psychological, Social and Epidemiological Studies. New York: Grune and Stratton, 1977.

3631.   Seixas, F.A., Ed. Currents in Alcoholism. Volume 4. Psychiatric, Psychological, Social and Epidemiological Studies. New York: Grune and Stratton, 1978.

3632. Seixas, Frank. A Possible Effect of Major Efforts to Treat
           Established Alcoholism: Initiating an Epidemic of Health.
           Preventive Medicine, 3(1): 86-96, 1974.

3633. Seixas, J. Children from Alcoholic Families. In: Alcoholism:
           Development, Consequences and Interventions. Eds.
           N.J. Estes and M.E. Heinemann. St. Louis, Missouri:
           Mosby, 1977, pages 153-161.

3634. Seixas, Judith S. Living with a Parent Who Drinks too Much.
           New York: Greenwillow Books, 1979.

3635. Sekei, L. Rabota po Preduprezhdenivu Kureniya i Potrebleniya
           Spiritnykh Napitkoy Mlodezh'yu Vengrii. (Work on
           Prevention of Smoking and Use of Alcoholic Beverages by the
           Youth of Hungary.) Trudy Tsentralnogo Nauchno-
           Issledovatelskogo Instituta Sanitarnogo Prosveshcheniia,
           Moscow, 3: 181-185, 1972.

3636. Selby, J.B. Pot and Booze. New England Journal of Medicine,
           280: 1077, 1969.

3637. Self, Charles R. and Seixas, Frank A. Drinking, Drugs and
           Driving. Pamphlet. Yonkers, New York: H.K. Simon Co.,
           Inc., 1973, pages 1-13.

3638. Seliger, R.V. Its Smarter Not to Drink. Pamphlet. Evanston,
           Illinois: School and College Service, 1969.

3639. Seliger, R.V., Gerber, S.R., Shupe, L.M. and Hearn, C.A. High
           School Hurdles. Evanston, Illinois: School and College
           Service, 1968.

3640. Sells, Saul B. and Simpson, D. Dwayne. Evaluation of Treatment
           Outcome for Youths in the Drug Abuse Reporting Program:
           A Follow-Up Study. In: Youth Drug Abuse: Problems,
           Issues and Treatment. Eds. G.M. Beschner and
           A.S. Friedman. Lexington, Massachusetts: D.C. Heath,
           1979, pages 571-628.

3641. Seltzer, H.S. Severe Drug-Induced Hypoglycemia: A Review.
           Comprehensive Therapy, 5(4): 21-29, 1979.

3642. Selzer, M.L. Alcoholism, Mental Illness, and Stress in 96
           Drivers Causing Fatal Accidents. Behavioral Science,
           14(1): 1-10, 1969.

3643. Selzer, M.L. and Weiss, S. Alcoholism and Traffic Fatalities:
           Study in Futility. Americal Journal of Psychiatry, 122:
           762-767, 1966.

3644. Semple, B.M. and Yarrow, A. Health Education, Alcohol, and
           Alcoholism in Scotland. Health Bulletin, 32(1): 31-34,
           1974.

3645. Senseman, L.A. The Housewife's Secret Illness: How to Recognize
        the Female Alcoholic. Rhode Island Medical Journal, 49:
        40-42, 1966.

3646. Seppälä, V. Tanssi ja Alkoholi Vähäkyrössä. (Dancing and
        Alcohol in Vähäkyrö.) Alkoholikysymys, Helsinki, 33:
        238-251, 1965.

3647. Serdahely, W.J. and Behunin, O. Drug Education: Reducing or
        Increasing Drug Consumption? Journal of Alcohol and Drug
        Education, 23(1): 8-19, 1977.

3648. Serdahely, William J. A Factual Approach to Drug Education and
        Its Effects on Drug Consumption. Journal of Alcohol and
        Drug Education, 26(1): 63-38, 1980.

3649. Serin, S. L'Alcoolisme des Enfants. (Alcoholism in Children.)
        Bulletin de l'Academie Nationale de Médecine, Paris, 138:
        324-327, 1954.

3650. Service de Santé de la Jeunesse, Genève. (Youth Health Service)
        Éducation pour la Santé: Le Travail en Équipe à l'École.
        (Health Education: Teamwork at School.) Sozial- und
        Präventivmedzin, Zürich, 22: 225-228, 1977.

3651. Seryes, O. Intérêt des Boissons non Alcoolisées du Type Soda
        pour la Jeunesse. (Importance of Nonalcoholic Sodalike
        Drinks for Youth.) Marseille Médical, 93: 814-815, 1956.

3652. Sexton, Brendan and Sexton, Patricia Cayo. Reaching Out:
        Helping Young People in Trouble. New York: Agathon, 1975.

3653. Shain, M. Cannabis, Alcohol, and the Family. In: Sociological
        Aspects of Drug Dependence. Ed. C. Winick. Cleveland,
        Ohio: CRC Press, 1974, pages 133-153.

3654. Shain, Martin, Riddell, William and Kilth, Heather Lee.
        Influence, Choice and Drugs: Toward a Systematic Approach
        to the Prevention of Substance Abuse. Lexington,
        Massachusetts: Lexington Books, 1977.

3655. Shanlkin, M. Choices for the Future: Alcohol and Pregnancy.
        Leaflet. Madison, Wisconsin: Clearinghouse for Alcohol
        and Other Drug Information, 1979.

3656. Shapiro, Jim, Chairperson - Panel Workshop F. Issue: Can We
        Separate Fact from Myth in Primary Prevention? Defining
        Prevention and Translating It into Workable Ideas and
        Programs. American Journal of Drug and Alcohol Abuse,
        3(1): 87-91, 1976.

3657. Shapiro, R.D. Alcohol, Tobacco and Illicit Drug Use among
        Adolescents. International Journal of the Addictions, 10:
        387-390, 1975.

3658.   Sharoff, R.L. Character Problems and Their Relation to Drug
        Abuse. American Journal of Psychoanalysis, 29(2): 186-193,
        1969.

3659.   Shastin, N. Influence of Alcohol on Conditioned Reflexes.
        (Russian Text) Fiziologicheskii Zhurna SSSR Imeni I.M.
        Sechenova, Moscow, 30: 472-477, 1941.

3660.   Shaw, J.S. Have Some (Legal) Madiera, M'dear? Campus Drinking
        is Changing. College and University Business, 56(1): 46-
        47, 1974.

3661.   Shea, H.H. and Senseman, L.A. The Workshop on Alcohol
        Education--A Report. Rhode Island Medical Journal, 40:
        304-305, 1957.

3662.   Sheppard, M.A., Goodstadt, M.S., Torrance, G. and Fieldstone, M.
        Alcohol Education: Ten Lesson Plans for Grades 9 and 10.
        Toronto, Ontario: Addiction Research Foundation, 1978.

3663.   Sheppard, M.A., Goodstadt, M.S., Torrance, G. and Fieldstone, M.
        Alcohol Education: Ten Lesson Plans for Grades 7 and 8.
        Toronto, Ontario: Addiction Research Foundation, 1978.

3664.   Sheppard, Margaret A. Barriers to the Implementation of a New
        School-Based Alcohol Education Program. Toronto, Ontario:
        Alcoholism and Drug Addiction Research Foundation, 1980.

3665.   Sherbini, Isam. Prevention--A Way of Life. In: Papers
        Presented at the 23rd International Institute on the
        Prevention and Treatment of Alcoholism. Dresden, June 6-
        10, 1977. Eds. E.J. Tongue and I. Moos. Lausanne,
        Switzerland: International Council on Alcohol and
        Addictions, 1977, pages 331-338.

3666.   Sherman, M.J. Abstention: An Exploratory Analysis of Reference
        Group Behavior and Non-Use of Alcohol among Negro Male
        Collegiates. Master's Thesis. Durham, North Carolina:
        Duke University, 1966.

3667.   Shick, J.F.E., Dorus, W. and Hughes, P.H. Adolescent Drug
        Using Groups in Chicago Parks. Drug and Alcohol
        Dependence, Lausanne, 3: 199-210, 1978.

3668.   Shick, J. Fred, Dorus, Walter and Hughes, Patrick. Adolescent
        Drug Using Groups in the Natural Setting. In: Drug
        Abuse: Modern Trends, Issues and Perspectives Proceedings
        of the Second National Drug Abuse Conference, Inc., New
        Orleans, Louisiana, 1975. Comp.: A. Schecter, H. Alksne
        and E. Kaufman. New York: Marcel Dekker, Inc., 1978,
        pages 36-51.

3669. Shick, J. Fred and Wiebel, W. Wayne. Congregation Sites for
       Youthful Multiple Drug Users: Locations for
       Epidemiological Research and Intervention. Drug and
       Alcohol Dependence, Lausanne, 7(1): 63-79, 1981.

3670. Shimmel, G.M., Lee, E.E. and Fishman, R. Emerging Trends of
       Alcohol Use and Abuse among Urban Teenagers. New York:
       School of Health Sciences, Hunter College, 1975.

3671. Shiretorova, D. Ch. O Roli Khronicheskoi Alkogol'noi
       Intoksikatsii v Razvitii Insul'tov u Bol'nykh Molodogo
       Vozrasta. (On the Role of Chronic Alcohol Intoxication in
       the Development of Insults in Young Patients.) In:
       Tretii Vseros. S'yezd Nevropatologov i Psikhiatrov,
       Kazan'. Tom 3. Tezisy i Doklady. (The Third All-Russian
       Congress of Neuropathologists and Psychiatrists, Kazan'.
       Volume 3. Thesis and Proceedings.) Moskva, 1974, pages
       90-94.

3672. Shoham, S. Giora, Rahav, G., Esformes, Y., Blau, Joanna,
       Kaplinsky, Nava, Markovsky, R. and Wolf, B. Differential
       Patterns of Drug Involvement among Israeli Youth. Bulletin
       on Narcotics, 30(4): 17-33, 1978.

3673. Shoham, S.C., Rahav, G., Esformes, Y., Markovski, R., Chard, F.
       and Kaplinsky, N. Some Parameters of the Use of Alcohol
       by Israeli Youth and Its Relationship to Their Involvement
       with Cannabis and Tobacco. Drug and Alcohol Dependence,
       Lausanne, 6: 263-272, 1980.

3674. Shore, J.H. and VonFumetti, B. Three Alcohol Programs for
       American Indians. American Journal of Psychiatry, 128(11):
       1450-1454, 1972.

3675. Short, James, Tennyson, Ray and Howard, Kenneth. Behavior
       Dimensions of Gang Delinquency. American Sociological
       Review, 1(28): 411-428, 1963.

3676. Short, James F. Street Corner Groups and Patterns of
       Delinquency. In: Readings in Juvenile Delinquency. Ed.
       R. Cavan. New York: J.B. Lippincott, 1969, pages 204-221.

3677. Shulamith, L., Straussner, A., Weinstein, D.L. and Hernandez, R.
       Effects of Alcoholism on the Family System. Health and
       Social Work, 4(4): 111-127, 1979.

3678. Schults, S.D. and Layne, N.R., Jr. Age and BAC When Arrested
       for Drunken Driving and Public Drunkenness. Journal of
       Studies on Alcohol, 40: 492-495, 1979.

3679.   Shurygin, G.I. Ob Osobennostyakh Psikhicheskogo Razvitiya Detei
        ot Materei, Stradayushchikh Kronicheskim Alkoholizmom.
        (Characteristics of Mental Development of Children of
        Alcoholic Mothers.) Pediatriya, Moskva, 11: 71-73, 1974.

3680.   Siegelmann, M. Family Background of Alcoholics: Some Research
        Considerations. Annals of the New York Academy of
        Science, 197: 226-229, 1972.

3681.   Siegrist, J. Teen-Age Alcoholism. Paper Presented for U.S.
        Senate Alcoholism and Narcotics Subcommittee Hearings,
        February 3-5, 1976.

3682.   Siegrist, J. Teen-Age Alcoholism: A Problem? Milwaukee,
        Wisconsin: Paper Presented at Youth and Alcohol Forum,
        Annual Conference of the National Council of Alcoholism,
        April 28, 1975.

3683.   Sielicka, M. Alkoholizm Wśród Mlodziezy. (Alcoholism among
        Adolescents.) Polski Tygodnik Lekarski, Warsaw, 16: 1907-
        1909, 1961.

3684.   Sijlbing, G. and Van-De-Wal, H.J. Alcoholgebruik Door Jonge
        Mensen. (Alcohol Consumption by Young People.) Feiten,
        Amsterdam, 16(2): 34-36, 1980.

3685.   Sikorska-Godwod, C. O Niektórych Zespolach Schizofrenopodobnych
        w Przebiegu Alkoholizmu Przewleklego Wczesnego. (On Some
        Schizophrenialike Syndromes in Early Chronic Alcoholism.)
        Neurologia-Neurocirugia Psiquiatria, Polska, 6: 923-932,
        1956.

3686.   Silberberg, C.G. An Investigation of Family Interaction
        Patterns: Similarities and Differences among Families
        with Adolescents Designated Normal, Emotionally Disturbed
        or Drug Abusing. Doctoral Dissertation (University
        Microfilms No. 77-6537). Bryn Mawr, Pennsylvania: Bryn
        Mawr College, 1976.

3687.   Silver, R. Reaching Out to the Alcoholic and the Family.
        Pamphlet. Center City, Minnesota: Hazelden, 1977.

3688.   Silverman, I., Lief, V.F. and Shah, R.K. Migration and Alcohol
        Use: A Careers Analysis. International Journal of the
        Addictions, 6(2): 195-213, 1971.

3689.   Silverstein, Alvin and Silverstein, Virginia B. Alcoholism.
        Philadelphia, Pennsylvania: J.B. Lippincott, Co., 1975.

3690.   Simmons, Ozzie G. Ambivalence and the Learning of Drinking
        Behavior in a Peruvian Community. American Anthropology,
        62: 1018-1027, 1960. (Also in: Society, Culture and
        Drinking Practice. Eds. D.J. Pittman and C.R. Snyder.
        New York: Wiley, 1962, pages 37-47.

3691. Simmons, Ozzie G. The Sociocultural Integration of Alcohol Use:
      A Peruvian Study. Quarterly Journal of Studies on Alcohol,
      29: 152-171, 1968.

3692. Simmonds, Robert M. Drug Abuse: A Problem of Socialization.
      Journal of Drug Education, 8(4): 299-303, 1978.

3693. Simonds, J.F. and Kashani, J. Drug Abuse and Criminal Behavior
      in Delinquent Boys Committed to a Training School.
      American Journal of Psychiatry, 136: 1444-1448, 1979.

3694. Simonds, John F. and Kashani, Javad. Specific Drug Use and
      Violence in Delinquent Boys. American Journal of Drug and
      Alcohol Abuse, 7(3 & 4): 305,322, 1980.

3695. Simpson, M.L. and Koenig, F.W. The Use of the Semantic
      Differential Technique in Drug Education Research: An
      Example and Some Suggestions. Journal of Drug Education,
      5(3): 251-259, 1975.

3696. Sinacore, J.S. Alcohol Education. Paper Presented at the NIMH-
      NHTSA Planning Meeting on a K-12 Curriculum in Alcohol
      Abuse and Traffic Safety, Washington, D.C., February 23-24,
      1971.

3697. Singerman, J. Teaching the Alcohol Problem. Science Teacher,
      14: 122-123, 140, 1947.

3698. Singh, B.K. State Characteristics and Admissions to Drug
      Treatment Programs. Journal of Drug Issues, 9(3): 413-
      423, 1979.

3699. Singh, J. and Lal, H., Eds. New Aspects of Analytical and
      Clinical Toxicology. Volume 4. New York: Stratton, 1974.

3700. Singh, R.N. and Haddy, L.E. Alcohol Consumption and the
      Students' Use of Hallucinogenic Drugs. West Virginia
      Medical Journal, 69(4): 88-90, 1973.

3701. Single, E., Kandel, D. and Faust, R. Patterns of Multiple Drug
      Use in High School. Journal of Health and Social
      Behavior, 15(4): 344-357, 1974.

3702. Single, E., Kandel, D. and Johnson, B.D. The Reliability and
      Validity of Drug Use Responses in a Large Scale
      Longitudinal Survey. Journal of Drug Issues, 5(4): 426-
      443, 1975.

3703. Sinnett, E.R., Wampler, K.S. and Harvey, W.M. Consistency of
      Patterns of Drug Use. Psychological Reports, 31: 143-152,
      1972.

3704. Sjöberg, C. Addiction in Sweden. Journal of Drug Issues, 5: 12-21, 1975.

3705. Sjoberg, Lennart and Olsson, Gudrun. Volitional Problems in Carrying through a Difficult Decision: The Case of Drug Addiction. Drug and Alcohol Dependence, Lausanne, 7(2): 177-191, 1981.

3706. Skála, J. Die Problematik des Alkoholismus die Organization Seiner Therapie und die Evidenz der Alkoholiker in der Tschechoslowakei. (The Problems of Alcoholism, the Organization of Its Treatment and the Evidence of Alcoholics in Czechoslovakia.) Zeitschrift Aertzliche Fortbilting, Jena, 53: 613-617, 1959.

3707. Skála, Jaroslav. Czechoslovakia's Response to Alcoholism. In: World Dialogue on Alcohol and Drug Dependence. Ed. E.D. Whitney. Boston, Massachusetts: Beacon Press, 1970, pages 90-115.

3708. Skiffington, E.W. and Brown, P.M. Personal, Home and School Factors Related to Eleventh Graders' Drug Attitudes. International Journal of the Addictions, 16(5): 879-892, 1981.

3709. Skolnick, J.H. Religious Affiliation and Drinking Behavior. Quarterly Journal of Studies on Alcohol, 19: 452-470, 1958.

3710. Skolnick, Jerome H. The Stumbling Block: A Sociological Study of the Relationship between Selected Religious Norms and Drinking Behavior. Doctoral Dissertation. New Haven, Connecituct: Yale University, 1957.

3711. Skolungdomens Alkohol-, Narkotika-, Tobaksoch Sniffningsvanor 1979. (Drinking, Smoking, Sniffing and Drug Use among School Children 1979). Alkohol och Narkotika, 74(3): 5-9, 1980.

3712. Skuja, A.T., Wood, D. and Bucky, S.F. Reported Drinking among Posttreatment Alcohol Abusers: A Preliminary Report. American Journal of Drug and Alcohol Abuse, 3(3): 473-483, 1976.

3713. Skvortsov, Ye. S. Metodicheskiye Rekomendatsii po Organizatsii Antialkogol'nogo Prosveshcheniya v Shkole. (Recommended Methods for the Setup of Antialcohol Education in Schools.) Moskva, 1978.

3714. Skvortsov, Ye. S. Ob Antialkogol'noi Propagande v Shkole. (Antialcohol Propaganda in School.) Zdravookhranenie Rossiiskoi Federatsii, Moscow, (5): 26-29, 1978.

3715.   Skyum-Nielsen, S. Unge Maends Alkoholvaner: En Undersøgelse i
        Københavnsområdet. Socialforskningsinstituttets
        Publikationer, 8. (Young Men's Alcohol Habits: An
        Investigation in the Copenhagen Region.) The Publication
        No. 8 of the Danish National Institute of Social Research.
        Copenhagen, Denmark: Kommission hos Teknisk, 1962.

3716.   Slater, A.D. A Study of the Use of Alcoholic Beverages among
        High-School Students in Utah. Quarterly Journal of Studies
        on Alcohol, 13: 78-86, 1952.

3717.   Slavney, P.R. and Grau, J.G. Fetal Alcohol Damage and
        Schizophrenia. Journal of Clinical Psychiatry, 39(10):
        782-783, 1978.

3718.   Sliepcevich, E.M. School Health Education Study: A Summary
        Report. Washington: School Health Education Study, 1964.

3719.   Sloboda, S.B. The Children of Alcoholics: A Neglected Problem.
        Hospital and Community Psychiatry, 25(9): 605-606, 1974.

3720.   Slomanson, W.R. Emergence of the "Tender Years" Doctrine: Too
        Young to Drink, But Capable of Escaping the Civil
        Consequences? Pepperdine Law Review, 8: 1-19, 1977.

3721.   Smart, R.G. Alcohol and Drug Use by Young Adults. In: North
        American Association of Alcoholism Programs. Selected
        Papers Presented at the General Sessions of the 20th
        Annual Meeting September 14-19, 1969. Vancouver, British
        Columbia, pages 37-44, no date.

3722.   Smart, R.G. Alcohol Consumption and Anxiety in College Students.
        Journal of General Psychology, 78: 35-39, 1968.

3723.   Smart, R.G. Alcohol Misuse and Alcoholism among Young People.
        In: Defining Adolescent Alcohol Use: Implications for a
        Definition of Adolescent Alcoholism. Chairman: M. Keller.
        Symposium Presented at the Meeting of the National Council
        on Alcoholism, Washington, May 5-7, 1976. (Also in:
        Defining Adolescent Alcohol Use: Implications Toward a
        Definition of Adolescent Alcoholism. Proceedings of a
        Conference. Washington, D.C., 1976. Eds. P.A. O'Gorman,
        S. Stringfield and I. Smith. New York: National Council
        on Alcoholism, 1977, pages 221-232.

3724.   Smart, R.G. Availability and the Prevention of Alcohol-Related
        Problems. In: Normative Approaches to the Prevention of
        Alcohol Abuse and Alcoholism. Proceedings of a Symposium,
        April 26-28, 1977, San Diego, California. (NIAAA Research
        Monograph No. 3). Eds. T.C. Harford, D.A. Parker and
        L. Light. Washington, D.C.: U.S. Government Printing
        Office, pages 123-146. (DHEW Publication No. ADM 79-847)

3725.   Smart, R.G.   Changes in Alcoholic Beverage Sales after Reductions
         in the Legal Drinking Age.   American Journal of Drug and
         Alcohol Abuse, 4: 101-108, 1977.

3726.   Smart, R.G.   Drinking and Drinking Problems among Young People.
         Toronto, Ontario: Addiction Research Foundation, 1975.

3727.   Smart, R.G.   Drinking Problems and Treatment for Them among Young
         Teenagers.   Canadian Mental Health, 28(3): 13-16, 1980.

3728.   Smart, R.G.   Illicit Drug Use in Canada: A Review of Current
         Epidemiology with Clues for Prevention.   International
         Journal of the Addictions, 6(3): 383-405, 1971.

3729.   Smart, R.G.   Marihuana and Driving Risk among College Students.
         Journal of Safety Research, 6(4): 155-158, 1974.

3730.   Smart, R.G.   The New Drinkers: Teenage Use and Abuse of Alcohol.
         (Addiction Research Foundation Program Rep. Ser. No. 4)
         Toronto, Ontario: Addiction Research Foundation, 1976;
         Second Edition, 1980.   (Also as: The New Drinkers:
         Teenage Use and Abuse of Alcohol.   Addiction, 23(1): 2-23,
         1976.   Excerpts from The New Drinkers.)

3731.   Smart, R.G.   Perceived Availability and the Use of Drugs.
         Bulletin on Narcotics, 29: 59-63, 1977.

3732.   Smart, R.G.   Priorities in Minimizing Alcohol Problems among
         Young People.   In: Youth, Alcohol and Social Policy.
         Eds. H.T. Blane and M.E. Chafetz.   New York: Plenum
         Press, 1979, pages 229-261.

3733.   Smart, R.G.   Problem Drinking among High School Students in
         Ontario.   Substudy No. 919.   Toronto, Ontario: Addiction
         Research Foindation, 1977.

3734.   Smart, R.G.   Some Current Studies of Psychoactive and
         Hallucinogenic Drug Use.   Canadian Journal of Behavioral
         Science, 2: 232-245, 1970.

3735.   Smart, R.G.   Some Recent Studies of Teenage Alcoholism and
         Problem Drinking.   In: Phenomenology and Treatment of
         Alcoholism.   Eds. W.E. Fann, I. Karacan, A.D. Pokorny,
         and R.L. Williams.   New York: SP Medical and Scientific
         Books, 1980, pages 127-138.

3736.   Smart, R.G.   Sources of Drug Information for High School
         Students: Changes between 1968 and 1970.   Toronto,
         Ontario: Addiction Research Foundation, 1975.

3737. Smart, R.G. Variationen des Gesetzlichen Mindestalters für den
       Erwerb Alkoholischer Getränke und ihre Auswirkungen für den
       Alkoholkonsum im Allgemeinen und im Kraftfahrzeugverkehr.
       (Variations of the Minimum Legal Age for the Acquisition of
       Alcoholic Beverages and Their Effect on Alcohol Consumption
       in General and in Motor Vehicle Traffic. Blutalkohol,
       Hamburg, 15: 161-175, 1978.

3738. Smart, R.G., Bennett, C. and Fejer, D. A Controlled Study of the
       Peer Group Approach to Drug Education. Toronto, Ontario:
       Addiction Research Foundation, 1975.

3739. Smart, R.G. and Blair, N.L. Test-Retest Reliability and Validity
       Information for a High School Drug Use Questionnaire.
       Drug and Alcohol Dependence, Lausanne, 3: 265-271, 1978.

3740. Smart, R.G. and Fejer, D. Drug Education: Current Issues,
       Future Directions. (Series No. 3) Toronto, Ontario:
       Addiction Research Foundation, 1974.

3741. Smart, R.G. and Fejer, D. Drug Use among Adolescents and Their
       Parents: Closing the Generation Gap in Mood Modification.
       Journal of Abnormal Psychology, 79(2): 153-160, 1972.

3742. Smart, R.G. and Fejer, D. Drug Use and Driving Risk among High
       School Students. Accident Analysis and Prevention, Oxford,
       8: 33-38, 1976.

3743. Smart, R.G. and Fejer, D. Illicit LSD Users: Their Social
       Backgrounds, Drug Use and Psychopathology. Journal of
       Health and Social Behavior, 10: 297-308, 1969.

3744. Smart, R.G. and Fejer, D. Recent Trends in Illicit Drug Use
       among Adolescents. Published by the Authority of the
       Honorable John Munro, Minister of National Health and
       Welfare. Toronto, Ontario: Addiction Research Foundation,
       1971.

3745. Smart, R.G. and Fejer, D. Relationships between Parental and
       Adolescent Drug Use. In: Drug Abuse: Current Concepts
       and Research. Ed. W. Keup. Springfield, Illinois:
       Charles C. Thomas, 1972, pages 146-153.

3746. Smart, R.G. and Fejer, D. Six Years of Cross-Sectional Surveys
       of Student Drug Use in Toronto. Bulletin on Narcotics,
       27(2): 11-22, 1975.

3747. Smart, R.G., Fejer, D. and White, J. The Extent of Drug Use in
       Metropolitan Toronto Schools: A Study of Changes from
       1968 to 1970. Addictions, 18(1): 1-17, 1971.

3748. Smart, R.G. and Goodstadt, M.S. Alcohol and Drug Use among
       Ontario Students in 1977: Preliminary Findings.
       (Substudy No. 889). Toronto, Ontario: Addiction Research
       Foundation, 1977.

3749. Smart, R.G. and Goodstadt, M.S. Effects of Reducing the Legal
       Alcohol-Purchasing Age on Drinking and Drinking Problems.
       Journal of Studies on Alcohol, 38: 1313-1323, 1977.

3750. Smart, R.G. and Goodstadt, M.S. Effects of Reducing the Legal
       Alcohol-Purchasing Age on Drinking and Drinking Problems:
       A Review of Empirical Studies. Pamphlet. New Brunswick,
       New Jersey: Rutgers Center of Alcohol Studies, 1977.

3751. Smart, R.G. and Goodstadt, M.S. Effects of Reducing the Legal
       Drinking Age on Drinking and Drinking Problems: A Review
       of Empirical Studies. Washington, D.C.: Papers Presented
       at NCA Forum, May, 1976.

3752. Smart, R.G., Goodstadt, M.S. and Sone, I.J. Alcohol and Drug
       Use among Ontario Students in 1977. Pamphlet. Toronto,
       Ontario: Addiction Research Foundation, 1977.

3753. Smart, R.G., LaForest, L. and Whitehead, P.C. The Epidemiology
       of Drug Use in Three Canadian Cities. British Journal of
       Addiction, 66: 293-299, 1971.

3754. Smart, R.G., LaForest, L. and Whitehead, P.C. L'épidémiologie
       de l'Usage des Drogues au Sein de Trois Populations
       Etudiantes. (The Epidemiology of Drug Use among Three
       Student Populations.) Toxicomanies, 3: 213-226, 1970.

3755. Smart, R.G. and Schmidt, W. Drinking and Problems from Drinking
       After a Reduction in the Minimum Drinking Age. British
       Journal of Addiction, 70: 347-358, 1975.

3756. Smart, R.G. and Schmidt, W. Physiological Impairment and
       Personality Factors in Traffic Accidents of Alcoholics.
       Quarterly Journal of Studies on Alcohol, 30(2): 440-445,
       1969.

3757. Smart, R.G. and Whitehead, P.C. The Prevention of Drug Abuse by
       Lowering per Capita Consumption: Distributions of
       Consumptions in Samples of Canadian Adults and British
       University Students. Bulletin on Narcotics, 25: 49-55,
       1973.

3758. Smart, Reginald. Addiction, Dependency, Abuse, or Use: Which
       Are We Studying with Epidemiology? In: Drug Use:
       Epidemiological and Sociological Approaches. Eds.
       E. Josephson and E.E. Carroll. Washington, D.C.:
       Hemisphere Publishing, 1974, pages 23-42.

3759. Smart, Reginald and Krakowski, Mark. The Nature and Frequency
       of Drug Content in Magazines and on Television. Journal
       of Alcohol and Drug Education, 18(3): 16-22, 1973.

3760.   Smart, Reginald G. Drug Problems and Their Correlates among High
         School Students. Toronto, Ontario: Addiction Research
         Foundation, 1978.

3761.   Smart, Reginald G. Drug Use among High School Students. In:
         Drug Abuse--Data and Debate. Springfield, Illinois:
         Charles C. Thomas, 1970, pages 153-168.

3762.   Smart, Reginald G. High School Drug Use: A Survey with
         Implications for Education. In: Resource Book for Drug
         Abuse Education (2nd Edition). Rockville, Maryland:
         National Clearinghouse for Drug Abuse Information, 1972,
         pages 13-18.

3763.   Smart, Reginald G. Young Alcoholics in Treatment: Their
         Characteristics and Recovery Rates at Follow-Up.
         Alcoholism: Clinical and Experimental Research, 3(1): 19-
         23, 1979.

3764.   Smart, Reginald G. and Fejer, Dianne. Changes in Drug Use in
         Toronto High School Students between 1972 and 1974.
         (Substudy No. 631) Toronto, Ontario: Addiction Research
         Foundation, 1974.

3765.   Smart, Reginald G. and Fejer, Dianne. Credibility of Sources of
         Drug Information for High School Students. Journal of
         Drug Issues, 2: 8-18, 1972.

3766.   Smart, Reginald G., Fejer, Dianne and White, W. James. Trends
         in Drug Use among Metropolitan Toronto High School
         Students: 1968-1972. Addictions, 20(1): 62-72, 1973.
         (Also as: Trends in Drug Use among Metropolitan Toronto
         High School Students: 1968-1972. Pamphlet. Toronto,
         Ontario: Addiction Research Foundation, 1973.)

3767.   Smart, Reginald G. and Finley, Joan. Changes in Drinking Age and
         Per Capita Beer Consumption in Ten Canadian Provinces.
         Toronto, Ontario: Addiction Research Foundation, 1974.
         (Also in: Addictive Diseases, 2(3): 393-402, 1976.)

3768.   Smart, Reginald G. and Finley, Joan. Increases in Youthful
         Admissions to Alcoholism Treatment in Ontario. Drug and
         Alcohol Dependence, Lausanne, 1: 83-87, 1975-76.

3769.   Smart, Reginald G. and Gray, Gaye. Parental and Peer Influences
         as Correlates of Problem Drinking among High School
         Students. The International Journal of the Addictions,
         14(7): 905-917, 1979.

3770.   Smart, Reginald G. and Gray, Gaye. Parental and Peer Influences
         as Correlates of Problem Drinking among High-School
         Students. Toronto, Ontario: Addiction Research
         Foundation, 1977.

3771. Smart, Reginald G., Gray, Gaye and Bennett, Clif. Predictors of
       Drinking and Signs of Heavy Drinking among High School
       Students. (Substudy No. 741) Toronto, Ontario: Addiction
       Research Foundation, 1976. (Also in International Journal
       of the Addictions, 13(7): 1079-1094, 1978.)

3772. Smart, Reginald G. and Liban, Carolyn B. Cannabis Use and
       Alcohol Problems among Adults and Students. Drug and
       Alcohol Dependence, Lausanne, 6(3): 141-147, 1980.

3773. Smith, A.J. What I'd Teach My Children about Alcohol. Leaflet.
       New York: National Council on Alcoholism, 1969.

3774. Smith, B.C. Drug Use on a University Campus. Journal of the
       American College Health Association, 18(5): 360-365, 1970.

3775. Smith, D., Levy, S.J. and Striar, D.E. Treatment Services for
       Youthful Drug Users. In: Youth Drug Abuse: Problems,
       Issues and Treatment. Eds. G.M. Beschner and
       A.S. Friedman. Lexington, Massachusetts: D.C. Heath,
       1979, pages 537-569.

3776. Smith, David and Gay, George. Management of Drug Abuse
       Emergencies. In: Management of Adolescent Drug Misuse:
       Clinical, Psychological, and Legal Perspectives. Ed.
       James Gamage. Beloit, Wisconsin: STASH Press, 1973,
       pages 24-41.

3777. Smith, David E. Youth and Drug Abuse. In: Mind Drugs. Ed.
       M. Hyde. New York: McGraw-Hill, 1968, pages 16-24.

3778. Smith, David E. and Luce, J. Love Needs Care: A History of
       San Francisco's Haight-Ashbury Free Medical Clinic and
       Its Pioneer Role in Treating Drug Abuse Problems (1st
       Edition). Boston, Massachusetts: Little, Brown and
       Company, 1971.

3779. Smith, David R. An Instrument for Evaluating Attitudes toward
       Drinking. School Health Review, 2(2): 12-13, 1971.

3780. Smith, D.W. Contemporary Patterns of Youth and Drug Abuse. In:
       Mind Drugs (4th Edition). Ed. M.O. Hyde. New York:
       McGraw-Hill, 1980, pages 9-32.

3781. Smith, Gene M. and Fogg, Charles P. Psychological Antecedents of
       Teenage Drug Use. In: Research in Community and Mental
       Health, Volume I. Ed. Roberta G. Simmons. Greenwich,
       Connecticut: JAI Press, Inc., 1979, pages 87-102.

3782. Smith, H.W. and Meyer, F.J. Parent and Teacher Attitudes toward
       and Knowledge of Drug Abuse. Journal of School Health,
       44(3): 152-155, 1974.

3783.   Smith, J.A.   Up Your Spirits: Everything You Wanted to Know
        about Alcohol but Were Not Quite Sober Enough (or too
        Scared) to Ask. New York: Atheneum/SMI, 1978.

3784.   Smith, M.E. Problems Related to Alcohol Consumption in Young
        People. Central African Journal of Medicine, 25(1); 15-
        19, 1979.

3785.   Smith, Thomas J. Drinking-Driving Patterns at Night: Baseline
        Roadside Survey of the Fairfax Alcohol Safety Action
        Project. (DOT-HS-067-1-087) Charlottesville: Virginia
        Highway Research Council, Highway Safety Division, 1974.

3786.   Smithers (Christopher D.) Foundation. Alcohol Education in the
        Private Schools. Pamphlet. New York, 1960.

3787.   Smithers (Christopher D.) Foundation. Alcoholism: A Family
        Illness. New York, 1969.

3788.   Smithers (Christopher D.) Foundation. Preventing Alcoholism.
        (Second printing) New York, 1974.

3789.   Smithers (Christopher D.) Foundation. Understanding Alcoholism:
        For the Patient, the Family and the Employer. New York:
        Charles Scribner and Sons, 1968.

3790.   Smithurst, B.A. and Armstrong, J.L. Social Background of 171
        Women Attending a Female Venereal Disease Clinic in
        Brisbane. Medical Journal of Australia, 62: 339-343,
        1975.

3791.   Snyder, A. First Step. New York: Holt, Rinehart and Winston,
        1975.

3792.   Snyder, A. My Name is Davy--I'm an Alcoholic. New York: New
        American Library, 1977.

3793.   Snyder, Anne. Kids and Drinking. Minneapolis, Minnesota:
        CompCare Publications, 1977.

3794.   Snyder, Charles. Culture and Jewish Sobriety: The Ingroup-
        Outgroup Factor. In: Society, Culture and Drinking
        Patterns. Eds. D.J. Pittman and C.R. Snyder, New York:
        Wiley, 1962, pages 188-225.

3795.   Sobel, R. and Underhill, R.N. Family Disorganization and
        Teenage Auto Accidents. Journal of Safety Research, 8:
        8-18, 1976.

3796.   Social Drinking--Debit or Credit? Leaflet. Evanston, Illinois:
        Signal Press, 1971.

3797. Soden, Edward W. The Probation Officer and the Alcoholic Client.
       Journal of Drug Issues, 5: 242-247, 1975.

3798. Sokol, Robert J., Miller, Sheldon I. and Reed, George. Alcohol
       Abuse During Pregnancy: An Epidemiologic Study.
       Alcoholism, Clinical and Experimental Research, 4(2): 135-
       145, 1980.

3799. Sokolov, A.A. Profilaktike Pravonarushenii Nesovershennoletnikh-
       -Bol'she Vnimaniya. (Prophylaxis against Juvenile
       Delinquency Needs More Attention.) Sovetskoe Gosudarstvoi
       i Pravo, Moscow, 5: 88-90, 1964.

3800. Sokolov, I.S. O Protivoalkogol'noy Propagande v SSSR i v
       Kapitalisticheskikh Stranakh. (On Antialcohol Propaganda
       in the U.S.S.R. and in the Capitalistic Countries.)
       Sovetskoe Zdravookhranenie, Moscow, 20(2): 25-30, 1961.

3801. Solbrig. Alkohol und Jugendpflege. (Alcohol and Youth.)
       Concordia, 22: 14-19, 1915.

3802. Söllner, H. Besonderheiten des Jugendalkoholismus. (Special
       Characteristics of Adolescent Alcoholism.) Öffentliche
       Gesundheitswenson, Stuttgart, 39: 27-28, 1977.

3803. Solms, H. Gesundheitliche und Gesellschaftliche Auswirkungen
       der Alkoholprobeme in der Schweiz. (Health and Social
       Effects of Alcohol-Related Problems in Switzerland.) In:
       Prophylaxe des Alkoholismus. (Prevention of Alcoholism.)
       Eds. R. Battegay and M. Wieser. Bern: Verlag Hans Huber,
       1979, pages 58-70.

3804. Somekh, D. Factors Contributing to Self-Reported Drug Use among
       London Undergraduates. Drug and Alcohol Dependence,
       Lausanne, 3: 289-299, 1978.

3805. Sorosiak, F.M., Thomas, L.E. and Balet, F.N. Adolescent Drug
       Use: An Analysis. Psychological Reports, 38: 211-221,
       1976.

3806. Soueif, M.I., El-Sayed, A.M., Hannourah, M.A. and Darweesh, Z.A.
       The Non-Medical Use of Psychoactive Substances among Male
       Secondary School Students in Egypt: An Epidemiological
       Study. Drug and Alcohol Dependence, Lausanne, 5: 235-238,
       1980.

3807. South Carolina Department of Education. The Story of Alcohol:
       A Resource and Guidebook for Teachers. Columbia, South
       Carolina, 1957.

3808. South Carolina Department of Education. The Story of Alcohol.
       Pamphlet. Columbia, South Carolina, 1967.

3809. South Dakota Department of Public Instruction. Alcohol and
          Narcotics Education. Pierre, South Dakota, no date.

3810. South Dakota Division of Alcoholism. Strictly for Teenagers.
          Leaflet. Pierre, South Dakota, no date.

3811. Southerby, N. and Southerby, A. Twelve Young Women: How They
          Became Alcohol and Drug Dependent in their Painful Struggle
          toward Adulthood. Long Beach, California: N. Southerby,
          1975.

3812. Southern Area Alcohol Education and Training Program. Alcohol
          Education and Training Resources in the Southern Area.
          Atlanta, Georgia, 1976.

3813. Southern Area Alcohol Education and Training Program. Theory in
          Practice: A Compendium of Alcohol Education and Training
          Programs. Pamphlet. Atlanta, Georgia, no date.

3814. Southwick, William. Children of Alcoholics. In: Papers
          Presented at the 6th International Institute on the
          Prevention and Treatment of Drug Dependence, Hamburg,
          Germany, June 28-July 2, 1976. Lausanne, Switzerland:
          International Council on Alcohol and Addictions, 1979,
          pages 455-459.

3815. Sower, C. Teen-Age Drinking and the School. In: Mental Health
          Aspects of Alcohol Education. Boston: Massachusetts
          Office of the Commissioner on Alcoholism, Massachusetts
          Department of Mental Health, 1959.

3816. Sower, C. Teen-Age Drinking as Group Behavior: Implications
          for Research. Quarterly Journal of Studies on Alcohol,
          20: 655-668, 1959.

3817. Spalding, Willard B. and Montague, John. Alcohol and Human
          Affairs. Yonkers, New York: World Book Company, 1949.

3818. Spandl, O.P. Schuler und Alkohol. (Students and Alcohol.)
          Offentliche Gesundheitswenson, 42(Suppl. 1): 37-44, 1980.

3819. Sparks, B. Voices. New York: Times Books, no date.

3820. Spevack, Michael Gerald. Drugs and the Adolescent High School
          Student: A Three Year Survey Study. Doctoral
          Dissertation. Canada: McGill University, 1973.

3821. Spieker, G. Dissimilarities among Alcoholics and Drug Abusers.
          In: International Conference on Alcoholism and Drug Abuse,
          San Juan, Puerto Rico, November, 1973. Lausanne,
          Switzerland: International Council on Alcohol and
          Addictions, 1974, pages 194-203.

3822.   Spieker, G. and Mouzakitis, C.M.   Alcohol Abuse and Child Abuse
         and Neglect: An Inquiry into Alcohol Abusers' Behavior
         toward Children.   Paper Presented at the 27th Annual
         Meeting of the Alcohol and Drug Problems Association of
         North America, New Orleans, Louisiana, September 12-16,
         1976.

3823.   Spieker, G. and Sarver, C.R.   Alcohol and Crime.   British Journal
         of Alcohol Abuse and Alcoholism, 13: 184-189, 1978.

3824.   Spieker, Gisela.   Family Violence and Alcohol Abuse.   In: Papers
         Presented at the 24th International Congress on the
         Prevention and Treatment of Alcoholism, Zurich, June, 1978.
         Lausanne, Switzerland: International Council on Alcohol
         and Addictions, 1978, pages 335-342.

3825.   Spielholz, J.B. and Krimmel, H.E.   Teenage Drinking.   Pamphlet.
         Olympia: Washington State Department of Health, Alcoholism
         Section, no date.

3826.   Spielmann, F.E.   A Compilation of Anti-Alcoholic Measures in
         Germany.   Scientific Temperance Journal, 49: 38-41, 1941.

3827.   Spratto, G.R.   A Statement Concerning the Use of Alcohol.
         Journal of School Health, 42(4): 212-213, 1972.

3828.   The Spread of Alcoholism.   The Washington Post: A16, January 5,
         1974.

3829.   Spreng, M.   Vom Einfluss der Trunksucht der Eltern auf die
         Entwicklung der Kinder. Aus dem Blickfeld der Fürsorgerin
         Gesehen.   (Concerning the Influence of Parental Alcoholism
         on Children's Development.   From the Viewpoint of the
         Social Caseworker.)   Bern: Schule für Soziale Arbeit,
         1958.

3830.   Stacey, B. and Davies, J.   Drinking Behavior in Childhood and
         Adolescence: An Evaluative Review.   British Journal of
         Addiction, 65(3): 203-212, 1970.

3831.   Stacey, B. and Davies, J.   Teenagers and Alcohol.   Health
         Bulletin, Edinborough, 31(6): 318-319, 1973.

3832.   Stacey, B. and Davies, J.   The Teenage Drinker.   Journal of
         Alcohol and Drug Education, 18(4): 1-8, 1973.

3833.   Staitch, G.   Temperence Instruction in European Schools.
         International Congress against Alcoholism, 15: 299-310,
         1921.

3834.   Stancak, A.   Krivka Pracovnej Vykonnosti v Bourdonovej Skúške pod
        Vplyvom Alkoholu a Dexfenmetrazínu.   (The Effect of Alcohol
        and Dexphenmetrazine on the Performance Efficiency Curve in
        the Bourdon Test.)   Activitas Nervosa Superior, Prague, 5:
        189-190, 1963.

3835.   Stanton, M.D.   A Critique of Kaufman's "Myth and Reality in the
        Family Patterns and Treatment of Substance Abusers."
        American Journal of Drug and Alcohol Abuse, 7(3&4): 281-
        289, 1980.

3836.   Stanton, M.D.   The Woman Substance Abuser within a Family
        Concept.   In: The Woman Next Door.   Summary Proceedings of
        a Symposium on the Subject of Drugs and the Modern Woman
        Held at the Institute of Pennsylvania Hospital,
        February 15-16, 1980.   Eds. C. D'Amanda and M. Korcok.
        Hollywood, Florida: U.S. Journal of Alcohol and Drug
        Dependence, 1980, pages 21-26.

3837.   Stanton, M. Duncan.   Some Overlooked Aspects of the Family and
        Drug Abuse.   In: Drug Abuse from the Family Perspective.
        Ed. Barbara Gray Ellis.   Washington, D.C.:   U.S. Government
        Printing Office, 1980, pages 1-17.

3838.   Starland, V.D.   An Education Program Module: For Blacks
        Concerned with Alcohol and Drug Abuse.   In: Drug Problems
        of the 70's, Solutions for the 80's.   Ed. R. Faulkinberry.
        Lafayette, Louisiana: Endac Enterprises/Print Media, 1980,
        pages 296-300.

3839.   State Liquor Laws Relative to Legal Age for Drinking.   Journal of
        Alcohol Education, 12(3): 34-35, 1966.

3840.   State Programs on Alcoholism and their Relationships to Programs
        of Alcohol Education in the Publicly Supported Schools and
        Colleges.   New York: Licensed Beverage Industries, 1957.

3841.   State Regulations Governing Drinking by Minors Reported.   Journal
        of Alcohol and Drug Education, 21(2): 17, 1976.

3842.   Statement Concerning the Use of Alcohol.   Journal of School
        Health, 42(4): 212, 1972.

3843.   Statewide Conference in Connecticut.   Journal of Alcohol
        Education, 13(1): 18-19, 1967.

3844.   Statewide Study Sheds New Light on the Role of Alcohol in Fatal
        Traffic Crashes.   The Bottom Line on Alcohol in Society,
        4(4): 21-23, 1981.

3845.   Staulcup, H., Kenward, K. and Frigo, D.   A Review of Federal
        Primary Alcoholism Prevention Projects.   Journal of Studies
        on Alcohol, 40: 943-968, 1979.

3846. Steele, E.W. Some Ideas about the Educator's Responsibility for Teaching about Alcohol. A.A.I.A.N. Newsletter, 5(1): 19-22, 1959.

3847. Stefanic, W.D. Teen-Age Drinker Drivers. Mutual Insurance Bulletin, 60(10): 4-6, 1973.

3848. Steffenhagen, R.A., McAree, C.P. and Nixon, H.L. Drug Use among College Females: Socio-Demographic and Social Psychological Correlates. International Journal of the Addictions, 7(2): 285-303, 1972.

3849. Steffenhagen, R.A., McAree, C.P. and Persing, B.F. Socio-Demographic Variables Associated with Drug Use at a New England College. International Journal of Social Psychiatry, 17(4), 1971.

3850. Steffenhagen, R.A., Polich, J.M. and Lash, S. Alienation, Delinquency and Patterns of Drug Use. International Journal of Social Psychiatry, 24: 125-137, 1978.

3851. Stein, K.B., Soskin, W.F. and Korchin, S.J. Drug Use among Disaffected High School Youth. Journal of Drug Education, 5(3): 193-203, 1975.

3852. Steiner, G. Teenage Abuse of Alcohol. New York State School Nurse/Teacher Association Journal, 7(2): 10-11, 1976.

3853. Steinglass, P. The Alcoholic Family in the Interaction Laboratory. Journal of Nervous and Mental Diseases, 167: 428-436, 1979.

3854. Steinglass, P. Assessing Families in Their Own Homes. American Journal of Psychiatry, 137: 1523-1529, 1980.

3855. Steinglass, P. A Life History Model of the Alcoholic Family. Family Process, 19: 211-226, 1980.

3856. Steinglass, Peter. The Impact of Alcoholism on the Family: Relationship between Degree of Alcoholism and Psychiatric Symptomatology. Journal of Studies on Alcohol, 42(3): 288-303, 1981.

3857. Stenmark, D.E., Kinder, B.N. and Milne, L.D. Drug-Related Attitudes and Knowledge of Pharmacy Students and College Undergraduates. International Journal of the Addictions, 12: 153-160, 1977.

3858. Stenmark, D.E., Wackwitz, J.H., Pelfrey, M.C. and Dougherty, F. Substance Use among Juvenile Offenders: Relationships to Parental Substance Use and Demographic Characteristics. Addictive Diseases, 1(1): 43-54, 1974.

3859.   Stepién, H.   Wśród Dzieci i Młodziezy.   (Preventive Action among
          Children and Adolescents.)   Problemy Alkoholizmu, Warsaw,
          26(3): 4, 8, 1979.

3860.   Sterling, J.W.   A Comparative Examination of Two Modes of
          Intoxication--An Exploratory Study of Glue Sniffing.
          Journal of Criminal Law and Criminology, 55, 94-99, 1964.

3861.   Sterling-Smith, Robert.   Alcohol, Marijuana and Other Drug
          Patterns among Operators Involved in Fatal Motor Vehicle
          Accidents.   In: Alcohol, Drugs and Traffic Safety.
          Proceedings of the Sixth International Conference on
          Alcohol, Drugs and Traffic Safety, Toronto, September 8-13,
          1974.   Eds. S. Israelstam and S. Lambert.   Toronto:
          Addiction Research Foundation of Ontario, 1975, pages 93-
          105.

3862.   Sterling-Smith, Robert and Graham, David.   Marihuana and Driver
          Behaviors: Historic and Social Observations among Fatal
          Accident Operators and a Control Sample.   Final Report to
          the National Highway Safety Administration.   Washington,
          D.C.:   Department of Transportation, 1976.

3863.   Sterne, M.W., Pittman, D.J. and Coe, T.   Teen-Agers, Drinking,
          and the Law: A Study of Arrest Trends for Alcohol-Related
          Offenses.   Crime and Delinquency, 11: 78-85, 1965.

3864.   Sterne, Muriel W. and Pittman, David J.   Alcohol Abuse and the
          Black Family.   In: Alcohol Abuse and Black America.   Ed.
          F.D. Harper.   Alexandria, Virginia: Douglass Publishers,
          Inc., 1976, pages 177-185.

3865.   Sterne, Muriel W. and Pittman, David J.   Drinking Patterns in
          the Ghetto.   Volume I.   St. Louis, Missouri: Washington
          University, 1972.

3866.   Stevens, Susan M.   Alcohol and World View: A Study of
          Possamaquoddy Alcohol Use.   Journal of Studies on Alcohol,
          Suppl. No. 9: 122-142, 1981.

3867.   Stevenson, G.S.   Education and the Control of Alcoholism.
          Diseases of the Nervous System, 3: 238-243, 1942.

3868.   Stewart, M.A., DeBlois, C.S. and Cummings, C.   Psychiatric
          Disorder in the Parents of Hyperactive Boys and Those with
          Conduct Disorder.   Journal of Child Psychology and
          Psychiatry, 21: 283-292, 1980.

3869.   Stewart, M.A., DeBlois, C. S. and Singer, S.   Alcoholism and
          Hyperactivity Revisited: A Preliminary Report.   Currents
          in Alcoholism, Volume 5.   Biomedical Issues and Clinical
          Effects of Alcoholism.   Ed. M. Galanter.   New York: Grune
          and Stratton, 1979, pages 349-357.

3870. Stewart, W.F.R. Drink, Drugs and the Family. London: National
       Society for the Prevention of Cruelty to Children,
       Developments Department, 1971.

3871. Štichová, E. and Kokrdová, Z. Pití Alkoholických Nápoju a
       Koureni u Žáku 6. až. 9. Tříd ZDŠ v Okrese Klatovy.
       (Drinking of Alcoholic Beverages and Smoking by Students
       in the 6th through 9th Grades of Elementary Schools in
       the Klatovy District.) Protialkoholicky Obzor, Bratislava,
       9: 113-115, 1974.

3872. Stickgold, Arthur and Brovar, A. Undesirable Sequelae of Drug
       Abuse Education. Contemporary Drug Problems, 7(1): 99-
       115, 1978.

3873. Stimmer, F. Ein Drei-Phasen-Modell zur Soziogenese der
       Alkoholabhängigkeit Männlicher Jugendlicher: Ein Beitrag
       zur Psychiatrischen Familiensoziologie. (A Three-Phase
       Model for Sociogenesis of Alcohol Dependence among Young
       Men: A Contribution to Psychiatric Sociology of the
       Family.) In: Jugend und Alkohol: Trinkmuster,
       Suchtentwicklung und Therapie. (Youth and Alcohol:
       Drinking Patterns, Addiction Development and Therapy.)
       Eds. H. Berger, A. Legnaro ahd K.-H. Reuband. Stuttgart:
       W. Kohlhammer, 1980, pages 94-114.

3874. Stimmer, F. Jugendalkoholismus: Eine Familiensoziologische
       Untersuchung zur Genese der Alkoholabhängigkeit Männlicher
       Jugendlicher. (Alcoholism among Youth: A Sociological
       Family Study on the Development of Alcohol Dependence
       among Young Men.) Berlin: Duncker and Humblot, 1978.

3875. Stober, B. Alkohol-Missbrauch bei Kindern und Jugendlichen.
       (Alcohol Misuse in Children and Adolescents.) Fortschritte
       der Medizin, Leipzig, 96: 1917-1922, 1978.

3876. Stoddard, C.F. The Present Status of Provision for Public
       School Instruction in the United States as to Alcoholic
       Drinks and Other Narcotics. International Zeitschrift
       Alkoholismus, 37: 129-139, 1929.

3877. Stoddard, C.F. Prohibition and Youth. Scientific Temperance
       Journal, 34: 121-130, 1925.

3878. Stoddard, C.F. The Relation of Juvenile Temperance Teaching to
       National Progress. International Congress against
       Alcoholism, 12: 37-42, 1909.

3879. Stoddard, C.F. Scientific Temperance Instruction in the Public
       Schools of the U.S. International Congress against
       Alcoholism, 15: 311-317, 1921.

3880.   Stoeffler, V.R.   Physicians Should Identify Teenage Alcoholism.
        Michigan Medicine, 75(8): 443-444, 1976.

3881.   Stokes, J.P.   Personality Traits and Attitudes and Their
        Relationship to Student Drug Using Behavior.   Doctoral
        Dissertation (University Microfilms No. 73-08230).
        University of Illinois at Chicago Circle, 1972.   (Also in:
        International Journal of the Addictions, 9(2): 267-287,
        1974.

3882.   Stokvis, B., Ed.   Proceedings of the Fifth International Congress
        of Psychotherapy, Vienna, 1961.   Basel: Karger, 1963.

3883.   Storm, Thomas and Cutler, R.E.   The Role of Research in Alcohol
        and Drug Education.   Journal of Alcohol and Drug Education,
        20(2): 5-11, 1975.

3884.   Stott, D.H.   Saving Children from Delinquency.   New York:
        Philosophical Library, 1953.

3885.   Stowell, W.L.   Alcohol and Children.   Journal of Inebriety, 29:
        287-289, 1907.

3886.   Stoyanov, S. and Zamimova, S.   A Case of Alcohol Delirium in a
        14-Year-Old Boy.   Nevrologiya Psikhiatriya i
        Nevrokhirurgiya, Sofia, 11: 133-136, 1972.

3887.   Strachan, J.G.   Recovery from Alcoholism.   Vancouver: Mitchell,
        1975.

3888.   Strassburger, F. and Strassburger, Z.   Measurement of Attitudes
        toward Alcohol and Their Relation to Personality Variables.
        Journal of Consulting Psychology, 29(5): 440-445, 1965.

3889.   Straus, R.   Alcohol.   In: Contemporary Social Problems (2nd
        Edition).   Eds. R.K. Merton and R.A. Nisbet.   New York:
        Harcourt, 1966, pages 236-280.

3890.   Straus, R.   Alcohol and Society.   Psychiatric Annals, 3(10): 8-
        107, 1973.

3891.   Straus, R.   Conceptualizing Alcoholism and Problem Drinking.
        In: Defining Adolescent Alcohol Use: Implication for a
        Definition of Adolescent Alcoholism.   Chair.: M. Keller.
        Symposium Presented at the Meeting of the National Council
        on Alcoholism, Washington, May 5-7, 1976.

3892.   Straus, R.   Drinking in College in the Perspective of Social
        Change.   In: The Domesticated Drug: Drinking among
        Collegians.   Ed. G.L. Maddox.   New Haven: College and
        University Press, 1970, pages 27-44.

3893.   Straus, R.   The Life Record of an Alcoholic.   Quarterly Journal
        of Studies on Alcohol, 34(4): 1212-1219, 1973.

3894. Straus, R. Yale Plan on Alcoholism: A Co-Ordinated Approach to
       the Problem. Yale Scientific Magazine, 24(4): 7-8, 26,
       28, 32, 1950.

3895. Straus, Robert. The Challenge of Reconceptualization. In:
       Research Priorities on Alcohol. Proceedings of a
       Symposium Sponsored by the Rutgers Center of Alcohol
       Studies and Rutgers University. Ed. Mark Keller. New
       Jersey: Journal of Studies on Alcohol, Supplement No. 8,
       1979, pages 279-288.

3896. Straus, Robert. Problem Drinking in the Perspective of Social
       Change. In: Alcohol and Alcohol Problems. Eds.
       W.J. Filstead, J.J. Rossi and M. Keller. Cambridge,
       Massachusetts: Ballinger, 1976, pages 29-56.

3897. Straus, Robert and Bacon, Selden. Drinking in College. New
       Haven: Yale University Press, 1953. (Reprint:
       Westport, Connecticut: Greenwood Press, 1973.)

3898. Straus, Robert and Bacon, Selden D. To Drink or Not to Drink.
       In: Drinking and Intoxication: Selected Readings in
       Social Attitudes and Controls. Ed. R.G. McCarthy. New
       Haven: College and University Press, 1959, pages 220-231.

3899. Straus, Robert and Bacon, Selden D. The Problems of Drinking in
       College. In: Society, Culture and Drinking Patterns.
       Eds. D.J. Pittman and C.R. Snyder. New York: Wiley,
       1962, pages 246-258.

3900. Straussner, S.L., Ashenberg, Kitman C., Strausser, J. and
       Demos, E.S. The Alcoholic Housewife. Focus on Women,
       1(1): 15-32, 1980.

3901. Straussner, S.L., Weinstein, D.L. and Hernandez, R. Effects of
       Alcoholism on the Family System. Health and Social Work,
       4(4): 112-127, 1979.

3902. Strayer, Robert. A Study of the Negro Alcoholic. Quarterly
       Journal of Studies on Alcohol, 22: 111-123, 1961.

3903. Streesman, Adele E. Psychiatric Aspects of Alcoholism. In:
       Alcoholism and Family Casework: Theory and Practice.
       Ed. M.B. Bailey. New York: Community Council of Greater
       New York, 1968, pages 25-30.

3904. Streissguth, A.P., Herman, C.S. and Smith, D.W. Intelligence,
       Behavior, and Dysmorphogenesis in the Fetal Alcohol
       Syndrome: A Report on 20 Patients. Journal of Pediatrics,
       92: 363-367, 1978.

3905. Streit, F. Parents and Problems. Pamphlets. Highland Park,
       New Jersey: Essence Publications, 1978. (Revised 1979)

3906.   Streit, Fred, Halsted, Donald L. and Pascale, Pietro J.
        Differences among Youthful Users and Nonusers of Drugs
        Based on Their Perceptions of Parental Behavior.
        International Journal of the Addictions, 9(5): 749-755,
        1974.

3907.   Streit, F. and Nicolich, M.J. Myths Versus Data on American
        Indian Drug Abuse. Journal of Drug Education, 7: 117-122,
        1977.

3908.   Strickler, Daniel P., Bradlyn, Andrew S. and Maxwell, Wayne A.
        Teaching Moderate Drinking Behaviors to Young Adult Heavy
        Drinkers: The Effects of Three Training Procedures.
        Addictive Behaviors, 6(4): 355-364, 1981.

3909.   Strickler, D.P., Dobbs, S.D. and Maxwell, W.A. The Influence of
        Setting on Drinking Behaviors: The Laboratory Vs. the
        Barroom. Addictive Behaviors, 4: 339-344, 1979.

3910.   Strimbu, J.L., Schoenfeldt, L.F. and Sims, O.S. Sex Differences
        in College Student Drug Use. Journal of College Student
        Personnel, 14(6): 507-510, 1973.

3911.   Strimbu, J.L. and Sims, O.S., Jr. A University System Drug
        Profile. International Journal of the Addictions, 9: 569-
        583, 1974.

3912.   Strimbu, Jerry, Schoenfeldt, Lyle and Sims, O. Drug Usage in
        College Students as a Function of Racial Classification
        and Minority Group Status. Research in Higher Education,
        1: 263-272, 1973.

3913.   Stroup, A.L. and Robins, L.N. Elementary School Predictors of
        High School Dropout among Black Males. Sociology of
        Education, 45(2): 212-222, 1972.

3914.   Strug, David L. Social Functions of an Alcoholism Treatment
        Program. Journal of Studies on Alcohol, Supplement No. 9:
        207-216, 1981.

3915.   Strunk, P. Alkoholismus bei Jugendlichen. (Alcoholism in
        Adolescents.) Zeitschrift fuer Allgemeinmedizen,
        Stuttgart, 53: 1521-1524, 1977.

3916.   Stuart, R.B. Teaching Facts about Drugs: Pushing or Preventing.
        Journal of Educational Psychology, 66(2): 189-201, 1974.

3917.   Studenski, P. Liquor Consumption among the American Youth: A
        Study of the Drinking Habits of Certain Segments of the
        American Youth. (Report of the Social Study Committee of
        the National Conference of State Liquor Administrators).
        Presented to the Conference, Mackinac Island, Michigan,
        July 20, 1937.

3918. Student Survey. Anti-Saloon League: American Issue Press (Westerville, Ohio): 57-78, 1930.

3919. Study Relationship of Teen Drinking to Middle Aged Problem Drinking. Traffic Safety, 75(1): 21, 1975.

3920. Study Shows that Youth are Adopting Adult Drinking-Driving Patterns. Traffic Safety, 75(4): 7, 1975.

3921. Stumphauzer, Jerome S. A Behavior Analysis Questionnaire for Adolescent Drinkers. Psychological Reports, 47: 641-642, 1980.

3922. Stumphauzer, Jerome S. Learning to Drink: Adolescents and Alcohol. Addictive Behaviors, 5(4): 277-283, 1980.

3923. Sturner, W. and Garriott, J. Deaths Involving Propoxyphene: A Study of 41 Cases Over a Two-Year Period. Journal of the American Medical Association, 223(10): 1125-1130, 1973.

3924. Styk, J. Sledovanie Postojov Adolescentov k Alkoholu a Alkoholizmu. (Study of Adolescent's Attitudes toward Alcohol and Alcoholism.) Protialkoholicky Obzor, Bratislava, 3: 116-118, 1968.

3925. Successfully Kicking the Habit: Developing a Drug Prevention Curriculum. Nation's Schools, 87(2): 56-57, 1971.

3926. Suchman, E.A. The "Hang-Loose" Ethic and the Spirit of Drug Use. Journal of Health and Social Behavior, 9: 146-155, 1968.

3927. Suffet, F. and Brotman, R. Female Drug Users: Some Observations. International Journal of the Addictions, 11(1): 19-33, 1976.

3928. Sulzbacher, S.L. and Edgar, E. Drug and Alcohol Abuse Education: Opinions of School Principals. Journal of School Health, 45: 468-469, 1975.

3929. Summary of Recommendations from the 1967 Teenage Institute. Journal of Alcohol Education, 14(1): 16-19, 1968.

3930. Summer Courses in Alcohol Problems and Hygiene for Public School Teachers. Tirfing, (10): 97-100, 1916.

3931. Sund, A. Personality Inventories as Selective and Prognostic Criteria. Military Medicine, 136(2): 97-104, 1971.

3932. Sundberg, N. Folkhögskolan och Alkohol- och Narkotikafrågorna. (The County College and Problems of Alcohol and Narcotics.) Alkohol och Narkotica, 68: 128-129, 1974.

3933.   Sundberg, N.   Undervisningens Betydelse i Nykterhetsarbetet.
        (The Importance of Education in Abstinence Work.)
        Tirfing, 42: 133-140, 1948.

3934.   Sundet, O.   School Knowledge and Point of View about the Alcohol
        Problem.   Tirfing, 32: 18-25, 1938.

3935.   Sunnyside School District, Tucson, Arizona.   Resource for
        Learning in Health Education, Grades 1-12.   Arlington,
        Virginia: ERIC Document Reproduction Service, no date.

3936.   Sunter, J.P., Heath, A.B. and Ranasinghe, H.   Alcohol Associated
        Mortality in Newcastle Upon Tyne.   Medical Science Law,
        18(2): 84-89, 1978.

3937.   Susman, J., Ed.   Drug Use and Social Policy.   New York: AMS
        Press, 1972.

3938.   Svensson, H.G.   Temperance Instruction in High Schools.
        Tirfing, 34: 165-173, 1940.

3939.   Swanson, A.Q. and Christenson, S.J.   Women and Drug Use: An
        Annotated Bibliography.   Madison, Wisconsin: Student
        Association for the Study of Halluconogens, 1974.

3940.   Swanson, D.W.   Adult Sexual Abuse of Children: The Man and
        Circumstances.   Diseases of the Nervous System, 29: 677-
        683, 1968.

3941.   Swanson, D.W., Bratrude, A.P. and Brown, E.M.   Alcohol Abuse in
        a Population of Indian Children.   Diseases of the Nervous
        System, 32(12): 835-842, 1971.

3942.   Swart, J.C.   Adolescent Alcohol Abuse and Social Control.
        Doctoral Dissertation (University Microfilm No. 7927876).
        University of Washington, 1979.

3943.   Sweet, Robert E.   The Teenage Institute, Guide to Total
        Commitment.   Ohio's Health, 24(9): 27-30, 1972.

3944.   Świecicki, A.   Consumption of Alcoholic Drinks by Pupils and
        Students of Primary, Secondary and High Schools in Polish
        Cities.   British Journal of Addiction, 62: 357-366, 1967.

3945.   Świecicki, A.   Dzieci i Pomoc Udzielana Dzieciom z Rodzin
        Alkoholików i Rodzin Grupy Kontrolnej.   (Children and
        Assistance Given to Children from Alcoholic Families and
        Control Families.)   Problemy Alkoholizmu, Warsaw, 15(8):
        1-4, 1967.

3946. Świecicki, A. Poziom Poinformowania Rodziców i Wychowawcow o
       Spozyciu Napojow Alkoholwych Przez Uczniów Szkól
       Warszawskich. (Levels of Information of Parents and
       Educators on the Consumption of Alcohol by School Children
       in Warsaw.) Problemy Alkoholizmu, Warsaw, 14(3&4): 4-8,
       1966.

3947. Świecicki, A. Przystosowanie Spoleczne Doroslych Dzieci z Rodzin
       Alkoholików i nie Alkoholików: Badania Retrospektywne
       Obejmujace Okres 10 Lat. (Adult Adjustment of Children
       from Alcoholic and Nonalcoholic Families: A 10-Year
       Follow-Up Study.) Problemy Alkoholizmu, Warsaw, 17(2): 1-
       7, 1969.

3948. Świecicki, A. Spozycie Alkoholu Przez Uczniów Szkól
       Podstawowych, Średnich i Wyzszych w Niektórych Miastach w
       Polsce. (Alcohol Consumption by Students in Public
       Schools, Colleges and Univerisites in Some Towns in
       Poland.) Problemy Alkoholizmu, Warsaw, 14(9&10): 6-8,
       1966. (Also as: Consumption of Alcoholic Drinks by Pupils
       and Students of Primary, Secondary and High Schools in
       Polish Cities. British Journal of Addiction, 62: 357-366,
       1967.)

3949. Świecicki, A. Teenagers and Drinking in Poland. The Drinking
       and Drug Practices Surveyor, (6): 4-6, 1972.

3950. Swift, Pamela. High School Drunks. The Washington Post (Parade
       Section): 14, February 9, 1975

3951. Swinehart, James W. Public Information Programs Related to
       Alcohol, Drugs and Traffic Safety. In: Alcohol, Drugs
       and Traffic Safety. Eds. S. Israelstam and S. Lambert.
       Toronto, Ontario: Addiction Research Foundation, 1975,
       pages 799-811.

3952. Swinyard, C.A., Chaube, S. and Sutton, D.B. Neurological and
       Behavioral Aspects of Transcendental Meditation Relevant to
       Alcoholism: A Review. Annals of the New York Academy of
       Sciences: 233: 162-173, 1974.

3953. Swisher, John and Horan, John. Pennsylvania State University
       Evaluation Scales. In: Accountability in Drug Education:
       A Model for Evaluation. Eds. L.A. Abrams, E.F. Garfield
       and J.D. Swisher. Washington, D.C.: Drug Abuse Council,
       1973, pages 87-99.

3954. Switzerland. Federal Commission against Alcoholism.
       Jugendalkoholismus in der Schweiz. (Alcoholism among
       Youth in Switzerland.) Fursorger, 44: 13, 1976.

3955.   Szakács, F., Faragó, K. and Szuszky, J.   "Maradj Józan, Hogy
        Ember Maradhass!" Vizsgálatok az Alkoholizmus elleni
        Propaganda Köréböl. ("Remain Sober in Order to Remain
        Human!" Study from the Domain of Antialcoholism
        Propaganda.) Alkohologia, Budapest, 4: 86-99, 1973.

3956.   Szapocnik, Jose, Ladner, Robert A. and Scopetta, Mercedes A.
        Youth Drug Abuse and Subjective Distress in a Hispanic
        Population. In: Youth Drug Abuse: Problems, Issues and
        Treatment. Eds. G.M. Beschner and A.S. Friedman. Toronto,
        Ontario: Lexington Books, D.C. Heath and Co., 1979, pages
        493-511.

3957.   Szasz, Thomas. The Ethics of Addiction. In: Alcoholism and
        Other Drugs: Perspectives on Use, Abuse, Treatment and
        Prevention. Eds. P.C. Whitehead, C.F. Grindstaff and
        C.L. Boydell. Toronto, Ontario: Holt, Rinehard and
        Winston, 1973, pages 229-236.

3958.   Szeniec, M. Młodzieżowa Prasa o Alkoholizmu Wizerunki
        Najcześciej Mgliste. (Youth Magazines on Alcoholism: The
        Images are Mostly Hazy.) Problemy Alkoholizmu, Warsaw,
        23(7&8): 27-28, 1976.

3959.   Szewczyk, H., Jahnig, H. The Problem of Drug Misuse in the
        German Democratic Republic. Journal of Drug Issues, 5(1):
        89-91, 1975.

3960.   Szamosi, J. Alkoholvergiftungen im Kindesalter. (Alcohol
        Poisoning in Childhood.) Zeitschrift fuer
        Kinderheilkunde, Vienna, 99: 356-365, 1967.

3961.   Szamosi, J. A Gyermekkori Alkoholmérgezés és Therápiája.
        (Alcohol Intoxication in Childhood and Its Treatment.)
        Gyermekgyógyászat, Budapest, 14: 81-88, 1963.

T

3962. Tächner, K.-L. Social Data and Personality Factors of Clinically Treated Young Drug Users. British Journal of the Addictions, 69: 67-74, 1974.

3963. Tagung "Jugend und Alkohol." (Conference on "Youth and Alcohol.") Jugendschutz, 11: 63-64, 1966.

3964. Tähkä, V. Juoppouden Psykodynaamisesta Etiologiasta. (On the Psychodynamic Etiology of Drunkenness.) Alkoholipolitiikka, Helsingfor, (6): 175-182, 1954.

3965. Tähkä, V. Om Dryckenskapens Psykodynamiska Etiologi. (On the Psychodynamic Etiology of Drunkenness.) Alkoholipolitiikka, Helsingfor, (4): 103-110, 1954.

3966. Taintor, Zebulon, C. What the Schools Can do to Promote Mental Health. The Journal of School Health, 46(2): 86-90, 1976.

3967. Takman, J. Promiskuösa, Prostituerade och Alkoholiserade Flickor? (Promiscuous, Prostituted and Alcoholic Girls?) Sociala Meddelanden: 389-398, 1962.

3968. Takman, J. Thinner-, Alkohol- och Tablettmissbruk Bland Barn Och Ungdom: Socialmedicinska Synpunkter. (Thinner, Alcohol and Drug Misuse in Children and Adolescents: Sociomedical Aspects.) Nordisk Medicin, Copenhagen, 70: 899-903, 1963.

3969. Tamerin, J.S. The Psychotherapy of Alcoholic Women. In: Practical Approaches to Alcoholism Psychotherapy. Eds. S. Zimberg, J. Wallace and S.B. Blume. New York: Plenum, 1978, pages 183-203.

3970. Tani, N., Haga, H., Horii, T., Fukui, K. and Kato, N. (A Survey of Concern for Drinking and Alcoholics. Fourth Report: Senior High School Students.) [Japanese Text] Japanese Journal of Studies on Alcohol, 13: 135-142, 1978.

3971. Tani, N., Haga, H. and Kato, N. (A Survey of Concern about Drinking and Alcoholics. First Report: Students of Junior High School.) [Japanese Text] Japanese Journal of Studies on Alcohol, 10: 35-40, 1975.

3972. Taschner, K.L., Richtberg, W. and Schmidt, K. Sociale und Psychologische Schrittmacher des Jugendalkoholismus. (Social and Psychological Harbingers of Alcoholism in Youth.) In: Papers Presented at the 23rd International Institute on the Prevention and Treatment of Alcoholism, Dresden, June 6-10, 1977. Eds. E.J. Tongue and I. Moos. Lausanne, Switzerland: International Council on Alcohol and Addictions, 1977, pages 217-226.

3973. Taubert, D.S. Alcohol: The No. 1 Drug. Pamphlet. Madison, Wisconsin: Substance Abuse Clearinghouse, no date.

3974. Taubert, S., Yoast, R., Diulio, J. and Lenox, L. Middle School Drug Series. (Revised Edition) Five Pamphlets. Madison: Wisconsin Clearinghouse for Alcohol and Other Drug Information, 1979.

3975. Taylor, J.F. Personality Correlates of Abstinence and Moderate Drinking. Ohio Research Quarterly, 3: 343-346, 1972.

3976. Taylor, Michael and Abrams, Richard. Manic States: A Genetic Study of Early and Late Onset Affecture Disorders. Archives of General Psychiatry, 28(5): 656-658, 1973.

3977. Taylor, R.W. Education for the Prevention of Alcoholism in Australia. Report on Alcohol, 30(4): 5-13, 1972.

3978. Teaching about Drinking. Pamphlet. Alcohol, Drug Abuse and Mental Health Administration. Rockville, Maryland: National Clearinghouse for Alcohol Education, 1974. (DHEW Publication No. ADM 74-45)

3979. Teaching about Drugs. (A Curriculum Guide, K-12) Kent, Ohio: American School Health Association, 1971.

3980. The Teachings of Alcohol in School Books. (Editorial) Quarterly Journal of Inebriety, 28: 133-136, 1906.

3981. Teaching of Hygiene and Temperance in Public Schools. (Notes) British Journal of Inebriety, 4: 192-193, 1907.

3982. Tec, N. A Clarification of the Relationship between Alcohol and
       Marijuana. British Journal of Addiction, 68: 191-195,
       1973.

3983. Tec, Nechama. Grass is Green in Suburbia: A Sociological Study
       of Adolescent Usage of Illicit Drugs. Roslyn Heights, New
       York: Libra Publishers, 1974.

3984. Teed, R.D. The Effect of Interpersonal Contact with Female
       Alcoholics on the Attitudes of Counseling Students.
       Doctoral Dissertation (University Microfilms No.
       68-15,018). Tempe: Arizona State University, 1968.

3985. Teen Drinking, Drug Use Up. The Washington Post, 6, May 13,
       1976.

3986. Teenage Drinking Widespread, Solons Hear. California Alcoholism
       Review and Treatment Digest, 7(6): 62, 64, 66, 68, 1964.

3987. Teenage Traits Indicate Potential Alcoholism. New Jersey Council
       News, 30(1): 4, 1973.

3988. Teens Urged to Take Initiative in Solving Own Alcohol Problems.
       Journal of Alcohol and Drug Education, 20(3): 48-49, 1975.

3989. Teicher, Joseph D., Sinay, Ruth D. and Stumphauser, Jerome S.
       Behavior Therapy and Alcohol Abuse in Adolescents. In:
       Scientific Proceedings in Summary Form. One Hundred
       Twenty-Eighth Annual Meeting of the American Psychiatric
       Asociation, Washington, D.C., 1975, pages 36-37.

3990. Teicher, Joseph D., Sinay, Ruth D. and Stumphauzer, Jerome S.
       Training Community-Based Paraprofessionals as Behavior
       Therapists with Families of Alcohol-Abusing Adolescents.
       American Journal of Psychiatry, 133(7): 847-850, 1976.

3991. Teirich, H.R. Zum Alkoholproblem im Leben des Mannes. (The
       Problem of Alcoholism in the Life of the Male.)
       Psychologische Berater, 4: 325-329, 1952.

3992. Tennant, F. Dependency Traits among Parents of Drug Abusers.
       Journal of Drug Education, 6(1): 83-88, 1976.

3993. Tennant, F.S., Jr. and Detels, R. Relationship of Alcohol,
       Cigarette, and Drug Abuse in Adulthood with Alcohol,
       Cigarette and Coffee Consumption in Childhood. Preventive
       Medicine, 5: 70-77, 1976.

3994. Tennant, F.S., Jr., Detels, R. and Clark, V. Some Childhood
       Antecedents of Drug and Alcohol Abuse. American Journal
       of Epidemiology, 102(5): 377-385, 1975.

3995. Tennant, F.S., Jr. and La-Cour, J. Children at High Risk for
          Addiction and Alcoholism: Identification and Intervention.
          <u>Pediatric Nursing</u>, <u>6</u>: 26-27, 1980.

3996. Tennant, Forest S., Jr. Childhood Antecedents of Drug and
          Alcohol Abuse. Proceedings of the Thirty-Seventh Annual
          Scientific Meeting, Committee on Problems of Drug
          Dependence, Washington, D.C., May 19-21, 1975.

3997. Tennes, K. and Blackard, C. Maternal Alcohol Consumption,
          Birth Weight and Minor Physical Anomalies. <u>American
          Journal of Obstetrics and Gynecology</u>, <u>138</u>(7): 774-780,
          1980.

3998. Tevis, B. Relationships of Information and Attitudes Concerning
          Alcohol to the Drinking Behavior of Tenth Grade Students in
          Selected "Wet" and "Dry" Areas of Texas. New York, New
          York: Paper Presented at 48th Annual Convention of the
          American School Health Association, October, 1974.

3999. Tevis, B. and Tuck, M. Relationships of Information and
          Attitudes Concerning Alcohol to the Drinking Behavior of
          Tenth Grade Students in Selected "Wet" and "Dry" Areas of
          Texas. <u>Journal of Alcohol and Drug Education</u>, <u>22</u>(1): 5-
          13, 1976.

4000. Texas Alcohol Narcotics Education. <u>Alcohol...Narcotics
          Education</u>. Pamphlet. Dallas, Texas: TANE Press, 1971.

4001. Texas Alcohol Narcotics Education. <u>The Alcohol-Narcotics
          Problem: A Handbook for Teachers</u>. (Third Revised Edition)
          Dallas, Texas: TANE Press, 1966.

4002. Texas Alcohol Narcotics Education. <u>Give Yourself a Break</u>.
          Dallas, Texas: TANE Press, 1971.

4003. Texas Alcohol Narcotics Education. <u>A Student Supplement to the
          Problem: Alcohol...Narcotics</u>. Pamphlet. Dallas, Texas:
          TANE Press, 1965.

4004. Texas Alcohol Narcotics Education. <u>The Problem: Alcohol--
          Narcotics: A Handbook for Teachers</u>. (Fourth Revised
          Edition, Standard Third) Dallas, Texas: TANE Press,
          1969.

4005. Texas Commission on Alcoholism. <u>Alcohol Education in the Public
          Schools</u>. Pamphlet. Austin, Texas, no date.

4006. Texas Commission on Alcoholism. <u>Thinking about Drinking: An
          Alcohol Education Resource for Teachers</u>. Austin, Texas,
          1974.

4007. Thierman, Toby, Kern, Joseph C. and Paul, Stewart R. Alcoholism Education in the Undergraduate Curriculum. Journal of Drug Education, 6(2): 153-164, 1976.

4008. Thomas, Robert K. The History of North American Indian Alcohol Use as a Community-Based Phenomenon. Journal of Studies on Alcohol, Supplement No. 9: 29-39, 1981.

4009. Thompson, J.C. Blueprint for Colorado Schools in Alcohol, Drug and Tobacco Education. Journal of School Health, 39(10): 711-712, 1969.

4010. Thomson, W.O., Imrie, C.W. and Joffe, S.N. Letter: Alcohol-Associated Pancreatitis in a 15-Year-Old. Lancet, 2(7947): 1256, 1975.

4011. Thorarinsson, A.A. Mortality among Men Alcoholics in Iceland, 1951-1974. Journal of Studies on Alcohol, 40(7): 704-718, 1979.

4012. Thorn, Elizabeth B. Problems in Affecting Attitudinal Changes through an Alcohol Education Program. Journal of Alcohol Education, 12(3): 13-21, 1966.

4013. Thornburg, H.D. Adolescent and Drugs: An Overview. Journal of School Health, 43(10): 640-644, 1973.

4014. Thornton, R.Y. Sale of Liquor to Minors. Oregon Law Review, 13: 261-262, 1934.

4015. Throckmorton, Adel F. Approaches to Alcohol Education. Alcohol Education for Kansas Schools. Topeka, Kansas: State Superintendent of Public Instruction, 1951.

4016. Tidsskriftet Besøker et Godtemplar-Ungdomslag. (Visit to the Good Templars Youth Organization.) Norsk Tidsskrift EdruSpørsm, 30(4): 20-22, 1978.

4017. Tinklenberg, J.R., Murphy, P.L., Murphy, P., Darley, C.F., Roth, W.T. and Kopell, B.S. Drug Involvement in Criminal Assaults by Adolescents. Archives of General Psychiatry, 30(5): 685-689, 1974.

4018. Tinklenberg, J.R., Roth, W.T., Kopell, B.S. and Murphy, P. Cannabis and Alcohol Effects on Assaultiveness in Adolescent Delinquents. Annals of the New York Academy of Sciences, 282: 85-94, 1976.

4019. Tinklenberg, J.R. and Woodrow, K.M. Drug Use among Youthful Assaultive and Sexual Offenders. Research Publication of the Association for Research in Nervous and Mental Diseases, 52: 209-224, 1974.

4020. Tinklenberg, Jared. Alcohol and Violence. In: Alcoholism:
       Progress in Research and Treatment. Eds. P.G. Bourne and
       R. Fox. New York: Academic Press, 1973, pages 195-210.

4021. Tinklenberg, Jared. Drugs and Crime. In: Drug Use in America:
       Problems in Perspective. Appendix. Volume I. Patterns
       and Consequences of Drug Use. U.S. National Commission on
       Marihuana and Drug Abuse. Washington, D.C.: U.S.
       Government Printing Office, 1973, pages 242-299.

4022. Tittmar, H.G. Contact: The Help It Offers. British Journal of
       Alcohol and Alcoholism, 15(1): 26-27, 1980.

4023. Tobias, J.J. and Wax, J. Youthful Drinking Patterns in the
       Suburbs. Adolescence, 8(29): 113-118, 1973.

4024. Todd, F. Problems of Teaching about Alcohol. In: Alcohol
       Education for Teenagers: Proceedings of a Workshop.
       Newport, Rhode Island, April 5-7, 1965, pages 11-14.

4025. Todd, F. The Teacher. In: Alcohol Education. Proceedings of
       a Conference, U.S. Department of Health, Education and
       Welfare, March 29, 1966. Washington, D.C.: U.S.
       Government Printing Office, 1967, pages 38-41.

4026. Todd, F. Teaching about Alcohol. New York: McGraw-Hill, 1964.

4027. Toennies, J.E. Effectiveness of Selected Treatments in a Drug
       Education Program for University Freshmen. Doctoral
       Dissertation (University Microfilms No. 72-18919). Indiana
       University, 1971.

4028. Tolor, A. and Tamerin, J.S. The Question of a Genetic Basis for
       Alcoholism: Comment on the Study by Goodwin et al. and a
       Response. Quarterly Journal of Studies on Alcohol, 34:
       1341-1347, 1973.

4029. Tomasic, Roman. Court Based Referral Programs for Alcoholic and
       Drug Dependent Persons. Journal of Drug Issues, 7: 377-
       384, 1977.

4030. Tongue, E.J. and Moos, I., Eds. Papers Presented at the 23rd
       International Institute on the Prevention and Treatment of
       Alcoholism, Dresden, June 6-10, 1977. Lausanne,
       Switzerland: International Council on Alcohol and
       Addictions, 1977.

4031. Topics of the Day. Great Boom in Student Drinking. Teetotal
       Enforcement in Colleges Appears to be Crumbling.
       Literary Digest, 123(10): 3-6, 1937.

4032. Toohey, J.V. An Analysis of Drug Use Behavior at Five
       American Universities. Journal of School Health, 41(9):
       464-468, 1971.

4033. Toohey, Jack V. and Dezelsky, Thomas L. A Six-Year Analysis of
       Patterns in Non-Medical Drug Use Behavior. Journal of
       School Health, 48(1); 672-679, 1978.

4034. Topper, M.D. Drinking Patterns, Culture Change, Sociability,
       and Navajo "Adolescents." Addictive Diseases, 1(10):
       97-116, 1974.

4035. Topper, Martin. The Drinker's Story: An Important but Often
       Forgotten Source of Data. Journal of Studies on Alcohol,
       Supplement No. 9: 73-86, 1981.

4036. Torts--Negligence--Social Host Who Furnishes Alcoholic Beverages
       to Minors May be Held Liable for Minor's Negligent Acts.
       Rutgers Camden Law, 8: 719-723, 1977.

4037. Town to Combat Teenage Drinking. The Narragansett Times: 1, 7
       January 15, 1976.

4038. Toyoda, K. (Drinking Patterns of Students and Their Families,
       and the Interrelationship among Them.) [Japanese Text]
       Japanese Journal of Studies on Alcohol, 11: 67-72, 1976.

4039. Traffic Accident Facts. Traffic Safety, 73(9): 8-11, 1973.

4040. Training Children to become Inebriates. Journal of Inebriety,
       30: 63-66, 1908.

4041. Training for Living, Inc. Sex Education Can Help Stop Drug
       Abuse. Pamphlet. Mattituck, New York: TFL Press, 1977.

4042. Trainor, D. Father's Drinking Disturbs Family Harmony. The
       Journal, 2(10): 4, 1973.

4043. Tramer, M. Psychohygiene des Alkoholismus. (Psychohygiene of
       Alcoholism.) Schweizerische Medizinische Wochenschrift
       Journal Suisse de Medecine, Basel, 72: 15-17, 1942.

4044. Traub, S. Perceptions of Marijuana and Its Effects: A
       Comparison of Users and Nonusers. British Journal of
       Addiction, 72(1): 67-74, 1977.

4045. Treanor, William and Van Houten, Therese. Survey of Alcohol
       Related Problems among Runaway Youth Seen in Runaway
       Centers. Washington, D.C.: National Youth Alternatives
       Project, Inc., 1976.

4046. Treiman, B.R. and Sami, D. Youth and Alcohol: A Selective
         Annotated Bibliography. Prepared for the Office of
         Alcoholism, State of California. Berkeley: Social
         Research Group, School of Public Health, University of
         California, 1977.

4047. Trice, H.M. and Belasko, J.A. The Aging Collegian: Drinking
         Pathologies among Executive and Professional Alumni. In:
         The Domesticated Drug: Drinking among Collegians. Ed.
         G.L. Maddox. New Haven, Connecticut: College and
         University Press, 1970, pages 218-233.

4048. Trice, H.M., Lodahl, J.B. and Bailey, P.L. Differential Social
         Support among U.S. University Students for the Use of
         Various Drugs. In: International Conference on
         Alcoholism and Drug Abuse, San Juan, Puerto Rico,
         November, 1973. Lausanne, Switzerland: International
         Council on Alcohol and Addictions, 1974, pages 433-435.

4049. Trice, Harrison and Beyer, Janice. Women Employees and Job-
         Based Alcoholism Programs. Journal of Drug Issues, 9(3):
         371-385, 1979.

4050. Trice, Harrison M. and Beyer, Janice M. A Sociological
         Property of Drugs: Acceptance of Users of Alcohol and
         Other Drugs among University Graduates. Journal of
         Studies on Alcohol, 38(1): 58-74, 1977.

4051. Trillat, J. La Jeunesse et l'Alcoolisme: Action Éducative du
         Haut Comité d'Étude et d'Information sur 'Alcoolisme de
         France. (Youth and Alcoholism: The Educational Act of the
         High Committee of Research and Information on Alcoholism in
         France.) Revue de l'Alcoolisme, 22: 59-63, 1976.

4052. Trillat, J. Principles of Current French Policy for the
         Prevention of Alcoholism. The Alcoholism Digest Annual,
         5: 27-34, 1976-1977.

4053. Triplett, June L. and Arneson, Sara W. Children of Alcoholic
         Parents: A Neglected Issue. Journal of School Health,
         48(10): 596-599, 1978.

4054. Trivers, James. I Can Stop Any Time I Want. Englewood Cliffs,
         New Jersey: Prentice Hall, 1974.

4055. Troszyński, M. Wpływ Alkoholizmu Rodziców na Rozwój ich
         Potpmstwa. (The Influence of Parental Alcoholism on the
         Development of Progeny.) Problemy Alkoholizmu, Warsaw,
         23(3): 5, 18, 1976.

4056. Trotter, A.B., Gozali, J. and Cunningham, L.J. Family
Participation in the Treatment of Alcoholism. Personnel
and Guidance Journal, 48(2): 140-143, 1969.

4057. Trout, Michael D. Diagnosis of Infant Abuse and Neglect by
Alcohol Abuse Counselors: An Observational Model. The
Catalyst, 1(3); 28-34, 1980.

4058. Trow, Jess E. and Shanelaris, Peter J. "This Is What We Want to
Know" Say New Hampshire Youth. Journal of Alcohol
Education, 14(1): 35-37, 1968.

4059. Truckenbrodt, H. Die Kindesmisshandlung und ihre Folgen.
(Child Abuse and Its Consequences.) Öffentliche
Gesundheitswenson, Stuttgart, 41: 835-838, 1979.

4060. Trygg-Helenius, A. Temperance Effort in Juvenile Societies
throughout the World. International Congress Against
Alcoholism, 12: 67-77, 1909.

4061. Tuchmann, E. Rehabilitation of Alcoholics at Kalksburg
(Austria). British Journal of the Addictions, 61: 59-70,
1965.

4062. Tudor, Cynthia G., Peterson, D.M. and Elifson, Kirk W. An
Examination of the Relationship between Peer and Parental
Influences and Adolescent Drug Use. Adolescence, 15(60):
783-798, 1980.

4063. Turek, A. Dzieci Pacjentów Poradni Odwykowej. (Children of
Patients Who Underwent Alcoholism Treatment.) Problemy
Alkoholizmu, Warsaw, 26(5): 9-10, 1979.

4064. Türk, E. Möglichkeiten des Padagogen bei der Verhutung und
Eindämmung des Alkoholmissbrauchs im Gymnasium.
(Possibilities for Teachers to Prevent and Check Alcohol
Misuse in High Schools.) Offentliche Gesundheitswenson,
Stuttgart, 39: 40-43, 1977.

4065. Turnauer, M.S. A Comparison of High School Driver Education
Students' Attitudes as Measured by the Mann Inventory and
Vincent Attitude Scale after Receiving Two Types of
Alcohol Instruction at Selected Illinois High Schools.
Doctoral Dissertation (University Microfilms No. 74-6290).
Southern Illinois University, 1973.

4066. Turner, Carol and Willis, Robert. The Relationship of College
Students' Use of Marijuana to Parental Attitudes and Drug-
Taking Behavior. International Journal of the Addictions,
15(7): 1103-1112, 1980.

4067. Turner, G. The Fetal Alcohol Syndrome. Editorial. Medical
Journal of Australia, 1(1): 18-19, 1978.

4068. Turner, R. Alcohol Education. School and Society, 97: 415-416,
            1969.

4069. Turner, T.J. and McClure, L. Alcohol and Drug Use by Queensland
            School Children. Brisbaine, Queensland Department of
            Education, 1975.

4070. Twenty-Four States Stop Drinking Age in Three-Year Period.
            Alcohol and Health Notes (Experimental Issue): 1, 5, 1973.

4071. Tyler, H.E. Where Prayer and Purpose Meet: The WCTU Story.
            Evanston, Illinois: Signal Press, 1949.

U

4072. Uchalik, D.C. A Comparison of Questionnaire and Self-Monitored
Reports of Alcohol Intake in a Nonalcoholic Population.
Addictive Behaviors, Oxford, 4: 409-413, 1979.

4073. Ulff-Moller, B. Drug Use among Youth in Denmark in the Spring of
1968. Danish Medical Bulletin, 18(5): 105-111, 1971.

4074. Ullis, K. Adolescent Alcoholism. Paper Presented at the
American Public Health Association Annual Meeting, San
Francisco, California, November 7, 1973.

4075. Ullman, A.D. Ethnic Differences in the First Drinking Experience.
Social Problems, 8(1): 45-56, 1960.

4076. Ullman, A.D. The First Drinking Experiences of Addictive and
"Normal" Drinkers. Quarterly Journal of Studies on Alcohol,
14: 181-191, 1953.

4077. Ullman, A.D. Sociocultural Backgrounds of Alcoholism. Annals of
the American Academy of Political and Social Sciences, 315:
48-54, 1958.

4078. Ullman, Albert D. First Drinking Experience as Related to Age and
Sex. In: Society, Culture and Drinking Patterns. Eds.
D.J. Pittman and C.R. Snyder. New York: Wiley, 1962, pages
259-268.

4079. Ullman, Albert D. Sex Differences in the First Drinking
Experience. Quarterly Journal of Studies on Alcohol, 18:
229-239, 1957.

4080. Ullrich, H. Jugendkriminalität und Alkohol. (Juvenile
Delinquency and Alcohol.) Kriminalistik, Köln, 20: 239-241,
1966.

4081. Umunna, Ifekandu. The Drinking Culture of a Nigerian Community.
       Quarterly Journal of Studies on Alcohol, 28(3): 529-537,
       1967.

4082. Underage Drinking Offenses Studied. Journal of Alcohol and Drug
       Education, 24(2): 70-71, 1979.

4083. Underage Drinking: Quarterly Notes. Journal of Alcoholism,
       8(2): 46, 1973.

4084. Undervisning i Alkoholspørsmalet i Ungdomensskolen: En Mate a
       Gjennomføre Den På. (Instruction in the Alcohol Question
       in High School: A Way to Achieve It.) Norsk Tidsskrift
       AlkSpørsm, 19: 222-225, 1967.

4085. Unger, Robert A. The Treatment of Adolescent Alcoholism. Social
       Casework, 59(1): 27-35, 1978.

4086. Ungerleider, J.T. and Bowen, H.L. Drug Abuse and the Schools.
       American Journal of Psychiatry, 125: 1691-1697, 1969.

4087. United Methodist Church. Alcohol and You. Washington, D.C.,
       1976.

4088. United States Congress and Senate, Committee on Human Resources,
       Subcommittee on Alcoholism and Drug Abuse. Alcohol and
       Drug Abuse Education Programs, 1977. Hearings, 95th
       Congress, First Session, March 24-25, 1977. Washington,
       D.C.: U.S. Government Printing Office, 1977.

4089. United States Congress and Senate, Special Subcommittee on
       Alcoholism and Narcotics. Alcoholism and Narcotics.
       Hearings before the Special Subcommittee on Alcoholism and
       Narcotics of the Committee on Labor and Public Welfare
       (of the) United States Senate, 91st Congress, First and
       Second Sessions in Inquiry into the Problem of Alcoholism
       and Narcotics. Washington, D.C.: U.S. Government
       Printing Office, 1970.

4090. United States Congress and Senate, Special Subcommittee on
       Alcoholism and Narcotics. Comprehensive Alcohol Abuse and
       Alcoholism Prevention, Treatment, and Rehabilitation Act
       Amendments, 1973. Hearings before the Special Subcommittee
       on Alcoholism and Narcotics of the Committee on Labor and
       Public Welfare of the United States, 93rd Congress, First
       Session. Washington, D.C.: U.S. Government Printing
       Office, 1973.

4091. United States Congress and Senate, Special Subcommittee on
       Alcoholism and Narcotics. The Impact of Alcoholism.
       Hearings before the Special Subcommittee on Alcoholism and
       Narcotics of the Committee on Labor and Public Welfare (of
       the) United States Senate, 91st Congress, First Session on
       Examination of the Impact of Alcoholism. Washington, D.C.:
       U.S. Government Printing Office, 1970.

4092.   United States Congress and Senate, Special Subcommittee on
         Alcoholism and Narcotics. Narcotics and Alcoholism.
         Hearings before the Special Subcommittee on Alcoholism and
         Narcotics of the Committee on Labor and Public Welfare of
         the United States, 92nd Congress, First Session.
         Washington, D.C.: U.S. Government Printing Office, 1971.

4093.   United States Congress and Senate, Subcommittee on Alcoholism
         and Narcotics. Alcohol Abuse among Women: Special
         Problems and Unmet Needs. Hearings before the Subcommittee
         on Alcoholism and Narcotics of the Committee on Labor and
         Public Welfare of the United States, 94th Congress, First
         Session. Washington, D.C.: U.S. Government Printing
         Office, 1976.

4094.   United States Department of Health, Education and Welfare.
         Alcohol and Health. First Special Report to the U.S.
         Congress from the Secretary of Health, Education and
         Welfare. Washington, D.C.: U.S. Government Printing
         Office, 1971.

4095.   United States Department of Health, Education and Welfare.
         Alcohol and Health: New Knowledge. Second Special Report
         to the U.S. Congress from the Secretary of Health,
         Education and Welfare, Washington, D.C.: U.S. Government
         Printing Office, 1974.

4096.   United States Department of Health and Human Services. Alcohol
         and Health. Fourth Special Report to the U.S. Congress on
         Alcohol and Health from the Secretary of Health and Human
         Services, January, 1981. Washington, D.C.: U.S.
         Government Printing Office, 1981.

4097.   United States Department of Health, Education and Welfare.
         Alcohol and Health. Third Special Report to the U.S.
         Congress on Alcohol and Health from the Secretary of
         Health, Education and Welfare, June, 1978. Washington,
         D.C.: U.S. Government Printing Office, 1978.

4098.   United States Department of Health, Education and Welfare.
         Thinking about Drinking. Washington, D.C.: U.S.
         Government Printing Office, 1968. (Reprinted 1975, 1978)
         (DHEW Publication No. ADM 75-27 ADM 78-27)

4099.   United States Department of Health, Education and Welfare.
         Secretary's Committee on Alcoholism. Alcohol Education.
         Proceedings of a Conference, March 29, 1966. Washington,
         D.C.: U.S. Government Printing Office, 1967.

4100.   United States Department of Justice, Division of Research and
         Public Information. Alcohol, Hygiene and the Public
         Schools. Washington, D.C.: U.S. Government Printing
         Office, 1931.

4101. United States Department of Transportation. Alcohol and Highway
          Safety. A Report to the Congress from the Secretary of
          Transportation. Washington, D.C.: U.S. Department of
          Transportation, 1968.

4102. United States Department of Transportation. Young Americans:
          Drinking, Driving, Dying. Washington, D.C., 1974

4103. United States Health Services Administration. Approaches to
          Adolescent Health Care in the 1970's. Pamphlet.
          Washington, D.C.: U.S. Government Printing Office, 1975.

4104. United States Jaycees. All in the Family: Understanding How We
          Teach and Influence Children about Alcohol. Pamphlet.
          Tulsa, Oklahoma, 1975.

4105. United States Jaycees. Booze Package. Pamphlet. Tulsa,
          Olkahoma, 1973.

4106. United States Jaycees. Drinking Myths: A Guided Tour through
          Folklore, Fantasy, Humbug and Hogwash. Pamphlet. Tulsa,
          Olkahoma, 1975.

4107. United States National Commission on Marihuana and Drug Abuse.
          Drug Use in America: Problem in Perspective. Washington,
          D.C.: U.S. Government Printing Office, 1973.

4108. United States National Commission on Marihuana and Drug Abuse.
          Drug Use in America: Problem in Perspective. Appendix.
          Volume II: Social Responses to Drug Use. Washington,
          D.C.: U.S. Government Printing Office, 1973.

4109. United States National Commission on Marihuana and Drug Abuse.
          Drug Use in America: Problem in Perspective. Appendix.
          Volume III. The Legal System and Drug Control.
          Washington, D.C.: U.S. Government Printing Office, 1973.

4110. United States National Commission on Marihuana and Drug Abuse.
          Marihuana: A Signal of Misunderstanding. Volume II. The
          Technical Papers of the First Report of the National
          Commission on Marihuana and Drug Abuse. Washington, D.C.:
          U.S. Government Printing Office, 1972.

4111. United States Office of Education. Kids and Alcohol: Facts and
          Ideas about Drinking and Not Drinking. Pamphlet.
          Washington, D.C.: U.S. Government Printing Office, 1976.

4112. United States Office of Education. A Teacher Manual for Use with
          Jackson Junior High: A Film Series for Grades Five through
          Eight on Alcohol Education. Pamphlet. Washington, D.C.:
          U.S. Government Printing Office, 1976.

4113.   United States Office of Education. <u>Temperance Instruction</u>.
            Washington, D.C.: U.S. Government Printing Office, 1902.

4114.   United States Office of Education. <u>Temperance Instruction in
            Public Schools and the Liquor Question</u>. Washington, D.C.:
            U.S. Government Printing Office, 1905.

4115.   United States Office of Education and the United States National
            Institute on Alcohol Abuse and Alcoholism. <u>Alcohol:
            Pleasures and Problems</u>. Pamphlet. Washington, D.C.:
            U.S. Government Printing Office, 1976.

4116.   United States Office of Education and the United States National
            Institute on Alcohol Abuse and Alcoholism. <u>Dial
            A-L-C-O-H-O-L and Jackson Junior High: Adult Group Leader
            Guide</u>. Pamphlet. Washington, D.C.: U.S. Government
            Printing Office, 1977.

4117.   United States Office of Education and the United States National
            Institute on Alcohol Abuse and Alcoholism. <u>A Teacher
            Manual Use for Use with Dial A-L-C-O-H-O-L: A Film Series
            for Grades Nine through Twelve on Alcohol Education</u>.
            Pamphlet. Washington, D.C.: U.S. Government Printing
            Office, 1976.

4118.   United States Office of Education and the United States National
            Institute on Alcohol Abuse and Alcoholism. <u>Teacher
            Training in Alcohol Education Using the Two Film Series
            Jackson Junior High and Dial A-L-C-O-H-O-L</u>. Pamphlet.
            Cambridge, Massachusetts: Abt Associates, no date.

4119.   University of Kansas Department of Sociology and Anthropology.
            Attitudes of High School Students toward Alcoholic
            Beverages. New York: Sheppard Foundation, 1956.

4120.   University of Melbourne, Department of Medicine, St. Vincent's
            Hospital. Symposium: Alcohol and the Family. Presented
            at the Third Summer School of Alcohol Studies, January 26,
            1968. Melbourne, Australia, 1968.

4121.   The University of Michigan Highway Safety Research Institute.
            Michigan Fatal Accidents Involving Alcohol, 1968-1976.
            <u>The Highway Safety Research Institute</u>, $\underline{8}$(5): 1-12, 1978.

4122.   University of Wisconsin, Bureau of Economics, Sociology and
            Anthropology. Attitudes of High School Students toward
            Alcoholic Beverages. New York: Sheppard Foundation, 1956.

4123.   Unkovic, Charles. A Contemporary Study of Jewish Alcoholism.
            <u>The Alcoholism Digest Annual</u>, $\underline{4}$: 7-13, 1975-1976.

4124. Unsworth, M. Drinking Habits of People in War-Time: As Seen by the Salvation Army Officer. British Journal of Inebriety, 39: 60-64, 1942.

4125. Unterberger, Hilma and DiCicco, Lena. Alcohol Education Re-Evaluated. The Bulletin of the National Association of Secondary School Principals, 52(326): 15-29, 1968.

4126. Unterberger, Hilma and DiCicco, Lena. Alcohol Education Reevaluated. Pamphlet. Rockville, Maryland: U.S. National Center for Prevention and Control of Alcoholism: 1968.

4127. Unterberger, Hilma and DiCicco, Lena. Alcohol Education through Small Group Discussion. Journal of Alcohol Education, 14(1): 1-12, 1968.

4128. Uppal, G.S., Babst, D.V. and Schmeidler, J. Assessing Age-of-Onset Data on Substance Use among New York State Public Secondary School Students. American Journal of Drug and Alcohol Abuse, 4: 505-515, 1977.

4129. Utah Congress of Parents and Teachers. Alcohol Education: A Community Involvement Manual. Pamphlet. Chicago, Illinois: National Congress of Parents and Teachers, 1977.

4130. Utah State Superintendent of Public Instruction. Junior High School Health Guide. Salt Lake City, Utah, 1965.

4131. Utah State Superintendent of Public Instruction. Senior High School Health Guide. Salt Lake City, Utah, 1968.

4132. Utrata, R. Z Historie Protialkoholní Výchovy. (History of Anitalcohol Education.) Československa Psychiatrie, 61: 125-127, 1965.

4133. Uusitalo, A. Päihdeilmiön Sosiaaliset ja Kulttuuriin Liittyvät Tekijät. (Social and Cultural Factors in Alcohol and Drug Abuse among Minors.) Lapsi Ja Nuoriso, Lastensuojelun Keskusliitto, 30(10): 296-298, 317, 1971.

V

4134. Vaaramo, A. Alkohol und Jugend. (Alcohol and Youth.)
International Congress against Alcoholism, 22: 197-202,
1941.

4135. Valentine, Paul W. Drug, Alcohol Abuse above Average in D.C.
The Washington Post, C1, C2, June 6, 1975.

4136. Vaillant, G.E., Sobowale, N.C. and McArthur, C. Some Psychologic
Vulnerabilities of Physicians. New England Journal of
Medicine, 287: 372-375, 1972.

4137. Validity of Statutes Forbidding Sale of Liquor to Students. Law
Notes, 18: 232, 1915.

4138. Valles, J. From Social Drinking to Alcoholism. Dallas: Texas
Alcohol and Narcotics Education, 1969.

4139. Valtasaari, A. Some Aspects of Temperance Education in the
Secondary Schools. Alkoholikysymys, Helsinki, 5: 7-21,
1937.

4140. Vamosi, M. Einige Tatsachen über das Trinken von Kindern und
Jugendlichen Analyse und Schlussfolgerungen aus
Verschiedenen Untersuchungen. (Some Data Concerning
Drinking by Children and Youth--Analysis and Conclusions of
Different Studies.) Suchtgefahren, Hamburg, 18(2): 4-9,
1972.

4141. Van Amberg, R.J. A Study of Fifty Women Patients Hospitalized
for Alcohol Addiction. Diseases of the Nervous System,
4: 246-251, 1943.

4142. Van-Dalen, W.E. Alkoholvoorlichting als Prioriteit? (Alcohol
Education as a Priority?) Tijdschrift voor Alcohol, Drugs
en Andere Psychotrope Stoffen, The Hague, 7(1): 38-40,
1981.

4143. Vander Kooi, R.C. An Analysis of Drinking Practices and Problems among Male Undergraduates at a Midwestern University. Master's Thesis. Kalamazoo, Michigan: Western Michigan University, 1961.

4144. Van der Wal, H.J. Drinking Habits among Dutch Youth. Fifteenth International Institute on the Prevention and Treatment of Alcoholism, 1: 57-60, 1969.

4145. Van Houten, Therese and Golembiewski, Gary. Adolescent Life Stress as a Predicator of Alcohol Abuse and/or Runaway Behavior. Washington, D.C.: National Youth Alternatives Project, 1978.

4146. The Varieties of Drug Experience. Trans-Action, 5(9): 5-6, 1968.

4147. Varma, V.K. and Dang, R. Non-Medical Drug Use amongst Non-Student Youth in India. Drug and Alcohol Dependence, Lausanne, 5: 457-465, 1980.

4148. Vatutin, N.T. and Veligotskaya, T.N. K Diagnostike Infarkta Miokarda na fone Ostroi Alkogol'noi Intoksikatsii u Bol'nykh Molodogo Vozrasta. (Diagnosis of Myocardia Infarction against the Background of Acute Alcohol Intoxication in Young Patients.) Terapevticheskii Arkhiv, Moscow, 49(4): 114-115, 1977.

4149. Vaucleroy, de. Education Antialcoolique de la Jeunesse. (Education against Alcohol for the Young.) International Congress against Alcoholism, 14: 446-450, 1921.

4150. Vaz, E.W. Middle-Class Adolescents: Self-Reported Delinquency and Youth-Culture Activities. Canadian Review of Sociological Anthropology, 2: 52-70, 1965.

4151. Vaz, Edmund. Delinquency and the Youth Culture: Upper- and Middle-Class Boys. Journal of Criminal Law, Criminology and Police Science, 60(1): 33-46, 1969. (Also in: Deviant Behavior and Social Reaction. Eds. C.L. Boydell, C.F. Grindstaff and P.C. Whitehead. Toronto, Ontario: Holt, Rinehart and Winston, 1972, pages 212-231.)

4152. Vaziri, H. Fréquence de l'Oligophrénie, de la Psychopathie et de l'Alcoolisme dans 79 Familles de Schizophrènes. (The Incidence of Oligophrenia, Psychopathy and Alcoholism in 79 Families of Schizophrenics.) Schweizer Archiv für Neurologie and Psychiatrie, 87: 160-177, 1961.

4153. Velazques, A.P. Drinking among Junior High School Students. Master's Thesis. Baltimore, Maryland: Johns Hopkins University, 1973.

4154.   Velleman, Jim and Lawrence, Ted. Do Drinking Parents Make Teen
            Addicts? Survey by Students Turns Up a Shocker. Science
            Digest: Adventure in Science and Discovery: 47-56, 1970.

4155.   Vermes, H.G. and Vermes, J.C. Helping Youth Avoid Four Great
            Dangers: Smoking, Drinking, VD, Narcotics Addiction. New
            York: Association Press, 1965.

4156.   Vermont Department of Education. Alcohol Education in Vermont.
            Supplementary Report No. 52-13, July 10, 1951-June 30,
            1952. Burlington, Vermont, 1952.

4157.   Vermont Department of Education. With Focus on Youth. Pamphlet.
            Montpelier, Vermont, 1956.

4158.   Vermont Department of Education. The Role of Elementary Schools
            in Alcohol Education. Montpelier, Vermont, 1957.

4159.   Vermont Department of Education. The Role of Parents in Alcohol
            Problems. Pamphlet. Montpelier, Vermont, 1957.

4160.   Vener, A.M. and Stewart, C.S. Adolescent Sexual Behavior in
            Middle America Revisited, 1970-1973. Journal of Marriage
            and the Family, 36(4): 728-735, 1974.

4161.   Viamontes, J.A. and Powell, B.J. Demographic Characteristics of
            Black and White Male Alcoholics. International Journal of
            Addiction, 9(3): 489-494, 1974.

4162.   Vicary, J.R. Relating and Comparing Affective Education and
            Addictions Prevention. Toronto, Ontario: Addiction
            Research Foundation, 1979.

4163.   Viel, B., Donoso, S., Salcedo, D., Rojas, P., Varela, A. and
            Alessandri, R. Alcoholism and Socioeconomic Status,
            Hepatic Damage, and Arteriosclerosis: Study of 777
            Autopsied Men in Santiago, Chile. Archive of Internal
            Medicine, 117(1): 84-91, 1966.

4164.   Viesselman, J.O., Spalt, L.H. and Tuason, V.B. Psychiatric
            Disorders in a Community Mental Health Center. II. Who
            Gets Readmitted. Comprehensive Psychiatry, 16(5): 485-
            494, 1975.

4165.   Vincent, M.L. A Comparison of the Drug Habits and Attitudes of
            Alcohol and Marijuana Users. Journal of Drug Education,
            2(2): 149-170, 1972.

4166.   Vine, L. and Cousins, T. Gateway to Addiction: A Study of the
            Drinking Behavior of Young People within the County of
            Avon. Journal of Alcoholism, 9(3): 94-96, 1974.

4167. Vingilis, E. Drinking and Driving among Ontario Students in 1979 and Changes from 1977. (Substudy No. 1011) Toronto, Ontario: Addiction Research Foundation, 1980.

4168. Vingilis, E. A Literature Review of the Young Drinking Offender. Is He a Problem Drinker? British Journal of Addiction, 76(1): 27-46, 1981.

4169. Vingilis, Evelyn and Smart, Reginald G. Effects of Raising the Legal Drinking Age in Ontario. British Journal of Addiction, 76(4): 415-424, 1981.

4170. Virginia Department of Education, Health and Physical Education Service. Health Education: Grades 7-12. Richmond, Virginia, 1971.

4171. Virkkunen, M. Alcoholism and Antisocial Personality. Acta Psychiatrica Scandinavica, 59(5): 493-501, 1979.

4172. Virkkunen, M. Incest Offenses and Alcoholism. Medicine, Science, and the Law, 14(2): 124-128, 1974.

4173. Virkkunen, M. Juopumuspidatykset ja Uusintarikollisuus Nuorilla Rikoksentekijoilla. (Drunkenness Offenses and Recidivism in Juvenile Delinquents.) Alkoholikysymys, Helsinki, 2: 58-62, 1975.

4174. Virkkunen, Matti. Arrests for Drunkenness and Recidivism in Juvenile Delinquents. British Journal of Addiction, 72: 201-204, 1977.

4175. Vissing, Y.M. How Do the Schools View Substance Education and Prevention? Journal of Drug Education, 8: 267-277, 1978.

4176. Vitols, M.M. Culture Patterns of Drinking in Negro and White Alcoholics. Diseases of the Nervous System, 29: 391-394, 1968.

4177. Vivaldo, J.C. Alcoholismo y Dipsomania en un Débil Mental Congenito. Algunas Consideraciones. Prensa Médica Argentia, 27: 1587-1594, 1940.

4178. Voas, R.B. Alcohol, Drugs and Young Drivers. Washington, D.C.: Traffic Safety Program, Office of Driver and Pedestrian Programs, U.S. Department of Transportation, 1974.

4179. Voas, Robert. Roadside Surveys, Demographics and BACs of Drivers. In: Alcohol, Drugs and Traffic Safety. Proceedings of the Sixth International Conference on Alcohol, Drugs and Traffic Safety, Toronto, September 8-13, 1974. Eds. S. Israelstam and S. Lambert. Toronto, Ontario: Addiction Research Foundaton, 1975, pages 21-31.

4180. Vodrážka, R. Výzkum Zdravotního Uvědoměni Mládeže v Otázkách
       Alkoholismu. (Studies on Health Knowledge among Young
       People in Relation to Alcoholism.) Československe
       Zdravotnictvi, Prague, 7: 453-456, 1959.

4181. Voegtlin, W.L. The Conditioned Reflex Treatment of Chronic
       Alcohlism. Hygeia, 26: 628-629, 662-665, 1948.

4182. Vogt, Irmgard. Jugendlicher Alkoholkonsum und Familienmilieu.
       (Drinking by Adolescents and the Family Environment.) In:
       Papers Presented at the 24th International Congress on the
       Prevention and Treatment of Alcoholism, Zurich, June, 1978.
       Ed. E.J. Tongue. Lausanne, Switzerland: International
       Council on Alcohol and Addictions, 1978, pages 203-216.

4183. Vojtik, V. On the Problems of Toxicomania in Prague Youth.
       Ceskoslovenska Psychiatrie, 68: 204-213, 1972.

4184. Voipio, M. The Effects of the Liberalization of Alcohol
       Legislation in Finland. In: International Congress on
       Alcoholism and Drug Dependence, February 23-28, 1975,
       31st. Volume III. Proceedings. Eds. B. Blair, V. Pawlak,
       E. Tongue and C. Zwicky. Lausanne, Switzerland:
       International Council on Alcohol and Addictions, 1975,
       pages 584-592.

4185. Voipio, M. Raittiusopetuksen Ongelmia. (Curriculum Problems in
       Alcohol Education.) Alkoholikysymys, Helsinki, 39: 72-81,
       1971.

4186. Voipio, Martti R. The Prospects for Adequate Education about
       Alcohol and Alcoholism (A Contribution to the Discussions).
       Journal of Alcohol Education, 14(3): 1-8, 1969.

4187. Von Taschner, K.L., Richtberg, W. and Schmidt, K. Soziale und
       Psychologische Schrittmacher des Jugendalkohismus. In:
       Papers Presented at the 23rd International Institute on
       the Prevention and Treatment of Alcoholism. Dresden,
       June 6-10, 1977. Eds. E.J. Tongue and I. Moos. Lausanne,
       Switzerland: International Council on Alcohol and
       Addictions, 1977, pages 217-226.

4188. Vrba, Z. Alkohol ve Školních Osnovách. (Alcohol in School
       Curricula.) Protialkoholiky Obzor, Bratislava, 5: 113-
       114, 1970.

4189. Vyhňák, M. Alkoholismus a Jeho Vliv na Kriminalitu, Její
       Recidivu a na Páchání Trestné Činnosti v Dopravě, Mládeže
       a Trestné Činy Násilné Povahy. (Alcoholism and Its
       Influence on Criminality and Recidivism, on Traffic
       Offenses, Juvenile Delinquency and Crimes of Violence.)
       Protialkoholicky Obzor, Bratislava, 8: 105-116, 1973.

W

4190. Wagenaar, Alexander C. Legal Minimum Drinking Age Changes in the United States: 1970-1981. Alcohol Health and Research World, 6(2): 21-26, 1981-1982.

4191. Wagner, R.S. Sarah T.: Portrait of a Teenage Alcoholic. Toronto, Ontario: Ballantine Books, A Division of Random House, Inc., and Ballantine Books, Ltd., 1975.

4192. Wahl, C.W. Some Antecedent Factors in the Family Histories of 109 Alcoholics. Quarterly Journal of Studies on Alcohol, 17(4): 643-654, 1956.

4193. Wakely, C. Temperance Teaching in Schools in England. International Congress against Alcoholism, 14: 450-456, 1921.

4194. Waldron, Ingrid and Eyer, Joseph. Socioeconomic Causes of the Recent Rise in Death Rates for 15-24-Year-Olds. Social Science and Medicine, 9: 383-396, 1975.

4195. Walfish, S., Stenmark, D.E., Wentz, D., Myers, C. and Linares, D. Alcohol-Related Advertisement in a College Newspaper. International Journal of Addiction, 16(5): 941-946, 1981.

4196. Walker, Betty A., Jasinska, Magda D. and Carnes, Earl F. Adolescent Alcohol Abuse: A Review of the Literature. Journal of Alcohol and Drug Education, 23(3): 51-65, 1978.

4197. Wall, Helge. Unconventional Treatment Models for Young Drug Dependents. Journal of Drug Issues, 10: 441-452, 1980.

4198. Wallack, L. A Decade of the San Mateo Annual Student Census of Drug Use--Final Report. Drinking and Drug Practices Surveyor, 13: 27, 1977.

4199.   Wallack, L. San Mateo Annual Student Census of Drug Use, 1976:
        A Brief Review. The Drinking and Drug Practices Surveyor,
        12: 31-32, 1976.

4200.   Waller, J. Factors Associated with Alcohol and Responsibility
        for Fatal Highway Crashes. Quarterly Journal of Studies
        on Alcohol, 33(1): 160-170, 1972.

4201.   Waller, J.A. Fact and Fiction about Accidental Injury.
        Northwestern Medicine, 67: 451-457, 1968.

4202.   Waller, J.A. High "Accident" Risk among Middle-Aged Drivers and
        Pedestrians. Geriatrics, 21(12): 125-137, 1966.

4203.   Waller, J.A., King, E.M., Nielson, G. and Turkel, H.W. Alcohol
        and Other Factors in California Highway Fatalities.
        Forensic Science, 14(4): 429-444, 1969.

4204.   Waller, J.A., Lamborn, K.R. and Steffenhagen, R.A. Marihuana
        and Driving among Teenagers: Reported Use Patterns,
        Effects, and Experiences Related to Driving. Accident
        Analysis and Prevention, Oxford, 6: 141-161, 1974.

4205.   Waller, J.A. and Turkel, H.W. Alcoholism and Traffic Deaths.
        New England Journal of Medicine, 275(10): 532-536, 1966.

4206.   Waller, Julian. Alcohol and Unintentional Injury. In: The
        Biology of Alcoholism. Volume 4. Social Aspects of
        Alcoholism. Eds. B. Kissin and H. Begleiter. New York:
        Plenum Press, 1976, pages 307-351.

4207.   Waller, Julian. Epidemiologic Issues about Alcohol, Other Drugs
        and Highway Safety. In: Alcohol, Drugs and Traffic
        Safety. Proceedings of the Sixth International Conference
        on Alcohol, Drugs and Traffic Safety, Toronto, September 8-
        13, 1974. Eds. S. Israelstam and S. Lambert. Toronto,
        Ontario: Addiction Research Foundation, 1975, pages 3-11.

4208.   Waller, Patricia. Drinking and Highway Safety. In: Drinking:
        Alcohol in American Society--Issues and Current Research.
        Eds. J.A. Ewing and B.A. Rouse. Chicago, Illinois:
        Nelson-Hall, 1978, pages 117-136.

4209.   Walsh, D. Alcoholism in Ireland Today. Irish Journal of Medical
        Science (Supplement): 58-65, 1975.

4210.   Walsh, D. Alcoholism in the Republic of Ireland. British
        Journal of Psychiatry, 115(526): 1021-1025, 1969.

4211.   Walsh, Robert E. and Negri, Gloria. $82M to Fight Drunk
        Drivers. The Morning Globe (Boston), February 28, 1973.

4212.   Walshe-Brennan, K.S. The Roots of Child Crime. Nursing Mirror,
        143(9): 66-68, 1976.

4213.   Walters, O.S. The Religious Background of Fifty Alcoholics.
        Quarterly Journal of Studies on Alcohol, 18: 405-416, 1957.

4214.   Walters, P., Goethals, G.W. and Pope, H.G. Drug Use and Life-
        Style among 500 College Undergraduates. Archives of
        General Psychiatry, 26: 92-96, 1972.

4215.   Walton, R.G. Smoking and Alcoholism: A Brief Report. American
        Journal of Psychiatry, 128(11): 1455-1456, 1972.

4216.   Wanberg, K.W. and Horn, J.L. Alcoholism Syndromes Related to
        Sociological Classifications. International Journal of
        the Addictions, 8(1): 99-120, 1973.

4217.   Wangenheim, K.H. Liquor Sale to Minors: Yugoslav Law.
        Quarterly Journal of Studies on Alcohol, 25: 153, 1964.

4218.   Wanner, Eric. Power and Inhibition: A Revision of the Magical
        Potency Theory. In: The Drinking Man. Eds.
        D.C. McClelland, W.N. Davis, R. Kalin and E. Wanner. New
        York: The Free Press, 1972, pages 73-98.

4219.   Wanner, O. Ursachen der Trunksucht. (Causes of Alcoholism.)
        Fürsorger, 22: 33-46, 1954.

4220.   Ward, D.A. Alcoholism: Introduction to Theory and Treatment.
        Dubuque, Iowa: Kendall and Hunt, 1980.

4221.   Ward, David A. Evidence for Controlled Drinking in Diagnosed
        Alcoholics: A Critical Analysis of the Goodwin et al.
        Adoption Study. Journal of Drug Issues, 8: 373-378, 1978.

4222.   Warder, J. and Ross, C.J. Age and Alcoholism. British Journal
        of Addiction, 66(1): 45-51, 1971.

4223.   Warder, J. and Ross, C.J. Alcoholism and Its Treatment in
        Scotland: A Critical Review. British Journal of
        Addiction, 66(2): 110-122, 1971.

4224.   Warheit, George J., Arey, Sandra A. and Swanson, Edith. Patterns
        of Drug Use: An Epidemiologic Overview. Journal of Drug
        Issues, 6: 223-237, 1976.

4225.   Warner, H.S. Alcohol Trends in College Life. Washington, D.C.:
        Methodist Episcopal Church, 1938. (Also in: The
        Domesticated Drug: Drinking among Collegians. Ed.
        G.L. Maddox. New Haven, Connecticut: College and
        University Press, 1970, pages 45-80.)

4226. Warner, H.S. An Evolution in Understanding the Problem of Alcohol: A History of College Idealism. Boston, Massachusetts: Christopher, 1966.

4227. Warren, R.A., Simpson, H.M., Pagé-Valin, L. and Collard, D. Point Zero Eight and the Change in Drinking Age: One Step Forward and Two Steps Backward? Ottawa, Ontario: Traffic Injury Research Foundation of Canada, 1977.

4228. Warrington, John. A Programme for Educating the Young about Alcohol. Journal of Alcoholism, 9(2): 73-75, 1974.

4229. Washington, R. Public Health Viewpoint: The Present Crisis in Alcohol and Drug Abuse Education for Youth--Lack of Consistency. In: Sixth Annual West Virginia School of Alcohol and Drug Abuse Studies. Morgantown, West Virginia, June 14-19, 1970.

4230. Washington Department of Social and Health Services. Teenage Drinking, A Stepping Stone to Other Drug Usage. Pamphlet. Olympia, Washington, no date.

4231. Washington Liquor Control Board. Take a Sober Look at Drinking. Olympia, Washington, 1966.

4232. Washington Office of Public Instruction. Health Education Guide to Better Health. Olympia, Washington, 1966.

4233. Wattenberg, W.W. and Moir, J.B. A Study of Teen-Agers Arrested for Drunkenness. Quarterly Journal of Studies on Alcohol, 17: 426-436, 1956.

4234. Wattenberg, William W. and Moir, John B. Teen-Age Drinkers. A Research Project Conducted Under the Auspices of the Social Science Research Center of Wayne University on a Grant from the Michigan State Board of Alcoholism. Lansing, Michigan, 1955.

4235. Watter, J.A. Factors Associated with Alcohol and Responsibility for Fatal Highway Crashes. Quarterly Journal of Studies on Alcohol, 33(1): 160-170, 1972.

4236. Wciórka, J., Chlopocka, M., Lisowska, J., Nowacka, L. and Rybakowski, J. Przyczynek do Badań nad Alcoholizmem Wśród Mlodzieży. (Additional Note to Studies on Alcoholism among Youth.) Problemy Alkoholizmu, Warsaw, 20(5): 4-6, 1972.

4237. Webb, R.A.J. New South Wales Drug Education Programme. Medical Journal of Australia, 52(2): 269-271, 1972.

4238. Webb, R.A.J., Egger, Gary J. and Reynolds, Ingrid. Prediction and Prevention of Drug Abuse. Journal of Drug Education, 8(3): 221-230, 1978.

4239.   Weber, W.   Gefährdung durch Alkohol bei 10- bis 14jährigen
        Jungen.   (Risk of Problem Drinking in Youths Aged 10-14.)
        Suchtgefahren, Hamburg, 25: 136-139, 1979.

4240.   Wechsler, H.   Alcohol Intoxication and Drug Use among Teen-Agers.
        Journal of Studies on Alcohol, 37: 1672-1677, 1976.

4241.   Wechsler, H.   Marihuana, Alcohol and Public Policy.   New England
        Journal of Medicine, 287: 515-516, 1972.

4242.   Wechsler, H.   Patterns of Alcohol Consumption among the Young:
        High School, College and General Population Studies.   In:
        Youth, Alcohol, and Social Policy.   Eds. H.T. Blane and
        M.E. Chafetz.   New York: Plenum, 1979, pages 39-58.

4243.   Wechsler, H., Kasey, E.H., Thum, D. and Demone, H.W., Jr.
        Alcohol Level and Home Accidents.   Public Health Reports,
        84(12): 1043-1050, 1969.

4244.   Wechsler, H. and McFadden, M.   Drinking among College Students
        in New England: Extent, Social Correlates and Consequences
        of Alcohol Use.   Journal of Studies on Alcohol, 40: 969-
        996, 1979.

4245.   Wechsler, H. and McFadden, M.   Sex Differences in Adolescent
        Alcohol and Drug Use: A Disappearing Phenomenon.   Journal
        of Studies on Alcohol, 37(9): 1291-1301, 1976.

4246.   Wechsler, H., McFadden, M. and Rohman, M.   Drinking and Drug Use
        among College Students in New England.   Journal of the
        American College Health Association, 28: 275-279, 1980.

4247.   Wechsler, H. and Thum, D.   Alcohol and Drug Use among Teenagers:
        A Questionnaire Study.   In: Proceedings of the Second
        Annual Alcoholism Conference of the NIAAA.   Ed. M. Chafetz.
        Rockville, Maryland: National Institute on Alcoholism and
        Alcohol Abuse, 1973, pages 33-46.

4248.   Wechsler, H. and Thum, D.   Teen-Age Drinking, Drug Use and Social
        Correlates.   Quarterly Journal of Studies on Alcohol,
        34(4): 1220-1227, 1973.

4249.   Wechsler, H., Thum, D., Demone, H.W. and Dwinnell, J.   Social
        Characteristics and Blood Alcohol Level: Measurement of
        Subgroup Differences.   Quarterly Journal of Studies on
        Alcohol, 33: 132-147, 1972.

4250.   Wechsler, Henry, Ed.   Minimum-Drinking-Age Laws: An Evaluation.
        Lexington, Massachusetts: D.C. Heath and Company, 1980.

4251. Wechsler, Henry and Rohman, Mary. Extensive Users of Alcohol among College Students. Journal of Studies on Alcohol, 42(1): 149-155, 1981. (Also in: American Journal of Drug and Alcohol Abuse, 8(1): 27-37, 1981.)

4252. Wechsler, Henry and Rohman, Mary E. Patterns of Drug Use among New England College Students. American Journal of Drug and Alcohol Abuse, 8(1): 27-37, 1981.

4253. Wedel, K.W. Jugend und Sucht unter Besonderer Berücksichtigung der Prophylaxe: Prophylaxe in der Bundeswehr. (Youth and Addiction: Prevention in the German Army.) Suchtgefahren, Hamburg, 24: 101-105, 1978.

4254. Weeber, Stan. DWI Repeaters and Non-Repeaters: A Comparison. Journal of Alcohol and Drug Education, 26(3): 1-9, 1981.

4255. Weeks, C.C. Introduction of Temperance Teaching in All Training Institutions for Future Teachers in All Countries. International Review Against Alcoholism, 39: 150-155, 1931.

4256. Wegscheider, S. The Family Trap...No One Escapes from a Chemically Dependent Family. Pamphlet. Minneapolis, Minnesota: Johnson Institute, 1976.

4257. Wegscheider, S. From the Family Trap to Family Freedom. Alcoholism: The National Magazine, 1(3): 36-39, 1981.

4258. Weidmann, M., Ladewig, D., Faust, V., Gastpar, M., Heise, H., Hobi, V., Mayer-Boss, S. and Wyss, P. Drogengebrauch von Basler Schülern--Ein Beitrag zur Epidemiologie. (Drug Use of Basel Students--A Contribution to Epidemiology.) Schweizerische Medizinische Wochenschrift Journal Suisse de Medecine, Basel, 103: 121-126, 1973.

4259. Weil, Andrew. The Natural Mind. Boston, Massachusetts: Houghton Mifflin, 1972.

4260. Weinberg, L.M., Brasitus, T.A. and Lefkowitch, J.H. Fluctuating Kayser-Fleischer-Like Rings in a Jaundiced Patient. Archives of Internal Medicine, 141(2): 246-247, 1981.

4261. Weiner, J.B. Drinking. New York: Norton, 1976.

4262. Weiner, S., Tamerin, J.S., Steinglass, P. and Mendelson, J.H. Familial Patterns in Chronic Alcoholism: A Study of a Father and Son during Experimental Intoxication. American Journal of Orthopsychiatry, 40: 356-357, 1970.

4263. Weingarten, Nicholes. Treating Adolescent Drug Abuse as a Symptom of Dysfunction in the Family. In: Drug Abuse from the Family Perspective. Ed. Barbara Gray Ellis. Washington, D.C.: U.S. Government Printing Office, 1980, pages 57-62.

4264.   Weinstein, Martin. Changes in Drug Usage and Associated
         Personality Traits among College Students. International
         Journal of the Addictions, 13(4): 683-688, 1978.

4265.   Weir, W.R. Alcohol and Alcoholism Education: Attitude
         Development and Change. Journal of Alcohol Education,
         15(1): 1-8, 1969. (Also in: Inventory: A Quarterly
         Journal on Alcohol and Alcoholism, 20(4): 5-9, 19, 1971.

4266.   Weir, W.R. Counseling Youth Whose Parents are Alcoholic: A
         Means to an End as Well as an End in Itself. Journal of
         Alcohol Education, 16(1): 13-19, 1970.

4267.   Weir, W.R. A Program of Alcohol Education and Counseling for
         High School Students with and without a Family Alcohol
         Problem. Doctoral Dissertation (University Microfilms No.
         68-6797). Grand Forks: The University of North Dakota,
         1967.

4268.   Weiss, Mildred H. What We Should Know about Alcohol: A Manual
         for Teachers and Group Leaders to Accompany Slides for
         Alcohol Education. Cleveland, Ohio: Cleveland Health
         Museum, 1957.

4269.   Weissbach, Theodore A. and Vogler, Roger E. Implications of a
         Social Learning Approach to the Prevention and Treatment of
         Alcohol Abuse. Contemporary Drug Problems, 6(4): 553-568,
         1977.

4270.   Weitman, M., Scheble, R., Johnson, K.G. and Abbey, H. Survey of
         Adolescent Drug Use. III. Correlations among Use of Drugs.
         American Journal of Public Health, 62(2): 166-170, 1972.

4271.   Weitman, M., Scheble, R.O. and Johnson, K.G. Survey of
         Adolescent Drug Use. IV. Patterns of Drug Use. American
         Journal of Public Health, 64(5): 417-421, 1974.

4272.   Well-Being. Morristown, New Jersey: Silver Burdett, 1972.

4273.   Wellborn, Charles. Introduction (Drugs and Religion). Journal
         of Drug Issues, 7: 217-218, 1977.

4274.   Wellisch, David, DeAngelis, G.G. and Bond, Doug. Family
         Treatment of the Homosexual Adolescent Drug Abuser: On
         Being Gay in a Sad Family. In: Family Therapy of Drug and
         Alcohol Abuse. Eds. E. Kaufman and P.N. Kaufman. New York:
         Gardner Press, 1979, pages 105-114.

4275.   Wellisch, D. and Hays, J.R. A Cross-Cultural Study of the
         Prevalence and Correlates of Student Drug Use in the United
         States and Mexico. Bulletin on Narcotics, 26(1): 31-42,
         1974.

4276. Wellman, M. Towards an Etiology of Alcoholism: Why Young Men Drink too Much. Canadian Medical Association Journal, 73: 717-725, 1955.

4277. Wells, B. and Stacey, B.G. Social and Psychological Features of Young Drug Misusers. British Journal of Addiction, 71: 243-251, 1976.

4278. Welner, A., Welner, Z. and Fishman, R. Psychiatric Adolescent Inpatients: Eight- to Ten-Year Follow-Up. Archive of General Psychiatry, 36: 698-700, 1979.

4279. Welsh, Tina. Alateens Talk about Their Troubles. The Washington Star News (Teen Section), 7, April 20, 1974.

4280. Welter, H. Alkoholmissbrauch und Alkoholismus junger Menschen. (Alcohol Misuse and Alcoholism among Young People.) Jugendwohl, Freiburg, 44: 399-405, 1963.

4281. Wenger, P. History of a Drinking Habit in 400 Inmates of a Penal Institution. New York State Journal of Medicine, 44: 1898-1904, 1944.

4282. West, D.J. The Young Offender. Harmondsworth, Middlesex: Penguin, 1967.

4283. Westermeyer, J. Drink, Options Regarding Alcohol Use among the Chippewa. American Journal of Orthopsychiatry, 42: 398-403, 1972.

4284. Westermeyer, J., Doheny, S. and Stone, B. An Assessment of Hospital Care for the Alcoholic Patient. Alcoholism, Zagreb, 2(1): 53-57, 1978.

4285. Westermeyer, J. and Walzer, V. Sociopathy and Drug Use in a Young Psychiatric Population. Diseases of the Nervous System, 36: 673-677, 1975.

4286. West Germans Worried about Teenage Alcoholism. (International Comments) Journal of the American Medical Association, 238: 1855, 1977.

4287. Westling, A. On the Correlation of the Consumption of Alcoholic Drinks with Some Sexual Phenomenon of Finnish Male Students. International Journal of Sexology, 7: 109-115, 1954.

4288. Westwood, M., Cohen, M.I. and McNamara, H. Serum δ-Glutamyl Transpeptidase Activity: A Chemical Determinant of Alcohol Consumption during Adolescence. Pediatrics, 62: 560-562, 1978.

4289. When Young Drivers Drink. Journal of American Insurance, 50(2): 10-11, 1974.

4290.   Whiddon, T. and Halpin, G.   Relationships between Drug Knowledge
        and Drug Attitudes for Students in Large, Intermediate and
        Small Schools.   Research Quarterly, 48: 191-195, 1977.

4291.   Whiddon, Thomas Rodney, Jr.   A Comparative Study of Drug
        Knowledge, Attitudes toward Drugs, and Use of Drugs among
        Twelfth Grade Students in Class I, II, and III Schools in
        Western Montana.   Doctoral Dissertation (University
        Microfilms No. 75-26200).   University of Montana, 1975.

4292.   Whipple, Dorothy V.   Is the Grass Greener? Answers to Questions
        about Drugs.   Washington: Robert B. Luce, Inc., 1971.

4293.   White, Exie P.   Bibliography and Evaluation of Books and
        Pamphlets on Alcohol Education.   (University of Nebraska
        Publication No. 156; Contributions to Education No. 23.)
        Lincoln, Nebraska, 1947.

4294.   White, R.E. and Biron, R.M.   A Manual of Evaluation Guidelines
        for CASPAR: A Model Program in Alcohol Education.
        Prepared for National Institute on Alcohol Abuse and
        Alcoholism.   Springfield, Virginia: National Technical
        Information Service, 1979.

4295.   White, R.E. and Biron, R.M.   A Manual of Evaluation Guidelines
        for CASPAR, a Model Program in Alcohol Education (Grades 7-
        120.   Somerville, Massachusetts: CASPAR Alcohol Education
        Program, 1979.

4296.   White, Robert E. and Biron, Ronald M.   A Manual of Evaluation
        Guidelines for CASPAR: A Model Program in Alcohol
        Education.   Prepared for Urban and Rural Systems Associates
        of San Francisco under Contract No. ADM-281-0004 with the
        National Institute on Alcohol Abuse and Alcoholism, May,
        1979.   Somerville, Massachusetts: CASPAR Alcohol Education
        Program, 1979.

4297.   White, S.B. and Clayton, C.A.   Some Effects of Alcohol, Age of
        Driver, and Estimated Speed on the Likelihood of Driver
        Injury.   Accident Analysis and Prevention, Oxford, 4: 59-
        66, 1972.

4298.   Whitehead, M.   A Fresh Look at Scottish Health Education.
        International Journal of Health Education, 21: 253-257,
        1978.

4299.   Whitehead, P.C.   Alcohol and Young Drivers: Impact and
        Implications of Lowering the Drinking Age.   Ottawa, Canada:
        Department of National Health and Welfare, Non-Medical Use
        of Drugs Directorate, 1977.

4300.   Whitehead, P.C.   Collision Behavior of Young Drivers: A Response
        to Zylman.   Journal of Studies on Alcohol, 37(3): 402-408,
        1976.

4301. Whitehead, P.C. Drug Use among Adolescent Students in Halifax.
       Halifax: Youth Agency, Province of Nova Scotia, 1969.

4302. Whitehead, P.C. The Epidemiology of Drug Use in a Canadian City
       at Two Points in Time: Halifax, 1969-1970. British Journal
       of Addiction, 66: 301-314, 1971.

4303. Whitehead, P.C. The Incidence of Drug Use among Halifax
       Adolescents. British Journal of Addiction, 65: 159-165,
       1970.

4304. Whitehead, P.C. Multidrug Use: Supplementary Perspectives.
       International Journal of the Addictions, 9(2): 185-204,
       1974.

4305. Whitehead, P.C. Research Strategies to Evaluate the Impact of
       Changes in the Legal Drinking Age. In: Minimum-Drinking-
       Age Laws. Ed. H. Wechsler. Lexington, Massachusetts:
       D.C. Heath and Company, 1980, pages 73-91.

4306. Whitehead, P.C. Young Drivers' Involvement in Traffic Accidents
       with Specific Relation to the Abuse of Alcohol and Other
       Drugs. Paper Presented to the Seventh Annual Conference
       of the Canada Safety Council, Vancouver, British Columbia,
       October, 1975.

4307. Whitehead, P.C. and Brook, R. Social and Drug Using Background
       of Drug Users Seeking Help: Some Implications for
       Treatment. International Journal of Addiction, 8: 75-85,
       1973.

4308. Whitehead, P.C., Craig, J., Langford, N., MacArthur, C.
       Stanton, B. and Ferrence, R.G. Collision Behavior of Young
       Drivers: Impact of the Change in the Age of Majority.
       Journal of Studies on Alcohol, 36: 1208-1223, 1975.

4309. Whitehead, P.C. and Ferrence, R.G. Alcohol and Other Drugs
       Related to Young Drivers' Traffic Accident Involvement.
       Journal of Safety Research, 8: 65-72, 1976.

4310. Whitehead, P.C., Smart, R.G. and Laforest, L. Multiple Drug Use
       among Marijuana Smokers in Eastern Canada. International
       Journal of the Addictions, 7: 179-190, 1972.

4311. Whitehead, Paul, Craig, John, Langford, Nanci, MacArthur, Carol
       and Stanton, Bruce. The Impact of the Change in the
       Drinking Age on the Collision Behavior of Young Drivers.
       In: Alcohol, Drugs and Traffic Safety. Proceedings of the
       Sixth International Conference on Alcohol, Drugs and
       Traffic Safety, Toronto, September 8-13, 1974. Eds.
       S. Israelstam and S. lambert. Toronto: Addiction Research
       Foundation of Ontario, 1975, pages 771-774.

4312.   Whitehead, Paul and Smart, Reginald. Epidemiological Aspects of
        Drug Use and Implications for the Prevention of Drug Abuse.
        In: Deviant Behavior and Social Reaction. Eds.
        C.L. Boydell, C.F. Grindstaff and P.C. Whitehead. Toronto,
        Ontario: Holt, Rinehart and Winston, 1972, pages 369-375.

4313.   Whitehead, Paul and Smart, Reginald. Validity and Reliability
        of Self-Reported Drug Use. Paper Presented at the First
        International Conference on Student Drug Surveys, Newark,
        New Jersey, September, 1971. (Also in: Deviant Behavior
        and Social Reaction. Eds. C.L. Boydell, C.F. Grindstaff
        and P.C. Whitehead. Toronto, Ontario: Holt, Rinehart and
        Winston, 1972, pages 354-359. Also in: Canadian Journal of
        Criminology and Corrections, 14(1): 83-89, 1972.

4314.   Whitehead, Paul C. Alcohol Control Policy: The Canadian
        Perspective. British Journal on Alcohol and Alcoholism,
        13(4): 190-197, 1978.

4315.   Whitehead, Paul C. Effects of Changing Alcohol Control Measures.
        Revised version of a paper presented to the International
        Session of the North American Congress on Alcohol and Drug
        Problems, San Francisco, December, 1974. (Also as: Effects
        of Changing Alcohol Control Measures. (Substudy No. 649).
        Toronto, Ontario: Addiction Research Foundation, 1975.
        Also in: Alcoholism Digest Annual, 3: 16-19, 1974-1975).

4316.   Whitehead, Paul C. Effects of Liberalizing Alcohol Control
        Measures. Addictive Behaviors, 1(3): 197-202, 1976.

4317.   Whitehead, Paul C. The Epidemiology of a Specific Alcohol-
        Related Problem: Case Studies in Analytic Epidemiology.
        In: Epidemiology of Drug-Related Problems in Canada, 1975.
        (Workshop Proceedings.) Ottawa, Ontario: Health and
        Welfare, 1976, pages 69-87.

4318.   Whitehead, Paul C. The Prevention of Alcoholism: Divergences
        and Convergences of Two Approaches. Addictive Diseases,
        1(4): 431-443, 1975.

4319.   Whitehead, Paul C. and Aharan, Charles H. Drug-Using Attitudes:
        Their Distributions and Implications for Prevention.
        Canadian Journal of Public Health, 65: 301-304, 1974.

4320.   Whitehead, Paul C. and Cabral, Robert M. Scaling the Sequence
        of Drug Using Behaviour: A Test of the Stepping Stone
        Hypothesis. Presented at the National Academy of Science
        National Research Council Committee on Problems of Drug
        Dependence, Mexico City, March, 1974. Drug Forum, 8(2), no
        pages, 1974.

4321.   Whitehead, Paul C. and Ferrence, Roberta G. Women and Children
        Last: Implications of General Trends in the Consumption of
        Alcoholic Beverages on Alcohol-Related Problems among Women
        and Young People. (Substudy No. 773) Toronto, Ontario:
        Addiction Research Foundation, 1976. (Also in: Alcoholism
        Problems in Women and Children. Eds. M. Greenblatt and
        M. Schuckit. New York: Grune and Stratton, 1976, pages
        163-194.)

4322.   Whitehead, Paul C., Grindstaff, Carl F. and Boydell, Craig L.,
        Eds. Alcohol and Other Drugs: Perspectives on Use, Abuse,
        Treatment and Prevention. Toronto, Ontario: Holt,
        Rinehart and Winston, 1973.

4323.   Whitfield, C.L. Children of Alcoholics: Treatment Issues.
        Maryland State Medical Journal, 29(6): 86-91, 1980. (Also
        in: Services for Children of Alcoholics. Symposium held
        on September 24-26, 1979 at Silver Spring, Maryland. U.S.
        National Institute on Alcohol Abuse and Alcoholism.
        [Research Monograph No. 4] Washington, D.C.: U.S.
        Government Printing Office, 1981, pages 66-80. [DHHS
        Publication No. ADM 81-1007])

4324.   Whitlock, F.A., Armstrong, J.L., Tonge, J.I., O'Reilly, M.J.,
        Davison, A., Johnston, N.G. and Biltoft, R.P. The Drinking
        Driver or the Driving Drinker? Alcohol, Alcoholism and
        Other Factors in Road Accidents. Medical Journal of
        Australia, 2(1): 5-16, 1971.

4325.   Whitlow, C.M. The Prevalence of Smoking and Drinking among High
        School Pupils. School and Society, 36: 177-178, 1932.

4326.   Whitman, H. What Are We For? Bismarck, North Dakota:
        Commission on Alcoholism, no date.

4327.   Whitney, E.D., Ed. A World Dialogue on Alcohol and Drug
        Dependence. Boston, Massachusetts: Beacon Press, 1970.

4328.   Whittaker, James O. Alcohol Use and the American Indian--Some
        Sociocultural Lessons about the Naure of Alcoholism.
        British Journal on Alcohol and Alcoholism, 14(3): 140-147,
        1979.

4329.   Who Will Help Teenage Alcohol Abusers? Patient Care: 88-103,
        September 15, 1975.

4330.   Widseth, J.C. Reported Dependent Behaviors toward Mother and Use
        of Alcohol in Delinquent Girls. Doctoral Dissertation
        (University Microfilms No. 72-25,354). Boston University
        Graduate School, 1972.

4331.   Widseth, J.C. and Mayer, J. Drinking Behavior and Attitudes
        toward Alcohol in Delinquent Girls. International Journal
        of Addictions, 6: 453-461, 1971.

4332.   Wieder, Herbert and Kaplan, Eugene H.   Drug Use in Adolescents:
        Psychodynamic Meaning and Pharmacogenic Effects.   In: The
        Psychology of Adolescence.   Ed. Aaron H. Esman.   New York:
        International Universities Press, Inc., 1975, pages 348-374.

4333.   Wiener, R.S.P.   Drugs and Schoolchildren.   London: Longman
        Group, Ltd., 1970.

4334.   Wieser, S.   Das Trinkverhalten der Deutschen: Eine Medizin-
        Soziologische Untersuchung.   (The Drinking Behavior of
        Germans: A Medicosociological Study.)   Herford: Nikolai,
        1973.

4335.   Wightman, W.-C.-M.   Preparation for Temerance Teaching of
        Leaders of Bands of Hope Juvenile Lodges.   International
        Congress against Alcoholism, 16: 372-386, 1922.

4336.   Wilbur, Richard S.   The Battle against Drug Dependency within
        the Military.   Journal of Drug Issues, 4: 11-31, 1974.

4337.   Wilkerson, D.   Fast Track to Nowhere.   Old Tappan, New Jersey:
        Spire Books, 1979.

4338.   Wilkerson, D.   Sipping Saints.   Old Tappan, New Jersey: Revell,
        1978.

4339.   Wilkerson, D. and Wilkerson, D.   The Untapped Generation.   Grand
        Rapids, Michigan: Zondervan, 1971.

4340.   Wilkinson, P., Kornaczewski, A., Rankin, J.G. and
        Santamaria, J.N.   Physical Disease in Alcoholism: Initial
        Survey of 1,000 Patients.   Medical Journal of Australia,
        1(23): 1217-1223, 1971.

4341.   Wilkinson, P., Santamaria, J.N., Rankin, J.G. and Martin, D.
        Epidemiology of Alcoholism: Social Data and Drinking
        Patterns of a Sample of Australian Alcoholics.   Medical
        Journal of Australia, 1(20): 1020-1025, 1969.

4342.   Wilkinson, R.   The Prevention of Drinking Problems: Alcohol
        Control and Cultural Influences.   New York: Oxford
        University Presss, 1970.

4343.   Williams, A.F.   College Problem Drinkers: A Personality Profile.
        In: The Domesticated Drug: Drinking among Collegians.
        Ed. G.L. Maddox.   New Haven, Connecticut: College and
        University Press, 1970, pages 343-360.

4344.   Williams, A.F.   Psychological Needs and Social Drinking of
        College Students.   Boston: Massachusetts Department of
        Public Health, no date.   (Also in: Quarterly Journal of
        Studies on Alcohol, 29: 355-363, 1968.

4345. Williams, A.F. Self-Concepts of College Problem Drinkers: I.
       A Comparison with Alcoholics. Quarterly Journal of Studies
       on Alcohol, 26: 586-594, 1965.

4346. Williams, A.F. Self-Concepts of College Problem Drinkers: II.
       Heilbrun Need Scales. Quarterly Journal of Studies on
       Alcohol, 28(2): 267-276, 1976.

4347. Williams, A.F. Social Drinking, Anxiety, and Depression.
       Journal of Personality and Social Psychology, 3: 689-693,
       1966.

4348. Williams, A.F. Validation of a College Problem-Drinking Scale.
       Journal of Projective Techniques, 31: 33-40, 1967.

4349. Williams, A.F., Rich, R.F., Zador, P.L. and Robertson, L.S. The
       Legal Minimum Drinking Age and Fatal Motor Vehicle Crashes.
       Journal of Legal Studies, 4: 219-239, 1975.

4350. Williams, Allan. The Alcoholic Personality. In: The Biology
       of Alcoholism. Volume 4. Social Aspects of Alcoholism.
       Eds. B. Kissin and H. Begleiter. New York: Plenum Press,
       1976, pages 243-275.

4351. Williams, Allan F., DiCicco, Lena M. and Unterberger, Hilma.
       Philosophy and Evaluation of an Alcohol Education Program.
       Quarterly Journal of Studies on Alcohol, 29(3): 685-702,
       1968.

4352. Williams, Allan F., McCourt, William F. and Schneider, Lawrence.
       Personality Self-Descriptions of Alcoholics and Heavy
       Drinkers. Quarterly Journal of Studies on Alcohol, 32:
       310-317, 1971.

4353. Williams, A.T., Burns, F.H. and Morey, S. Prevalence of
       Alcoholism in a Sydney Teaching Hospital: Some Aspects.
       Medical Journal of Australia, 2(14): 608-611, 1978.

4354. Williams, C. Should the Young be Educated in the Use and Abuse
       of Alcohol? British Journal of Addiction, 56: 49-52, 1960.

4355. Williams, C.O. The Value of Temperance Education in the Schools.
       Scientific Temperance Journal, 38: 70-87, 1929.

4356. Williams, E.Y. The Anxiety Syndrome in Alcoholism. Psychiatric
       Quarterly, 24: 782-787, 1950.

4357. Williams, G. Prys. Off Licenses in Supermarkets Open a New Door
       to Liquor for Many. Journal of Alcoholism, 10(3): 122-131,
       1975.

4358.   Williams, John M.   The Relationship between Assertiveness,
          Conformity and Drug Use.   Journal of Drug Education, 11(1):
          47-51, 1981.

4359.   Williams, K.H.   Intervention with Children of Alcoholics.   In:
          Services for Children of Alcoholics.   Symposium held on
          September 24-26, 1979 at Silver Spring, Maryland.   U.S.
          National Institute on Alcohol Abuse and Alcoholism.
          Research Monograph No. 4.   Washington, D.C.:   U.S.
          Government Printing Office, 1981, pages 60-65.   (DHHS
          Publication No. ADM 81-1007)

4360.   Williams, R.J.   Alcoholism Prevention and Reality.   Comment on
          the Article by M.E. Chafetz.   Quarterly Journal of Studies
          on Alcohol, 28: 350, 1967.

4361.   Williams, T.A.   How Inebriety Might be Prevented by Early
          Education.   Pedagogical Seminary, 16: 195-204, 1909.

4362.   Willis, A.   Our Greatest Enemy: Beverage Alcohol.   New York:
          Exposition, 1958.

4363.   Willson, John Paul.   The Nature and Extent of Drug Use among
          Students at a Comprehensive Suburban High School.   Journal
          of Drug Education, 9(1): 11-20, 1979.

4364.   Wilsnack, Richard W. and Wilsnack, Sharon C.   Drinking and Denial
          of Social Obligations among Adolescent Boys.   Journal of
          Studies on Alcohol, 41(11): 1118-1133, 1980.

4365.   Wilsnack, Richard W. and Wilsnack, Sharon C.   Sex Roles and
          Drinking among Adolescent Girls.   Journal of Studies on
          Alcohol, 39(11): 1855-1874, 1978.   (Also in: Youth,
          Alcohol and Social Policy.   Eds. H.T. Blane and
          M.E. Chafetz.   New York: Plenum Press, 1979, pages 183-
          227.)

4366.   Wilsnack, Sharon.   The Impact of Sex Roles on Women's Alcohol Use
          and Abuse.   In: Alcoholism Problems in Women and Children.
          Eds. M. Greenblatt and M. Schuckit.   New York: Grune and
          Stratton, 1976, pages 37-63.

4367.   Wilson, C.   The Family.   In: Camberwell Council on Alcoholism:
          Women and Alcohol.   New York: Tavistock Publications, 1980,
          pages 101-132.

4368.   Wilson, C., Ed.   The Pharmacological and Epidemiological Aspects
          of Adolescent Drug Dependence.   Oxford, England: Pergamon
          Press, 1968.

4369.   Wilson, C.W.M.   Drug Dependence or Drug Abuse.   In: The
          Pharmacological and Epidemiological Aspects of Adolescent
          Drug Dependence.   Ed. C. Wilson.   Oxford, England:
          Pergamon Press, 1968, pages 141-158.

4370.   Wilson, Clare and Orford, Jim. Children of Alcoholics. Report
        of a Preliminary Study and Comments on the Literature.
        Journal of Studies on Alcohol, 39(1): 121-142, 1978. (Also
        in: International Journal of Rehabilitation Research, 3(1):
        94-96, 1980).

4371.   Wilson, M.S. Do College Girls Conform to the Standards of Their
        Parents? Marriage and Family, 15: 207-208, 1953.

4372.   Wilson, R.A. and Smith, B.B. Putting Drug Education in Its
        Place: Toward a Realistic Policy. In: Communication
        Research and Drug Education. Ed. R.E. Ostman. Beverly
        Hills, California: Sage Publications, 1976, pages 301-316.

4373.   Wilson, R.A. and Smith, B.B. Taking the Guesswork Out of Drug
        Education: Utilizing a Drug Survey in the Development of a
        High-Risk Profile and Target Programs. Journal of Drug
        Issues, 4: 29-41, 1973.

4374.   Wilson, R.W., Wingender, M.K., Redican, K.J. and Hettler, W.
        Effects of the Health Hazard Appraisal Inventory on
        Practices of College Students. Health Education, 11: 28-30,
        1980.

4375.   Wilson, S. Should You Offer Teenagers Drinks in Your Home?
        Leaflet. Harrisburg: Pennsylvania Council on Alcohol
        Problems, no date. (Also in: Reader's Digest, no pages,
        December, 1964.)

4376.   Wilson, W.J. Say When. New York: Paulist Press, 1978.

4377.   Wiltse, F.L., Sr. Exploring Alcohol and Alcoholism:
        Instructor's Manual and Student Workbook. Sycamore,
        Illinois: Kishwaukee Publishing Company, 1978.

4378.   Winburn, G.M. and Hays, J.R. Dropouts: A Study of Drug Use.
        Journal of Drug Education, 4(2): 249-254, 1974.

4379.   Windham, G.O. Community Attitudes toward Alcohol Education. In:
        Proceedings of the Fourth Southeastern School of Alcohol
        Studies. Athens, Georgia: University of Georgia Center for
        Continuing Education, 1964.

4380.   Windham, Gerald, Preston, James and Armstrong, Harold. The High
        School Student in Mississippi and Beverage Alcohol. Journal
        of Alcohol Education, 13(1): 1-12, 1967.

4381.   Windsor, R.A. Mood Modifying Substance Usage among 4-H and non-
        4-H Youth in Illinois. Journal of Drug Education, 3(3):
        261-273, 1973.

4382.   Windsor, R.A.   Relationships between Mood Modifying Substance
         Usage, Attitude and Alienation among 4-H and non-4-H Youth.
         Doctoral Dissertation (University Microfilms No. 73-17,669).
         University of Illinois at Urbana-Champaign, 1973.

4383.   Winfree, L. Thomas, Beasley, Richard and Cary, Karl R.   The
         Initiation and Avoidance of Drugs by Adolescents in the
         Southwest.   Journal of Drug Education, 11(4): 327-340, 1981.

4384.   Winfree, L. Thomas, Jr., Theis, Harold E. and Griffiths, Curt T.
         Drug Use in Rural America: A Cross-Cultural Examination of
         Complementary Social Deviance Theories.   Youth and Society,
         12(4): 465-489, 1981.

4385.   Wingard, J.A., Huba, G.J. and Bentler, P.M.   A Longitudinal
         Analysis of Personality Structure and Adolescent Substance
         Use.   Personality and Individual Differences, 1: 259-272,
         1980.

4386.   Winick, Charles.   A Sociological Theory of the Genesis of Drug
         Dependence.   In: Sociological Aspects of Drug Dependence.
         Ed. Charles Winick.   Cleveland, Ohio: CRC Press, Inc.,
         1974, especially pages 3-13.

4387.   Winn, Mitchell.   The Drug Alternative.   Washington: American
         Alliance for Health, Physical Education and Recreation,
         1974.

4388.   Winokur, G.   Alcoholism in Adoptees Raised Apart from Biologic
         Alcoholic Parents.   In: Alcoholism Problems in Women and
         Children.   Eds. M. Greenblatt and M. Schuckit.   New York:
         Grune and Stratton, 1976, pages 239-249.

4389.   Winokur, G., Cadoret, R., Baker, M. and Dorzab, J.   Depression
         Spectrum Disease Versus Pure Depressive Disease: Some
         Further Data.   British Journal of Psychiatry, 127: 75-77,
         1975.

4390.   Winokur, G., Rimmer, J. and Reich, T.   Alcoholism.   IV. Is There
         More than One Type of Alcoholism?   British Journal of
         Psychiatry, 118(546): 525-531, 1971.

4391.   Winokur, George and Clayton, Paula.   Family History Studies.
         II. Sex Differences and Alcoholism in Primary Affective
         Illness.   The British Journal of Psychiatry, 113(500): 973-
         979, 1967.

4392.   Winston Products for Education.   Authoritative Instructional Aids
         on Alcohol, Drugs, and Narcotics: Ecology and Environment;
         Tobacco and Smoking; Venereal Disease.   San Diego:
         California: Authoritative Instructional Aids, 1971.

4393.   Winston, S. and Butler, M.   Negro Bootleggers in Eastern North
         Carolina.   American Sociological Review, 8: 692-697, 1943.

4394.   Winter, D.G.   The Need for Power in College Men: Action
        Correlates and Relationship to Drinking.   In: The Drinking
        Man.   Eds. D.C. McClelland, W.N. Davis, R. Kalin and
        E. Wanner.   New York: The Free Press, 1972, pages 99-119.

4395.   Winter, E.   Früherkennung und Prophylaxe von Medikamenten- und
        Alkoholmissbrauch.   (Early Detection and Prevention of Drug
        and Alcohol Misuse.)   Zeitschrift fur Äertzliche
        Fortbilking, Jena, 74: 132-134, 1980.

4396.   Winters, A.   Alternatives for the Problem Drinker: A.A. Is Not
        the Only Way.   New York: Drake, 1978.

4397.   Winters, A.   Drinkwatchers.   Haverstraw, New York: Gullistan,
        1977.

4398.   Wisconsin Department of Health and Social Services, Bureau of
        Alcohol and Other Drug Abuse.   Youth, Alcohol and the Law:
        Final Report: Wisconsin, 1933-1978.   Madison, Wisconsin:
        Bureau of Alcohol and Other Drug Abuse, 1978.

4399.   Wisconsin Legislative Council.   Staff Memorandum to the Youthful
        Drinking and Driving Committee.   Madison, Wisconsin, 1962.

4400.   Wisconsin University.   Attitudes of High School Students toward
        Beverage Alcohol.   New York: The Mrs. John S. Sheppard
        Foundation, 1956.

4401.   Wiseman, Jacqueline.   Sober Comportment: Patterns and
        Perspectives on Alcohol Addiction.   Journal of Studies on
        Alcohol, 42(1): 106-126, 1981.

4402.   Witt, S.   Untersuchungen über den Alkoholkonsum von Kindern und
        Jugendlichen.   (Studies on the Alcohol Consumption of
        Children and Adolescents.)   Nachrictenblatt der Deutscher
        Vereinigung fuer Fursorge, 55: 185-187, 1975.

4403.   Wittenborn, J.R., Smith, Jean Paul and Wittenborn, Sarah A., Eds.
        Communication and Drug Abuse: Proceedings of the Second
        Rutgers Symposium on Drug Abuse.   Springfield, Illinois:
        Charles C. Thomas, 1970.

4404.   Wittenborn, John R., Brill, Henry, Smith, Jean Paul and
        Wittenborn, Sarah, Eds.   Drugs and Youth.   Proceedings of
        the Rutgers Symposium on Drug Abuse.   Springfield, Illinois:
        Charles C. Thomas, 1969.

4405.   Woititz, J.G.   The Education Aspect of Servicing the Children of
        Alcoholics.   In: Services for Children of Alcoholics.
        Symposium held on September 24-26, 1979 at Silver Spring,
        Maryland.   U.S. National Institute on Alcohol Abuse and
        Alcoholism.   Research Monograph No. 4.   Washington, D.C.:
        U.S. Government Printing Office, 1981, pages 186-191.   (DHHS
        Publication No. ADM 81-1007)

4406. Woititz, J.G. A Study of Self-Esteem in Children of Alcoholics.
         Doctoral Dissertation (University Microfilms No. 77-13,299).
         New Brunswick, New Jersey: Rutgers University, 1976.

4407. Woititz, Janet G. Alcoholism and the Family: A Survey of the
         Literature. Journal of Alcohol and Drug Education, 23(2):
         18-23, 1978.

4408. Woititz, Janet Geringer. Adult Children of Alcoholics: A
         Treatment Issue. Focus on Alcohol and Drug Issues, 6(4):
         10-11, 1981.

4409. Wolf, A.S. Homicide and Blackout in Alaskan Natives: A Report
         and Reproduction of Five Cases. Journal of Studies on
         Alcohol, 41(5): 456-462, 1980.

4410. Wolf, Barry M. The Struggling Adolescent: A Social
         Phenomenological Study of Adolescent Substance Abuse.
         Journal of Alcohol and Drug Education, 26(3): 51-61, 1981.

4411. Wolf, I. Emotions and Teen-Age Drinking. Bulletin of the
         Association for the Advancement of Instruction about Alcohol
         and Narcotics, 6: 3-11, 1960.

4412. Wolf, Irving. Youth and Alcohol. In: Interpreting Current
         Knowledge about Alcohol and Alcoholism to a College
         Community. Proceedings of Conference, May 28-30, 1963,
         Albany, New York. Ed. Richard Reynolds. Albany: New York
         State Department of Mental Health, 1963, pages 21-31.

4413. Wolfe, A.C. and Chapman, M.M. High School Student Drinking and
         Driving Behavior. Hit Lab Reports (Highway Safety Research
         Institute, University of Michigan), 4(4): 6-13, 1973.

4414. Wolfe, A.C. and Chapman, M.M. 1970-71 Washtenaw County High
         School Survey on Drinking and Driving. Ann Arbor, Michigan:
         University of Michigan, Highway Safety Research Institute,
         1972.

4415. Wolfe, A.C. and Chapman, M.M. Washtenaw County High School
         Students: 1971 and 1973 ASAP Surveys. Final Report.
         (Report No. UM-HSRI-AL-73-12; DOT Publication No. HS-801-
         047) Ann Arbor, Michigan: University of Michigan, Highway
         Safety Research Institute, 1973.

4416. Wolfe, Arthur C. Characteristics of Late-Night and Weekend
         Drivers: Results of the U.S. National Roadside Breath-
         Testing Survey and Several Local Surveys. In: Alcohol,
         Drugs and Traffic Safety. Proceedings of the Sixth
         International Conference on Alcohol, Drugs and Traffic
         Safety, Toronto, September 8-13, 1974. Eds. S. Israelstam
         and S. Lambert. Toronto, Ontario: Addiction Research
         Foundation, 1975, pages 41-49.

4417.   Wolfe, Arthur C. and Chapman, Marion M. An Analysis of Drinking
        and Driving Survey Data. HIT Lab Reports, 4(4): 1-5, 1973.

4418.   Wolff, P.O. Conceptos Modernos Sobre la Lucha Contra el
        Alcoholismo. (Modern Concepts on the Fight against
        Alcoholism.) Boletin del Instituto Internacional Americano
        de Proteccion a la Infancia, 22(4): 1-16, 1948.

4419.   Wolfgang, Marvin. Violence in the Family. In: Violence. Eds.
        I.L. Kutash, S.B. Kutash and L.B. Schlesinger. San
        Francisco: Jossey Bass, 1978, pages 238-253.

4420.   Wolin, S.J., Bennett, L.A., Noonan, D.L. and Teitelbaum, M.A.
        Disrupted Family Rituals: A Factor in the Intergenerational
        Transmission of Alcoholism. Journal of Studies on Alcohol,
        41: 199-214, 1980.

4421.   Wolin, Steven J., Bennett, Linda A., Noonan, Denise L. and
        Teitebaum, Martha A. Family Rituals and the Transmission of
        Alcoholism. Digest of Alcoholism Theory and Application,
        1(1): 7-17, 1981.

4422.   Wolkon, G.H., Jasso, N.K., Gallagher, S. and Cohn, P. The "Hang-
        Loose" Ethic and Drug Use Revisited. (Research Note)
        International Journal of the Addictions, 9(6): 909-918,
        1974.

4423.   Wolter, H.J. and Fuhrmann, B. Alkohol-Bedingte Delinquenz
        Jugendlicher und Heranwachsender in Hamburg. (Alcohol-
        Linked Delinquency among Adolescents and Young Adults in
        Hamburg.) Kriminalist, Duesseldorf, 10/12: 528-532, 1978.

4424.   Women Alcoholics: What Can Be Done to Help Them. Good
        Housekeeping, 170: 157-159, 1970.

4425.   Wood, Abigail. My Parents Drink Too Much. Seventeen, 30(4):
        168-170, 1971.

4426.   Wood, Howard P. and Duffy, Edward L. Psychological Factors in
        Alcoholic Women. American Journal of Psychiatry, 123: 341-
        345, 1966.

4427.   Woodhead, G.S. Alcohol and the Undergraduate. British Journal
        of Inebriety, 10: 194-196, 1913.

4428.   Woodside, A.G., Bearden, W.O. and Ronkainen, I. Images on
        Serving Marijuana, Alcoholic Beverages and Soft Drinks.
        Journal of Psychology, 96: 11-14, 1977.

4429.   Woodside, M. Women Drinkers Admitted to Holloway Prison During
        February 1960: A Pilot Survey. British Journal of
        Criminology, 1: 221-235, 1961.

4430.   Worden, Mark. Popular and Unpopular Prevention. Journal of
            Drug Issues, 9(3): 425-433, 1979.

4431.   Works, D.A. Statement on 18 Year Old Drinking. Journal of
            Alcohol Education, 18(3): 14-15, 1973.

4432.   Workshop on Alcohol Education, May 25-27, 1959. Minneapolis:
            University of Minnesota, Center of Continuation Study of
            the General Extension Division, 1959. (Not for General
            Distribution.)

4433.   World Health Organization. Problems Related to Alcohol
            Consumption: The Changing Situation. Geneva, Switzerland,
            1980. (WHO Technical Report Series No. 650)

4434.   World Health Organization. Youths and Drugs: Report of a WHO
            Study Group. Geneva, Switzerland, 1973. (WHO Technical
            Report Series No. 516)

4435.   World Health Organization. Regional Office for Europe. The
            Child and the Adolescent in Society. Report on a WHO
            Conference, Athens, September 26-30, 1978. Copenhagen:
            Regional Office for Europe. World Health Organization,
            1979.

4436.   Worthley,Mary G. Handbook on Alcohol. For College and High
            School Students. Rochester, New Hampshire: Record Press,
            1955.

4437.   Wortis, Herman and Sillman, Leonard R. Studies of Compulsive
            Drinkers. Part 1. Case Histories. Eds. J.F. Cushman and
            C. Landis. New Haven, Connecticut: Hillhouse Press, 1946.

4438.   Wrenn, C.G. and Schwarzrock, S. Facts and Fantasies about
            Alcohol. Circle Pines, Minnesota: American Guidance
            Service, 1971.

4439.   Wright, H.B. A Better High. Springfield, Illinois: Research
            and Education on Alcohol and Drugs, 1978.

4440.   Wright, Joseph S. The Psychology and Personality of Addicts.
            Adolescence, 12(47): 399-403, 1977.

4441.   Wurmser, L. Psychoanalytic Considerations of the Etiology of
            Compulsive Drug Use. Journal of the American Psychoanalytic
            Association, 22(4): 820-843, 1974.

4442.   Wyatt, P.D. Alcohol Education: An Exploratory Study of Teacher
            Opinions and Drinking Practices. Doctoral Dissertation
            (Univesity Microfilms No. 73-12,905). University of the
            Pacific, 1972.

Y

4443. Yablonsky, Lewis. The Violent Gang. Baltimore, Maryland: Penguin Books, 1970.

4444. Yankelovich, Skelly and White, Inc. Drugs and Youth. Pamphlet. Washington, D.C.: Drug Abuse Council, Inc., 1976.

4445. Yankelovich, Skelly and White, Inc. Students and Drugs. Vol. I. Executive Summary. Vol. II. Detailed Findings. New York: Yankelovich, Skelly and White, 1975.

4446. Yoakum, Charles. Many States Reconsidering Lowered Drinking Age Laws. Traffic Safety, 79(7): 17, 1979.

4447. Yolles, Stanley F. Forward. In: Mind Drugs. Ed. M. Hyde. New York: McGraw-Hill, 1968, pages 5-7.

4448. Yorke, E. Help in the Anti-Alcohol Struggle by Means of Home and School Educations. International Congress against Alcoholism, 10: 136-137, 1906

4449. Youcha, G.A. A Dangerous Pleasure. New York: Hawthorn Books, 1978.

4450. Young Alcoholics. Medical Journal of Australia, 1: 1251, 1969.

4451. Young Drinkers. Lancet, 1: 142, 1973.

4452. The Young Drinkers: Teenagers and Alcohol. Pamphlet. Hollywood, Florida: Health Communications, 1978.

4453. Young, G.W. The Perceptual Accuracy of Certain Student Personnel Administrators when Estimating the Drinking Behavior of College Men at a Selected University. Doctoral Dissertation (University Microfilms No. 67-00320). Tallahasee: Florida State University, 1966.

4454.   Young, H.T.P.   Parental Alcoholism as a Factor in Adolescent
        Crime. British Journal of Inebriety, 35: 93-113, 1938.

4455.   Young, Leontine. Wednesday's Children. New York: McGraw-Hill,
        1964.

4456.   Young People and Alcohol. Drinking Practices, Drinking Problems,
        Initiatives in Prevention and Treatment. Alcohol Health
        and Research World, 2-10, Summer, 1975.

4457.   Young People in Licensed Premises. Justice of the Peace, 108:
        39, 1944.

4458.   Ungdom Alkohol. (Youth and Alcohol.) Stockholm: Svenska
        Utbildningsförlaget, 1972.

4459.   Youth and Alcohol. (Swedish Text.) Tirfing, 40: 27-31, 1946.

4460.   Youth Discussion. ASAP Newsletter, 2(1): 3, 1973.

4461.   Youth Drinking on the Rise. Montgomery County Sentinel,
        (Supplement): 3, 4, April 1, 1976.

4462.   Youth Market Boosts Pop Wine Sales. Report on Alcohol, 34(3):
        20-27, 1976.

4463.   Youth See Drinking as a Symbol of Adulthood. Journal of Alcohol
        and Drug Abuse, 22(1): 22, 1976.

Z

4464. Záčková, Z. Alkohol a Kriminalita Mládeže. (Alcohol and Criminality of Young People.) Protialkoholicky Obzor, Bratislava, 5: 40-42, 1970.

4465. Zaczkiewicz, H. Alkoholizm Wśród Dzieci w Wieku Szkolnym. (Alcoholism among School-Aged Children.) Problemy Alkoholizmu, Warsaw, 22(12): 11-14, 1974.

4466. Zakrzewski, P. Młodociani Alkoholicy. (Adolescent Alcoholics.) Problemy Alkoholizmu, Warsaw, 26(2): 9-10, 16, 1979.

4467. Zakrzewski, P. Młodociani Pacjenci Izby Wyrtzeźweiń. Cz. 1. Analiza Socjologiczna. (Adolescent Patients at Sobering-Up Stations. Part 1. Sociological Analysis.) Problemy Alkoholizmu, Warsaw, 25(2): 7-8, 22, 1978.

4468. Zakrzewski, P. Zawarcie Małżeństwa Przez Młodych Alkoholików. (The End of Marriages of Young Alcoholics.) Problemy Alkoholizmu, Warsaw, 22(10): 4-7, 1974.

4469. Zanini, Antonio Carlos, Moraes, Ester de Camargo Fonseca, Akerman, Bernardo, Aizenstein, Moacyr and Salgado, Paulo Eduardo de Toledo. Concept and Use of Psychoactive Drugs among University Students in the San Paulo Area. Drug Forum, 6(2): 85-99, 1977.

4470. Zaporozhchenko, V.G. Na Povestke Dnia--Profilaktika Alkogolizma u Detei i Podrostkov. (Agenda--Prevention of Alcoholism in Children and Adolescents.) Zdravookhranenie Rossiiskoi Federatsii, Moscow, 12: 38-39, 1978.

4471. Zappela, D.G. Recent Concepts Regarding Alcohol and Alcohol Education. The Journal of School Health, 27: 303-310, 1957.

4472. Zax, M., Gardner, E.A. and Hart, W.T. A Survey of the Prevalence of Alcoholism in Monroe County, New York, 1961. Quarterly Journal of Studies on Alcohol, 28: 316-327, 1967.

4473.   Zax, M., Cowen, E.L., Budin, W. and Biggs, C.F.   The Social
        Desirability of Trait Descriptive Terms: Applications to
        an Alcoholic Sample.   Journal of Social Psychology, 56: 21-
        27, 1962.

4474.   Zelhart, Paul, Shurr, Bryce and Brown, Peggy.   The Drinking
        Driver: Identification of High Risk Alcoholics.   In:
        Alcohol, Drugs and Traffic Safety.   Proceedings of the
        Sixth International Conference on Alcohol, Drugs and Traffic
        Safety, Toronto, September 8-13, 1974.   Eds. S. Israelstam
        and S. Lambert.   Toronto, Ontario: Addiction Research
        Foundation, 1975, pages 181-189.

4475.   Ziegler-Driscoll, G.   Family Treatment with Parent Addict
        Families.   In: A Multicultural View of Drug Abuse:
        Proceedings of the National Drug Abuse Conference, 1977.
        Eds. D.E. Smith, S.M. Anderson, M. Buxton, N. Gottlieb,
        W. Harvey and T. Chung.   Cambridge, Massachusetts:
        Schenkman, 1978, pages 389-396.

4476.   Ziegler-Driscoll, G.   The Similarities in Families of Drug
        Dependents and Alcoholics.   In: Family Therapy of Drug
        and Alcohol Abuse.   Eds. E. Kaufman and P. Kaufman.   New
        York: Gardner, 1979, pages 19-39.

4477.   Zielinski, J.   The Anti-Alcohol Campaign in Poland.   Quarterly
        Journal of Studies on Alcohol, 30(1): 173-177, 1969.

4478.   Zimberg, S.   Alcoholism: Prevalence in General Hospital
        Emergency Room and Walk-In Clinic.   New York State Journal
        of Medicine, 79(10): 1533-1536, 1979.

4479.   Zimberg, S.   New York State Task Force on Alcohol Problems.
        Position Paper on Treatment.   New York State Journal of
        Medicine, 75(10): 1794-1798, 1975.

4480.   Zimberg, S., Wallace, J. and Blume, S.B., Eds.   Practical
        Approaches to Alcoholism Psychotherapy.   New York: Plenum,
        1978.

4481.   Zimering, Stanley and McCreery, Marianne.   The Alcoholic Teacher:
        A Growing Concern of the Next Decade.   Journal of Drug
        Education, 8(3): 253-260, 1978.

4482.   Zinberg, N.E.   Teen-Age Alcoholism and Drug Abuse.   New England
        Journal of Medicine, 294: 56, 1976.

4483.   Zinberg, Norman.   The Social Setting as a Control Mechanism in
        Intoxicant Use.   In: Theories on Drug Abuse: Selected
        Contemporary Problems.   (Research Monograph Series 30) U.S.
        National Institute on Drug Abuse.   Eds. Dan Lettieri,
        Mollie Sayers and Helen Pearson.   Rockville, Maryland, 1980,
        pages 236-244.   (DHEW Publication No. ADM 80-967)

4484. Zinberg, Norman and Harding, Wayne. Control and Intoxicant Use:
       A Theoretical Practical Overview. Journal of Drug Issues,
       9(2): 121-143, 1979.

4485. Zinberg, Norman E., Harding, Wayne M. and Apsler, Robert. What
       Is Drug Abuse? Journal of Drug Issues, 8: 9-36, 1978.

4486. Ziomkowski, Laurence, Mulder, Rodney and Williams, Donald. Drug
       Use Variations between Delinquent and Nondelinquent Youth.
       Intellect, 104(2367): 36-38, 1975.

4487. Zmrhal. Temperance Instruction in European Schools.
       International Congress against Alcoholism, 15: 296-298,
       1921.

4488. Zourbas, J., Senecal, J. and Touffet, R. L'alcoolisation des
       Jeunes et l'Information à l'École. (Intoxication among
       Youth and Alcohol Education in the Schools.) Revue de
       l'Alcoolisme, 25: 121-136, 1979.

4489. Zourbas, J., Touffet, R., Lhuissier, P., Kerbellec, P. and
       Delaporte, L. Nalyse Épidémiologique de Trois Enquêtes sur
       l'Alcoolisation des Jeunes. (Epidemiological Analysis of
       Three Surveys on Alcoholism in Youth.) Ouest Médical,
       France, 31: 1271-1275, 1978.

4490. Zucchi, M. Il Comportamento di Fronte All'Alcool Nell'età dello
       Sviluppo in Alcuni Casi di Alcoolismo ad Inizio
       Relativamente Tardivo. (Behavior with Respect to Alcohol
       during Developmental Years in Several Cases of Alcoholism of
       Relatively Late Beginning.) Neuropsichiatria, Genova, 15:
       635-674, 1960.

4491. Zucker, R.A. Developmental Aspects of Drinking through the
       Young Adult Years. In: Youth, Alcohol and Social Policy.
       Eds. H.T. Blane and M.E. Chafetz. New York: Plenum, 1979.

4492. Zucker, R.A. Heavy Drinking and Affiliative Motivation among
       Adolescents. St. Louis, Missouri: Paper presented at the
       1970 Southwestern Psychological Association Meetings,
       April, 1970.

4493. Zucker, R.A. Implications of Recent Adolescent Drinking Research
       for Programs of Primary Prevention and Education. San
       Francisco, California: Paper presented at the meetings of
       the North American Congress on Alcohol and Drug Problems--
       Prevention Section, December, 1974.

4494. Zucker, R.A. Parental Influences upon Drinking Patterns of Their
       Children. In: Alcoholism Problems in Women and Children.
       Eds. M. Greenblatt and M. Schuckit. New York: Grune and
       Stratton, 1976, pages 211-238.

4495. Zucker, R.A. Problem Drinking in Adolescence. American Family
       Physician, 121: 103-106, 1975.

4496. Zucker, R.A. Sex Role Identity Patterns and Drinking Behavior
       of Adolescents. Quarterly Journal of Studies on Alcohol,
       29: 868-884, 1968.

4497. Zucker, R.A. and Barron, F.H. Parental Behaviors Associated
       with Problem Drinking and Antisocial Behavior among
       Adolescent Males. In: Proceedings of the First Annual
       Alcoholism Conference of the National Institute on Alcohol
       Abuse and Alcoholism. Ed. M. Chafetz. Washington, D.C.:
       U.S. Government Printing Office, 1973, pages 276-296.

4498. Zucker, R.A., Battistich, V.A. and Langer, G.B. Sexual
       Behavior, Sex Role Adaptation and Drinking in Young Women.
       Journal of Studies on Alcohol, 42(5): 457-465, 1981.

4499. Zucker, R.A. and Devoe, C.I. Life History Characteristics
       Associated with Problem Drinking and Antisocial Behavior in
       Adolescent Girls: A Comparison with Male Findings. In:
       Life History Research in Psychopathology. Vol. 4. Eds.
       R.D. Wirt, G. Winokur and M. Roff. Minneapolis: The
       University of Minnesota Press, 1975, pages 109-134.

4500. Zucker, R.A. and Fillmore, K.M. Motivational Factors and
       Problem Drinking among Adolescents. Paper presented at
       28th International Congress on Alcohol and Alcoholism,
       Washington, D.C., September 17, 1968.

4501. Zucker, R.A. and Van Horn, H. Sibling Social Structure and Oral
       Behavior: Drinking and Smoking in Adolescence. Quarterly
       Journal of Studies on Alcohol, 33: 193-197, 1972.

4502. Zuckerman, M., Bone, R., Neary, R., Mangelsdorff, D. and
       Brustman, B. What is the Sensation Seeker? Personality
       Trait and Experience Correlates of the Sensation-Seeking
       Scales. Journal of Consulting and Clinical Psychology,
       39: 308-321, 1972.

4503. Zvolsky, P. Prognóza Léčebného Úspěchu u Alkoholiků v Závislosti
       na Věku. (The Age Factor in the Outcome of the Treatment
       of Alcoholics.) Československa Psychiatrie, Praha, 58: 321-
       323, 1962.

4504. Zylman, R. Accidents, Alcohol and Single-Cause Explanations:
       Lessons from the Grand Rapids Study. Quarterly Journal of
       Studies on Alcohol, 29 (Supplement No. 4): 212-233, 1968.

4505. Zylman, R. Collision Behavior of Young Drivers: Comment on the
       Study by Whitehead et al. Journal of Studies on Alcohol,
       37: 393-401, 1976.

4506. Zylman, R. The Consequences of Lower Legal Drinking Ages on
       Alcohol-Related Crash Involvement of Young People. Journal
       of Traffic Safety Education, 24(2): 13-15, 18, 1977.

4507. Zylman, R. Drinking Practices among Youth are Changing
       Regardless of Legal Drinking Age. Journal of Traffic Safety
       Education, 24(1): 31-32, 37, 1976.

4508. Zylman, R. Drinking and Driving After It's Legal to Drink at 18:
       Is the Problem Real? Journal of Alcohol and Drug Education,
       20(1): 48-52, 1974.

4509. Zylman, R. Drinking and Driving: After It's Legal to Drink at
       18. Police Chief, 41(11): 18, 20-21, 1974.

4510. Zylman, R. Fatal Crashes among Michigan Youth Following
       Reduction of Legal Drinking Age. Quarterly Journal of
       Studies on Alcohol, 35: 283-286, 1974.

4511. Zylman, R. Response. Quarterly Journal of Studies on Alcohol,
       36: 173-177, 1975.

4512. Zylman, R. Teenagers and Alcohol. American Association of
       Automotive Medicine Quarterly, 1: 26-27, 1974.

4513. Zylman, R. When It became Legal to Drink at 18 in Massachusetts
       and Maine: What Happened? Police Chief, 43(1): 56-59,
       1976.

4514. Zylman, R. When it became Legal to Drink at 18 in Michigan:
       What Happened? Journal of Traffic Safety Education, 21(3):
       15-16, 38, 1974.

4515. Zylman, R. When It is Legal to Drink at 18: What Should We
       Expect? Journal of Traffic Safety Education, 20(4): 9-19,
       35, 1973.

4516. Zylman, Richard. Age is More Important than Alcohol in the
       Collision-Involvement of Young and Old Drivers. Journal of
       Traffic Safety Education, 20(1): 7-8, 34, 1972. (Also in:
       Journal of Alcohol and Drug Education, 18(2): 1-5, 1973.

4517. Zylman, Richard. Alcohol Related Traffic Deaths. The Alcoholism
       Digest Annual, 2: 31-33, 1973-1974.

4518. Zylman, Richard. Drinking-Driving and Fatal Crashes: A New
       Perspective. Journal of Alcohol and Drug Education, 21(1):
       1-10, 1975.

4519. Zylman, Richard. Youth, Alcohol and Collision Involvement. In:
       Proceedings of the Joint Conference on Alcohol Abuse and
       Alcoholism, February 21-23, 1972. U.S. Law Enforcement
       Assistance Administration. Washington, D.C.: U.S.
       Government Printing Office, 1972, pages 109-139. (DHEW
       Publication No. HSM 73-9051) (Also in: Journal of Traffic
       Safety, 5: 58-72, 1973.)

Addendum

A

4520. Aaron, Paul and Musto, David. Temperance and Prohibition in America: A Historical Overview. In: Alcohol and Public Policy: Beyond the Shadow of Prohibition. Eds. M.H. Moore and D.R. Gerstein. Washington, D.C.: National Academy Press, 1981, pages 127-181.

4521. Adler, I. and Kandel, D.B. Cross-Cultural Perspectives on Developmental States in Adolescent Drug Use. Journal of Studies on Alcohol, 42(9): 701-715, 1981.

4522. Alcoholism among Adolescents. Psychiatric Opinion, 12(3): no pages, March, 1975.

4523. Anderson, S.C. Alcoholic Women: Personality Traits During Adolescence. American Journal of Drug and Alcohol Abuse, 8(2): 239-248, 1981.

4524. Andersson, P. and Farm, I. En Alkoholenkät--Och Vad Sen Da'? En Modell för Alkoholundervisning i A'k 6. (An Alcohol Inquiry--And What Then? A Model for Alcohol Instruction in the Sixth Grade [Age 13].) Alkohol och Narkotica, 74(8): 8-18, 1980.

4525. Anumonye, Amechi. Drug Use among Young People in Lagos, Nigeria. Bulletin on Narcotics, 18(3): 38-45, 1981.

4526. Arthur, G.L., Sisson, P.J. and Natson, S. Drug Survey: A Knowledge and Attitude Inventory of Youth in a Typical High School in Georgia. Journal of Drug Education, 3: 79-84, 1973.

4527. Auleytner, W. Zagrożenie i Wychowanie. (The Alcohol Hazard and Education.) Problemy Alkoholizmu, Warsaw, 27(12): 5, 1980.

4528. Bach, Paul J. and Borstein, Phillip H. A Social Learning
      Rationale and Suggestions for Behavioral Treatment with
      American Indian Alcohol Abusers. Addictive Behaviors,
      6(1): 75-81, 1981.

4529. Barnard, C.P. Families, Alcoholism and Therapy. Springfield,
      Illinois: Charles C. Thomas, 1981.

4530. Barnes, Grace, Sokolow, Lloyd and Welte, John. Alcohol Use
      among College Students in New York State. Buffalo, New
      York: Research Institute on Alcoholism, 1981.

4531. Batlegay, R., Muhlemann, R. and Zehner, R. Consumption Patterns
      of Alcohol, Tobacco and Drugs, Taking into Account Different
      Environmental Factors in a Sample of 4,082 20-Year-Old
      Healthy Swiss Males. In: Papers Presented at the 20th
      International Institute on the Prevention and Treatment of
      Alcoholism, Manchester, England. Lausanne, Switzerland:
      International Council on Alcohol and Addictions, 1974,
      pages 162-164.

4532. Baynes, Bill. Prevention with Pizzazz. Alcoholism: The National
      Magazine, 2(3): 34-35, 1982.

4533. Beauchamp, Dan E. The Paradox of Alcohol Policy: The Case of
      the 1969 Alcohol Act in England. In: Alcohol and Public
      Policy: Beyond the Shadows of Prohibition. Eds.
      M.H. Moore and D.R. Gerstein. Washington, D.C.: National
      Academy Press, 1981, pages 225-254.

4534. Beauvais, Fred. Preventing Drug Abuse among American Indian
      Young People. Fort Collins, Colorado: Psychological
      Department at Colorado State University, 1980.

4535. Beck, Kenneth H. Driving While Under the Influence of Alcohol:
      Relationship to Attitudes and Beliefs in a College
      Population. American Journal of Drug and Alcohol Abuse,
      8(3): 377-388, 1981.

4536.   Benson, C.S.   Coping and Support among Daughters of Alcoholics.
        Doctoral Dissertation (University Microfilms No. 8029210).
        Indiana University, 1980.

4537.   Berger, H. and Legnaro, A.   Die Karriere von Jugendlichen zum
        Alkoholiker.   (The Development of Alcoholism among Youth.)
        In: Jugend und Alkohol: Trinkmuster, Suchtentwicklung und
        Therapie.   (Youth and Alcohol: Drinking Patterns,
        Addiction Development and Therapy.)   Eds. H. Berger,
        A. Legnaro and K.-H. Reuband.   Stuttgart: W. Kohlhammer,
        1980, pages 115-137.

4538.   Berger, H., Legnaro, A. and Reuband, K.-H., Eds. Jugend und Alkohol:
        Trinkmuster, Suchtentwicklung und Therapie.   (Youth and
        Alcohol: Drinking Patterns, Addiction Development and
        Therapy.)   Stuttgart: W. Kohlhammer, 1980.

4539.   Black, Claudia.   Don't Talk--The Family Law.   Focus: On Alcohol
        and Drug Issues, 6(4): 6-7, 1981.

4540.   Black, Claudia.   Why Johnny Can't Learn about Alcoholism.
        Alcoholism: The National Magazine, 2(3): 30, 1982.

4541.   Black, R.M., Mayer, J. and Zaklan, A.   The Relationship between
        Opiate Abuse and Child Abuse and Neglect.   In: Critical
        Concerns in the Field of Drug Abuse: Proceedings of the
        Third National Drug Abuse Conference, Inc., New York, 1976.
        Eds. A. Schecter, H. Alksne and E. Kaufman.   New York:
        Marcel Dekker, 1978, pages 755-758.

4542.   Bowen, Murray.   A Family Systems Approach to Alcoholism.
        Addictions, 21(2): 28-39, 1974.

4543.   Bozhanov, A.   Prouchvane na Tyutyunopusheneto, Alkoholnata i
        Medikamentoznata Upotreba i Zloupotreba sred Uchenitsi ot
        Gorniya Uchilishchen Kurs.   (Investigation of Smoking,
        Alcohol and Drug Use among Secondary School Students.)
        Khigiyena, (4): 343-348, 1980.

4544.   Braucht, G.N.   Psychosocial Research on Teenage Drinking: Past
        and Future.   In: Drugs and the Youth Culture.   (Sage
        Annual Reviews of Drug and Alcohol Abuse, Volume 4.)   Eds.
        F.R. Scarpitti and S.K. Datesman.   Beverly Hills,
        California: Sage Publications, 1980, pages 109-143.

4545.   Breed, Lawrence A. and Defoe James R.   Comic Book Supercharacters
        and Their Role in Alcohol Education.   Journal of Alcohol and
        Drug Education, 27(1): 1-13, 1981.

4546.   Brown, David B. and Saeed, Maghsoodloo.   A Study of Alcohol
        Involvement in Young Driver Accidents with the Lowering of
        the Legal Age of Drinking in Alabama.   Accident Analysis
        and Prevention, 13(4): 319-322, 1981.

C

4547. Cadden, J.J. and Harrison-Ross, P. Alcoholism in American Youth: The Scope and Treatment of the Problem. In: Papers Presented at the 20th International Institute on the Prevention and Treatment of Alcoholism, Manchester, England. Ed. B. Hore. Lausanne, Switzerland: International Council on Alcohol and Addictions, 1974, pages 78-81.

4548. Castro, Maria Elena and Valencia, Maredo. Drug Consumption among the Student Population of Mexico City and Its Metropolitan Area: Subgroup Affected and the Distribution of Users. Bulletin on Narcotics, 18(3): 29-37, 1981.

4549. Catanzaro, R.J., Pisani, V.D., Fox, R. and Kennedy, E.R. Familization Therapy: An Alternative to Traditional Mental Health Care. Diseases of the Nervous System, 34: 212-218, 1973.

4550. Children of Alcoholics. Professional, 10(1): no pages, 1964.

4551. Clark, Alfred W. and Prolisko, Andrew. Social-Role Correlates of Driving Accidents. Human Factors, 21(6): 655-659, 1979.

4552. Coleman, S.B. Cross-Cultural Approaches to Addict Families. Journal of Drug Education, 9(4): 293-299, 1979.

4553. Coleman, S.B. An Endangered Species: The Female as Addict or Member of an Addict Family. Journal of Marital and Family Therapy, 5, 1979.

4554. Coombs, Robert H. Drug Abuse as a Career. Journal of Drug Issues, 11(4): 369-387, 1981.

4555. Couturier, C. Tabac, Alcool, Drogue en Milieu Scolaire. (Tobacco, Alcohol and Drugs in the School.) Doctoral Dissertation. Universite de Rennes, 1979.

D

4556. Davis, D.M., Gonzalez, V. and Piat, J. Follow-Up of Adolescent Psychiatric Inpatients. Southern Medical Journal, 73: 1215-1217, 1980.

4557. Deitch, R. Alcohol Education and Research Council. Lancet, 1: 622, 1981.

4558. Dembo, Richard, Babst, Dean V., Burgos, Wilham and Schmeidler, James. Survival Orientation and the Drug User Experience of a Sample of Inner City Junior High School Youths. International Journal of the Addictions, 16(6): 1031-1047, 1981.

4559. Deschner, Jeanne P., Plain, Michael D., Terhune, Gerald K. and Williamson, Celia. Development of the DDI: A Seriousness Scale for Delinquency. Evaluation Review, 5(6): 788-809, 1981.

4560. Deutsch, C. Teachers Help Children to Cope. Focus: On Alcohol and Drug Issues, 2(3): 24-26, 1979.

4561. DiCicco, L. Children of Alcoholic Parents: Issues of Identification. In: Services for Children of Alcoholics. Symposium held on September 24-26, 1979, at Silver Spring, Maryland. National Institute on Alcohol Abuse and Alcoholism. (Research Monograph No. 4). Washington, D.C.: U.S. Government Printing Office, 1981, pages 44-59.

4562. Djurstedt, B. Den nya Läroplanen och ANT-Undervisningen. (The New Curriculum and ANT [Alcohol, Narcotics and Tobacco] Instruction. Alkohol och Narkotica, 74(8): 1-4, 1980.

4563. Drinking Age Law Reduces Accidents Arrest. The Bottom Line on Alcohol in Society, 4(4): 23, 1981.

E

4564. Ecke, S.A. The Role of the Significant Other in Alcoholism. Doctoral Dissertation (University Microfilms No. 8023573). United States International University, 1980.

4565. Erschreckender Test in Aachen: So Leicht Kommen Kinder an Alkohol. (A Frightening Test in Aachen: How Easily Children Can Acquire Alcoholic Beverages.) Münchener Medizinische Wochenschrift, 122: 1563, 1980.

4566. Fahrenkrug, H. Sociologische Aspekte Sozial Integrierten
        Alkoholkonsums im Jugendalter. (Sociologial Aspects of
        Youth's Socially Integrated Alcohol Consumption.) In:
        Jugend und Alkohol: Trinkmuster, Suchtentwicklung und
        Therapie. (Youth and Alcohol: Drinking Patterns, Addiction
        Development and Therapy.) Eds. H. Berger, A. Legnaro and
        K.-H. Reuband. Stuttgart: W. Kohlhammer, 1980, pages 11-
        21.

4567. Fauman, M.A. and Fauman, B.J. Chronic Phencyclidine (PCP) Abuse:
        A Psychiatric Perspective. Journal of Psychedelic Drugs,
        12: 307-315, 1980.

4568. Feldhege, F.-J. Entstehungsbedingungen und
        Behandlungsmöglichkeiten des Jugendalkoholismus aus
        Verhaltenstherapeutischer Sicht. (Causes and Treatment
        Possibilities of Alcoholism among Youth from a Behavioral
        Therapy Point of View.) In: Jugend und Alkohol:
        Trinkmuster, Suchtentwicklung und Therapie. (Youth and
        Alcohol: Drinking Patterns, Addiction Development and
        Therapy.) Eds. H. Berger, A. Legnaro and K.-H. Reuband.
        Stuttgart: W. Kohlhammer, 1980, pages 175-196.

4569. Fine, E. Observations of Young Children from Alcoholic Homes.
        Philadelphia, Pennsylvania: West Philadelphia Community
        Mental Health Consortium, 1975.

4570. Finn, Peter. Hey Teach! Do You Drink? Journal of School
        Health, 51(8): 538-542, 1981.

4571. Foster, W. Let's Include the Child in Family Therapy.
        Alcoholism: A National Magazine, 1(4): 14, 1981.

4572. Frazier, Charles F. and Potter, Roberto H. Alcohol and Drug
        Offenders in the Juvenile Justice System: Are There
        Differentials in Handling? Journal of Drug Issues, 12(1):
        89-102, 1982.

G

4573. Gerber, C. Kind und Alkohol: Materialien zur Alkoholprophylaxe:
      Informationen, Überlegungen und Anregungen fur Schule,
      Kinder-und Jugendarbeit. (Alcohol and the Child: Materials
      Concerning Alcohol Prevention: Information, Reflections
      and Suggestions for Schools, Children and Young Working
      People.) Bern: Blaukreuz Verlag, 1979.

4574. Globetti, G. and Alsikafi, M. Prevention of Alcohol Problems--
      Some Findings on the Alcohol Education Model. In: Papers
      Presented at the 20th International Institute of the
      Prevention and Treatment of Alcoholism, Manchester, England.
      Ed. B. Hore. Lausanne, Switzerland: International Council
      of Alcohol and Addictions, 1974, pages 180-185.

4575. Glynn, Thomas J., Ed. Drugs and the Family. National Institute
      of Drug Abuse. Research Issue No. 29. Published in
      Cooperation with the Department of Health and Human Services
      and the National Institute on Drug Abuse (Contract
      #271-80-3720). Washington, D.C.: U.S. Government Printing
      Office, 1981. (DHHS Publication No. ADM 81-1151)

4576. Glynn, T.J. From Family to Peer: A Review of Transitions of
      Influence among Drug Using Youth. Journal of Youth and
      Adolescence, 10(4), 1981.

4577. Gottlieb, Nancy. What Happen to the "Forgotten Children"? Focus:
      on Alcohol and Drug Issues, 6(4): 17, 19, 1981.

4578. Greiner, I. Der Junge Alkoholkranke und Seine Behandlung im
      Fachkrankenhaus. (Young Alcoholics and Their Treatment at
      a Specialized Hospital.) In: Jugend und Alkohol:
      Trinkmuster, Suchtentwicklung und Therapie. (Youth and
      Alcohol: Drinking Patterns, Addiction Development and
      Therapy.) Eds. H. Berger, A. Legnaro and K.-H. Reuband.
      Stuttgart: W. Kohlhammer, 1980, pages 159-174.

H

4579. Hashway, R.M., Hesse, S., Nutile, K. and Taylor, H. Preliminary
Results of a Longitudinal Study of Collegiate Alcohol
Abuse. Journal of the American College Health Association,
28: 362-363, 1980.

4580. Hochheimer, John L. Reducing Alcohol Abuse: A Critical Review
of Educational Strategies. In: Alcohol and Public Policy:
Beyond the Shadows of Prohibition. Eds. M.H. Moore and
D.R. Gerstein. Washington, D.C.: National Academy Press,
1981, pages 286-335.

4581. Hoikkala, Tommi. Heikki Katajisto: Suomen Nuoriso ja Alkoholi
Joukkotiedotuksessa. Karpon Ohjelma ja Sanomalehdisto.
(Finnish Youth and Drinking in the Mass Media.)
Alkoholipolitiikka, Helsingfor, 46(3): 110-119, 1981.

4582. Hoikkala, Tommi. Ylioppilaskokelaiden Alkoholikasitykset.
(Conceptions of Alcohol by Upper Secondary School Students
Sitting for the Matriculation Examination.)
Alkoholipolitiikka, Helsingfor, 46(4): 205-212, 1981.

4583. Hore, Brian, Ed. Papers Presented at the 20th International
Institute on the Prevention and Treatment of Alcoholism
and Addiction. Lausanne, Switzerland: International
Council on Alcoholism and Addiction, 1974.

4584. Huba, G.J. and Bentler, P.M. The Role of Peer and Adult Models
for Drug Taking at Different Stages in Adolescence.
Journal of Youth and Adolescence, 9(5): 449-465, 1980.

4585. Hyman, Merton M. Weighting for Populations at Risk and
Standardizing for Age in Alcohol Research. Journal of
Studies on Alcohol, 42(7): 579-593, 1981.

4586. The Impact of Alcohol Beverage Advertising: Landmark Study by MSU Professors. The Bottom Line on Alcohol in Society, 4(4): 2-17, 1981.

4587. Inciardi, J.A. Youths, Drugs, and Street Crime. In: Drugs and the Youth Culture. (Sage Annual Reviews of Drug and Alcohol Abuse. Volume 4.) Eds. F.R. Scarpitti and S.K. Datesman. Beverly Hills, California: Sage Publications, 1980, pages 175-204.

4588. Irgens-Jensen, O. Bergensungdommens bruk av Stoffer, Alkohol og Tobakk 1971-1979. (Use of Drugs, Alcohol and Tobacco among Youth in Bergen 1971-1979.) Oslo: Statens Institutt for Alkoholforskning, 1980.

4589. It's Never Too Late to Share a Secret. Alcoholism: The National Magazine, 2(2): 34-36, 1981.

4590. Iverson, D.C. and Roberts, T.E. The Juvenile Intervention Program: Results of the Process, Impact and Outcome Evaluations. Journal of Drug Education, 10: 289-300, 1980.

4591. Jackson, N., Carlisi, J., Greenway, C. and Zalesnick, M. Age of Initial Drug Experimentation among White and Non-White Ethnics. The International Journal of the Addictions, 16(8): 1373-1386, 1981.

4592. Jacob, T., Ritchey, D., Cvitkovic, J.F. and Blane, H.T. Communication Styles of Alcoholic and Nonalcoholic Families When Drinking and Not Drinking. Journal of Studies on Alcohol, 42(5): 466-482, 1981.

4593. Jaquith, Susan M. Adolescent Marijuana and Alcohol Use. Criminology, 19(2): 271-280, 1981.

4594. Jenner, C. Zur Entwicklung der Alkoholabhängigkeit bei Jugendlichen und bei Frauen. (Development of Alcoholism among Youth and Women.) Österreichische Artzeitung, Vienna, 33: 693-696, 1978.

4595. Johnson, Bruce D. Marijuana: The Intervening Variable between Alcohol/Cigarette Use and Hard Drug Use. In: Papers Presented at the 20th International Institute on the Prevention and Treatment of Alcoholism, Manchester, England. Ed. B. Hore. Lausanne, Switzerland: International Council on Alcohol and Addictions, 1974, pages 138-146.

4596. Johnson, Nancy. Drinking Age Increase Leads to Traffic Crash Decrease. Alcohol Health and Research World, 6(2): 22-23, 1981-82.

4597. Johnston, Lloyd D. Review of General Population Surveys of Drug Abuse. WHO Offset Publication No. 52. Geneva, Switzerland: World Health Organization, 1980.

4598.   Johnston, Lloyd D., Bachman, Jerald G. and O'Malley, Patrick M.
        Highlights from Student Drug Use in America 1975-1980.
        The University of Michigan Institute for Social Research.
        Rockville, Maryland: Alcohol, Drug Abuse and Mental Health
        Administration, 1980. (DHHS Publication No. ADM 1-1066)

4599.   Johnston, Lloyd D., Bachman, Jerald G. and O'Malley, Patrick M.
        Monitoring the Future: Questionnaire Responses from the
        Nation's High School Seniors 1979. Ann Arbor, Michigan:
        The University of Michigan's Survey Research Center and
        Institute for Social Research, 1980.

4600.   Johnston, Lloyd D., Bachman, Jerald G. and O'Malley, Patrick M.
        1979 Highlights: Drugs and the Nation's High School
        Students: Five Year National Trends. Published in
        Cooperation with the Department of Health and Human
        Services and the National Institute on Drug Abuse.
        Rockville, Maryland: Alcohol, Drug Abuse and Mental Health
        Administration, 1979 (reprinted 1980). (DHHS Publication
        No. ADM 81-930)

4601.   Johnston, Lloyd D. and O'Malley, Patrick M. Drugs and the
        Nation's High School Students. In: Drug Abuse in the
        Modern World: A Perspective for the Eighties. Eds.
        G.G. Nahas and H.C. Frick. New York: Pergamon Press,
        1981, pages 87-98.

K

4602. Kline, F.G., Morrison, A.J., Miller, P.V. and Fredin, E.S.
Adolescents and Alcohol Information: An Exploration of
Audience Needs and Media Effects. In: Papers Presented
at the 20th International Institute on the Prevention and
Treatment of Alcoholism, Manchester, England. Ed. B. Hore.
Lausanne, Switzerland: International Council of Alcohol
and Addictions, 1974, pages 185-196.

4603. Kohler-Palmersheim, R. Soziale Merkmale von Jungen Alkoholikern.
(Social Traits of Young Alcoholics.) In: Jugend und
Alkohol: Trinkmuster, Suchtentwicklung und Therapie.
(Youth and Alcohol: Drinking Patterns, Addiction
Development and Therapy.) Eds. H. Berger, A. Legnaro and
K.-H. Reuband. Stuttgart: W. Kohlhammer, 1980, pages 138-
148.

4604. Korcok, Milan. Children of Alcoholics Comprise by Share of
Society's Future. Focus on Alcohol and Drug Issues, 6(4):
2-3, 1981.

4605. Korcok, Milan. Many Children Overcome Difficulties. Focus: On
Alcohol and Drug Issues, 6(4): 20, 24, 1981.

_____L

4606. Landes, S. The Children of Alcoholics: Program Needs and
       Implications Derived from Experience within the Adolescent
       Alcohol Abuse Treatment Program--The Door, New York City,
       A Multiservice Center for Youth. In: Services for
       Children of Alcoholics. Symposium held on September 24-26,
       1979 at Silver Spring, Maryland. U.S. National Institute
       on Alcohol Abuse and Alcoholism. Research Monograph No. 4.
       Washington, D.C.: U.S. Government Printing Office, 1981,
       pages 110-130. (DHHS Publication No. ADM 81-1007)

4607. Leane, A. and Roche, D. Developmental Disorder in the Children
       of Male Alcoholics. In: Papers Presented at the 20th
       International Intitute on the Prevention and Treatment of
       Alcoholism, Manchester, England. Ed. B. Hore. Lausanne,
       Switzerland: International Council on Alcohol and
       Addictions, 1974, pages 82-91.

4608. Leczenie i Rehabilitacja Młodocianych Alkoholików. I. Stan
       Świadzcen dla Alkoholików w Finlandii. (Treatment and
       Rehabilitation of Adolescent Alcoholics. I. The Health
       Service System for Alcoholics in Finland.) Problemy
       Alkoholizmu, Warsaw, 27(11): 19-21, 1980.

4609. Lerner, Rokelle. Growing Up in an Alcoholic Home--What's It
       Like? Focus: On Alcohol and Drug Issues, 6(4): 12-15, 1981.

4610. Liccione, William James. The Relative Influence of Significant
       Others on Adolescent Drinking: An Exploratory Study.
       Journal of Alcohol and Drug Education, 26(1): 55-62, 1980.

4611. Lillis, Robert P., William, Timothy P., Chupka, Joyce Q. and
       Williford, William R. Highway Safety Considerations in
       Raising the Minimum Legal Age for Purchase of Alcoholic
       Beverages to Nineteen in New York State. In: Raising the
       Minimum Purchasing Age for Alcoholic Beverages: Highway
       Safety Considerations. Albany, New York: Division of
       Alcoholism and Alcohol Abuse, 1982, pages 1-11.

4612. Litt, Iris.   Substance Abuse among Adolescent Females.   Focus on
         Women: Journal of Addiction and Health, 2(2): 61-71,
         1981.

4613. Lund, M.   Omaha Area Council on Alcoholism, Omaha, Nebraska.
         In: Services for Children of Alcoholics.   Symposium held
         on September 24-26, 1979 at Silver Spring, Maryland.   U.S.
         National Institute on Alcohol Abuse and Alcoholism.
         Research Monograph No. 4.   Washington, D.C.: U.S.
         Government Printing Office, 1981, pages 131-137.   (DHHS
         Publication No. ADM 81-1007)

4614. MacAndrew, Craig. An Examination of the Relevance of the Individual Differences (A-Trait) Formulation of the Tension-Reduction Theory to the Etiology of Alcohol Abuse in Young Males. Addictive Behaviors: An International Journal, 7(1): 39-46, 1982.

4615. McCarthy, D. Evaluation Guidelines for the University of Massachusetts Model: A University-Based Alcohol Education Project. Prepared for National Institute on Alcohol Abuse and Alcoholism (PB No. 80-210594). Springfield, Virginia: National Technical Information Service, 1979.

4616. Martin, G.L., Newman, I.M. and Hanus, R.D. Inconsistencies in the Evaluation of Selected Alcohol Education Materials. Journal of Drug Education, 11: 53-60, 1981.

4617. Maryland Department of Health and Mental Hygiene, Drug Abuse Administration, Office of Special Services, Division of Management Information Services. 1980 Maryland Adolescent Survey: Report on Alcohol Use. Annapolis, Maryland, 1981.

4618. Maryland Department of Health and Mental Hygiene, Drug Abuse Administration, Office of Special Services, Division of Management Information Services. 1980 Maryland Adolescent Survey: Report on Drug Knowledge and Attitudes. Annapolis, Maryland, 1981.

4619. Mayer, J. and Black, R. Child Abuse and Neglect in Families with an Alcohol or Opiate Addicted Parent. Child Abuse and Neglect, 1: 85-98, 1977.

4620. Milgram, Gail Gleason. Alcoholism in the Family: Implication for the School System. Focus on Alcohol and Drug Issues, 6(4): 4-5, 22, 1981.

4621. Mills, Kenneth C., Pfaffenberger, Bryan and McCarty, Dennis.
       Guidelines for Alcohol Abuse Prevention on the College
       Campus: Overcoming the Barriers to Program Success.
       Journal of Higher Education, 52(4): no pages, 1981.

4622. Moore, Mark H. and Gerstein, Dean R., Eds. Alcohol and Public
       Policy: Beyond the Shadow of Prohibition. Washington,
       D.C.: National Academy Press, 1981.

4623. Morehouse, E.R. Working with Children of Alcoholic Parents in
       an Outpatient Alcoholism Treatment Facility and in the
       Schools, Department of Community Mental Health, Westchester
       County, New York. In: Services for Children of Alcoholics.
       Symposium held on September 24-26, 1979 at Silver Spring,
       Maryland. U.S. National Institute on Alcohol Abuse and
       Alcoholism. Research Monograph No. 4. Washington, D.C.:
       U.S. Government Printing Office, 1981, pages 138-151.
       (DHHS Publication No. ADM 81-1007)

4624. Morrissey, Elizabeth R. The Measurement of Multiple Drug Use
       and Its Relationship to the Patterning of Alcohol Intake.
       American Journal of Drug and Alcohol Abuse, 8(3): 311-328,
       1981.

4625. Müller, R. Entwicklung Jugendlichen Trinkverhaltens in
       Unterschiedlichen Trinkkulturen: Alkoholkonsum in der
       Schweiz. (Development of Drinking Behavior among Youth in
       Different Drinking Cultures: Alcohol Consumption in
       Switzerland.) In: Jugend und Alkohol: Trinkmuster,
       Suchtentwicklung und Therapie. (Youth and Alcohol:
       Drinking Patterns, Addiction Development and Therapy.) Eds.
       H. Berger, A. Legnaro and K.-H. Reuband. Stuttgart:
       W. Kohlhammer, 1980, pages 42-60.

4626. Muller, W. New Directions: The Family Center Youth Program,
       Human Relations Center, Inc., Santa Barbara, California.
       In: Services for Children of Alcoholics. Symposium held
       on September 24-26, 1979 at Silver Spring, Maryland. U.S.
       National Institute on Alcohol Abuse and Alcoholism.
       Research Monograph No. 4. Washington, D.C.: U.S.
       Government Printing Office, 1981, pages 152-163. (DHHS
       Publication No. ADM 81-1007)

4627. National Institute on Alcohol Abuse and Alcoholism. Alcohol and
       the Family. Pamphlet. Rockville, Maryland: National
       Clearinghouse for Alcohol Information, 1980.

4628. National Institute on Alcohol Abuse and Alcoholism. General
       Conclusions and Recommendations (of the Symposium). In:
       Services for Children of Alcoholics. Symposium held on
       September 24-26, 1979 at Silver Spring, Maryland. U.S.
       National Institute on Alcohol Abuse and Alcoholism.
       Research Monograph No. 4. Washington, D.C.: U.S.
       Government Printing Office, 1981, pages 39-41. (DHHS
       Publication No. ADM 81-1007)

4629. National Institute on Alcohol Abuse and Alcoholism.
       Identification (of the Children of Alcoholics). In:
       Services for Children of Alcoholics. Symposium held on
       September 24-26, 1979, Silver Spring, Maryland. U.S.
       National Institute on Alcohol Abuse and Alcoholism.
       Research Monograph No. 4. Washington, D.C.: U.S.
       Government Printing Office, 1981, pages 7-16. (DHHS
       Publication No. ADM 81-1007)

4630. National Institute on Alcohol Abuse and Alcoholism.
       Intervention (with the Children of Alcoholics). In:
       Services for Children of Alcoholics. Symposium held on
       September 24-26, 1979 at Silver Spring, Maryland. U.S.
       National Institute on Alcohol Abuse and Alcoholism.
       Research Monograph No. 4. Washington, D.C.: U.S.
       Government Printing Office, 1981, pages 17-22. (DHHS
       Publication No. ADM 81-1007)

4631. National Institute on Alcohol Abuse and Alcoholism. Prevention
       (Issues Applying to Children of Alcoholics). In: Services
       for Children of Alcoholics. Symposium held on September 24-
       26, 1979 at Silver Spring, Maryland. U.S. National
       Institute on Alcohol Abuse and Alcoholism. Research
       Monograph No. 4. Washington, D.C.: U.S. Government
       Printing Office, 1981, pages 30-38. (DHHS Publication No.
       ADM 81-1007)

4632. National Institute on Alcohol Abuse and Alcoholism. Services for
       Children of Alcoholics. Symposium held on September 24-26,
       1979 at Silver Spring, Maryland. Research Monograph No. 4.
       Washington, D.C.: U.S. Government Printing Office, 1981.
       (DHHS Publication No. ADM 81-1007)

4633. National Institute on Alcohol Abuse and Alcoholism. Treatment
       (of the Children of Alcoholics). In: Services for
       Children of Alcoholics. Symposium held on September 24-26,
       1979 at Silver Spring, Maryland. U.S. National Institute
       on Alcohol Abuse and Alcoholism. Research Monograph No. 4.
       Washington, D.C.: U.S. Government Printing Office, 1981,
       pages 23-29. (DHHS Publication No. ADM 81-1007)

4634. National Institute on Drug Abuse. Adolescent Marijuana Abusers
       and Their Families. NIDA Research Monograph No. 40.
       Published in cooperation with the U.S. Department of Health
       and Human Services. Washington, D.C.: U.S. Government
       Printing Office, 1981. (DHHS Publication No. ADM 81-1168)

4635. National Institute on Drug Abuse. The Door: A Model Youth
       Center. Treatment Program Monograph Series. Published in
       cooperation with the U.S. Department of Health and Human
       Services. Washington, D.C.: U.S. Government Printing
       Office, 1981. (DHHS Publication No. ADM 81-1132)

4636. National Institute on Drug Abuse. Drugs and the Family. Ed.
       T.J. Glynn. Research Issue No. 29. Published in
       cooperation with the U.S. Department of Health and Human
       Services. Rockville Maryland, 1981. (DHHS Publication
       No. ADM 81-1151)

4637. National Institute on Drug Abuse. Highlights from: Student
       Drug Use in America: 1975-1980. Published in cooperation
       with the U.S. Department of Health and Human Services.
       Rockville, Maryland: Alcohol, Drug Abuse and Mental Health
       Administration, 1980. (DHHS Publication No. ADM 81-1066)

4638. National Institute on Drug Abuse. 1979 Highlights: Drugs and
       the Nation's High School Students: Five Year National
       Trends. Published in cooperation with the U.S. Department
       of Health and Human Services. Rockville, Maryland:
       Alcohol, Drug Abuse and Mental Health Administration, 1979
       (reprinted 1980). (DHHS Publication No. ADM 81-930)

4639. National Institute on Drug Abuse. Young Men and Drugs in
       Manhattan: A Causal Analysis. NIDA Monograph No. 39.
       Published in cooperation with the Department of Health and
       Human Services. Rockville, Maryland: Alcohol, Drug Abuse
       and Mental Health Administration, 1981. (DHHS Publication
       No. ADM 81-1167)

4640. National Institute on Drug Abuse Services Research Report.
       Drug Abuse Patterns among Young Polydrug Users and Urban
       Appalachian Youths. Published in cooperation with the U.S.
       Department of Health and Human Services. Rockville,
       Maryland: Alcohol, Drug Abuse and Mental Health
       Administration, 1980. (DHHS Publication No. ADM 80-1002)

4641. New York Division of Alcoholism and Alcohol Abuse. Raising the
       Minimum Purchase Age for Alcoholic Beverages: Highway
       Safety Considerations. Albany, New York, 1982.

P

4642. Partanen, Juha. Teesaja Valistuksesta. (Thesis about Alcohol
       Education). Alkoholipolitiikka, Helsingfor, 46(4); 161-
       168, 1981.

4643. Pekkala, Junno, Manninen, Jouka, Nieminen, Tuula and
       Nylund Marjukka. Valistus Alkoholipotiittisena Keinona.
       (Education as an Alcohol Policy Measure.)
       Alkoholipolitiikka, Helsingor, 46(4): 157-160, 1981.

4644. Rachal, J. Valley, Guess, L. Lynn, Hubbard, Robert L., Maisto, Stephen A., Cavanaugh, Elizabeth R., Waddell, Richard and Benrud, Charles H. Adolescent Drinking Behavior. Volume 1. The Extent and Nature of Adolescent Alcohol and Drug Use: The 1974 and 1978 National Sample Studies. Prepared for National Institute on Alcohol Abuse and Alcoholism. Research Triangle Park, North Carolina: Research Triangle Institute, 1980. (DHHS Publication No. ADM 281-76-0019)

4645. Reed, David S. Reducing the Cost of Drinking and Driving. In: Alcohol and Public Policy: Beyond the Shadows of Prohibition. Eds. M.H. Moore and D.R. Gerstein. Washington, D.C.: National Academy Press, 1981, pages 336-387.

4646. Reilly, D.M. Family Factors in the Etiology and Treatment of Youthful Drug Abuse. Family Therapy, 2(2): 149-171, 1976.

4647. Richards, Tarpley. Reestablish Some Old Ties for the Sake of the Children. Focus: On Alcohol and Drug Issues, 6(4): 23, 1981.

4648. Richard, Tarpley. Working with Children of an Alcoholic Mother. Alcohol Health and Research World, 3(3): 22-24, 1979.

4649. Rittenhouse, Joan Dunne. Drugs in the School: The Shape of Drug Abuse among American Youth in the Seventies. In: Drug Abuse in the Modern World: A Perspective for the Eighties. Eds. G.G. Nahas and H.C. Frick. New York: Pergamon Press, 1981, pages 99-105.

4650. Rosellini, Gayle. Starting in Kindergarten: Here's Looking at You. Alcoholism: The National Magazine, 2(3): 27-29, 1982.

4651.   Rutherford, D.   Public Education and Information.   In: <u>Papers</u>
        <u>Presented at the 20th International Institute on the</u>
        <u>Prevention and Treatment of Alcoholism, Manchester, England.</u>
        Ed. B. Hore.   Lausanne, Switzerland: International Council
        on Alcohol and Addictions, 1974, pages 71-78.

4652. Santo, Yoav, Farley, Edward C. and Friedman, Alfred S.
        Highlights from the National Youth Polydrug Study. In:
        Drug Abuse Patterns among Young Polydrug Users and Urban
        Appalachian Youths. Published in cooperation with the
        U.S. Department of Health and Human Services. Rockville,
        Maryland: Alcohol, Drug Abuse and Mental Health
        Administration, 1980. (DHHS Publication No. ADM 80-1002)

4653. Segal, Bernard. Family Background, Personality Characteristics
        and Use of Drugs, Alcohol or Non-Use of Either among
        College Students. In: Papers Presented at the 20th
        International Institute on the Prevention and Treatment of
        Alcoholism, Manchester, England. Ed. B. Hore. Lausanne,
        Switzerland: International Council on Alcohol and
        Addictions, 1974, pages 165-170.

4654. Seidler, Gary. Psychological Study Would Fill Gaps. Focus: On
        Alcohol and Drug Issues, 6(4): 21, 23, 1981.

4655. Seidler, Gary. Ten Million New Alcoholics Coming Down the Road.
        Focus: On Alcohol and Drug Issues, 6(4): 9, 1981.

4656. Sheppard, Margaret A., Goodstadt, Michael S. and Goodwin, Chan.
        Drug Education in Ontario Schools: Content and Processes.
        Journal of Drug Education, 11(4): 317-326, 1981.

4657. Singh, Santosh and Preet, Kamal. Drug Abuse Amongst School and
        College Students in Punjab. Child Psychiatry Quarterly,
        14(1): 5-11, 1981.

4658. Smart, R.G. and Liban, C.B. The Need for Attitude Changes
        Concerning Drinking and Drinking Problems. Journal of
        Alcohol and Drug Education, 27(1): 47-61, 1981.

4659. Smart, R.G. and Murray, G.F. A Review of Trends in Alcohol and
         Cannabis Use among Young People. Bulletin on Narcotics,
         32(4): 77-90, 1981.

4660. Strack, Jay. Drugs and Drinking: The All American Cop-Out.
         Nashville, Tennessee: Thomas Nelson Publishers, 1979.

T

4661. Tarnai, John, Magnusson-Fagan, Nancy J., Hopkins, Ronald H., Mauss, Armand L. and Eichberger, Monica. On Re-Tooling the Teachers: An Evaluation of Teacher Training in Alcohol Education. Journal of Alcohol and Drug Education, 27(1): 34-46, 1981.

4662. Torda, C. Comments on the Character Structure and Psychodynamic Processes of Heroin Addicts. Perceptual and Motor Skills, 27: 143-146, 1968.

W

4663. Watkins, Virginia McCoy and McCoy, Clyde B. Drug Use among
       Urban Appalachian Youths. In: Drug Abuse Patterns among
       Young Polydrug Users and Urban Appalachian Youths.
       Published in cooperation with the U.S. Department of Health
       and Human Services. Rockville, Maryland: Alcohol, Drug
       Abuse and Mental Health Administration, 1980. (DHHS
       Publication No. ADM 80-1002)

4664. Webb, N.L., Pratt, T.C., Linn, M.W. and Carmichael, J.S. Focus
       on the Family as a Factor in Differential Treatment Outcome.
       The International Journal of the Addictions, 13(5): 783-795,
       1978.

4665. Wells, Kathleen. Adolescents' Attributions for Delinquent
       Behavior. Personality and Social Psychology Bulletin,
       6(1): 63-67, 1980.

4666. Wilkinson, D. Adrian. Legal and Ethical Implications of
       Treatment of Minors. Social Science and Medicine: 1-5,
       1981.

Index

(continued on next page)

About the Compiler

GRACE M. BARNES is a Research Scientist III in the Division of Alcoholism and Alcohol Abuse in New York State's Research Institute on Alcoholism. She also compiled the Greenwood Press bibliography *Alcohol and the Elderly* (1980), and has written articles on alcohol use and abuse that have appeared in *The Journal of School Health, Adolescence,* and the *Journal of Studies on Alcohol.*